Theories of
development

International Library of Sociology

Founded by Karl Mannheim

Editor: John Rex, University of Aston in Birmingham

Arbor Scientiae
Arbor Vitae

A catalogue of the books available in the International Library
of Sociology and other series of Social Science books published
by Routledge & Kegan Paul will be found at the end of this
volume.

Theories of development

P.W. Preston

Routledge & Kegan Paul
London, Boston, Melbourne and Henley

First published in 1982
by Routledge & Kegan Paul Ltd
39 Store Street, London WC1E 7DD,
9 Park Street, Boston, Mass. 02108, USA,
296 Beaconsfield Parade, Middle Park,
Melbourne, 3206, Australia and
Broadway House, Newtown Road,
Henley-on-Thames, Oxon RG9 1EN
Printed in Great Britain by
Redwood Burn Ltd, Trowbridge, Wiltshire
© P.W. Preston 1982

Library of Congress Cataloging in Publication Data

Preston, P.W.
Theories of development.
(International library of sociology)
Bibliography: p.
Includes index.
1. Underdeveloped areas. 2. Economic development -
Social aspects. 3. Planning. I. Title II. Series.
HN980.P73 1982   307'.14   82-7660
ISBN 0-7100-9055-2   AACR2

pd
3-17-84

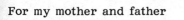

For my mother and father

Contents

Acknowledgments

An earlier version of this text was prepared as a PhD thesis under the supervision of Aidan Foster-Carter in the Department of Sociology of the University of Leeds. I should like to thank Aidan for his generous encouragement and gently made corrections. Thereafter I would thank those teachers I had as an undergraduate in the Departments of Sociology and Philosophy at Leeds. Bob Lorman and Steve McGilp at Gloucestershire College of Art and Design encouraged me when my interests in matters of social theorizing first stirred; as did my friends of those days. Throughout my time in Leeds my girlfriend Rose has provided invaluable support for my efforts.

Abbreviations

DC	Developed country
ECLA	United Nations Economic Commission for Latin America
ERP	European Recovery Programme
FRELIMO	Frente de Libertaçao de Moçambique
GNP	Gross national product
H-D	Harrod-Domar
IBRD	International Bank for Reconstruction and Development
ICOR	Incremental capital output ratio
IMF	International Monetary Fund
MPLA	Movimento Popular de Libertaçao de Angola
NIST	Neo-institutional social theory
NL	New Left
PAIGC	Partido Africano de Independencia de Guine e Cabo Verde
SDS	Students for Democratic Society
SPD	Social Democratic Party (West Germany)
SNCC	Student Non-violent Coordinating Committee
UDC	Underdeveloped country
UNCTAD	United Nations Conferences on Trade and Development
IBRD	International Bank for Reconstruction and Development
UNRRA	United Nations Relief and Rehabilitation Administration

Part I

Prologue

1 The scope and concerns of the study

A POINT OF DEPARTURE

It has been observed that the so called 'discovery of the Third World' is as significant for present-day social theory as was that nineteenth-century 'discovery of industrialization' for the classical theorists of political economy and the 'founding fathers' of sociology. It is towards an elucidation of this claim that our study may be taken to be directed. It is an underlying assumption that if it is true that the discovery of the Third World in some way recapitulates the experience of the nineteenth-century theorists, then it is not unreasonable to suppose that the 'career' of 'development studies' will provide a series of unequivocal, undisguised, non-routinized, examples of social theorizing in action. The particular 'object' of our inquiry is taken as the 'career' of 'development studies', and this history we treat in the hope of uncovering and displaying something of the nature of social theorizing.

1.0 THE CONSTITUTION OF THE 'OBJECT' OF STUDY AND THE METHOD APPROPRIATE THERETO

The matter of the constitution of our 'object'[1] will serve to offer a preliminary statement, an over-view, of the way in which we shall treat the history of the period. It will also offer a programme for the study and establish the legitimacy of the enterprise. Having treated the 'object' of study, we will consider the method to be used.

As we want to claim that the theorist bestows coherence upon the period selected by virtue of the questions he is moved to raise, then it seems clear that this construction of an 'object' is itself a process. The particular interests of the theorist are lodged within the frame of his discipline, itself lodged within history. The 'object' of inquiry is a distillate of particular interests, disciplinary constraints and the common sense of the society of which the scholar is a member. Rather than simply announce the 'object' of the study, we will review, albeit in a simple fashion, this process.

In this work the period treated is bounded by two wars. This presents the period both formally, i.e. two dates, and commonsensically. Thus the start is indicated by the end of the Second World War, and the end point by the defeat of the USA in Viet-

nam. Now if this identifies the period formally, then the substantive issues/problems shaping it - that is, the criteria of
selection and coherence - are the changes in approach to problems of the development of the Third World. This aspect we take
to represent the experience of the discipline of 'development
studies', given our particular interest in argument strategies.

1.1

This matter of the changes in approach to development is the
key to the constitution of the 'object' of study. It permits our
inquiries to begin with the ideas of the practitioners themselves.
Thus if we ask to what extent is it legitimate to pick out theories of development as a discrete realm of discourse, or how
much is it a new separate discipline, and when did it start and
why, then we can identify three general sorts of answers. These
will provide the material, lodged within the dates noted, which
with the addition of our own questions will constitute our
'object'.

On the question of the independence and theoretical novelty
of the discipline of 'development studies', the three views are:
first, that it is not proper to single out 'development studies' as
the whole enterprise properly belongs to a positive science of
economics; second, that it is proper to single out 'development
studies' and that, moreover, they have good reason to be regarded as the basis of the first adequate economics; and third,
that it is an error to single out 'development studies' as these
concerns and questions should be subsumed within the study of
the historical development of the world capitalist system.

1.11

So, first, it may be argued that it is an error to single out
'development studies' as being anything other than a sub-
specialism of positive economic science. The purist Bauer[2]
adopts such a position. He seems to want to deny that 'development studies' and theories are especially novel in the light of
the efforts of colonial governments, which he takes to have been
pursuing development for many years, and the corresponding
intellectual reflection upon these matters. Any novelty development theories might have is that of being wrongheaded and generally mistaken in diagnoses and prescriptions. Bauer is critical
of aid and planning, arguing that neither are necessary conditions of development. Economics in the end is a form of technical assistance.

That economics is to be seen as a science, and that the proper
exchange of economics and the problems of the Third World is
one of the application/extension of the established, proven,
tools of the former to the circumstances of the latter, is generally taken for granted by those we can identify as taking this

line on the matter of the status of 'development studies'. However, those who take this line do not, in the main, adopt Bauer's
purism. The 'conventional wisdom' of 'development studies',
established in the immediate post-war period, is, as we shall see,
in its initial presentation quite clearly Keynesian. It is this that
Bauer rails against.

It is characteristic of the work in this early period of those
who would follow the general theoretical line indicated, that it
pursues what we can call an ideology of 'authoritative interventionism'. That 'development' was taken to be a technical matter
we have noted, but further, it was also assumed that the experts of the presently developed nations had access to the
requisite technical expertise. A relationship of super- and sub-
ordination was thus legitimated, and responsibility for the future
reserved for the technical experts of the developed nations and
their agents.

1,12

The second view on the matter of the disciplinary status of 'development studies' can be seen to be evidenced in the work of a
fairly diverse group of writers. In general we can suggest that
they would take it to be proper to single out 'development
studies', but it should be noted that there would be differences
in the strengths of their respective claims. The representatives
of our second view might be presented most conveniently as
three groups: together they encompass work on the fringe of
the economic orthodoxy detailed above, through to work on the
fringe of marxian schemes.

The first may be introduced by reference to Seers's 1963
article.[3] In it he denies that the orthodoxy of economics is of
any use when treating the economies of the Third World. Attention must be paid, on the one hand, to the institutional and
social context of the economies in question, and, on the other,
to their location in the world economy. The emphasis on 'situat-
ing' analysis is taken up by Streeten,[4] who is not only the
most philosophically sophisticated member of this group, but can
also be taken as Myrdal's exegetist.

Streeten advances the claim that 'development studies' only
got going after the end of the Second World War. The occasion
for this involves two sets of reasons: (1) problems of resources
and people are taken to be urgent in view of the population explosion and soluble in the light of the success of post-war Western European recovery; (2) political change, in the form of the
rise of the new states of the Third World and the start of the
Cold War, increases the concern of the 'West' for the 'proper'
development of these areas. The earlier, Keynesian-derived
efforts of the orthodox are taken to be a theoretically misconceived departure. The concepts used by 'development studies'
must necessarily be fashioned in the problem-situation of the
Third World societies themselves. The Streeten/Myrdal line is

resolutely problem-centred, and the wider implications of their efforts are not systematically developed. Whether they take themselves to have extended/revised/replaced the economic orthodoxy is not made clear; indeed their problem-centred scheme of 'institutional social theory' would probably dismiss the issue as uninteresting.

The second strand to be picked out is largely inspired by Latin American work. The theorist Prebisch makes the first break with the orthodox when in 1949 he rejects the Ricardian notion of international specialization which had justified Latin America's role in the world economy being restricted to that of primary product exporter. Prebisch advocates industrialization behind protective tariff barriers. The policy change is mirrored in theoretical revision: the equilibrium model of the orthodoxy is set aside in favour of a 'structuralist' analysis which takes the putative national economy to be a concatenation of 'residues', 'enclaves', and 'parasitic forms'. Later the gradual failure of ECLA reformism occasions a reworking of these views. In the middle and late 1960s the notions used were 'institutional' and 'structural' economics. According to Girvan,[5] the revision entailed (a) adding an historical aspect to structural and institutional method, and (b) giving the synthesis the empirical content necessary to generate a full theory of underdevelopment.

From Furtado,[6] Girvan draws an interesting point vis à vis the status of economics. Furtado comes to see the Latin American debate as resolving the issue of whether one or two economics were required to treat respectively 'rich' and 'poor'. The answer is that we are treating a world-historical system and that consequently one economics is needed - and it is to be found in the tradition exemplified in Furtado's own career. That the school of dependency economics began as a reaction against the economic orthodoxy was due to the latter's being inapplicable to the circumstances of the Third World, but now it transpires that the orthodoxy makes no sense in the circumstances of the rich either! If 'development studies' is seen as a product of the post-war period, then it is surely independent of the orthodoxy of economics which is now regarded as chimerical.

The third group of those who would affirm the novelty of 'development studies' are represented pre-eminently by A.G. Frank, though their views in this context are oddly insubstantial. In brief, to the above-noted dependency line there is to be added an influx of marxian notions which serves to produce what Leys[7] terms a 'left UDT/dependency'. The phrasing is deliberate and serves to indicate that the theoretical realm of underdevelopment theory/dependency is not abandoned, rather a political re-orientation takes place. However, in contrast to the two above-noted threads, each of which would grant 'development studies' a measure of autonomy, the marxist infusion is in a sense self-annihilating. It shifts from a political radicalization of common themes to a renunciation of its own perspective as being, ultimately, 'bourgeois' in theoretical character and liable, therefore, to 're-absorption'. The most recent messages from this group commend the adoption of a thoroughgoingly 'marxist' standpoint.

1.13

The third view on this matter of the independence and theoretical novelty of 'development studies' adopts the strategy of subsuming its concerns and questions within the very much broader framework of the analysis of the historical development of the world capitalist system. This view is exemplified, paradigmatically, in the work of those who regard themselves as either marxists or as working in a tradition of social theory which counts Marx as its most distinguished figure.

The major line of marxian analysis of the Third World is usually associated with Baran and the notion of 'dependency', where this connotes the subordinate incorporation of peripheral areas in the world economy. But if this can be regarded as the 'conventional wisdom' of the marxists, then it is also a disputed wisdom. The renaissance of marxian scholarship is recent. In the 'West' it is strongly associated with the 'New Left', and its initial engagement with the Third World was via the co-optation of 'liberation struggles' to the efforts of the New Left. The subsequent exchange between this circumstance-specific renewal and established traditions of theorizing within marxism, on the one hand, and, on the other, a dawning appreciation of the complexity of debate in respect of 'development', has produced, if not a theoretical Babel, then at least a highly complex discussion that has, as one centre, the question of the precise nature of a properly marxian analysis of the Third World. It is in this area of inquiry that we find the most ambitious efforts to theorize the matter of 'development'.

1.2

We have now taken note of the formal limits of our period of study, and have considered the various distinguishable efforts of the practitioners themselves - ordered around the matter of disciplinary status, itself called forth by our interest in argument forms. To this technical issue we must add a broader interest, both to give shape to the inquiry and to acknowledge recent debate within social science as to the precise nature of the endeavour.

We have noted above that we are interested in the idea that the 'career' of development studies might provide a series of examples of social theorizing in action, and that consequently it might be expected to illuminate the matter of the way in which social theorizing is to be done. We take the proper centre of such inquiry to be located within the ambit of the concerns of the marxian renaissance of scholarship to which we have referred.

The 'object' of our study, the 'career' of 'development studies' in the period 1945-75, is taken (in the light of the above report of the practitioners' views) to have involved, at least in the earlier efforts, the attempt to constitute an autonomous discipline; which project collapses under the combined weight of events, its own implausibility and its success in occasioning refinement in argument. The 'career' of 'development studies' is not taken to be the whole of the story of the renewal of marxian scholarship, but it might quite reasonably be taken to be a major part of the process of reconstituting that tradition of critical social inquiry exemplified in the work of Marx. Generally, the 'career' of 'development studies' is seen as an emergent sequence, such that a narrowly technical engagement gives way to a richer and increasingly subtle exercise in social theorizing.

1.3

Having reviewed the process of the construction of our 'object' of inquiry, we can here indicate the method of analysis appropriate thereto. Indeed, this method has been anticipated in the foregoing, both explicitly, in the references to the process of 'object' construction, where the mention of 'distillates' of various interests reveals a sociology-of-knowledge-informed approach, and implicitly - as will become clear a little later - in that the constitution of the 'object' by the theorist is taken to be determined by the resources available to the theorist. We claim that presumptions about the nature of a proper analysis are integral to the constitution of the 'object' of inquiry.

Having indicated that the 'objects' of social theoretical inquiry are here taken to be socially produced, and having reviewed the process of the constitution of our own 'object' in a fashion which reveals it to comprise a series of efforts to make sense of the exchange of rich and poor nations, it will come as no surprise that the notion of ideology figures centrally in our work. In line with the anticipations noted above, it appears both as an analytic technique and as a notion encompassing our presuppositions in respect of explanatory propriety.

First, it presents itself in the guise of the analytic stance of the sociology of knowledge. Thus the particular elements of the history of 'development studies' are treated by means of the preparation of sociology-of-knowledge-informed critiques. As our 'object' of study was taken as a distillate of various elements, so too are the various distinguishable efforts within 'development studies'. In particular, we consider 'exemplars' taken as representatives of 'schools', and of their work ask after: its milieu, the political demands made upon it, and the body of theoretical resources used. Clearly, this treatment presents these exemplars as producing ideologies, as this would be ordinarily and pejoratively understood. However, the reconsideration of the legacy of Marx within the social sciences has also seen a reconsideration of the notion of ideology, and here is our second area of use.

That we might properly use a notion of ideology as the methodological key to social theorizing can be established in a preliminary fashion by recalling recent interest in language. Thus, after MacIntyre,[8] we can argue that if it is true that thinking goes on by the use of our commonly accepted language ('language is practical consciousness', as Marx puts it), then the limits of my world equal the limits of the explanations available to me. The explanations available to me will be limited to those that I do accept, or could accept if they were spelt out to me. Now if this is my ideology, then clearly it is not going to be an elaborated scheme taken on board as a result of consumer choice amongst proffered alternatives, but rather it is a taken-for-granted body of knowledge which expresses some sort of structured/constituting relationship of self, social location, and explanations.

At this point the issue broadens in a fashion that introduces presently debated topics in social theory. The scope of these matters, and the idea of the non-arbitrariness of ideology, can be introduced by referring to the work of Giddens.[9]

In respect of the question of the nature of social theorizing and its proper method, Giddens approaches an answer via the 'debate with positivism'. Three streams are run together: (i) hermeneutics, the concern with understanding; (ii) phenomenology, the creation of everday life in the routine detail of social life, that is, in interaction; (iii) analytic philosophy, with its affirmation of the centrality of language to any adequate explanation of the social. The thrust of the effort is towards the presentation of an elaborated notion of praxis, where Marx is taken as an undeveloped counter-tradition to the orthodox 'Durksonian' scheme. This extension of the notion of praxis serves to elucidate the claim that men make their own histories and lives, but not as they choose. The extension proceeds via four steps: (a) it is granted that language equals reality; (b) it is noted that realities do change; (c) this introduces the process of making structures and the idea of the dual nature of structure as product and ground of interaction; (d) finally, language as the ground and vehicle of action reflects asymmetries of power inherent in action.

Now there seem to be two elements in all this. One is that ideas about the nature of language provide the basis of an analogy – thus as we have speech/language, so we have action and interaction, that is, the production of social life and an established structure that is over and above individuals and is the expression of and basis of action. The use of this analogy serves, it seems, to provide Giddens with the means whereby a sociological general theory of the construction of the social world might be envisaged. In addition to this, 'language' entails an ontology. Thus if 'language' constitutes the social world, then any relationist epistemology – that is, one involving centrally a subject object dualism – is denied. subject and object interpene-

trate, and 'explanations' become the central concern of social
scientific effort.

1.4

We now have an 'object' of inquiry, and have presented a methodological notion that seems appropriate to it. A history of the
'career' of 'development studies' might now be prepared. However, to proceed thus would be presently inappropriate. We
have constituted our 'object' by taking note of the debates, internal to 'development studies', in respect of the status of their
endeavour. This particular 'reading' of their work was occasioned by our interest in argument-construction; but these
interests are themselves to be lodged within the frame of the
discipline of learning governing our study. The constitution of
the 'object' of study is determined, in part, by the resources
available to the theorist, and these resources represent our
reading of that recent debate in social theory noted with Giddens
above. Given, then, that we shall treat the history of 'development studies' in the period indicated with a view to uncovering
the characteristic argument forms of the distinguishable efforts,
and moreover do so in the hope of illuminating the nature of
social theorizing itself, it seems appropriate to offer some preliminary statements in respect of our conception of social theory.

2.0 RECEIVED WISDOM: SOME SUPPOSITIONS OF OUR STUDY

These remarks are offered as an introduction to those theoretical
issues with which we are concerned: it is this cluster of problems which constitutes the formal counterpoint to the historical
material presented in the study. At the outset we have three
areas of concern: first, the question of the nature of the theorist's involvement with his work; second, the broader issue of
the nature of the exchange between theorists and their social
surroundings; and finally, the more abstract matter of the
nature of social theorizing, taken paradigmatically as 'ideology
construction', and the problems of this conception.

2.1

Hawthorn, in his history of sociological thought, remarks that
all eighteenth- and nineteenth-century theorists had a moral
model of man as a reference point around which data, explanations, and arguments were organized. Confronted with a given
theorist, we should proceed, advises Hawthorn, by asking 'what
exactly did he consider as a defensible social, political and moral
order? ....for it is that which most directly informed analysis.'[10] This is interesting for two reasons.

In the first place it lets us link, in an intuitively persuasive
way, theorist and theory; in that an element of the self-image
of the theorist is included as a basic organizing element of the
theorist's product. If we regard this as a piece of 'moral psychology', then we can extend it by looking at the notion of
integrity. This we can take to comprise two elements, one being
the demand for consistency in formulation of moral statements,
the other being the requirement of continuity of personal identity. The requirement of consistency in statements is general
to intellectual discourse, but the necessary link to personal self-
image would seem to be novel to moral discourse. The hoary old
problem of value freedom is 'solved' in that it is denied that this
is, at base, a coherent notion; that a person is thoroughly involved in what is being said is not a defect to be regretted and
removed, rather it is a necessary condition of that discourse
being moral discourse. Interesting support for this view comes
from Gellner, who makes social theorizing (though he does not
use this term) the attempt to make sense of novel and disturbing social situations. Thus sociology is seen as a nineteenth-
century invention in the face of the rise of the 'modern world'.
The 'transition' (a continuing and pervasive phenomenon for
Gellner) is marked by a loss of identity; this is, he says, 'the
very paradigm of a moral problem'.[11]
    The second point raised by Hawthorn is the closely related
question of the manner in which we take such a model of man to
be inserted into theorizing. Now Hawthorn builds, at the end of
his study, what he calls a 'typology of intentions' derived from
those theorists he has looked at. The first such 'intention', both
logically and historically, has been to account for man's place in
the 'scheme of things' in such a way as to distinguish man from
some external realm; or as he puts it, 'man is in some sense separate from nature'.[12] This first 'intention' is the base of all
subsequent theorizing; consequently he argues that: 'Only when
one has convinced oneself of the properties and possibilities of
human nature ... can one convince oneself of the properties and
possibilities of man's relation to society.'[13] To this we can say
that we want to agree that a model of man is central to theorizing.
But we would deny that this model emerges ex nihilo into the
mind of the theorist, or that it can be used as Hawthorn rather
seems to suggest: that is, first decide what social atoms are and
then how they fit together. Hawthorn's voluntaristic phrasing
invites a slide into regarding moral vision as the organizing
principle of the theorist's effort. But the point we wish to urge
is that moral vision is only one element of the organization of the
theorist's effort; the other part is his membership of a community of scholars, and here criteria of evidence, insight and moral
propriety are given. The theorist's activity is expressive within a given (albeit not fixed) frame.
    Reference to the 'disciplinary frame' invites the extension of
these remarks into the vexed area of the relationship of theorists
to their historical society, and the constitution of the problems

they approach. As the individual theorist is to be lodged in his
discipline, so that community is to be seen as lodged in history.
The matter of the extent to which models of man might be determined by specific historico-social locations is taken up in chapter
2 when we discuss the idea of 'development'.

2.2

With regard to the question of the nature of the engagement of
the theorist with the wider social world, the tripartite scheme
of 'interests' presented here by Fay must now, one supposes,
be widely known. Fay is concerned with the relationship of conceptions of social theorizing and political practice: thus he
reports that 'I am claiming that implicit in the theories of knowledge which I examine ... is a certain conception of the relation
between knowledge and action, and that such a conception, when
elaborated in the context of social life, is a political theory.'[14]
The three 'varieties' of reason, with their attendant politics,
can be presented, in brief, as follows: (1) the instrumental
knowledge of natural science, with its positivistic extension into
the realm of the social in the guise of 'policy science'; (2) the
interpretative appreciation of the webs of meaning-constitutive
social rules, and its political practice which revolves around
notions of broken communication; (3) the critical, lodged firmly
within the humanist and marxist traditions, and characterized
by its emancipatory engagement. Fay takes this line of thought
to be the only candidate for a plausible social science.
    This tripartite division is reworked in a sociological context by
Bauman,[15] who proposes to distinguish, on the one hand,
(1) Durksonian sociology, and (2) the existential critiques of
that orthodoxy. Yet these two are adjudged to remain the same,
in this sense: they are both committed to a notion of 'truth' as
describing things 'as they really are' and providing thereby a
firm basis for action. The 'true description of the facts' is the
arbiter of debate. In this tradition of social philosophizing such
a stance is taken as submission to positivism. Horkheimer and
Adorno[16] have traced the historical/intellectual route whereby
the open-ended and emancipatory reason of the Enlightenment
collapses into a restricted descriptivism. The historical base for
this is indicated by Goldmann[17], who argues, in his essay on
the Enlightenment, that a triumphant bourgeoisie did not need
or want critical negative philosophy; what they did need was a
positive philosophy which affirmed, by its moral dis-engagement
and technical manipulative mode of reasoning, the emergent
status quo. To these two Bauman contrasts (3) emancipatory
reason; it is characterized as not seeking to describe the world
taken for granted, but rather as trying to fracture that common
sense. It aims, we are told, to promote 'historical' at the expense of 'natural' reasoning, and Marx is taken to provide the
most advanced example of such 'historical' reasoning.

The nature of the 'engagement' of the theorist will concern us throughout our substantive analyses, as we observe the various strategies of self-deception on offer, and it is a matter to which we shall return in our concluding remarks.

The difference between those theorists' efforts which aim, on the one hand, to 'describe the world' and those which, on the other hand, endeavour primarily to 'express a response to the world' has occasioned extensive debate in respect of the matter of validation/authentication. We can take note of this for two reasons: (1) it points up the difference between orthodox and critical theory introduced above, and (2) it lets us sharpen a hitherto implicit commitment to the notion of a critical stance, by introducing a distinction between 'deployment' and 'grounding'.

Both Fay and Bauman note that the confirmation of the efforts of the critical theorist is, in part, accomplished by the theorist's product becoming a significant cultural object. In the case of the work of the natural scientist, the community of experts does the testing in accordance with the criteria of validity current in the community, and if approved, the product is released for use by the population at large. But in the case of the efforts of the critical theorist, testing within the community of experts is preliminary to the test of historical relevance. Thus Bauman notes, 'Authentication - becoming true in the process - can occur only in the realm of praxis, of which the institutionalized, partial discourse of professional scientists constitutes only the initial stage.'[18] This revision of the orthodox scheme of science is indeed radical, but it seems to me that it grants too much to the orthodox in that 'grounding' a theoretical effort is still taken to be the business of the expert and, more importantly, the initial stage. As will become clear in our substantive analyses, we take a more jaundiced view of the matter of building theoretical efforts; social theories we take to be constructed, at particular times, in particular places, and with specific intent. The matter of their 'grounding' is technical and secondary. The orthodox interest in epistemology - including the revisions/extensions proposed by Bauman and Fay - is implicitly demoted, and the practical question of ranking competing ideologies comes to the fore. This is a matter of the plausibility of various efforts at explanation, and seems to be a wider issue than orthodox schemes usually treat.

2.3

If we return to the familiar area of the matter of 'grounding', we can approach our conception of the business of social theory. We do so in the context of academic discourse, and we present the claim that the construction of ideologies, ordinarily understood, is the paradigm of what it is to be engaged with society in a social-theoretical manner. To put this another way, if we are asked what is it to do social theory, we reply: it is to be involved in constructing ideologies.

Hollis and Nell concern themselves with this problem of 'grounding' in their book 'Rational Economic Man'. They distinguish three sorts of model – predictive, programming, and production – and they describe their respective functions. Thus, 'a production model gives conditions for the system to continue, a programming model shows how to improve performance, and a prediction model forecasts whether the conditions will in fact be met or the improvement forthcoming'.[19] The models present a story in logical time – a blueprint to which reality can be adapted, or by means of which it can be altered. Hollis and Nell go on to point to two areas of debate with regard to the career of such a story in logical time: thus it will be taken up and used (1) if it is a sound theory (and this is made to be a technical matter for the scholarly group in question), and (2) if it is recognizably a solution to perceived problems.

The issue of 'grounding' is presented in epistemic guise. Hollis and Nell affirm a 'conceptual rationalism' and introduce it as follows: 'positivism civilized logic making it a human invention, but only to insist on the utter bruteness of the independent facts. Pragmatism civilized the facts too. A true belief is true only insofar as it coheres with all others we choose to believe at the time.'[20] Yet as pragmatism is right to say that facts are theory-laden, so Hollis and Nell argue that we must regard theories as independent.

Theories are independent in that they are derived from necessary truths which 'introduce central concepts which define the subject and scope of theories'.[21] They go on to claim that 'a sound theory is a system of necessary truths whose application is a contingent matter'.[22] These necessary truths are 'real definitions'; that is, they tell us what a thing essentially is if it is to count as that sort of thing. It is to be distinguished (we are reminded) from the usual trio of lexical, stipulative, and persuasive definitions.

Setting aside, for the moment, the questions that occur in respect of this scheme,[23] we can go on to note that the practical test of such a rationalist theory is going to be dependent upon the richness and problem-appropriateness of its assumptions. It is pointed out that in contrast to positivism (which says: Never mind the assumptions, what about the successful predictions?), rationalism urges that sound theory depends upon its assumptions. With regard to economics, Hollis and Nell proceed to dismantle the orthodoxy: its empiricist positivist prop is useless, and its assumptions fantastic. A set of assumptions underpinning classical marxian economics is advanced instead.

If we turn to Marx, we can extend this discussion of rationalism by invoking the work of Rockmore, who is concerned to treat the relationship of philosophy and science in Marx. In the course of this analysis he finds that he is able to offer some conclusions on the structure of Marx's work: thus he takes the effort to be constituted by a set of philosophical ideas. Rockmore argues that: 'Three of the Marxian philosophy's distinctive characteristics are

monism, a categorical scheme, and philosophic anthropology, all
of which are general features of 19th century philosophy.'[24]
It is the second aspect which interests us here. What is the
character of the 'categorical' approach detected in Marx? First,
it is a matter of procedure; in the 'Grundrisse', claims Rockmore,[25]

> Marx suggested that there are only two approaches to exper-
> ience: either one can begin with concrete or real existence,
> then progress to abstract relations in order finally to recon-
> stitute the real in terms of abstract concepts; or conversely,
> one can begin from abstract categories, such as population,
> in order to reconstitute the real directly.

It is the latter procedure that is affirmed by Marx as correct.
Second, as regards the nature of these categories, they are out
of the Hegelian school with the important difference that they
are not permitted to become fixed; 'on Marx's view categories
correspond to actual social relations ...and need to be revised
as society changes'.[26] Third, in respect of the deployment of
these ideas, the categorical element continues to be central and
presents itself as the land/labour/capital set: of this Rockmore
notes, 'First it presents a series of categories adequate for the
interpretation of any and all aspects of capitalistic economy.
Second the inner arrangement is hierarchical.'[27] This hierarchy revolves around the notion of alienated labour, derived in
turn from philosophical anthropology - Marx's model of man.
    If we now ask how we produce a social-theoretical analysis of
some set of circumstances, then we may answer provisionally
that it involves the 'deployment of a morally informed categorical frame' whose product might properly, and non-pejoratively,
be regarded as an ideological schema serving to legitimate and
order action in the world. Now this pitches the matter at a general level, one of 'broad treatments'. However, we do not want
to restrict the 'ideological' to this realm. Following Giddens,[28]
'ideology' is not taken as a discrete realm of discourse; rather
we say discourse can be more or less ideologically elaborated.
Social-theoretical engagement, as we have detailed it here with
references to Marx and classical political economy, we take to be
the paradigm of ideologically elaborated discourse.
    This view, as will become clear, informs our substantive anal-
yses of the 'schools' of 'development studies'. Producing
sociology-of-knowledge-informed studies, ordered around the
distinction between conception and intent, is a critical strategy
that derives quite obviously from our notion of ideology construction. It should also be clear that this is a fairly low-level
use of the idea of critique. At this point we can introduce an
extension to our core conception of social-theoretical engagement:
Habermas and the extended notion of critique used in that tradition of thought. Here the ideas of democracy, critique and
ideology-ranking come together, in that the latter pair suppose

an ideal speech situation which in turn supposes a democratic
society.
   We can now draw out a wider view of social theorizing; we take
social theorizing to be involved with the construction, criticism,
and comparative ranking of ideological schemas.

3.0 A PROGRAMME FOR THE REST OF THE STUDY

Our 'object' of inquiry is the 'career' of 'development studies'
in the period 1945-75, and we treat this history in the hope of
displaying something of the nature of social theorizing. Our
approach to this history involves the construction of an emergent
series/critique of the body of work in question, and it revolves
around the issue of the status of 'development studies' as a discipline of learning. Three general views are identified. The
earliest regarded development as a technical matter of the appropriate application of the established procedures of economics,
where economics was taken as a 'positive science'. We have labelled these theorists 'the positivists', and their work is considered in Part II of the study. The efforts characteristic of the
'middle period' adopted varieties of 'sociologized' economics, and
lodged claims for the independence and novelty of 'development
studies'. These theorists we have called 'the radicals' and they
are treated in Part III of the study. To complete the substantive
work, we look at the efforts of the most recent 'school', who
deny the independence and novelty of 'development studies' and
subsume its concerns in a wider historico-economic schema which
revolves around the idea of a world capitalist system. These we
label 'the marxists' and their work is treated in Part IV of the
study.
   Throughout the presentation of this historical material, which
treats the constitution of various ideological efforts[29] in a
sociology-of-knowledge-informed fashion, a series of theoretical
issues will be taken note of; these revolve around those three
themes we have introduced. In Part V of the study we present
some concluding remarks on the matter of social theorizing itself,
and on the more immediate question of the nature of the engagement of the 'Western' scholar with matters of the Third World.
   Before we begin this programme there remains one task that
can usefully be accomplished at this stage. Routinely, in texts
of a general nature treating matters of the Third World, there is
some self-disclosure on the part of the writer of ideological or
value positions taken. Now in this case, as we have argued that
social theorizing is necessarily and crucially engaged, something
more than pro-forma declarations seems to be called for. We will
therefore present, in chapter 2, a statement in respect of the
idea of development that is supposed in this study.

2   The idea of development

INTRODUCTION

The idea of 'development' tends to be presented in the literature
of 'development studies' as a technical notion; so 'development'
is taken as entailing (or as evidenced by) the accretion of some
set of characteristics. In what is arguably the crudest version
of the stance, these characteristics are virtually taken as a set
of artefacts. Thus 'modernization theory', in its undisguised
formulations, sees the process of development as the business of
the acquisition by the underdeveloped countries of the traits and
characteristics of the developed countries. Of course, it is true
that the orthodox lines in 'development studies' do not all display this transposition of the politico-ethical into the technical
in quite such a transparent fashion; indeed, the switch can be
made quite subtly. In the case of Myrdal's 'Fabianism', for example, the issues arising from the fact that to affirm a notion of
'development' is to affirm a politico-ethical stance are not dismissed. Rather, they are set aside; a notion of 'crisis politics'
is invoked, and it is asserted that in these circumstances the
course we must take is obvious. One may hazard that the Myrdalian claim to the obviousness of the propriety of the engagement
of 'development studies' represents the response of the mainstream of the discipline.
   It will be the business of this chapter, at its most general
level, to recall attention to the engagement entailed by deploying the notion of 'development'; we hope to make it clear that
'development' is a politico-ethical notion and not a technical one.
To put this another way, 'development' is not the simple accretion of some set of artefacts, cultural/industrial/social, it is
rather the instantiation of a politico-ethical orientation. It may
present itself 'in reality' as the accumulation of artefacts, but it
would be naive to reduce it to that accumulation.
   There are more particular interests to be pursued. Most triv-
ially, we offer an essay in ideological self-disclosure. The more
interesting questions revolve around two matters. First, as regards social theorizing per se, we have declared that the paradigm case of social-theoretical argument is the construction of an
ideological schema where this construction involves the 'deployment of a morally informed categorical frame'. We take this politico-ethical (moral) aspect of theorizing to be given, at least in
its general outline. So what is this moral core? We will here present an abstract treatment focusing upon the origins and scope

of the idea of progress. The notion of 'development' can be regarded as either the discipline ('development studies') - specific
instantiation of the idea of progress - or (rather more loosely)
as a simple synonym. As a detailed investigation of usage would
be required to establish the former reading, we have tended to
regard 'development' as a synonym for 'progress'.

A matter which flows from the above-noted views is our second
concern. If it is true that the politico-ethical aspect of theorizing is in some way given, then how should we approach treatments of the matters of the Third World: in particular, are we
not inevitably committing ourselves to a fixed stance and opening ourselves thereby to charges of one-sided insensitivity to
the views of the people of the Third World themselves? We follow
up these issues by anticipating[1] our substantive analyses.
Thus we take these substantive efforts as exercises in social
theorizing and consequently as morally informed. We can treat
these stances as variations upon our already identified core set
of ideas and offer a series of instantiations of the notion of progress. The issue of the one-sidedness or otherwise of our
politico-ethical stance towards matters of the Third World is investigated through the various instances of the idea of progress.

1.0 THE ORIGINS OF THE IDEA OF PROGRESS

We begin with the origins of the idea of progress in intellectual
history and we note two approaches. The general ideas will be
presented by using Passmore's philosophical history.[2] Passmore relates the career of the notions involved as a history of
ideas; tracing the shifts in argument and the various problems
thrown up, faced, evaded or simply not seen. The context of
these ideas we will note using Pollard's sociology-of-knowledge-
informed history.[3]

The idea of progress is modern, which is to say, it belongs to
the post-Renaissance period of European history. But if it is a
modern notion, then it can also be seen as one recent manoeuvre
in an even longer argument - that which Passmore identifies as
treating the idea of the perfectibility of man. It is reported that
the notions of perfection are based in Greek philosophy and are
taken up by Christian theologians. The Christian intervention
entailed the denial of the possibility of perfection here on earth
in favour of preparation for perfection in some after-life. But in
the fourteenth century the Renaissance humanists present a
notion drawn from a reinterpreted Aristotle, that of civic perfection.

The impact of Renaissance humanism - its ethic, its science
and its success - results in a shift of gravity of discussions of
perfection which Passmore sums up under three points: (a) perfection comes to be defined in natural not metaphysical terms;
(b) it is now seen that it has to be gained with the help of one's
fellows rather than with God's grace or individual effort;

(c) there is a shift in focus from an unrealizable purity of motive towards doing the maximum of good. This shift also involves the view that the contemplative life is that of the scholar/scientist and not that of the mystic, and it is the rise of science that is taken by progressives of the time as the key to subsequent change.

The idea of progress emerges in the eighteenth century and its emergence can be viewed in two ways. In the first place, as an idea, it may be interpreted as an answer to the problem presented by Locke. Thus in the course of the theoretical shift just noted the ideas of perfectibility and perfection are divorced. The general doctrine is reformulated such that all men are capable of being perfected and to a limitless degree. If it is asked how, then the candidate is plain: that is education, and Locke shows that it can do the job. This lays the ground for discussions of education and social action in the eighteenth and nineteenth centuries. However, the classic texts of education fail to confront a problem that Marx will point out, that the educator needs educating. Locke may have established that man can be perfected, but the gap between perfectibility and actually being perfected has to be bridged.

If secular perfectibilism lacked the metaphysical guarantor of a God, then the position was retrieved by two steps; in the first the educator is made subsidiary to a method; in the second he is abolished altogether. The first step was to conceive of human history in such a way that it guaranteed that man will continue to improve his condition; if this is done, then the occasional errors of educators, law-givers or whatever can be set aside as unimportant. We arrive at the idea of progress. Passmore goes on to relate that this idea was argued for in part inductively; for example, it was pointed out that the optics of Newton were superior to those of Descartes, but the major discovery of the early modern philosophers was method.

The second view of the emergence of the idea of progress involves taking note that the focus on method reflects the social expectations of the theorist in alliance with commerce. Thus Pollard points out that these ideas were not taken up in a vacuum. The advance of science is not a result of its sudden evident superiority coupled with a new tolerance on the part of the Church. Rather, the advance depended upon the support of powerful groups. Pollard's summary is familiar: 'it was the New Men of Europe, the merchants and traders and manufacturers ... whose experience tallied with the new philosophy and whose needs called forth the new science'.[4] Passmore notes that the Enlightenment thinkers were confident that a science of man had been established and would be used. Why this confidence? The self-perception of the Enlightenment thinkers involved their emergence as a new and distinct social group: they were a self-conscious community, seeing themselves as the natural governors of society through an equally natural alliance with the commercial classes. As Passmore puts it, 'overt power to the middle class, actual power to the intellectuals'.[5] Progress is evident in history, appropriate to the present, and underpinned by reason.

This optimism reaches a peak in the work of the philosophes, and thereafter declines and becomes diffuse. The idea of progress is generally accepted through the nineteenth century, but is presented by various groups in various countries. The intellectual and social career of the notion, so to say, is very complex. Greatly simplifying matters, we can again offer a two-fold reading. Thus, first, treating the history of ideas side, we can note that as an idea the notion of secular progress lacks a guarantor and that the response to this, after the unsatisfactory nature of the focus on method is seen, is to abolish the educator altogether and to invoke guarantors in the shape of history and biology. Thus we have theories of progress as natural development. With Darwin we can associate a range of evolutionisms, but the initial precision of formulation tends, in the social-theoretical versions, to the descriptive general. Historical guarantors are first presented by Leibniz. Themes of unfolding by means of dialectic present social mechanisms and are better explanations. A central nineteenth-century figure here is Marx.

If we turn to the second reading, the social responses, then the alliance of commerce with science is seen as restrictedly progressive given the incompatibility of an open-ended progressive method oriented to the closure implied in the establishment of the bourgeois state. The response is the search for a new motor of progress, and in Marx the endemic conflict of bourgeois and working class is grasped in his class dialectic. On the part of the bourgeoisie, the progressiveness of science in respect of the social is curbed, and classic political economy becomes social science.

We have now traced the origin and career of the idea of progress from its inception in Greek philosophy to the forms taken by the nineteenth-century theorists of industrialization. The range of debate relevant to present social matters we take to be fixed at this time: so we inherit, on the one hand, the marxian-classical conceptions of progress, and, on the other, those of orthodox social science. The range of subsequent variation (with national sociologies, particular streams of thought, etc.) we do not wish to consider. Instead, with regard to the career of the idea of progress we shift directly to our own area of interest; that is, the post-war career of 'development studies'. Before doing that, however, we consider the scope of the idea of progress.

2.0 THE SCOPE OF THE IDEA OF PROGRESS

We have noted the route whereby the idea of the individual pursuit of perfection was transformed into naturally guaranteed social progress. We have also seen that as this key idea of the

tradition of political thought we inhabit was in point of formation
it simultaneously assumed two forms: the one pursuing the core,
now taken as a radical line, and the other endeavouring to fix
change either in place by invoking schemes of overweening generality or in a mundane realm (cf. Hawthorn where, in the USA
in particular, progress is equated with increasing consumption).
We can now turn to consider the ethico-political substance of
these two lines. This will let us treat the issue of the scope of
the idea of progress.

That there are two such distinguishable lines in political theory is a familiar claim and there are diverse characterizations
of their respective substance. Berlin, for example, distinguishes
'positive' and 'negative' ideas of liberty, where the former is
pernicious and characterized thus:[6]

> I wish above all, to be conscious of myself as a thinking, will-
> ing, active being, bearing responsibility for my choices and
> able to explain them by reference to my own ideas and pur-
> poses. I feel free to the degree that I believe this to be true
> and enslaved to the degree that I am made to realize that it is
> not.

This passage is quoted with approval by Macpherson[7], whose
work we will here rely on.

The drift of Macpherson's work is that we can separate out
two traditions of politico-moral thought and argue that the more
familiar scheme is unsatisfactory and should be revised to meet
the criticisms of the overshadowed counter-tradition. We can
approach the argument - which presents itself in many aspects -
via the distinction that can be drawn between 'powers' and
'power'.

The use of the notion of power in treatments of political conflict
is familiar, and Lukes[8] analyses power in this fashion. Lukes
makes the core of the idea of power, 'power over' and contrasts
this with orthodox schemes which focus on voluntaristic decision-
making. But Macpherson objects to the use of what he sees as
the restricted starting point of political conflict. This focuses
upon the issues of the source of power, but Macpherson wants
to claim that concern for the purpose of power is a richer orientation. It is one that reintroduces classical notions of developmental power: 'power to be', an ethical notion, and the base of
the idea of 'powers' in contrast to 'power', a descriptive notion.
With this schema, Macpherson turns to consider what he takes to
be the justificatory theorem of Western capitalism, that is liberal
democracy.

The justificatory claims of liberal democracy, to maximize men's
power(s), involves, it is claimed, a vacillation between the two
notions of power. It is argued that the democratic notions (that
is, 'powers') are extra-liberal and attempt to link with pre-
seventeenth-century notions of man which made his activities
intrinsically valuable: the Aristotelian derived scheme of civic

virtue and flowering of natural capacities. This is the ethical
concept of powers, and includes access to whatever external
means are needed for their exercise. Limitation of access constitutes, therefore, a diminution of ethical powers. The descriptive, liberal, concept of power includes a man's natural
powers plus whatever gains he has made by controlling the
powers of others. A man's power is just that which he presently
has. The conflation of the two concepts of power, the one treating man as concerned to develop intrinsic skills and valuable
thereby, and the other treating man as consumer, is attempted
in response to intellectual and social events by J.S. Mill. Mill
attempts to introduce the ethical concept, but into a liberal capitalist theory. The descriptive concept of power is used in analysis (of the liberal market economy), and the ethical in justifi-
cations (of the claimed result of maximization of individual and
social good). But the two notions of power are incompatible, and
the power that liberal democracy claims to maximize is not that
which it in fact maximizes.

With regard to the scope of the notion of progress we can, in
the light of Macpherson's analyses, identify the two limiting
cases that we inherit from the nineteenth century. On the one
hand, the efforts of a victorious bourgeoisie to fix their position
produces the doctrine of liberal democracy, taken by Macpherson
to be a fundamentally incoherent conflation of two models of man:
the liberal regarding him as an infinitely desirous consumer, and
the democratic seeing him as possessed of natural talents and
attributes – the development of which is his proper nature. On
the other hand (and in terms of Passmore's history of ideas representing the more plausible central line of reasoning), we have
what is now seen as the radical line, that is the democratic, with
its model of man as a rational doer rather than consumer.

3.0 THE IDEA OF DEVELOPMENT IN TREATMENTS OF MATTERS
OF THE THIRD WORLD

When the question of sensitivity to value assumptions in the context of stances adopted toward Third World matters usually
arises, it does so in terms of claims to the crudity of some stance
or other. That is to say, discussion seems to proceed by regular
steps; first the identification of some set of assumptions, followed by the lodging of claims in respect of their impropriety,
and finally the indication of some set of counter-claims. The central question at issue never seems to be confronted directly;
that is, the question 'just what is a proper politico-ethical stance'
does not appear.

In the light of our discussions of the origin and scope of the
idea of progress this is perhaps unsurprising; and for two
reasons. First, the notion appears on all occasions (inevitably)
in some specific practical context, as an element of some ideological intervention in the world. This, we can suppose, suggests

to disputants that present consideration of the idea should treat
present instances of the idea; that is, focus on the lines taken
within current debate in respect of practical theoretical engagements. Second, it is clear that to approach the matter abstractly
would involve much very complex argument, and, moreover,
argument whose major reference points within established work
would be given by the concerns of moral philosophers rather
than those of the social theorists. Thus much unnecessary work
could ensue.

We shall follow the routine strategy and approach an answer
to the core question of the nature of a proper stance by offering reasons for the exclusion of certain presently affirmed lines.
We will, however, in the light of our insistence that 'development' be taken as an ethico-political and not a technical term,
formalize the procedure to some extent so as to take some account
of the more abstract aspects involved. In respect of each instantiation of the idea of progress we ask two questions. How close
is it to the core of the idea of progress, as discussed above?
And how does it stand methodologically with respect to definition
of a 'crude' effort?

We want a definition of a 'crude' effort, so as to be able to
order (methodological) discussion, and we can construct such a
definition by negating what we take to be a subtle effort. A
'crude' effort would be characterized most easily in this light as
one that was un-reflective in both conception and intent, and
which failed to treat the implications of the idea of 'the social
construction of social theory'.

The sociology-of-knowledge-informed terms present themselves
in our required definition as the notions of europomorphism and
europocentrism. The first we can understand as the affirmation
of the priority of what are held to be typically European categories of thought,[9] and the second we can take to be the
affirmation of the priority of the material and practical interests
of the 'West'. With this we can now move on to treat the broad
distinguishable instances of the idea of progress in the post-war
'career' of 'development studies'. These instances are given to
us by the programme identified in chapter 1: 'positivist', 'radical', and 'marxist'.

3.1

The first instantiation of the notion of progress we take to be
presented by that 'school' we have labelled 'positivist'. We hold
this to belong to what Ehrensaft[10] has dubbed the 'pre-Seers
consensus' and it may be seen to comprise two versions -- an
earlier UK/UN flavoured effort, and a later distinctly US schema --
of a basic idea of authoritative intervention. If we unpack this
notion of authoritative intervention, which we see as analogous
to Fay's 'policy science', we come up with a scheme of analysis/
engagement which takes the exchange of the theorist/world to be

in essence the knowing manipulation of the latter by the former.
Typically, an empiricist epistemology which holds 'theory' to be
a complex summary statement of the correspondences of events
and reports is used. The methodology of the scheme is that of
modelling. Although the theorists usually lodge disclaimers in
respect of the status they would wish to accord these models,
they are (given their formalism, empiricism and technical manipulative intent) inevitably more or less scientistic. Theorists
adopt the role of experts, and the procedure for any practical
analysis involves the disaggregation of abstract models to fit
given circumstances.

With regard to the ideological function of this scheme, we can
identify the legitimation of a relationship of super- and sub-
ordination whereby the 'development' of the present underdeveloped countries is ordered by the experts of the developed
countries and their agents. 'Development' or progress is understood as a technical matter, and taken as elicited by this authoritative intervention and as presenting itself in indices of
economic growth. Progress is equated with growth.

That the notion of progress used by the early 'positivist'
school is, in the light of our treatment of the origin and scope
of the idea, firmly lodged within the (now dominant) peripheral
line should be clear. The idea of progress is presented in narrowly materialistic guise and is to be secured by orthodox social
science.

Where then does this instantiation of the idea of progress
stand vis à vis our definition of what it is to adopt a 'crude'
approach? Evidently it is close enough to be worth noting; the
theorists of the orthodoxy would reply to a question in respect of
the propriety of their efforts with a dual affirmation. The present extent of the line's reflexivity we will treat in chapters 3 and
4. Here we can offer a sketch of an answer in the form of notes
on its history. (It is the English theorists whom we have particularly in mind here).

(1) As regards the issue of reflexivity, we can identify a long
history of presumption in this regard which cuts across a spec-
trum of issues: from questions of participation in government to
questions of rationality itself; from regarding colonies as reser-
voirs of resources for the home economy to treating them as
responsibilities to be discharged. Probably the most uncompro-
mising general statement appears in the late nineteenth-century
jingoistic themes of the complete superiority of Western man in
contrast to the childish natives. These images are called forth
not as a result of the exchange between people of the Third
World and Westerners, but by the politics of colonialism. Sachs
points out that the image of the 'native' shifts from the time of
the philosophes, who used it as a model of man untainted by
civilization's vices, towards the routine deprecatory view of the
late nineteenth century. Sachs notes: 'after the French Revolution of 1789 the noble savage ceased to be indispensable to the
development of European ideas, and furthermore the race for the

colonies resulted in a hardening of attitudes on the part of Europeans'.[11] As an ideology it assumes that the colonial powers have a 'civilizing mission' - and if we wanted an elaborated, paradigmatic, model of a 'crude' approach this is presumably the place to start gathering material.

(2) Subsequently, this stance relaxes, and Hetherington reports that the period 1920-40 sees a clear shift in position from the above exploitation to a notion of responsibility, where this entailed ideas of eventual independence. Curiously, it was German demands for return of their colonies which prodded the British into action.[12] Hetherington notes: 'In the 1920s the colonies were still largely thought of as an extension of Great Britain. ...By the 1930s the eventual separation of the African colonies from Great Britain could be envisaged.'[13]

(3) There is a further softening of the position in the case of the orthodoxy of the immediate post-war period; and whilst it would be clearly unreasonable to link in any very direct fashion those we have called the 'positivists' with the jingoists associated with (1) above, there is, none the less, a clear family resemblance. The modern version of this stance, whose character we noted above, would deny that its effort was un-reflexive if by this it is granted that an error of some sort is being made. Thus both 'growth' and 'modernization' theorists argue or assume that the developed 'West' just is the model, and that orthodox economics are scientific and thereby applicable generally. It is at this point that critics of the orthodoxy become suspicious that what is in progress is a largely verbal shift, akin to replacing 'backward' with 'developing', and that what we have is a sophisticated reformulation of the jingoistic scheme. It is pointed out that orthodox economics is not scientific in the sense its practitioners would like to claim, and nor is the history of the 'West' a programme for subsequent nation states - the idea of 'recapitulation' is taken as a nonsense.

We hold the view that the idea of progress affirmed by this 'school' is, of the three we shall consider, the most impoverished. Furthermore, we take the theoretical engagement of this 'school' to be the least plausible of those we shall consider, and this we would hope to make clear in our subsequent substantive analyses.

3.2

The second instantiation of the idea of progress we take to be presented by the efforts of that group of theorists we have labelled 'radicals'. All begin with orthodox economics (Myrdal, Furtado and Frank are our 'exemplars' here) and reject it for what has been called 'sociologized economics'. Progress is no longer associated with economic growth, called forth by the application of the technical expertise of the economists, but is conceived more broadly: it becomes equated with ordered social reform.

For present purposes we can collapse Frank and Furtado into one; that is, read their differences as being due to Frank's polemics. This being so, we have two schemes to note: Myrdal's 'world welfarism' and Latin American 'dependency'. Of them, we may note that both are interventionist schemes, seeing the theorist's business as the production of knowledge of an instrumental kind. Nevertheless, it is also true that their conceptions of social-theoretical engagement, though different, are markedly richer than those of the economics-dominated orthodoxy.

We can trace the links and revisions around three important points. (1) Problem specificity: the claims of the orthodox to be applying or extending a generally applicable intellectual (scientific) scheme is denied. Thus NIST[14] is piecemeal, sceptical, empiricist and insists upon the pursuit of realism in models. This in turn attaches to the key idea that concepts have ecologies; which is to say that they only work in certain circumstances and, contrariwise, knowledge of the problem situation is a prerequisite of the construction of appropriate concepts. The general methodological dictum is the pursuit of problem-specific formulations and not general theories. Similarly 'dependency' rejects the claims of the orthodox and, through a series of steps (which we uncover in the career of Furtado) a methodology which treats structural, institutional and historical factors emerges. 'Dependency' resembles NIST in that it began as an attempt to theorize the situation of the Latin American economies, that is, it sought to be relevant: but paradoxically it ends – with Furtado – by claiming to be the first generally adequate economics, in contradistinction to the limited scope of the orthodoxy. (2) Valuation: the claims of the orthodoxy to neutrality of expert status are denied, but in different fashions. Both NIST and 'dependency' respond to their engagement in the social processes of which they write; but their proposals in this respect differ, and their doing so we may take to reflect their circumstances. Thus Myrdal's efforts lodge within the experience of 'decolonization' and concern themselves with reworking long-established colonial relationships. Power is to be handed over; there is a continuity of governmental procedure, and 'development' is to be ordered authoritatively. Myrdal writes for the reasonable men in charge of the new states' planning machinery. Ehrensaft rightly calls the entire scheme 'Fabian'. With 'dependency' the position is rather different: the pursuit of relevance which moved early 'dependency' work admits of a range of development that is different to that permitted by the injunction to problem-specificity which informed NIST. 'Dependency' has a more orthodox frame than NIST; and this, when coupled with the stance's evidently politically blocked circumstances (for in Latin America, at this time, the reasonable men are, typically, not in control of the state), issues in a drift to generality. Thus we have the claim to have replaced the orthodoxy on a general level. (Frank, we might note, offers here a third version, the shift to political activism.) (3) Scientism: we have noted that Furtado remains

close to orthodoxy, so too does Myrdal. Both NIST and 'dependency' are empiricist interventionisms, though their theorizing is
suffused with an appreciation of the social character of both
that which they study and their study of it. Indeed, much of
what is theoretically characteristic of these efforts flows from
the tension between the restrictions they place upon themselves
by their respective acknowledgments of the dictates of the orthodox conceptions of science and its extension to the social, on
the one hand, and their continuing and central urge to practical
engagement, on the other.

Progress is conceived of as ordered social reform. If we ask
where they fit in respect of our treatment of the idea of progress, then the answer is that clearly they remain within the
(now dominant) peripheral line which attaches to orthodox social
science. However, that said, we can add that if it is desired to
construct a policy science in the area of 'development studies'
then these efforts must be regarded as prime candidates. In
particular, Myrdal's 'Fabianism' can be readily seen as subtle,
humane and plausible.

That the orthodoxy could conceivably be seen as 'crude' was
made plausible by offering a series of stages; jingoistic, revised,
present. With NIST and 'dependency' the matter is a little more
difficult. So, as regards the location of these approaches to
'development' in connection with our definition of a 'crude'
approach, we may note that in respect of intent both would reject any suggestion of favouring the interests of the metropolitan centres, claiming that their interest is the establishment of
new economies, not the reinforcement or sustaining of subordinate incorporation. We can note that in neither case has this
intent been questioned: there is no suggestion, as there was
with the orthodoxy above, that their efforts might be taken as
(self-deluding) reformulations of a narrow and unreflective
orthodoxy. Both operate within the injunction of 'nationalist
developmentalism'.

As regards the matter of conception and our definition of the
'crude', whereby self-serving categories of analysis are blandly
assumed to apply generally, both NIST and 'dependency' would
deny that their schemes could be regarded as 'crude'. The replies would be different, but both would be rather ambiguous.
Furtado claims to transcend and encompass the orthodoxy,
which is taken to be cleansed and properly established. Myrdal
too looks to establish a defensible procedure, but in doing so
professes to resolve problems of valuation by lodging appeals to
'obviousness'.

With Furtado we shall note (this is presented in chapter 6) a
progression in his work, from a scientistic pursuit of a typology
of models of economies and their sectors to the dynamic scheme
of 'dependency' with its 'structural/institutional/historical'
method. Furtado, having begun with the pursuit of relevance,
claims that this 'dependency' scheme offers a generally adequate
economics, in contradistinction to the untenable claims of the

orthodox. That is to say, Furtado thus lodges himself within a
realm of discourse that transcends and encompasses the orthodoxy, which we have taken to be the remote inheritor of the
imperialist jingoistic view of the superiority of 'Western' man -
the paradigmatically 'crude' approach to theorizing the exchange
of 'rich' and 'poor'. Furtado's denial of europomorphism is emergent; '*now* we have a generally adequate economics'. It seems to
be an ambiguous effort, whose ambiguity revolves around granting the notion of a generally adequate economics; it is this that
seems to link Furtado to the interventionist orthodoxy. In his
work 'dependency' shifts from a problem-specific politically
informed orientation to a general, 'scientific' one: a wrong idea
of social science and a typically orthodox one.

   With Myrdal, if we look for evidence of sensitivity to the problems arising from conceiving social theorizing to be socially constructed then we can find it, simply because matters of valuation
constitute a point of departure in his work; this is made clear by
his exegetist, Streeten. This evidence of reflexivity is related to
the basis of a denial of europomorphism. Myrdal would claim that
his effort is free of any taint of the wrongful importation of foreign concepts or dispositions, as his epistemic starting point was
the idea of concepts having ecologies and his procedure was
problem-specific. In terms of the dispositions, the position taken
would be one of the obviousness of welfarism in crisis politics.
Once again this is an ambiguous effort in that the epistemology
is unpersuasive, as is the idea that appealing to the obviousness
of courses of action in times of crisis is a satisfactory resolution
of the problems attendant upon deploying the politico-ethical
notion of 'development'. Myrdal may thus claim to be free of the
taint of unreflexiveness, but to the extent that his effort is
Fabian it must be tainted, as Fabianism is evidently a circumstance-specific policy science. However, even if we grant this,
NIST constitutes a marked distancing from what is implied by
our definition of the 'crude', and from the orthodoxy treated
above.

   We take the idea of progress affirmed by this group, in their
different ways, to be the most readily accepted notion. That it
represents the common sense of much of 'development studies' is
an immediate suspicion. It is a considerably richer idea of progress than that adopted by the orthodox, yet it remains within
that (now dominant) peripheral line of the history of the idea of
progress. As regards the theoretical engagement of these theorists, we confront (in NIST especially) what must be the common sense of 'development studies': pragmatic, humane and
concerned with governmental ordering of 'development'. Its
plausibility should not, however, blind us to its defects.

3.3

We have argued above that the efforts of the classical political economists, and in particular Marx, constitute the best model of what it is to argue social-theoretically. We have also claimed that the marxian tradition continues the main trend from the career of the idea of progress, that is, by presenting such notions as democracy and the 'free development of all', and treating its occasion/realization as having a natural guarantor in the historical dialectic of class. We now consider this school of social thought as they present themselves in the post-war career of 'development studies'; that is, we look at the group labelled 'neo-marxist'.

We treat 'neo-marxism' in the established fashion, taking it as a specimen of social-theoretical engagement and not as self-evidently coterminous with a 'marxian analysis of the Third World'. 'Neo-marxism' constitutes our third instantiation of the idea of progress; it attempts to recover the submerged counter-tradition of politico-ethical thinking, that is, the radical democratic scheme that presents man as a 'doer' rather than a 'consumer'. Additionally, 'neo-marxism' seeks to present a scheme of theorizing which is reflexive at the level of the totality (in contrast to, say, NIST whose reflexivity was a partial refinement of technique in a generally orthodox scheme), and thereby to locate itself in the social processes it seeks to understand and effect.

Generally, we take the classical-marxian mode of inquiry to be engaged: its value orientation suffuses it and requires effective deployment. The notion of the unity of theory and practice demands that moral engagement be practically developed and, with regard to this practicality, it adopts a categorical analysis of its social situation. It is thus apparent that it is the antithesis of a 'crude' effort. The self-deluding accommodation to the demands of the status quo evidenced by the orthodox is rejected in favour of an explicitly revolutionary praxis. Yet, although it may be the anti-thesis of 'crude', it does not thereby lay claim to some position from which it can be free of the circumstances of its construction and thus general in application. It is thorough-goingly reflexive and therefore locates itself self-consciously in society and history. It is this reflexivity that is the basis of its denials of any approximation to the 'crude'. That position is turned inside out. Thus it would claim to be the most fruitful mode of analysis and always practical. The history of marxian analyses should, in the light of this conception of it, appear as a history of the circumstances of theorizing. Marxian theorizing, we would claim, should always appear as circumstance-specific and problem-centred; and if it does not, then we may suspect that something has gone awry.

Palma identifies three major efforts of marxian analysis of the exchange of 'rich' and 'poor'. (a) The efforts of Marx and Engels themselves who, reports Palma, treat 'capitalism as a historically

progressive system ...which will spread through the backward
nations by a continual process of destruction and replacement of
pre-capitalist structures'.[15] (b) the efforts of the original
theorists of imperialism, schemes presented in the circumstances
of attempts to grasp Russia's situation as a 'backward' state.
Capitalism is taken as progressive, but altered in its effects by
the dictates of monopoly, and by the 1920s the emphasis has
switched to the idea that post-colonial change might be blocked
by metropolitan monopoly capital and local bourgeoisie. (c) the
'neo-marxism' of the post Second World War period: capitalism is
no longer taken as progressive; in the metropolitan centres
crisis management seems to offer to guarantee an irrational long-
evity, and the peripheral areas are condemned to subordinate
incorporation. The political implications for the 'poor' are of dis-
engagement from world capitalism and the pursuit of planned
socialism.

Thus in respect of what Palma identifies as the third marxian
attempt to grasp the relations of centres/peripheries of world
capitalism we confront the last group of theorists to appear in
our reconstruction of the post-war career of 'development studies': the 'neo-marxists'. In respect of this group we may note
that we treat the major efforts: that is, the orthodoxy of 'neo-
marxism', as it were. Palma distinguishes three lines; a Baran-
inspired line; a revision of ECLA (he cites Furtado), and a third
in the work of Cardoso. We treat the first of these.

In respect of the idea of progress affirmed by the 'neo-
marxists', we can report that it is the broadest of those instanced in the career of 'development studies'. It is also integral to
their analyses. Thus with Baran, the 'father' of this approach,
a notion of economic surplus is used and social forms are ranked
according to how humane is its allocation. Monopoly capitalism
with its militarism, imperialism, and consumerism is deemed
irrational. The impact of monopoly capitalism in its peripheral
areas is indicated by noting its misuse of economic surplus: subordinate incorporation results and the possibility of an autonomous capitalism and thereafter some higher social form is blocked.
The whole is an argument for socialist planning as a political
alternative route to economic and social rationality. With the peripheral areas this requires dis-engagement and in Frank this is
read straightforwardly as socialist revolution.

The extent to which this 'neo-marxism' is actually marxist is a
matter of sharp debate. The critics on the left tend to suggest
that the schemes of the 'father', Baran, are those of an 'idealist
left-wing Keynesian': aggregative economics coupled with the
sentiments of a liberal reformer. Again, in this line, Palma notes
of Frank that his effort is orthodox in that it tries to build a
'mechanico-formal' model of the underdeveloped areas of the periphery. The extent to which their efforts manage to be problem-
specific and reflexive is thus called into question; there is, it
seems, suspicion of a retrogressive collapse towards the descrip-
tive-general.

This raises a crucial and difficult issue: how close does 'neo-marxism' come to being classical marxian social-theoretical engagement? The question spills over from being a simple report on where 'neo-marxism' sits in terms of our career of the idea of progress, or our definition of the 'crude', and raises issues which anticipate directly the central concerns of our concluding chapters. The matter of the precise nature of a social-theoretical inquiry and the proper limits of the efforts of the Western academic in respect of questions about the Third World we shall leav : until these final chapters. However, for present purposes we would affirm that 'neo-marxism' has the richest idea of progress and deploys the subtlest scheme of analysis as it treats the world historical development of the capitalist system.

4.0 CONCLUDING NOTE: SOME CRITICISMS REBUTTED

It might be objected that having at the outset of the chapter decried the habit of lodging pro forma statements of values, we have proceeded to offer just such a statement, and moreover a somewhat grandiose one. We reply that in what is a complex and densely considered area any brief treatment of these issues is liable to appear unsatisfactory in this way. However, we do extend the treatment of the politico-ethical into the substantive material that is to be our concern, and in these substantive histories the issue of the theorist's engagement recurs.

In respect of the politico-ethical material presented, it might be objected that we are guilty of an embarrassing derivative simplicity and would have done well to have left these matters to those whose academic business they are. We reply that this appeal to intellectual compartmentalism is typically orthodox and is a prejudice we do not share. Confronting matters of the Third World entails a breadth of treatment and thus the slighting observation that we are borrowing from the work of others is simply fatuous – of course we are, what else is there to do? And, in any case, the orthodox have their 'philosophical underpinnings', whether they acknowledge them or not.

These two lines of objection can come together in a claim that our effort here is over-general, and that the idea of progress appears in countless forms. This last point is true, but we would reply that we have tried to trace the career of the idea of progress and to present its scope. We have tried to identify the notions available to the classic political economists and the founding fathers of sociology in the nineteenth century. Subsequent variation – national sociologies, or particular streams of thought or schools of social theorists – we have not treated; rather we have confronted the matter of the instantiation of the idea of progress in the post-war career of 'development studies'. We have established, it is hoped, that 'development' has to be taken as a politico-ethical notion and not a technical one; this stance entails acknowledging a distinct range of issues in respect of social theory which are not within the usual realm of the orthodox.

Part II

The 'positivists'

INTRODUCTORY REMARKS

The period we now treat is that which encompasses the 'pre-Seers consensus' referred to by Ehrensaft:[1] this 'consensus' is the theme which is most prominent in 'development studies' up until, roughly, the mid-1960s, and it may be conveniently termed 'positivist'. We take it to comprise two distinguishable streams: an earlier, somewhat general, statement, exemplified in the 1951 UN report,[2] and a subsequent rather more distinctly US effort that elaborates this line. Each line is presented in a separate chapter.

Historically, the division of the period treated in Part II flows from our view of the behaviour of the developed areas to the non-developed areas. We can explain, briefly, as follows. From Brookfield we draw the observation that aid flows to the Third World did not become significant until the mid-1950s; prior to that 'international development aid remained quite small'.[3] Thus for some ten years after the end of the Second World War the developed nations with, in the 'West' certainly, all the experience of a remarkable recovery of economic health, did little, it seems. That they might have been expected to be more active is indicated in Brookfield's observation that 'development' had been on the Allies' 'agenda' since 1942 when the Japanese conquered South-East Asia and promoted locals into 'government'.[4] Yet if the inaction is perhaps curious, then the occasion for activity is illustrative of much of the rationale and spirit of the developed areas' involvement in the Third World. According to Zeylstra,[5] it was the distribution of aid by the USSR in 1954 that provoked the USA into raising aid expenditure.

Thus in the period 1943-55 aid is largely internal to the developed areas and it is only from 1955 that the attention of the 'rich' turns outwards to the Third World. Implicitly, then, in this first period of the establishment of the orthodoxy of 'development studies' the demands of nascent Third World nationalisms and the few 'new nations' established in this period are downgraded in importance. And historically we have the start of the efforts of the Allies to come to agreement about the ordering of the post-war economic and political world. After the arrival of the USSR on the aid scene, and after the declarations of the Bandung Conference, the eyes of the theorists turned outwards, and the demands of nationalist developmentalism were acknowledged in the doctrines of modernization.

In chapter 3 we treat the earlier efforts, and from this period
we take as a central event the institution of Marshall Aid and the
European Recovery Programme. This lets us present what we
take to be the essential idea of the 'positivist' orthodoxy, that
is, 'intervention'. This idea we unpack and this permits us to
identify as the practical core of orthodox 'intervention' the three
principles of (1) growth, both as theory and as doctrine; (2)
planning; (3) aid. These three, we will argue, may be taken to
constitute the skeleton of 'positivist' development theory from
its inception, in the wake of the Second World War, to its 'flowering' at the time of the Kennedy administration. The theoretical
products of this time may be characterized loosely as the response of specialists to quickly moving events. Notions of 'growth'
were constructed out of existing economic doctrine and used as
general theories whereby dealings with 'client' states might be
legitimated. The period is dominated, intellectually, by 'positive
economic science'; the other members of the family of the human
sciences are cast in the role of 'under-labourers'.
   In chapter 4 we consider the circumstances surrounding aid
competition with the USSR: the 'Cold War' bulks large in this
period. At this time, reports Brookfield, the economists felt that
they had solved the problem of growth; and the notion of 'modernization' allows acknowledgment of differences in basic circumstances of the non-developed and, simultaneously, affirms the
pattern of life of rich nations as the model. 'Confidence in the
inevitability of progress rose steadily from 1945 to a peak around
1960',[6] argues Brookfield. The time of Kennedy's 'new frontier'
is taken to mark the high tide of positivist conceit, and thereafter the collapse is general.
   In chapter 4 we treat two main lines of inquiry: (1) the revision of the essentially pessimistic message of Harrod-Domar by
Solow and the emergence of a neo-classical theory of growth
which identifies the process as natural, self-regulating, and self-
sustaining; (2) the concomitant relative emancipation of the
sociologist from the status of 'under-labourer'. The treatment of
'non-economic aspects' of economic growth broadens into something entailing more of a 'master-scientist' role for the sociologist
with ideas of 'modernization'. The themes in economics, sociology
and the other human sciences are blended by Rostow in a widely
influential book which we note in order to return from abstract
to concrete issues.
   In chapter 1 we presented the notion of ideology as our methodological key to these substantive efforts. Here we can indicate
how that key is to be used. Thus Dobb,[7] observing that the
history of economic thought reveals that 'history conditions theories', asks how this is so. He answers in terms of a dialectic
between current practice and presently accepted theory, both
having their own dynamic. Current practice throws up problems[8] that are shaped by their social context, of which he
notes that 'this context itself is a complex mixture and interaction of accepted ideas and systems of thought ... and the

problems presented by current events and practical situations'. [9]
Conversely, 'thought' is not to be taken as a passive recipient of
problems presented to it: 'current problems are something created as much by thought-inspired human action upon an existing
situation as by the given objective (but changing) situation itself'. [10] The source of the medium of criticism, theoretical
language, is the body of existing theory reworked as seems
appropriate. Consequently, 'new ideas are necessarily shaped in
part by the antithetical relation in which they stand to the
old'. [11]

This presents the exchange of theorists and circumstances in
a relatively simple sociology-of-knowledge fashion. We make
practical use of the schema by organizing our substantive analyses around the sequence: milieu, those most general explanations available to the theorist, the 'limits of the thinkable';
demands, the political and problem-relevant expectations made
of the theorist; resources, the intellectual resources available
to the theorist, namely the constructs of the various specialist
disciplines; and finally the product, the completed effort itself.
We may note, finally, that whilst this sequence is the key to our
procedure in respect of our analyses of the distinguishable
efforts we treat, it is not followed slavishly. And indeed in these
analyses the sequence is submerged in the looser scheme of the
dialectic of the dynamic of society (milieu, demands) and the dynamic of theory (resources, products).

3 The crystallization of the positivist orthodoxy, 1943-55

1.0 DYNAMIC OF SOCIETY: THE OCCASION OF THEORIZING

We will begin with some details of the broad history of the period. What we want to identify primarily is (1) the backdrop to the pronouncements of the economic orthodoxy of the early post-war era. From this, (2) we will go on to identify the fundamental structure of that interventionist schema, treating the notions of growth, planning, and aid. This treatment is complemented by (3) notes on the initial efforts of the orthodoxy to extend their theorizing into the realm of matters of the Third World.

This 'backdrop' to the emergence of the first efforts of 'development theory' is complex, and our treatment will rely heavily on the work of a small group of historians and economists. The central historical event is a crisis of enormous proportions, the Second World War, and through this period the rivalries of the USA and UK are played out. Around the figure of Keynes the two sides manoeuvre for advantage, until with the abrupt ending of 'Lend-Lease' in 1945 the power of the UK is curbed and, in Kiernan's phrase, 'it was America's turn to be carried up to the mountain top and shown the kingdoms of the earth'.[1] We can identify three elements in this backdrop: these are (1) issues of economic theorizing and the rise of Keynesianism, (2) matters of the multiple conflicts of the 'Big Three', and (3) the reconstruction of Western Europe and Marshall Aid.

1.1 Economic theory and the Keynesian revolution

From the discussions of the so called 'Keynesian revolution' we draw three points. First, the inter-war period sees the occasion of the Great Depression, an event which could not happen according to neo-classical doctrine. Second, there is the impact of the apparent contrast of the success of the USSR's planned economy; and third, there is the radical overhaul of neo-classicism effected by Keynes.

The economic historian, and Keynesian, Clairmonte,[2] traces the history of the disintegration of economic liberalism. The point of departure of his study is an inquiry into the extent to which 'British Integral Liberalism', 'Ricardianism', or the 'classical approach' might be taken to be a part of the ideological superstructure of the emergent bourgeoisie of British capitalism in the wake of the Napoleonic wars. It is taken to be just that:

'Ricardianism' is an aggressive doctrine of and for the bourgeoisie. This line is familiar: it is detailed, for example, by Hobsbawm.[3] It is noted that the actual period of genuinely free
trade was brief, and that it was the dominant position of the
British economy in world trade that permitted the reification of
notions of liberalism into a self-serving and enclosed formal system.

Now whilst the doctrines of liberalism suited (for a while) the
situation of the UK, their relevance to the problems of other
areas was far from evident. In fact, the disintegration of liberalism may be taken to have started very early. Indeed, it is to the
strategic requirements of the new American republic that Clairmonte traces the criticisms that he argues culminate in Keynes.
The views of Hamilton with regard to the nurturing of local
industries are taken to be a formative influence upon List, of
whom it is observed that 'underlining the pitfalls of integral
liberalism he emerges as the leading protagonist of purposive
policy interventionism'.[4]

If the fall of economic liberalism is taken to be protracted,
then its demise in the 1930s is seen to be unequivocal, thereafter,
claims Clairmonte, 'we see the mushrooming of every species of
restrictionism with the concomitant proliferation of massive aggre-
gations of power and increasing state intrusion'.[5] However,
so far as the neo-classical doctrinaires were concerned, it was
not the mechanisms of the market that had been shown to be at
fault; rather, it was interference with them. This illusion is
located (on the part of UK theorists at least) by Clairmonte in
the familiar misapprehension of the UK economy in the period
1870-1914: what is taken as a golden age is, in fact, a period of
industrial decline masked by receipts from the empire.

To this phenomenon of justificatory ideas parting company with
reality is added an element hinted at by Lichtheim:[6] that is,
the spectre of Bolshevism. If the issue for the West and Third
World is now how rather than whether to plan, as Clairmonte
would claim, then in his view:[7]

it was basically the irrepressible and unprecedented tempo of
industrial and scientific advance in those formerly funereal
half-Asian, half-European nations of the Tsarist empire within
forty years, two disastrous wars, encirclement and uncon-
cealed hostility, which dramatised the viability of the planning
mechanism ....The seminal fact is that the impact of Soviet
planning left its ineradicable impress on the economic policies
of many countries.

This line is confirmed by Kurihara's investigation of the impact of history on Keynesian theory. Two events are cited,
'namely (a) the establishment of the first centrally planned
economy in Russia, after World War 1 and (b) the Great Depression of the 1930s'.[8] Kurihara takes Keynes to have plotted a
middle course through the alternatives of laissez-faire and auth-

oritarian intervention. As regards the theses established by
Keynes, three are identified as flowing from the experience of
Depression and Bolshevism. They are: (1) the notion of depression equilibrium; (2) deficit finance and the idea of the multiplier; and (3) the compatibility of full employment and liberty.

(1) In the 1930s the economic orthodoxy rested upon the work
of the 'equilibrium theorists', men such as Jevons, Marshall,
Walras, and Pareto. Setting marxists and socialists to one side,
amongst the criticisms voiced, Sraffa (in 1926) had argued, in
effect, that the notion of 'perfect competition' was untenable as
each firm not merely competes, but seeks to differentiate itself
in the market. Ruling out 'perfect competition' denies the possibility of a general theory of equilibrium; it thus cuts at the
heart of the project of the orthodox neo-classical theorists.
Attempts at repair by Robinson ('imperfect competition') and
Chamberlin ('monopolistic competition') in 1933 are deemed by
the economic historian Napoleoni to have failed. The contribution
of Keynes to this debate is introduced thus:[9]

> Parallel with the revision of the theory of market forms an-
> other criticism was levelled at the theory of economic equil-
> ibrium. This criticism concerned the statement that a
> competitive economy, left to itself, will automatically achieve
> the full employment of resources in general and of the labour
> force in particular.

Keynes shows that it is perfectly possible for economies to go
into depression equilibrium whereby factors of production were
so used that optimum configurations were not achieved. The neo-
classical scheme argued that this was impossible.

(2) The question follows, what conditions if any will ensure
full employment? The answers to this question provide for a new
idea of the government's role in the economy. The laissez-faire
scheme had been attacked on three points: (a) unemployment,
(b) misuse of available resources, and (c) trend to monopoly.
Policy proposals flow from this view: generally, if the level of
total expenditure falls below that necessary to sustain full employment, then the short-fall is to be made up by government
spending. This in turn rests on the two notions of the 'multiplier'
and 'deficit financing'. Thus the role for a government is sharply
altered in line with revision of the established conception of the
market.

(3) This counter-cyclical role with regard to unemployment
does not necessarily alter any fundamentals in the system. Policy
proposals which might flow from charges of misuse of resources
or maldistribution of income would involve more radical change.
So Keynes reassured doubters that full employment policies did
not entail significant diminution of ordinarily understood liberties
(though we might note that the political import of Keynes has
been regarded as deeply ambiguous).

What we can take from all this is the observation that the work

of Keynes grows out of two circumstances: first, the situation
of protected monopoly capitalism working at greatly reduced
capacity whilst simultaneously having massive unemployment,
and the concurrent manifest theoretical absurdity of the rump of
British integral liberalism; second, the combined encouragement
and awful warning of the apparently successful efforts at planning in the USSR.[10] To this we may add that with Keynes, the
economic orthodoxy was very sharply overhauled, resulting in a
style of government intervention that for many years after the
war was taken to have tamed the system's periodic crises.

1.2 The political and economic context for post-war thinking about development

Having looked at the roots of the Keynesian enterprise, we now
go on to indicate the initial set of political factors which gave
form to those subsequent efforts to make use of it in guiding
policy with regard to 'development'. The crucial considerations
here revolve around the determination of the US to order the
post-war world in a fashion acceptable to itself. The gist of this
element of our study is that the US, under the guise of an enlightened liberalism[11] and couched in the internationalist
rhetoric associated with (most familiarly) the UN organization,
established in the period 1943-7 its economic hegemony over the
'West'. The first schemes of help for developing countries operated within this frame, the 'Pax Americana'.
    Of the war aims of the USA, Kolko argues that three issues
dominated US thinking in the period 1943-5:[12]

> First was the question of the left which is to say, the disin-
> tegration of the pre-war social systems and the growth of
> revolutionary movements and political upheaval everywhere in
> the world. Next was the problem of the Soviet Union, which
> at times appeared very much connected with the issue of the
> left. Finally there was the issue of Great Britain, invariably
> set in the context of the future of the world economy and its
> present and future relationship to the US.

It is argued that the Americans, once they were in the war,
quickly began to establish a series of economic war aims. This
task is reported as falling to the Department of State under
Cordell Hull, a disciple of Wilson's laissez-faire liberalism and a
man marked, as was Keynes, by the experience of the depression.
Yet Hull drew opposing conclusions: tariff blocks and controls
were the road to economic ruin and war, and the solution was
laissez-faire. Kolko wryly notes: 'The identification of the interests of the world and future peace with Hull's doctrines and
American prosperity looked more and more like the classic pursuit of national self-interest in an ill-fitting wrapper of internationalist rhetoric.'[13]

It is reported that there were two major elements in US thinking, finance and relief/trade. The discussion of finance was
initiated in 1942 with a British submission prepared by Keynes,
envisaging the growth of world trade with an international fund
to smooth over deficits and channel investment money through
the world economy. To this, the US replied with the White plan
(White was number two in the US Treasury), and debate revolved around the control of these proposed institutions and the
ground rules of their operation. The debate continued right up
to July 1944 and Bretton Woods: the British eventually agreeing,
having removed the most blatantly pro-US elements. However,
the IMF and IBRD were 'far closer in their principles to the US
scheme than any other'.[14] Bretton Woods established the US
view of the post-war economy, that is, one run by business on
business principles.

As regards trade/relief, Kolko takes the view that UNRRA,
set up in late 1943, was seen as a temporary necessity and was
only ever incidental to the pursuit of US interests. The overall
view was that 'emergency reconstruction and relief programs
would exist, but they would be temporary and solved essentially
as a by-product of the creation of a rational world economy'.[15]
These notes, derived mainly from the work of Kolko, serve to
correct the common-sense view of this period which would have
it that the USA and UK were in close harmony and that only the
recalcitrant behaviour of the USSR prevented the establishment
of a new world order.[16]

In respect of the relations between 'East' and 'West', Fleming[17] argues persuasively for all his brittle moralism, that
the period of the 'Grand Alliance' was a wholly untypical episode
in the history of these relations. Lichtheim too speaks of the
struggle between 'communism and anti-communism which had
been going on all over Europe since 1917'.[18] Kolko traces the
evolution of US thinking through the war and subsequent occupation of Europe, and corrects in persuasive detail the orthodox
notion of the westward surge of godless communism. In relating
the history of the Western allies' occupation of Italy (a crucial
precedent), France, Belgium and Greece (a brutal example), it
is clearly established that the Western allies did not lend their
support to local democratic groups (which usually included communist elements), but instead imposed governments and leaders
acceptable to themselves. Truman's later (March 1947) declar-
ation of 'cold war' effectively fixes the division of Europe into
two occupied camps.

By the end of the war the USA had committed itself to organizing a counter-revolution: 'the old order of pre-war capitalism
and oligarchy with which the US identified ... was dying in the
colonial world and a dependent China; it committed suicide in
Eastern Europe, and the US could refurbish it in temporarily
acceptable ways only in Western Europe'.[19] Kolko continues:[20]

Only the US had the power to engage fully in international counter-revolution and sustain the forces of conservatism for prolonged periods and it was this militant intervention into the affairs of literally every area of the world that set the pattern for post-war politics. By 1945 Washington's decision to undertake that role was an unquestioned postulate in America's plans for the future of its power in the world.

The style in which the USA was later to approach matters of development was also clear. Again Kolko: 'America's foreign policy at the end of World War II necessitated the ability and desire to employ loans, credits and investments everywhere to create a world economic order to its own desires.'[21] We shall see that 'growth theories' flowing out of an authoritative and instrumentalist stance were clearly theoretically congruent with this dominating political need. It is clear that Streeten's choice of Marshall Aid as one of the roots of 'development theory' is apposite; the European Recovery Programme (ERP) evidently encapsulates a wealth of tensions, and it is to the history of post-war Europe that we now turn.

1.3 The economic recovery of Western Europe

Streeten[22] argues that it was the dramatic recovery of Europe's economy that lent credence to the notion that deliberate intervention in an economic system to raise its level of activity was possible. Postan[23] confirms this reading of the response to European recovery; at the outset he declares that 'the unique feature of the post-war economy in the West is growth'. He identifies four phases. The first being 'de-mobilization and readjustment' as economies are shifted off war footings, during 1945-8. Postan notes that it was not until 1948 that the majority of European nations recovered economically to their 1939 levels.[24] The second phase identified is that of 'recovery proper', dated 1948-53, the period when the dominant economic/political pattern of the post-war period was established. Internal factors are cited, in particular measures to control inflation. Turning to external factors, Postan reveals the orthodoxy of his views; thus he says: 'By far the most dramatic, as well as the most effective contribution to recovery was the announcement[25] in the summer of 1947 ... of the so-called "Marshall Plan".'[26]

The nature of the ERP can now be considered. The views of the US government may be approached via the views of an academic proponent of the ERP, Seymour Harris. In 1948 Harris produced a book with the title, 'The European Recovery Programme'. At the time he was Professor of Economics at Harvard, and we may take him to represent the Keynesian element in the USA establishment. In the justification of ERP, crisis in Europe and fear of communism figure prominently. Thus Harris says,[27]

Self-interest rather than charity inspired ERP. Frightened
by the onward movement of communism, which feeds on
distress, the American people rallied to the support of the
Marshall Plan ... Americans realized also that economic recovery in Western Europe would rebound favourably on the
American economy.

In addition, Harris notes the pressure of particular US
economic groups which had surpluses on their hands, for
example farmers. The mixture of both political and economic
aspects is evident.

Politically the major event of this period was the promulgation of the 'Truman Doctrine', which was presented in a speech
to Congress on 12 March 1947. Its essence was that political
change was to be arrested: 'Truman spoke for the bulk of
American conservatives and allied himself with reaction around
the globe.'[28] The Marshall Plan followed on from this stance,
and in Western Europe the aid administration's powers were
used, reports Fleming, 'to discourage social reform ... the
effect of our economic intervention in Europe has been not only
to oust communists from the governments but to put the socialists
out or decrease their influence'.[29]

The second area indicated by Harris is that of economics and
economic theory (which Harris treats in that he attempts to
settle doubts about the propriety and efficacy of ERP). In
respect of the economics, Zeylstra's remark is instructive:
'For the first time the Truman Doctrine contained a concept of
international aid based on the need to promote a suitable rate of
growth in the receiving countries, a prototype thus of modern
development aid.'[30] Zeylstra passes by the use of 'to promote'
and 'rate of growth' without comment, his target being development aid. But as we have seen with Keynes, that growth could
be described theoretically and actually promoted as a matter of
policy were the greater novelties. Yet Zeylstra's words reveal
both the essence of the orthodox notion that specific policy-
guided interventions could be made to secure a targeted growth
rate and the fact that such ideas have become a part of the
common coin of 'development studies'.

We can complete this brief review of ERP by taking note of the
views of those who explicitly run together economics and politics.
Postan, for example, tends to let the politics take care of themselves: a 'neutral' treatment - ERP was a source of finance. Yet
we have seen with Kolko that the issue of the manner in which
European reconstruction would be effected was by no means
simply a technical matter of finance. The questions of the post-
war shape of Europe and the division of Germany were closely
bound up with issues of reparations, reconstruction, and access
for the USA to European markets. The USA consistently opposed
the breaking up of Germany or using its industry to supply
European reconstruction. The USA had surplus capacity and
finance and needed to use it. In Europe, Kolko reports that the

divergence of views with regard to the nature of the post-war
world and the role and form of bodies such as IMF or IBRD, between the USA and its allies grew progressively more acute. By
the end of the war there was no agreement, and the USA imposed
its own views as and when it could.

Returning to Postan's history, we can note that he sketches
the backdrop and novelty of the post-war period in comparison
to the depression years. The story in Postan's hands is not so
much one of design as of a dam bursting. Thus he says of the
potential for recovery in Europe that: 'shortages of goods had
been accumulating for years, the needs of reconstruction were
great and urgent, the reserves of unemployed resources were
immense'.[31] It is pointed out that a surge of activity was to be
expected. It is the fact that following this understandable surge
growth is sustained that is novel. Postan goes on: 'In all European countries economic growth became a universal creed and a
common expectation to which governments were expected to
conform.'[32] The pre-war economic policy orthodoxy had
stressed financial probity; that growth was preferred and that
policies were fashioned to that end in the novelty of the post
war, post-Keynes period. Thus at the back of European doctrines of growth there is 'a confluence of tributaries, the
policy of high aggregate demand and full employment, the welfare state, the defence of the west, obligations to under-developed
countries and American pressures and influences'.[33] From all
this it is clear that the extension of post-war interventionist
techniques to matters of the development of the Third World
was something other than the straightforward exercise which
studies of that time seem to have taken it to be. The extraction from this tangled web of a simple 'programme for development' has been dismissively labelled by Brookfield as the pursuit
of a 'development vending machine: you put in the money, press
the button and get growth'.[34] However, whilst the enterprise
may have been ill-conceived, even naive, it none the less has
an elegant and deeply persuasive model of explanation at the
back of it. In our next section we will try to draw this out.

1.4 Summary

The above we take to outline the environment from which the
early post-war orthodoxy, subsequently deployed in treating
matters of the development of the Third World, emerged. The
history presents, albeit perhaps in an overly general style, the
'structure of the possible' for the post-war theorists. The possibilities opened by the theoretical work of Keynes are squeezed
between the twin pressures of popular (left) demand and US
determination to hold the line against change. Ordered reconstruction and development is now taken to be within the grasp
of governments, but the ruling factor in any such efforts is
the overwhelming economic and military power of the US. Inter-

ventionist activity is subsumed, paradoxically, under the imposed rubric of economic liberalism.

The shift from this point to the treatment of the Third World
can be effected by citing the work of Streeten, who argues that
the subject 'development studies' has its origins in two general
sets of thoughts: problems of resources and people are taken to
be urgent in view of the population explosion and soluble in the
light of the success of post-war European recovery; second,
political change in the form of the rise of new states in the
Third World and the Cold War increases the concern of the
'West' for the 'proper' development of these areas. The Marshall
Plan is thus an appropriate symbol for the start of 'development studies'. More technically, we see that out of the set of
descriptions/explanations available to theorists in the wake of
depression, war and Cold War, the demands of the reform and
defence of Western capitalism crystallize out three novel theoretical devices. Thus the explanatory theory, the overarching
and legitimating construction that permits and guides action
oriented to development problems, is found in 'growth theory'.
This will be our first concern below; our second will be the
elucidation of the schemes and techniques whereby intervention
is organized, that is, planning. Finally as a corollary of one
and two, we look at the matter of the execution of such intervention schemes as may be prepared; that is, aid.

2.0 DYNAMIC OF THEORY I: THE NATURE OF THE ORTHODOXY
- THE NOTION OF 'INTERVENTION'

Our treatment rests on the claim that out of the mélange of theoretical possibility identified by Keynes, political necessity as
established principally by the US, and example provided by
European recovery, the theorists of the orthodoxy distil an
intellectually coherent and politically relevant scheme. As
Zeylstra puts it, 'when finally the economists made common cause
with the politicians ... this happened not only because the latter
seized and exploited ideas of the former, but also as the outcome of the economists' own course of theoretical thinking'.[35]
More familiarly, Zeylstra remarks that, 'Since Keynes the economists had grown familiar with normative theory, with identifying
themselves with the problems of the political scientist and the
public administrator.'[36] Thus the distillate, so to say, of
the period was a variety of 'policy science'.

The term 'policy science' we take from Fay who uses it to designate the assumed product of mainstream social science, such
that in response to the question 'why have a social science?' -
the answer is made that it permits the rational ordering of
decisions in complex modern societies; or, more bluntly, it 'will
enable men to control their social environment'.[37] It is clear
that our notion of 'intervention' as a label summing up the orthodoxy of this time is apposite, and, further, we may claim that

it designates the substantive core of this 'conventional wisdom'.
If we take the notion of 'intervention' and unpack it, we can
make a preliminary identification of what the idea presupposes
and entails. Thus if we take any particular occasion of an intervention then it might be understood as a 'deliberate action whose
objective is to bring about a particular change in some array and
thereby achieve or approach a preferred state of affairs'. Here
we seem to have three basic elements: the supposition that (1)
there is something to be acted upon, an object; (2) that it will
respond, and in a predictable fashion; and (3) the idea that the
intervention is accomplished by an actor in a precise manner
according to some clear set of expectations.

There are two related points to note in this. First, that the
story above requires that the actor confront (or constitute for
his present purposes) an object; that is, there is implicit in
the ordinary notion of intervention a subject-object dualism.
Now, whether this dualism is taken as a moment in some more
general procedure or as a fixed assumption is a matter of the
wider philosophy of science into which a particular theorist's
object drops. We can see this more clearly if we go on to look at
another element from above, that of a predictable response. For
'critical theory' the products of the thinker are finally 'authen-
ticated' by their being taken up by groups within society. That
is, the critical theorist is in the business of making sense, and
this being so the element of 'subject-object' is but a moment in a
longer all-embracing process of theoreticians' meditations and
their dissemination and translation - or not - into practice. On
the other hand, so far as empiricist positivism is concerned, the
dualism is a fixed assumption. There is an array of objects and
(relatively)[38] detached from them the actor, whose intervention
alters in some way that array of objects. That there are objects
whose behaviour is amenable to intervention such that its result
is knowable beforehand entails empiricist positivism subscribing
to an idea of the exchange between theorists and reality as
issuing in description in terms of causes, rather than, as with
'critical theory', tendencies. The products of the empiricist
thinker are 'validated' by their corresponding to the facts. In
general we can claim that positivism as a variety of empiricism
entails an ontology of things, separate from other things.[39]

If the above is true, then clearly the 'interventions' of the
critical theorist are not those of the orthodox empiricist positivist.
Those of the former are interpretative-directive (moral persuasion, broadly) whilst those of the latter are causal-descriptive
(manipulation of objects), and in some measure these ideals of
explanation flow from the monistic/dualistic metaphysics affirmed.

Related to this is the matter of our second observation upon
our 'definition', and this concerns the form of explanation required by the demand for/pursuit of causal explanations. It is
clear that for an intervention to be successful it must be a knowing intervention, that is, in the right place, at the right time
and of the right kind. Thus manipulative intervention demands a

general set of explanations which will tell the actor or agent how
the object in question behaves in the absence of intervention
and in the presence of specified interventions. In ordinary par-
lance, what is needed is a 'theory'; but it is not that simple.
The role and status of 'theory' and 'models' and so on, on the
one hand, and political and social practice, on the other, and
the nature of their relationship are much debated questions.
Here we shall be content with noting a few views from economists
which, as we are interested at present in establishing the nature
of the set of explanations of the inhabitants of the orthodoxy is
both appropriate and a legitimate temporary evasion of these
difficult problems.

From Napoleoni's history we draw the important example of
'deductive empiricism'. Robbins published in 1932 a book which
argued that economics is to be seen as a science which derives
its propositions from a set of particular (obvious) assumptions.
These are 'certain simple and indisputable facts of experience
relating to the way in which the scarcity of goods, which is the
subject of economics, is actually revealed in everyday life'.[40]
The method follows: 'if these premises are accepted as corresponding to reality, the generalizations economics achieves by
way of deduction also correspond to reality'.[41] The situation
is thus of a deductive core erected upon a bed of formally expressed commonplaces, issuing in complex descriptions of reality,
and having remote consequences (deduced) taken as true of
reality. Napoleoni reports that Robbins's 'deductive empiricism'
was the methodological counterpart of equilibrium economics and
that it was an influential text in the years before the Second
World War.

The general drift of subsequent reflection upon the grounding
and procedures of economics within the mainstream would seem
to be one of a relaxation of this strict line. There is a shift from
'deductive empiricism' to what Hindess dubs 'epistemology of
models', where realism is crucial. In respect of 'growth theory',
Harrod plays a central role. Of this work, Robinson notes that
he falls into the familiar and unhappy procedure of deriving policy prescriptions of great precision from premises of great
abstractness. Thus she writes: 'There is a big gap between
Mr Harrod's ingenious and instructive manipulation of his three
G's and the conditions of any actual economy.'[42]

In 1953 Friedman[43] published a famous text wherein he
argues that the realism of model-builders' assumptions is not an
interesting question; instead, economists should look to the success or otherwise of the predictions made from them. Developing
this line with reference to Popper, Hutchison has argued[44] that
economics can at last 'grow out of' its apriorism: the task would
become the improvement of the predictions routinely made in
social life, a collection as it were of extremely sophisticated rules
of thumb.

Yet in general it would seem that these arguments are overly
subtle; work within economics repeatedly collapses into a common

sense that is straightforwardly empiricist, even though it might
be an attenuated strain compared to Robbins. Thus Solow[45]
has proposed to regard growth theory as a parable whereby
typical economic relations may be displayed; and it is within the
empiricist frame that economics sought to fashion the stratagems
for intervention demanded by political events. What they came
up with, and refined to great levels of sophistication and politico-
social generality, was 'growth theory'.

2.1 Growth theory: 'intervention' legitimated

We begin with the origins of growth theory in Keynes's work.
We have already seen how Keynes effects a sharp reformulation
of neo-classicism; his effort, organized around the pressing
need (both practical and intellectual) to resolve the problem of
treatment of unemployment, offers a challenge to neo-classicism
at several points as we have seen. However, whilst Keynes's
analyois iooued in oonoluoiono diotinotly unpalatable to neo
classicism, he none the less remained within the ambit of neo-
classicism. It is only later (e.g. Robinson, 1962) that the idea
that Keynes has re-invented political economy is entertained.
    Against this background Harrod produces his essay of 1939
and the fuller collection of 1948. Kurihara notes that Harrod
(with Domar later) 'established growth economics as a going concern on the foundations of Keynes's saving-investment theory',[46]
and helps us further by offering a summary of the shift in em-
phaois and orientation effected by Harrod.[47]

> If Keynes effected the transition from micro-analysis (with
> emphasis on profit maximization for the firm à la Marshallian
> price theory) to macro-analysis (with emphasis on employ-
> ment maximization for the whole economy à la General Theory),
> then Harrod can be credited with effecting the post-Keynesian
> transition from short run macro-statics to long run macro-
> dynamics. Harrod emphasized the long run importance of the
> growth-promoting, capacity-increasing aspect of saving,
> whereas Keynes had concentrated on the employment-impeding,
> demand-decreasing aspect of saving; Harrod also emphasized
> investment both as a cause and as an effect of capacity ex-
> pansion, whereas Keynes has treated investment mainly as a
> source of effective demand.

It would now be appropriate to look at the H-D[48] model in a
little detail and to take note of one major subsequent change.
The influence of the H-D model has been extensive: Brookfield
notes that it was this theory that 'underlay the growth policies
actually put into effect'.[49] Looking at the model will let us
grasp the narrowness of its origin and form; for example,
Zeylstra describes it, quite accurately, as a 'by-product of the
Keynesian revolution in income and employment theory'.[50] The

theory of growth is not an easy area for the non-specialist to
penetrate; for example, Brookfield remarks that the division of
efforts into two schools is a 'rather fine distinction ... of greater
importance to economists than to users of their work'.[51] Yet
Jones notes that from H-D's work 'radically different conclusions
have emerged'.[52] Thus Brookfield's remark entails either his
having misread the import of the technical debate or his tacit
agreement with Zeylstra, who has the 'politicians' taking what
they wanted out of the work of the economists. He says, 'Once
confronted with reality in the developing countries the economists began arguing among themselves about aid theories and
strategies they preferred leaving to the politicians the opportunity of adhering to the most convenient opinions.'[53] However
the results of theorizing have been used, it is the case that two
'schools' may be identified. Thus Kregel[54] distinguishes two
lines of thought, both revolving around H-D, but with one
descending from neo-classical equilibrium theory, whilst the other
derives from classical economics via Keynes and Kalecki. This
reading is supported, in emphatic terms, by Jones who reports
that the 'Cambridge school' including Kaldor, Robinson and
Sraffa has heavily and persistently criticized the neo-classical
schemes represented by Solow and Samuelson at MIT, at Cambridge, Mass. Earlier it is noted that 'theories of growth have
generated bitter controversy':[55] and when Solow's 1956 reworking of H-D's problem is looked at it is not hard to see why.

   Harrod's work is in the style of Keynes, as regards terminology, assumptions and techniques. His essay focuses on 'the
necessary conditions for equilibrium between aggregate saving
and investment in a dynamic economy'.[56] The basic proposition
is that Ga=s/v where 'Ga' is the actual rate of growth of National
Income, 's' is marginal propensity to save and 'v' is the marginal
capital-output ratio. This 'fundamental relation' [57] can define
a growth path if it can be linked to a statement of the entrepreneur's estimations. The notion of 'warranted growth' is introduced, it seems, to fulfil the Keynesian role of entrepreneur.
The entrepreneur invests, and his investment today depends
upon his estimation of tomorrow's possibilities.[58] If he is to be
reassured that his reading of the economy is correct, then Ga
will have to be equal to Gw. In addition to Ga and Gw, Harrod
has Gn, which is the 'natural' rate of growth flowing from given
rises in population.

   If these are put together we have the first major conclusion to
issue from his work thus: 'If, by coincidence, the actual rate of
growth equalled the warranted rate, which itself equalled the
rate of growth of the labour force, then steady growth at full
employment would occur.'[59] Harrod thinks it extremely unlikely,[60] and as Jones says 'this conclusion is thoroughly
Keynesian in spirit: there is no reason to believe that full employment equilibrium will be attained'.[61] This being the case,
it is noted that all subsequent growth theory has been aimed at
evading Harrod's thesis.[62]

The second line of thought on growth models comes from the USA and falls into the tradition of neo-classicism. It is this line that is most used; it is the 'dominant method of growth economics'.[63] It may be taken to begin with a paper by Solow (1956) which was aimed explicitly at the first of Harrod's 'problems', the difficulty of 'getting on target'; but in the course of his paper both 'problems' are treated. Solow's theory is constructed in the same fashion as Harrod's; that is, he begins with a series of assumptions and derives a set of conclusions relevant to practice.

The notable features of his model for our purposes, are the impact his assumptions have on it in comparison to Harrod's assumptions. In fact he contrives to by-pass all the problems presented by Harrod's model. In Harrod the role of entrepreneurial expectation is, following Keynes, of major significance as a source of instability in the system, yet Solow simply chops out entrepreneurial expectation. The other major change concerns the type of production function used, the way capital and labour are fitted into the model. Solow used a scheme whose import is that warranted and natural rates of growth coincide automatically; the 'first Harrod problem' thus disappears.[64]

Solow's model (or parable) inverts Harrod: the growth path is not only obtainable, but economies tend to move towards it. Cigno sums it up: 'This model projects the image of a well-ordered and stable society, whose prosperity depends on the thriftiness, inventiveness and technical skill of its members, and where everyone is rewarded according to his contribution to the common good.'[65]

We now turn to some criticisms of the H-D procedure. If the foregoing presents the emergence of the formal explanatory core of the early post-war orthodoxy, now we may ask (1) how does it translate into practice (in rich areas, in poor areas) and (2) what are the fundamental problems (if any) of going about things in this way? We may answer that as regards the precise form and associated problems of H-D's extension to matters of the Third World, this is a topic for section 3 of this chapter, and for chapter 4. The relevance to situations of 'rich' we will touch upon in Part III when we look at the disintegration of the orthodoxy. Here we pursue the question of the use of models as the typical frame of the explanatory-justificatory schemes governing 'intervention'. We want to argue (1) that the H-D model not only is not a developed social theory, but cannot be turned into one; (2) that the H-D model must be regarded as an elaboration of common sense, and as it claims to be something more than this it is thus ideological in a pejorative sense.

(1) That the H-D model is not a developed social theory is readily apparent; it does not claim to be one. However, (as Brookfield, Jones, Streeten and others note) it does underlie the policies put into effect. If this is so, then we can say that it is a poor place to start. We can recall our characterization of social

theory and indicate how, in comparison, the H-D model fails to make sense. Social theorizing, it was suggested, can be seen as the deployment of a morally informed categorical scheme where the categories are (for the theorist) given and value-sloped, and the moral involvement is self-defining and secondary. Now in contrast to the product we might envisage flowing from such an exercise, the H-D effort is defective in two areas. It is 'intrinsically' defective in that it is unreflective. H-D theorists are making a moral intervention in the world and this is not an acknowledged part of their effort. Claims to 'value freedom' are not credible, and equally unsatisfactory are pro forma statements. The second defect - 'extrinsic', as it were - of the H-D model is that its style compounds the errors encouraged by its unreflectiveness. We note three points.

(a) Streeten points out that the formal mode adopted invites a slide from the possibly true claim that 'economic facts' are accessible, quantifiable and manipulable to the wholly false claim that 'economic facts' are somehow 'objective' in a way that political, social or moral considerations are not. It is noted that 'though logically fallacious this type of reasoning which attempts to substitute "objective" criteria for political choices provides an intellectual escape mechanism from difficult or unpleasant political decisions'.[66] But, it might be objected, thus far H-D are possibly being held responsible for the sins of those who have used their work; is this not unreasonable? (b) However, the dominant style of economic theorizing (out of which background they came) lodged claims to factual adequacy. Thus Robbins (1932) presents his 'deductive-empiricism': 'the admissibility of the premises on which economic science is built cannot, according to Robbins, be doubted since these are simple and obvious propositions ... they are the object of our everyday experience'.[67] (c) The tradition of economics as a deductive science, (coupled with Streeten's note in respect of the tendency to equate quantification with objectivity), plus desire of theorists in government to provide policy-informing analyses, issues in an environment that can be seen to be conducive to reading H-D models as, if not reporting fact, then close to it, or (in the same line but with minimal commitment) as helpful in uncovering it.

(2) What then is the status of H-D? Hindess[68] points out that in mathematics a 'model' is a precisely specified set of rules relating one area of mathematical discourse to another. This is a 'paradigm case of a theory in which the concept of model has a definite and rigorously defined function'.[69] From here on (thinks Hindess, if we have understood him right), things get worse.

In positivist philosophy of science this intra-theoretic relation is altered; a model now details the relation between theoretical machineries and the real world, a set of observations. Hindess takes this to be the substitution of analogies for models. Indeed, claims to the use of models in natural science are taken to be few and implausible.

In the realm of the social sciences the notion of model reaches
its nadir. Bauman (1972) and Lévi-Strauss (1968) are cited.
Bauman is quoted as saying: 'theorising consists in modelling
reality. Theories *are* models'.[70] Hindess comments: 'In these
lines we have a concise statement of what might be called the
epistemology of model building.'[71] He then delineates, with
reference to prior discussions of the role of models in mathematical logic, the consequences of this view. The precisely formulated correspondences of elements of theoretical realms in
mathematical logic, or the rigour of the (eventually unsatisfactory) positivist attempt to explicate the relation of theory and
observation, are abandoned. Citing Lévi-Strauss, he comments
that now 'theoretical activity consists in the construction of
models that are similar in certain "essential" respects to the empirical domain in question. But how similar is similar and how
does one choose amongst the multiplicity of possible models?'[72]
It is concluded that: 'at its best the epistemology of model building would result in a complex and sophisticated theoretical construct resting on an arbitrary and merely plausible foundation
in resemblance'.[73]
    Returning to the status of H-D, it seems to be fairly clear that
the scheme operates within the ambit of the epistemology of
models. Recalling our references to the procedures of Robbins's
'deductive empiricism', we can compare them with those of the
epistemology of models. Hindess notes of these that 'the epistemology of model building is an epistemology in which scientific
knowledge is said to be produced through the construction and
manipulation of models'.[74] 'Models are obtained through a
double process of abstraction and simplification and they may be
subject to an "experimental" manipulation... knowledge may be
produced through the experimental manipulation of formal systems'.[75] At the end of the day, models, conceived so, reduce
to the status of persuasive metaphor. The theorist begins from
some formalized element of common sense, be it the common sense
of society or the common sense of the discipline, and thither he
eventually returns.
    As a general theory providing legitimation for 'intervention',
'growth theory', based on H-D models and theories of development derived therefrom, would seem to be untenable. However,
whilst the effort is unsatisfactory in a technical sense, its ideological role remains serviceable.
    Touching upon the ideological role of H-D, we may recall from
Postan that governments were caught up in a tide of opinion and
only then did doctrines of growth emerge. What began as a solution to problems of unemployment - that is, a relatively specific
remedy - was extended and transformed into a fully-fledged, if
unclearly spelt out, social doctrine. In the 'rich' world it underpinned 'social democracy', and with regard to the Third World it
attained its most florid guise in the work of Rostow with his
'stages of growth'.
    Putting a date to the emergence of the doctrine of growth is a

little difficult. From Brookfield we have the following: 'The
quasi-religion of economic growth has had its origins in the "long
boom" experienced most joyfully in the West.'[76] Postan, we
have seen, dates 'recovery proper' as beginning in 1948, and
the 'boom' takes off with the Korean war. By 1958 Galbraith is
using 'growth' in the sense of 'doctrine'. In 1959 Kurihara pub-
lishes an exposition, so presumably the notion itself is earlier.
The 1951 UN report of Lewis et al. is cited by Kurihara as the
first fruits of the Keynesian approach in regard to matters of
development. Thus we may say the doctrine emerges between
1951 and 1958, the period (as Postan puts it) of the West's most
'robust' growth.[77]

2.2 Planning: 'intervention' organized

Now we move from matters of legitimation to those of organization,
that is, planning. The conceptual relation is straightforward, in
outline at least. Thus, given that we have a 'theory', based on
growth models, we need to have an idea of how to go about using
the theory. How do we organize, initiate, monitor and control
our 'intervention'? How do we plan? Indeed, can we?

With regard to the theoretical possibility of planning, we may
begin by noting that it is possible with the notion of 'planning'
(as with any other term in the social science lexicon) to distinguish a range of meanings. To offer even a preliminary exposition of the term's conceptual and historical range would be a
long and, more pertinently, often irrelevant task at present. We
shall begin where our discussion so far indicates that we should,
that is, with economics and economic theory.

The debate about the possibility of planning begins, it has
been argued, not with Marx and Engels (who advocated but did
not treat the notion of a 'planned economy'), but with an Austrian
economist, Von Mises, who in the 1920s argued that a planned
economy could not work rationally. The gist of his argument is
that, separating the economy from its institutional frame, it is
the economy's job to allocate scarce resources between competing
ends. This requires precise indices of scarcity, or else choices
would be ungrounded. The only way to get these indices is to
allow market determination of price. Thus an economy with no
market cannot provide any index of scarcity and so cannot rationally allocate scarce resources.

Unfortunately for Von Mises, a reply was to be found in established equilibrium theory. The answer follows from Walrasian
analysis of 'price'. Common-sensically, 'price' is the rate at which
goods are exchanged; they may additionally be expressed via a
'standard', say, relative to the price of gold. Walras's system
goes rather deeper and issues in the entirely non-intuitive as-
sertion that, from the general character of the system, 'price'
can be established prior to - indeed independently of - any
involvement with the market. Napoleoni, who provides this

analysis, sums up his treatment by noting that 'the price of one good in terms of another can be determined at least in theory as the rate of technological and psychological equivalence of the two goods whether or not an actual act of exchange takes place in a market'.[78] More directly,[79]

if one accepts that the mechanism which determines the choices of individuals, that is, the mechanism that generates relative prices, can be put in the form of a system of equations, then one has to accept, at least in principle that given the terms of the problem the prices can be calculated without any need for a market.

Subsequent debate revolved around the practical possibility of planning. Thus Hayek and Robbins objected that the Walrasian equations would take so much time and data as to be unusable for practical purposes, whereas Lange and Dobb both defended the notion. Lange opposes Von Mises yet grants much of the force of the criticisms of Robbins and Hayek. In doing so he reproduces, says Napoleoni, a mechanism rather like the market. Dobb's line points to a distinction between the efficient use of presently available goods on the one hand, and on the other to the longer-term problem of raising the productive capacity of an economy; planning is thus conceived as an instrument for accumulation rather than another style of allocation.

The history prepared by Turner and Collis[80] of notions of economic planning fills out the above treatment in that it permits us to add two further notes. First, they distinguish, both as practical and as theoretical efforts, between 'imperative' and 'indicative' planning. The former identifies those conceptions thrown up by socialist thinkers, and the latter one those patterns of government intervention developed by the 'West'. The former seeks to replace the market, whilst the latter seeks to reduce the possibilities for market disequilibrium. The second note to be made is that the history of theorizing on these matters (whether imperative or indicative), has been marked by the elaboration of sophisticated modelling, forecasting, gaming, etc., techniques.

What this brief sketch establishes for our purposes is that the required notion of planning was not wholly novel, nor incoherent, for the orthodoxy; and (recalling Clairmonte) it was increasingly an element of the actual behaviour of capitalist enterprise in that era of concentration. None the less, the notion, cutting at the heart of the dogma of the market, was not uncontested.[81]

We now consider institutional change. Above we have seen how the idea of 'intervention' elicits the idea of planning and how that idea was a contested element of established economic theory, available for use when required for the construction of theories of development. We now come at the same issue, the emergence of planning, from a different direction and show how the notion's

theoretical availability was translated, ambiguously, into practice as an element of the 'Keynesian revolution' as further
shaped by the emergence of doctrines of growth.

Brookfield notes that a contributory factor in the rise of the
preoccupation with 'growth' was the 'reconstruction of capitalism', specifically monopoly forms of enterprises and a recasting
of the relationship of state and industry. Writing as some sort
of a marxist, he properly notes that 'there is nothing new about
the partnership between capital and state';[82] what is novel is
its respectability and organization. The aspect of 'respectability'
is well expressed in Clairmonte's work, as when, discussing the
emergence of interventionism, he remarks that: 'By the end of
the thirties the Keynesian approach to problems of economic
stabilisation and full employment had become generalized.'[83]
Now this is a bold claim: and whilst with regard to subsequently
established war economies it is arguably true,[84] with regard
to post-war capitalist economies of the 'West' it is arguably false.
Indeed, Clairmonte notes that between 1950 and 1954 there was
a stream of US government reports stressing market principles,
and Robinson (1962) notes that Keynesianism was only ever
patchily taken up.

That Clairmonte can make his bold, if anxious, claim reflects,
as we shall see in chapter 4, the optimism of the period. Here
we can record that legislative innovation accompanies the emergence of the doctrine of growth. The doctrine is itself novel but,
says Postan, 'even more fundamental were the legislative and
institutional innovations introduced by individual governments in
their pursuit of economic development'.[85] After that gesture
to theory, he notes the practical counterpart, saying: 'If immediately after the war France was almost alone in trying to
work out and to enforce a central "plan", eventually most governments equipped themselves with machineries and policies for
the concerted planning of economic growth.'[86]

The theoretical basis for these changes from pre-war attitudes
was Keynesian; and in the 'West' these new machineries have
taken the form of varieties of indicative planning devices. The
extent and style of adoption varies; so in the USA acknowledgment of a Keynesian-style role of government was, at least
ideologically, more fraught. Thus Harris, talking of the ERP,
notes that it points out an uncomfortable gap between US ideals
of market forces and actual US practice. Some see this tension
as resolved in favour of the status quo; thus Sweezy argues
that with the Kennedy period the reformism of Keynes was finally
extinguished.[87] However any debate about the career of
Keynesianism is resolved, it remains the case that in matters of
respectability and organization the work of Keynes legitimated
and permitted a reworking of the relationship of state and industry, and a reworking of public attitudes thereto. Keynesianism, we have tried to point out, was the particular intellectual/
ideological form in which a prior political need to 'intervene'
manifested itself.

2.3 Aid: the lowest tier, 'intervention' implemented

Thus far we have looked at the legitimation of the idea of 'intervention' in the construction of growth theories which serve (or
purport to) the purpose of telling the intervening agent how a
given system might be understood to behave. The 'might' is not
unimportant, as we noted that the claim of model-users and
economists with regard to the status of these models was problematic. We intimated that even if the claim to deductive-empirical
scientific status was not lodged then it was very easy to slide
from regarding a model as a heuristic device to seeing it as a,
maybe imperfect, statement about an external, given, reality.
  Subsequently we pursued the matter of the organization of
intervention: if we know in principle how our target system
behaves, then we need as a next step to be clear as to how,
precisely, we may approach and manipulate it. This requirement
of 'intervention' we took to have spawned the interest we noted,
amongst theoreticians and practitioners, in planning. The planner, our agent, seeks to establish mechanisms for the organization of specific interventions. This role is subject to two polar
interpretations; the master scientist and the under-labourer.
Both are out of the same school of interventionism, and thus
shifting from one to the other represents a change of emphasis
within an approach, rather than any change of line. Waterson
plots this, as a historical shift, very well.[88] Treating the
period of the late 1960s, he argues that the style of 'planning
from the top down' gives way to the inverse style, that is 'planning from the bottom up', where the pursuit of straightforwardly
given opportunities is substituted for the pursuit of more general ideologically derived objectives of development. Yet, whatever the style and whatever the mix of the above two elements,
in the end the planner writes plans: blueprints for 'interventions'.
  We thus reach the third stage of 'intervention': from legitimation, through organization, to implementation. Aid - which
generically we can take to be specific, piecemeal interventions
in the system having the aim of contriving a preferred state of
affairs - may be in the form of 'one-off jobs', a part of a sequence, a programme, a set, etc. Here we look at questions of
the origins and principles of aid, and the extension of interest
to the Third World.
  The sources of the idea of aid can be placed in the nature of
the ideology of growth; that is, aid is a logical consequence of
growth models. As regards the origin of present conceptions of
aid as a practical activity, most theorists point to the immediate
post-war period.[89] The usual conception of this time is most
clearly expressed by Mikesell when he writes that: '(i) aid
theories provide an analytic framework for determining the
amount and timing of the aid and the policies which must be
followed by the recipient country for (ii) achieving a given target rate of growth which can be sustained without further external assistance'.[90]

Zeylstra identifies two sources of interest for aid-giving, though these reflect wider differences than he explicitly notes between US and European interests. Thus we have noted a split between H-D et al. and Solow et al., and here we may add a historical aspect to the divergence. Mikesell argues that:[91]

the vast bulk of French and British foreign aid is directed toward their respective community of nations. Unlike the US, Britain and France have not had to develop a special rationale in terms of either Free World security or universal human-itarianism for obtaining public support for their aid programs.

Zeylstra's first source is aid to allies, exemplified by the ERP, by means of which the USA disbursed aid to sixteen European nations. White[92], in his politically sensitive treatment of aid, identifies the period 1948-52 (original ERP programme years) as the time of the first phase in the career of the notion of aid. The second phase represents a geographical extension: thus as ERP secured allies in Europe, so aid will secure allies in Asia, 1952-6. These two periods constitute what we have taken as the period of 'internal orientation' on the part of Western theorists and agencies. With the shift of aid to the Asian sphere, its per-ceived task is broadened, and the notion of development comes to the fore rather than reconstruction. The notion becomes dif-fuse. This process is further advanced when, in the wake of the 1955 Bandung Conference's advocacy of the claims of the 'non-aligned', the USSR emerges as a source of aid. The division of the world into two camps is thus broken and the Third World becomes a realm of competition. Aid is no longer to allies, but is rather a contract; demands that recipients become allies are no longer tenable; rather, a development ideology is propounded. As Streeten puts it, 'growth according to their respective West-ern and Eastern recipes was held out as the reward for keeping out of the other camp'.[93] This set of events we take to mark the switch from 'internal' to 'external' focus in regard to growth.

The second source of interest in aid-giving identified by Zeylstra is the 'decolonization' process. This is taken to have been split into two periods. The first was the more or less en-forced withdrawal from Asian and Arab lands. The problem of 'off-loading' remaining areas, principally in Africa, in an ordered manner was then confronted. The result is that from 1957 to 1964 (the period of ordered withdrawal) aid flows are linked to the transfer of power from colonial to indigenous regimes with whom agreements relating to development are made.

The above indicates the divergent sources of interest in, and consequent character of, the notion of aid. Identifying a core to such an idea is difficult, yet Zeylstra attempts this. (In his case it is to fix a measure against which practice may be judged; for our purposes, it is to reveal the character of the notion in the light of our idea of 'intervention'.) Zeylstra attempts to con-struct his criterial definition out of an examination of ordinary

usage; thus he says the analysis 'needs a concept defined
strictly according to the purpose that is expressed by it'.[94]
Five criteria of what is to count as international development aid
are identified.
(a) 'cooperation with a foreign state or autonomous political
unit':[95] here he acknowledges the problematical nature of the
state; de facto authority over an area is a sufficient condition,
de jure not a necessary one. Zeylstra begins here – not an obvious starting point, as one of his concerns is to locate the idea
of aid within the corpus of Western categories surrounding the
nineteenth-century rise of industrial states: the relevance of
this set of notions he questions. Polemically, he reduces 'development aid' to a 'missionary inspiration to propagate the western
way of life'.[96] The thrust of this critique we have treated in
chapter 2, when we asked, in effect, what else?
(b) 'With the object of assisting that state or autonomous political unit in furthering its economic growth and social purpose:'[97] the linking of questions of 'statehood' to notions of
'progress' is probably correct; we have intimated above that the
present form of the 'idea of progress' is 'growth', understood as
a doctrine. The ambiguity here, of which Zeylstra seems to be
aware, lies between propounding 'progress' (taken as integral
to Western thought) and the notion of 'development' on the one
hand, and on the other 'growth' seen as a post-war bastard
form of 'progress': an 'intervention' indeed designed to buy off
conflict!
(c) 'The peoples to be assisted should be completely responsible
for their countries' economic and social development.'[98] Here
there is a hint at the formal aspect of aid: the development aid
should be planned, assistance is targeted, it is not like flinging
fertilizer about and hoping. Thus a functioning government
machine is a necessary condition of receipt of aid.
(d) 'The decision to offer assistance, however, should not be
dominated by the wish to create... advantages [n.b. for donor]
intentionally.'[99] Aid is not an export-credit guarantee, for
instance (as the 'left' correctly perceived the Marshall Plan to
be). Advantages accruing to the donor should be secondary.
This is the moral aspect of 'aiding', as Zeylstra sees it; the
effort ought not to flow from an instrumental stance but from an
ethic of ends.
(e) 'Insofar as development cooperation refers to economic development, presuming its efficacy presupposes that development,
growth, progress, are not predetermined elements of a "given
reality", but subject to human effort.'[100] Zeylstra talks of
'effort', not control; he hedges on extent to which human input
to history is taken as being effective. A naive view of planning
would approach, say, a Fabian/liberal ideal of replacement of
politics. The converse would be a thoroughgoing determinism.
It is the mix of these two and the resulting claims for extent of
human power (both theoretically, and as a practical historical
possibility for the present) that is the difficult question here.

Zeylstra dodges it. That this is the crucial element he indeed recognizes, noting that 'in all social fields attention became focussed on the role human effort played as a creative element'.[101]

This final criterion, (e), is in fact the basis of any aid effort, whilst the other four list in idealist fashion the ordinary-language derived definition of aid. That such a definition may be of use in examining the practical record of donors becomes clear when we add that this arguably rather empty analysis follows an explicit setting aside of familiar political notions of aid. For the present, we note that Zeylstra offers the beginnings of a formal definition of aid, what we would expect to derive from 'intervention' ((c) and (e), and (a) in that it pursues clarity in exchange), and couples it with an odd acknowledgment of his status as a Western theorist ((a), (b), and (d)). The criticisms aimed at the notions of progress/state/development are in some sense moral, the notions are taken to be problematical in some way. That they are not absolutes we may grant; that they are thereby negotiable in any significant or immediate sense, seems to us to be a false conclusion (as we say in chapter 2).

The foregoing indicates the practical sources of interest in aid and its scope as a concept guiding action. (It is not a report on how it has been used. This is White's procedure; of his own effort he notes that it looks at 'the many ways in which the many different sorts of resource called "aid" have been used'.[102]) It will now be appropriate to ask how the orthodox notion was deployed via à vis matters of the development of the Third World. Here we use the work of White; his 'empiricist' approach to aid easily reveals the facts brute-relative to our present concerns. We ask how does aid sit with orthodox economics? The answer, to anticipate, is: very closely, with 'supplemental theories' whereby specific interventions are aimed at unsatisfactory areas of the recipient's economic system.

White's procedure presents problems, thus his 'empiricism', although declared, is flawed. He seemingly deploys an aprioristic categorization to types of aid theories and entirely fails to see how the most familiar type of theory, in his own estimation, flows from the fundamental 'intervention' orientation of the conventional wisdom. Thus he says of his first category, 'supplemental','that [it] predominates in most of the literature on aid', [103] and he goes on: 'this in itself is a phenomenon which requires explanation. In principle the four categories are indeed of equal status.'[104] Setting aside the question of what this last remark entails for his declared 'nominalism', we may ask whether his answer to his own question is adequate. His answer is that in the 'ideas market' supplemental theories were in demand. In contrast, Zeylstra's effort here is richer: he also shows the element of political demand, but goes on to note that the theories produced were developed out of existing economic-theory resources. It seems safe to assert that thinkers pursue consistency even if they are operating in a market for ideas. The failure of

White to relate supplementary theories of aid to the dominant
orthodoxies' ethos flows, it would seem, from his insensitivity to
the role of theory in social science.

White begins his report as follows: 'The starting point of
supplemental theories is the identification of some key factor of
the development process.'[105] We can note that White does not
split the intervention sequence into three parts as we have
done, consequently he criticizes supplemental schemes for being
more than descriptions of how aid works, saying; 'they are
essentially theories about the role of savings or foreign exchange or skills or institutions in development, not about aid as
such, and it is from a view about the role of savings etc. that
they prescribe rather than describe the role of aid'.[106] If he
regarded aid as the third leg of an intervention sequence then
this criticism could not arise, because the wholly formal aspect
of description is effected by the 'growth model' stage of the
treatment. A second point from the above is that the view noted
fits with our examination of the notion of 'intervention', but we
may ask: why 'key factor' and not 'key factors'? Is this simply
an accident of intellectual history in the sense that a theory,
H-D, liable to single-factor interpretation, was available on the
shelf when called for? Or might there be an intrinsic tendency
in this interventionist line towards identifying a 'key factor' out
of some wider preliminary set? If the realm of the social is regarded as a field of interactions behaving analogously to natural
science 'causes', then the possibility of identifying one element
that just is the crucial element is open. It follows from the
principle of economy in explanation, as a logical possibility.
However, on the face of it White's explanation seems more plausible; presumably the confidence of the theorists did not extend
to their being prepared to claim that their models were that
accurate. If that estimation is correct, then a sociology of knowledge and/or psychological explanation is to be sought for this
habit of producing 'key' factors.

White notes that in the 1950s and early 1960s this 'key factor'
was usually savings. He goes on to say that by the mid-1960s
'single factor' approaches were falling out of favour. Supplemental theories were revised, he tells us, by adding 'transfer of
organisation' to the development brew, and this was significant.
'The emphasis shifted from resources for development to institutions of development and to the forms of social organisation
most likely to stimulate development.'[107] The significance of
this is taken to be two-fold. First, 'assistance' becomes 'leverage'; and second, expectations of impact of aid veer from en-
hancement of local trends to effecting of fundamental changes
in recipient states' social orders.

Two points arise from this. First, the shift from 'help' to
'leverage' is non-existent. White takes 'leverage' to be a late
1960s notion, whereas with Harris we have noted its being an
element of ERP. It also rather goes against what he has to say
with respect to history of aid. Thus his phase II (early 1950s)

sees the US offering aid to allies in Asia to fight communism;
surely that counts as 'leverage'? The second point is rather more
significant. We may ask whether White is lumping together US
modernization theory with Streeten/Myrdal 'institutional economics'. Clearly they have resemblances, yet we wish to distinguish them. A little light is thrown on this with White's next
claim: 'The two dominant influences in the construction of
growth models as a basis for supplemental theories have been
the H-D model ... and W.W. Rostow's theory of the stages of
economic growth.'[108] Now it is clear that 'institutional economists' (if they include Seers, Streeten, Myrdal, etc.) do move
away from any H-D/Rostow line. This latter line leads straight
to the Kennedy 'high tide' period. Thus we may suggest that
Rostow (abusing much work on ICOR, according to Brookfield)
combines the H-D model, as adjusted by Solow such that growth
is 'natural' and not unlikely, with US proselytizing, in modernization theory. In this case there are indeed two lines to be
distinguished, and it is not clear that White does this.

We began this subsection by asking how the principles of
development aid looked at sat with the economic orthodoxy. We
answer that the relation is close in the case of supplemental
theories of aid, in that aid is: (1) seen as a specific intervention, this assumes the guise of an implication of H-D model,
though that model is later heavily revised in very many ways
(see Mikesell); (2) seen as being of short duration, vulgarly
Rostow's 'take-off'; (3) seen as resulting in the raising of the
economic system to a new higher level of activity where growth
is self-sustaining.

2.4 Summary of section 2

Beginning with the notion of 'intervention', we have tried to
display the nature of the early post-war orthodoxy of 'development studies'. We have argued that political demand lodged
within the theoretical context of the Keynesian revolution, as
indicated in Part I, called forth the policy-scientific notion of
ordered growth.

'Intervention', we argued, required a tripartite treatment.
(1) Legitimation, a general theorem, and this we saw as being
provided by 'growth theory'. (2) Action must be ordered; here
we looked at ideas of planning, both those lodged in the history
of economic debate, and those called forth by Keynesian recasting of the role of government. (3) Aid: the final stage in
the interventionist scheme, that is, implementation.

Now we have had something to say about these issues as they
present themselves in the context of treatments of matters of
the Third World, but thus far only in passing. We now turn
directly to the question of the application of this general strategy and set of assumptions to the issue of the development of
the Third World.

3.0 DYNAMIC OF THEORY II: EARLY PRACTICE, KEYNES EXPORTED

In the earlier parts of this chapter we have looked at the pre-occupations of the politically dominant groups of the 'West' and at the subsequent efforts, on their behalf, of economic theorists. Now we must look at examples of this orientation at work with issues of Third World development. Thus we now effect the shift from historical résumé and analytic exegesis to critical reporting: we look at Keynesianism in action.

Kurihara provides the lever when he observes that: 'The UN 1951 publication "Measures for the economic development of underdeveloped countries" was an eloquent testimony to the new post-war, post-Keynesian hope of raising the living standards of economically backward countries through deliberate action.'[109] This provides a starting point, but then we are given two specific preliminaries. Kurihara remarks: 'that UN report could not, I believe, have been written prior to the appearance of Harrod's "Dynamic Economics" or possibly without Joan Robinson's challenging suggestion that Harrod's growth theory should be applied a fortiori to capital-poor under-developed economies'.[110]

Harrod's work we have already taken note of and here we are concerned with applications, so we begin with Joan Robinson. The suggestion to which Kurihara refers[111] is to be found in her 1949 review of Harrod's essays. In the course of the review she has occasion to ask just what is meant by the notion of a 'warranted rate of growth'. The answer involves the familiar Keynesian terms - saving, investment, capital, etc. The relevance of all this to the situation of 'under-developed countries' is the realization that the notion of 'unemployment' used in developed areas is not suitable to the situation of under-developed countries, more useful is 'marxian unemployment'.[112]

This is of interest to us, not for any purposes of economic analysis, but because it clearly leads into the central issue for these Keynesian-inspired economists, that is, how to plot the behaviour of economic factors and indicators in a Keynesian-informed way when the economies being treated are so radically different to those of the industrialized nations. The major report that follows up Robinson's remarks in the sense of centring the work on 'employment' is the 1951 UN report of Lewis et al.

3.1 The 1951 UN report

We may quote, as they do, from their brief from the UN Economic and Social Council; thus they are instructed to prepare 'a report on unemployment and under-employment... [in under-developed countries], and the national and international measures required to reduce such unemployment and under-employment'.[113] The authors admit to having problems in 'interpreting the term "under-developed countries",'[114] but apparently they find the use of the notions of employment straightforward, thus they first list and review the four types of unemployment found in under-developed countries. However, there is an implicit appreciation here of Robinson's point, for they redefine their task as focusing on 'economic development rather than upon unemployment'.[115] Their treatment involves looking at: (1) preconditions of progress; thus they see as a necessary condition 'proper' cultural orientations. Here we may note that the committee's narrow intellectual background is revealed in that what distinguishes under-developed countries from developed countries is labelled/dismissed as 'pre-requisites'. They go on (2) and note the role of the government, though here the Keynesianism is blurred as its task is presented as passive and enabling. The effort rests on the analogy of under-developed countries' governments facing development and developed countries' governments facing depression.

Now matters technical are treated; thus (3) domestic saving is dealt with, and here they offer a tacit definition of their assumed goal. They note that developed countries' rate of capital formation is 10 per cent of national income, whereas the rate for under-developed countries is only 5 per cent of national income. The question is how to raise the rate of capital-formation. In White's pejorative phrase, this tends to 'gappery' or supplemental thinking, thus aid is seen to be one way of plugging this gap. Several techniques are discussed, and what is most interesting is how matters of economics and politics are casually jumbled together. In para. III they observe that 'people of middle and higher incomes in many UDCs are well known for their tendency to conspicuous consumption and there is no doubt that a fall in their consumption would be in the public interest'.[116] The authors neither pretend to be neutral social scientists nor do they come out and explicitly argue a case, as our notion of social theory requires. Rather they take the role of 'experts' and argue a case against a backdrop of unexamined, unacknowledged, assumptions.

The intellectual link between Robinson and Lewis et al.'s work - revealing the project of the 'extension' of Keynes - can be seen most clearly in the latter's treatment of deficit financing and inflation. Asking about the use of idle resources, they go straight on to 'considering the possibility of creating capital by employing the under-employed to work for wages on public works ... if this labour were employed on public works, capital would be created without any fall in either output or total consumption'.[117] Having presented the rationale, they go on to contrast the situation in developed countries, where governments can create money and lift employment rates and activity rates via the multiplier, with the situation in under-developed countries. Here, they say, 'the process is not so simple';[118] they note a propensity to import and pressure for inflation as the system cannot respond to a rise in demand from consumers. This is an interesting area and here we may cite the work of

V.K.R.V. Rao, a contemporary critic, whose treatment is distinctly sharper. His view is that the Keynesian approach breaks
down.[119]

Rao's critique begins by rehearsing the main points of Keynesian theory. It is noted that Keynes was mostly concerned with
'the problem of involuntary unemployment in the richer countries'[120] and that 'the remedies he puts forward, viz. cheap
money, deficit financing, redistributive taxation, and public
investment have all become current coin in national economic
policies with full employment as the major objective'.[121] This
general set of notions, this newly (re)constituted common sense
of economics, has been applied (as might be expected) to various
circumstances, in particular those of the under-developed
country. Rao notes:[122]

> unfortunately Keynes did not formulate the economic problem
> of the UDCs .... the result has been a rather unintelligent
> application .... thus it is common ground with most writers
> on the economics of UDCs that what was required for their
> economic development was an increase in the purchasing power
> of the people. Deficit financing and created money have
> figured in practically all the plans.

Rao goes on to consider the presumptions of the Keynesian
scheme; that is, he asks in what particular circumstances do
these concepts make sense? It is then indicated how these concepts are inadequate to the situation of a UDC (India is taken
as illustrative case). Rao focuses his attention on the matter of
'employment' and asks what are the conditions in which the
'multiplier' will work? The answer is, immediately, 'involuntary
unemployment', and thereafter the free market economy which
this phenomenon presupposes. That the economies of under-
developed countries can be said to have 'involuntary unemployment' is not obvious. Rao recalls that Robinson ('Essays in the
Theory of Employment') has introduced the term 'disguised unemployment' and that this might be thought appropriate to under-
developed countries; but this would be wrong. Robinson's
'disguised unemployment' flows from a decline in demand, whereas under-developed countries have always operated at a low
activity level; so 'disguised unemployment' is normal, thus we
might even properly speak of 'voluntary unemployment'. Anyhow,
a presumption of the 'multiplier' thus does not hold and 'the
multiplier principle as enunciated by Keynes does not operate in
regard to the problem of diminishing unemployment and increasing output in an under-developed country'.[123] Of course,
policy based on these assumptions will not be helpful either;
indeed, the simple extension of Keynesian ideas is taken to have
done a great deal of harm. In this Brookfield concurs, reporting
that these early attempts to apply Keynes 'proved disastrous'.[124]
Interestingly, Rao suggests, finally, that the work of the classical economists might prove a more rewarding area of intellectual
inquiry.

Returning to the 1951 UN report, it goes on to treat (4) planning. We are given an anodyne definition of planning as 'concerned with the proper disposal of resources between different
uses'.[125] That Lewis et al. are advocates of planning should
not surprise anyone. However, we note their 'defence' (for they
do offer one) as it illuminates the aside made by Robinson in her
review of Harrod (where she noted that Harrod executes a familiar and unhappy manoeuvre of argument: namely, 'It is a
common vice of present-day economic argument to jump from a
highly abstract piece of analysis straight to prescriptions for
policy, without going through the intermediate stage of examining how far the assumptions in the analysis fit the facts of
the actual situation').[126]

The 'experts' (as the UN and Kurihara (1954) describe them)
say that economics provides two general principles. First, the
notion of the margin: thus 'resources should be used in such a
way that a transfer of marginal units from one use to another
could not increase welfare'.[127] Now this is the 'welfare economics' version of the neo-classical notion of an optimum config-
uration, and as such it is acceptable. But they go on to make
the following claim, that the corollary is that one should not
think of any single industry or economic activity as more important than any other and should not therefore concentrate all
resources in one particular part of the economy'.[128] The shift
from a piece of neo-classical formalism to a policy injunction is
abrupt. The corollary, as thus far reported, is either a simple
equiform methodological note issuing in the dubiously derived
conclusion that a wholly unlikely situation ('all resources') is
prohibited, or it is the set-up for the introduction of a clearly
unrelated, non-consequential, policy prescription. They go on:
'Progress must be made on all fronts simultaneously';[129] and
this, if it means 'balanced growth', does not follow from the
simple statement of Paretian optimum. Robinson's point would
seem to be confirmed.

The second principle of policy the 'experts' take to flow
from the substantive difference between micro- and macro-level
changes in the system. Thus 'large movements of resources
within the economy will have effects which are disproportionately
different from marginal movements'.[130] The planning dictum
apparently derived from this is that if marginal adjustments do
not look promising, try structural ones. The justification drawn
from theory of this rule of thumb looks strained, and indeed the
rule of thumb with which we have been presented looks trivial.
However, this 'argument' is then used as a hay-maker for neo-
classical economics. Thus if it is structural changes we are
looking at, then micro-economics of marginalism are of secondary
importance. Further, as quantification is so difficult at these
aggregative levels and as data differs from one UDC to another,
it is not possible to offer any general rules governing economic
planning: 'those who are responsible must soak themselves
thoroughly in the facts of each particular case and must then

use their best judgment as to what will be the most desirable
directions of movement'.[131] This is one of the more breath-
takingly optimistic sections of this report. The orthodoxy from
which Keynesianism sprang is cast off entirely and replaced by
the planner's 'best judgment'. Indeed, it calls for nothing less
than carte blanche for the economic planner.

There are two further elements of the 1951 UN report to note.
Thus (5) the report looks at terms of trade. On this they affirm
a loose internationalism that is in accord with the style to be
expected of a UN study, and, more pointedly, fits with American
notions of the proper development of post-war trade. They
affirm that international trade is important to all; and as regards cyclical fluctuations in the trade cycle, long-term decline
in terms of trade, and protectionist measures by the developed,
the 'experts' are sure that the DCs can sort these problems out.

Finally, (6) we come to the matter of external sources of capital. Here we see two points of interest. First, they answer the
question of the extent to which capital is needed from abroad by
seeking to indicate a quantity. This, they grant, is difficult, so
why do they do it? It meets the orthodox desire for precision,
and falls into line worked by C. Clarke and S. Kuznets. The
immediate thought must be that they are arguing in the light of
the experience of Marshall Aid where large sums were shifted
about. This impression is reinforced when, discussing the government's role as provider of infrastructure, they go on to say:
'we do not suggest that aid should be given unconditionally to
under-developed countries. This would not be wise. Each grant
should be linked to a specific function, and there should be
international verification that the funds are used only for the
purposes for which they have been granted'.[132] Thus aid is
targeted and monitored according to 'wise' prescriptions. This
is what we would expect to find: it is the practical expression of
a 'policy science', and indeed it is how the Marshall Plan worked,
at least at first.

3.2 An early general statement: Arthur Lewis

The above critical exposition of the 1951 UN report had as its
objective the elucidation of its Keynesian inspiration and com-
mensurability with an interventionist ideal. It was one of the
earliest efforts to make sense of the matter of the Third World.
We can further pursue the question of the 'export of Keynes'
with the theorist Lewis, who in 1955 published a formal treatise
on the development of the under-developed countries.

Lewis[133] declares in the book's preface that he is not presenting original ideas, but offering a framework for studying
economic development. 'A book of this kind', he says,[134]

seemed to be necessary because the theory of economic growth
once more engages worldwide interest, and because no com-

prehensive treatise on the subject has been published for
about a century. The last great book covering this wide range
was J.S. Mill's 'Principles of Political Economy' published in
1848.

Lewis begins by identifying his subject as 'the growth of output per head of population'.[135] His method is a combination
(unspecified) of the deductive pursuit of consistency of formulation of statements (the familiar realm of economics, he says)
and what he calls 'evolutionary' study. We must 'apply the
inductive method to historical data'.[136] That this empiricism
is to be taken as inferior to that of the natural sciences is a
point Lewis makes, and he calls for modesty of conclusion when
predicting how far 'changes which occurred in the wealthier
countries as they developed may be expected to repeat themselves in the poorer countries if they develop'.[137]
     The level of the inquiry is announced early: thus causal ex-
planation is assumed but not pursued, rather a general level of
'proximate cause' is fastened on. There are three such 'proximate causes', Lewis tells us, with which we can grasp these
matters of growth and development. These are: first, the 'effort
to economise',[138] which notion Lewis uses to characterize the
DCs: included within it, or as illustrations of it, are experiment-
ation, risk-taking, mobility, and specialization. We can take it
as straightforwardly descriptive of his world. Its liability to
criticisms developed with the notions of over-simplification,
aggregation, and value insensitivity, is evident. The second
cause which Lewis cites is the increase of knowledge and its
application. We can regard this as a simple corollary of the first
point; thus Gellner remarks that 'science is the mode of cog-
nition of industrial society'.[139] Finally we are reminded that
growth depends upon increasing the amount of capital; which is
vacuous, except that it reads development as an economic matter.
     From these three elements Lewis sketches a procedure of un-
packing; thus he shifts closer to 'history', asking why do these
'proximate causes' operate in some societies more strongly than
in others. He takes this sequence to be one of a search for consistency - just what environment is conducive to economic
growth? These questions are then reformulated to focus on the
evolutionary aspects: how do 'environments' change, becoming
more or less conducive to economic growth? This is the area of
historical research and social scientific interest.
     Lewis, it seems, is fixed in the economist's deductive empiri-
cism. The trio of 'proximate causes' are simply presented; they
are obvious, and with hindsight clearly of no greater status than
any other group's taken-for-granted assumptions. For our immediate purposes, we note that they reduce to an affirmation of
the common sense of the orthodoxy plus an emphasis on the role
of capital. We can go on to look at what he has to say about capital; the comments on social/cultural preconditions we will leave
until chapter 4, when we look at the rise of the wider social

scientific contribution in the guise of 'modernization theory'.
With regard to the issue of capital, Lewis is concerned to look
at (a) the amount of capital required for economic growth, (b)
sources of savings, and (c) the process of investment.

(a) Lewis begins with a weak claim: 'economic growth is associated with an increase in capital per head';[140] and as regards
the matters of quantification he acknowledges the work of Clarke
and Kuznets as pioneers. The work begins with ICOR, taken as
embracing two generally accepted generalizations: that ICOR is
constant at the margin, and that in developed countries it is
3:1. The question becomes how can this be shifted to situation
of under-developed countries. The debate revolves around the
issue of whether ICOR is higher or lower in under-developed
countries. Lewis looks at the debate, which is couched in the
familiar aggregative mechanics of economics, and concludes that
'we do not know what the marginal capital income ratio is in any
UDC ... all the same, if for want of anything better we use the
ratio which has been found for industrial countries, it is easy
enough to see why income grows so slowly in the less developed
countries' [141] Briefly, rates of investment as a percentage of
national income are lower than in developed countries; the conclusion is that 'this in turn raises the question of how rapidly
capital formation can be accelerated'.[142]

(b) Looking for sources, Lewis begins with the claim: 'The
proposition which we have established in the preceding section
is that investment is necessary to economic growth',[143] and
here we may note that the relation between growth and capital
has shifted from 'association' to 'necessity' via an admittedly inadequate route that is, ICOR and the discussion attached thereto. Lewis has not established this link, either empirically or
conceptually; though that is where the link is, in his presumed
Keynesianism. However, from this claim Lewis remarks that: 'it
follows in a passive sense'[144] that saving is necessary for
growth because savings have to be equal to investment. Quite
what he means by 'passive sense' is not clear: it follows within
the logic of neo-classical economics, but the issue which he goes
on to treat, as to whether and how they are in balance, is more
particularly Keynesian. He remarks that 'we have therefore come
to analyse separately the forces determining saving and the
forces determining investment'.[145] Either way, the problem for
under-developed countries, as Lewis sees it at this point, is a
lack of savings to finance investment. Given this requirement
for savings, and having ruled out deficit financing, he asks
about sources, identifying two: first, domestic, such as hoards,
taxation, banking and profits, etc.; and second, external finance,
a supplement to local efforts.

(c) Under the heading 'investment' Lewis discusses some institutional preconditions of economic growth. He makes note of such
financial arrangements as 'limited liability', 'flexible bank lending
policy', 'easy marketability of investments' and so on. The list
presented of preconditions is that of the superficial character-

istics of a post-war Keynesian-run economy plus descriptions of various mechanisms peculiar to the industrial 'West', modified where it seems appropriate to 'fit' the under-developed country situations.

Let us now, briefly, consider Lewis's strategy in his version of the 'export of Keynes'. Most generally it is clear that Lewis argues out of a 'school': he writes 'explanation-in-the-light-of-x', where x happens to be that set of Keynesian-derived ideas treating growth which centre on the role of capital. So how does this differ from the preliminary notes on the notion of 'social theory' presented in Part I of this study? (i) Epistemologically the effort is taken to be empiricist, and consequently it gets confused. Much pertinent detail is taken note of, but the material lacks any plausible frame of explanation. The material appears to be all 'on a level', and elements of the text are not distinguished according to role, or at least not in any obvious fashion. Consequently, the material presents itself as very largely descriptive in character. The general form assumed is deductive, and this requires that its starting points be taken as facts: high-level generalizations, from which an explanatory model is made. The model, correctly manipulated, will generate remote conclusions and these will be taken as drawn from and corresponding to facts where the latter set can then inform policy decisions. We have argued above that this is an implausible scheme; and when we add to this a set of starting points that so resemble common sense, that the resultant material should present itself as orthodoxly descriptive should come as no surprise. (ii) With engagement, the orthodox take the role of the 'expert' and conceive of their role as analogous to that of the natural scientist. The class or group they represent is consequently not clearly identified and nor, inevitably, are the implications of their relation to a social group spelt out. Thus the whole 'realm of valuation' is sidestepped, indeed the orthodox is supposed; what we have is 'policy science'. (iii) In the light of the preceding two notes we add one on theory. In Lewis's scheme the role of theory is, to our mind, mishandled. For Lewis, the role of theory is passive: it is an assemblage of deductions from evident truths, it is a kind of scaffolding for getting from familiar As to unfamiliar and hopefully policy-relevant Bs. Grounded in social facts, the edifice helps uncover others. Contrariwise, the notion of social theory which we introduced in our Prologue made theory a more central phenomenon. We took theorizing to be concerned with actively displaying the nature of the social construction of explanation; that is, we placed stress on the business of 'making sense'. Theory was taken as a moral intervention in the world, not just an attempt to model it.

3.3 Concluding note

The work of Lewis we take to be an exemplar of the positivistic empiricism of orthodox policy science. He begins with assumptions

of a superficially formal kind, adds in aggregated empirical
notions and builds abstract models. The return to the practical-
empirical is effected by the removal of simplifying assumptions.
This procedure admits of a wide variety of treatments of any
particular problem. Assumptions may be varied, aggregated
notions varied, and procedures of stepping down to 'reality'
varied. This amount of intrinsic 'slack' in the procedure permits
the pursuit of a practical problem to be so ordered as to produce a favoured 'sort' of answer for the theoretician's 'client'.
We may note that this is not science, however loosely that is
defined. Solow's rewrite of the H-D model throws up into clear
relief the question of the precise status of this style of modelling.

However, we should not stress this aspect of the orthodoxy to
the exclusion of all else. The effort was not monolithic, and nor
was it fruitless; indeed the reverse is the case. Evidently these
theorists were sensitive to (i) the difficulties of shifting established tools to the Third World and (ii) the complexity of the
problems themselves. Given the demand that they produce something by way of a 'development theory', their procedure was
both what we would expect, thus their theories reveal their intellectual roots, and sensible in that they apparently began with
the world-as-it-was and sought to identify its possibilities. That
they misconceived their starting point, or miscast it theoretically,
is pointed out by Streeten and it is a view we would echo.

4 The positivist high tide: 'modernization theory'

1.0 INTRODUCTION

Chapters 3 and 4 comprise one part of this study and the relationship of these two elements may be expressed in the claim
that what is at issue is a revision of the legitimating theorem of
'intervention'. Thus 'modernization theory' replaces 'growth
theory' as the orthodoxy of 'development studies', and does so
within the context of cold war competition between super-powers
for influence in the Third World.

We will begin by taking note of the then current political pre-
occupations of the USA, the principal actor in this period. In
chapter 3 the historical material presented focused upon the pre-
war revisions of Keynes, the wartime alliances, and the economic
role of the ERP in European reconstruction. Here we must start
with the more general counterpart to Marshall Aid, that is, the
Truman Doctrine and the so-called 'cold war'. It will be our contention that 'modernization theory' is the ideological child of the
cold war: US theorists, operating within the ambit of the notion
of 'containment', seek to secure allies for the US within the
Third World. Competition with the USSR necessitates the dis-
guising of self-interest; thus the US offers 'modernization' and
membership of the 'free world' as against 'socialism'. It is here
that we find the moral core of 'modernization', and from this
point we seek to show how this evaluative core is given analytic
and descriptive substance by examining the efforts of economics
and the wider group of the social sciences.

Following our note on the 'cold war', we develop the line of
Keynesian theorizing that we have already come across as it experiences further refinement and general reformulation vis à vis
Third World development. The 'debate with Harrod' is noted as
one aspect of the wider process of the emasculation of Keynes
and the reconstitution of neo-classical economics. Specifically in
relation to matters of the Third World, we observe the continued
reliance on growth models, and note that they become elaborate
in their pursuit of realism.

The elements of economics constitute one thread of theoretical
or disciplinary work that carries over from chapter 3. There is
another, in so far as it was latent in the efforts of Lewis et al.[1]
and Lewis,[2] and this concerns the rise in importance of the
contribution made by the wider group of the social sciences. It
is here that we can plot the elaboration of the 'modernization'
scheme through the use of a series of dichotomies serving to

elucidate the one overarching distinction between 'traditional' and 'modern' societies.

Following the discussion of the occasion and character of 'modernization', we go on to investigate the impact of the work of Rostow as a legitimating theorem for 'intervention'.[3] We consider the way in which he uses the theoretical resources available to him to fashion, in response to political demand, his own widely influential scheme of 'modernization'.

Having presented a review of the material via its critics, and a review of the work of Rostow, we take note that the career of 'modernization' can be taken to traverse a series of 'stages' and that as its gaudiest manifestation, in Rostow, achieves widespread notice, so too does an almost unremarked line of revision point to a reintroduction of the concerns of classical political theorizing.

By this time it is also clear that the world of 'cold war' is not that of elaborated 'modernization', in two senses. First, the ideology of 'modernization' is broader and less stridently enunciated than Truman's 'cold war', and second, the 'reality' of the world situation is no longer that of the cold war era. In particular, US paramountcy has already given way, even if not yet in the perceptions of the US government, to a more complex pattern. Thus as 'modernization' reached its apogee in the Kennedy years, its assumptions and thus formulations became wholly implausible.

2.0 DYNAMIC OF SOCIETY: THE OCCASION OF 'MODERNIZATION'

The period covered by this chapter, in so far as 'themes' attach to otherwise identified historical periods or events, runs from the mid-1950s to the mid-1960s. We begin by following White[4] in distinguishing between the loci of interest on the part of the theorists. Thus chapter 3 treated the interventionist orthodoxy in its internally oriented phase. Here development was construed along lines taken as identified in the episode of the Marshall Plan, and we went on to treat what we termed the 'export' of Keynesianism to the Third World. White's second phase is the subject of the present chapter; here the theorist's attention is firmly directed to matters of the character, dynamics and directions of change of the societies of the Third World. White, whose study is concerned with the politics of aid, identifies the Bandung Conference as marking this shift.

Until 1953 the USSR is taken to have regarded the world as split into hostile camps; hence 'non-alignment' was viewed with disfavour. With Stalin's death there was a relaxation in that stance which coincided with a 'thaw' in the 'cold war' proper. White records that in July 1953 the first sign of a new line was the USSR's pledge of one million dollars to a UN aid programme. This shift was reinforced by the Bandung Conference of 1955

which asserted, on the part of a group of Asian and African
countries, the notion of 'non-alignment' and anti-colonialism. In
1956 Khrushchev, in a report to the 20th Party Congress,[5]
announced the USSR's willingness to offer aid to 'developing'
countries. This offer saw practical expression in that in the wake
of the USA's withdrawal of financial support for Nasser's Aswan
High Dam the USSR stepped in.

As a consequence of these events there opened up, with regard to aid-giving, 'a grey area between the two camps which
constituted an area of competition'.[6] Henceforth aid, the clear-
est example of concern with the Third World on the part of the
rich, was not distributed solely by the US and on condition of
military alliance against the Soviets. The situation was now competitive and as this political situation changed, so too did the
conception of the precise role of aid. Thus whereas Marshall Aid
had had clearly defined objectives and (hypothesized) mechanisms,
aid to the Third World had neither. Initially, in White's phase of
'US hegemony', aid was used to strengthen allies in Asia; so
when the question was raised as to what this aid was supposed
to achieve, a foreign-policy-derived answer was available. As
regards the mechanisms of aid-impact upon recipients, these
issues could be lost in the cold war objectives. Yet when the
USSR came upon the scene, and when the notion of 'non-
alignment' was promulgated, it became more difficult to justify
aid in terms of donors' foreign policy objectives. The emphasis
shifted to the developmental aspects, and thus were mechanisms
of aid-impact brought to the fore.

This competitive aid-giving took the form of offers of, on the
one hand, 'socialism' and, on the other, membership of the 'free
world' with its capitalist free market. With the USA the latter
scheme was presented within the ambit of development studies
as 'modernization theory'. Where in chapter 3 we followed the
crystallization of Keynesian-derived 'growth theory', here in
chapter 4 we trace the construction of 'modernization theory'.
Broader and blander than 'growth theory', it was the ideological
by-product of the globalist stance of 'containment' created by
the USA in the wake of the disintegration of the wartime Grand
Alliance. Those who asked after the 'how' and the 'why' of aid-
giving could now be given an answer.

2.1

The history of the period leading up to and embracing the business of aid competition and the production of 'modernization
theory' may be reviewed at this point. We begin with a sketch of
the occasion and immediate consequences of the end of the wartime Grand Alliance.

The story of this dissolution and partition of Europe reflects
the fact that the USSR and USA had become pre-eminent world
powers. Lichtheim notes that at the same time a de facto agree-

ment between the two was reached: essentially a realpolitik
approach to respective spheres, with a corollary that peripheral
areas were not worth a major war. This being the case, such
states were subject to the disciplines of the alliance leaders.
This view was established early: Kolko, following the same line,
notes that even before the 'collapse' of the British in Greece in
1947 and the subsequent establishment of bipolarity, 'neither
the Americans, British, nor Russians were willing to permit
democracy to run its course anywhere in Europe at the cost of
damaging their vital strategic and economic interests'.[7]

Aron's[8] treatment of the USA, in the first half of his work,
is aimed at elucidating the nature of its diplomacy. Here he suggests the interesting idea that after the end of the Second World
War the nature of the 'inter-state system', as he terms it,
changed. What had been a European-style negotiation between
states – a sort of diplomatic free market, its theory flowing from
Machiavelli – becomes a bipolar situation where two 'great powers'
confront and accommodate each other's interests. So in this
period the style of USA 'inter-state' activity is – with regard to
its allies – that of generalship. This requires the consent or
acquiescence of those so organized.

It seems, on the face of it, that the notion of bipolar diplomacy, if it does not actually entail 'interventionism', is certainly
thus disposed. Ronald Steel quotes De Gaulle as remarking of
the USA in the late 1950s, that they had developed 'a taste for
intervention'.[9]

The career of the orthodoxy which we have subsumed under
the label of 'intervention' thus parallels, with 'development
studies' as 'modernization theory', the period of bipolar diplomacy and US paramountcy. The disintegration of the US position
and (says Aron) bipolarity in diplomacy is reflected in the disintegration of orthodox interventionist optimism: so it has been
observed that 'as the conditions which gave rise to modernization
theory have changed .... the flow of new "theories" of modernization also seems to have ebbed'.[10]

Granting this post-war de facto agreement over European partition, the question arises as to the precise nature of the 'cold
war'. Aron presents three readings. One flowing from the notion
of fundamental and irreconcilable hostility of the two systems.
We could take Fleming to follow this line, arguing as he does
that it was only the size of the Red Army that stopped the Western allies from seriously considering 'rolling back'[11] the Soviets.
Within this fundamental hostility, 'cold war' expresses the situation of there being just two 'great powers'. The second reading is the common-sense notion of war carried out by all means
short of war; yet Aron, in the end, prefers a third notion which
takes from both and adds a significant measure of historical
specificity. Thus the 'cold war' was precisely that period we so
designate, and it represented merely an unusual heightening of
the tensions inherent in what he dubs the 'inter-state system'.
This conclusion represents his version of a 'realist' history,

which is to say that he focuses on the behaviour of ruling groups
within a system of diplomatic-strategic meanings (rather than by
explaining their actions in terms of economic interests, say).
This being the case, bipolarity represents, for Aron, a change
in style, or perception of role, and 'cold war' hysteria is taken
as a mask for acceptance of the new perceptions. This line is
followed by Lichtheim when he argues that 'cold war' and 'coexistence' were 'two sides of the same coin'. [12]

One element of both Aron's and Lichtheim's treatments is thus
the reduction of the 'cold war' to the status of a grandiose 'PR
job', designed to placate the US public. Caute[13], in his history of the 'cold war', indicates that its inception and development owed not a little to matters of party politics in the US. Yet
to implicitly deny the 'cold war' a broader relevance seems misleading. Kolko details the economic interests of the USA during
the war and argues that it was whilst the war was in progress
that the USA prepared for its global role. If this is true, then
the 'cold war' was more than 'PR' for a change of diplomatic
style: it was an integral element of a clearly articulated resistance to the 'left' in general and the USSR in particular.

2.2

However, this is a debate about proper historical explanation
which we need not pursue at this time. Rather, we must focus
on what we take to be the background to the genesis of 'modernization theory': that is, the rhetoric and practice of cold war,
the US policy of 'containment', and the results of that policy. In
preferring this route into these matters, we follow our methodological dictum with regard to 'available explanations'. It is here
that we must start, though we follow Kolko in matters of substance. One other apparent omission may be noted, and this is
our treatment of the USSR. The behaviour of the USSR is not
closely examined. In terms of the efforts of the orthodoxy the
USSR appears as a shadowy 'other' against which US ideology,
in part, defines itself.

US concern was initially focused upon Europe in the wake of
wartime upheaval, both the occupation of Eastern Europe by the
Soviets and the activities of the 'left' in Western Europe. Subsequently, attention is extended to the Third World in a period
of disintegration of formal European empires. That the interests
of the USA, Western Europe, and Third World are divergent
throughout this episode, we here take for granted (this is taken
up more fully in chapter 5); a 'modernizer' would not, affirming
instead an elaborate scheme which collapses divergent interests
into those of the US in a style redolent of Secretary Hull (whom
we met in chapter 3).

The domestic political background to the inauguration of 'containment', in the announcement of the Truman Doctrine, is described by Caute.[14] It is noted that when Truman came to power, 'federal and state statute books were already bristling with anti-communist legislation. All that was required, and conspicuously lacking under F.D. Roosevelt, was the will to enforce it.' This political will came to be provided in the period immediately following the end of the war, when Truman came under increasing pressure from the right and gave ground to it. Truman's response to this is seen by Caute to have been governed by considerations of party advantage; thus he sought to steal the vote-catcher of the Republicans. It is noted that 'It was Truman and Clark (his Attorney General) who produced the loyalty program, who codified the association of dissent with disloyalty and legitimized guilt by association.'[15] This is important to note in that it indicates that the period's excesses are not to be laid solely at McCarthy's door. By 1947 red-baiting, as an integral element of the US political scene, was well under way.

But all this, it may be said, is simply a matter of style; and indeed it is in a sense. Thus in Western Europe the prevailing political tone was anti-communist without there being a witch-hunt. However, we can reply that our interest is in the manner of production of 'modernization theory': with what intellectual raw materials, and under what political circumstances and pressures. Thus the climate of opinion in the USA is of interest for more than stylistic reasons.

Hawthorn[16] offers an illuminating viewpoint on this issue. Arguing from the use of a liberal eighteenth-century constitution for essentially conservative ends at the time of the establishment of the Republic, he suggests that the equation of dissent with disloyalty was latent in US legitimating ideologies; whereas for Europeans this was not, generally, the case. This, when coupled with what Kiernan describes as a 'mystic faith in its special destiny'[17] on the part of the orthodoxy of US thought, may be seen to have been given expression in all levels of discourse. Steel offers a slice of this ideology in sentimental guise when he posits in the 'ordinary American' 'an instinct to help those less fortunate and permit them to emulate and perhaps one day achieve the virtues of our own society'.[18] These sentiments, when expressed at the level of political rhetoric and in the context of a contrast with supposed views of the USSR, issue in the following absurdity: Truman in March 1947 averred that 'the earth is deeply divided between free and captive peoples'.[19] This stance has obvious implications, and these were picked up and elaborated by the period's 'organic intellectuals'. Yet this was, arguably, a deeply ambiguous service: Caute has the liberal intelligentsia collapsing in front of 'cold war' red-baiting. Not only did they not (with a few honourable exceptions) resist the witch-hunt and maintain their scholars' stance of critical evaluation, but they contributed their own two-pennorth in the form of celebrations of the USA as exemplar of modern society. In the period of the late 1940s and early 1950s, when the first efforts in the direction of 'modernization theory' were being undertaken, the model of the modern was not merely the image of the USA writ large, but an image suffused with the demands of the 'patriotic imperative'.[20] It was the business of the USA to reconstruct the world in its own image. And where is the ambiguity in this service? It is identified by Caute[21] when he makes the claim that 'it was the liberals rather than the reactionary right ... who set the USA on the disastrously interventionist and egotistical course that culminated in the horror of the Vietnam war'.[22]

Turning to 'structural' matters, we may note that the debate about the extent to which US diplomacy flowed from economic interest is one that is pursued by Aron in debate with those he terms 'para-marxists'. However, we do not need to pursue the detail of this debate. Rather we note that the ideology of the USA, whatever its precise well-springs, did equate: (a) the interests of the USA, (b) functioning liberal market economies, (c) resistance to communism, and (d) the future prosperity of the world. This doctrinal package was labelled 'the Free World', and as Caute notes 'Soviet policy challenged America's claim'.[23] Peace and stability thus required, it seemed, the continuous presence of the USA as guarantor of the 'Free World'. It was Truman's 12 March 1947 address to Congress that officially launched the doctrine of 'containment'; what the US government attempted to do was to proscribe any change not agreed by it.

Here Aron distinguishes concept from doctrine: the concept was the defensive expression of the competition of USA and USSR, whereas the doctrine was its expression in policy. Again Aron's Weberian-derived focus on 'ideas' lets him present the antagonism of USA and USSR as latent in the US idea-system and as being called forth by the political activities of the USSR; for example, the Sovietization of Eastern Europe, or Korea 1950-3.[24] This line of argument lets Aron distinguish, against the 'para-marxists', between 'imperial' and 'imperialism'. So the USA may be imperial in its behaviour, but it is not imperialist: its power and sway were extended in response to political vacuum in the inter-state system consequent upon the collapse of old Europe and the political aggressiveness of the USSR, and not in pursuit of economic objectives. This evades the 'para-marxists', but Aron cannot sustain his case: he goes on to argue that revision of the concept opens up a slide in the US position. Thus:[25]

> the concept of containment was in fact expanded into a doctrine of international order, and this doctrine was calculated to lead to imperial or even imperialist intervention, or to put it another way intervention in order to uphold a government favourable to the institutions and ideologies of the US, even against its people's aspirations.

Aron's Weberianism issues here in an acknowledgment of those brute-relative historical facts that are the raw materials for the 'para-marxists'[26] and the 'given' context for the constructors of 'modernization-theory'.

If US domestic politics and the demands of an ideology of economic liberalism are two of the roots of the promulgation of the 'containment' doctrine, then its full development bids us take note of the manner in which the initial outlines of the post-war political map were drawn. The notion of 'containment' was at first directed to Western Europe and its objectives secured via the disbursement of dollars; that is, the Marshall Plan. From this point the doctrine broadened, both geographically and practically. In Western Europe it acquired a military aspect with the Formation of NATO in 1949 in the wake of the left-wing coup in Czechoslovakia of the year before. Its geographical extent was made general with the onset of the Korean War of 1950-3.

The list of US activities under the 'containment' notion is familiar, with the stationing of permanently based armies in Western Europe and the removal of left influence as far as possible. The US undertook military interventions in East and South-East Asia, in Central America, Southern Europe, and Central Africa; covert interventions in the Philippines, Indonesia, the Middle East, Latin America and Southern Europe. The detail we need not pursue here.[27]

We may conclude by noting that the ideology and practical activity of the USA are thus not in doubt, in so far as they constitute the climate within which 'modernization theory' was to be constructed and developed.

2.3

It is to the fashioning of the intellectual counterparts of the new US expansionism that we now turn. The resources available to the theorists comprised two major areas. First, the efforts of the economists: hesitantly rediscovering the work of their classical progenitors, they confront the problems attendant upon the scale and complexity of the macro-economics of growth. Second - initially a residual group, but subsequently aspiring to the status of 'master scientists' of this particular area of social science - we have the sociologists, historians, psychologists, and so on, whose efforts constituted 'modernization theory'. The work of the economists we will briefly review, noting their internal disputes and continued optimism. The work of the theorists of development who produce 'modernization' we will pay more attention to, looking at the genesis and form of their central concepts.

3.0 DYNAMIC OF THEORY I: FURTHER DEVELOPMENTS IN THE WORK OF THE ECONOMISTS

Jones remarks of the history of growth economics that it may be characterized as being a sustained effort to evade the unpalatable implications of Harrod's work. Thus he says that whilst Harrod's conclusion is that 'there is no reason to believe that full employment equilibrium growth will be attained ... much of the literature on the theory of growth in the last twenty years is capable of being interpreted as a sustained attempt to weaken this conclusion'.[28]

This debate around Harrod and the possibilities of growth may also be seen as an element of a wider debate around the implications of the work of Keynes for economics in general. Two tendencies may be identified. First, the 'new Cambridge school' ('new' to distinguish it from the Cambridge school of Marshall), which seems to have taken Keynes to have re-invented political economy, understood as a style of social theory. And second, the continued neo-classical line, promoted by scholars at Cambridge, Massachusetts, which takes Keynes to be assimilable to the neo-classical line, where economics is taken to be a matter of the construction of economic-analytic calculi. Jones observes: 'few controversies in the history of economic thought have been conducted with so much vigour and, at times, virulence as the series of interconnected debates between the two Cambridges on the concept of "capital" and the process of economic growth and technical change'.[29]

With regard to this wider debate, we will not here pursue any of its technical aspects; rather, we will make just two notes. First, and in anticipation of matters to be raised later, we note that the intellectual roots of the 'new Cambridge school' are to be traced both to the work of Keynes and his circle of students and to the work of the classical economists; particularly, it seems, Ricardo whose collected papers were edited by Sraffa. This 'broader' vision of the school extends to their taking Marx seriously (thus Kregel regards Marx as the first modern economist to treat the system dynamically), and to a preference for what Jones calls 'grand theory': a blend of sociological, historical and economic analysis. Robinson sums up the impact of Keynes thus: 'The Keynesian revolution has destroyed the old soporific doctrines.... We are left in the uncomfortable situation of having to think for ourselves.'[30]

The second point concerns the 'gradual emasculation of Keynes's vision to conform with the neo-classical method of thinking'.[31] Though resisted by the 'new Cambridge school', this indeed seems to be the fate of Keynesian thought with regard to its general impact on thinking about economics. Sweezy argues that whilst Keynes looked radical at a time when radical solutions were perceived to be required, the post-war working-up of the formal aspects of Keynes's schemes have permitted the social reformism to drop away.[32] As regards the USA, Graham[33]

argues that with the 'cold war' there was a change in the liberal
position away from the redistribution of wealth to the doctrine
of growth. There was a collapse towards the 'end of ideology
thesis', which is seen as the ideology of an exhausted liberalism
perceiving a political choice of cautious reformism or irrelevant
socialism. The choice of 'planning', advocated in the 1930s, was
no longer mentioned. Sweezy sees the post-war development of
Keynesianism as being characterized by absorption: the creed of
growth coupled with techniques of demand management now en-
hances the stability of that status quo which Keynes criticized.
Keynesianism, remarks Sweezy, 'is now used in order to bulwark
the system, not to reform it'.[34] Others have gone further and
identified a fundamental political ambiguity in the 'General
Theory'. The stress on job-creation evoked fascist admiration.
Subsequently, the US Democratic Party has been criticized for
basing full employment on continual preparations for war. Critics
from the left have advanced the notion of a 'permanent arms
economy'.
   Both these aspects may be seen in the behaviour of the Kennedy administration. Sweezy thinks that 'the victory of what I
would call the New Keynesianism, often called the "New Economics", came really with the Kennedy administration'.[35] He
goes on to say that the celebration of that victory came in June
1964, when Treasury Secretary Dillon gave a speech to the
Harvard Business School which used the notion of a proper level
of unemployment; thereby removing the heart from Keynesianism.
Dillon is a figure praised by Seymour Harris, an advisor to
Kennedy: the ambiguity and emasculation is brought out when
Harris comments upon the administration's record. Thus he observes: 'Perhaps the most important factor in the lag of welfare
programs has been the rising demands of the military. Defence,
space and related expenditures accounted for about 75% of the
increase of expenditures under Kennedy through fiscal year
1964.'[36]
   Returning to the narrower area of growth economics, we shall
again eschew any involvement with technical detail. We have seen
in chapter 3 that with the semi-formal mode of reasoning adopted
by orthodox economics the possibilities for theoretical novelties
are extensive. It will not help our study to attempt to pursue
the economists through their labyrinth, for, as Brookfield remarks, 'growth theory quickly became highly elaborated and
often esoteric: contact with the real world was not often established'.[37]
   If there is any simple way of characterizing the change in
economics between 'growth theory' and 'modernization theory'
relevant work, it is encapsulated in Solow's neo-classical model
of growth where the pessimistic assumptions of Harrod are simply
struck out. Economic growth is made freely available (in theory)
to those who would have it. Clearly, in terms of aid-donor competition, this is both more usable (e.g. by administrations) and
saleable to recipient governments.

From Mikesell we may draw the observation that from their inception growth models underwent a two-fold development.
Initially taken as presenting an oversimplified model of the
growth process, they have 'become more complex by the introduction of larger numbers of economic and non-economic factors
and have borrowed heavily from theories dealing with the process of social and institutional change'.[38] So models have become both more complex and less narrowly economic. Another
way of regarding the development of growth models is to say
that there have been continuing efforts to translate into the
mould of the economic calculus matters external to that calculus
yet transparently relevant to the issue of growth. Thus Mikesell
notes of the Cobb-Douglas model (a familiar starting point for
neo-classical-style work) that it 'fails to include a number of
important determinants of growth such as technical progress'.[39]
He then goes on to report on the work of an economist who, looking at technical change, executes the following intellectual manoeuvre: 'one approach is to assume that technological change
represents that part of the growth of output which cannot be
explained by the growth of capital and/or labour'.[40] The matter is thereby reduced to a relationship between established
economic concepts, and may be translated into algebraic form and
then manipulated as one more element of the model.
    This pursuit of greater realism in modelling by means of piece-
meal emendation of simpler growth models now regarded as unsatisfactory in this or that aspect has produced the vast and
obscure literature referred to by Brookfield. Indeed, the point
is that this conception of the task of the theorist investigating
development, and this intellectual procedure, lend themselves
uniquely to the elaboration of scholastic detail. With the use of
a mechanistic logic, coupled with a subtle notation, fine distinctions can be made ever finer simply by the use of established
methods. These thoughts[41] we will pursue in Part III when we
look at the work of Streeten. Here we can simply note that within economics at this stage the slide from economics understood
as the manipulation of formal machineries towards economics
taken as actually involved in the world is under way. The distinction between economic growth theories and theories of social
and economic change grows increasingly blurred; it is to the
latter that we now turn.

4.0 DYNAMIC OF THEORY II: 'MODERNIZATION THEORY', A
NEW MASTER SCIENTIST

Theories of social and economic change constitute our second
area of substantive interest carried over from the previous
chapter. Now whilst there these matters were touched upon very
briefly and almost in passing, here we trace the emancipation of
the broad range of the social sciences from their early status as
'under-labourers' to economics. In general we can say that

where chapter 3 traced the construction and deployment of
'growth models', in this chapter we see the resources of a wider
set of disciplines being plundered for elements which might flesh
out a theory of 'modernization'.

4.1

With regard to the origins of 'modernization theory', Tipps makes
the very general observation that its origins can be placed in
'the response of American political elites and intellectuals to the
international setting of the post Second World War era'.[42] Indeed, he goes on to say that this was the first time that substantial resources had been deployed in making systematic sense
of the world beyond the US borders. This surge of interest presented social scientists with novel demands, and we are offered
a quasi-Kuhnian explanation for the variety of conceptual
schemes offered. They provided 'surrogates for a tradition of
inquiry into the problems of these societies which was almost
entirely lacking'.[43] Without an established literature, theorists plundered their disciplines' histories in search of a general
paradigm. So 'modernization' is 'deeply rooted in the perspective
of developmentalism', claims Tipps,[44] citing Nisbet.
    Further sociology of knowledge information on the genesis of
'modernization' may be found in Tipps's ideological critique of
the thesis. A résumé of the criticisms of 'modernization' is begun
by noting the charge of ethnocentricity. The modernization
theorists talk of 'traditional' and 'modern' where nineteenth-
century evolutionists, from whom comes 'modernization's' theoretical underpinning, spoke of 'civilization' and 'barbarism'. This
is deemed to be a cosmetic change; 'modernization' remains a
style of evaluation which measures a society's progress/status
by 'its proximity to the institutions and values of Western, and
particularly Anglo-American, societies'.[45]
    In addition to the use of the model of the modern-as-Western,
plus the use of the dichotomous style of nineteenth-century
evolutionists, the 'modernization' scheme was shaped by peculiarly American pressures. Tipps notes that 'the idea of modernization is primarily an American idea, developed by American
social scientists in the period after the Second World War and
reaching the height of its popularity in the middle years of the
1960s'.[46] He goes on to note that: 'Two features of this period
stand out: a widespread attitude of complacency toward American
society and the expansion of American interest throughout the
world.'[47] This complacency has its counterpart in social theory.
Thus Hawthorn sees US sociology in the early 1960s deploying a
familiar mixture of normative functionalism, social psychology
and empirical survey analysis, but against the rather new question of the 'possibilities of stable change'.[48] He goes on to take
note that: 'the answers were curiously soothing. Industrial
societies, it was claimed, were all converging towards a common

destination dictated by the technical and organisational imperatives of advanced industrialisation.'[49] Kerr (1960) advances
the notion of a 'logic of industrialization'. The fate of the Third
World was one of disintegration and reformation in line with this
'logic'. Hawthorn reads this view in the light of US intellectual
traditions in social thought, and current preoccupations and
problems. He notes: 'in such a way contemporary history was
assimilated to the foreshortened historical understanding in
American social thought so that the diverse peculiarities of other
societies and the worrying features of America itself could always be explained away'.[50] A related strand of thought
'establishes' the propriety of the US style of democracy; one
thinks of Lipset's 'Political Man' and also Taylor's critique of its
'cheating' argument style.[51]

Tipps notes that the increase of research was designed to increase the 'flow of information concerning these societies in the
US and especially in official circles'.[52] It is this demand for
what Fay would call policy science that is at back of 'modernization'. However, from this point Tipps's argument shades off
into confusion and ambiguity. It is argued that an 'ideological'
critique is not enough to throw over the thesis of 'modernization';
yet in so far as these theorists lay claims to value-free work and
claim for their results generality, they provide the lever to
topple the whole edifice. As Fay points out,[53] to uncover the
ideological nature of a stance that denies such a character in
favour of claims to the status of (natural) science, is to deal it
a mortal blow: it collapses into ideology ordinarily understood.

Paralleling these issues, Tipps goes on to remark that there
is no reason to suppose that the notion of 'modernization' itself
is 'inherently incompatible with a variety of ethnocentrisms, or
that a revolutionary or socialist version of modernization theory
could not be developed'.[54] Our commentator, we may assume,
has grasped (albeit unconsciously) the idea that 'modernization'
as an evaluative stance is proper in so far as it takes a stance.
However, the conclusion that a 'left-modernization' is possible is
not helpful. 'Modernization' is clearly 'policy science', and unless
we want to construct a positivistic 'left' philosophy of social
development, 'modernization' has no place in it.[55] That Tipps
can consider the idea reflects his empiricist distinction between
fact and value. To carry over the wholly proper idea of moral
engagement and call that 'modernization' would be a needless
and obfuscating stretching of the notion of 'modernization'. The
empiricist frame and narrow notion of ideology used by Tipps
are the cause of his eventual confusion. It is claimed of 'modernization' that 'Far from it being a universally applicable schema...
modernization theory reflects a particular phase in the development of single society, that of the US.'[56] It is this aspect of
the matter, the clearly situation-bound character of 'modernization', that not only establishes Tipps's thesis to the effect
that 'modernization' needs replacing rather than adjusting, but
also provides the stance's continuing interest: that is, it dis-

plays clearly the essential character of social theorizing as the business of making sense. Our commentator misses the point of what his critique of ideology provides him with.

4.2

Thus far we have looked at 'modernization' as being a (primarily American) ideology. But what of its character and typical mode of argument? In order to discover the form of 'modernization', we will rely upon the work of – in the main – recent critics. What follows is a brief review, serving only to identify the typical argument form of the 'modernization' scheme.

Brookfield begins his treatment of 'modernization' by taking note of the general matter of strategies of explanation; thus he says that he is writing 'about dichotomies in the theory of development'.[57] The whole episode of 'modernization' is taken as characterized by its adherence to a dichotomous characterization of the issue of development. It is this strategy for grasping the exchange of 'rich' and 'poor' that is Brookfield's target. He argues that, having conceptualized the general circumstances in terms of the dichotomy 'traditional society/modern society', theorists of the school then proceed to attempt to elucidate matters by deploying a further set of dichotomous constructs: familiarly, dual economy, agricultural and industrial sectors, community and association, and so on. What Brookfield wants to show is that the dichotomies used are a linked set and, in toto, an unhelpful set. That they are linked may be established in two ways: 'analytically', by reporting on work derived from Parsons's 'pattern variables', and 'associatively', by reporting upon the diverse efforts of those seeking descriptive characterizations of traditional/modern. That they are an unhelpful set is a matter of noting the inadequacies of their argument forms. We shall follow in rough outline this scheme of Brookfield's.

(I) Linked set: analytic/associative

Brookfield observes, rightly, that 'modernization theory' is, in contrast to 'growth theory', a broader based effort: it embraces contributions from a variety of sources. Four are noted in his treatment: 'The "acculturation" thesis of anthropology was an important element; others included Talcott Parsons' theories of "action" and of social change, notions of the plural society originating with Furnivall, theory in political science on the evolution of nationalism.'[58] Other critics offer variations of such a 'list' of contributions to the 'modernization' scheme; yet all would follow Brookfield's view that these contributions are channelled through 'a particular view of change which is essentially dualistic'.[59]

Huntington offers the view of the characteristic terms of debate in the late 1950s and early 1960s, 'tradition' and 'modernity', that

'these categories were, of course, the latest manifestation of a
Great Dichotomy between more primitive and more advanced
societies which has been a common feature of Western social
thought for the past one hundred years'.[60] So we can note,
as do Huntington and Brookfield: Maine's status/contract, Durkheim's mechanical/organic, Tönnies's gemeinschaft/gesellschaft
or Weber's traditional/rational. Doubtless a search of the literature would reveal other similar orientating metaphors. The
argument strategy of 'modernization' has been summed up as
follows: 'The bridge across the Great Dichotomy between modern
and traditional societies is the Grand Process of Modernization.'[61]
     Of this dichotomy, Huntington claims that the modern set of
notions attempting to flesh out the before/after metaphor origin-
ate with Parsons's and Shils's 'pattern variables', 'and the subsequent extension of these from "choices" confronting an actor
to characterizations of social systems'.[62] The 'pattern variables' appear in simple forms in early 'modernization' work. Thus
Bernstein notes, as an example of 'an occasionally useful eclecticism',[63] Hoselitz's 1952 work 'The Progress of the Under-
developed Areas', which includes essays from Gerschenkron,
Watnick and Hirschman. In Hoselitz's essay, 'Social Structure
and Economic Growth' we find a systematized dualism; that is,
seeking to characterize 'tradition' and 'modernity' the 'pattern
variables' are invoked. Three out of five are taken to be pertinent. Hilal summarizes:[64]

> Thus, while developed societies are characterized by univer-
> salism, achievement orientation and role specificity, under-
> developed countries have the opposite properties of
> particularism, ascriptiveness and role diffuseness. Once this
> is stated it becomes easy to see that development consists in
> the acquisition of the first set of characteristics and the loss
> of the opposite set.

Here the dichotomies which purport to elucidate the nature of
the major bifurcation are clearly a linked set. In the instances
where the 'pattern variables' are invoked, they gesture to an
'analytical' linkage. But more often than not we find that, whilst
the Parsonian scheme is cited, the set of dichotomies are linked
only in so far as they belong to one group of efforts to produce
a descriptive and general model of 'tradition' versus 'modern'.
The linkage is rather 'associative'.
     The pursuit of a descriptive/general scheme of evolution had
one ready consequence; as Roxborough notes, it 'usually led to
the formulation of a series of stages of development'.[65] In
A.G. Frank's famed critique of 'modernization' dualism ('Sociology of Development and Underdevelopment of Sociology') the
Parsonian-derived scheme of Hoselitz using the 'pattern variables'
is one of two versions of the general line which Frank dubs the
'Ideal-typical index approach'. The other is stage theory: here
Rostow is cited, and his work we treat below. As regards Frank's

'magisterial'[66] critique, we find that he identifies three lines
within the orthodoxy of modernization, and attacks them all in
turn under the headings of empirical, theoretical, and policy
inadequacy. Thus he observes that there is a 'deep similarity
in the extent of the three modes' empirical inaccuracy, theoretical inadequacy and policy ineffectiveness'.[67] He argues that
this reveals similarities in argument strategy. So the ideal typical index approach is taken to be concerned with setting up the
characteristics of development, diffusionism with how the characteristics of the 'modern' are transmitted to the 'traditional',
against what obstacles; finally the psychological approach, a
'Freudianised Weber',[68] treats the absorption of these stances
by groups/individuals within the 'traditional' societies.

We can move beyond Frank's attacks by noting Hilal's extended
version of this critical stance. Here there is reference to Parsons's 'neo-evolutionism', described as a very general scheme
which provides 'an assurance of stability and a semblance of
order in a situation of apparent rapid change'.[69] Hilal thinks
Parsons's scheme is 'little more than useless',[70] but ideologically its usofulness might be appreciated if we recall Hawthorn's
characterization of US sociology as being concerned above all
with the issue of stable change. Extended to the Third World,
this scheme came up with the following: 'Non-industrial societies
... would if they were not already doing so experience a differ-
entiation of structures the more efficiently to meet the imperatives dictated by economic development'.[71] So the 'modernization' schemes reflected this reassuring and optimistic view;
and, as Rhodes notes, this dualism of 'tradition' and 'modernity',
lodged in an evolutionist frame, suited the dispositions of the
US theorists. The effects of colonialism were ignored, the inhabitants of the Third World made responsible for their own
conditions, and the possibility of revolutionary change discounted. 'Thus the substitution of an evolutionary for a truly
historical perspective had very convenient ideological consequences.'[72] The convenience of some of these ideological
consequences - if this is the right way to cast it - can be seen
clearly in the work of Rostow, explicitly a 'non-communist
manifesto'.

It seems clear that what we have in these 'modernization'
schemes is an effort to effect a descriptive general policy science
which not only characterizes the process and goal of 'modernization' in a fashion appropriate to the needs of current political
demand, but also seeks to identify specific points of intervention
within the 'target' systems.

(II) An unhelpful set

From the above lines of critique/characterization we can perhaps
pick out two areas of criticism which usefully relate to issues
pursued in this study. So we look at the particular issue of dualism, in two areas. First, economic dualism, which attempts to

provide a single theory of economics - in contradistinction to the 'classic' dualists, who advanced claims for distinct schemes treating 'rich' and 'poor'. Second, we look at the sociological dualisms of 'traditional/modern' societies, attacked by many. Following this, we add a note on the more general issue of attempts to construct descriptive general models. There we register what for us is the crucial problem with 'modernization' formulations.

Brookfield notes that it 'is a matter of simple observation that the economies of a great many developing countries are organised in two parts ... almost as though they formed two different societies and economies'.[73] That this general observation is plausible is confirmed by Frank. In a critique of the dual society thesis he observes that: 'Evident inequalities of income and differences in culture have led many observers to see "dual" societies and economies in the underdeveloped countries.'[74] It is the shift from common-sense-informed observation/description to generalized models that purport to explain that occasions the mendacious confusion attacked by theorists like Frank or Griffin. That the shift is illegitimate is not something which it is entirely clear that Brookfield has grasped, even though he makes reference to arguments for recasting the manner in which the work is conceived rather than simply continually making piecemeal revisions.

The thesis of the dual economy is taken as presented by Boeke and Furnivall, both writing before the Second World War. It is reported that Boeke, who anticipates Furnivall, takes Western economics to be inapplicable in the circumstances of colonial dependencies; and that 'two sets of economic principles are required'.[75] Brookfield continues by noting that 'the central problem in understanding a tropical dependency, he [Boeke] argued, arises from the contact between the two social and economic systems'.[76] It is this view which anticipates the familiar, dual economy-society thesis, but it also informs a line of more particularly economic thought on these matters. 'Classic' dualism is rejected in the attempt to construct a single economics.

'The essence of the theory of economic dualism is the attempt to combine in one system theory for an advanced and for a backward economy',[77] where the two 'sectors' are characterized in the usual way. 'The primitive statement of economic dualism is the ... paper of W.A. Lewis (1954) on "Economic development with unlimited supplies of labour". Though not formally a dual-economy model, Lewis's formulation concerns two coexistent sectors and the conditions governing the supply of labour to the growing industrial sector from the agricultural.'[78] Now, according to Brookfield, this type of orthodox-formulated investigation of the exchange between a 'modern sector' and a 'non modern sector' was extensively treated through the 1950s. It is reported that these 'models of economic dualism are growth models and this characteristic has become more pronounced in the 1960s'.[79] These efforts parallel, it would seem, the more familiar 'sociological' schemes.

But where is the interest in all this? Clearly this note goes no way to elucidating what is evidently a complex debate within a area of economics. Yet our remarks do serve to call attention to this aspect of the history of economic thinking on such matters; and the debate is of interest in that it anticipates a remark made by a noted 'dependency' theorist, Girvan.[80] The latter, having reviewed the work of Furtado, observes that here the old debate about whether one or two economics are needed can be resolved. The orthodox scheme (which would embrace an economic dualism) is found wanting, but not in favour of the two schemes of economics: quite the reverse. Now that 'dependency' has established an economics adequate to the dependent economies (Latin America in particular) it can also be seen that this scheme is appropriate to the economies of the developed areas. The orthodoxy is now rejected as demonstrably inadequate to its own and the circumstances of Third World economies. There is now one economics, 'dependency'. This argument we treat in a later chapter, where we will detail the confusions between conceptual progressivity in natural science and ideology ranking in the social that give rise to it.

Turning to sociological dualisms and the concern with 'The bridge across the Great Dichotomy',[81] we can codify some of the criticisms that have been brought against 'modernization'. We can move from what we take to be the more obvious to the rather more subtle criticisms.

We can begin with objections to the characterizations made of the two central notions used, 'modern' and 'traditional'. As regards the former element of the dichotomy, it has been strongly argued that the characterization of the 'modern' is highly dubious. The well-known use of Parsons's 'pattern variables' is criticized with all the familiar points brought against that scheme: thus it is ahistorical, static, neglecting of class and matters of conflict and power. Frank, treating the 'Ideal Typical Index Approach', confronts Hoselitz's Parsonian-inspired characterization of the modern with a series of rhetorical, commonsense fact-presenting questions and shows it to be untenable. It is an empirically unsatisfactory description. This line is followed by Hilal: speaking of the ideal-typological approach, he observes that: 'In its dominant version it is unrepentantly empiricist.'[82] There is, the same author continues, a 'distinct tendency to compile check lists of attributes'.[83] These criticisms apply also to characterizations of 'traditional'. Hilal quite rightly questions the 'meaningfulness' of this approach.[84]

There is a further line of criticism made of the category 'traditional'; and if we follow this, we can open up the issue of residual categories and note some of the difficulties associated with them. We can agree that the category 'modern', even if characterizations produced are faulty, does at least stand in some sort of clear and direct relationship to the material circumstances it would grasp. And even, to go one step further, if we note that abstracting and generalizing are faulty procedures we can grant that with 'modern' the procedure is at least minimally plausible. This is not so with 'tradition'. This concept is constructed not by abstraction and generalization, but by spelling out the particulars in which it is supposed that the non-developed fail to measure up to the model of the 'modern'. This collection of deficiencies presents itself as the model of traditional society. As Huntington notes: 'Dichotomies which combine "positive" concepts and residual ones . . . are highly dangerous analytically. In point of fact, they are not properly dichotomies at all.'[85] It is from this fundamental incoherence that the errors flow, because this dichotomous formulation has the effect of masking the implausibility of the 'modernization' theorists' argument strategy. They attempt to model the interaction of two specific circumstances (objects). But we can see that in the usual natural-science-aping syntax the argument appears to be curiously circular: we have a fairly clear end point in presently experienced modern society, but the putative start point is merely a 'negative image' of the end point and not actually independent or different at all. If, on the other hand, the pretence to the status of (natural) science were dropped in favour of an explicitly argued case, then this problem would not arise. In the literature of criticism of this specimen of 'development studies' this argument is not usually pushed through. Thus Bernstein, who sees (as do the others) the over-generality of the concept 'traditional', writes that 'The first objection to be noted concerns the methodological procedure by which the traditional is simply defined negatively in relation to the modern so that ... differences between empirical societies allocated to the residual category of the traditional are ignored.'[86] He starts off in the right direction and then disappears up the familiar side-street.

Two related points can be presented here. One concerns 'dice-loading' and the other 'collapsing arguments'. As regards 'dice-loading', we would argue that a dichotomous construct that affirms one category and identifies the other as a concatenation of non-prime category elements is immediately value-skewed. Consider the idea of the 'non-medical use of drugs'. This is a term which purports to allow the cool-headed discussion of social drug use, in particular recreational use. It is taken to be a movement forward from simple condemnation. But we can ask, just when and by whom was the model of medical use established as prime case against which other uses might be classified? Clearly, when the dichotomy 'medical/non-medical' is written in full, then the implicit criticism of any drug use that is other than prime case - that is, which is not legitimated by an authoritative medical practitioner for approved use - is revealed. The expression 'non-medical use of drugs' is presented as non-judgmental, a basis for free and equal discussion. Clearly it is not; and generally, if value-skew is either not acknowledged or, because the particular skew is clothed in 'common sense' as with

our example, not seen, then we get simple bias. In the case of
our example, we move from a situation of outright condemnation,
which is relatively easy to attack, to a situation of disguised
condemnation, which is very much harder to attack. The point
of all this is fairly clear: the notion of 'modernization', as it presents itself in its usual scientistic formulations, tends, to our
mind, to simple bias in the same way. The 'modern' is taken as
the self-evidently given, and the non-modern constitute so many
deviations from it. A proper approach to matters of theorizing
the exchange of 'rich' and 'poor' involves, as we argued in Part
I, explicitly arguing a case. To the extent that 'modernization
theory' neglects the reflexive posture attendant upon arguing a
case it must be judged to be 'low-grade ideology'.

The second point concerns 'collapsing arguments'. We draw
this line of criticism from Huntington. It is noted that the characterizations of 'modern' and 'traditional' are unsatisfactory, but
in comparison with the idea of 'modernization' they are lucid and
clear. Criticizing the scheme for ambiguity in respect of claims
(are these actual stages or ideal types?) it is remarked that
'Inevitably, also, the dual character of the concepts undermined
the conceptual dichotomy.'[87] The problem is that all societies
display 'traditional' and 'modern' characteristics, which is no
problem if it is static descriptions that are required. But,
'Viewed as a theory of history or change, however, the addition
of a transitional category tended to exclude the traditional and
modern stages from the historical process.'[88] The two notions
'traditional' and 'modern' come to represent, it is claimed, the
start and end of history. 'But if all real societies are transitional
societies a theory is needed which will explain the forms and
processes of change at work in transitional societies. This is
just what the dichotomic theory failed to provide.'[89] This is
surely a crucial attack: the fundamental argument-strategy of
'modernization', the elucidation of change across a general dichotomy by means of invoking a series of particular dichotomies,
fails when the scheme is brought to bear on 'the world'. The
scheme is unable to grasp change, or transition, and can only
offer static comparisons in abstract and ahistorical terms. This
is not just an empirical inadequacy but is rather a fundamental
conceptual incapacity.

In respect of 'values' we can note a (familiar) instance of value-
skew in 'modernization'. Thus, in respect of Rostow's stage
theory, Frank notes that the scheme supposes a 'primitive starting point' from which even the presently developed are taken to
have emerged. Frank thinks this is fallacious: 'This entire
approach to economic development and cultural change attributes
a history to the developed countries but denies all history to the
under-developed ones.'[90] The presently 'rich' have the history of their emergence, whilst the 'poor' have yet to move, so
to say, and consequently have no history. Griffin follows Frank
in regarding this as ludicrous, observing that classifying Third
World countries 'as "traditional societies" begs the issue'.[91]

Both Frank and Griffin argue that, far from the Third World
countries having been 'traditional' and unchanging in a way that
could plausibly be taken to leave them with 'no history', it is
precisely their history that explains their present: in particular,
the centuries-long exchange of peripheral with metropolitan
areas. Again the 'modernization' scheme is condemned as theoretically incapable of treating what, on any account, would be
taken to be part of the common sense of an inquiry. The formulation 'traditional/modern' is thus skewed in that it rules out
consideration of the part played by the 'rich' in creating the
present circumstances of the 'poor'.
    Finally, in pursuit of the Brookfield-inspired claim that the
categories of 'modernization' are an unhelpful set, we can turn
to the matter of descriptive general models. The above treatment is a review of 'modernization' and its critics which rests
largely within the terms of their debate, and within these terms
the charges of the critics we would grant. However, in order to
link with our general interest in argument-construction we have
to note that, for us, the trouble with 'modernization' - taking it
as an exercise in social theorizing - is that it has an impoverished (and arguably disingenuous) conception of a proper and
fruitful analysis. The scheme takes the proper mode of inquiry
to be the establishment of policy-scientific general models,
which descriptively characterize the structure of the society in
question in such a fashion as to permit manipulative interventions governed by an authoritative 'objective' knowledge. This
is the effort's strategic error; thereafter its adherents are liable
to criticisms which attach to the use of residual categories,
skewed arguments, and collapsing dualisms which we have noted
above. Their fundamental strategy is clearly grasped by Hilal:
first define 'modern', then in opposition 'non-modern', and 'modernization' is the route between them. The rest is just detail,
which may or may not be intrinsically interesting. Smith follows
this and identifies the same uniform theme at back of the various
schemes of 'modernization': 'Ultimately, the various societies with
their different cultures and modernizing routes can be analysed
in terms of an ideal-type of these trends. They constitute so
many "deviations" from the general direction of these trends, so
many variant patterns on a common theme.'[92]

5.0 DYNAMIC OF THEORY III: THE APOGEE OF 'MODERN-
IZATION'

We conclude with a brief mention of Rostow: a figure we associate with the apogee of 'modernization', and evidence of the
re-emergence of a counter-tradition to 'positivistic' social science.
We proceed by noting that the episode of 'modernization's' 'career'
can be itself described as a series of 'stages', and that Rostow
appears in the period of the maximum celebration of 'modernization'. Having taken note of why Rostow's effort was so popular,

we finish with a reference to what seems to be an almost unremarked development: that is, the 'revisionist-modernization-
theorist's' explorations in the realm of what Gellner[93] calls
'classical political philosophy'.

5.1

What we might call the 'initial phase of modernization' can be
made to parallel the pre-1955 period of US dominance in aid-
giving. According to White's history, it is the occasion of the
extension of the Marshall Aid doctrine to similarly distressed
areas in the Third World. It aims to secure allies for the USA,
and in so far as an articulated theory was concerned a version
of the Harrod-Domar model (as core) plus a range of 'non-
economic factors', was in use. The particular 'factor' that linked
the Harrod-Domar core to political requirements was what Kolko
identifies in US European policy: the equation of economic health
with lowering of liability to communist 'infection'. In practice,
prior to 1950, flows of aid remained small and what there was
went mostly to South-East Asia where 'aid policy ... was vir
tually indistinguishable from strategic policy'.[94] This orientation continues to inform inquiry into the matter of the
development of the Third World. But around 1956 there is a
change.

The second phase, which we might label the 'phase of the
elaboration of modernization' (1956-61, say), sees the invention
of 'modernization'. It was in 1955 that the Bandung Conference
affirmed the principle of 'non-alignment'. Together with the
entry (as White reports it) of the USSR into the realm of aid-
giving, this constitutes the political occasion of a shift in legitimating theorems. This change in the politics of aid necessitates
changes in its presentation and thus theorizing. The themes of
legitimation, in US work, shift from foreign policy objectives
couched in 'cold war' terms, to the encouragement of 'development'. So 'containment' is revised and 'modernization' within the
ambit of the 'free world' is offered to counteract the USSR's
offers of 'socialism'. The theoretical counterpart is a concern,
as we have seen, for the explication of the matter of stable
change; and the US intellectual scene produces general, systematic, theories of the emergence and character of industrial life.
Systems functionalism, as the general paradigm, permits detailed
empirical work, intermediate level (project) theorizing and very
general schemes of societal development.

The third phase, which is notable for its optimism, we can
label the 'phase of the apogee of modernization'. This peak coincides with the Kennedy administration, and it declines slowly as
the USA sinks into the Vietnam quagmire and as 'development'
fails to materialize. The first root of the optimistic formulation
of 'modernization' would seem to be lodged in the Kennedy administration's foreign policy efforts. Thus the Truman Doctrine is

re-affirmed in the Inaugural Address, and according to Graham[95] foreign policy becomes the only area of operation for an
administration that is stymied at home. After the fiasco of the
Bay of Pigs, the Cuban missile crisis is taken (wrongly, according to Young[96]) as a vindication of 'crisis management'. None
the less, the chance for Kennedy to recoup his political fortunes
lay, thinks Kiernan,[97] in Vietnam. These 'New Frontiersmen'
are characterized by Nolting (the US ambassador in Vietnam,
1961-3) as being 'very gung-ho fellows, wanting to get things
straightened up in a hurry, clear up the mess. We've got the
power and we've got the know how and we can do it.'[98] If
this is one root, then the other is to be found, on White's
account, in the shift of aid debate to the level of the general.
   Here there are two political considerations. At the end of the
1950s there was a surge of decolonization, of mostly Black
African states. This surge of decolonization occasioned a reworking of accepted notions of aid, as the character of Black
African states was evidently more fragile than had been the case
in the earlier colonial withdrawal from Asia. There is a double
shift, from regarding aid-flows as unusual and transitory phenomena to seeing aid as both continuing and proper. By the end
of the 1950s, White reports, the provision of aid and its efficacy
were taken for granted; it was all 'self-evidently desirable'.[99]
The reinforcing political circumstance was the aid-recipients'
response to the US/European debate, in the wake of the Cuban
episode, on 'sharing the burden' of defending the interests of
the 'free world'. This is taken to have looked rather like a
'donors club' and it is recorded that the aid-recipients responded
by trying to shift the debate to the UN where they had a voice.
White sees this as having the effect of wrenching aid-giving out
of various local and evolving contexts and fixing debate at a
very general level. The impact on theorizing was unfortunate,
thinks White, because 'it had to be assumed, falsely, that the
objectives were self-evident and accepted; that is, that the
nature of the development process and of the aspirations of those
who sought to promote such a process was not in dispute'.[100]
It is into this context of optimism, and non-controversiality,
that Rostow's work is introduced.

5.2

We can now turn to Rostow, whose 'Stages' might be taken to
encapsulate the theoretical elements looked at in Part II as a
whole. Thus the core of the Rostovian scheme is, it would seem,
the Harrod-Domar model. Mikesell notes that 'Rostow was considerably influenced by the Harrod-Domar model in his definitions
of take-off in terms of the critical rate of investment required
for the achievement of a level of income and savings sufficient
to assure self-contained growth.'[101] Brookfield would agree
with this, and adds a remark on an area of work in economics

that we have not treated; this is the quantitative work which
parallels the more formal elaborations of Harrod-Domar models.
It is reported that there was 'a spell of quite profound research
into the capital/output ratio'.[102] The suggestion is that Rostow takes the theoretical position of the Harrod-Domar model,
adopts the quantitative work on ICOR, and comes up with the
notion of 'take-off'.

Now, if the core of the Rostovian effort is the growth model
work of the economists, then its frame – its general theory of
change – is a neo-evolutionary scheme. Essentially dualistic,
Rostow presents five 'stages'. The fifth is the model of the USA,
and the first is a combined residual and antithetical concept to
set against the model of the USA. The remaining three, centring
on 'take-off', treat the transition from 'tradition' to 'modernity'.
That this sort of descriptive, general, dualistic characterization
is unsatisfactory as an explanation of change has been argued
above.

A detailed exposition/critique of the Rostovian effort we will
eschew providing: it has been done before on numerous occasions, and the bones of this particular debate are surely picked
clean. We do want to make one point (arising from our interest
in argument strategies) which is not often made in treatments of
'modernization'. But before that we can ask: just why was Rostow's work so popular?

Hagen, in a review of Rostow's scheme, notes that the 'conception of stages of economic growth almost immediately captured
the attention of laymen.... It was given serious though not generally favourable attention by social scientists as well.'[103] It
is with the 'laymen' that we should concern ourselves, noting
that the term must include primarily government circles who
were, after all, involved in these matters. A sketch of an
answer to the question of the popularity of the Rostovian scheme
can be presented in terms of 'ideological-fitness'. This analogy
comes from design problems, where a 'design problem' is a matter
of fitting functional requirements to the possibilities of the materials and the constraints of the environment. So we ask: how
does Rostow's mélange of proffered explanations sit with the
political needs of those embroiled in matters of development? We
can identify two broad areas which serve to illuminate Rostow's
peculiar suitability: the timing and origin of his message, on
the one hand, and, on the other, the optimistic generality of its
content.

Rostow's 'Stages' is the pre-eminent theory of development
through the early 1960s. The work was first presented in a 1956
essay, in the 'Economic Journal', 'The Take-Off into Self-sustained
Growth', and represented in its familiar form in 1960. Thus its
initial publication coincides with the shift from US hegemony in
aid-giving and subsequent search for an elaborated theory of
'modernization' during White's phase of aid-donor competition.
In the 1960 publication the anti-communist theme and the core
message of the Harrod-Domar model fit Rostow into the mould of

the 'New Frontier'. It is here that we find the highest expression of the notions of 'interventionism'. Rostow was a part of
this establishment; and as the pronouncements of the most
powerful state on Earth are of understandable interest to others,
then the work of one of its members may be expected to be studied for clues as to that government's likely activities.

The counterpart is the message's acceptability. In the 1960s,
as we have just seen, a confluence of factors effectively shifted
international discussion of aid and development on to a very general level. Debate came to focus on the 'rules of the game'; and
this being the case, questions about what aid was actually for,
how it was supposed to work, and what existing conceptions
supposed and entailed, all dropped away. In its place, as White
argued, there was a presumption of 'self-evidence'. Here the
descriptive, unreflective generality of the Rostovian scheme was,
we can suggest, wholly appropriate. This point is made, if in
passing, by Hagen: 'Undoubtedly one of the causes of the wide
popularity of Rostow's book is the perception conveyed by it
that there is order in this uncertain world; that once a certain
sequence is entered upon, economic growth will follow.'[104] In
addition to the acceptability at the level of the general, so to say,
we can discern in the Rostovian effort some more immediate
attractions. Thus if we imagine the circumstances of international
conferences and so on, then we can see that the period for
'take-off' proposed by Rostow (twenty years) was such as to be
(a) conceivable and (b) long enough not to be oppressive.
Equally, the mechanism of 'take-off' - the creation of a rise in
ICOR from 5 per cent to 10 per cent, which is taken from Lewis
in particular - is obviously quantifiable; so targets can be set
for aid-flows, growth rates and the rest. Brookfield summarizes
the scheme's persuasiveness as follows:[105]

> It seemed to give every country an equal chance; it 'explained'
> the advantage of the developed countries; it offered a clear
> path to progress - without spelling this out in detail; it iden-
> tified the requirements for advance with the virtues of the
> West; it suggested comfortingly that the communist countries
> were in fact following Western recipes, with a difference; it
> debunked the historical theories of Marx.

5.3

The Rostovian schema we take to be the gaudiest manifestation
of 'modernization' in the phase of its apogee: Baran and Hobsbawm speak of a mixture of 'coffee house sociology and political
speculation'.[106] But at the same time we find stirrings of a
fruitful line of revision. We take Gellner to exemplify this line.

Gellner writes from within the school of Popperian liberalism,
and we may provisionally label him a 'phase four, revisionist,
modernization theorist'. We can see how his treatment of 'social

change' is adequate to the importance of the debate as practical
social theorizing, and sensitive to its intellectual complexity and
disciplinary import.

We may approach these matters by noting that Gellner takes a
different line, with regard to the internal logic of the various
basic metaphors of change, than does Rostow. In particular, his
conception of the ideological role of such metaphors is to be
noted. Gellner's 'neo-episodic' conception of change - where the
interests and metaphors expressed by the classical evolutionists,
treating the broad sweep of history, are reworked into a less
ambitious theory focused upon a circumscribed object, a discrete historical episode - does not easily correspond to the evolutionist scheme of Rostow. Thus Gellner's notion is essentially
an element of an attempt at an explicit moral ordering of the
world, which procedure is necessarily tentative and self-
involving. The Rostovian pursuit, on the other hand, is of a
general descriptive scheme; along with other 'modernization'
theorists, it is 'recipe' knowledge that is sought.

Gellner begins by noting that 'men generally have a view of
the nature of their society. They also have views concerning
what validates the society's arrangements. The two things, image
and validation, never are and cannot be wholly distinct.'[107]
Three explanations/legitimations are presented, each taken as
expressive of a fundamental metaphor of progress. Of these, the
simplest is taken as identifying 'one episode, one transition from
one bad state of affairs to one good state'.[108] We are given
the example of the explanation offered by the Enlightenment
thinkers, the device of the 'social contract'. These seventeenth-
and eighteenth-century views (their predecessors are unspecified) are taken to be sociologically impoverished, and thus
unsatisfactory, given their demanding role. A richer and en-
during schema is generated by nineteenth-century thinkers and
is the familiar evolutionist type, validating society in terms of
an all-embracing and permanent process: transition as such. The
metaphor's persuasiveness Gellner locates in its nineteenth-
century incorporation into common sense as the general theory
of the (natural) progress (of the West). These schemes are
objected to on the ground that they tend to confuse history and
mechanism: thus a period is taken (wrongly) to be explained
when it is slotted into some wider postulated series. Marx is
excepted in so far as he presents a mechanism of change and
thus offers a genuine explanation. Gellner also takes exception,
as we might expect, to the latent determinism of evolutionist
schemes, arguing that it tends to squeeze out the moral agent.
Finally, he adds that anyway, as a simple matter of fact, these
efforts do not fit the situation of the Third World and so are
largely irrelevant to today's problems.

Gellner's third conception of 'social change' is his own and he
constructs it from basics. He begins by observing that the conditions of the legitimacy of a social order are its being (i) industrialized or modernizing and (ii) non-colonial. This is taken to

be both a matter of fact and, as it happens, a correct political philosophy. He reformulates it thus: 'the diffusion of industrialism, carried out by national units is the dominant event of our time. This is an "episode", however large and fundamental it may be.'[109] Gellner attaches to his revised, focused, evolutionism the practical conclusion of his Popperian liberalism; and so as the key to 'the transition' we have the affirmation of science and its method. Analogously, in the realm of politics (and presumably only for the Third World) he advocates the rule of the modernizing elite.

If the foregoing indicates how the notion of 'social change' may be taken to be able to encapsulate the complex issues thrown up in the efforts of the post-war period to grasp this matter of 'development' (and does so in a way which reveals the intellectual impoverishment of the run of the mill 'modernization-theorists'), then we may note, as a corollary, a general point with regard to the matter of social theory itself. Thus Gellner, after presenting the two core elements of what he takes to be a presently relevant political philosophy, goes on to make the remarkable claim that 'the heir of "classical" political theory is now sociology'.[110] The task of political theory is here taken to be the formulation of descriptions of society in terms of which action is informed; or briefly, the construction of ideologies. If it is to be a good ideology then it must necessarily take cognizance of how societies function and change, thus it will be sociological. Gellner takes the business of sociology in the nineteenth century to have been the rendering intelligible of the novel, and morally problematical, process of industrialization. He notes that; 'the emergence of industrial society is the prime concern of sociology'.[111] If we recall our paraphrasing of Hilal vis à vis the 'discovery' of the Third World, we can note that Gellner goes on to say that:[112]

> when industrialization had happened only once, those who had been through it tended to confuse it with what may have been accidental or once-only concomitants of its first occurrence. Now, the repetitions provided by new combinations of circumstances, and the attempt to understand and facilitate the process in new places, also throw light on its earlier occurrence in the West.

The old problem of political philosophy – that is, the 'problem of order' – is now overthrown in favour of investigation of the bases of industrial society.

It is with Gellner that we see how the fruitful legacy of 'modernization' may be taken to have been established. The line from a narrow, Keynesian-derived 'growth theory' via the ideological naiveté of early and elaborated 'modernization' to this explicit acknowledgment of the richness and complexity of the problem of development is completed. The fruit, erroneous formulations aside, is a rediscovery of 'social theory', what Gellner calls 'classical' political philosophy.

It is our view that particular marxian-inspired schemes of social theorizing are the appropriate vehicles for further inquiry of this sort. These we will come to. At this point Gellner's remarks invite a review of the then contemporary efforts at similarly theoretically 'rich' treatments of the Third World, but this is an area we cannot here review.

It must, finally, be noted that if Gellner points to a 'better' modernization than the run of the mill efforts, then he does so, arguably, because he inhabits a different, European, intellectual tradition. Quite how important this fact is will become clearer in the course of the next chapter when we look at 'decolonization' and the work of the theorists of 'neo-institutionalism'.

Part III

The 'radicals'

INTRODUCTORY REMARKS

In Part II we looked at the 'positivists' within the 'career' of 'development studies', the dominant school within the immediate post-war, 'cold war', period. Now we turn to an examination of the contributions to, and results of, the partial disintegration of this position. Again we must recall that we are treating a web of events in the real world and theoretical responses amongst academics and practitioners, mediated by political demands and disciplinary traditions. We are dealing with themes: and, more particularly, with one theme picked out of the web of the history of the 1960s. The 'positivist' orthodoxy does not simply go away and nor does this period of the 'radicals' end neatly with the resurgence of marxian scholarship. The three periods overlap, and theorists change their roles as we change our questions.

The material of Part II offers our second distinguishable answer to the question of the independence and novelty of the efforts of 'development studies': in their differing fashions the lines treated here would claim to see 'development studies' as independent and novel, and as constituting a clear advance over earlier work. Thus Part III confronts two problem areas: the independence and theoretical novelty or otherwise of 'development studies'; and the matter of ranking competing efforts.

In Part III, the 'positivist conventional wisdom' is subjected to a three-fold critique. The three critiques have it in common that they deny the possibility of separating matters of economy, on the one hand, from matters of society, on the other. The familiar calculus of the economists is inadequate to those tasks which are typically those of 'development studies'. This denial takes its starting point in different places for the three critiques and issues in distinctive, though related, analyses.

The 'European line', we term 'neo-institutional social theory' and take it to form a distinctive alternative to orthodox lines. In terms of noted practitioners we exchange Lewis (chapter 3) and Rostow (chapter 4) for Myrdal, Seers and Streeten (whom we meet in chapter 5). The key to the scheme is expressed by Seers[1] in his 1963 article, where he denies that orthodox economics is of any use in treating the typical problems of the Third World. Attention must be paid to the social and institutional context and to the world economic context within which these economies function.

The 'Latin American line' is taken by Girvan[2] to begin with

the rejection of Ricardian-derived notions of international
specialization, in favour of industrialization, by Prebisch.[3]
Girvan argues that in the late 1960s the schemes in use were
institutional economics, which we have noted above, and structuralist economics, the genesis of which we can locate in a
reaction to monetarist explanations of inflation.[4] The denial of
such monetarist explanations focused attention on issues of
economic structure. The consummation of this trend, argues
Girvan,[5] 'took the forms of adding (I) an historical perspective and analysis to the structural and institutional method, (II)
giving the historical/structural/institutional method the kind of
theoretical and empirical content needed to construct a general
theory of dependence and under-development'.[6]

The third line may be exemplified by A.G. Frank and 'underdevelopment theory'. In general it may be argued that the
under-development theory line deals with more or less the same
phenomena as do dependency theorists with the difference that
the notion of dependency is located within a functioning world
capitalist system with the analytical stress on 'capitalism', that
is, criticism is couched in marxian terms. Ehrensaft takes this
to be simply a difference of interpretation of the same phenomena, and we may note that the precise status of these underdevelopment theory efforts has been a matter of sharp debate
amongst theorists.

These three reactions to the orthodoxy will be treated in Part
III as we have treated previously noted theoretical efforts, that
is, we indicate the genesis of the critiques and then go on to
'unpack' them in order to reveal their characteristic argument
forms. On this matter of the genesis of the critiques we may
observe that hitherto, in accordance with our methodological
programme, we have tried to plot the way in which given sets
of resources have been selectively plundered and reworked in
response to particular political demands. But in Part III the political demands are not unequivocally 'positive'; they are rather
to some extent 'critical'. The clients for whom the theorists prepare their efforts are not those of Part II; that is, the nature of
the political demand informing the critiques is of a different
order to that informing the efforts of the orthodox. The nature
of the revisions made in the political demands will be a matter of
no little concern. In addition to this, and corresponding to the
shift in character of the political demand, there is a reconsideration of the 'positivist' orthodoxy because it forms the object
over against which the critiques, at least in part, are defined.
Here we may perhaps indicate a reason why the resultant critiques all partake of a single family of concepts.

The program for Part III will be as follows: chapter 5 will treat
the ideology of the 'neo-institutionalists', and chapter 6 will
treat the varieties of dependency and under-development theory.

5 The contribution of the 'neo-institutionalists'

1.0 DYNAMIC OF SOCIETY I: AN UNDERLYING DIVERGENCE

Here we look at the general milieu within which the neo-institutionalists worked. We may begin with a point made by Nafziger in respect of the sources of critiques of the dominant, 'economics-positivist', notions of development. He observes that; 'Fundamental criticism of existing conceptions of reality in development studies originated in Latin America and continental Europe, and to a lesser extent in Asia and Africa, all with some "inside" perspective on the weakness of dependent economies, rather than in the U.S.'[1] That these criticisms emerged outside of the US we may take, granting the sociology of knowledge as a premise, to reflect differences in the situations of the various actors. In this descriptive vein we can record briefly two complex trends running through this period. On the one hand, we find an economically reconstructed Western Europe divesting itself of formal colonial empires, and, on the other, we see the 'interventionist' creed of the USA reaching its apogee with Kennedy's 'New Frontier', and the subsequent full expression of that, namely Johnson's 'Great Society'.

Of this post-war career of the US Mandel[2] observes that 'never in human history has a country exercised global power comparable to the U.S. at the end of the Second World War. No power ever lost absolute supremacy so quickly. The "American Century" did not last ten years.' Citing Mandel recalls that this discussion might, in contrast to the descriptive treatment above, be cast in the form of an inquiry in respect of meaning-systems; that is, ideologies. Further, it is clear that the discussion is ideologically alive; thus the nature of the relationship of the USA to western Europe and likely changes in that relationship are matters of present concern and differing interpretations.

The former descriptive line is pursued by Schurmann, who notes that up to the mid-1960s the position of the USA seemed secure: 'then it seemed as if American economic and military power were virtually unlimited'.[3] Yet as early as 1968 the position is seen as crumbling; inflation, unemployment and a weakening dollar are cited. Schurmann presents all this as an introduction to treating the gradual process whereby the ideology of US supremacy became untenable. He claims that:[4]

From the end of World War II till 1968, the vision of the American Empire rested on three fundamental assumptions: (1) that

only America had the strategic military power to protect the
free world from attack by the Eurasian heartland communist
nations, Russia and China; (2) that the powerful American
economy was the foundation of all other capitalist and free
world economies; and (3) that the political power of the
American government alone was capable of organising region-
ally the free world.

Schurmann then goes on to indicate how these assumptions lost
credibility. He follows Kiernan's treatment, which focuses on
'shifts in economic strength'.[5] Two of these are noted: the
resource drain of the 'imperial style', and the gradual encroach-
ment of Western European and Japanese competition. With regard to the former, Kiernan notes that notwithstanding that up
until 1972 the USA 'maintained a surplus on exchange of goods
and services'[6] the drain of maintaining the role of 'world
policeman' has outweighed this. This outflow peaked with the
commitment in Vietnam. With regard to the latter point, the
effective refurbishment of Western Europe and Japan under US
hegemony has raised up competitors who have forced the USA
to open up its own economy and have competed effectively in
the world economy generally. As evidence of the loss on the
part of the USA of organizing power within the 'West', Schurmann presents the refusal of Western European nations to send
troops to Vietnam.
    That there was a divergence in the circumstances of the US
and Western Europe is clearly a claim that our quoted sources
would make. The plausibility of their analyses may be open to
question, yet to note this simply serves to introduce the second
aspect we noted with Mandel; which is that the relationship between the USA and Western Europe is a significant part of current political debate. That this is the case bids us recall that
even if we can retrospectively identify what might be taken to
be early signs of the diminution of US power and the divergence
of USA and Western European interests, it is still the case that
this disintegration of US hegemony is far from being 'obvious'.
The minimum we can safely take from this (here unexamined)
debate is that there has been a recovery of European economic
power. Finally, and most important for our purpose, common
perceptions of the relationship between the USA and Western
Europe have changed sharply and have worked to render problematical that which for most of the post-war period has been
taken for granted.
    All this historical material, the substance of continuing de-
bate, we present in order to indicate the broad divergence of
US and Western European interests. That is, we are not interested in constructing a detailed résumé of the post-war history
of the relationship and the comparative performances of the USA
and Western Europe; rather, we wish to indicate the most general milieu within which European theorists operated. Further
than this, it is with the issue of 'decolonization' that we meet

the proximate cause of the sharp and unequivocal divergence
that may be observed in the realm of development studies between US theory and that of Europeans. We take 'decolonization'
to represent a peculiarly European exchange with the Third
World. It invokes traditions and histories of which the USA has
no real counterpart. For example, it provides (we may hazard)
at least an element of that moral core necessary to any social
theory. So where the US, in dealings with under-developed
countries, invoked the 'patriotic imperative' and presented it in
the guise of 'modernization theory', Europeans are in a position
to invoke a tradition of 'stewardship'. This may, indeed, be
just as hypocritical in the end as the core of 'modernization
theory'; but it is also arguably richer and more subtle in its
conception of the relationship of the parties involved, and of
the possibilities for change inherent in those circumstances.

It is around this idea that the episode of 'decolonization' was
a peculiarly Western European experience, and that as such it
called forth distinctive efforts of theorizing, that we shall organize the rest of our inquiry. If we ask what it is for circumstances to 'call forth' a theoretical response, we can answer in
our sociology of knowledge terms. Thus the problem (ordinarily
understood) is of withdrawal from formal empire, and the circumstances of the problem comprise the espousal of notions of
democracy and current exploitation which it is desired to continue. The practical solution is that pattern of handover, or
withdrawal in favour of local elites, identified as 'decolonization'.
The theorist's problem, running alongside and informing the
practical problem is to grasp/interpret/organize/legitimate this
practical solution. To do this he not only has the accepted situation (milieu) plus political demand (the problem ordinarily
understood), but he also has his own intellectual discipline with
its own dynamic. Thus he tackles the given problem with and in
reaction to the established notions of his discipline.

2.0 DYNAMIC OF SOCIETY II: GREATER DIVERGENCE

Within the framework of the general divergence of interests of
the USA and Western Europe, we now focus our attention upon
those local circumstances which encompass the emergence of a
European reply to 'modernization theory'. Our principal claim,
or point of departure, is that the episode of 'decolonization' was
a peculiarly Western European experience and that, as such, it
called forth a distinctive effort of theorizing. The corollary to
this view is that the particular character of the work of Seers/
Myrdal/Streeten can be illuminated by taking the episode of decolonization as formative. The actual argument-forms which are
developed and intellectual traditions which are evoked, we can
consider below (in section 3).

In section 2 we treat the theme of the dynamic of society,
taking 'decolonization' as the 'best' solution to the problem of

withdrawal from empire. We show how it emerges from the experience and routine of colonial government. This is accomplished
by first noting the 'fact' of nationalisms, and then abstractly
considering the reponse of the colonial power. A range of responses are imputed to the colonial power and the ideal is taken
to be minimum necessary change. Historically, we see various
responses. It is the minimum change effected in withdrawal from
sub-Saharan Africa by the UK and France that is taken as the
paradigm of 'decolonization'. We also note that this set of circumstances was subsequently accorded the status of a general
model of the relationship of newly independent and ex-colonial
powers. From this point we continue in section 2.1 and effect a
shift from matters of the dynamic of society to those of the dynamic of theory. We consider the notion that 'decolonization'
presents the form of a theory legitimating it; that is, that practice leads to the solution of its own problems. We present an
argument to this effect by comparing the forms that the practice
of intervention takes in the US context and in the Western European context.

The episode of the decline of the European empires is one of
the more obvious features of the history of the twentieth century. Indeed, Barraclough makes it fairly central. He argues
that 'the history of the present century has been marked at one
and the same time by the impact of the West on Asia and Africa
and by the revolt of Asia and Africa against the West'.[7] He
goes on to say that 'when the 20th century opened, European
power in Asia and Africa stood at its zenith ... sixty years
later only the vestiges of European domination remained.'[8]
Barraclough discusses the revolt of the subject peoples against
the 'West' in terms of European expansionism calling forth a
reaction - that reaction being organized around what (he notes)
has been called Europe's greatest, and most ambiguous, export
- nationalism.

With the rise of nationalisms within subject-territories, the
colonial powers faced the problem of contriving a response. The
general problem for them, we can suggest (impute), is of identifying: (i) a creative response to nationalist pressure for autonomy, where such calls are defined (at least in part) by the very
presence of the colonial power; and (ii) a similar creative response in respect of the related calls for the initiation of 'development', where this is taken (at a minimum) as being something
rather different to simple incorporation in a colonial economy.
That 'autonomy', both political and economic, is so defined by
the nationalists makes the colonial power's problems of evading
its demands distinctly awkward. The interests of one party are,
on the face of it, wholly incompatible with those of the other.
The most general principle governing the entire episode must be,
for the colonial power, that of minimum necessary change to the
status quo. Now in addition to these objectives, which we can
plausibly impute to the colonial power, the immediately available
mechanisms and philosophy of response are going to be that

principle which informs government practice; that is, 'intervention', what Skillen[9] calls 'statism', the view that it is the business of government to order matters in and of society.

Can we identify any minimum requirements of this response to the pressure of 'nationalist developmentalism'? Consider first the colonial situation. At one limit it issues in the total incorporation of the subject people, both economically and culturally, and at the behest of the colonizers. Power will reside with the colonizers and be relinquished only when nothing untoward can follow from their relinquishing power. Here perhaps is the location of the conservative colonist's equation of political and organizational sophistication with experience of government and administration; issuing, as Worsley[10] notes, in the line that 'the natives are not ready to look after their own affairs yet'. But clearly on this view the transfer of power can be infinitely delayed, and 'troublemakers' can be treated with repression. The other limit will be a speedy acquiescence to nationalisms and an ordered withdrawal; with a variety of stances accommodating to the pressures of nationalism in between. If we turn to the end result of withdrawal, we find the reverse of incorporation, that is, genuine autonomy - governmental, administrative, economic, cultural. Power resides in the hands of the 'new' elite (this is a specific form of handover), and the ex-colonial power is involved only to the extent that the 'new' elite, from time to time, deems to be appropriate. Thus we have a symmetrical frame of possibility - from repression through accommodation to acquiescence.

Within that frame of limits, and given our imputed problem for the colonial power, we could now sketch out a series of theory-derived responses open to the colonial power.[11] However, if the question is of the minimum necessary requirements of response to 'nationalist developmentalism' for a particular area, then we confront an empirical question. Here the question of 'minimum requirements' is a matter of a historically specific set of changes in historically specific established relationships. The circumstances of European withdrawal from empire provide a series of 'answers' in respect of minimum requirements of responses.

We can follow Zeylstra and White in distinguishing an early and a late phase of the withdrawal (this is, of course, to exclude the issue of 'white dominions' altogether). In the first phase, completed more or less by 1956 with the independence of Tunisia and Morocco, there was accomplished the withdrawal from Asian and Arab lands. The second, later phase covered the withdrawal from sub-Saharan Africa. The early phase reveals some of the variety of methods of accomplishing withdrawal. On the one hand the UK withdrew from the Indian sub-continent, Ceylon and Burma by January 1948. In respect of the withdrawal from India/Pakistan, the colonial power at one point declared in advance an intention to withdraw by a particular date so that rival nationalist groupings would settle. Grimal notes that 'Both the rapidity of the solution and its clear-cut nature astonished international opinion.'[12] On the other hand, we can note the forcible ejection of the French from Indo-China and the Dutch from the East Indies. In both instances metropolitan governments decided after the war to re-establish their authority over colonial territories. However, the war itself had seen their essentially precarious holds fatally loosened. Both efforts collapsed into bloody wars before returning powers were beaten off. Indeed, Grimal reports that it was in no small measure the wars of independence that created distinctly national states where before there had been a disparate and maybe only loosely associated collection of groups within the colonial territories.

The later phase also offers distinguishable 'answers' to the problem of 'nationalist developmentalism': thus the French in Algeria fight a bloody war and are ejected in much the same way as they were from Indo-China. The Belgians and, with a different prelude, the Portuguese present another style - that of 'precipitate withdrawal'. In southern Africa varieties of colonization linger. But, as for the rest, we note the ordered process of 'decolonozation'.

Both White[13] and Zeylstra[14] use the phase I/phase II distinction we have thus far followed. We must now ask why, and with what degree of propriety. The establishment of independent states in this first phase was, reports Zeylstra, taken as marking the end of any financial or other responsibilities toward ex-colonies by sometime colonial powers. This is fairly obviously the case with the UK, and Zeylstra indeed makes this clear. However, he also wants us to believe that this is generally the case for all phase I withdrawals - but he offers no supporting evidence. White, who also uses this phasing, again mentions the UK withdrawal from Asia, but adds in respect of the other colonial powers that: 'Further east, countries such as Indonesia had won their independence in circumstances which had led to a sharp diminution of relations with the former colonial power.'[15] Here is the first problem in respect of this phasing: that phase I is characterized generally by a cutting off of aid and other responsibilities by colonial powers is not established. It is true of the UK; but whilst it may be plausible in the case of other colonial powers, they offer no evidence other than its plausibility. For two empiricists, this is no good.

Phase II is established as a contrast to Phase I. Here, both White and Zeylstra agree, the withdrawal of colonial power was marked by its being orderly and part of a scheme which entailed the assumption of long-term responsibilities to aid in 'nation-building'. Again, we note that this is offered as a general characterization. But this is preposterous: we can shatter this claim by intoning Algeria, Congo, Angola, etc. None the less, to the extent that it is possible to present the withdrawal from Africa as being in not a few cases ordered and peaceable and entailing long-term commitments to new nations, it is evident that White and Zeylstra have hit upon something worth noting.

In the arguments and histories presented by Zeylstra and
White there is thus a double failure. This issues in the conclusion that the distinction they aimed to draw between phases I
and II, in terms of the nature of the post-independence relationship of new nations to their old colonial masters, is not tenable.
There is no such distinction to be drawn. How important is this
for their general views? In our opinion, not very. Both writers
fail to secure their points simply because they adopt an empiricist approach and try to present perfectly sensible theoretical
notes as being derived from reading history. White's 'nominalism' fails him in that his effort to derive his theory from the
facts results in a ludicrous misrepresentation of those facts;
and Zeylstra's effort is a hopelessly transparent attempt to make
the UK example serve all cases, which clearly it does not.

However, given our abstract sketch of the possibilities for
reworking a challenged relationship and the imputed wishes of
the colonial power, we can measure history (the 'facts') against
this ideal of a programmed response of minimum change. Zeylstra in fact presents this programme as it was manifest in withdrawal from English and French 'Black Africa'; yet failing to
see how the procedure flows from the unhindered 'logic of the
situation', he takes it to be an adventitious bit of history need-
ing interpretation. We are able to take, then, the ordered withdrawal from Anglo-French sub-Saharan Africa as being a classic
accommodating response on the part of the colonial powers. It is
this style of withdrawal for which we reserve the theoretical-
descriptive term 'decolonization'. That we take 'decolonization'
to be a particular variety of withdrawal is both reasonable (in
the light of our above 'abstract' arguments) and banal in the
light of history. Who would wish to use the same term to designate the withdrawal of, say, the Dutch from Indonesia and the
British from Africa? The former power ejected; the latter instal-
ling what Hargreaves[16] might call 'collaborators'.

The distinction drawn between phases I and II is thus unhelpful and unnecessary. We can grant that the withdrawal from
Anglo-French sub-Saharan Africa entailed a peculiar sort of
relationship. It is both the 'best solution' and the paradigm from
which other withdrawals more or less diverge. In place of White
and Zeylstra's two 'phases' we substitute two categories of response, the 'best' and the 'rest'.

We can bring out the particular character of 'decolonization'
by quoting from White and Zeylstra. While using the distinction
that we have criticized, White observes that:[17]

In Africa the transition for most territories was less abrupt.
Administrative structures remained intact. There was an expectation of a continuing flow of communication, and of resources. The need for external resources to develop relatively
backward economies seemed much clearer in Africa than it had
in Asia.

Zeylstra, concerned with the relationship between withdrawal
and provision of aid, argues that only in one area were development programmes initiated prior to independence: this was in
sub-Saharan Africa. His desire to let geographical and chron-
ological differences serve as a basis for an emergent characterization of development-aid programmes leads him to this obfuscating looseness - 'sub-Saharan Africa'. What he means is the
Anglo-French withdrawal from Black Africa. Yet he clearly picks
up the essential novelty. He observes:[18]

> Assistance to colonies was integrated in a systematically plan-
> ned decolonization. There, assistance became identical with
> preparation for the acceptance of responsibility for one's own
> country's destiny - a long term process, in the course of
> which at some time or other sovereignty was being transferred
> as a necessary condition for its completion. This kind of de-
> colonization [i.e. withdrawal] ... cannot be imagined as
> resulting only from a loss of political power and prestige. On
> the contrary it must have its roots in a colonial policy in-
> cluding concern with the welfare of the subject peoples. His-
> torically seen it must have been a logical consequence of an
> idea embedded in the rationale of colonialism.

We observed above that our point of departure was that 'decolonization' was uniquely European, and might be taken as
formative for Seers et al. That it is unique we should have
established prima facie above. We must now turn to the 'formative' aspect, for this is our principal concern - and not, as
might be supposed from the length of these reflections, the
elucidation of a theoretical history of the process of withdrawal
from empire in general and 'decolonization' in particular. Prior
to that, however, there remains one final task. This is to note,
with White, that the pattern of inter-state relations made manifest in the withdrawal of decolonization was, by the end of the
1950s, taken as the norm. White reports, after noting the particular character of aid to his 'phase II' recipients, that: 'from
the late 1950s onwards first the newly independent countries,
and then other developing countries as well, came to *expect* aid,
which thus became more diffused, more diversified, and more
closely integrated into long-term policy making'.[19] White presents this as simply a 'generalization' of the 'phase II' African
situation, though he is not specific: presumably he would argue
that the behaviour of one colonial government towards its client
would be enough to establish a precedent which might then be
invoked. If the precedent was set thus, the general expectation
he takes to have been reinforced by Nixon's (1957) reception in
Latin America when he was abused, in part, because the US had
'neglected' Latin America. The model established in Africa was
most visibly and dramatically brought out in the Indian exchange
crisis of 1957-8. Here the Indian development programme ran
into finance problems and was bailed out by the Aid India Con-

sortium of rich trading partners. White observes: 'The India
Consortium was the first and perhaps most ambitious collective
attempt by a group of donors to underwrite a national development strategy.... [he adds] The precedent had an almost immediate impact on aid to Pakistan, for which a similar consortium
was established in 1960.'[20] Whether this bit of history should
be regarded simply as a result of 'accidents of history' (as
White rather suspects) or as some sort of 'unconscious' realization on the part of the 'new nations' that their precise status
was close to the model of decolonization and that this was the
appropriate starting point for their relations with the rich, is
not a matter we will pursue – though it is the obvious question
in the light of the above discussion. Rather, we shall content
ourselves with noting that the relationship inherent in 'decolonization' did in fact become the norm. White goes on to note that
it was fixed in the period 1961-5, when a combination of US and
Third World pressure invited all concerned to take for granted
what had thus far been established.

Given that the pattern of 'decolonization' became the paradigm
of the exchange between rich and poor nations, we may turn to
Zeylstra and pick out its particular characteristics; and in observing these we may see how close they come to a speculative
'cashing' of the 'argument from colonial interest' we noted above.
In this respect, we may say that, given the presumed interest
of the colonial power, then within the African context it is clear
that withdrawal could be reduced (in line with 'statist' ideology)
to a 'transfer of sovereignty' that would be a sham: simply a
replacement of role incumbents within a continuing frame of
practice and expectation.

We can detail the characteristics of 'decolonization' as follows:
(i) the withdrawal was accomplished in an ordered manner; that
is, within the ambit of existing resources, both intellectual and
organizational; (ii) the withdrawal was legitimated by reference
to the notion of stewardship, which was available to the African
elite for transformation into notions such as 'father of the nation';
(iii) the withdrawal was taken as an element of a longer-term
process of 'nation-building'.

Putting all this another way, what we may claim is that there
are certain resources available within the actual experience of
the colonial episode which may, in concert with the colonial
power's intellectual tradition and present world economic/political
situation, be taken to have contributed to the form of the process of 'decolonization'. We can order the resources and opportunities which the colonial episode itself presents to the de-
colonizers according to the schema of 'intervention' we have
presented; thus we may fuse theory and practice and present
this exchange in a historically specific guise as the response of
real people to real, practical problems. We are thereby able to
indicate how a characteristic orientation to problems of development is generated. In sum, the situation expresses the form of
its appropriate theory.

2.1 DYNAMIC OF THEORY I: DECOLONIZATION AND ITS LEGITIMATING THEOREM

In order to show that the situation expresses the form of its
appropriate theory with the persuasiveness necessary to convince a sceptic we would have to write a detailed history of the
period detailing the circumstances, behaviour and utterances
of the main actors. A weaker demonstration of our claim would
be to offer a comparison. In section 2.1 we compare the form
the practice of 'intervention' takes in the US context with 'modernization theory', and in the Western European line with 'neo-
institutionalist social theory', and attempt to show how the given
problem shapes the articulation of the invoked theory. Crudely,
'neo-institutionalist social theory' evolves out of an ongoing
situation whereas 'modernization theory' is cobbled together in
response to a developing situation. Section 2.1 is therefore
transitional between 2.0, which dealt with the dynamic of society,
and section 3.0, which will treat the dynamic of theory. In sum
we have three elements: (2.11) the possibilities inherent in the
colonial situation, or experience itself; (2.12) the possibilities
inherent in the established mode of government, 'statism'; (2.13)
the resultant practical form/theoretical explanation of the process of decolonization. This we take to be exemplified in the
efforts of Seers, Streeten and Myrdal. We elucidate these three
aspects in contrast to US efforts.

2.11

Having cast section 2 in the form of asking after the colonial
powers' view of the pressure for withdrawal from empire, it is
appropriate to focus on their established colonial practices as
the first source of resources available to them in fashioning a
response.
    We can identify an available moral core for any response to
'nationalist developmentalism' in the notion of 'stewardship'. We
can follow Grimal in granting that, in general, 'the colonial policies of the European countries were not deliberately directed
towards emancipation'[21] and add that none the less within
their relationship was the possibility of invoking, if need be, a
progressive schema.[22] The various European colonial powers
took different lines; but in the case of the UK, the notion of
leading dependencies towards independence was established in
the cases of the 'white dominions', and then taken as general.
Co-option of locals to colonial governments clearly placed a transfer of power on the list of possibilities. Grimal notes that this
was all ordered by the UK; thus 'progress towards autonomy
had to be cautious and controlled, leading towards a solution
that could satisfy both the principles of self-determination and
the interests of the home country'.[23] This 'moral dualism' is
reflected in the behaviour of the other colonial powers. Accord-

ing to their espoused 'democratic' principles they were obliged
to talk in terms of colonialism benefiting subject peoples. They
nevertheless searched for ways of protecting their interests in
face of calls for self-government. The French vacillated between
the policies of assimilation and association, and the Dutch, after
rather belatedly introducing the 'moral policy' in 1902, invented
the doctrine of 'synthesis' in 1922. This supposedly involved
fusing 'the best of the east' with 'the best of the west': it was
never clear just what this meant.

Very generally then - and arguably very much as an incidental
to straightforward exploitation - the Europeans did acknowledge
the minimum notions required by their putative ideologies of
democracy. A slow movement towards some sort of emancipation
was envisaged, and this conception was available when, after
the Second World War, demands for independence became pressing. Thus we may observe that the moral core of this European
style of 'intervention' is not that which informed US efforts. The
moral core of modernization theory lay in the cowed response of
liberals to red-baiting politicians; the result was a florid celebration of the 'patriotic imperative'.[24] The moral core of
European efforts we can take to invoke the colonial episode -
'stewardship' - and a notion of 'proper development' which
issues out of the long exchange between colonial power and subject people; in comparison we can presume it to be richer and
more subtle than anything flowing from a relationship struck up
under the banner of the 'free world' and the 'fight against international communism'.[25]

That the European exchange with colonial areas was more
immediately rich in usable notions and data we may take to be a
simple function of social exchange over a period of time. The
colonial authorities and subject people will necessarily come to
share some ideas through shared experience. Thus it is usually
suggested that the result of this interchange is evident, for
example, in political and social ideas of the new elite. More generally, as Grimal puts it, 'the district officers, who maintained
the peace and subjected the inhabitants to such measures as the
taking of a regular population census, the levying of taxes ...
served in the long run to build up a communal identity'[26] -
and that 'identity' served not only subject peoples but also colonial power when it came to reworking their relationship with
their dependencies.

Here we may recall White's work and draw out another difference in the European and US experiences. White observes that
when the USA endeavoured to extend aid and containment from
Western Europe, where it worked well, to the Third World - in
particular South-East Asia - two factors militated against success:[27]

Firstly the status of the Asian allies as client states was far
plainer to see. Secondly and more significantly the immediate
task of the aid was harder to identify ... Aid had become a

form of generalized support, the purpose of which was described slightingly by its critics as being to 'shore-up' weak
regimes.

If we recall White's four proximate causes of the success of Marshall Aid - (a) volume of aid, (b) clear task, (c) political con-
gruence of objectives, and (d) shared culture - then we can see
that in South-East Asia the USA was short of (b), (d) and
arguably (c). In contrast, for European and colonial areas (b),
(c) and (d) were less obtrusively problematical.

Finally we may note a third resource which the actual experience of the colonial episode made available when 'decolonization'
had to be programmed and theorized. This is the simple practical experience of the territories coupled with the habit of
liberal reformism. A US counterpart to the practical experience
is difficult to identify from their involvement with Latin American states, and Hawthorn[28] does not identify any habit of reformism in US government/academic relations.

2.12

If the above represents the resources immediately available within the situation of moves to withdraw from the colonial relationship, and if they are clearly available to Europeans and not to
the USA, then the prism through which these lines are focused
is common to both. This is, the government habit, or style, or
ontological mode, of 'intervention'.

2.13

Here we indicate how the resources of the situation present
themselves in the exchange with theory. The available notion of
'stewardship' and the partial incorporation of subject people in
terms of ideas and material interests issues in the legitimating
notion of 'transfer of sovereignty'. For the colonial power, this
is the logical consequence of the notion of 'stewardship', and
for the indigenous 'replacement' elite it is the assumption of
that role of 'stewardship' in the guise of the leader as 'father
of the nation'. This all represents a loose summation of historical
events: abstractly, it reduces to the minimum change desired
by the colonial power if we present it as being simply a change
of role incumbents. The extent to which the 'transfer of sovereignty' is other than this simple change of political personnel is
a matter for empirical observation of the various cases.[29] As
to the USA, the alien nature of its 'intervention' was noted by
Kiernan when he observed that the host nation's armed forces
often were seen as the most 'progressive social formation'. Hence,
as a result supplies of arms became equated with 'nation-building'.
The notion of transfer of sovereignty is not an option for US
theorists.

The legitimating notion of transfer of sovereignty, with its consequence for the role of the new government being that of 'building a nation', couples up with the practical experience of territories and liberal-democratic reformism to present the organizational principles of neo-institutionalism as 'obviously' appropriate to the task. The established patterns of colonial and metropolitan administrative activity are broadened and deepened into 'nation-building', and social theory of neo-institutionalism presents itself as uniquely suited to the task. Administered national development requires the possibility of translating economic models into 'circumstance-relevant' programmes, and systemic analysis is ideal. Both new elite and colonial power can agree that their task is largely one of 'system construction' - a technical task. Subsequent matters of implementation are piecemeal: projects, programmes, plans and so on. Thus theory and procedure 'grow out of' practice for Europeans where for the USA this was not possible.

We can summarize as follows: with 'neo-institutionalists' the political content of the calls for 'intervention' has shifted from confronting expansionist communism, as was the case with modernization theory, towards the project of reworking established colonial relationships. The effort as a whole is, not unexpectedly, informed by a different set of ideas. As regards the moral core of modernization theory, we noted that it was formed by cowed liberals in the situation of red-baiting and presented in the context of donor-competition with the USSR. The moral core of European efforts is formed in response to pressures of 'nationalist developmentalism', and invokes traditions of 'stewardship' integral to (if latent within, for the most part) the colonial situation. Generally, the European theorists invoke a moral tradition of social reformism. The sets of resources used by the two groups of theorists can also be distinguished; where modernization theory had recourse to structural functionalism and an emasculated Keynesianism, the 'neo-institutionalist social theorists' have recourse to the experience of the colonial episode, and a distinct European tradition of social thought: the latter being characterized with reference to a relationship with government that disposes them to practical policy-making rather than to the elaboration of formal schemes of great generality. To put this another way (this point we may call the methodological context): the US theorists pursued if not quite a 'general theory', then a set of policy-relevant pieces of work presented using that syntax. The Europeans, using essentially the same sociological and economic ideas, within the same empiricist epistemology, produce piecemeal studies. This we may take, following Hawthorn, to be a function of the relationship of the two groups of theorists to their respective government machines. It is for these reasons that we take the episode of 'decolonization' to be formative for Europeans.

3.0 DYNAMIC OF THEORY II: THE PROXIMATE INTELLECTUAL
SOURCE OF THE EUROPEAN EFFORTS

3.1 What is 'institutional' economics?

Institutionalism we take to be a particular approach to economics; in brief, it is a 'sociologized economics'. That is, notions
drawn from economics are considered with reference to their
social assumptions. Economies, as functioning social systems, are
considered, rather than the elaborate calculi of abstract models.
We take institutionalism to be reformist in character, and carefully non-marxian; here we may cite Myrdal and Galbraith, but
the line traces back to Veblen. It is, by and large, a European
tradition, though it has received its most elaborate and familiar
presentation in the work of the theorists of the New Deal. We
will present our exposition of the origins and preliminary characterization of institutionalism through the work of Gruchy, who
(falsely) assimilates all institutionalist thinking to a single, US,
school. What is crucial in all this is institutionalism's character
as a 'sociologized-economics' and its association with economic
and social crisis.
    Here we look at 'institutionalism' in its most prominent, New
Deal, guise. Otis Graham,[30] in a history of planning experi-
ments in the USA, establishes that within US government and
academic worlds there has been pressure for the establishment
of some sort of 'directed capitalism'. Graham cites Roosevelt's
New Deal as the response/solution of one variety of liberalism to
the catastrophe of the depression. This history is presented as
the story of a conflict between government, big business and
academics on the one hand, and, on the other, an alliance of
smaller business, miscellaneous pressure groups and Congress
pressing to maintain the status quo. In nuce, Graham's thesis is
that whilst Capitol Hill needs planners, unfortunately all it has
got are interest groups, lobbyists, and power-brokers; that is
the 'Broker State', as he dubs it.
    This theme is familiar: thus in the post-Second World War
period the names of Galbraith and Myrdal come readily to mind.
Yet their criticisms and those of the 'New Dealers' are by no
means novel. Gruchy[31] sees Galbraith and Myrdal (and others)
as 'neo-institutionalists', invoking an older, pre-Second World
War tradition of 'institutional theory'. This inter-war period is
characterized by Myrdal as requiring practical theorizing. He
observes: 'The Great Depression and the practical problems
raised in its wake rescued me from my critical philosophy and
restored my scientific productivity.'[32] It is at this juncture
that Myrdal coincides most closely with the pre-war US institutionalists (notwithstanding that he is at some pains to distance
himself from this tradition and to recount his intellectual biography in terms of Swedish scholars, as we shall see below).
We can take the US tradition as the 'mainstream', and as such

this line is older than Gruchy makes it.

Dorfman argues that the background to institutional economics involves 'a slice of the whole development of civilisation in the U.S. since the end of the Civil War'.[33] He traces the emergence of the school out of the conflict engendered by the rapid US industrialization of the last third of the nineteenth century. Tracing the flux of the debate[34] he observes that at the turn of the century the 'narrow practicality'[35] of the business community found its champion in Jevons and the 'marginalist revolution', subsequently developed into the neo-classical line by Marshall. This was the target against which Veblen 'launched his barbs'; Dorfman adds 'it was at this point that institutionalism, as we know it, reached maturity'.[36]

If the key figure in the pre-First World War effort was Veblen, then it seems that through the 1920s and 1930s there were a series of American theorists following similar lines of inquiry (including, according to Gruchy, Rexwell Tugwell who is cited by Graham as a key figure of the 'New Deal' and the 'father' of US planning). A number of economists are noted who have it in common that 'the economic system is analysed within the framework of the total culture of which the economic system is a part'.[37] Methodologically they subscribed to a general evolutionary paradigm, and their relations with the other social sciences were eclectic. Gruchy goes on to say that the 'institutionalists of the 1920s and 1930s were mainly interested in how to prevent depressions and how to stabilize economic activity at a full employment level ... the main issue was the "social control of business"'.[38]

Gruchy is at some pains throughout his lengthy study to apologize for the 'radical' tone of the theorists he treats, and he disavows on behalf of Veblen's later followers the marxian 'flavour' of that theorist's work. Indeed, Dorfman notes that 'the view of Marx and his disciples as "pre-Darwinian" - to use Veblen's term - is a major negative characteristic of institutionalists and serves to differentiate them from most of the critics of the dominant economics'.[39] This is both rather ambiguous and, recalling Myrdal on Marx, interesting. It is ambiguous in that it does not say anything about these other critics of the 'conventional wisdom' - and the context of the remark is not such as to lead us to suppose that he has marxist critics in mind. This being so, that the institutionalists felt obliged to attack Marx must indicate that they saw affinities between his work and their own, and that they were anxious to deflect an obvious line of attack from the orthodox. As regards Myrdal's sensitivity to marxian critique, we may note that its anticipations go right back to Veblen. Further than this, Gruchy observes that the US theorists never fully developed their evolutionary schema of economics; and Gordon, after proposing Schumpeter as the theorist who actually did proceed to 'fill-out' the institutionalists' programme, suggests that the reason that institutionalists would hesitate to accept Schumpeter as a co-worker is precisely the

extent of his critique. Thus Gordon observes that he 'took the
entire story of capitalist evolution and possible decline as his
province. American institutionalists, I think it is fair to say,
have not been willing to go this far in their institutionalism.'[40]
   If institutionalism had a European theoretical input to a US
situation, then that imported aspect was rapidly domesticated.
Thus Veblen's marxian elements were quickly struck out and replaced with a Deweyite pragmatism.[41] Institutionalism was
thereby taken into the US university scene which, says Gruchy,
'provided more academic opportunity for the dissemination of the
economics of dissent than was the case in Western Europe'.[42]
Now this is a misleading remark: 'institutionalism' is the 'economics of dissent' and has been presented as specifically American.
None the less it lets us see how Gruchy makes his tacit claim
that institutionalism is the only dissenting economics.
   Western European critical lines are represented by the Fabians,
on the one hand, and Keynes, on the other. The former are
taken by Gruchy to resemble the institutionalists but are dismissed as secondary to Veblen; and Keynes is presented as
'depression-relevant' and subsequently just irrelevant. The post-
war emasculation of Keynes is not treated and nor is the work of
the 'new Cambridge School'. Gruchy simply equates the work of
Keynes with the Keynesianism of orthodox government regulation
of the economy. Partly, we may hazard, this flows from a desire
to separate the institutionalists, who were concerned as Gruchy
noted above with full employment, from Keynes - just as the
institutionalists themselves have been anxious to eschew any
connections with the marxian tradition - and partly we could
take it to be a reflection of the fate of Keynes in the US. But,
more interestingly, it derives, we can suggest, from Gruchy's
apparent haste to 'de-radicalize' his radicals. Thus he presents
the exchange of event and theory in a simplistic manner; he
observes 'Keynesian economics and economic policy proposals
have come to have diminishing acceptance as post-World War Two
problems have come to the surface'.[43] All of which makes
theory a simple response to event. In the case of Keynes, this
ignores the element of the active 'killing-off' of the reformer,
detailed by Sweezy,[44] and in the case of the neo-institutionalists it permits the presentation of Myrdal and Galbraith as
neutral scientists. Gruchy wants them to have it all ways - the
richness and relevance of a developed political economy and the
'untainted' status of a natural scientist.[45] Gruchy's apology
for the radical roots of the ideas he propounds is captured in
his observing of the neo-institutionalists that they differ from
Veblen, in that 'whereas Veblen looked forward to the demise of
the private enterprise system the neo-institutionalists think in
terms of preserving this system'.[46]
   In the end, the drift of Gruchy's effort coincides with that of
Graham in regarding the options open to the government of a
developed state as being limited, and the choice - for reasonable
men - as a foregone conclusion. A return to laissez-faire is taken

as nonsensical, the Broker State is out-moded, and the only
remaining choice is of a centrist-planning ideal; a 'regulated
capitalism'.

The foregoing has presented 'institutionalism' in a historical
guise as the response of reform-minded liberals to the various
problems thrown up by the developing industrial society in
which they found themselves. The institutionalists have often,
it seems, been dismissed as 'generalists', and thus either not
suited to, or, alternatively, rather difficult for, scholarly treatment. Clearly, their disposition to 'generality' flows from their
construction of an ideology of planning. This we take to be
based upon either (as, say, in case of Western Europe and the
UK) the gradual accretion not of government powers of intervention, but of established areas of intervention, or (as, say,
in the case of the USA) upon fewer areas of intervention and
a more clearly argued case for these patterns of activity. The
tradition is resolutely problem-centred, and the core of the
stance is picked out by Gordon. He notes that the institutional
line is not easy to define and offers a set of criteria: 'the term
"institutional" economics suggests to me a series of propositions
which, taken together add up to a particular way of approaching the study of economics'.[47] He offers the following: that
economic behaviour is 'strongly conditioned by the institutional
environment',[48] and that the 'process of mutual interaction is
an evolutionary one'.[49] Gordon introduces 'conflict' in several
ways, thus in a criterion which seems to echo the circumstances
of depression he notes the key role of 'the (largely conflicting)
conditions imposed by modern technology and by the pecuniary
institutions of modern capitalism'.[50] Conflict is the business
of economics rather than any harmonious equilibrium, and that
this is indeed the case opens the door to the requirement of
'social control of economic activity'.[51] The principle of 'rational
economic action' is denied. He concludes his summation by noting
the argument that: 'Granted the preceding assumptions, much of
orthodox economic theory is either wrong or irrelevant because
it makes demonstrably false assumptions and does not ask the
really important questions.'[52]

3.2 Myrdal and institutionalism

Gruchy claims Myrdal for this (essentially US, so far as he is
concerned) tradition in quite unequivocal terms. Thus, after
observing that 'among European economists none is better known
today in the U.S. than the eminent Swedish economist Gunnar
Myrdal', he goes on to characterize his works as follows: 'Myrdal's main interest has been in the analysis of the developing
economic process and the movement towards more fully integrated or planned economies in the western world and elsewhere.'[53] Now whilst we can easily grant a general resemblance,
it is not clear that Gruchy is not being somewhat misleading.

Myrdal describes his intellectual roots as Swedish, recalling that
his early intellectual milieu was dominated by Wicksell and the
analysis of dynamic economic processes. Myrdal also notes Cas-
sel's influence: 'There was, I felt, a healthy realism in his
approach to economic problems, a desire to avoid metaphysical
speculation and get down to facts and figures.'[54] This 'practicality' is emphasized. Myrdal distinguishes his generation
from the preceding one by noting that they were familiar with
crises, the Great War, inflation and recession, so he notes that:
'when they faced undesirable situations, such as unemployment,
they had fewer inhibitions than the older generation to think
constructively about measures which would mitigate them'.[55]
All this contributes, we may hazard, a retrospective reading of
his own career. But in addition to these intellectual sources
there is one seminal experience. After recalling that his work
was running into the sands over the issue of 'values', he records:[56]

> Meanwhile the happy 'twenties had ended. The gathering
> Great Depression and the practical economic problems raised
> in its wake rescued me from my critical philosophy and re-
> stored my scientific productivity. My outer life had already
> placed forcefully before me that important phenomena: Social
> Crisis, and I have remained, with the rest of the world,
> under that sign ever since.

From what Myrdal has to say in his biographical postscript, it
seems as if his work comes to resemble that of the US institutionalists only in so far as there was a common practical orientation.
Myrdal notes that he received the work of Keynes with pleasure,
but no great surprise. As for the US institutionalists, he reports coming into contact with them and adds that their naive
empiricism helped him clear up a few points in respect of 'value'.
The core of the resemblance is the treatment of social crisis
through government intervention, with the disciplinary corollary
of practicality in research. Around this convergence, called
forth by the historically common experience of the depression,
the various theorists take their different stances. Thus, whilst
there is undoubtedly a family resemblance, the precise nature of
the resemblance is a matter requiring detailed comparison.
Gruchy's assimilation of Myrdal to a US school must be denied.

The substantive material we can briefly note. Myrdal's writings
are very extensive and often apparently repetitive; and as we
shall not treat them in any detail here, we offer a sketch to
show how his style and line do coincide with the institutionalists
we have noted above. Myrdal is taken by Gruchy to react against
the equilibrium theory orthodoxy of 1900-29 in favour of 'a new
economics of integration oriented around the concept of a cumulative process of development'.[57] The motor of the social
dynamic is derived from Wicksell. Where Wicksell uses the notion
of a 'moving equilibrium' such that divergence on the part of the

economy from its 'ideal track' was self-correcting, Myrdal, on
the other hand - rather like Harrod - sees a continuing divergence. Once some given direction of social change is instituted,
a process of 'circular cumulative causation' tends to reinforce
that disposition to change. In addition to this general theoretical
revision, Myrdal introduces people and groups into his schema,
treating them naturalistically: they become causal agents of
change. On the most general level an evolutionary schema is
invoked, whereby the present result of the process of cumulative
causation is the modern organizational welfare state, perfected
in the 'West' as a series of national welfare states. The next,
'logical' step is therefore the establishment of 'the world welfare
state'.[58]

In respect of the states of the Third World, Myrdal applies
his notion of cumulative change to their particular situation vis
à vis the world economy. With regard to internal institutional
structures, his conclusions are notoriously pessimistic. The
Third World states are locked into a debilitating position in the
world economy and are internally crippled by 'outmoded' social
forms. The remedy - if there is one - is to use the weapon of
nationalistic planning to shift the economy into an upward dynamic; as he says, 'what in fact we all mean by development is
the movement upward of the whole social system'.[59] Thus we
come to Myrdal's focus on the state and, in view of the manifest
inadequacy of his identified agent to meet his theories' requirements, the 'soft state'.

To pursue Myrdal through his voluminous writings would be
exhausting and unhelpful. Rather we may recall our characterization of institutionalism as the crisis-occasioned ideology of
the planner and ask after the nature of the method of analysis
used by Myrdal, taken as our representative neo-institutionalist.
Three issues present themselves: (1) the use of social science
resources by theorists of neo-institutionalism; (2) the treatment
of 'values', that is, of the role of the theorist; and (3) the related policy line, that is, planning and the 'soft state'. Our
treatment of these issues will focus upon the work of Paul
Streeten, who may be regarded as the principal English exponent of the work of Myrdal. Additionally, his own work falls within the ambit of neo-institutionalism, and he helpfully adopts the
guise of a philosophically sophisticated empiricism. To put this
another way, we can say that Streeten's work both interprets
Myrdal to us and is, of itself, too sophisticated to ignore.

3.3 The strategic use of the resources of the social sciences

Mikesell[60] has noted that the early efforts of the economists,
built around the core of 'growth theories', have undergone a
two-fold change: the models have become more complex as more
variables have been introduced, and there has been a greater
use made of the resources of the wider circle of the social

sciences. There has been, in a nutshell, a pursuit of greater
realism in modelling. In this context we can recall the institutionalists' concern for realism and empirical research, in contrast
(as Gordon argued) to the 'metaphysics' of the neo-classicists.
However, rather than continue with a general style of exegesis,
we can turn to Streeten for specimens of work revealing the use
made by institutionalists of the resources of social science. His
substantive conclusions are not our concern here.

Streeten presents no general theory. In contrast, the theorists of 'modernization', deploying their conceptual armoury of
dualisms to the 'Grand Process of Modernization'[61] did couch
their efforts in such terms to a greater or lesser extent. Streeten
evidently feels no obligation to present a 'general theory' or to
couch his contributions to 'development studies' in that syntax.
Whether Streeten regards this pursuit of 'the general' as properly empiricist and as amenable to full elaboration and presentation (given time), or whether he takes it as a forlorn hope
like Mikesell – 'I do not believe that a realistic *general* model of
economic and social development is possible, at least one which
would be worth very much from the standpoint of prediction
and control'[62] – is a matter that need not concern us now.
Here we may simply observe that Streeten works out of the
institutionalists' frame, taking it for granted. Thus his work is
piecemeal, sceptical, empiricist and concerned with realistic modelling; and whilst he does not present, or pursue, a general
theory, he uses the data and more particularly the concepts of
social science in order to get clear the outlines and character of
the economy he happens to be concerned with. Given the Myrdalian project of 'development', Streeten is thereby able to identify
the nature of the changes that can be initiated given the existing
institutional frame, and subsequently identify the necessary conditions of further, more radical change. He exemplifies Gordon's
observation of institutionalism: that is, that in the end it adds
up to 'a particular way of approaching the study of economics'.[63]

Streeten's empiricism and institutionalist line are confirmed
when he observes that 'the bias in our view of economic and
social reality enters before the model building begins, at the
level where concepts are formed'.[64] And in this respect concept-formation is taken as the bringing together under a concept
of a mass of data. Aggregation and isolation of data, says Street-
en, let us separate out sets of data (concepts). Streeten reveals
his general orientation to theorizing thus: 'All thought presupposes implicit or explicit model building and model using. Rigorous abstraction, simplification and quantification are necessary
conditions of analysis and policy.'[65] Clearly, Streeten sub-
scribes to what Hindess has called the 'epistemology of model
building'.[66] In this sense we have a sophisticated empiricism
confronting the naive efforts of the early orthodox schemes. As
Streeten puts it, 'it is of the essence of what is sometimes called
the institutional approach to probe into the psychological, social,
political and cultural justification for the formation of certain
concepts'.[67]

We consider first a general statement on the formation of concepts: the essay entitled 'The Use and Abuse of Models in Development Studies'. In this essay, it is claimed that model-building typically reveals four 'systematic biases'. The first of these concerns the decision as to what counts as a variable and what counts as a parameter.

Streeten observes that 'the separation of parameters' from variables in Western orthodox models is partly determined by what is appropriate for advanced industrial nations, partly by ideology and vested interest, and partly by convenience of analysis'.[68] He develops this point in terms of spelling out the functional conditions of any economic concept being a realistic concept. In contradistinction to the orthodox myth of the (imagined) world of laissez-faire constituting a universally relevant ideal, Streeten bids us focus on the context of whatever problem engages us. The problem will reveal what is to count as parameter and what as variable. From these points he derives the moral of specificity; thus he says: 'to be useful models will have to be, at least initially, much more specific to individual cases and much less general and "theoretical"'.[69]

Using this distinction - parameters/variables - Streeten goes on to characterize and counterpose to his own position the views of the orthodox and of the marxists. The orthodox treat economic variables (ordinarily understood) and eschew meddling with 'attitudes'; the marxists suppose such meddling is unnecessary. Thus these two very different analyses are taken to manifest a convergence-in-neglect of the 'social aspects' of development. This is a curious argument. In construction it seems to involve the conflation of two distinct matters: (1) that of the habit of the orthodox of preferring inherited and now irrelevant concepts to the more difficult job of fashioning their own (the notion of the 'conventional wisdom'); and (2) that of the manner of treatment of parameters (which is the key to his critique of that orthodoxy). In point this argument rather seems to be designed both to draw the sting of his critique of the orthodox and to distance himself from any marxian line by means of an almost reflex side-swipe.

Streeten's second source of bias invokes the notion of fashion.[70] His reference lets him juxtapose the pursuit of various putative 'strategic' factors of growth with an (unspecified) problem-relevant and catholic analysis. That one factor has been picked out of complex reality at some time or other and peddled as 'the' answer to development is justly ridiculed; but that the pursuit of a single strategic factor is in itself a misconceived endeavour Streeten does not establish. He observes: 'It soon became obvious however that numerous other conditions both account for past growth in advanced countries and are required for development in "U.D.C's". But instead of embarking on a careful analysis of the necessary direction and coordination of policies in particular cases a new one-factor analysis has tended to replace the old.'[71]

Again, it rather seems as if two issues are being conflated. The first is the ordering of explanatory principles: do we necessarily do this hierarchically (reducing, in the extreme, to the priority of one notion); or, at the other limit, are all explanatory concepts of equal weight? The second is the habit of disciplines of having 'fashions'. Running these together, Streeten implies that explanatory equality is obviously the line to follow, but in no sense does he establish this. Rather, he ridicules the former - hierarchical - view by invoking academic fashion.[72]

Streeten's third source of bias resembles the above. He presents it as the habit of shifting from regarding some facet of the development situation as being a necessary condition to seeing it as a sufficient condition. He dubs this 'illegitimate isolation'. Thus, from the stance of propriety of analysis of the system-as-a-whole, he is able to indicate the foolishness of aid missions descending, investigating and then reporting in terms of proposals to treat this or that aspect in the expectation that the rest of the system will then respond favourably.

Streeten's fourth source of bias in modelling we can take to indicate another use of social science - that is its data. This third error represents a more immediately recognizable institutionalist point; thus he observes: 'Almost all concepts formed by aggregation suitable for analysing Western economies must be carefully considered before they can be applied to under developed economies.'[73] He does not, of course, object to aggregative concepts per se, but to the use of such concepts where their functional prerequisites are absent; or in brief, where they do not make sense. This use of familiar notions in unfamiliar and unsuitable situations entails, so Streeten claims, a 'category mistake'. This is Gilbert Ryle's notion, and is usually taken as indicating a particular quality of 'wrong-ness' in the use of a concept. Thus for Streeten, to treat the lack of 'regular gainful employment' of some Third World peasant as a matter of unemployment would be to commit a category error.

Of this notion of 'category error' we may note two things. First, that it is very suggestive and seems, on the face of it, to be a logician's analogue of familiar ideas of ideological stance. Here a plausible question can be shown to be foolish when all its presuppositions as to what is the case are displayed. In terms of 'ideologies', this is familiar to social science: indeed, divining the ideological stance of an author is virtually a reflex habit in this area. What is noted in general is that as ideologies 'order' the world they also establish that some questions are sensible and others necessarily foolish. The borrowing from Ryle seems to repeat this strategy/situation at an abstract level of argument form. However, and this is our second point, philosophers have looked rather askance at the notion. So what does Streeten add to his discussion of the functional requisites of empirical concept deployment by invoking the notion 'category error'?

Streeten's image of empirical concepts in model-building entails them being attenuated replicas of reality. The concept is a model

in itself. Given this schema of concept construction, then it
seems obvious that whilst an attenuated version of some aspect
of 'reality A' may be useful in 'reality A', it will not be in 'reality B'. Streeten's analysis of 'unemployment' presents this
strategy of argument. Yet a shift of concept from 'home' to
'foreign' context where it simply will not work seems to be just
an error in the use of a concept: a misuse of a notion flowing
from empirical ignorance of the novel situation. There does not
seem to be any reason to regard the misuse of the notion 'employment' in some Third World country as being a 'category
error', where this is some peculiarly philosophical type of error.
Streeten's use of the term does not, then, seem to advance
matters.

We can now try to summarize the uses made of the resources
of social science by the institutionalists, via the particular work
of Streeten. Streeten takes empirical concepts to be simplifying
abstractions of raw data - aggregative isolations from experience.
Thus a subtle grasp of the data of economy A, B or C is a necessary condition of concept-formation and subsequently model-
making. A poor grasp of data will result in a greater likelihood
of the construction of inadequate concepts. Thus facts discipline
concepts. Epistemologically, fine-grain social science data is
thus necessary to Streeten, so as to be able to (1) construct
concepts; it is also used to (2) check concepts. Here Streeten's
notion of 'bias' indicates errors of which he is familiar. His
identification of these is sociology-of-knowledge-informed. Thus
the use of the notion of 'unemployment' in a poor economy A, B
or C is a mistake - a mistake in modelling, which flows from
ignorance of the facts of the situation. This 'checking' use is
presented, by Streeten, as being in a sense 'formal' - Ryle is
invoked. But these are not philosophical objections; rather they
seem to be a variety of ideologically sensitive objection. Thus
he reports that the concepts of the orthodoxy are inadequate in
respect of model-construction, yet they are functionally adequate
in the sense that they serve the interests of the status quo.
Thus at the level of concepts, or logical geography, Streeten
deploys a style of criticism often used in social science to attack
ideological stances.

Methodologically, as he takes empirical concepts to be abstractions from particular concrete situations, he is able to ask of
any concept: just what is the empirical situation from which it
abstracts? Rephrased, we see that as his economics are lodged
within an institutionalist frame, then his concepts (in so far as
they are 'social' and not just 'economic') are borrowings from the
conceptual store of social science. Social science data establishes
the possibility of realistic concepts, whilst social science concepts
provide the governing frame for concept-formation. All this follows the institutionalists' problem-centred empiricism, in contrast
to the abstract-formal style of the neo-classical orthodoxy.
Coupled up to their ideology of planning, this reveals the source
and impetus in their work to the construction of realistic models.

There is a related procedural/methodological point here. Since social science (concepts and data) provide a technique of testing the adequacy of data, and as Streeten takes economies A, B or C to be intimately lodged within some institutional frame, the habit of thought of social science is used to generate criticisms. It both orders the data brought to bear on concepts suspected of being unrealistic, and is the point of departure of critical speculations, a source of questions to put to otherwise 'innocent' data. Thus the thoroughly sceptical nature of social science is used. Rather than accepting that which is 'taken for granted' or 'obvious', etc., social science is invoked. There is a final note to be made, a corollary of the scepticism just noted, and this is the habit of reflexive criticism. Streeten, and the institutionalists, regard their own discipline through the eyes of a sociologist of knowledge.

3.4 The treatment of 'values': the role of the theorist

Myrdal describes Streeten as 'a friend of much intellectual affinity',[74] and it is through Streeten's exegesis that we shall approach this matter of 'values'. As regards the role of the theorist, Streeten presents Myrdal as posing a three-fold question: 'can one be at the same time objective, practical and idealistic?' To this he adds, revealingly, that Myrdal's career 'looks almost like a series of attempts to extort from concrete problems ... the replies to these and similar fundamental questions'.[75]

Myrdal reports that the issue of 'values' arose in the context of academic work in Sweden. The orthodox preached 'value-neutrality' whilst clearly having an impact in the realm of practical politics. These early efforts Myrdal comes to disavow. Their relevance is overtaken by the depression and concurrently he comes to regard his critiques of the orthodox as wrong-headed: simply a naive empiricism resting on the principled strivings of the theorist after value-neutrality. It is through his experience of the US institutionalists that this is brought home. Myrdal records that: 'By their naive empiricism which was flagrant they forced me to become aware of the need for a rational method of introducing value premises into economic research'.[76] He cannot, he reports, resolve the issue. However, the depression presents a solution in that its demanding urgency shrinks such critical problems; and in fact the value consensus of 'social crisis' provides the answer. Myrdal sums up the matter thus:[77]

> The crux of the matter is, of course, that when the old liberal postulate of harmony of interests is renounced, political conclusions - and ultimately theoretical research - must be founded on explicit value premises which must be concrete and take into account the actual conflict of interests between different social groups. However, in a situation experienced as crisis, it is a matter of empirical fact that interests con-

verge and that conflicts of valuation disappear. Political conclusions can then be drawn from value premises which are
homogenous and defined in concrete terms.

Thus is Myrdal's dilemma resolved by practical activity within
the context of social crisis; this is a 'solution' which Myrdal has
hung on to. It is out of this 'practical' orientation that the distinctively Myrdalian treatment of 'values' is constructed. Street-
en reports that in 'An American Dilemma' (begun in 1938)
'Myrdal draws a distinction between "programmes" and "prognosis"', and adds that 'these two key concepts open the door to
his approach to the whole problem of value'. [78]
    Streeten defines a programme as 'a plan of intended action ...
it consists of certain objectives or ends, and rules about the
manner in which these objectives are to be pursued'. [79] The
complementary concept is that of prognosis, defined thus: 'By
prognosis is meant a forecast of the probable or possible course
of events.' [80] Here we can see how the Myrdalian solution to
the fact/value problem flows out of the position of centrality
given to a certain type of practical activity. Streeten notes that
the distinction is 'related to the more familiar one between analysis and policy'. [81] It is also like the split between means and
ends, but it is not the same. Where the means/ends split lets
the practitioners of the conventional wisdom shunt off matters of
'value' into the given ends and thereafter treat means as a technical issue, Streeten sees the programme/prognosis split as pre-
venting such an escape manoeuvre. He observes, 'This complex
of desired ends, means and procedures ... all of which is conditioned by valuations, one may call "programme".' [82] The core
of this Myrdal/Streeten line as regards the practical efforts of
the theorist is a denial of the orthodox means/ends split in the
context of a certain sort of theorizing activity. The programme,
by definition, includes both means and ends. It is thus a counter-
stance that rules out the 'conventional wisdom' line, rather than
any direct criticism of that line. The style of validation that it
would have applied to itself are the tests of realism and relevance.
Realism because it claims to produce a better model of what in
fact is the case, in contrast with 'conventional wisdom'; and
relevance because the whole effort takes as its point of departure
a reading of some problem inherent in social crisis (as opposed
to matters of the formal elaboration of now irrelevant equilibrium
notions).
    The relationship of programmes and prognosis is dialectical: 'A
programme without a prognosis is an impotent utopian dream. On
the other hand, a prognosis without programmes is *necessarily*
incomplete. Prognosis depends upon programmes in two distinct
ways. First and obviously, the programmes of others are data
for the social observer and theorist.' [83] This is a fairly trivial
point requiring theorists to note that group beliefs are causally
effective (a naturalistic treatment of 'meanings'). He goes on:
'Second, and perhaps less obviously, the observer and theorist

himself has something like a programme which determines his analysis and prognosis.'[84] Here is the acknowledgment that the theorist is a person; thus the theorist is bound by the discipline of learning, rules of evidence, procedures for bringing data under concepts, and problems of bias. In sum, all these are areas where the claims of the orthodox to 'value-free' endeavours break down. We may note, however, that the necessity of which Streeten speaks is restricted. Where we see theory as necessarily linked to practice via the specified agent of the theory's execution, Streeten sees theory linked to practice via the truth-degrading chains of personhood. Streeten sees the link to practice as essentially problematical and not as enabling.

Streeten observes that: 'In social analysis valuations enter not only at the ultumate (or initial) stage in decision about sets of given ends, but at every stage. People do not attach value only to ultimate ends ... and they are not indifferent between the means which promote those ends.'[85] Indeed, this may well be true, yet it illustrates once again the fact of Streeten's orientation in all this discussion. We want to say that 'valuation' enters from the moment that we actually speak - language is 'value-sloped'. Streeten's actors, bestowing or attaching 'value', are working in a moral market-place. This is a restricted view: what Streeten is talking about are the ideologically informed 'lines' which we take on issues. If we recall his starting point for all this exegesis, that is the relationship of fact to value, then we can see that his empiricism is untouched and the disjunction between 'is' and 'ought' is affirmed. What is being done is that the related notions of analysis/policy and means/ends are being reorganized within the model of the essentially unproblematical activity of the crisis theorist.

If Streeten is affirming the disjunction between fact and value, then how does his subsequent discussion of 'values' in social theory differ from that of the 'conventional wisdom', or from that we might get from critical theory? It seems that he takes the 'conventional wisdom' to be splitting fact from value and thereafter separating them. Thus there are statements of fact and there are statements of valuation; the two sets are distinct, and particular statements of fact can be linked with any statements of value that you choose. But we have seen that this is untenable (in chapter 2) and issues in moral nihilism. Streeten's course rather seems to entail that, after granting the split, the two sets of propositions be taken as closely related. Thus valuation inevitably adheres to factual description. The relation is not a necessary one - rather it is contingent, but a general fact. If Streeten is a consistent empiricist then presumably these 'adherences' are regarded as the products of habit. Fact and value are thus split, but then paired. For critical theory, the position is different again: fact and value, properly regarded, are simply fused. Thus people do not go around habitually attaching value. Rather, they just inhabit a value-suffused world, and statements of fact are 'brute-relative' to some context.

None of all this denies the obvious fact of day-to-day living, which is that we can and do distinguish between judgments of fact and judgments of value, rather the issue is how this common-place is taken up into theory and what conclusions are then drawn from it. Presented thus, we can suggest that Streeten is taking the 'conventional wisdom' to be adhering to an ideal of value-neutral study, and as wilfully refusing to acknowledge what the routine practice of theorizing reveals. That is, that a value-neutral study is impossible – valuations just do keep getting caught up. Streeten then seems to be saying that far from resisting this and the subsequent job of making a list of deviations from the ideal, as brute reality forces itself upon the observer, the list of deviations should be systematized and embraced. Thus a new conception of the job of the observer and theory is posited. To this end, Streeten follows Myrdal and constructs a sophisticated scheme of 'value-seepage', endeavouring to minimize the seepage in some places (for example by advocating 'reflexive' theorizing), and at others granting it; for example, theory is 'value-relevant' because it has a purpose and we had best declare it at the outset.

What we would want to do, affirming the notion of 'social theory' as the deployment of a morally informed categorical frame, is to go further than Streeten and deny the propriety (and efficacy[86]) of the conception of 'ideal plus list' and make value-suffused practical activity the paradigm of the exchange of theorist and his world. Whatever rules-of-thumb governing the construction of theories we are to establish – and Streeten's list is just that in the end – the unavoidable nature of 'social theory' is that it is a morally informed, moral intervention in the world. Indeed, if we recall our approval of Gellner's[87] idea of the rediscovery in 'development theory' of classic political philosophy, then we can see that the moral core of 'social theory' is not something to be regretted, rather it is the well-spring of the whole effort.

Streeten continues his exegesis in a revealing way when he asks, given all this 'value-seepage', whether or not we can continue with social science or must we 'plunge at once into valuation and ideologies'.[88] He answers in terms dismissive of the study of 'ideologies' and in line with his interventionist disposition. Thus he says: 'To be useful and truthful, the social scientist, and in particular the economists, should start with the actual political attitudes of people, or groups of people, not with their rationalizations and pseudo-theoretical ideologies.'[89] The task of the scientist is to grasp the form-of-life of groups. Streeten seems to advocate a psychological hermeneutics; thus such an effort is not a matter of the elaboration of formal system, 'it is more like the exercise of artistic imagination and sympathetic understanding'.[90] In sum, we may say, the social scientist perfects a mechanics of social interaction. With Myrdal, this is slotted into an evolutionist frame which takes the present task of society to be the construction of a rationally managed system.

The whole is evidently the ideology of a planner: authoritative
rule by the reasonable in the interests of the general good. Much
of what is said with regard to the execution of practical research
(i.e. familiarly empirical study) is eminently sensible, but the
whole is deformed by the refusal to acknowledge that the effort
is fundamentally ideological.

As regards the 'institutionalist' treatment of the related issues
of valuation and the role of the theorist, we can summarize
thus. (1) We have seen that whilst Myrdal poses the 'problem of
values' in theoretical terms, derived from a debate with his intellectual mentors, he fails to resolve the issues. (2) He goes on
to offer a parallel solution whereby he resolves the matter practically, in 'crisis politics' - the nature of 'crisis politics' is taken
to be such as to obviate any great problem with 'values'. (3) What
he now has to say about 'values' flows from his practical activity;
that is, 'crisis politics' lets basic values be assumed, and thereafter the problem is simply of removal of idiosyncratic valuations,
or bias, or 'seepages'. (4) He adopts the stance of a 'reasonable
man' and takes his procedure, with its element of mea culpa and
various rules of thumb, to be fundamentally sound. (5) The
whole is an empiricist scheme: not a naive empiricism, and
equally with Myrdal not, perhaps, very sophisticated either.
Yet with Streeten the effort becomes indeed a highly subtle
approach.

3.5 Policy - planning and the 'soft-state'

Myrdal, like the other institutionalists, argues out of reaction
to the 'conventional wisdom' of neo-classicism and the experience
of the depression to the rational necessity of 'planning'. As
Gruchy noted, the issue for institutionalists was the 'social control of business'[91] and the agent of control was to be the state.
Myrdal reveals this as the core of his theories' practical engagement when he observes that:[92]

> what a state needs, and what politics is about, is precisely a
> macro-plan for inducing changes, simultaneously, in a great
> number of conditions, not only in the economic, and doing
> it in a way so as to coordinate all these changes in order to
> reach a maximum development effect of efforts and sacrifices.
> This may, in popular terms, be a definition of what we should
> mean by planning.

Observing that the situation in the Third World simply does
not measure up to these requirements of his theory, Myrdal invokes the notion of the 'soft state': an encapsulating term for
the extent to which reality diverges from the requirements of
theory. It is explicated thus: 'By that term I want to characterize a general lack of social discipline.'[93] He then presents a
detailed list of the failings of the typical[94] Third World state,

and concludes that his observations 'should rightly lead up to an investigation of the *policy issue* of by what means the "soft state" can be changed into more of a "strong state".... This is, in my view, *the most important task* to be fulfilled in order to make possible rapid development.'[95] Without all this, planning for development is futile. However, we should not be down-hearted: 'To begin with the problem must be discussed honestly and effectively, *as a problem of planning*' (my emphasis).[96]

Myrdal is rather pessimistic about the chances of the Third World putting its own house in order. He has reason to be, since his policy proposals take the form of a vague injunction: 'the under-developed countries have to struggle on a broad front to make their states less soft'.[97] But the agents of this reform are never clearly identified, much less openly discussed. The role of the presently developed is ambiguous - the use of 'lever-age' to press for more 'social discipline' is advocated, yet this in turn rests on the assumption of power of liberal-progressives in the governments of the developed nations. In respect of the Third World states, Myrdal has observed that little can be done before 'the power structure has been changed by evolution or revolution'.[98] The reform of the political and social structures of the underdeveloped, plus changes in orientation on the part of the developed, are made the prerequisites of planning the development of the Third World. And it seems that it is the 'planners', the reasonable men, who must press for these reforms.

We can make a series of objections to this: (1) Perhaps the most familiar objection to be brought against this line of argument is the one we can dub the 'tactical'. Such critics ask why a part of the problem - the present nature of the state - should be made into a vehicle of the solution of these problems. They add that this 'mystery' is not to be resolved via the internal renewal of the state through the gradual extension of the area held by 'reasonable men'. This line of criticism we will not pursue.

(2) An alternative line of criticism can be generated if we re-call the matter of engagement. We noted above the argument that theorizing is incoherent without an identified agent of the exe-cution of the theory. Analysis thus entails prescription, in that a 'complete' analysis necessarily involves some suppositions and suggestions as to mechanisms for the execution of the solution presented in analysis. Theories are not simply constructed for somebody: they involve as a necessary assumption 'somebody' acting as the theory supposes/suggests. With no identified agent the theory simply does not touch the ground.

So who, or what, is Myrdal's 'agent'? We can approach the identification of his 'agent' via his stance on 'values'. Myrdal does not pursue 'value-neutrality',[99] so much as a '*virtuous non-partisanship*'. Two techniques support the pursuit of this goal. On the one hand, Myrdal wears his 'values' on his sleeve, which, claiming these are both general and obvious, he seems to take to deflect criticism of ideological taint (which it does not, of course). On the other hand, the elimination of anything that

militates against realistic modelling of development. This latter
aspect is the elimination of 'value-seepage', which quasi-medical
metaphor is wholly appropriate. This pursuit of technically
rational social knowledge, free from ideology, and his tacit
granting of the need to identify an agent – which he does in
affirming the value principle 'development' – issues in the identification of the state as the agent of execution of his theory.
But what sort of a commitment is this? Can we call this an unsatisfactory minimum commitment?

Let us recall Bauman's[100] jibe at Berger and Luckmann; their
'actor', around whom they display their sociology of knowledge,
is not a human but an epistemic being, established as the minimum necessary link with reality for that exercise in idealistic
theorizing which they are disposed to present. The essential
historical and social specificity of any exercise in the sociology
of knowledge is ignored, and we have an idealist abstraction
from common sense whose only acknowledged link with reality is
an actor devoid of any characteristics. The 'actor' serves as the
necessary condition of their theorizing, but plays no role in it.
The 'actor's' presence simply satisfies a technical requirement of
the logic of theorizing.

So, is Myrdal's 'state' an epistemic phenomenon – called forth
by the demands of the logic of theorizing, and thus to be taken
as satisfying a technical requirement – or is it any identifiable
state in the real world? What then is the nature of an adequate
analysis of the state? For our part that must be answered in
terms of a marxian analysis – but for Myrdal? It is claimed that
his methodology is essentially the pursuit of realism in modelling;
the facts come first. Thus in respect of the 'state', we should
expect the discussion of, and around, the state to be predomin-
antly concerned with how it is. But the reverse is the case, here
Myrdal's treatment of the state is dominated by his notion of the
'soft state' – where this is transparently a measure of the divergence of reality from the requirements of theory. Thus his
analysis is dominated by how the state ought to be. In considering his treatment of the issue, of state, it seems to be the case
that Myrdal, having just established by moral and practical
reflection how the world is and how it ought to be, then proceeds to search for an agent. The agent he invokes is made in
his own image. It is the embodiment of the pursuit of the general
public good; and, as we have noted, the 'soft state' is to be discussed as a 'problem of planning'.[101] Myrdal does not begin
his analysis of the state from, as we would expect, how it is,
rather he begins from how it has to be if Myrdalian theory is to
be executed.

The reforming state is a necessary condition of the deployment
of the Myrdalian scheme; Myrdal's 'state' is the minimum necessary acknowledgment of the logical requirement to identify an
agent of theory-expectation. This agent of Myrdal's derives
from the requirements of the logic of theorizing in the particular
context of Myrdal's pursuit of a 'virtuous non-partisanship', and

not from any historically specific analysis of the nature of the
state in Third World society.
   The Myrdalian scheme thus touches the ground only in a technical sense. Whether this invalidates the entire effort - that is,
whether there is a requirement in theorizing for the 'agent' to
be realistic (so to say) - we have not asked. Clearly, the use of
a technical grounding only must reduce the plausibility of any
policy proposals that are stronger than tentative; and as Myrdal
makes the 'state' the core and key to the implementation of his
effort, then this technical grounding seems to be insufficient.
His 'state' does not seem able to carry the weight the general
argument requires it to. What we are saying, then, is that the
Myrdalian 'state' must be taken as insufficient to carry the argument; and therefore, as the basis of practical policy-making,
unsatisfactory. The prior question of whether or not the Myrdalian 'state' is enough to meet properly the demands of the logic of
theorizing we do not know. We can note, however, that if the
Myrdalian state is a device for the evasion of political commitment,
which is a jibe made by some (and not only marxists), then this
would seem to imply that Myrdal is pursuing a theory which is
not grounded: that is to say, a perfectly irrelevant theory. And
that notion certainly does look incoherent.
   (3) We can construct another approach to these matters if we
recall Passmore's[102] remarks on the pursuit of knowledge and
the manner of its dissemination and use, in the light of the ideal
of progress.
   The notion of the perfectibility of man comes down to us, so
Passmore argues, from the ancient Greeks. Prior to the Renaissance such discussions of perfectibility were couched in metaphysical or theological terms, and concerned the pursuit of a
goal - that is, the state of perfection. Locke transforms the idea,
arguing that men are capable of being improved by moral education, that is, social action. This is the idea that was influential
in the eighteenth and nineteenth centuries: the focus is on the
role of education, and the process of improvement. However, a
damaging criticism of this line is to point out that the educator
is a member of corrupt society and presumably corrupt also.
Marx will accuse Locke and his followers of forgetting the matter
of the education of the educator. This opens up the search for
a guarantor - if Locke has established the possibility of the moral
advancement of the citizens and their society, the question becomes one of securing the fact.
   Two lines of argument flow from this point. The first, presented by the philosophes (very much aware of their own novel
social status), argued for the rule of the best - a version of the
Platonic 'philosopher-king' idea. Thus Passmore observes that
'Helvetius, a convinced Lockian, is the founding father of modern governmentalism',[103] and that he focused on the role of
the state. But this does not meet Marx's question - the matter of
control is not here resolved. Passmore presents this line as
moving via Bentham and J.S. Mill (who were experienced in

government, unlike the philosophes) down to the Fabians and
their stress on legislation. The second line, on the other hand,
has recourse to the model of the natural sciences. Here the need
for a guarantor was focused upon a method. The extension of
the method of natural science into the realm of the social was entailed, as was the dissemination and use of the resultant knowledge. The notion of 'progress' is presented, and progress is
taken to be normal in so far as it is not blocked by sinister
partial interest. However, this line fails also; for the dissemination of scientific knowledge is problematical, as is the expectation that any knowledge will be acted upon. The method of
natural science is no guarantee of progress in society. (The
further extension of the argument involves taking the question
of a guarantor completely out of the hands of anybody: thus we
have determinist schemes, the social determinism of rationalists
from Leibniz down to Marx and the natural determinisms of
Darwinian evolutionisms. We need not pursue these.)

What then of Myrdal? He refers to himself as 'a student in the
great liberal tradition of the Enlightenment'[104] and cites the
state as the agent of progress. If we follow Passmore's argument
then clearly Myrdal follows the Locke-Helvetius-Mill line down to
Fabianism. Indeed Ehrensaft[105] dismissively labels him as just
that, a Fabian. If we allow Passmore's arguments, then it is
clear that Myrdal's use of the state as agent of development is
unsatisfactory in that it cannot, in theory, meet the demands of
securing progress. Variations on the idea of the 'philosopher-
king' have in the main been rejected. In addition to this, there
is also discernible in Myrdal an element of line two; that is, the
invoking of the method of science. Not only is this evident in
the relatively unsurprising sense that it is entailed by his rejection of the centrality of the notion of ideology, and his constant harping on the question of the elimination of bias; but it is
also revealed - if we follow Passmore - in his appeal to the pro-
gressive-minded, reasonable men. The idea that there is an ever-
growing reservoir of knowledge that is free from ideological
taint represents the direct and obvious argument from the model
of science. Myrdal invoking the steady, diverse, broad-fronted
pressure of the reasonable men represents the corollary, which
is the argument from the supposedly self-evident propriety and
superiority of properly transmitted scientific knowledge. Myrdal's
belief in the power of reflexive institutional theory echoes the
belief of the philosophes in the power of rational argument - and
this is the most optimistic aspect of an argument from science.

In Myrdal these two elements (we noted) are run together; in
that the state, invoked as the agent of development (that is,
progress), is also the locus of (social) scientific method. The
state is served and staffed by reasonable men bent on the pursuit of the general public good. This is revealed in the quotation
we have noted already: 'What the state needs, and what politics
is about, is precisely a macro-plan for inducing changes.... This
may in popular terms, be a definition of what we should mean by

planning.'[106] But the state as guarantor of progress is unsatisfactory. The explication of the role of the state reveals the
failure to secure 'progress'; and the method of science as guarantor is equally unhelpful. The adoption of this as key does not
secure 'progress'.

In summary, we note that above we argued that the Myrdalian
'state' is an epistemic device to secure a grounded theory; and
that, as such, it represents a minimum response to the demands
of the logic of theorizing. We argued that the Myrdalian treatment of the state conflicted with the avowed method of the pursuit of realism in modelling, and that the notion was too weak to
carry the load the general argument required it to. (We further
suggested at this point that here was the site of a possible collapse into incoherence for the entire effort - but we did not try
to secure this argument.) To these points we added that, even
setting aside doubts as to the adequacy of the Myrdalian state,
the state combined with the method of science was insufficient
to secure 'development' (for reasons Passmore has presented).

These notes are about Myrdal's argument strategies. From our
criticisms it does not follow that anything by way of statements
of (brute-relative) facts made by Myrdal are necessarily false
(or uninteresting). Whether or not Myrdal's 'facts' are right is
a matter of 'checking the facts'. Our point is that even if he has
got the facts straight, his argument is deeply flawed, as we have
seen, and this is a reason for doubting any derived policy proposals.

4.0 DYNAMIC OF THEORY III: THE STATUS OF NEO-INSTITUTIONAL SOCIAL THEORY

In the introductory remarks to this part we made reference to
the broad context of inquiry into which this particular effort
slotted. Noting that the institutionalists have lodged claims to
the effect that their endeavours constitute an independent and
adequate development studies, in contradiction to the products
of the 'conventional wisdom' (where this comprises both 'growth
theory' and 'modernization theory'), we indicated that we would
consider this claim. In the light of our above researches we are
now able to redeem this promise. In section 4.1 we treat the
question: to what extent can neo-institutional social theory be
taken as establishing an independent development studies? In
part 4.2 we ask to what extent can neo-institutionalist work be
taken to represent a theoretical advance over the material of the
'conventional wisdom'.

4.1

We can introduce our analyses by asking whether or not neo-
institutional social theory can be taken as establishing an inde-

pendent development studies. This seems to be roughly the
burden of Streeten's work. It is partially granted by Ehrensaft
in his history, when he distinguishes a 'pre-Seers consensus',
static and wrong-headed, from subsequent movement towards an
adequate theory of development. Streeten observes that 'Awareness of a problem of development is remarkably recent. The
academic literature, the public debate, voluntary and official
agencies and institutions and policies are not more than twenty
years old.'[107] He goes on to locate the source of this rise in
interest in two related sets of circumstances: (1) problems of
resources and poverty are taken to be urgent in view of the
population explosion, and soluble in the light of the success of
post-war European recovery; (2) political change in the form of
the rise of 'new nations' of the Third World within the context of
'cold war' occasions concern for the 'proper' development of
these 'new nations'. Streeten goes on to remark that 'The psychological, political and even military origins of our interest in
development have coloured the approach and the content of development studies.'[108] Streeten makes these remarks in line
with the 'reflexive' aspect of his general orientations. In addition,
we have seen that the orthodoxy of neo-classicism forms a theoretical object against which 'neo-institutional social theory' is
defined, and the Keynesian-derived growth models are assimilated to that orthodoxy. The method of neo-institutional social
theory entails the pursuit of realistic models of developing
economies; bias is to be purged, and in this light the early
efforts of the 'conventional wisdom' are taken as a theoretically
misconceived departure.

Yet, even if we grant all this, precisely what follows is not
clear. Let us then pose the question in regard to career of development studies: in what sense is an institutionalist scheme
independent? If we ask whether the practitioners of neo-institutional social theory are independent of orthodox economics, then
we have to report that with regard to neo-classicism they take
themselves to encompass and surpass that scheme. The result is
that they reconstitute a general political economics, which is distinct from both marxian radicalism and orthodox narrowness. But
for us the question of their relative independence reduces to a
question of intent and style of analysis. We have noted above,
with both Gordon and Gruchy, that neo-institutionalism is a
style of approaching economics that lodges the economic system
within an institutional framework. It is thereby more immediately
plausible in the context of the Third World, but none the less
any genuine theoretical novelty must be restricted. Following on
from this, we can say that even if the mode of analysis is richer
(which it must be, to the extent that it treats institutional aspects), then the intent remains the same. That is, just as 'conventional wisdom' is an economics designed to legitimate/
organize intervention by an authoritative state to promote development, then so too does neo-institutional social theory aim to
legitimate/organize authoritative state intervention. Further, in

the light of the refusal of neo-institutional social theory to
acknowledge its status as ideology, it must be accounted (along
with the growth and modernization theories) as itself ideological
in the pejorative sense; that is, blind to significant elements of
its own nature. In the light of our interest in the elucidation of
the nature of 'social theory' (a morally informed categorical
frame), neo-institutional social theory, for all its greater subtlety,
remains firmly within the framework of the orthodox.

But what would the theorists of neo-institutional social theory
say to this question of ours? It seems likely that they would both
deny that the question is especially interesting (in that their
ideology disposes them to affirm a practical bent, thus implicitly
eschewing what could be seen as academic-departmental scholas-
ticism) or that it is particularly difficult to answer, in that they
would affirm their orientation to these matters as being manifestly
more adequate to the novel problems of the post-war world than
the efforts of the 'conventional wisdom'.

If political economics is an empirical (indeed, problem-centred)
science, conceived in an empiricist vein, then theirs is at least
potentially an adequate political economics in contradistinction to
the efforts of the orthodoxy. Yet this self-conception to our mind
lodges them firmly within the realm of the orthodox, even if we
grant their greater plausibility. Can we then take neo-institutionalism to provide the basis for an independent development studies?
It seems as if the question does not make very good sense because, in sum, we have to say that neo-institutionalist social
theory is a problem-centred European line of thought, within
social science, whose intent is the legitimation/organization of
authoritative interventions. If the exchange of the rich and poor
nations is properly conceived as a matter of 'intervention', then
neo-institutional social theory does have claims to be the most
subtle intervention to date. But to our mind that relation is improper and, in the end, untenable. Again, if we take development studies to be about the pursuit of a 'science' of 'Third
World' society, then neo-institutional social theory has claims to
some approximation to that ideal, but to our mind this goal is
absurd.

4.2

Setting aside the matter of the independence of an institutionalist
development studies, we turn to the major question, which is:
Can we take neo-institutional theory to represent a theoretical
advance over modernization theory and any Harrod-Domar-
informed orthodoxy?

This question raises the prior issue of theory. Can we, having
indicated that we take neo-institutional social theory and modernization and the early orthodoxy built around Harrod-Domar to be
ideologies, rank ideologies? If ideologies can be ranked, then
how? Here we offer a brief answer, before going on to consider

Seers and Ehrensaft and the relative positions of the ideologies we have thus far met.

Bernstein offers an answer to the question of ranking ideologies which focuses on the aspect of argument. (This is in contrast to, say, Goldmann,[109] who takes explanatory scope; thus the 'better' ideology is the one that explains the narrower one. Or again in contrast to Mannheim, who focuses on the relativism of points of view.) Bernstein observes that 'ideologies are based on beliefs and interpretations which purport to be true or valid. These beliefs and interpretations are consequently subject to rational criticism.'[110] How these 'rational criticisms' are to be ordered, or how we might judge between one ideology and another, becomes a complex issue to be treated via a distinction between validation and authentication; between the discipline the community of scholars imposes, and thereafter the significance that comes to be attached to any cultural objects they may construct. Here we can note that our task is apparently easier, since all of the theories (ideologies) we have thus far looked at claim to be both (1) empiricist, that is, modelling themselves on the natural sciences and (2) aimed at legitimating/organizing/implementing authoritative interventions, where this requires a model of the world and a measurement/intervention technology; together these permit the theorist to 'go to work on the world'. So, out of the ideologies we have so far assembled, which is the best in regard to this essentially technical requirement?

With regard to those efforts which are built around the Harrod-Domar model, that is, the 'export-Keynes' and 'early modernization theory', we have to say that the neo-institutional social theory line does indeed constitute an advance. If we note the papers of Seers and Ehrensaft we can illustrate this – probably widely accepted – view. Both Seers and Ehrensaft operate within what Hindess has called the 'epistemology of model building'; that is, both conceive their task as the realization of realistic models of reality. We can see with the work of Seers that the institutionalists' line is strong. He argues the orthodox are simply 'out of touch', and his explanation of this is an amalgam of observation on the teaching and career pattern of economists which reduces to the claim that there is an incapacity of vision on the part of the orthodox which renders them incapable of seeing the world straight. The specific area of conceptual inadequacy follows the line we have noted with Streeten: the 'conventional wisdom' is inadequate to its object and objectives in that it represents a set of intellectual tools fashioned for use in the rich world and not the poor. Ehrensaft treats this in terms of a contrast between, on the one hand, the claims to generality on the part of the orthodox; and, on the other, the fact of their claims being situation-bound. The upshot is to open up the basis of a familiar line of criticism: 'when these assumptions are scrutinized, it is readily apparent that they describe conditions contrary to the typical case of world societies'.[111] We can suggest that, according to the criteria of adequacy that would be proposed by

the 'conventional wisdom', that the Harrod-Domar-informed theories of growth and of modernization are inadequate; and that,
in addition, the efforts of 'neo-institutional social theory' are
an advance. Henceforth the question of the 'best' ideology so
far is lodged in respect of neo-institutional social theory and
revisionist-modernization.

When we turn to a comparison between revisionist-modernization
and neo-institutional social theory, the problem of ranking becomes rather more problematical. If we take Gellner as a representative of a sophisticated revisionist-modernization and
compare his work - in so far as he presents a general theory of
process of development[112] - with that of Myrdal, then we can
observe a number of 'strategic' resemblances.

We have seen that Myrdal, in the course of the pursuit of progress (in the guise of development) invokes the state and (sec-
ondarily) the method of science as agents and guarantors of
progress. The particular agents of change were, upon observation, found to be the diffuse efforts of the 'reasonable men':
it was in these people that the possibilities inherent in the con
junction of social scientific knowledge and state intervention were
lodged. We indicated grounds for scepticism in respect of this
schema. Now if we turn to Gellner we find a similar conception
of the possibility of progress. Gellner regards the intervention
of the social theorist as constrained by the dual circumstances
of, on the one hand, the tendential yet overwhelmingly strong
movement of industrial- and science-based development (a world
historical phenomenon); and on the other hand, the restriction of
the nature of any theoretically informed grasp of the process to
the limits set by natural scientific method. The 'transition', as
Gellner calls the whole process, is to be accomplished with critical
reason as the guide towards the goal of 'being developed'.

Thus where Myrdal takes the state to guide the social dynamic
of 'cumulative causation' towards the goal of 'world-welfarism',
Gellner sees an essentially opaque process of transition, illuminated (from within, as it were) by the possibilities inherent in
scientific method and a very good, if rough, idea of the end-
situation of transition. Where Myrdal, describing himself as an
Enlightenment liberal, identifies the effective locus of human
intervention in the social science-informed intervention of the
state in the hands of the progressives, Gellner sees the locus of
human intervention in the 'transition' as bounded by the devel-
opment-orientated deployment of 'critical-rationalism'; a Popperian
liberalism whose roots are essentially seventeenth-century. As
Myrdal's effort fails, so too does Gellner's; the method of
science is no guarantor.

Both theorists are pessimistic. Gellner attempts to make this
a virtue of his stance; whereas Myrdal, notoriously, expects
little in the way of development. The strategies resemble each
other in this general form: thus (a) both affirm a notion of progress in the guise of development, and (b) both seek an agent to
act as guarantor; that is, they both fall short of accepting the

only cogent guarantor-strategy; which is to make progress 'natural' by involving notions of determinism. In terms of their 'meta-theories' it is difficult to identify any means whereby they may be, generally, ranked as development theories vis à vis each other.

Are we now in a position to answer our question vis à vis the relative sophistication and problem-adequacy of neo-institutional social theory and modernization theory? If we mean an advance in terms of practical efficacy, in the sense of the deployment of a more subtle set of concepts, or more adequate concepts in the light of some controlling idea of a 'science of (Third World) society', then the answer must be yes. We have argued for this above: the experience of withdrawal from empire as 'decolonization' and the European intellectual/governmental tradition provided resources which lent themselves more readily to a project of authoritative interventionism oriented to 'development' goals than did the resources of the US theorists of modernization. The crucial difference was identified as concerning the theorists' social milieu and the nature of the respective political demands; that is, the dynamic of society rather than the dynamic of theory. Indeed, these straightforwardly theoretical resources were largely shared. The European effort was thus adequate to its task. If we mean an advance in terms of the nature of theorizing, in the sense of a movement towards a notion of social theory as the 'deployment of a morally-informed categorical' frame and away from notions of social science as poor relation to natural science, then the general answer has to be no. There is no theoretical advance. Both neo-institutional social theory and modernization theory are ideologies, which are in conception empiricist and in intent authoritative-interventionist.

6 Disciplinary independence and theoretical progressivity

1.0 PREAMBLE

In the Introduction to Part III we noted that the material of the part presented us with two strategic issues. These were, first, the matter of the putative independence of 'development studies' from the body of the social sciences in general (and in particular from economics); and second, the related issue of the progressive theoretical status of those intellectual schemes considered in this section. As these two issues have not been resolved thus far in this section (i.e. in chapter 5), the logic of the study as a whole bids us acknowledge them here. Chapter 6 will be organized around these two theoretical issues.

Evidently this represents a change in our procedure from the more straightforward sociology of knowledge line followed before, but we can advance reasons for this. Thus, in addition to invoking the dictates of the logic of the structure of the study as a whole we can offer two points. First, if we recall that a sociology of knowledge treatment would require us to relate the dynamics of the exchange between historically conditioned political demand and relevant theoretical traditions, then it is clear that the results of such an analysis have been most competently anticipated by more than one writer, (e.g. O'Brien, 1975; Booth, 1975; Girvan, 1973). This being the case, there is little point in our presenting yet another variation on this relatively well-worn theme. Second, we can note that our study is of 'Western' theories. This raises the issue of the manner in which clearly Latin-American-inspired theoretical departures are to be incorporated in our text. In the absence of a fully prepared sociology of knowledge treatment, it seems appropriate to observe that within the general ambit of an interest in 'development' there seem to be some important shared concepts. Thus Girvan, treating the Caribbean school of 'dependency theorists', refers to the 'historical/structural/institutional method'.[1] Our interest, then, granting this note and in the light of the interest accorded these Latin American efforts by 'Western' theorists, may therefore be pitched quite reasonably at an abstract level.

In sum: we invoke the fact of the established exchange and (more particularly) the conceptual similarities of Latin American and 'Western' work, on the one hand, and, on the other, the fact that sociology of knowledge treatments have been executed in major respects already, as the basis of a decision to pitch this chapter at an abstract level and organize it around the related

issues of disciplinary independence and theoretical status, as
demanded by the logic of the study as a whole.

Having thus declared an intention to simplify the tasks of this
chapter, we will add one further simplification, and this refers
to the substantive attachments of the chapter. We noted in the
Introduction to Part III that our thematic treatment of these complex issues of the nature of the exchanges between theorist and
world required that theorists change their roles as we changed
our questions. That remark is nowhere more apposite than in
the present context. The debate we endeavour to capture for
our study ranges over a wide area, from the structuralist reformism of ECLA to the marxian-style polemics of A.G. Frank.
The simplification we adopt here is the association of 'dependency' with Furtado and 'underdevelopment theory' with Frank.
This lets us organize our questions/material thus: when we
treat 'disciplinary independence' we will focus upon 'dependency'
and Furtado; and when we treat the matter of 'progressivity in
conceptualization' we will focus upon 'underdevelopment theory'
and A.G. Frank.

2.0 DISCIPLINARY INDEPENDENCE

We can recall that chapter 5 treated, amongst other points the
question of whether NIST[2] established an independent and
adequate development studies. After noting and setting aside
the practitioners' self-images, and considering the intent and
form of their efforts, we answered that the question made little
sense; and that rather we would wish to say that 'NIST' established the most sophisticated scheme of 'authoritative interventionism' to date. A similar issue may be phrased as follows: does
'dependency' establish an independent and adequate development
studies? Anticipating a similar pattern of reply[3] to that just
noted, we can break down this question into two parts:
2.1 What is the form and intent of 'dependency'?; and
2.2 Does 'dependency' supersede conventional wisdom economics?

2.1 Form and intent

If we argue that NIST aimed at establishing a subtle and co-
operative 'authoritative interventionism' whose function was to
legitimate and order a withdrawal from formal empire, and which
subsequently became the model of the exchange of rich and poor
nations, then precisely what does 'dependency' function to legitimate and order? At first glance, and adopting the manner of
'ideology labelling' we have used above, the answer would seem
to be 'reactive (populist) interpretative interventionism'. This
line of argument we now consider.[4]

2.11 Sociology of knowledge sketch of 'dependency'

Resting on already existing work (Brookfield, Ehrensaft, Girvan, Oxaal, Furtado, DiMarco and others), we may present the circumstances of the emergence of 'dependency' in terms of the invocation of available resources within a general milieu in response to particular political demands. Now, if we are taking Furtado to exemplify the 'dependency' line, then our presentation of the position needs must be sequential in form. Furtado's work encompasses (i) the critical revisions to the orthodox views, initiated by Prebisch and developed by ECLA; (ii) the concern to rebut monetarist views with structuralist analyses of inflation, and (iii) the lodging of claims on behalf of 'dependency' to have replaced the orthodox in so far as that school represented a truly adequate economics.

  (i) Prebisch's early work grows out of the experience of the Latin American economies after the crisis of 1929 when their traditional economic mode, that of exporting primary products, was severely curtailed by the contraction in world trade. The measures initiated by governments to mitigate the impact of this loss of export markets had the incidental effect of initiating a process of import-substituting industrialization. After the end of the war, with a revival of credit lines to Latin America and of world trade, the now established process of industrialization was in need of a legitimating and ordering explanation; and Prebisch and ECLA provided it. The principal theoretical object against which Prebisch developed his views was the claim of traditional theories to the effect that international specialization conferred benefits upon all those involved. Clairmonte locates the establishment of this doctrine in the heyday of what he calls British Integral Liberalism - through the middle part of the nineteenth century. Against it Prebisch utilizes a version of the centre/periphery notion, which was a long-established motif not only in liberalism and marxism but also in indigenous Latin American anti-imperialist and anti-marxian writings. He argues that within the ambit of the orthodox theory, and pre-1929 status quo, Latin American economies were condemned to a secondary and relatively declining position. The solution was to pursue industrialization behind protective barriers. In the first instance the advocated policy was via import-substitution: precisely that pattern which had grown up in the wake of the crisis. In addition to this reworking of the conception of the position of Latin American economies within the world economy, there is a concurrent reworking of explanations of the nature of these peripheral economies. Here the equilibrium model of neo-classical orthodoxy is rejected, in favour of an empiricist-flavoured, pragmatic, and problem-oriented approach, namely structuralism. The structuralist effort takes off from an attempt to model the local situation. It thus presents a scheme whereby the putative single national economy is seen as split into a very loosely integrated set of quasi-autonomous 'sectors'; each of which represents either a residue of the historical process of

the expansion of European capitalism, or a present requirement
of the newly dominant capitalist centre (that is, the US). The
distinctively 'autonomous national economy' simply does not exist,
save as a concatenation of 'residues', 'enclaves', and various
'parasitic forms'. As O'Brien puts it, 'An underdeveloped country
is underdeveloped precisely because it consists of different
structures each with a specific type of behaviour.'[5]

(ii) The reformist structuralism propounded by ECLA belongs
to the first of what Furtado calls 'three easily identifiable periods'[6] in the economic history of post-war Latin America. The
first is characterized as one of rapid growth based upon favourable terms of trade, accumulated reserves from the war years,
and currencies strong enough to be able to withstand gradual
devaluation in the face of already active inflationary pressures.
By the end of the early 1960s the position was changed, and the
policy of industrialization via protected import-substitution was
apparently failing. Furtado[7] notes a sharp deterioration in the
terms of trade and a 'marked slackening' in the rate of growth.
On top of this, the experience of the Cuban revolution provoked
widespread questioning of the 'real significance of the region's
economic development'.[8] The deteriorating situation presented
itself to the ECLA school in the form of concern for market size
and international exchange. As Girvan puts it: 'ECLA thus pursued a two pronged strategy of pressure and persuasion in the
1960s: the first, on Latin American governments in favour of
regional integration, the second, on governments of the developed countries for more liberal trade and financial policies.'[9]

Setting aside matters of integration and trade, we can focus
on the topic of finance. Here the question of inflation provides
an issue whereby we can see, in the work of Furtado, a clear
example of the progressive reworking of the theoretical resource
established in the ECLA line. This change is anticipated, as
Brookfield points out, in the 1965 work published by Furtado in
the wake of the 1964 coup in Brazil. Here Furtado writes of the
'dialectic of capitalist development', where in his 1950s essay
collection he presents a 'theory of underdevelopment'; and the
whole expresses a shift from a simple additive treatment of social
aspects attendant on economic changes, towards a richer conception of structural change in the process of industrialization.[10]
The debate around the matter of inflation enables Furtado to
counterpose to the financial orthodoxy of monetarism (which regards inflation as a matter of the poor functioning of money flows,
and which diagnoses either demand or cost inflation) a structuralist analysis. Thus Furtado insists that even if these familiar
patterns of inflation did occur, then 'they were nearly always
responses to more deep seated pressures, or rather they reflected an adaptation effort within the framework of more complex
processes, whose main ingredients were structural inflexibility
and the determination to press ahead with a development policy.'[11]
This argument is unpacked in terms of the various responses
contrived by the sectors of the economy in endeavouring to avoid

the burden of financing the government's deficit. Thus Furtado deploys (not entirely consistently) notions such as 'basic inflationary pressures', 'propagation mechanisms', and 'decision centers', where these latter are the financial authorities and the point at which the monetarist arguments get started. In this debate with the orthodox, over a pressing practical problem, we see Furtado developing that which was latent in the reformist ECLA line into what might be dubbed an 'oppositional meaning system'.

(iii) It is out of this debate around the issues of the exchange between the Latin American countries and the metropolitan centres, within the context of continuing failure to achieve the establishment of autonomous economies, that the notion of 'dependency' as that which characterizes most fruitfully the situation of the Latin American economies crystallizes. Brookfield notes that 'Furtado's disenchantment with the ECLA industrialization policies became in time complete'.[12] His original approval was replaced by a view which explained the failure of industrialization policies in terms of the position of Latin American economies within a dual frame of external dependency and internal fixity of social and economic structures. In a 1976 work Furtado observes that:[13]

> there can be no doubt that development based on exports of raw materials and import-substituting industrialization has reached the limits of its possibilities, at least in the case of the region's largest countries. Similarly the institutional framework inherited from the colonial period, or established shortly after separation from the mother countries, seems to have exhausted its possibilities of adaptation to development needs. It is understandable then, that problems relating to structural reform should have become the region's foremost concern.

Having said that, Furtado goes on to list matters of international relations first - with the USA, with multi-national corporations, and with the world economy generally - after which he turns to questions of the economy and society of the peripheral economies and presents familiar structuralist and ECLA notions.

This represents the point at which the 'dependency' line fully emerges. Familiar structuralist themes are firmly lodged within an explanatory frame which locates crucial elements of the local problems beyond the underdeveloped state's immediate control.

2.12 Furtado and the emergence of the 'dependency' theorists' conception of a proper and fruitful analysis

Girvan has been quoted earlier as observing of Latin American work that:[14]

> the development in thought, generally, took the forms of (I) adding a historical perspective and analysis to the structural

and institutional method, (II) giving the historical/structural/
institutional method the kind of theoretical and empirical content needed to construct a general theory of dependence and
underdevelopment.

We shall pursue the matter of the 'dependency' theorists' conception of useful and proper analysis with this passage in mind.
We organize our questions thus:
(i)   What is Furtado's epistemology?
(ii)   What is the nature of Furtado's early formulations?
(iii) What are the post-1964 coup revisions?
(iv)   What is the nature of his late 1960s work?

(i) Furtado's epistemology and methodology Furtado's early
study, 'Development and Underdevelopment' (1964), begins with
a chapter on 'The theory of development in economic science'
which treats the issue methodologically and in terms of the history of ideas in economics. The chapter is revealing in several
ways, and in character most strongly recalls Myrdal's style of
inquiry. The handicap of using what Hindess dubs 'the epistemology of models' is again demonstrated. Furtado begins thus:[15]

> The theory of economic development endeavours to explain,
> from a macroeconomic point of view, the causes and mechan-
> isms of the persistent growth in productivity of the labour
> factor and the repercussions of this growth on the organization
> of production and on the distribution and utilization of the
> social product.

This is Furtado's reading of the work of the classical school, and
the presentation of his own area of inquiry. He continues:[16]

> That explanatory task is projected here on two planes. The
> first, in which abstract formulations prevail, comprises anal-
> ysis of the actual mechanisms of the process of growth ...
> building models or simplified schemes of existing economic sys-
> tems ... models based on stable relationships between calcu-
> lable variables deemed to be relevant and important.

Thus the classical line of treating the realm of the economic as
'determinate in the end' is here acknowledged, and simultaneously
transposed into the post-war, neo-classical informed, language
of the precise elucidation of mechanisms. Additionally, these
elucidations are taken as exercises in modelling reality; though
it is at this point that we encounter the first of those discon-
certing lurches that seem to characterize this style of analysis.
The phrase 'deemed to be' is unexpected and intriguing. It would
seem either to introduce the space for Furtado to distance himself from those technical efforts that he might want to disagree
with, or to permit the possibility of referring intellectual schemes
to the position of their producer - whether in the style of Seers,

or after the style of those who invoke the notion of ideology.
Whatever the reason for Furtado's remark, the 'deemed to be'
phrase sounds voluntaristic and is not the phrase to be expected
from a writer who took economics to be 'about the facts'.

Furtado continues: 'The second, the historical plane, comprises critical study in the light of a given reality and on the
basis of the categories defined by the abstract analysis.'[17]
Three points arise here. First, we have Furtado saying that
historical analysis is informed by categories 'defined by the abstract analysis'. But if we recall that these analyses are exercises in modelling 'existing economic systems', then it seems as
if Furtado is about to present a singularly unhistorical analysis.
Unless, that is, he lodges some claims to universality on behalf
of the abstract categories. This he does: there is, he says,
'some degree of universality pertaining to the definitions of
broad basic concepts whose explanatory validity, though limited,
has undeniable practical bearing'.[18] Abstractions from the
present are taken to have universal relevance. This would seem
to recall the apriorisitic line of Robbins, the formal 'spokesman'
of the neo-classical school. Thus from basic, 'obviously true'
generalizations, models can be built from which, via deductive
argument, other 'facts' are generated. This formalism sits uneasily with Furtado's disposition to affirm the problem-centredness of economics.

The second point is similar. Furtado argues that 'history' is
to be used to test the model. It is not enough, Furtado argues,
to build an abstract model: that model has to be seen to be able
to explain historical material. This lets the model be tested and
reworked as necessary, a routine part of this epistemology of
models scheme; but to what end? Furtado rejects the habit of
resting content with generality of the abstract - only to pursue,
it seems, a generality of the concrete. In contrast to the problem-
centredness of Myrdal, Furtado forever seems to be tugged at by
the neo-classical pretensions to scientific status; that is, generality in formulations is taken as the essence of the truly
scientific, and consequently the adopting of this style of argument is taken to secure claims to scientific status. It is a spurious argument; but in this early work it is one of which Furtado
has not yet purged himself.

Our third point again indicates Furtado's apparent confusion
as to the nature of the exchange between theorist and world. We
are told that all this model-testing is necessary 'in order to make
it valid from the point of view of a given reality'.[19] It is the
phrase 'point of view of a given reality' that is odd. Is this use
of *point of view of a* given reality' the same as the earlier 'critical study *in the light of a* given reality' (my emphases)? Are
we to take 'reality' to be a simple given for the theorist, or
something that is shaped by ideological orientation? Does Furtado
vacillate between the two stances?

From this plane of epistemological reflections Furtado descends
to the level of methodology. Here, amongst a series of pertinent

and acute points, the image of the natural sciences continues to sow confusion. This confusion revolves around the dilemma of the effort to integrate the pursuit of generality in statements (which Furtado evidently takes to be properly 'scientific') with the implications of the conflicting tendency of regarding economics as problem-relevant, and thereby specific – in terms of its explanatory mechanisms and content – to particular historical and socioeconomic circumstances. We can follow Furtado through one effort to resolve his dilemma. Thus after making reference to Ricardo's work, with its late concern for the matter of production in the light of the growing system of factory-based manufacture, Furtado presents the following observation: 'The question of the abstract or historical nature of the method used by the economist is not then independent of the problems concerning him.'[20] This, claims Furtado, permits the following split: a concern with production necessitates a historical approach, whereas concern with distribution permits the formal elaboration of general statements. This simple division of economics into two halves, each with its appropriate method, evidently makes Furtado uneasy for he promptly retreats. Thus: 'economic development is a phenomenon with clear cut historical aspects'.[21] Or again, whilst Furtado will grant that there is no complete and 'problem-neutral' economics, he asserts (as we have seen) that there is an established body of basic truths. Having thus secured economics as unitary and fundamentally scientific by virtue of a core of generally true propositions, he proceeds to make these claims otiose by rehearsing a point usually associated with Seers: 'It is because we are often forgetful of the limitations of that validity when approaching problems in concrete historic situations that we pass surreptitiously from the field of scientific speculation into that of dogma.'[22] It seems that economics is either scientific, general, and of no practical use; or it is useful, historically specific, and not 'general' in the way science ought to be. Clearly, the effort to encompass the scheme we treat with the 'double dynamic of society and discipline of learning' within the framework of an empiricist epistemology of models is, in the end, only productive of confusion.

(ii) Early formulations in Furtado's work First we consider problems of the pursuit of propriety. The tension between the goal of generality and the fact of problem-centredness is evident in the programmatic statement made in the Preface to Furtado's earliest collection of essays. These are from the period of the 1950s when he was on the staff of ECLA. Furtado observes that 'the most necessary effort to be made on the theoretical plane at the present stage consists of the progressive identification of factors that are specific for each structure. That effort will subsequently serve as a basis for establishing a typology of structures.'[23] It is the notion of the specificity of structures that seems to be the key to his efforts. Thus he notes in the Preface:[24]

The need for diagnosing the problems of national economic systems in various stages of underdevelopment led him [Furtado] to bring economic analysis closer to the historical method. Comparative study of similar problems on an abstract plane, within variants conditioned by different historical situations and dissimilar national contexts, progressively induced him to adopt a structural view of economic problems.

Now, 'relevance of context' in economic formulations is an idea we have met before; and in matters of treating the Third World it is probably most readily associated with Seers's 1963 article. It is within this tradition of a 'sociologized economics' that Furtado is working. It is a tradition that breeds confusion: while the sociology of knowledge line lets us discuss the exchange between society's demands and disciplinary resources in the process of the production of 'a theory', the present sub-tradition casts the effort within the shadow of a routine conception of 'natural science'. Hence Furtado's dilemma between 'problem-relevance' and 'scientifically proper generality', which he attempts to resolve by, on the one hand, invoking some (unspecified) set of fundamental concepts, and then, on the other, arguing that these must not be taken as a basis for a supposedly general economics (in the way the neo-classical writers did with the concepts pertinent to the marginalist analysis of an unregulated market). The affirmation of the idea of 'relevance of context', subsumed under the style of the natural sciences, results in the pursuit of a relevance being undertaken in the manner of disaggregation of models. The economic model, informed by these general concepts, is tailored to fit both local circumstances and local problems. These early efforts of Furtado remain within that empiricist and interventionist schema of the relationship of knowledge and politics that we have already met. Furtado, at this stage, is pursuing technical rational recipes for development.

We can further elucidate the character of Furtado's work by introducing the idea, invoked and referred to in previous chapters, that a given form of argument makes its own demands. That is, that a particular conception of logic of explanation will help to fashion the substantive explanations given. In respect of Furtado, we would want to claim that, once the idea of 'models of reality' is affirmed, then a particular sequence of theory-elaboration follows. As an introductory comparison, let us recall the subject of chapter 3 and the orthodox arguments of the economists. Here we saw that their form of argument - that is, quasi-formal, combining technical notions and the use of mathematical notations - lets them produce vast quantities of elaborate and arcane material almost mechanically. So if the raw material of their efforts is given by ideological notions and common-sense 'facts', then the general formal characteristics of the elaborated theory are a consequence of their conception of the proper manner of explanation. Similarly, if we recall the efforts of Myrdal and Streeten then we can see that their notion of adequacy of

explanation - realism in models - involved a characteristic use of
the resources of the social sciences, both in the construction of
concepts and in the ordering of those concepts. The upshot was
a problem-centred empiricism compatible with their ideological
predispositions and work interests.

In an analogous fashion, we can indicate how the construction
of the structuralist scheme is conditioned by the epistemology of
models approach and the ideas of specificity of structures and
typology of structures. Here the construction of a model involves
generalizing about, or simplifying from, some given situation:
thus the idea that a model is inevitably specific to that which it
is a model of is a ready deduction. Equally ready is the response
to this limited applicability: a set of models may be prepared,
both of differing present economies and of these same economies
through time. This historical set aspect requires a general meta-
theory in order to provide the means of constructing these
models of the past, and so as to provide an integrating frame
for all these models. Thus we see, for example, this sort of manoeuvre: 'The foregoing discussion reveals the close interdepend-
ence between the evolution of technology in industrialized
countries and the historic conditions of their economic development.'[25] The simple logic of the notion of model gets Furtado
this far, and routine historical ideas provide the substantive
resource. Thus a series of models can be built; but what of
present comparisons? The two dimensions are needed in order to
be able to generate any appropriate model. A full set of models
must be possible, as we operate under the dictates of the image
of natural sciences and the shibboleth of generality in formulation. Furtado builds in this aspect by generalizing from the
observation of the disintegrated nature of underdeveloped
countries' economies in contrast to the integrated nature of the
developed countries' economies. This observation of the under-
developed countries' economies as comprising disparate and quasi-
autonomous elements is presented using the notion of 'structure'.
Economies have structures, and these are specific to time and
place; the developed countries have such and such a structure
and the underdeveloped countries have another. Here is the
vehicle for comparing present economies.

Thus we have a way of making models of circumstances through
history (a sequence) and of models of circumstances existing
now (a collection). These two aspects are then integrated to
generate the full set of models, by invoking the available resource of the notion of 'Centre-Periphery' - giving the one total
system.

If we now ask just what does all this produce by way of a
'theory', we get, with Furtado, the following scheme. 'The advent of an industrial nucleus in 18th century Europe disrupted
the world economy of the time and eventually conditioned later
economic development in almost every region of the world. The
action of that powerful dynamic nucleus proceeded to operate in
three directions.'[26] First in Europe, second in the 'empty lands'

of the USA and Australia, and third 'towards the already inhabited regions, some of which were densely populated, whose
old economic systems were of various but invariably pre-capitalist types'.[27] Furtado continues: 'The effect of the impact of
capitalist expansion on the archaic structures varied from region
to region, being conditioned by local circumstances.'[28] Furthermore, 'the result was almost always to create hybrid structures'.[29] This notion is finally unpacked in an exercise of
historico-formal exegesis which details the nature of the presently
underdeveloped areas (in Latin America). 'Thus, three sectors
came to coexist within the economy: one was the "remnant" economy ... the second comprises activities directly connected with
foreign trade; the third consisted of activities directly connected
with the domestic market.'[30] Thus the 'theory' presented by
Furtado is elaborated as a series of interrelated models.

So far we have noted the way in which Furtado has pursued
his objective of working towards a 'typology of structures', and
we have seen how this flows out of the 'pursuit of relevance'
within the frame of the model of the natural sciences. This is
clear in so far as the 'typology' is concerned. But what of 'structure'? The notion would seem to be, for Furtado, expressive of
the level of analysis achieved when the general economic model is
tailored to fit specific circumstances. That records the matter
epistemologically/methodologically; however, we can further
elucidate the nature of Furtado's effort by considering the origins of the term.

In this case, it would seem that the term 'economic structure'
is designed as a revision of the orthodox style of analysis so as
to fit the situation of a UDC economy. Thus an 'economic structure' is taken as a set of sectors in just such and such a relationship; so Furtado can speak of 'simple underdeveloped structures'
having one or few dynamic sectors, and 'more complex under-
developed structures' having multiple dynamic sectors.[31] Yet
the use of the terms 'sector' and 'structure' are, at this juncture,
fluid. Speaking of underdeveloped countries, Furtado notes that
their situation is not basic, or original, but is created by the
'penetration of modern capitalistic structures into archaic structures'.[32] This penetration may be simple, as with enclave
development, or it may be more complex, thus: 'The most complex situation as in the Brazilian economy at the present time, is
that in which there are three sectors in the economy: a subsistence structure, a structure oriented mainly towards export and
an industrial nucleus connected with the domestic market.'[33]
Here it seems as if we have a different notion of what 'economic
structure' involves; it is not now a set of sectors in relationship,
but is rather something that each sector has. If we were to be
pernickety at this point we would have to write off these passages as hopelessly confused; yet more charitably (and interestingly) we can read them as marking the process of the transformation of an orthodox notion of sector into a form usable in
analysing an underdeveloped country's economy (which is seen

as disintegrated), and presenting thereby the issue of the manner in which quasi-autonomous sectors interact; hence 'structural' analysis.[34]

(iii) Revision in the middle period Thus far we have considered the notion of a structure having a specific character given by its location in, and career within, the world centre-periphery system. In addition we have seen that Furtado's acknowledgment of the familiar image of the natural sciences leads him to couch his inquiries in the style of a pursuit of a typology of structures. Thus comparative and historical inquiries enter Furtado's work at an early stage. We have seen also that they enter Furtado's work in the course of his effort to model realistically the economies of the underdeveloped countries. The term 'institutional' now enters this exegesis. In Furtado's early version (1964) the term was not in evidence, though a turn in this direction entails no sharp change in the analytical machineries thus far constructed. As we saw in chapter 5, the neo-institutionalist line was concerned, in certain aspects, with the pursuit of realism in modelling. With Furtado working in this same general area of 'sociologized economics', it is not very surprising that he should come to consider the institutional natures of given economic structures. That Furtado should move in this direction is also unsurprising if we recall the above sociology of knowledge presentation; which recorded that the early 1960s threw doubt upon the then ECLA line, both in regard to its technical points and in regard to its assumptions about 'development'. In addition, it was in this period that the neo-institutionalists began to establish their stance.

The introduction of the term 'institutional' occurs within the post-1964 coup context of a revision, by Furtado, of his position vis à vis the assumptions of the orthodox line in economics. Thus he is able to commend a marxian notion of dialectic, and see in it a notion of 'development' which can order efforts to grasp the movement of social change. Quite what sort of method Furtado ends up with is debatable: his own developing version of what Girvan will call the 'structural/historical/institutional method' seems to be equated with the core of a rehabilitated Marx. This in itself seems implausible; yet we may recall a similar discovery of Marx's notion of 'development' by Kregel, who observed that the work of Marx constituted the only genuinely dynamic treatment of economic growth and change.

This broadening in Furtado's conception of the process of development, and consequent adjustment in his notion of the model required, is evident in the passage that Brookfield[35] finds so significant:[36]

Economic development, being fundamentally a process of incorporating and diffusing new techniques, implies changes of a structural nature in both the systems of production and distribution of income. The way in which these changes take place

depends, to a large extent, on the degree of flexibility of
the institutional framework within which the economy operates.
And this flexibility is dependent on the greater or lesser capacity of the ruling classes to go beyond the natural limitations
of their ideological horizons.

Furtado goes on to sketch the history of the development of the
'West', and rehearses the view that the presently underdeveloped
were created by the irruption of capitalistic enterprise into their
archaic social forms. (This chapter, we may note, is entitled
'The Dialectic of Capitalist Development'.)

In this chapter we see how Furtado has 'broadened' his conception of what counts as a plausible explanation of development;
and how he has had recourse to classical political economy and
marxian lines[37] in order to produce a distinctive scheme which
presents, in outline, the now familiar 'dependency' argument.
Thus, in respect of the underdeveloped countries, he notes the
historical manner of their incorporation into the world capitalist
economy (whose nature he characterizes), and concludes that:[38]

> since the growth of these economies is basically dependent on
> the activities of the groups responsible for the accumulative
> process, the historical conditions, under which these groups
> emerged, and those under which they operate, must be con-
> sidered in each specific case if we are to distinguish the pos-
> sibilities for growth in a particular society with an under-
> developed structure within the capitalist dynamic.

(iv) The later work The 'dependency' theme is fully present in
a 1970 work, 'Economic Development of Latin America', wherein
we find a more precise and formal statement of the thesis that
the economic structure of Latin America is a result of the manner
of that continent's incorporation into and present role within the
world capitalist economy. The nature of Girvan's 'historical/
structural/institutional' method is exemplified in the thesis presented. Thus that which admits of a description (or disaggre-
gated modelling informed by generally true economic propositions)
in terms of economic structure also admits of a complementary
description in terms of a functionally necessary institutional
framework. Historical analysis provides data for examples and
the construction of a sequence of models; and further, borrowing
from classical economics and marxian traditions, an over-arching
frame which firmly locates the Latin American economies in the
dependent peripheral area of the world capitalist economy. Problems of 'development' are then treated in terms of the lack of fit
between, on the one hand, the possibilities for development provided by technological levels and, on the other, the restrictions
and possibilities attendant upon a given structural arrangement
and institutional circumstance.

Furtado's work ends with a chapter summarizing his argument
and identifying the necessary conditions of any future advance.

Here he observes, as we noted above:[39]

> There can be no doubt that development based on exports of
> raw materials and import substituting industrialization has
> reached the limits of its possibilities.... Similarly the insti-
> tutional framework inherited from the colonial period ... seems
> to have exhausted its possibilities of adaptation to develop-
> ment needs.

With that analysis, he notes it is not surprising that 'discussion
has focused increasingly on the means to be used for a structural
reconstruction'.[40]
These matters are listed in two sets. First, reference is made
to matters of external dependency. Thus we have: 're-entry of
the regional economies into the expanding lines of the international economy',[41] 'reshaping of economic relations with the
US',[42] and 're-shaping of relations with the big international
consortia'.[43] The second set of matters treats the internal
characteristics of the Latin American economies, and here Furtado presents a list of tasks appropriate to the state's ordering
of the necessary transformation of out-moded institutional forms
and economic structures. At this point Furtado has emerged to
present the familiar outline of 'dependency' theory.

2.13 Comparative ideological character

The foregoing discussion was designed to elucidate, through
looking at Furtado's work, the 'dependency' theorists' conception
of what counted as a proper and fruitful analysis; that is, we
were concerned with the form of their arguments. Now we must
turn briefly to the substance of these efforts in the sense of
asking after their intentions. Just why did they prepare these
distinctive views? Much of the answer to this question has been
given during the course of sections 2.11 and 2.12 so here we will
add a simple comparative summary of the ideological character of
'dependency' vis à vis those efforts that we have thus far treated.
In chapter 3 we treated the conception of development theory
which was instantiated in the early Keynesian-derived 'growth
theories'. We stressed the priority of Keynesian ideas, looking
at them set against the historical period of the depression and
their theoretical sources in neo-classicism. We noted their implications for the role of government and then went on to consider
their extension, via the work of Harrod, to the circumstances of
the Third World. The notion of the development of the Third
World was, in its turn, seen as a particular and secondary version of the general doctrine of growth; which notion saw its
genesis in the needs of the West's elite to combat 'the left' in
general and the USSR in particular. Formally, we argued that
the 'growth models' were conceived within an empiricist epistemology and that their function was to legitimate and organize an
'authoritative interventionism' (viewed as knowledgeable manip-

pulation of a subject economy in the light of the science of economics, essentially a technical matter). This is the effort's self-image. We can label it basic authoritative interventionism.

Following this, in chapter 4, we treated the conception of development theory produced by the circumstances and perceived interests of cold-war America: that is, 'modernization theory'. The political demand at back of the production of 'modernization theory' was two-fold: the doctrine of containment provided the moral core, but aid competition with the USSR necessitated a disguised presentation of this pursuit of self-interest. Thus we get the notion of the 'free world'. Given these demands, theorists had recourse to two areas of work: first, an emasculated Keynesianism, and second, structural-functionalism. There is a clear move from treating economic growth and its social aspects (as in chapter 3) to treating the matter of the growth of industrial society (as in chapter 4). 'Modernization theory' provides a revised and elaborated legitimating theory of authoritative intervention. Knowledgeable manipulation of a subject society in the light of the social sciences, this is its self-image. We label it elaborated authoritative interventionism.

In chapter 5 we looked at the efforts that the 'neo-institutionalists' made in attempting to comprehend 'development'. In the case of the 'neo-institutionalists', the political context of calls for 'intervention' has shifted from confronting a supposedly expansionist communism - as was the case with 'modernization theory' and, to a lesser extent, with 'growth theory' - towards the project of reworking long-established colonial relationships. The resources invoked by the 'neo-institutionalists' include: the actual experience of the colonial episode, a distinct European tradition of social thought, and a relationship with government that disposes them to practical policy-making rather than the elaboration of formal schemes of great generality. The product, 'neo-institutional social theory', is characteristically problem-centred, piecemeal and sceptical. It constitutes the effort to theorize the withdrawal from Black Africa which subsequently becomes the model of the exchange of rich and poor. Its self-image is of the pursuit of realistic models of a development process to be ordered and implemented by government direction. We label it co-operative revised (authoritative) interventionism.

So what of the school represented here by Furtado, that is, 'dependency'? We may begin by noting that the 'dependency' effort is to be located in the context of Latin American efforts at industrialization and the problems attendant thereon. Furtado's effort resembles that of Myrdal; there is (i) a pursuit of realistic models, though Furtado in his earlier work lays very much stress on the goal of a general set of models where Myrdal focuses simply on problem-relevance; (ii) a similarity in method of analysis; and (iii) agreement in granting the centrality of the role of the state in any underdeveloped country's search for development. Yet, where Myrdal's 'reasonable men' are in nominal control of the state, those to whom Furtado would 'naturally' turn

are either not in control of the state or, if they are, their grasp
on the levers of power is apparently tenuous. Thus rather than
there being 'liberal democratic' states there are typically right-
wing, probably military, regimes.

We can pursue this aspect of the agent of execution of Furtado's work as the key to uncovering its differences in character
from previously treated lines. This apparently politically un-
favourable situation results in Furtado detaching himself from
any direct identification with the 'reasonable men' in the way
that Myrdal does. Recognizing the precarious position of the
'reasonable men', he couches his analyses in more neutral terms;
he affects to illuminate the nature of Latin American economies
generally.

The natural agent of execution of a stance like Furtado's is
the body of reasonable men in control of the state; and in the
absence of any plausibility in this claim Furtado retreats into a
more non-committal posture. Myrdal confronts the matter of the
implausibility of his work by invoking the notion of the 'soft
state' - his agent is required to 'pull itself together'.

Even if there is no agent of execution identified by Furtado,
none the less the outline of the 'dependency' stance may be
noted. Thus as the national economy is integrated into the world
economy, and moreover operates at less than its potential capacity, the solution is the pursuit of autonomous and efficient
economic development. This position is unpacked into a series of
reform proposals. Furtado's work is, then, certainly in its early
form, another variety of authoritative interventionism; and whilst
the political aspects of the situation do come to the fore in later
work, this frame is not changed, though it is subtly re-
emphasized. Thus, whilst the early work affirms a rather routine
empiricism, there none the less remains a considerable tension
between this adopted frame and the demands of specific, practical analysis. When this is coupled with his awareness of being,
so to say, politically blocked, then the whole effort changes
character and takes on an interpretative aspect. We can catch
this in the Preface to the post-1964 coup 'Diagnosis of the Brazilian Crisis'. Here Furtado propounds the thesis of the supra-
rationality of the intellectual, who is thereby morally obliged to
present analyses which are free of group or class loyalty. This
looks at first glance like an extension of the Myrdalian position
or Fabianism gone mad; but it might be more fruitfully regarded
as flowing from the particular circumstances of Brazil, and Latin
America generally. This non-class-specific theorizing we can take
as nationalist, in so far as the entire effort is a reaction to the
theoretical and practical dominance of the 'West'; and latently
populist in that in its developed form it both presents a general,
non-class-specific recipe for national progress and calls for the
removal of present elite groups. We label it reactive (populist)
interpretative interventionism.

2.14 Is 'dependency' independent? Is it adequate?[44]

In the literature which treats 'dependency' there are two areas
of debate which bear upon these issues, (that is, if we exclude
all the multiplicity of technical points). Between 'dependency'
theorists and putative marxists there is a confused debate
around the matters of the proper nature of a marxian analysis of
the Third World; and the concomitant matter of the development
of a marxian line in a novel situation, which presents itself as a
prob em of 'up-dating' Marx. This area of debate we shall for
the moment set aside, and instead look at the argument between
proponents of 'dependency' and those workers who are content
to remain within the ambit of the orthodoxy.

In the case of this second debate there are two related questions. On the one hand, there is the manner of 'dependency's'
construction, that is, do we take 'dependency' as growing out of
the structuralist scheme, or as established over and against
structuralist positions? On the other the issue of the extent to
which 'dependency' can claim to be novel vis à vis the orthodox
economics.

The first point revolves around the following claims. (i) 'Dependency' is a reformulation of that which was inherent in the
first structuralist effort. Here, as we see in the particular case
of Furtado's intellectual evolution and as Pinto and Knakal argue,
'recent "dependency" formulations can be accomodated within
the terms of Prebisch's Centre-Periphery model' (noted in Girvan[45]). (ii) 'Dependency' is a new departure. Here the structuralism of the ECLA position is taken as a theoretical object
over against which the new position is developed in response to
changing circumstance. In this instance O'Brien provides our
example: 'The theory of dependency is the response to the perceived failure of national development through import substitution
industrialization and to a growing disillusionment with existing
development theory.'[46] Related to this is O'Brien's view of
the debate about 'dependency' and the orthodox economics; he
observes, 'In brief it is an attempt to establish a new paradigm.'[47]

The second question is exemplified in the exchange between
Girvan and Cumper. Girvan highlights the novelty of 'dependency' (somewhat inconsistently, perhaps, given his approval of
Pinto and Knakal's paper). But Cumper is at some pains both to
deny that 'dependency' supersedes orthodox economics, and to
establish that it is properly to be taken as the self-serving
ideology of a post-independence intelligentsia.

To our mind, both these debates - the manner of the establishment of 'dependency', and its nature once established - can be
taken as occasioned by the practical effort to establish an 'oppositional meaning system'; that is, to theorize the situation of
Latin American economies and societies in a theoretically autonomous and progressive form. However, this effort is presented
at the meta-theoretical level as a debate about disciplinary

independence and adequacy. The proponents of 'dependency'
lodge their claims in conventional (that is, disciplinary) terms.
This opens them up to the range of criticisms of their stance
and objections from the orthodox lodged by Cumper. Neither
party to these related debates is right. 'Dependency' is neither
(treating the practitioners' claims), on the one hand, the basis
for an 'adequate general economics' nor is it, on the other hand,
distinct from structuralism. Yet, as against its critics, it is not
a worthless by-product merely of self-aggrandisement.

So what is it? Let us rework the discussion and return to our
point of departure at the beginning of section 2.0. Given our
résumé of the establishment of 'dependency', our explication of
its argument form, and the comparative exercise in labelling;
does all this tend to establish 'dependency' as a candidate for
the descriptions of 'independent discipline' or 'adequate development studies'? The second term of description, which on the
face of it would seem to entail the former, is often applied by
commentators who simultaneously invoke a notion of theoretical
progressivity in setting up 'dependency' over an orthodoxy
which encompasses 'growth' and 'modernization' theories. Yet to
our mind, just as the question was inappropriate in regard to
'NIST' versus modernization theory, so it is inappropriate here.
'Dependency' can only be read as an ideology.

When we treated Myrdal and the neo-institutionalists, we asked
if they had prepared a scheme which was superior (in terms of
its grasp on the world) to the efforts of 'growth' and 'modernization' theory. 'Growth theory' was dismissed, for the present
issue, as crude. The comparison of 'NIST' and 'modernization
theory' revealed that, in terms of practical efficacy, 'NIST' was
superior to 'modernization theory' in that its background provided
for the establishment of a more subtle scheme, even though intellectual resources were largely common. As regards conceptual
advance, we felt there was none. Both 'NIST' and 'modernization
theory' remained in conception empiricist and in intent authoritative interventionisms. They were both exercises in what Fay
would call 'policy science'.

But what of 'dependency'? If we measure it against a notion of
ideology as the result of the deployment of morally informed
categorical frame, then we can note two issues. One is the matter
of reflexive consistency; that is, at its simplest, does the stance
in question grant that it is an ideology and shape itself accordingly (morally informed)? Second, what is the scope of its core
ideas (categorical frame)? Do they fit the job they are required
to do? This is a vast question; but here we simply want to see
if problems call forth theoretical forms.

We have already seen, in discussing Furtado's epistemological
ideas, that 'dependency' does not regard itself as an ideology
and indeed in many respects tries to ape the natural sciences.
In addition, 'dependency' fails to specify any agent of theory
execution; like Myrdal's effort, it floats uncomfortably above the
world. Thus far 'dependency' looks like more policy science.

However, if we ask after the core ideas of 'dependency' the
position changes somewhat. With 'NIST', as we presented it
through the work of Streeten, the key idea had been that of a
concept's having an ecology; that is, it was argued that a concept only worked within the context of just such and such a set
of institutional circumstances, and that realistic models needs
must be pragmatic, piecemeal, sceptical efforts. All this fitted,
as we saw, the 'decolonization' episode. If we ask whether or
not there is an analogous fruitful and novel core to 'dependency',
then we are bound to pick the idea of economic theorizing being
situation-specific. Thus the orthodox economics is judged to be
irrelevant and it is proposed that answers to Latin American
problems must be prepared with the peculiar characteristics of
Latin American economies to the fore. Evidently this line of argument bears no little resemblance to that of 'NIST', yet the context
and manner of its emergence make it difficult to regard as
straightforwardly policy scientific. Interventionist - yes, empiricist - yes; but also sensitive in its formulation to its own
circumstances,[48] even if (measured against our ideal definition
of ideology) the political sensitivity remains more or less latent.

   In sum, we can say that 'dependency' no more establishes an
independent and/or adequate development studies than did any
of its predecessors. It, too, is an ideology, an exercise in social
theorizing; and its nature can only be properly comprehended
via an understanding of its milieu, occasion of construction and
intellectual resource base.

2.2 'Dependency' and the supersession of the conventional wisdom: a problem misconstrued

Above (2.14) we made reference to the debate of Girvan and
Cumper in respect of the putative independence and theoretical
superiority of 'dependency' with regard to the 'conventional
wisdom' of economics. In respect of this debate, we observed
that it was occasioned by the project of propounding an 'oppositional meaning system' using the syntax of orthodox social
science. That is, Girvan did not present his exposition as the
why and wherefore of a novel ideological departure. Rather, he
claimed to be revealing the manner in which the orthodox notions
of a discipline came to be rendered liable to supersession. Here
we consider this debate; not so much because we take Girvan
and Cumper to be major figures in all this work, but rather because their exchange presents an accessible vehicle for treating
the theoretical point at issue.

   Girvan argues that the school of 'dependency' economics established not only an economics that was adequate to Latin
America, but also an economics that could be taken as generally
adequate.[49] This was in contrast to the hitherto unchallenged
economics of the developed world, which was now to be seen as
generally inadequate (which entails its being inadequate to the

economies of the rich nations themselves). This claim raises three issues that we wish to pursue.

(1) This is on the face of it a narrower issue than that treated in section 2.1; or, to put the matter another way, there seems to be a continual ambiguity in treatments of 'dependency' with regard to its proper disciplinary location. Are we treating economics, or some effort derived from the wider set of the social sciences? In the present situation Girvan would seem to be firmly locating 'dependency' within that tradition of thought called economics. If the conception of 'dependency' is thus restricted, then the issue of 'disciplinary independence' becomes that much more acute. In the above discussion (2.1), we approached these matters by asking: just what did 'dependency' function to legitimate and order? We still take that approach to be appropriate; but here Girvan's treatment has to be seen to open up the possibility of debating the issue of 'dependency' versus 'conventional wisdom' on a technical level. We find this to be an unhelpful level of debate; yet it is the terrain chosen by Girvan and Cumper. Technical debates within an agreed ideological frame make sense; technical debates across the boundaries of ideological frames produce nonsense.

(2) We are presented here with an example of intellectual expansionism. Girvan, having misread or misreported his ideological departure as scientific advance, goes on (in the light of the notion of generality of formulation) to claim for his effort an area of broad application (i.e. replacing the orthodox). Such a claim would be seen to be nonsensical if he had properly grasped the nature of his own effort as ideology. In addition, it is obvious that such a claim invites reply from the proponents of the orthodoxy in orthodox terms; that is, the fundamental points at issue, namely the disputes of the two ideologies, are missed or may be ignored.

(3) Girvan adds a final element of confusion in that he presents his views with reference to an established debate within economics. That is, Girvan takes the 'dependency' effort as resolving the issue of whether or not there is one general economics or two, one for the rich and one for the poor.

Thus we can see that the issues of disciplinary independence, intellectual expansionism, and the matter of the number of the sciences of economics, come together in the claims presented here by Girvan to the effect that 'dependency' has set economics on its feet. But rather than pursue these three questions for their own sake, which would involve us in much possibly irrelevant and unnecessary work, we will approach these issues only in so far as they are made manifest in the debate between Girvan and Cumper. This should ensure that our writings remain relevant to the job in hand, whilst at the same time acknowledging the importance of the matters presented by the dispute. In respect of the debate, our point of departure is the observation that the central axis of confusion is that between natural science (ordinarily understood) and ideology (understood as social theory).

If we first consider the work of Girvan, we can report that, building on the efforts of Sunkel and Furtado, he argues as follows. Out of the efforts to produce an indigenous economics, the notions of 'dependency' in fact present a solution to the issue of whether one or two economics are needed; in that comprehending the nature of the dependent subsystem must involve the comprehension of the entire system.[50] Thus far this is arguably trivial: we have simply rediscovered the concept of a 'world economy' that was present in the notion of 'imperialism', from which Prebisch derived the original 'Centre Periphery' motif.[51] Where the matter becomes other than trivial is in the claim that 'dependency' itself makes a distinctive (and implicitly seminal) contribution to the establishment of the proposed one economics of global capitalism. This is troubling for several reasons. First, the intellectual expansionism of the 'dependency' ideology entails that the efficacy of the 'structural/institutional/historical' method be affirmed. One can envisage the establishment of a project to generate a set of models of economies, the whole being subsumable under the premier concept of the capitalist world system. In reply, we would want to argue that the trio of concepts, fruitful as they are, is not enough to generate a general economics (whatever that might be); and that rather we should begin, philosophically, to build a political economy around the notion of production. Second, Girvan continues to use the syntax of orthodox social science; which matter is our present concern in so far as it is productive of confusion. In addition, it grants sense to the notion of a 'generally adequate economics', 'relevant and valid'[52] for rich and poor. But we may ask just what counts as a 'generally adequate economics'?[53]

If we now move on to consider Cumper's reply to Girvan's paper, we can see that Girvan's synthesizing generality is confronted with detailed criticism. There are broadly three lines of attack.

Cumper observes that Girvan's separation of 'dependency' into distinct Latin American and Caribbean lines is untenable. Girvan is charged with ignoring Seers, misrepresenting Lewis and forgetting about the impact of the collapse of the West Indian Federation and the Cuban Revolution. This mishandling of the detail serves to establish the distinction between Latin American and Caribbean schools. This is all, on the face of it, pertinent; but then Cumper destroys its critical force by noting that all that rests on this for Girvan is 'the scheme of his paper'.[54] This is trivial: Cumper is objecting to the simplifications which Girvan makes in order to be able to present a readily assimilable scheme. Moreover, Cumper adopts precisely the same sort of simplifying manoeuvre.

The matter of the rejected orthodoxy is pursued by Cumper. He presents a series of orthodox analytical techniques and asks, rhetorically, do the 'dependency' theorists reject this, or this, etc.? As an argument strategy it is unconvincing. Even within the misleading syntax adopted by Girvan, the proposed super-

session of orthodoxy cannot be taken to entail the wholesale rejection of the particular technical constructs of the 'conventional
wisdom'. In addition, if we consider that Cumper goes on to
lodge a sociology of knowledge critique of Girvan, it must be
open to the speculation that Cumper knows full well that what
Girvan wants to do is reject the orthodoxy qua ideology. This
line of attack from Cumper seems to be disingenuous.

Finally, Cumper launches a critique of Girvan which is informed by the notion of an 'ideology'; where this is taken in the
fairly narrow sense of the presentation of a self-serving schema.
It is suggested that 'dependency' is the ideology of an intellectual
in a post-independence state, wishing to secure his position as
an 'organic intellectual' at the expense of other intellectuals and
groups generally. The general points about the status of the
intelligentsia in newly independent states may well be true, but
Cumper undermines any force the attack might have by making
ideology the same as bias. Claiming that Girvan et al. are unprincipled careerists is an ad hominem argument that leads nowhere. Cumper grants this when he acknowledges a distinction
between origin and validity, such that the former does not entail
anything by way of truth or falsity for the latter. Cumper retreats at this point into claiming that he is simply interested in
sensitizing readers to 'ideological distortion'.

Against Cumper we would argue that bias cannot flow from an
ideological stance. Bias flows from prejudice, and that this is to
be regretted and extirpated is a trivial observation. If bias is
present in Girvan or his fellows' work, then it is unfortunate.
It is not enough to overturn their ideological stance.

The equation of ideology with bias crops up when Cumper
grants that his stance could be called ideological. He answers
that to go beyond this ideology-spotting routine requires a pragmatic test of what is or is not objective truth. Cumper proposes
a crude notion of consensus; thus the more who accept an idea,
the greater its likelihood of being objective. He further proposes
'track record': the more an analysis has been used operationally,
the more we can take it to be objective. Evidently these both
beg the question; orthodox views will be preferred and used by
people whose views are orthodox. That a view is orthodox says
nothing, on Cumper's own terms (origin/validity), about the
truth of that view. Additionally, we may observe that invoking
the notions of consensus and track record when treating a line
which deliberately opposes the orthodox seems singularly inappropriate. The observations which Cumper makes in the light of
the notion of ideology seem to run into the sand. The attack
finally has no point and no force.

We can now summarize this exchange. The essential tentative-
ness of the project in respect of which Girvan makes his expli-
catory report (that is, in our view, the construction of an
ideology), and the particular unfortunate syntax chosen (that
is, a quasi-natural-science revision of a discipline's concepts)
combine to present Cumper with a ready opportunity for 'missing

the point' and launching a thinly disguised counter-attack on
behalf of the orthodox. Girvan's presentation of the matter permits criticisms to be couched in orthodox vein - it does not require the orthodox to confront the fundamental (ideological)
issues at stake. The upshot is that Cumper is able to dismiss
'dependency' as a novel orientation, and condemn Girvan's paper
on and espousal of 'dependency' as slip-shod, untenable and
self-serving.

In general, it is our view that the matter of the relationship
of 'dependency' to the 'conventional wisdom' is a matter of comparing and contrasting the form and intent of two distinct
ideologies. Their comparative ranking is a difficult task, and
the way in which such an analysis might be accomplished will
exercise us through the rest of the study. What is clear is that
to cast the matter in empiricist terms, and pursue an argument
in respect of the supposed supersession of a technical scientific
discipline's notions by a new set of concepts, is to invite confusion.

2.3 Disciplinary independence - a chimera?

We began section 2 of this chapter by asking whether or not
'dependency' could be taken to establish an independent and/or
adequate development studies. Recalling the views in respect of
the nature of social theorizing propounded in the Prologue to
the study, we began a pursuit of an answer to our question by
asking what is the form and intent of 'dependency'. At the end
of that treatment, our disposition to regard 'dependency' as an
ideology was seen to be entirely plausible. With regard to the
exchange between practitioners of 'dependency' and their orthodox predecessors, we saw in the context of the Girvan-Cumper
debate that the issue of ranking the disparate efforts was
couched in terms of the dictates of the model of the natural
sciences. The particular metaphor borrowed to treat the process
of advancing this or that ideologically informed set of claims in
respect of development was that of a 'finally adequate theory',
in contradistinction to some orthodoxy or other. The model of
the natural sciences was borrowed, and disparate ideologies were
compared as though what was at issue was the construction of
some set of concepts adequate to an external, given object. An
independent and adequate discipline was taken to be one that
had both a particular object of study and an agreed and effective
investigatory procedure. We argued that this was a total misapprehension of the nature of the exchange between theoretical
lines in development studies, and that consequently all subsequent debate in respect of 'disciplinary independence' could only
be sterile and misleading.

In sum, it is our contention that the issue of 'disciplinary independence' is a chimera that is occasioned by a fundamental
misapprehension of the business of the development theorist.

3.0 PROGRESS IN CONCEPTUALIZATION

Thus far we have treated the matter of 'disciplinary independence' in the company of an exposition of 'dependency theory'.
The upshot of these discussions has been that 'dependency' is
to be properly taken as an ideology - like those efforts we have
looked at in earlier chapters - and that the issue of 'disciplinary
independence' is a chimera. The debate about all this can only
get off the ground if the social theorist involved invokes the
model of the natural sciences. But as we argued in our Prologue,
social theory is not a variation on natural science; consequently
the debate is sterile. Having thus resolved this issue and rejected the model of the natural sciences, we are left with the
sciences of the social as, properly regarded, being concerned
with the construction and analysis of ideologies. The question
which is raised in this part of the chapter is that, if social
theories are ideologies, then how are we to rank competing
schemas? We pursue this question in the company of 'underdevelopment theory'.

We first present two arguments which are familiar in the literature: the argument from a sequence, and the argument from
the identification of paradigms. We shall deny that these arguments help to establish either that there is progress in conceptualization within the history of social theorizing, or that there
has been progress in conceptualization within the ambit of development studies. Further, we shall argue that these lines of
inquiry (albeit informed by a genuine issue, viz. ranking ideologies) are misconceived, in that they begin with the model of the
natural sciences and search for social science analogues. They
fail to secure their objectives for precisely the same reasons as
those who pursue 'disciplinary independence': their goal is
illusory.[55]

After treating these two arguments, we go on to confront
directly the issue of ranking ideologies and through the medium
of a presentation of Frank's 'underdevelopment' work we offer a
series of preliminary and tentative remarks.

3.1 The argument from a sequence

We have seen in the case of Furtado's intellectual career how the
establishment of the 'dependency' view can quite properly be
regarded as an emergent sequence; that is, from the initial
centre-periphery notion presented by Prebisch the 'dependency'
position may be derived.[56] As Girvan puts it, noting the Prebisch formulation, 'The idea of the economic dependence of the
periphery is evidently implicit in this conceptualization.'[57] In
addition to this observation, we can note that latent within the
typical (favourable) commentary upon 'dependency' there is often
some sort of reference to this sequence, and the claim is implicitly
lodged that the mere existence of this sequence testifies to the

truth of the final product. We have, then, two elements to consider: on the one hand, the sequence, and, on the other, the
claims made for it or in the light of it. What we take to be the
typical and erroneous fusion of these matters is most accessibly
presented by Ehrensaft.

Ehrensaft begins by observing that 'During the last decade a
diverse stream of analyses emerged which taken together do
much *to update and correct* our perceptions of the Third World';
and he goes on to declare that 'my intention in this essay is to
give an *initial synthesis* of some of this new thinking.'[58] Already the phrasing (with our emphases) points up the plausibility of our general claims in regard to 'dependency's' expositors;
and Ehrensaft goes on to display quite unequivocally the typical
resolution of the matter of sequence and truth status. Thus he
declares:[59]

> The central proposition of this essay argues that the struc-
> tural position and interests of national bourgeoisies in Third
> World capitalist regimes block them from undertaking and
> carrying out these tasks of economic, political and cultural
> mobilization. *This proposition emerges in five steps from the
> new writings on Third World political economies. Each succes-
> sive step brings a closer approximation to actual societal re-
> lationships ... I will review these steps one by one, showing
> how each successive analysis builds intellectually on the ones
> which preceded* [our emphasis].

Ehrensaft here declares himself to be some sort of 'dependency'
theorist: a stance that he reduces to a 'central proposition',
which he states. The history of the post-war period is then reviewed in the light of this orientation. This procedure is familiar,
legitimate, and entirely his own affair. But to our mind, in making his presentation he commits a familiar and pernicious error,
and this is of general interest. The error seems to come when he
elects to relate the history of the establishment of his preferred
view in the mould of the supposed progressiveness of conceptualization of the natural sciences. When Ehrensaft writes that
his purpose is to 'explain why semi-industrialization occurs',[60]
we can note that it would seem to be the case that Ehrensaft takes
himself to be telling us something about how the world is; that is,
reporting on an empirical matter. This reading is reinforced by
his treatment of the sequence of notions which issues in 'dependency'. Of his history, he says that 'each successive step brings
us closer to approximation to actual societal relationships'.[61]
This presentation seems to invoke the model of the natural
sciences, as they are ordinarily understood. We are presented
with a scheme of increasingly accurate approximations to a reality
independent of the theorist's engagement.

Now whilst it may be argued that natural science conceptualizations are progressive to the extent that they approximate more
closely to an independent reality than their predecessors (and

presumably Ehrensaft would affirm this), we should note that
this formulation of the process of natural science work is both
(a) common-sensical and (b) in terms of the debates within the
philosophy of science, naive. Just what is going on within the
ambit of the natural sciences, how they may be demarcated, and
what ontological or epistemological commitments attach to any
one proposition of the natural sciences, are all matters of vigorous debate. Ehrensaft thus makes two assumptions: (i) that
the history of the formulations of the natural sciences is one of
increasingly subtle approximations to an independent reality;
and (ii) that the history of the formulations of the social sciences
is analogous to that of the natural sciences. Now, without reference to the debates within the philosophy of science, it can
be granted that assumption (i) is at the very least open to
question; and that assumption (ii) is widely denied. These remarks, let us note, attach to the idea which informs and structures Ehrensaft's entire argument, and from which it draws its
force. If they are called into question then so is the entire
Ehrensaftian project. It seems to us that Ehrensaft's argument
can be reduced to the status of a covert appeal to common sense
to support his schema. We can offer an alternative.

In contradistinction to what is seemingly assumed by Ehrensaft, we would wish to argue (setting aside matters of the nature
of the natural science effort) that with the social sciences there
is no reason to expect, or look for, this progressive tendency;
and that within the history of 'dependency' theory or any other
distinguishable school within the social sciences, there is no
need to cast expositions in this natural science-echoing style.

If we recall our schema of the sociology of knowledge, then we
see that the dynamic of theory is but one aspect of the production
of social theory (i.e. ideology); the other being the dynamic of
society. It is within the ambit of this second element that we can
locate those societal conflicts and changes that issue in the demands, made of theorists, to produce useful explanations. Quite
what the practical significance of autonomous developments in
theory might be we have not asked. Some role must be granted
to such intra-disciplinary developments if we are to give the
theorist a role broader than that of an apologist responding,
essentially passively, to the demands of whatever social group
he may feel beholden to. However, it is clear that (whatever the
solution to this question) the idea of the double dynamic of social
theory and social problem presents a sharply divergent picture
of the nature of social theorizing to that of Ehrensaft's natural-
science-informed common sense. More particularly, if social
theorizing entails some measure of 'social practicality' then it is
impossible to conceive of any progressivity of conceptualization
on the model of that supposed to be present in the natural
sciences. The notion of 'progressivity' is at least plausible in
respect of the natural sciences, but seems wholly improbable in
the realm of the social sciences. In this latter case, the only
'progressivity' would be within the frame of some 'social problem'

- that is, a specific exchange of theorist/world - and such 'progressivity' would be of a different sort to that which would be invoked in respect of natural scientific-type movement towards an ever more subtle grasp of a fixed and given reality.[62]

In sum, we have to say that: (i) Ehrensaft's pursuit of a progressive evolution of concepts towards a realistic economic sociology is, so far as we can determine, a misconceived project; (ii) there is no reason to suspect that such a progressive sequence exists; and (iii) there is reason, in the light of our arguments in respect of social theorizing, to suppose that it does not exist.

It is not enough for proponents of 'dependency' to point to a sequence of concept development and claim thereby that the present end point of the sequence is true, coherent and useful. Indeed, the reverse is the case; the identification of a sequence in a concept's history establishes nothing in respect of that concept's truthfulness, and to argue that it does is to draw wrongly upon a particular model of the natural sciences.

3.2 The argument from paradigms

We have noted and discussed above the notion that a sequence of argument, ECLA-Furtado-Frank, may be identified such that the end point may be regarded as some sort of theoretical consummation of this progressive sequence. We have dismissed that argument; but there is an analogous and related argument which treats the same material using a notion of 'paradigm shift', drawn from Kuhn, such that the complex and confused debate which lies between a start point of ECLA and an end point of Frank is taken as an instance of a 'paradigm shift'. We can take this to be used as an argument for theoretical progressivity, in that the notion 'paradigm shift' claims to encompass and render intelligible an intra-disciplinary process whereby a failing orthodoxy is superseded and replaced. How are we to regard this argument for theoretical progressivity?

With reference to Bernstein's work, we can review both the Kuhnian notion itself and the use made of that notion by social scientists. Kuhn is tagged by Bernstein as a 'post-empiricist', one of a number of philosophers of science who have attacked the (common-sense) idea of science as the incremental accumulation of facts which are subsequently ordered by theories. Kuhn's work endeavours to capture science as a social activity and as a set of procedures for apprehending the nature of their given object. Thus the Kuhnian notion of a 'paradigm' has two related senses. In the first, it denotes that set of very general shared assumptions whereby the scientific community constitute their activities; and second, it denotes a particular practical exemplification of their practices. Kuhn later revises his terminology such that the former sense is presented as 'disciplinary matrix' and the latter as 'exemplar'. Bernstein notes that whilst these revisions of terminology help to clear up some confusions, they do not help with one crucial issue. As he says, 'What is frequently forgotten or neglected is that a primary aim of his book is to help us understand what is distinctive about science.'[63] Bernstein thinks that what Kuhn has to say about 'paradigms' can apply quite happily to any other discipline of learning. Thus he remarks:[64]

> What he has to say about paradigms, their acceptance, the ways in which they are imposed, is just as true for the history of schools. There are many disciplines such as philosophy - which Kuhn distinguishes from science - where what Kuhn says about science is perfectly applicable.

If there is nothing distinct about the notion of a 'paradigm' when it is supposedly applied to the natural sciences, then to invoke it to illuminate events in social science is to present a vacuous explanation. The conceptual link-up with the natural sciences turns out to be non-existent, and all the talk of paradigm shifts and normal/revolutionary science advances the analysis of intra-disciplinary change in social science not as extensively as assumed. Additionally, we may note, it does not provide the long-sought-for route to scientific respectability for the social sciences. In all these arguments reference to 'paradigms' entails using an unstable metaphor.

So much for Kuhn himself; his work, Bernstein argues, is too ambiguous to be of any direct and immediate use. What then of the use made of Kuhn's work by social scientists? Bernstein discusses two 'mainstream social scientists', and after criticizing their misuse of Kuhn - which, it is argued, takes the form of reading the notion of 'paradigm' so very generally as to lose all contact with Kuhn's efforts[65] - suggests that a fundamental question is being begged. He observes that:[66]

> what is at issue is not only whether political science is or is not in a 'pre-paradigmatic' or 'paradigmatic' phase, but whether this very way of speaking is appropriate and illuminating ....
> If one thinks that political science is in a pre-paradigmatic stage, this suggests that surely a scientific paradigmatic stage must arise if we are patient and work toward it. But there is absolutely no warrant for such an inference on Kuhn's ground or any others.

In other words, to argue thus is to beg the question of the precise nature of social science. In all these debates reference to paradigms entails the obfuscation of crucial issues.

What are the implications of these remarks for the use of the notion of 'paradigms' in the social sciences? If we regard their use as either metaphorical or obfuscatory then two lines open up. In the first case, we can treat the use of the term 'paradigm' as marking the effort to express and give preliminary shape to the

participants' (and commentators') sense of the theoretical novelty
and importance of those new departures with which they are concerned. Thus, simply, it is one way whereby the totality of the
ECLA-Furtado-Frank line may be grasped/presented. Clearly,
if we could establish a suitably cautious (and, in particular, non-
natural science-referring) use of the terminology, then this
would be unobjectionable; if only because it would not be any
different in import from the way we ordinarily talk about new
'schools'. The other, second, use remains objectionable. Here
we may hazard that the term in question simply serves as an obfuscating notion whereby an essentially theoretically empty effort
may be passed off as coherent and/or novel. As regards the
'novel' reading, we could end up close to H. Bernstein's view of
the 'radicals' of development studies; which has it that they reduce to bourgeois orthodoxy plus moral outrage. The 'coherent'
reading might attach to those familiar scientistic efforts of orthodox social science whereby underdeveloped ideologies are loosely
disguised as efforts of science; that is, as being properly
scientific.

The foregoing discussion can be integrated into our preceding
remarks on the influence of the natural sciences. Thus if we con
sider the familiar debates within social science we can interpret
them in two ways: as inevitable and as transient.

Kuhn opts for transience - on, we may suggest, the analogy
of the established natural sciences - and then reworks the history
of the natural sciences on the model of the social sciences. Thus
he has 'pre-paradigm' debate (from the social sciences) issuing in
eventual 'paradigm' agreement (from natural sciences). There is
one story, a sort of 'unified theory' for the natural and the social
sciences. Reconstructing the argument strategy, we obtain the
following picture. Working one way, the empiricist's model of incremental science is denied in favour of suggestions drawn from
the image of the social sciences; thus natural science is seen as a
social activity. Working the other way, debate within the social
sciences is not taken to be endemic, and nor is social science
taken to be hopelessly polluted by bias and ideology. The core of
the natural science effort, the agreed apprehension of a unitary
truth of an external world, is made available to social science.
All social science has to do is sort out its agreed paradigm and
thereafter get on with it.

With regard to the search for an agreed paradigm, it is observed that parties to debates (i) sketch out differing and incompatible positions (this is routine in the social sciences); but
(ii) only bother to do this in the natural sciences when there is
debate or recourse to philosophy, and that this is extremely unusual in the natural science. The Kuhnian 'unified theory' then
presents us with the notion of pre-paradigm debate occasioning
the critical identification of hitherto taken-for-granted paradigms.
These exercises in the critical identification of the presently
assumed serve to permit or enable the construction of the new
and superseding paradigm.

If we now return to our start point and take debates within social science to be inevitable, and if we also affirm that these endless squabbles are not evidence of the futility of social science, then we are bound to ask for an explanation of the nature of social science that acknowledges and integrates into explanation that which is routinely observed of social science, viz. endless debate. Let us, therefore, embrace the notion of ideology and see what that entails. On the basis of arguments and discussions presented in preceding chapters we can report that the business of social science is the activity of making sense; and the history of social science efforts is the history of the various results of the double dynamic of society and discipline.

With regard to the particular exercise of constructing a theory, we can see that the theorist is (i) confronted with a problem presented by society (i.e. 'make sense of X') and (ii) has available a given set of disciplinary resources. The 'new theory' is developed out of a debate with existing theory according to the particular demands of the present problem. Thus established theory is revised in the light of the new problem; it is not simply extended.

It is at this point that the two lines coincide; so, paradigm shift in the social sciences and theory invention look to be the same thing.

To conclude, we can note that the treatment of intra-disciplinary change which uses the notion 'paradigm shift' represents, to our mind and in line with the observations of earlier parts of this chapter, the influence of the model of the natural sciences. It is our view that recourse to Kuhnian terminology does not advance our understanding of how 'schools' emerge and how they are constituted. Indeed, it obscures investigation of the more plausible view that revision of a set of concepts (within the realm of the social sciences) flows not from an improved apprehension of an independent reality, called forth by the 'anomalous behaviour' of that reality, but rather from the advancing of the claims of a novel ideology by a particular group in response to or in the light of changes within their social world.

The argument to theoretical progressivity is not secured by using the notion of paradigm shifts. That an established body of theoretical resources has been transmuted into a novel ideological form does not, of itself, establish the progressivity of that transmutation; and the question of the ranking of ideologies remains open.

To anticipate some questions which might be raised, we note that there are, in addition to the lines seen above, a whole set of versions of one familiar argument to the effect that progressivity entails you ditching your ideology in favour of my science. This is routine inter-ideology debate amongst the practitioners of the early efforts which we noted in the preceding chapters. We can safely ignore this style of argument.

Also related to this is the Bernstein/Leys/(Frank) argument to the effect that they have transcended simple radicalism by adopting marxism. On the face of it, this argument partakes of all the devices examined above. Progress in conceptualization is effected through transcending radicalism; where 'transcending' implies both a preparatory sequential movement and a distinct break. We are presented with what could be called the 'take-off into marxism'. Yet this must be regarded as largely a matter of biography, as the marxian line just is distinct – this debate, just what counts as a marxian line we leave to Part IV.

3.3 How do we rank ideologies?

3.31 Introductory note

The foregoing discussions issued in a rejection of the notions of sequential conceptual development and paradigm shifts as means whereby the adequacy of differing explanations could be judged. So how can we compare the theoretical status of various efforts? Thus far we have argued that all the substantive efforts with which we have concerned ourselves are to be taken as ideologies. How, then, do we rank ideologies?

 With Bernstein in chapter 5, we contented ourselves with noting simply that they could be ranked. We went on to observe that the efforts thus far treated (Keynesian 'growth', 'modernization theory', 'NIST') were all empiricist in conception and authoritative interventionisms in intent; that is, generally speaking, the same. This made questions of ranking fairly straightforward; that is, in line with simple (internal to the set) criteria of technical efficacy, even if these measures are illusory. But what if the ideologies are not generally 'the same', in the sense used; how then do we rank ideologies? We will pursue this question with A.G. Frank and 'underdevelopment theory'.

3.32 A.G. Frank and 'underdevelopment theory'

If we present a sociology of knowledge sketch of Frank's work, using our scheme of 'demands', 'resources' and 'product', then the picture we obtain is as follows.[67] Out of a general milieu of long-term foreign, and in particular US, dominance of the area and the experience of the Cuban revolution, Frank conceives the task of contributing to a revolutionary critique of orthodox theorizing and expectations. Brookfield speaks of Frank's 'most rapid conversion to radical ideologies'.[68] The available resources are three-fold. First, the orthodox economics of the neo-classical-dominated 'modernization' theories provide an object against which the new departure may be defined. Second, the analytical machineries are largely provided by the structuralist line associated with ECLA. These constitute the principal theoretical resource used by Frank, whilst the political reformism associated with ECLA provides another negative defining element of Frank's stance. Third, a simple strategic motaphor is borrowed from the marxism of Baran; that is, the notion of the debilitating metropolitan extraction of surplus from long-integrated peripheral areas. The product of this effort we here designate 'underdevelopment theory';[69] the situation of Latin American economies, and indeed those of the Third World generally, are to be explained in terms of their subordinate incorporation into the world capitalist system.

This product, Frank's 'manifesto', is expressed in a 1963 work (published in 1975) thus:[70]

> All serious study of the problems of development of under-developed areas and all serious intent to formulate policy for the elimination of underdevelopment and for the promotion of development must take into account, nay must begin with, this fundamental historical and structural cause of underdevelopment in capitalism. Indeed, all serious study of development must take into account the fundamental relation the development of development has had, and continues to have, with the development of underdevelopment. All serious study of capitalism, of its manifestations in the development of the metropole and of that in the underdevelopment of the periphery, and especially the study of the contemporary single world capitalist system and its development in the past and future, must begin with capitalism's unity and its fundamental internal contradiction, which has always and everywhere expressed itself in diffusion and exploitation, development and underdevelopment.

Ehrensaft labels Frank's effort 'satellitization', and remarks that 'Substantively, the satellitization approach deals with the same phenomena as does the structuralist. The difference consists largely in the interpretation given to these phenomena.'[71] Translating this observation out of its empiricist style, we can see that Ehrensaft is making the point that in conception Frank's effort resembles that of the structuralists ('dependency'), whilst in intent it does not.

As regards Frank's conceptual equipment in these early works, Ehrensaft's view appears to be correct. Ehrensaft quotes Frank from the essay 'The Development of Underdevelopment' to the effect that where he, Frank, differs from some other structuralists is that he is not ideologically blinkered. The implication being that, in respect of conception of analysis, there is a very much greater convergence of view than might otherwise be expected. Turning to this text, we find that it is indeed close to the 'dependency' style of analysis. Without going all the way through Frank's work to establish this, we can quote him directly. Thus he says, after considering the character of Brazilian economy and society, that 'the same historical and structural approach can also lead to a better development theory and policy'.[72] Any such product must be made by the peoples of the dependent states themselves. Frank goes on, 'to change their reality they

must understand it. For this reason I hope that better confirmation of these hypotheses and further pursuit of the proposed
historical, holistic and structural approach may help.'[73] In
addition, and at a more general level, Frank's approach resembles that of the 'dependency' line; in that, couched in the syntax of natural science, both efforts are conceived in 'epistemology of models' fashion.[74]

Turning to the matter of the intent of Frank's work, it is
clear that Ehrensaft is right in pointing to the ideological differences between Frank and 'dependency'.[75] However, it also
seems to be the case that Ehrensaft, bound up in his pursuit of
theoretical progressivity, entirely fails to grasp that the crucial
novelty of Frank's line resides precisely in his overt political
commitment. Frank's work is readily contrasted with previous
writers noted in this study. What is strikingly evident in the
Frank line is its political engagement; Frank makes his work's
political engagement not simply obvious, but central to his
effort.[76] Thus he declares 'These essays were written to contribute to the Revolution in Latin America and the world';[77]
and again, he argues that problems of underdevelopment can be
resolved 'with the only true development strategy: armed revolution and the construction of socialism'.[78]

In respect of this centrality of political engagement in Frank's
earlier work, we can ask (in the light of the notion of a theory
requiring an 'agent of execution'): just how is Frank's effort
supposed to fix on to the world? With Myrdal we identified the
reasonably acting state as agent of theory-execution, and the
notion of the 'soft state' as the apology for this view's implausibility. With Furtado we saw a similarly free-floating theory, that
required an enlightened nationalism from unspecified quarters.
What is the position with Frank? Frank's early work is, it may
be suggested, best regarded as that of a political pamphleteer,[79]
rather than as sociology, economics, political science, or whatever. If we read Frank as a pamphleteer then two points seem to
follow.

First, in contrast to earlier writers considered in this study,
the agent of theory-execution has a different status or presence
in Frank's work; that is, the idea of revolution enters Frank's
work very early on. In thus having a clear political aspect,
Frank's agent of theory-execution becomes omnipresent, rather
than being just one more element in some wider general scheme.
Myrdal, however, has a neo-institutionalist theory of Third
World society; additionally, affirming the value principle of
'development', he is obliged to identify a political agent of theory-
execution - thus we get the 'reasonable state'. Myrdal's agent is
called forth by the logic of theorizing, and is a minimum commit-
ment/engagement which is incapable of carrying the weight the
overall Myrdalian scheme requires of it. Frank in this early work
does not, to our mind, come armed with a general theory of
Third World society; rather he comes armed with a radical political commitment which presents him with a ready-made agent, viz.

the political activist, just as soon as he begins to sketch out his model of the situation.[80] Frank's agent is intrinsic rather than additional to his scheme. Whether the line is any more plausible than preceding efforts is another, albeit related, question.

The second point is related to the first. It concerns moral/ political commitment, and the syntax of the natural sciences. Frank, we want to say, presents his moral/political engagement as an empirical matter.[81] That is to say, he offers a program-matic statement in respect of the exchange of rich and poor and takes this to be liable to confirmation/disconfirmation in the light of future research - empirical research. Yet to our mind, Frank's orientation does not admit of empirical analysis; rather, it in-forms study and action. That Frank chooses to present his pol-itical stance in terms which do not invoke political philosophy or ethics, but instead in terms claiming to be routinely descriptive of how things are in respect of rich and poor, is simply an error. As Frank's agent was intrinsic, so his politics are taken for granted. Recalling our notion of social theorizing as the deploy-ment of a morally informed categorical frame, it is clear that Frank has time to acknowledge neither aspect; but he instead proceeds straight to the fray with a Schumpeterian 'vision',[82] the refinement and explication of which he thereafter (wrongly) takes to be a matter of empirical research and appropriate ad-justment.

In sum, it should be clearly noted that Frank does not develop a scholarly treatise nor even a half-way systematically presented piece of social science;[83] he does not try to. Given this, the criticisms of the limited nature of Frank's early efforts rather seem to miss the point. A political pamphleteer is not to be judged as a political philosopher, an economist or a sociologist, though he may well have recourse to (and, indeed, contribute to) the work of all three. The pamphleteer presents a critique; and we can regard this as an elementary exercise in ideology-making.

3.33 Ranking ideologies

Frank's work lets us present, unequivocally, one characteristic of all the various efforts we have thus far considered: that is, they are ideologies. Following Bernstein, who has pointed out that as ideologies claim to be pertinent to action in the world then they are liable to rational criticism, we can now ask; just how is such an examination to be carried out?

We may begin by offering a proximate answer to this question, based simply upon the procedures we have either invoked or supposed in the course of our foregoing discussions. We can then look at some of the interpretations of critical theory and ask whether we can accomplish any preliminary revisions of our schema.

If an exercise in 'social theorizing' comprises the 'deployment of a morally informed categorical frame' (which procedure, re-garded ideally, moves from the rationalistically conceived 'general' to an empirically relevant set of 'particulars'), then the resultant 'ideology' may be analysed in terms of the notions of 'conception' and 'intent'. The former line is how we have argued ideologies are constructed, and the latter line is how we have analysed completed products. If we now juxtapose these two approaches, we can develop and extend our manner of analysing completed efforts by invoking our slogan in respect of the manner of constructing ideological efforts. Thus, as regards 'conception', we ask how is this notion to be extended in the light of our slogan 'morally informed categorical frame'. Similarly, as regards 'intent', we ask how it might be extended. This is to read them as ideologies. But also they are exercises in argument construction, and liable, therefore, to the usual rules of intellectual discourse in respect of formal consistency and so on. This procedure generates what seems to be a set of criteria whereby an ideological effort might be evaluated. We present it as a 'checklist'.

As regards conception:

1 Does the effort in question display 'reflexive consistency'; that is, does it acknowledge that it is an ideology? There seem to be three sorts of 'reflexive consistency'.

(a) Reflexive Consistency I (Internal). Does the effort in question acknowledge its own value engagement? Does it demonstrate an awareness of being a value-suffused product? Claims to the status of natural science objectivity are simply fatuous; similarly, pro-forma declarations are not enough. On the other hand, Mannheimian-style claims to the relativity of all value schemas are unacceptable.

(b) Reflexive Consistency II (External). Does the stance in question specify an agent of theory-execution whereby the effort can latch on to the world? This agent of theory-execution is understood to be integral to the stance; thus an agent that is simply an addendum designed to meet the requirements of the logic of theorizing will not do. Crudely, the effort has to be engaged. The plausibility of the schema, which will rest in part on the agent chosen and its supposed role, is another question.

(c) Reflexive Consistency III (General). Does the line in question explain itself? Is the effort itself compatible with the claims lodged in the effort? For example, Giddens reports, in respect of Habermas's treatment of the notion of ideology, that 'the concept of ideology, Habermas argued, did not just come into being with the rise of bourgeois society; it is actually only relevant to the conditions of public debate forged by that society'.[84] Thus Habermas inserts his concern for ideology into a historical schema which explains the occasion for his interest.

2 Does the stance in question display formal or conceptual consistency? This is the routine demand of all intellectual efforts, so we need not pursue it.

3 As regards the exchange between conception/intent, does the effort in question have recourse to a categorical frame whose explanatory scope is commensurate with the demands for explan-

ations flowing from the declared intent? That is, is the set of concepts used rich enough to cope with the ordinarily understood world, the practical starting point of the effort's engagement? Two examples will serve: Girvan seemingly invokes this when he speaks of those revisions of theory which gave 'the historical/ structural/institutional method the kind of theoretical and empirical content *needed to construct* a general theory of dependence and underdevelopment' (our emphasis).[85] The second example is of a failure: thus in respect of the great depression it is argued that the conceptual apparatus of the economic orthodoxy was incapable of treating the events. It was not a matter of the appropriate sub-areas of the discipline being undeveloped; rather, the economic orthodoxy denied that it could happen. Clearly, it was inadequate, conceptually, to its task of interpreting the economic world in such a manner as to permit rational action in respect of that world.

4 As regards the intent. The matter of 'intent' concerns the objectives and evaluations underpinning and guiding the effort. Generally, it seems as if we confront an issue of practicality.

(a) Intent (External). Is the posited intent tenable? Thus ideology, as we understand it, is not, for example, religion; it is essentially practical. In this light, if an ideology is intended to secure for its adherents/ agents, say, 'eternal cosmic wisdom', then we would wish to rank it lower than an ideology intended to secure, say, some piecemeal change in the distribution of economic power in society.

(b) Intent (Internal). Is the intent proper? That is, does the moral aspect of the effort's intent coincide with or diverge from typically 'Western' views? This question arises from those considerations of chapter 2 'The Idea of Development', wherein we postulated a general determinism in respect of the stances open to any 'Westerner'. An ideology affirming progress would have to be ranked higher than one denying it.

At this point the coupling of formal requirements to sociology of knowledge analyses, to generate a list of criteria whereby ideologies might be ranked, evidently begins to look strained. This issue of ranking takes us into matters of the philosophy of social science. Any further treatment of the matters must await specialist input: to that end, and in order to indicate how the discussion might be advanced from this point, we can introduce those interpreters of 'critical theory' mentioned above.

To begin this area of additional inquiry we must lodge a disclaimer. We are not presenting an introduction to Habermas's work. Out of the very wide-ranging and complex issues this theorist treats we are trying to pick out one area, that which extends our own immediate interests. The aspect of Habermas's work we are concerned with is the critique of ideology, and our investigations are very much of a preliminary nature. None the less we might note that the themes we tackle, in the context of Habermas's work, are occasioned by general issues of no little complexity and interest. Thus Bernstein argues that after the

self-conception of mainstream social science is challenged and
found wanting, a series of issues crop up: 'these cluster around
the interpretation and understanding of political and social reality' and, Bernstein adds, 'Looming in the background is the
central question of how one can rationally adjudicate among competing and conflicting interpretations.'[86]

With regard to this inquiry into ideology, we may note that it
is not to be taken as ideal-formal, but rather marxian-critical.
As Giddens puts it: 'Marx introduced a radically new perspective
into social theory. Henceforth the diagnosis of ideology became
a mode of penetrating beyond the consciousness of human actors,
and of uncovering the "real foundations" of their activity, this
being harnessed to the end of social transformation.'[87] This is
echoed by Bernstein: 'An ideology must be deciphered.'[88]
That this process of 'deciphering' is taken to be emancipatory is
revealed in Bernstein's detailing of the functions of ideology
critique. He begins with injunctions as to how it should proceed
in terms of providing descriptions of its object, and moves to
indicating how it should serve to actively dismantle its object:[00]

> The critique of ideology has several inter-related functions:
> (1) It must describe and accurately characterise the ideology,
> and be wary of caricature. (2) It seeks a depth interpretation
> of the ideology which will at once reveal how the ideology re-
> flects and distorts an underlying social and political reality.
> (3) It seeks to discover the material and psychological factors
> that reinforce and sustain it. (4) It seeks to isolate the fun-
> damental beliefs and interpretations that are the basis of the
> ideology, and to criticise them in order to expose their falsity.
> (5) It seeks to dissolve the legitimizing power of ideologies by
> overcoming resistance in the ideologies' defenders.

This describes a substantive task; above, we pursued formal
criteria.

If this tells us why we should conduct critiques of ideology and
in what areas we should develop our analyses, it does not tell us
how it is to be done. The answer from Habermas seems to be that
ideology critique is a matter of argumentation. This apparently
rather disappointing contribution is, characteristically, lodged
within a wider frame; that of a general theory of communication.
Here Habermas makes a distinction between 'speech action' and
'discourse', where the former supposes a consensus and the
latter is the realm of argumentation. This work is very abstract
and according to Bernstein,[90]

> what Habermas seeks to establish in his theory of communi-
> cative competence ... parallels what Marx sought to accomplish
> in his own critique of political economy. Marx argues that im-
> plicit in the concrete historical forms of alienation and ex-
> ploitation that now exist, are real dynamic potentialities for
> radically transforming this existing historical situation. In

a parallel manner Habermas argues that human discourse or speech - even in its systematically distorted forms - both pre-supposes and anticipates an ideal speech situation in which both the theoretical and practical conditions exist for unre-strained communication and dialogue.

This notion of an 'ideal speech situation' seems to serve two functions. First, it provides a regulative ideal for discourse; that is, when consensus has broken down and argumentation is occurring, there is a common or universal inherent goal of lang-uage which serves to regulate and order argument. It is rather analogous to, say, Popper's notion of objective truth, where this is taken as a regulative ideal of scientific endeavour: it is the goal we collectively agree to work towards. In Habermas's proposals for ideology critique, the 'ideal speech situation' plays the same role: it is the fixed point around which debate can be organized. Second, this equation of 'open debate' with 'open society', so to say, provides the integral value aspect of the work. As Marx fused matters of fact and value, so does Habermas, arguing that the fundamental structure of language supposes a free society.

More generally, ideology critique fits into a wider schema which serves to locate the theorist and his effort in the 'real world'; the metaphor invoked is that of the therapeutic ex-change of psychoanalysis. The scheme is presented as a tripartite process whereby the efforts of the critical theorist are 'authen-ticated'. We begin with the debate internal to the scholarly com-munity. Both Bauman and Bernstein read Habermas as making this the ambit of positive science (not positivist, they insist). Bauman observes: 'It is by the positive analysis of reality, which seeks its legitimation in the sedulous application of the ordinary fact-finding means of positive social science, that the hypotheses of critical knowledge, aimed at the restitution of undistorted communication are first advanced.'[91] This seems to be ambig-uous; for whilst we can grant that there is a 'moment' of disci-plinary engagement, the orthodox methods of social science are lodged within a view that denies the propriety of value-engage-ment. Yet by invoking 'ordinary fact-finding means of positive science' Bauman at once grants plausibility to orthodox claims, and seemingly reduces critical theorizing to a matter of an affirm-ation of the orthodox plus something. Bernstein even talks of causal analyses; which, recalling MacIntyre[92] on the appro-priate ambit of Humean causes, must be a nonsense.

The second stage of this process is the exchange between the theorist and his target. This encompasses a dialogue of theorist and target/subject, with the objective of transmitting to the sub-ject the habit of critical investigation of assumed common sense. Here the exchange is theorized by direct reference to the meta-phor of psychotherapy. Finally, the third stage sees the subject engaging in critical-theory-informed political activity. Thus crit-ical theories' efforts are authenticated to the extent that they become significant cultural objects.

There is much to question in these schemes. Yet our business is not a critical exposition of Habermas's scheme; it is rather the matter of ideology ranking. In this context we can offer two pre-liminary general conclusions.

(i) If we take competition between ideologies as being 'dis-torted communication', then invoking the notion of 'discourse' seems not inappropriate. But the question remains: just how helpful is it, in contrast to more familiar patterns of marxian-informed ideology critique? It is not immediately clear, in respect of ranking ideologies of development, that we gain all that much from Habermas's subtle schemes. Treating the clash of ideolog-ical lines as a matter for the deployment and counter-deployment of arguments would seem to be a very narrow treatment of these issues: for, after all, these are real political issues and exem-plify the conflicts of actual groups in society. Habermas, we may say, argues for the situation of mature Western capitalism and its social science and other ideologues/critics. Thus we derive themes of legitimation crisis.

(ii) In so far as we are treating, in our study, Western efforts to make sense of the Third World then Habermas's line helps us. In the sections above we have treated various stances which we took to be legitimating/ordering particular politically informed departures. The critique of ideology would seem to be a pre-requisite of any defensible and coherent conception of the nature of the exchange between the Third World as is, and Western ac-ademics with their social science.

The permissible intent and scope of the efforts of social science and academics remains an open question. The attempted export of techniques (growth theory), or recipes (modernization theory), or methods (neo-institutionalism), have been criticized in various ways. What has to be asked is, crudely: just what do Western social scientists think they can and should do in their discus-sions and writings on 'development studies'? Habermas offers a theory which locates the theorist in the world in a plausible fashion, and goes on to provide him with a specified job to do. This invitation to consider the precise role of theorist is probably Habermas's general lesson to us for the present. We will return to matters of 'critique' in chapter 8.

Part IV

The 'marxists'

INTRODUCTORY REMARKS

The relationship of Part IV to the study as a whole may be elucidated in three ways.

(a) Part IV may be taken to represent the third instantiation of the notion of progress in this 'career' of 'development studies'. Thus stage one,[1] dealt with in Part II, equated progress with securing economic growth; stage two, dealt with in Part III, equated progress with securing reasonable and rational programmes of social reform; and now with stage three we find progress equated with revolutionary change oriented towards the extension of democracy.

(b) Part IV represents our third distinguishable answer to the question of our Prologue as to the intellectual/disciplinary status of 'development studies'. Where the 'positivist conventional wisdom' of Part II answered that 'development studies' should be regarded as an element of, or application of, a primarily economics-based social science, and the 'radicals' of Part III that 'development studies' was both independent and novel with regard to a superseded economic conventional wisdom, the 'marxists' would submerge the interests of 'development studies' within a very much wider set of politico-historical concerns.

(c) Part IV may also be taken to represent the third stage in our reconstruction of the post-war 'career' of 'development studies'. That 'career' spans the period from the end of the Second World War to the end of the US war in South-East Asia. This encompasses the occasion for the establishment of US hegemony and the occasion for its dissolution. The efforts subsumed under the label 'development studies' reflect these wider issues. Thus stage one sees the establishment of an optimistic 'positivistic' line that peaks with Kennedy's 'New Frontier'; stage two sees a reaction and the emergence of various 'radical' schemes. Stage three sees the decline of consensus, the end of the post-war economic boom, the fatal embroilment of the US in Vietnam, and a rediscovery of marxian scholarship.

In sum, Part IV can be taken as providing the third instantiation of the notion of progress, the third distinguishable conception of the nature of 'development studies', and the third stage in our reconstruction of its post-war history.

7 Elements of the renewal of interest in marxian scholarship: the treatments of the Third World

1.0 INTRODUCTORY REMARKS

As regards the strategic issues that confront and thereby shape chapter 7, we may note that the renewal of interest in marxian scholarship that we will here refer to has been general; but our major interest at this juncture is in finding out what is to count as a marxian analysis of the Third World. We are isolating one aspect of the revival of scholarship and submitting it to a specific inquiry.

Our treatment differs from that which we would expect to produce if we followed the routine schema of milieu, demands, resources and product; in that whilst it takes off from a discussion of milieu, as is usual, it then presents the product (that is, 'neomarxism') via a review of typical criticisms of it, thereby sketching in some aspects of the issue of resources. Thus the matter of the proper nature of a marxian analysis of the Third World is kept central. We select our material and order it around our interest in the practical efforts of present-day theorists. The revision in procedure is, arguably, minor: instead of pursuing an extensive (and supposedly exhaustive) sociology of knowledge treatment of the newly presented marxian schemes, we offer a self-limiting inquiry that is compatible with the dictates of the logic of the study (a, b, and c, above) and our over-arching concerns in respect of the nature of social theorizing per se.

Three strategic issues confront us as we ask what is to count as a marxian analysis of the Third World.
(1) Dynamic of society: just what occasioned the resurgence of interest in marxian scholarship and analysis, and how were matters in and of the Third World involved?
(2) Dynamic of theory I: how has this renewal of interest in marxian work manifested itself in the context of discussions of the Third World; what have activists said?
(3) Dynamic of theory II: what is the scope of these discussions of the Third World within marxian scholarship; that is, what are the resources invoked, and how are they revised in works of scholarship?

2.0 DYNAMIC OF SOCIETY: THE OCCASION FOR THE RENEWAL OF INTEREST IN MARXIAN SCHOLARSHIP

Kay, writing in 1973, begins the preface to his book in the following way:[1]

186

Since 1968 the myth that *Capital* is unreadable has been exploded. Marxist literature, including Marx's own writings, now
proliferate as never before. This recrudescence has a real
basis in developments during the sixties: the collapse of consensus politics; the decomposition of the affluent society and
the failure of the Americans to win a decisive victory in Vietnam. It also has ideological roots, for as the world has moved
on academic social science has stood still.

The distinction drawn between 'real basis' and 'ideological roots'
seems both unnecessarily orthodox and somewhat ambiguous -
what is an ideological root? The metaphors seem confused; none
the less Kay provides us with a starting point. We will consider
the 'occasion for renewal' under two headings: first, looking at
the circumstances internal to the developed societies of the 'West'
(though New Left upheaval extended to Eastern Europe); and
then, second, we consider those events in the Third World which
permitted the co-option of the experience of revolutionary groups
by New Left thinkers.

2.1 Pressures for renewal of interest in Marx I: internal/immediate

If we approach these matters via the idea of the dissolution of
consensus politics, we can ask after the occasion of this dissolution. This is to present the New Left.[2] We can here note
some of the main elements in their activities and doctrines: that
is, we offer a very tentative sociology of knowledge note. It is
tentative for two reasons: one, that for our present purposes
we require little more; and two, the history of the 1960s and
early 1970s is too new, too undigested (indeed it is largely un-
written).

The dissolution of consensus was abrupt and surprising.
Birnbaum, writing in 1969, observes that 'It was only yesterday
that we were assured that our western societies were immune to
severe disruptions.'[3] He goes on to report that liberals saw a
secure pluralism, socialists a solidly engineered consent, and
conservatives a vulgar consumerism. Interestingly, he also
mentions radicals, taking them to perceive an iron cage of bur-
eaucratic rationality. Birnbaum asks, 'What were the signs we
missed?'[4] and answers:[5]

> In the first place, of course, we under-estimated the signif-
> icance of the Third World's struggle against the older and
> newer forms of imperialism, or rather, its multiple meaning
> and consequences. On one level the success of the Algerians
> and Cubans in liberating themselves ... caused the imperialist
> powers to change their strategies. The French and British
> (with the West Germans in tow) abandoned military occupation
> for economic penetration and manipulation ... The US, by

contrast, after the Cuban trauma went over to ever more
naked military intervention in the Third World, culminating in
the Vietnamese horror.

The example of the wars of liberation are one side of the experience of the Third World coin; the other is the reflexive self-
examination occasioned by Vietnam. Thus it is said, 'mobilization
for the war in Vietnam has exposed for all the world to see ...
the brutal visage of our ambiguous society: a monstrous technological apparatus tended by moral dwarfs'.[6] Birnbaum pushes
his point home: 'what has occurred is not a distortion but the
ultimate truth about our relation to the world'.[7] In the USA the
collapse of consensus and the gradual awakening of critical
scholarship from the predominant quietude of the Eisenhower era
is intimately bound up with the experience of Vietnam, but it has
for the US radicals a domestic anticipation/parallel in the Civil
Rights Movement.
We can note here one or two significant points in respect of
the genesis of civil rights in the USA. The first was the Supreme
Court desegregation of schools decision in 1954, and the second
was the Greensboro actions of 1960 where a sit-in at a Woolworth's
lunch counter snowballed into very large demonstrations. Students came into the South to aid civil rights activities. Goode
reports that:[8]

> The first organisation of the sixties to address itself to these
> mundane problems was the Student Non-violent Coordinating
> Committee .... The SNCC represented the earliest actual
> appearance of the New Left. It was established in 1960 to or-
> ganise the numerous white and black civil rights workers who
> had gone to work with the people in the south.

Goode traces the efforts of SNCC-associated groups, seeing them
absorbed by the status quo and eventually issuing in the radical
positions of Stokely Carmichael and Black Power. In 1962 SDS is
inaugurated at Michigan and advances the notions of participation
and community; and community-based initiatives become widespread.
Goode notes a third strand, the attention paid to reform of the
universities. Here we may note with Birnbaum that the New Left
became, to a very significant extent 'transmuted into a youth
movement'.[9] Birnbaum also avers that 'At the moment Herbert
Marcuse ... is the most influential of New Left thinkers on both
continents.'[10] We may now turn to the situation of that other
continent.
Statera, in what appears to be a Mannheimian-informed analysis of European student movements, argues that the prototype
was German. In particular, he cites the students of the Free
University of Berlin.[11] This institution, Statera reports, was
established as a propaganda exercise aimed at the University in
East Berlin (Humboldt), and its constitution was extremely lib-

eral. Through the late 1940s and 1950s its organizational liberties were increasingly brought into line with those of other
universities in West Germany. This was the immediate occasion
of protest - the loss of institutional liberties. Concomitantly, in
1959 the SPD revised its marxian constitution and expelled the
German students union (also called SDS), which promptly became the sole repository for socialism in Germany.[12]

From this point the scope of protest was ever-widening. Statera remarks that: 'Both chronologically and ideologically West
Berlin was the birthplace of European student protest.'[13]
'Vietnam was the crucial issue; but from the attack on American
imperialism protest extended to the repressive nature of capitalism, to authoritarianism, to the "manipulation of consciousness".'[14] In Germany Statera reports that Rudi Dutschke presented a Marcusian view; in France, Daniel Cohn-Bendit simplified the anti-authoritarian aspect, and Marcuse was run together
with Sartre and Fanon. It was in France that the New Left/
Student Movement attained its European apotheosis. From an
occupation of administrative offices in Nanterre by a few hundred
radicals, France moved to the verge of revolution. Gross reports,
'It was in fact precisely in the social science departments at
Nanterre that the revolutionary student movement was born.'[15]
He continues,[16]

> In May 1968 the student movement in France mobilized tens of
> thousands of students and acted as the detonator and catalyst
> of a chain reaction which eventually brought 10 million workers
> out on strike, thus precipitating a situation in which, for the
> first time in the history of an advanced capitalist country, a
> revolution might have been possible.

Young, treating the matter of the core identity of the New Left,
grants that much crystallized around the universities. Thus he
says: 'The structure of the University was viewed, in its paternalism and hierarchy, as a microcosm of power in the larger
society. Its authoritarianism might be less naked, its elites less
irresponsible but such organisations still appeared essentially
undemocratic.'[17]

The loss of institutional liberties which occasioned trouble in
West Berlin was one factor amongst others in a wider trend.
Thus all the treatments of 'student protest' that we have con-
sulted refer to the massive expansion in student numbers in the
1950s and 1960s. Provision for these extra numbers seems to
have been uneven; thus in Italy at Rome University and in Paris
at Nanterre there were very large numbers and a low level of
provision. More generally, it seems to be the case that authoritarianism and hierarchical patterns of organization predominated.
A final, often-noted, matter of the universities themselves was
the shift from 'scholarship' to 'expertise': notions of the pursuit
of liberal scholarship gave way to demands that universities provide skilled experts. At this point the issue of the role of the

university in late capitalist societies was raised.

Much of the ideology of the New Left seems to have revolved around the notions of technical-rational knowledge and its increasingly central role in society. Statera notes that: 'False consciousness, manipulated consensus, authoritarianism, and imperialism were concepts which gave shape to the developing utopia of the German students.'[18] Again,[19]

> Authoritarianism and repression were regarded as dominant themes in the social, political and cultural life of industrial societies whose aim is to establish an immutable order both internally and internationally. The extra-parliamentary opposition, and the students above all, could therefore become the counterpart, on the internal political level, of the Vietcong.

To summarize: thus far we have considered the New Left in America and in Europe. In the US we identified three themes: (a) Third World/Vietnam; (b) race/poverty; (c) university expansion and the slide from scholarship to expertise. In Europe we identified two themes: (i) Third World/Vietnam; (ii) university reform. Birnbaum's reference to Marcuse as pre-eminent figure is appropriate. Marcuse links matters of the Third World, the revision of Marx and the analysis of mature capitalism. Similarly influential figures are Debray and Fanon. We will come back to their work after reviewing the circumstances of the Third World through this period of the New Left. We can ask just what was going on in the Third World that resulted in the incorporation of the Third World as an aspect of the ideology of the New Left? Our interest lies neither in the elucidation of the doctrines of Third World*ism*, nor in the presentation of some general ('neutral') history of the period. Rather, we are interested in noting those events which rendered the experience of the Third World assimilable to the New Left ideology. Additionally, we should note that the division between Pressures for Renewal I and II reflects our particular interests, rather than any judgment on the relative strengths of the various elements taken into the New Left positions.

2.2 Pressures for renewal of interest in Marx II: external/adoptive

In the works of not a few students of African and Third World affairs there is a pervasive sense of disappointment, of promise unfulfilled. This is perhaps unsurprising. It is not restricted to members of the New Left. Hargreaves writes: 'During the 1950s many who wrote enthusiastically about the triumph of "African Nationalism" were excited by the creative possibilities of the period'.[20] But it is clear from the works of Davidson that such optimism was misplaced. Far from it being the case that nationalist elites were inevitably innovative, they were, if anything, the

reverse; and circumstances conspired to reinforce any such
tendencies. Hargreaves's remark that 'European expectations in
the later 1970s are less euphoric'[21] is apposite. His further
observation that 'hopes for vital and authentically African political life have receded even further'[22] may be taken to reflect
the naiveté of the original hopes, rather than any unproblematic
judgment upon the dynamism (or otherwise) of present African
societies.

Davidson analyses the circumstances of decolonization with
reference to the particular expectations of the principal actors
(groups). Thus he distinguishes the 'few' from the 'many'. The
former are the Western-educated elite; of these, those present
around the turn of the century, in the full flood of jingoistic
'new imperialism', established the basis of the subsequently
successful line of response. Davidson makes this their legacy:
'That influence established the world of the European nation
state as the manifest destiny of the colonial state ... so that
decolonization, when it came, was bound and fettered within the
terms of this nationalism.'[23] As for the latter group, the 'many',
Davidson reports that they were detached from the nationalists
and made a variety of accommodating responses to colonial rule.
During the years of the great slump and the Second World War,
the 'many' saw their established practices totally swept away.
Davidson notes, 'Every feature of dislocation stamped into the
African scene by the great depression was enlarged and sharp-
ened: the impoverishment of rural populations, the flight to
urban slums and shanty towns, the dismantlement of traditional
communities.'[24]

The two groups came together, briefly, in the early post-war
period. 'The new parties mobilized the clamour in the streets.
They became movements of mass support or mass acclaim. They
did not become movements of mass participation. The distinction
is important.'[25] The interests of the nationalists in political
power and the interests of the masses in social reform came together;[26]

> This convergence of the 1950's between struggle for nation-
> hood, the 'national struggle', and struggle for social gains,
> the 'social struggle', thus occurred as a mutual opportunism.
> The nationalists needed the masses and the masses needed the
> nationalists, but for purposes by no means necessarily iden-
> tical.

This is the gap that Davidson sees opening up later, so that the
new ruling group quickly comes to stand in the same relationship to the masses as did the old colonial authority. The imported
model collapsed and Davidson, adding that this is not surprising,
locates the historical interest elsewhere: 'in the working out of
confrontation between the colonial heritage and the pre-colonial
heritage ... and ... the resultant development of ideas concerned
with searching for a different model'.[27]

Davidson argues that the spectacle of corrupted elite groups and successions of military coups led to the recognition that any affirmation of the notion of democracy would entail a sharp revision in political theory and practice.[28] This new politics slowly began to emerge. It proposed ditching elite-ordered capitalist nation-building in favour of an identification by leaders with the problems of the masses. 'This new politics ... became known as the politics of liberation. Its development after 1966 occurred in many forms.'[29] The examples of the independent states of Tanzania and Somalia are cited; and the efforts of the then non-independent are noted. Thus Cabral and PAIGC, Mondlance and FRELIMO, and the MPLA in Angola are listed. Of them, Davidson observes that they 'may be said to have been the first in Africa to have fully indigenized a marxist analysis .... But what their evolution really displayed was an African politics of mass participation in a mature phase.'[30]

The struggle against a repressive and often brutal and unjustifiable colonial authority; the creative revision of democratic/ socialist/marxist theorems; the identification with the masses, with the corollary of the affirmation of the centrality of social reform; all these, it would seem, are the bases whereby activity within the Third World might be embraced by radicals in the developed nations. Both Hargreaves and Davidson focus their attention on sub-Saharan Africa, but the claim may be extended to the Third World in general. Thus Chaliand follows Davidson in making Cabral and PAIGC genuinely revolutionary; he also adds China, Korea, Vietnam and Cuba as places where political and social revolution has occurred. We can note Chaliand's agreement with Davidson in respect of the distinction between social and political, and of the crucial nature of the social struggle. The precise contents of Chaliand's list we will not debate. There is a further matter to note, and this is the manner in which revolutionary struggle in the Third World was taken on board by the New Left.

The clue has been offered by Birnbaum: the circumstances of war. The experiences of Vietnam, Algeria and Cuba are central to the manner of co-option by the New Left of the experience of groups in the Third World. Chaliand treats it as myth-making; he observes:[31]

A sort of Third World euphoria began to be felt at the close of the 1950's, during the Algerian war, and it was soon given a boost by the radical turn of events in the Cuban revolution in 1960-61 ... the Algerian revolution, geographically so close to Europe, came to symbolize the anticolonialist struggle.

In the case of Vietnam: 'The war in Vietnam embodies the very model of the Third World myth: a war of the people victoriously resisting the most powerful imperialism.'[32] In sum, we may say that it would seem to be the case that the pervasive activism of the New Left, when confronted with genuinely relevant events

in the lurid light of the circumstance of brutal warfare, issued
in an anguished, and inevitably over-emphatic, co-option of the
proffered lessons: hence Chaliand's 'myth'.
Of the myth, Chaliand notes:[33]

> Third Worldism saw the revolutionary potential of the Third
> World as deriving from two main factors: on the one hand, the
> grinding, humiliating poverty of the masses, and the contra-
> dictions that produced it, and on the other hand, the crisis
> that could not fail to erupt in industrial countries, once rev-
> olutionary regimes put a stop to their pillage of Third World
> materials.

He adds that 'Third Worldism was a phenomenon born of the crisis of Stalinism and fed by a policy of peaceful coexistence. It
prospered in the 1960's because of the new hopes in the spread
of socialist revolution in and by the Third World. But it has
turned out to be a myth.'[34] Myth it may have been, and Chaliand's argument is persuasive. Yet this is not to say that the
original impulse to embrace these novel contributions to theor
izing/reforming mature capitalism were wrong-headed. They were
not, as we see below.
   Our general interest in Part IV is in identifying the proper
nature of a marxian analysis of the Third World. It would be
appropriate to begin with the efforts most closely associated with
the general renewal of interest in marxian scholarship: theorists
associated with or embraced by the New Left. This will be our
point of departure for considering some of the various post-war
efforts to present a marxian analysis of the Third World.

3.0 DYNAMIC OF THEORY I: NEW LEFT THEORIZING AND THE
THIRD WORLD

Young, who argues that 'it would be quite erroneous to suppose
that the NL was ever a marxist movement',[35] tends to follow
Chaliand in regarding the co-option by the New Left of struggles
in the Third World as (at best) ill-advised. He is less sympathetic to the root of the interest than is Chaliand; though iron-
ically his style of inquiry ought to make it easy to answer the
question of why the co-option was attempted, because he uses
sociology of knowledge descriptions and concerns himself with
how the New Left constructed their ideological efforts. Young
reports that:[36]

> Factually and ideologically the division between the urban ad-
> vanced sector and peasant society was a world wide division
> that cut across national boundaries. An imagery was needed
> to express this opposition, and the images of Fanon and Mao
> were combined with dreams of a Third World peasant revolution
> strangling and dispossessing the exploitative metropolitan

areas. In the West this was an imagery compounded of roman-
ticism, guilt, compassion and pure misunderstanding about the
relationship between the peasants and their liberators.... The
character of these superficial identifications can, it is also
argued, be explained in their association with a more generalized attack on Western values, mounted both by the counter-
culture and black American writers, in common with both
African and Asian theorists and Western metropolitan intellectuals like Sartre.

3.1 Are there significant analogies?

We may begin a reply to Young's dismissive line by inquiring
into the similarities between New Left and Third World work and
circumstances. Are there significant analogies upon which the
attempted co-option might be seen to have been based, or was
the whole episode simply and essentially a fatuous passing intellectual fashion? Above (in 2.2) we offered general remarks relevant to this question; here we are trying to be a little more
specific. The following would seem to be the central analogies:
(i) the struggle against a repressive and unjustifiable authority;
(ii) the centrality of the task of social reform; (iii) the creative
revision of marxian/democratic/socialist theorems. We shall consider each of these areas of analogy in turn, and refute Young's
claims that the attempted co-option was foolish. (Our position,
however, is a comment upon one aspect of the occasion of renewal of interest in marxian scholarship, and not a commitment
to Third Worldism.)
    (i) The struggle against a repressive and unjustifiable auth-
ority. That this circumstance holds (or held) in the colonial
territories ought not to be in doubt. With Davidson in the case
of Africa, and Frank in the case of Latin America, we have seen
the suggestion that the history of the exchange of rich and poor
nations has been one of the largely unprincipled exploitation of
the latter by the former. An exchange that, so Davidson and
Frank report, resulted in the complete destruction of pre-contact
social forms and the absorption of the native population into
colonial forms of life. Fanon (recalling the style of our chapter 5
characterization of the options open to the colonial power confronted by 'nationalist developmentalism') characterizes the
relationship of colonial power and native thus: 'The colonial world
is a world cut in two. The dividing line, the frontiers are shown
by barracks and police stations.'[37] Fanon goes on to distinguish
between the circumstances of the exercise of power in metropolitan and colonial areas:[38]

> In the capitalist countries a multitude of moral teachers, coun-
> sellors and 'bewilderers' separate the exploited from those in
> power. In the colonial countries on the contrary the policeman
> and the soldier, by their immediate presence and their frequent

and direct action maintain contact with the native and advise
him by means of rifle-butts and napalm not to budge. It is
obvious here that the agents of government speak the language
of pure force.

The bifurcation of the colonial world is absolute: 'This world
divided into compartments, this world cut in two is inhabited by
two different species.'[39] Fanon treats the matter of repression:
that the colonial authorities' behaviour is unjustifiable he takes
to be luminously self-evident, and we can follow the historians
we have cited and grant that claim. The question that is crucial
is: to what extent can it be argued that the mass of the people
in the rich nations stand in relation to their rulers as the natives to the colonial authorities? This is the claimed analogy.

In New Left sources, the slenderness of the analogy is granted
(tacitly) in so far as notions of repression are presented less in
terms of economic disparities and mechanisms of force and more
in cultural terms. Thus we have notions of, say, 'repressive tolerance' or the 'engineering of consent'. The precise extent and
nature of the comparison's implausibility as an analogy is a
matter for debate. At the most general level, it may be observed
both that the majority in the nations of the West do inhabit inegalitarian, unequal, class societies, and that their absolute
level of living is far superior to that of the mass of people in the
UDCs. The resemblance seems to be one of form rather than substance. On the other hand, the issue is easier to tackle in respect of the linked point about justifiability, since this is more
of a formal matter anyway. That the behaviour of the colonial
authorities is (was) unjustifiable we granted above. What, then,
of the theorems of legitimation presented in and for the rich
nations? Here we can observe that the balance of the argument
lies heavily in the left's favour. The New Left's critique of the
pretensions to liberal scholarship of Western universities are a
case in point; the critique of the slide from scholarship to expertise is clearly of continuing relevance. More generally, the justifying theorems of Western nations - 'liberal democracy' - have
been effectively demolished by Macpherson, whose arguments we
rehearsed in chapter 2. In the case of the justifiability of authority in metropolitan and colonial areas, the analogy is, to our
mind, a significant one.

(ii) The centrality of the task of social reform. This point requires that we make clear the distinctions between the stances of
the New Left and the reformist or social democratic left, on the
one hand, and on the other, between episodes of decolonization
and revolutionary wars of liberation.

Young distinguishes between an 'old' New Left and a 'new' New
Left. One could associate the 'old' New Left with the bourgeois
nationalist episodes of decolonization. Hargreaves apparently
does this when he speaks of the disappointment of those who
looked to fruitful collaboration (seen above, 2.2). Pursuing this
line, we would then wish to associate the 'new' New Left with the

experience of the revolutionary wars of liberation. But this might
be held to involve a wrong association, based upon an unjustifiable fusion of 'old' New Left and reformist elements. Both the
'old' and the 'new' New Left looked to both social and political
change. But as Davidson has argued in respect of the African
situation, the coincidence of interest on the part of nationalist
elites and impoverished masses was brief and unusual. The interests of those two colonial groups are taken to be divergent.
Thus the disillusionment of the reformers is explained;[40] as is
the attention given by the New Left to the wars of liberation,
where mass social reform is made integral to political activity.

Davidson treats these matters in broad historical terms. Distinguishing the 'few' and the 'many', he observes of the populist
nationalist movements of the early post-Second World War years
that 'this convergence of the 1950's between struggle for nation-
hood ... and struggle for social gains ... occurred as a mutual
opportunism'.[41] This gap then opened up. Davidson is un-
surprised, and compares the post-independence confusion of
Africa with the period following the dissolution of the Austro-
Hungarian empire. He concludes:[42]

> Once again it was shown that this way of solving the national
> problem could not solve the social problem; that the colonial
> state turned nation state could not be usefully reformed, but
> must be revolutionized; and that only a clear priority to the
> solving of the social problem by whatever means the future
> might reveal, would be able to fulfil the promises of national
> freedom.

This affirmation of the centrality of the 'social problem' - that is,
of the circumstances of the mass as opposed to the elite - is seen
by Davidson as the key to real change. Both the abandonment
of notions of elite-ordered modernization, and the acknowledgment that the genuine pursuit of democracy would entail sharp
revisions of conception and strategy: 'the politics of liberation'.[43]

Davidson's list of those states attempting new departures has
been noted; so too has Chaliand's scepticism. Thus Chaliand
reports that the 'term socialism has been widely abused.'[44]
There have been many bourgeois revolutions and 'these regimes
differ markedly from the three or four really radical revolutions
that have occurred in the Third World since the end of World War
Two: in China, North Korea, Vietnam, and Cuba.'[45] This,
however, seems to be a difficult line of inquiry. Sets of lists can
always be disputed, the more so when those nation states likely
to be listed are also those where any changes in policies are
going to be accompanied by elaborate revisions of justificatory
schemas. What we want to take from all this is the association of
democracy in the Third World with 'liberation politics', which
attempts to fuse matters of social reform and political organization.
There is undoubtedly such a distinction to be drawn, and for the

present this is all we need. Just how and where it should be
drawn in practice need not detain us. Rather, we ask: how
plausible is the analogy between such New Left-cited 'liberation
politics' and the nature of New Left political activity and doctrinal statement?

Young's work shows how confused was the brew of social criticism labelled the New Left. We can pick out some elements. Thus
organizationally and generationally there is 'a vision of young
activists facing middle aged quietist leaderships'.[46] Young
picks out the SNCC and Committee of 100 as key groups in the
New Left, and of them reports that 'Both were infused with an
anarchistic spirit of decentralism, direct action at centres of
power, propaganda of the deed, non-cooperation with unjust
laws, and symbolic revolution.'[47] The movement regarded itself as a community and as an alternative in embryo. Young goes
on: 'The dominant NL themes of the mid-1960's were those which
linked decentralization and community decision making in a par-
ticipatory democracy.'[48]

With the New Left there is an internal/external distinction that
can be tentatively made in order to help grasp what they were
about. Thus the 'internal' aspect of their line was the 'existen-
tialist' insistence on authenticity. All the while, with the New
Left, political action was interpreted as integral to life in general; 'personal liberation' was taken to be firmly bound up with
'social liberation', and political activity ordinarily understood
was removed from the centre of the stage. We may compare this
with, say, Fanon on the social-psychological redemptive value of
revolutionary violence - when the black revolutionist kills a white
settler he destroys two men, etc. Or again, Debray's elucidation
of the dictum that 'it is the duty of the revolutionary to make the
revolution'. None the less, political action ordinarily understood
(albeit reworked) is fully present in the New Left, and here is
the 'external' aspect. Thus the New Left as a political movement
pursues notions of community/participation/democracy in the
areas of civil rights and poverty programmes, in university reform and in the anti-war movement. Similarly, the guerrilla movements pursue a goal of independent and democratic statehood.
States of affairs rather than states of mind. The analogy invoked,
or claimed, equates 'liberation' in the colonial or neo-colonial
territories, with its concern for the 'social question', with 'par-
ticipatory democracy' and libertarian/socialist ideas about people
taking control of their own lives. The analogy would seem to be
a good one.

(iii) The creative revision of democratic/socialist/marxian theorems. Cranston, touching upon this issue, remarks that 'this
association of the New Left with the reformulation of Marxism may
account in part for its appeal'[49]. This seems to be a grudging
acknowledgment of the obvious. More informative is Young's report that, 'It is rather amongst the dissident communists of the
West ... that the intellectual origins of the New Left are usually
first discerned .... Searching for a third way beyond the 'empty

cant' of current liberalism, and the Marxist-Stalinist orthodoxies.'[50] Young regards this searching as issuing in a catholic
internationalism, and notes that: 'In particular Third World
movements did not seem to be slavishly following previous revolutionary models.'[51] Here, then, is one acknowledgment of a
clear similarity between New Left and liberation movements: both
affirmed notions of democracy/socialism/marxism, and both
offered substantial revisions to the established orthodoxies.

This is a claim that can either be left at this simple level or
extended into a detailed debate. We will leave any consideration
of the revisions made by Fanon and Debray until later; here we
can note that both are taken to be idiosyncratic in their marx-
ism(s). Thus of Fanon, Caute says that '[he] was not a marxist
in any traditional sense'.[52] Blackburn, noting the influence of
Cuba on Debray, argues that: 'What above all distinguishes these
writings is their relentlessly Leninist focus on making the revolution, as a political technical and military problem.'[53]

As regards the New Left, we have seen that Young takes them
to be non-marxian and follows Statera in regarding the decline of
the New Left as associated with its turning towards marxian formulations. Young discusses the available languages of dissent
and takes marxism as ready-made. He argues thus:[54]

> The NL has often been interpreted as a further revision of
> Marxist ideas.... Of course any search for a new revolutionary
> strategy had inevitably involved dialogue with Marx.... But it
> would be quite erroneous to suppose that the NL was ever a
> 'marxist' movement.

Young grants its interest, but feels that: 'the principal impression remaining is of wide ranging ideological eclecticism'.[55]
This lack of any clear and coherent self-image is cited as the
root cause of the eventual collapse of the New Left. Young continues, 'The crude conceptualizations that later emerged, the
piecemeal strategies, were an inevitable counterpart to the anti-
intellectualism, pragmatism and moralism of the movement; as a
result they left a vacuum that would be filled by concepts and
strategies drawn from dated or external models.'[56] Hence the
collapse into marxism. In reply, we can note that, even granting
all the diffuseness of the New Left elements, if it had a core then
that core was a libertarian marxist humanism. Claiming otherwise
is simply tendentious, and indeed this last quotation from Young
rather tends to contradict the earlier ones cited above.

If we compare the revisions to respective orthodoxies on the
part of the New Left and Fanon/Debray, we get something like
the following: presented diagramatically.

Revision	Fanon/Debray	New Left
Activism	Orthodox CP line dropped in favour of vanguardist activism.	Orthodox political channels ignored in favour of direct action.
Violence	Orthodox ambiguity dropped in favour of a central affirmation of role of violence.	Un-orthodox direct action becomes increasingly violent.
Agency of Change	Proletariat dropped in favour of peasantry and lumpenproletariat.	Proletariat dropped in favour of marginal groups.
Organization and strategy	Military/political are fused, and liberation is to be formative for the new nation.	Means exemplify ends: the monolithic party is eschewed for anarchistically diffuse activity.
Moralism	Voluntarist making of the socialist revolution Redemptive violence of zero sum game.	Self and social liberation are taken to be inter-linked.
Practicality	Cuba/Algerian focus	University/anti-war focus

On these bases the claimed analogy between 'liberation politics' and New Left efforts must be seen to be plausible. It is here that the general renewal of interest in marxian scholarship and radical interest in the Third World coincided. From this point the marxian interest in the Third World generated its own momentum, so to say; and from here on the material we treat becomes increasingly specialist and increasingly technical. Now as this matter of the revision of Marx is of general interest to us, we will consider further those revisions effected by the early theorists of the Third World, Fanon and Debray. In addition to the issue of the production of circumstance-relevant general statements, attempted by Fanon and Debray, we must note that the particular notion of 'learning the lessons of experience' will exercise us.

3.2 Theorists, practitioners, interpreters: Fanon and Debray

3.21

We may now turn to the doctrines of these early theorists of the circumstances of the Third World. We begin by noting that both Debray and Fanon[57] are reporting on the lessons of experience. With Dobb we presented one unpacking of the view that social

theorizing was essentially a matter of the construction of ideological schemas. We made use of a model of the theorist which
permitted analysis of social-theoretical efforts under the four
headings of milieu, demand, resources and product. The theorist was presented as responding to political demands to provide
interpretative guides to action. This raises, familiarly, questions
of validation and notions of a process theory of truth. But also
it is evident that if we regard theorizing as a social activity
then we can introduce matters pertaining to time-scales. Theory
and event can be related in more than one fashion.[58] Most
simply (and naively), we have the following implied scheme: (a)
circumstances; (b) produced theory; (c) event, called forth by
theory-informed action; (d) new circumstance.

Continuing in this simple fashion, another way in which theory
and event may be related is presented by the case of Debray,
who is taken by Minogue to be the exponent of the Cuban revolutionary process. The distinctive revisions of Marx that are
made here revolve around the practical activity of being a revolutionary. Minogue comments: 'It is here - in the area where
theory is related to practice - that the Cuban revolution has
made its major contribution to Marxism.'[59] Minogue goes on to
explain as follows:[60]

> Che's Marxism, like everything else about him, is concrete and
> practical. We hear little about historical epochs and very little
> analysis of class relations. We do hear a great deal about the
> guerilla. Developed into a theory[61] the guerilla generates
> the idea of the foco, the process of revolutionary detonation
> by which a small band of guerillas set up a centre of attraction
> in the sierras and bring the capitalist or neo-colonialist re-
> gimes to its knees. It is essential to this theory, certainly as
> developed by Debray that the foco be regarded as simultan-
> eously military and political.

Minogue reports that those who generalize from the case of
Cuba use 'inductive reasoning' and produce false theories as a
result. Minogue argues thus: if we see marxism as a social
phenomenon, then its history is marked by its heretics. They
are the ones who have disregarded established party lines and
gone ahead and forged new schemes of revolution. This is seen
as presenting the problem of general theoretical interpretation:
'each change has been followed by a development of theory which
purports to learn the lessons of the new experience'.[62] Now
clearly learning these lessons is a real task, and thus Minogue
has a genuine point. Yet he hints that the task is of adapting
dogma (where this is taken in its usual pejorative sense) to new
circumstances. Arguing thus begs the interesting question of
how these lessons are learnt.

Debray reports on his own efforts as follows:[63]

We are never completely contemporaneous with our present.
History advances in disguise; it appears on stage wearing the
mask of the preceding scene, and we tend to lose the meaning
of the play. Each time the curtain rises continuity has to be
re-established. The blame, of course, is not history's, but
lies in our vision, encumbered with memory and images learned
in the past. We see the past superimposed on the present,
even when the present is a revolution.

Now if we compare this with our simple schema of theorizing then
clearly Debray is emphasizing the 'retrospective' aspect. This is
concerned with making sense after the event; whereas the above
schema was forward-looking, whilst invoking the past as an
inevitable/enabling jumping-off point. Debray, in contrast, lays
a heavier stress on the idea of a 'conventional wisdom'. On the
radical intellectual as potential guerrilla, Debray recalls Castro's
view; thus,[64]

> the intellectual will try to grasp the present through precon-
> ceived ideological constructions and live it through books. He
> will be less able than others to invent, improvise, make do
> with available resources, decide instantly on bold moves when
> he is in a tight spot. Thinking that he already knows he will
> learn more slowly, display less flexibility.

Two points are involved here; one, the matter of the requisite
flexibility of mind required to interpret the lessons proffered by
events; and, two, the matter of the imaginative innovation of the
practitioner faced with responding to, rather than interpreting,
events.
   If we distinguish between the roles of, on the one hand, interpreters, and on the other, theorists and practitioners, then we
can present the following schema. Thus, the revision of theory
after the fact of revolution is, it seems, the interpreter's task.
Revision of theory before or during the revolutionary change
belongs to theorist and practitioner respectively. Minogue fails
to make this distinction, and he also offers a wrong criticism.
Thus he claims: 'The Russians, the Chinese, the Yugoslavs and
the Cubans have all indulged in this exercise. Its logic is of
course inductive. It consists in transporting the most striking
facts of the successful experience into abstract terms and generating theory from them.'[65] This is false; if the 'learning' is
done crudely then the argument strategy may be taken as inductive, but not the logic. A general objection to inductive
reasoning will not invalidate lessons drawn from the experience
simply because the elements of the experience picked out will be
selected in the light of established theorizing. The 'learning' is
not simply inductive. Indeed, returning to Minogue's 'adapting
dogma' jibe, we can reply that it might be better to see this sort
of 'learning' exercise - with, say, the case of Debray, with its
detailed elucidation/celebration of the Cuban episode - as casu-

istry. Indeed, at one point Debray quotes Althusser, 'Marxists
know that no tactic is possible which does not rest on some
strategy and no strategy which does not rest on some theory.'[66]
It might be said that this sentiment rather seems to go against
the above-noted emphases; a little like a denial of the role of
spontaneity, novelty, or plain fluke in practical activity, in order
to speed the re-absorption of the novel into the established canon.
Althusserian idealism and Cuban voluntarism sit uneasily in
Debray. None the less these remarks do confirm the point that
'learning the lessons of experience' involves an accommodating
adjustment to general conceptions, and not any simple process of
the elaboration of a revised set of generalizations. If Fanon and
Debray interpreted their respective experiences of revolutionary
guerrilla warfare, then we may ask: given that the term 'casu-
istry' implies accommodating doctrinal revisions, just what revisions of marxian work to they propose?

3.22

On the part of Guevara/Debray, taken as representatives for the
Cuban revolutionary experience, we have already had occasion to
note Minogue's summary: 'It is here - in the area where theory
is related to practice - that the Cuban revolution has made its
major contribution to Marxism.'[67] Let us turn to the work of
Debray and consider this contribution. We may note, incidentally,
that Minogue reports that this contribution 'was brought to its
fullest maturity in the writings of Regis Debray';[68] and Blackburn too observes that 'Debray is a faithful mirror of Cuban
Marxism.'[69] Debray is evidently an appropriate subject for us,
the more so in view of Blackburn's report that:[70]

> Debray left France in the early 'sixties partly because of the
> hopelessness and corruption of the French Left - underlined by
> the abject role of the French CP during the Algerian war. In
> the event he has contributed significantly to the re-birth of
> a revolutionary Left in Europe and North America by making
> available to them the experience of the Latin American guer-
> rillas.

We may begin this brief treatment of Debray by noting his
thoroughgoing practical intent. He is concerned both to interpret
and learn the lessons of Cuba and to present the actions/theories
of the revolutionists as practical activity. Blackburn notes this,
speaking of Debray's 'technics': a detailed concern for the nuts
and bolts of insurrection. But the matter is also slightly broader.
Debray is concerned to interpret the Cuban experience; so the
'history', as it were, is central and thereafter links are made to
established areas of debate. Debray is to be understood as interpreting the experience of Cuba to us, and not as proposing some
set of doctrinal revisions contrived by abstract reflection. We can
see this in the case of the matters of violence and voluntarism. In

the case of violence, Debray says: 'In semi-colonial countries, even more than in developed capitalist countries the State poses the decisive political problem.'[71] Hitherto that problem has been approached via the coup d'état, or by mass insurrectionary activity. Debray reads Castroism as having solved the problem of the appropriate strategy of active revolutionary action in Latin America; presented as the theory of the guerrilla foco. He argues as follows 'To sum up: the entire apparatus of organised violence belongs to the enemy .... What then is to be done?'[72]

The foregoing presents Debray's report of the Fidelists' appreciation of the particular circumstances of Cuba, and arguably of Latin America generally. It poses the central, crucial, issue of the appropriate creative response. Debray continues:[73]

> To Lenin's question, Fidelism replies in terms which are similar .... Under an autocratic regime only a minority organisation of professional revolutionaries, theoretically conscious and practically trained in all the skills of their profession can prepare a successful outcome for the revolutionary struggle of the masses. In Fidelist terms, this is the theory of the foco, of the insurrectionary centre.

3.23

If we turn to consider Fanon's work, in particular 'The Wretched of the Earth', we note immediately that it grows out of the experience of the Algerian war of independence. Caute reports that 'Algeria had belonged to France since 1830 and it was colonized in depth'.[74] When in 1957 the socialist premier, Mollet, gave way to nationalist pressures 'the scene was set for total war ... which spread from Algeria to France itself, decimated the Algerian people, brought down the Fourth Republic and raised the spectre of military rule or fascism in France.'[75] In 'The Wretched of the Earth', Fanon offers a general treatment of the Third World that is didactic, allusive, exhortative, 'diagnostic', as Worsley has it;[76] and which is steeped in Sartrean existentialism. Caute notes that: 'the wide canvas of the Third World is filled in with sweeping strokes of a brush exclusively dipped in African paint.... The Algerian revolution is implicitly treated as a model for all of Africa.'[77]

So much for the general occasion of theorizing; if we now note its character in terms of its appreciation of its circumstances and its response thereto, we have the following. (i) Fanon analyses the colonial scene in terms of a radical bifurcation of society; as we have seen, he speaks of a 'world divided into compartments... cut in two ... inhabited by two different species'.[78] (ii) Significant change is taken as a zero sum game. It extends to the notions of 'truth' and 'goodness'; here Fanon argues 'Truth is that which hurries on the break-up of the colonialist regime.... The good is quite simply that which is evil for "them".'[79] (iii) Fanon proposes that action should be ordered around the revo-

lutionary potential of the rural peasantry and the urban poor.
The reasons behind the affirmation of the need for violent
revolution are two-fold. First, this bifurcation of society leaves
all weapons in the hands of the colonial power. There is a
straightforwardly repressive government facing the indigenous
people; there is, it might otherwise be said, no area of 'civil
society'. Second, Fanon notes that the ease of co-option of elite
nationalists by the colonial regime entails that, if there is to be
progress, it needs must be achieved by violent means. Thus,
whilst granting the usual Leninist requirements vis à vis the
state, Fanon goes on to lay heavy stress on the unsatisfactory
character of the indigenous nationalist parties. Caute reports
this as the last step in Fanon's evolution as a social philosopher:
thus, 'First he had assailed prejudice and mystification; then he
had turned his fire against colonialism itself; now he recognised
that decolonization would only be authentically revolutionary if
it was also authentically socialist.'[80] The requirement of violence is derived, it appears, from the experience of radicals becoming absorbed by neo-colonial circumstances and from his
appreciation of the character of colonial Algeria. Thereafter, it
seems, violence is embraced as redemptive.

Fanon's proposals resemble Debray's: the nationalist party will
sooner or later throw off its genuine radicals, and these will
discover a home with the rural population. Fanon celebrates the
peasantry as the true source of revolutionary power and plots
their course through revolutionary war. We can here quote at
length:[81]

> The nationalist militant who has fled from the town in disgust
> at the demagogic and reformist manoeuvres of the leaders
> there, disappointed by political life, discovers in real action a
> new form of political activity which in no way resembles the
> old. These politics are the politics of leaders and organisers
> living inside history who take the lead with their brains and
> their muscles in the fight for freedom. These politics are
> national, revolutionary and social and these new facts which
> the native will come to know exist only in action. They are the
> essence of the fight which explodes the old colonial truths
> and reveals unexpected facets, which brings out new meanings
> and pinpoints the contradictions camouflaged by these facts.
> The people engaged in the struggle who because of it command
> and know these facts go forward, freed from colonialism and
> fore-warned of all attempts at mystification, inoculated against
> all national anthems. Violence alone, violence committed by the
> people, violence organised and educated by its leaders, makes
> it possible for the masses to understand social truths and
> gives the keys to them. Without that struggle, without that
> knowledge of the practice of action, there's nothing but a
> fancy dress parade and the blare of trumpets. There's nothing
> save a minimum of readaption, a few reforms at the top, a flag
> waving; and down there at the bottom an undivided mass, still
> living in the Middle Ages, endlessly marking time.

3. 24

We can now offer a comparative summary of the themes of Fanon
and Debray.
(1) The Fidelist appreciation of the character of the Third
World state is echoed by Fanon. The power of the ruling group
is centred on the state and there is no effective diffusion of
power through 'civil society'. The Fidelist reaction to this auto-
cracy is shared by Fanon: insurrectionary guerrilla violence and
the affirmation of home-grown models of action. Thus Debray,
arguing that the foco is the paradigm of an answer to the problem of the state in Latin America, goes on to insist upon the
locally developed links of military and political activity. He is at
pains to distinguish it from imported models which are not derived from the Cuban experience and which have not proved
successful. Fanon too insists upon local circumstance-relevant
solutions. In criticizing the bourgeois nationalist parties, he
observes: 'The notion of the party is a notion imported from the
mother country. This instrument of modern political warfare is
thrown down just as it is, without the slightest modification,
upon real life with all its infinite variations and lacks of balance.'[82]
(2) Having made this fundamental appraisal, much of the rest
is a matter of tactics. Here Debray offers the detail whilst Fanon
contents himself with the broadest of sketches. For Fidelism this
concerns the role of the guerrilla foco; the 'small motor' that
occasions the activity of the 'big motor' of the masses. Fanon too
offers a vanguardist schema, involving radical groups splinter-
ing from the nationalist party and finding their allies (and the
agent of change) in the rural peasantry. In Fanon's work there
is no counterpart to Debray's 'technics'; the language is more
general.
(3) Debray and Fanon resemble each other on the related point
of the dismissal of established radical views and groups. Thus
Debray rejects not only 'putschism' and 'mass action', but also
the line of the Communist Parties with regard to the preliminary
construction of a bourgeois nationalist state. Fanon follows this,
and both condemn established and orthodox aspirant rulers as
incompetent to the task of initiating autonomous national development.
(4) Both Fanon and Debray concern themselves wholly with the
pursuit of socialism. The circumstances of their theorizing are
such that the process with which they are concerned can be
treated as a zero sum game: hence the 'black and white' style of
their work. The corollary of this is their 'practicality': both are
absorbed in the circumstances of their respective struggles, and
general discussions of the conditions of successful action. The
realm of the 'orthodox left', the pursuit of a marxian science of
the social is, in their work, muted.[83] That the Cuban and
Algerian revolutions in fact represent 'creative responses' is
taken as evident from their success. Explanations of the con

ditions for success of insurrections do not go far beyond a description of the circumstances of which they treat the histories.

3.3 Summary note

Against Young, it is clear that the disposition of the New Left
thinkers to attempt the co-option of the 'liberation struggles' to
their own efforts was based on significant analogies in respect
both of circumstances and of analyses attempted. The events/
theorizing in the Third World provided a ready stock of 'examples' that could be drawn upon to illuminate the nature of
politics and the lines of attack upon the status quo. We have
looked at three such analogies: that of the struggle against repressive and unjustifiable authority; that of the affirmation of
the centrality of social reform; and, finally, the creative revision of socialist/democratic/marxian themes. Given the general
interests of this study, the matter of the third analogy was of
particular interest.

Fanon and Debray we took to present circumstance-particular
efforts of interpretative writing; though both shade off into
presenting work that is of the practitioner (partly this is a matter of their own involvement and partly of their reception by
wider, Western audiences, perhaps). Neither Fanon and Debray,[84] nor the New Left, offer any systematically elaborated
revision of marxian theory. Young, indeed, presents it as a
crucial failing of the New Left that it never established its own
distinct critical language, and instead rested content with the
ad hoc adoption of ready-made marxian notions.

Subsequent work has attempted a more systematic and coherent revision of Marx. We may note that given that the New Left
did regenerate an interest in Marx, the scholarly efforts at
revision/exposition/co-option have been widespread in the 'social
sciences'. These general and widespread debates we will not
attempt to review. Rather, again, we narrow our interest to
'development studies'. That our focus has become rather more
'technical' than above is further evidenced in the material we
consider. Whereas Fanon and Debray were both (a) anticipators
of our technical area of interest and (b) acknowledged influences
on the New Left as a whole, the figures of Baran, Sweezy and
Frank (to indicate some key writers) are known mainly to the
members of the specialist disciplines which treat development
matters. In sum, this chapter now shifts from treating widely
noted activists to treating comparatively unknown theorists, and
more particularly, Western, academic scholars.

The issue of the nature of a 'presently relevant marxism' is
here pursued as a theoretical matter; that is, not another exercise informed by the sociology of knowledge. With 'development
studies' the period sees: (a) the occasion of the presentation of
the claims of the 'neo-marxists' (to have established a marxian
political economy of mature capitalism and of the system's per-

ipheral areas, the Third World), and (b) a variety of denials of
these claims, where these denials revolve around the contention
that the 'neo-marxists' are not really marxists at all. We pursue
these matters in section 4.

4.0 DYNAMIC OF THEORY II: 'NEO-MARXISM'

4.1 From activists to scholars

In terms of the material we have to treat in this sub-section, the
most striking change from what has gone before is this: whereas
we have been concerned primarily with activists, now we are
faced with scholars. This distinction might at first glance seem
to be somewhat arbitrary, serving only to note a trivial fact in
respect of the biographies of the various writers whose work we
look at. Yet it is of rather more interest, and concomitantly more
defensible, if we recall our remarks on the temporal relation of
the engaged subject to his particular objects. Here we distinguished between: theorists, where we read them naively as operating 'before the fact': that is, as preparing recipes for action
that were subsequently to be followed; practitioners, who we took
to be those activists whose very behaviour occasions renewal in
established canons of thought (here the example of the Cuban
experience was to the fore); and interpreters, who we took to
be those writers concerned to learn the lessons of such practical
experience: we instanced Debray. Now given this, by using the
notion 'scholar' we are presenting, it seems, a variation of the
idea of 'interpreter'. We are implicitly distinguishing the circumstances of an 'interpreter', who, to a greater or lesser degree,
shares the experiences of those people whose activity he attempts
to interpret (the slide of role is towards that of spokesman); and
an 'interpreter' who does not directly share the experience of
those about whom he writes (the slide of role is towards commentator). The 'scholar' belongs to this second category. To put
this another way: it is one thing to tramp around the jungle
with people whose action you are trying to interpret to those you
think will be sympathetic; but it is quite another thing to discuss
in the comfort of (say) a university study those self-same people,
even if it is done with equivalent sympathy and interpretative
intent.
   The material we treat in this section is, generally, that of
scholars. In particular, it is the work of anglophone academics.
Just what the full implications of this 'reminder' might be taken
to be have not thus far been discovered. Evidently it involves
our disposition to consider the role of the academic social theorist in the context of the schema of social theorizing as involving
the construction, criticism and comparative ranking of ideological
schemes. These three are all tasks that can be plausibly allocated to the 'liberal academic', and if we invoke Habermas's
notion of an 'ideal speech situation', then it can be seen that the

critical role could count as a practical contribution to the pursuit
of democracy.

Putting a gloss on these remarks, it could be said that whilst
it is a familiar injunction in marxian writing to remember that
theorizing should be concrete and historically specific, it is
rather less obviously remembered that theorizing is both a concrete and historically specific activity. In this light it is possible
to distinguish between what it makes sense for one theorist to
say and what it makes sense for another to say, simply by virtue of their particular circumstances. Arising from this, and
noted below, is the matter of the 'slide to the general' that seems
to occur in (some) academic marxian scholarship. Deference is
paid, so it seems, to some model of 'properly marxian behaviour',
where this tends to collapse all radical activity into the one
mould of 'marxian revolution-making'. This has the effect of
suppressing reflexivity of theorizing. Thus, for example, we
get hugely elaborate, technical, scholarly analyses of this or
that issue which then conclude in a relatively few pages or para-
graphs that this or that is the proper political course. There
seems to be a crucial disjunction between behaviour, praxis
(which in this case is the pursuit of scholarship), and prescriptions for action (which in the case of those affirming the
model of 'properly marxian behaviour' looks like a generalized
recipe for class war). Reflexivity in theorizing, which here we
are taking as an injunction for the theorist to locate himself and
argue accordingly, would seem to entail that there can properly
be a diversity of contributions to the pursuit of democracy. The
corollary is that the 'liberal academic' should pursue critical theorizing because that is what is appropriate to academic practice.

We can offer a few examples of what we have in mind, by way
of illustration. It is clear that this change in the basic character
of the discussions referred to in our inquiries has been noted.
Negatively, it is invoked by Young when he criticizes the New
Left for: (1) facile borrowings of revolutionary models from liberation struggles – the Black Panthers being perhaps the 'best'
example of a group that failed to consider its own circumstances
and the scope of the practical activity open to it; (2) a catholicity of interest that led to the movement collapsing under the
weight of its own amorphousness; and (3) the failure to construct
an autonomous, self-locating and ordering, explanatory frame. In
sum, Young regards the New Left as never knowing where they
were, what they were doing, or where they were going. Conversely, others have taken a more positive view. Thus Foster-
Carter distinguishes 'marxism-as-theory' from 'marxism-as-
history'; which permits, amongst other things, the pointing up
of the fact that different concerns attach to the practice of abstract theorizing as opposed to practical 'politicking'. So Foster-
Carter distinguishes, for example, between the historical situation
of revolutionary struggle in the post-Second World War period,
on the one hand, and, on the other, academic efforts to make
sense of it. He notes 'neo-marxism as an academic phenomenon is

largely a response to the way in which people like Mao and Ho
have changed the world'.[85]

In certain cases we can see the vacillation between claims to
the role of scholar and claims to the role of activist. Typically,
these involve the 'slide to the general' that we mentioned above.
We see that the academics exemplify their circumstances in their
work. For instance, Brenner offers a detailed critique of the
argument strategy of the 'neo-marxian' work of Baran, Frank
and Wallerstein. This seems appropriate, though at the end of
this impressive essay Brenner offers a series of concluding remarks that fudge the distinctions that we are trying to point out.
He slides from exemplifying his circumstances (by presenting
detailed, historically informed work), which entails some view of
the contribution to the pursuit of democracy open to the scholar,
to apparently denying the specific character of his position and
efforts by suggesting that his work be judged according to how
it measures up to some implied general model of the proper behaviour of the 'marxian revolutionary'.

Another example of this 'exemplification/denial' movement can
be found in Taylor's[86] critique of Foster-Carter. Taylor con-
ducts a detailed critique of Foster-Carter, which we can best
regard as 'second order' analysis, internal to the discipline. The
concern Taylor displays for precision in formulation of claims
exemplifies his circumstances as an academic. Yet his notion of
the contribution he is making to the pursuit of democracy vitiates
this self-exemplification. Foster-Carter picks out Taylor's view
that he, Taylor, is helping provide revolutionaries with the best
possible, most advanced conceptual equipment. So a subtle and
complex analysis is to be linked to practice in a crude mechanical
fashion, one which implicitly grants that there is only one model
of revolutionary change.[87]

The change in the character of the discourses we must consider
can be exemplified in the case of Frank. The 'early' and the
'late' Frank can be compared in manner and tone, as he rejigs his
schemes in a fashion we can regard as rendering them compat-
ible/coherent with his circumstances. Frank moves from tending
to the role of spokesman towards that of commentator. The task
presents itself as the pursuit of an autonomous theoretical base.
In general terms, given the context of the recent history of substantive work in this area, this pursuit presents itself as the
attempt of 'dependency/underdevelopment theory' to secure for
itself an autonomous (Marx-derived) theoretical base.

The early work of Frank has been treated above (chapter 6). At
that time we noted the circumstances of production of the work;
that is, following Booth, that Frank was taken to have been
abruptly won over to the radical left view following experience of
Latin American conditions. We reported that Frank offered a
polemical critique of an orthodoxy that encompassed neo-classical
economics, the dependency line associated with ECLA, and the
traditional Latin American Communist Party lines. Affirming the
principles of historical, holistic and structural analysis, Frank

followed Baran in regarding the circumstances of the presently
'underdeveloped' as flowing from the debilitating metropolitan
extraction of surplus from these long-integrated peripheries.
The solution was the revolutionary removal of a historically incapable national bourgeoisie, and the socialist-governed pursuit
of an autonomous national development.

In his later work (1978), Frank recalls that he has contributed
to the formation of the 'dependency' school, and that his early
efforts have been heavily criticized for tending to the economistic
and lacking any genuinely dialectical analysis. Of the 1978 work,
Frank says that it represents 'an attempt to transcend the "dependence" approach, but without yet abandoning it or the focus
on underdevelopment, and to proceed on towards the integration
of dependence and underdevelopment within the world process of
accumulation'.[88] The book tackles a set of particular questions
of analysis: issues occasioned by the criticism of the earlier
work, though not flowing directly from them. The criticisms are
treated in an introductory chapter that indicates Frank's line of
research interest. Thus he declares, 'This book and these introductory questions to it are an attempt to break out of the vicious
circle of "development theory".'[89] The hoped-for replacement
is characterized in three ways. The first is by reference to
method:[90]

> To free ourselves from the irrelevance of narrowly limited neo-
> classical theory ... we may take the global historical vision of
> Adam Smith and the dialectical analysis of Karl Marx as points
> of departure in an attempt to advance toward a whole world
> encompassing holistic, real world historical, socially structural
> (and therefore in fact theoretically dialectical) theory of de-
> velopment and underdevelopment.

Second, as regards procedure, he says: 'This will require the
scientific examination of the historical evidence and record of
capitalist development and the better reading (in the sense of
Althusser) of Smith and Marx in the light of this evidence.'[91]
Third, Frank indicates the expected manner of emergence of the
product:[92]

> With this purpose and in this spirit we review the participation
> of Asia, Africa and Latin America in this world wide historical
> process; and we emphasize the subordinate dependence of
> these areas within the process of world capitalist development
> as the cause of their development of underdevelopment.

If, in order to fix the position of this later work of Frank in
relation to the earlier (characteristically underdevelopment theory) efforts, we consider the nature of the procedures noted
above, then what does it reveal? Clearly, there is no general
reconstruction being undertaken; there is no abstract consideration of the categorical framework of his effort. Rather he con-

tinues to use the syntax of the natural sciences: thus he seeks
to revise his theories with a closer, more detailed reading of history in the light of concepts that are already established in his
work – yet liable, he seems to claim, to relocation within a
subtler frame derived from Smith and Marx.

Frank's recent work seems to represent an intellectual/political
relocation. That which was characteristically Frankian is not so
much lost as partially submerged. To put this another way,
where Frank's earlier work grasped in one simplifying and synthesizing effort the 'answer' in respect of Latin America, it now
seems as if he is trying to work backwards, so to say, and discover those arguments that establish the 'answer'. Yet the
change of context introduces a subtle shift of emphasis. Frank
seeks not to uncover the arguments specific to his 'answer' in
respect of Latin America, but rather to uncover a set of arguments productive of a general 'answer'. In Frank's case the 'ex-
emplification/denial' manoeuvre entailed by the pursuit of a
'general answer' is made all the more easily by Frank's use of the
syntax of natural science.[93]

In sum: the discourse we now treat is that of (roughly speaking) scholars and not, as was the case, that of (roughly speaking) activists. Frank has exemplified this shift. He is an appropriate choice; not only for the intrinsic interest of the matters
arising from his work, but more pertinently because his early
(and indeed later) efforts constitute a familiar and central element of what must now be treated as the orthodoxy of this area
of development studies – that is, 'neo-marxism'.

4.2 The contested core of 'neo-marxism'

Thus far we have been considering the circumstances of the
theorist, noting the general constraints placed by particular
situations upon what it makes sense for the theorist in question
to say. Theorizing has been seen as a practical activity, and we
have had little to say about its eventual object. Now we dismiss
direct concern for the circumstances of theorizing – whether
particular workers are taken as activists or scholars, and what
difference it makes to them and to us – and we proceed to discuss their object, 'neo-marxism'. Our concern is now couched
in terms of intellectual history. We look at resources invoked
and matters arising therefrom.

We can begin with the useful essay by Palma on the character
of 'dependency'. Palma is interested in asking whether or not
'dependency' is a theory or a method, and in pointing out its
marxian background.[94] Where Palma uses the term 'dependency' it embraces Frank, Furtado and Cardoso, so his usage is
broader than the one adopted here.

Palma begins by noting the marxian programme of analysis of
the development of capitalism; he asks after the term 'imperialism' and reports that he finds it 'absolutely legitimate to use the

concept of imperialism to designate only those aspects of capitalist development which have related the fortunes of the advanced
and backward areas within the world capitalist system'.[95] Regarded thus (that is, taking note of the specific sense of 'imperialism' that Palma takes in order to get his treatment of 'dependency' underway), marxian interest in the relations between
centre and periphery may be divided[96] into three phases. Palma
quotes Sutcliffe:[97]

> One (prominent in Marx's and Engels's writings) involves
> plunder (of wealth and slaves) and exports of capitalist man-
> ufactures to the peripheral countries. The second (uppermost
> in Lenin's writing) involves the export of capital, competition
> for supplies of raw materials and the growth of monopoly. The
> third involves a more complex post-colonial dependency.

Given these three phases in theorizing about the relationship of
centre and periphery, Palma goes on to attach to each a particular view of the role of capitalism in backward nations. Thus for
Marx and Engels, capitalism appeared as a wholly progressive
force, even if the process of dismantling moribund social forms
was brutal and incidental to the exploitative interests of the
colonial forces. For Lenin capitalism appears as progressive in
underdeveloped areas, yet presently shackled by the demands
of the centres. The eventual outcome expected is the peripheral
development of a capitalism resembling that of the centres. Lenin's analysis is complex and is intertwined with debates on the
possibilities for capitalism in Russia. It is the third reading of
the role of capitalism in the peripheries that is of particular
interest to us: 'The third approach was first developed in the
1950s and "took off" with the publication in 1957 of Baran's "The
political economy of growth"; it is characterized by the acceptance, almost as an axiomatic truth, of the argument that no Third
World country can now expect to break out of a state of economic dependency and advance to an economic position beside the
major capitalist industrial powers'.[98]

Palma, treating 'dependency' as a school of approaches to political economy (where marxism is (a) the major school of political
economy and (b) the most significant substantive school treating
'dependency' and Latin America), distinguishes three varieties
of 'dependency' analysis: (1) Frank and notions of underdevelopment; (2) Furtado and ECLA revisions; and (3) Cardoso, who
is characterized as trying to produce a non-mechanico-formal
scheme. Now Furtado we have treated and Cardoso will come
to; here we look at the first, 'neo-marxian' line.

With regard to Frank and 'underdevelopment theory', Palma
offers a view that is more immediately familiar than the above
noted subsumption of a marxian approach in the tradition of political economy. Palma reports that:[99]

There is no doubt that the 'father' of this approach is Paul
Baran. His principal contribution to the general literature on
development (Baran 1957) continues the central line of marxist
thought regarding the contradictory character of the needs of
imperialism and the process of industrialization and general
economic development of the backward nations.

Along with Baran's work we need to mention Sweezy and Wallerstein, as well as Frank.

By briefly reviewing the efforts of these theorists we can
sketch the orthodoxy of this area of debate; that is, the 'neo-
marxian' schema. Our review is ordered around some criticisms
made of the 'neo-marxian' schema by those concerned with matters of theoretical status. That is, we construct the 'object'
'neo-marxism' with reference to those critics who specifically
deny that, amongst other things, 'neo-marxism' is marxian. This
seems an appropriate line, given our interest in what has been
taken as, or is to count as, a properly marxian analysis of the
Third World. Little of what we will say in respect of the con-
stitution/criticism of 'neo-marxism' will be new. Discussion has
been extensive, and here we rely upon it. First we will introduce six overlapping and cross-cutting criticisms which have
been made, and then we will go on to consider them in turn.

(1) Baran analyses the world capitalist system and claims to
identify a drift towards stagnation – both in the metropolitan
centres and in the dependent peripheral areas. Stagnation is
occasioned by an inability to utilize effectively the economic surplus generated by monopoly capitalism. It is here, critics com-
plain, that Baran's criticisms begin. He is taken to present an
essentially moral critique which revolves around the issue of
the extent of realization and allocation of societies' economic surplus. The evaluative moment of this theorizing is seen as preliminary to his economics. Criticism number one: objections to moral
critique.

(2) As regards the schema governing the exchange of centre
and periphery, the critics of 'neo-marxism' object to what they
see as a crude polemical inversion of the orthodox: the Third
World is not being developed but underdeveloped. As regards
the peripheral areas, Baran argues that the manner of their incorporation into the world capitalist system maintains their status
as underdeveloped, and that this is entailed by the misuse of
available surplus – excess consumption by indigenous elites, unproductive military expenditure, and transfers of profits (etc.),
to metropoles by multi-national corporations. So we have criticism number two: objections to the thesis in respect of the development of capitalism and peripheral underdevelopment.

(3) The notion of 'surplus' is central to Baran's work. A major
line of objection, from marxists, to this notion of 'economic surplus' has been that whilst it recalls Marx's notion of 'surplus
value', it has in fact very little to do with it. Thus we have
criticism number three: objections to the aggregative, 'left

Keynesian', notion of 'economic surplus'.
(4) A.G. Frank follows Baran and Frank's political conclusions
are that whereas the present situation offers the underdeveloped
only a prospect of continuing subordinate incorporation in the
world capitalist system and consequent misdevelopment, socialist
revolution offers the prospect of 'genuine', 'autonomous', development. Setting aside the appropriate objections to 'moral critique', 'historical thesis' and 'economistic concepts', here is
lodged a fourth objection in respect of the implied goal of the
'neo-marxians'. We have; criticism number four: objections to
the implicit model of development - just what is it?
(5) Wallerstein is taken to complete Frank. Thus Brenner reports
that: 'Wallerstein straightforwardly defines capitalism as a trade
based division of labour, and it is here that he locates the dynamic of the capitalist economic development.'[100] That the 'neo-
marxian' effort is economistic in that it totally fails to provide a
class analysis is a familiar complaint. Here, then, we note; criticism number five: objection to reduction of 'class' to 'market' -
it is neo-smithian.
(6) The political line which attaches to the Baran/Frank 'underdevelopment theory' approach follows from the above characteristics of analysis; the prerequisite of any development is the
disengagement from the world capitalist market and a prerequisite of this is the socialist revolutionary displacement of compro-
mised local bourgeoisies from power. Criticism number six: as
the analysis is implausible, so its proposals are unhelpful.
In sum, we may constitute the present 'object of debate' (that is,
'neo-marxism') according to its major elements as identified by its
critics. These six may be organized as follows: the aggregative
economic notion of surplus (3) entails an affirmation of an economistic scheme of society (5). This in turn involves a wrong
historical schema of the rise of capitalism, monopoly capitalism
and underdevelopment (2). The resultant model of what counts
as development is untenable (4) and the general moral critique
of capitalism is unhelpful (1). The political line which follows
from (1) to (5) is accordingly wrong-headed (and distracts
attention from questions of the present dynamic of capitalism in
these peripheral areas - and indeed generally).
   There is one note to be made in the context of this focus upon
criticisms which is that the 'neo-marxian' scheme is a richly developed one. Its critics tend to be scathing, suggesting that it
is a simple theoretical farrago. But even if they turned out to
be correct in their attacks, it would remain the case that 'neo-
marxism' constitutes the orthodoxy of radical thought in this
period. If the effort were quite so transparently futile it would
be difficult to understand the attention paid to it. One critic
lists the virtues of the line as follows: 'it stimulated the empirical study of institutional and structural mechanisms of underdevelopment .... And in the context of the early 1960's when
underdevelopment theory emerged as a militant critique of the
ruling ideas of developmentalism, its thrust was unquestionably

a progressive one.'[101] Leys adds that we should be careful to remember 'some of the intellectual deserts from which under-development theory rescued us'.[102]

We now turn to treat these objections. Here we can note that treatment of one or other of these 'objections' to the Baran-inspired line often involves carefully avoiding invoking the linked criticisms of linked notions. That is, the whole effort hangs together; and its elements overlap in such a way as to reveal that if it is all a farrago, then it is a very well integrated one.

4.21 Objections to the moral critique of capitalism

Some have claimed that Baran/Frank may be taken to present an essentially moral critique of monopoly capitalism and its claimed corollary underdevelopment. Such critiques, it is said, are neither marxian nor helpful.

In the case of Baran/Frank the issue of the moral critique of capitalism is coupled up with the issue of their notion of surplus. Culley reports that the concept of 'the potential economic sur-plus, is a most important one in Baran's discourse. It is primar-ily by an analysis of their potentialities that types of society ... are assessed.'[103] The notion of potential surplus is the meas-ure of general efficient functioning of the system and is estimated by noting (a) present excess consumption, (b) surplus lost in unproductive labour, (c) surplus lost through simple inefficiency and (d) surplus lost through unemployment. Culley notes, 'The Utopian nature of this conception is quite clear. It allows Baran and his followers to launch an attack upon capitalism as an ir-rational phenomenon with respect to his own ethical position.'[104] Culley takes Baran's effort to be humanistic, idealistic, relativ-istic and teleological: 'The similarity of their discussion with the nineteenth century Utopian socialists criticised by Marx and Engels is striking.'[105] Culley reduces Baran and Sweezy's in-vestigation to the status of an elaborate and disguised expression of disapproval. Bernstein follows this in respect of underdevel-opment theory: denying that underdevelopment theory is marxist, he speaks of, inter alia, 'the use of a moralistic and idealistic critique of capitalism based on a philosophical humanism, which condemns the objective efforts of the contradictory nature of capitalist development by reference to a utopia free of exploit-ation, oppression and dependence'.[106]

Having affirmed that we take social theorizing to involve the 'deployment of a morally informed categorical frame', we are ob-liged to pursue this matter. So we can perhaps elucidate these issues by proposing the following analogy. As Marcuse uses the trio Basic Repression/Surplus Repression/'Diminished Repres-sion' (where this is implied as holding for socialist society) to ground, in a psychological individualism, a moral critique of contemporary society, so Baran uses the trio Actual/Potential/Planned Surplus to ground, in an aggregative and reformist 'left Keynesianism', a moral critique of contemporary society.

Marcuse[107] presents the notions of repression/surplus repression. The argument strategy grants, it would seem, the (orthodox?) claim that in any society a measure of repression is necessary to establish social order. Marcuse begins with individuals as bundles of instinctual desires unhappily located in a hostile environment of scarcity. The unrepressed, autonomous, freely acting, individual is literally asocial. Having granted a minimum necessary 'amount' of repression, Marcuse then asks after the particular, historically specific, repression we have: it is, he reports, that which is required by the functioning capitalist society. To basic repression is added surplus repression.

Surplus repression (1) enables the growth of capitalist society's productivity, which effort simultaneously tends to the impoverishment of the quality of life; and (2) extracts a high price in terms of the suppression of the instinctual life of the human organism. The general and the particular reinforce each other. Two points now follow: (a) the whole system tends to collapse; as the opportunities for change rise (by virtue of success of capitalist production) so too does the level of SR needed to maintain the status quo. In terms of recent history, we can thus interpret the slide into fascism. (b) As capitalism has solved the problem of scarcity, SR could indeed be eased off.

It is clear that all this can be seen as a morally informed critique. It revolves around the idea of quality of life available to the inhabitants of the society in question. What they do have, and what they might have.

Reflecting upon the above-noted strategy of criticism, we can make the following points. Recalling the material of Part I of this study, we can contend that, in respect of valuation in social theorizing, what is at issue is not whether or not the effort is 'tainted' by valuation; because, as we have seen, there will necessarily be a significant aspect of valuation. Rather, the matter is one of the character of the valuations made, and the manner of their insertion into social theoretic efforts.

If the above-noted argument took as its moral reference point the schemes involved in Macpherson's 'reconstruction' of the notion of 'democracy', then it would be a moral reference point that we would wish to support. If it also inserted such notions via an explicit statement and in an appropriately secondary form, then the scheme would have a defensible core and a basis upon which to build an appropriate critique of present circumstance.

But in Marcuse's case he takes as a start point a psychological individualism that is, on the face of it, wholly problematical. A criticism of this start point could be mounted by invoking, say, Macpherson on Hobbes.[108] Now Hobbes strips away the social circumstances of bourgeois man and presents the result - grasping, acquisitive greed - as essential to man; which atom then has to be reintegrated into some sort of social whole. So with Marcuse, his start point offers a version of bourgeois man, avoiding work and pursuing, egoistically, sensual gratification, which atom is then reintegrated into a social whole. Marcuse's start point is apparently tainted; it is not defensible, because individualism is not. So, in this way, Marcuse's effort could be seen as ideological (pejorative) because it grants as a premise an incoherent and obfuscating notion.

With Baran we seem to have a similar pattern of argument. The notion of 'economic surplus', it is widely granted, is not marxian, even though it recalls the term 'surplus value'. Further, the notion of 'economic surplus' is redolent of Keynesian aggregative macro-economic analysis, and the treatment of society via the issue of the utilization of this surplus (whether rational or irrational) is similarly redolent of a 'liberal reformism'. Myrdal and Galbraith come to mind. It seems as if it could be argued that the key idea of Baran's scheme, that of 'economic surplus' is tainted in the same fashion as Marcuse's notion of 'surplus repression'. Charges of 'ideology-mongering' could be levelled in the same way.

That Baran's effort is critically engaged is not in doubt. Nor is it in doubt that the notion of 'economic surplus' will serve as a core element of a political economic analysis. What is at issue, for us, is the precise nature of the moral core of Baran's effort and the manner of its insertion into analysis.

We saw (with Rockmore in chapter 1) in the case of Marx's work that the moral core, a philosophical anthropology issuing in the notion of alienated labour, was central to the machinery of substantive, practical, analysis. Here is the key to our suspicions with regard to Baran: the evaluative stance, condemning the system's present irrationality of use of economic surplus and pointing to a possible rationally ordered future, is pitched at such a general level as to tend to be indistinguishable from any other 'liberal' critique. The related point (which comes up below, criticism 3) addresses the manner of insertion. It is suggested by Culley that Baran's economics is separate from the moral critique. The economics is seen as heuristic: a vehicle for cashing a moral stance that is presented, in a familiar manoeuvre, as a general scheme.

It might be replied, with regard to 'indistinguishability', that this shows how marxian critique has become a part of the culture (common sense) of the left; and does not, consequently, need spelling out in formal mode. But this seems dubious; and it is certainly a position that it would be difficult to grant, in a study predicated upon the existence of present reflection amongst practitioners as to the precise nature and status of social theorizing.

A better reply might be to invite critics to recall the circumstances of the effort's production; that is, the US in the late 1950s. Against that political background, and in contrast to 'modernization theory', Baran's effort must appear to be hugely sophisticated.

So, if we read the critics, Culley, Bernstein, et al., as objecting to 'moral critique' - where this is characterized as essentially

involving a surreptitious borrowing from the stance to be attacked - then we would wish to grant the argument some force. However, if the critics' attack embraces not just this 'surreptitious
borrowing', but all and any evaluative (moral) stance towards
social forms and issues, then we cannot agree. Following earlier
discussions (e.g. Myrdal), we would have to regard the critics
as pursuing the chimera of non-engaged theory.

4.22 Objections to the historical schema used

Our second point concerns criticisms of the thesis in respect of
the rise of capitalism and the creation of underdevelopment. Here
we invoke the work of Brenner; that is, his essay 'The Origins
of Capitalist Development: a Critique of Neo-Smithian Marxism'.
We may focus on three points. (a) Brenner says that 'neo-
marxian' theorists, in their efforts to explain the rise of capitalism, argue in a circular fashion. They assume the existence of
capitalistic social relations in their efforts to explain the rise of
capitalism. Brenner analyses Sweezy's work ('The transition from
feudalism to capitalism') by unpacking the proffered model and
asking after the plausibility and character of the assumptions
made in respect of the behaviour of the historical actors mentioned. He concludes that: 'Sweezy's entire account of the transition from feudalism to capitalism is based on the implicit
assumption that capitalism already exists.'[109] Sweezy's effort
is taken to reduce to the view that the transition from feudalism
to capitalism is a matter of the appropriate adjustment in society
to the demands of the market; yet the market is the sum of social
relations. Brenner reports:[110]

> In the last analysis, Sweezy's error is two-fold. It is to posit
> that the producers' relationship to the market determines their
> operation and development and, ultimately, their relationship
> to one another, rather than vice versa. Correlatively, it is to
> locate the system's potential for development in the capacities
> of its component *individual* units (thus the emphasis on moti-
> vations), rather than in the system as a whole - specifically,
> in the overall system of class relations of production which
> determine/condition the nature of the interrelationships be-
> tween the individual units and, in this manner, their oper-
> ation and development.

(b) Brenner argues that the entire 'neo-marxist' line in this
area of debate reduces to an inversion of Adam Smith. The 'neo-
marxists' follow Smith in equating capitalism with a trade-based
division of labour, where innovation (and thus growth/expansion)
is determined by market pressure. Class relations just follow on.
Brenner speaks of 'historical functionalism' and 'a classical form
of economic determinism', and takes this as wrong. Instead, he
wants to reduce economics to social (class) relations. The core

of the matter is the conjugation of class circumstances that trig-
ger and sustain the innovative dynamic of capitalism.
Wallerstein is singled out:[111]

> In Wallerstein's 'The modern world system' the Smithian theory
> embedded in Sweezy's analysis of the transition from feudal-
> ism to capitalism is made entirely explicit, and carried to its
> logical conclusion.... Thus Wallerstein straightforwardly de-
> fines capitalism as a trade based division of labour, and it is
> here that he locates the dynamic of capitalist economic devel-
> opment.

There is an economic determinism that 'pervades all aspects of
Wallerstein's theoretical framework'.[112]
To this, Brenner counterposes his own view. Resting upon
detailed historical exegesis, he affirms that: 'Neither development in the core nor underdevelopment in the periphery was
determined by surplus transfer. Economic development was a
qualitative process, which did not merely involve an accumulation of wealth in general, but was centrally focused on the
development of the productivity of labour.'[113]

> In short the uniquely successful development of capitalism in
> Western Europe was determined by a class system, a property
> system, a system of surplus extraction, in which the methods
> the extractors were obliged to use to increase their surplus
> corresponded to an unprecedented, though imperfect, degree
> to the needs of development of the productive forces'.[114]

It is in this conjunction that the search for an explanation of the
genesis of capitalism is to be found, not in any behaviour of an
abstractly regarded world market.
    Frank repeats this 'neo-marxian' line; development and under-
development are explained by reference to international trade-
based extraction of surplus, and not to the conjunctions of class
circumstances and technological possibility.
(c) With regard to the method of analysis of these theorists,
Brenner reports that their failure 'to discard the underlying
individualistic presuppositions'[115] of Smith's model has resulted
in their erecting a mirror version of it. Palma reports of Frank's
efforts that:[116]

> Probably still unduly influenced by his training as an econo-
> mist at the University of Chicago, he constructs a mechanico-
> formal model which is no more than a set of equations of
> general equilibrium (static and unhistorical), in which the
> extraction of the surplus takes place through a series of
> satellite-metropolis relationships, through which the surplus
> generated at each stage is syphoned off.

The historical material we cannot, and do not want to, follow.

We note it in order to indicate that there is a large area of discourse, apparently somewhat remote to development studies, that bears upon our concerns. The circularity, inversion of Smith and erection of a mechanico-formal model are matters closer to us. Palma, we have noted, has evinced an interest in political economy as an argument style, and has approved of Cardoso's problem-centred and specific methods. The pursuit of general theory is again shown to be ill-advised; yet the issue of the proper presentation and use of such general formulations remains to be resolved. The problem seems to be that general formulations are called forth by specific efforts and that thereafter they are taken to be analogous to natural science general formulations; efforts being made to develop and present them accordingly. The result being, in this case, the production of a mechanico-formal system which detracts from the original problem. Indeed, at worst, the initial problem-specificity is ignored and theorists proceed straightaway to the largely futile effort at the erection of general formulations, general theories.

4.23 Objections to the notion of 'economic surplus'

The material here largely overlaps with that of criticism number one; we have a slightly different focus. Thus there seem to be two main lines of criticism of the notion of 'economic surplus': (a) criticisms from within the ambit of the orthodox, that is, non-marxian economics; we will not pursue these, noting only that they involve charges of ambiguity and difficulty of measurement; and (b) criticisms in respect of the notion's theoretical status.

In respect of this latter line, it is argued that Baran's notion of surplus (and thus the notion used by the entire underdevelopment theory-marxian line) owes more to the aggregative economics of Keynes than it does to Marx. Sutcliffe reports that 'The conceptual difference is that Marx's "surplus value" is defined in relation to the ownership of property while Baran's "surplus" is defined more in relation to consumption needs. It is therefore to Baran something which exists in all societies.'[117] We can offer a preliminary elucidation of this distinction by calling upon the work of Culley once again. She argues thus:[118]

> In Capital the concepts of necessary and surplus labour are
> strictly economic concepts and are not derived from any extra-
> economic concept of human needs. For Marx, surplus value is
> the specifically capitalist mode of appropriation of surplus
> labour.... Surplus labour, that is, labour over and above
> necessary labour, exists in all modes of production, because
> the conditions of reproduction of the labourer are not equiv-
> alent to the conditions of reproduction of the economy....
> Necessary and surplus labour must always be defined in re-
> lation to a determinate mode of production. The precise form
> of surplus labour is determined by a definite mechanism of
> extraction.... For Marx, surplus value is the mode of appro-

priation of surplus labour specific to the capitalist mode of
production. *The concept of surplus value involves a mechan-*
ism requiring private property in the means of production and
separation of labour power from the objective conditions of
labour [our emphases].[119]

Culley's point is that the two versions of 'surplus' are quite
different in status and working. Baran's is an idealistic notion
derived from abstract notions of need. That is, his overall
scheme is a morally informed criticism; and his economics are
best taken as derived and heuristic, in the sense that they serve
to order the otherwise generated critique. Marx's concept, on
the other hand, is central to his economics and is firmly lodged
within that scheme of analysis: a scheme which claims to be a
thoroughly developed political economy, and which reveals the
dynamics of the system rather than simply offering a moral critique of it.

Culley's point, in the end, is this: both notions, 'economic
surplus' and 'surplus value', are taken as marxian political economy; but only Marx's notion actually is that. Baran's effort may
lay claim to justification elsewhere - in their moral sensitivity
and critique, or in the ease of assimilation of their lessons - but
they cannot lay claim to justification by virtue of being marxian-
informed political economy, because that, strictly, is what they
are not. Put another way, we might say that as Baran et al. begin with the desirability of change - rather than, as with Marx,
the real possibility - then to that extent their political economy
would seem to be impoverished. In the end we would pursue this
softer line, taking it to be compatible with our general orientation and as fitting within the scheme sketched out by Palma,
which treats these particular matters directly and in broad perspective.

4.24 Objections to the notion of 'development'

The notion of 'development' we take to be a synonym for 'progress'. Clearly, its use is prevalent in discussions of 'development studies'. Both in its general and in its local disciplinary
use, the notion partakes of the pre-eminently 'Western' set of
expectations/assumptions that attach to the notion of 'progress'.
'Progress' we take to have been conceptualized in the eighteenth
century; it is the heir to notions of perfectibility, and is taken
in its nineteenth-century variants as the guarantor of continued
improvement in man's affairs. The model of man affirmed is optimistic and the politics democratic, in Macpherson's sense. We
take Marx to have been firmly lodged in this emancipatory tradition. But if this is the core and heart of the notion, it is also
true that the idea has presented itself in different guises through
the post-war 'career' of 'development studies', initially as requiring the application of established economic techniques, or
subsequently as involving the reasonable pursuit of measured

social reform. However, it is with the Marxian work studied in
Part IV that the notion used in the 'career' of 'development
studies' begins to come close to the essence of the notion as we
have presented it. The question is: just how close do the 'neo-
marxists' come?

Phillips is not sure. The 'neo-marxists', arguing that peripheral countries are condemned to misdevelopment (underdevelopment) by virtue of their subordinate incorporation, affirm some
sort of notion of 'development' as 'autocentric capitalism'; which
they then indicate is impossible for peripheral areas to achieve,
thereby securing the necessity for socialism. Phillips sees this
stance as flowing from Baran et al.'s having to contrive a response to the apparent post-war success of capitalist centres in
solving their problems. Thus they pose 'a contradiction between
capitalism and development';[120] hence progress in the centres
could be taken to be 'not really' progress at all, and the situation
in the peripheries as obviously and inevitably other than development. Phillips takes this to (a) block all chance of change in
the centres, and (b) obscure the interesting question of the
nature of the capitalist dynamic in the peripheries.

So what of the notion of 'development' invoked? Phillips seems
to take it to be vacillating, nebulously idealist and in the end
narrow. Thus she argues:[121]

> The 'development' against which 'underdevelopment' is con-
> ceptualized has tended to become an amalgam of different
> concepts, such that the theories are *partly* drawing a contrast
> between the process of development in the advanced capitalist
> countries and in the underdeveloped countries, but *partly* a
> contrast between development in the underdeveloped countries
> and an idealized process of development which would ensure
> 'maximum utilisation of resources' or the 'most rational allo-
> cation of surplus'. What emerges is an ideal type of 'normal
> capitalist development' which serves as a measure by means of
> which we can recognise underdevelopment.

This vacillation conceals the problems which Phillips takes to
attach to the second element. Here, recalling the strictures noted
above on the concept of 'economic surplus', we can observe that
this element is taken as idealist and non-marxian. The final
point comes out of Phillips's remarks upon the sources of the
notion of 'development'. The radicals simply take what the orthodox assumed; a sort of nationalist capitalism, where the nation
state was the discrete unit in receipt of aid and planning interventions. The radicals take this in order to deny that it is possible. Phillips remarks that this naive idea set the terms for the
debates that followed.

In further discussing the radicals' dismissal of orthodox development initiatives, Phillips shares their scepticism but then
adds, 'this in no way undermines the argument that the development initiative was necessary as a means to overcoming

obstacles to the further accumulation of capital'.[122] Equally,
we may note that, granted the narrowness of the 'neo-marxian'
notion of 'development'; granted its idealism, as with 'economic
surplus', and granted the vacillation, it remains the case that
'neo-marxism' marked a signal advance upon preceding efforts.
We have cited Leys to this effect. It is not clear in the end just
what the line of criticism here exemplified in Phillips actually
achieves, when seen in the context of our history of the 'career'
of 'development studies'. More locally, so to say, the criticism
might be seen to have some force. As Kay argues, taking note
of the circumstances of production of underdevelopment theory
and the limitations imposed thereby, 'The radical critics ...
were so keen to prove the ideological point that underdevelopment was the product of capitalist exploitation, that they let the
crucial issue pass them by: capital created underdevelopment
not because it exploited the underdeveloped world, but because
it did not exploit it enough.'[123] This matter of the malintegra-
tion of the peripheries and the continuing dynamism of the
world system is tackled by Cardoso (cf. below). Any insistence,
by underdevelopment theory, on the irremediably disfigured
stasis of peripheral economies is perhaps best seen as polemical
over-statement.

4.25 Objections to the reduction of 'class' to 'market'

We have touched upon this material in noting criticism 2, treating the rise of capitalism. In particular, we referred to Brenner's
view that 'neo-marxism' is, in this matter, an 'inversion' of Adam
Smith.
    Pursuing this, we may note that Brenner argues that 'the
method of an entire line of writers in the marxist tradition has
led them to displace class relations from the centre of their analyses of economic development and underdevelopment'.[124] In
respect of Frank, the import of these shifts is presented as entailing a diversion of attention from issues of the inherent dynamism of the capitalist core to the exchange between centres and
peripheries; when, additionally, the world capitalist system's
dynamism is taken to be fuelled by exchange. Thus we have
Brenner's 'neo-Smithian' charge. Wallerstein is taken to system-
atize Frank, his scheme relying upon the 'immanent development
dynamic of unfettered world trade'.[125]
    Now these criticisms are indeed persuasive, and Palma offers
a particularly interesting reading of them.[126] Recalling
Brenner's analysis of Baran/Frank/Wallerstein, such that they
are taken to have provided a polemical inversion of Adam Smith's
scheme, Palma observes of Frank that he constructs a 'mechanico-formal model'[127] of the world historical dynamic of capitalism. Thus Palma presents a familiar criticism in a fashion that
calls attention to the issue of argument strategy. Recalling our
earlier notes on Palma in respect of the 'Is it really marxian?'
debate, here clearly is one point at which his conception of

political economy is being invoked. We return to this in section
4.3, where we briefly introduce Cardoso and the point picked up
by Palma; that is, specificity in engagement and eschewal of the
pursuit of the general.

4.26 An unhelpful politics

The above-noted criticisms have attached to the conceptual makeup of 'neo-marxism'. In nuce 'neo-marxism' has been charged
with a moralizing electicism that is, in the end, neither marxian
nor especially helpful in respect of matters of the Third World.
Here we can look briefly at the objections typically brought to
bear upon the politics which 'neo-marxism' propounds.

(a) It is claimed that 'neo-marxism' is Third Worldist and therefore naive in respect of the Third World. To this we may reply
that Third Worldism was not, as we saw above when discussing
Young, all that naive; nor was it unfounded.

(b) It is claimed that 'neo-marxism' rules out political activity
in the centre. To this we may reply that in so far as 'neo-
marxism' entails, or is associated with, an abandonment of orthodox notions of 'proletarian revolution', this is a measure of its
sophistication rather than anything else. Additionally, in so far
as (d) (below) is true, then 'neo-marxism' is an element of political activity in the centre. We have called Frank a pamphleteer
in his early work, and it is to be noted that much of his impact
has been on the perceptions which those in rich nations have of
the Third World. This is surely not inconsequential.

(c) It is claimed that 'neo-marxism' is liable, in Kay's phrase,
to 'conservative re-absorption'. This seems either trivial or
implicitly fantastic. In respect of its triviality, we can record
that there is no ideological effort that cannot be 'raided' by
those it would criticize. For example, Middlemas[128] makes use
of a simple 'class' notion in order to present his conservative
history of British politics in the twentieth century. Why criticize 'neo-marxism' for a general and inevitable problem? Alternatively, we may take the criticism and ask just what sort of
stance is being invoked in contrast to those 'liable to re-
absorption'. A political creed that was rigorously unacceptable
in the realm of the present - else how could it avoid 're-absorption' in some measure or other - would admit of no change in the
social system in question. Rigorous unacceptability of the creed
implies total disconnectedness of that creed; but if it is discon-
nected then how can it ever effect change. The only change in
the system permitted by a creed that is rigorously unacceptable
(that is, totally closed to re-absorption) would be total and
immediate change; and that is fantastic. The criticism of 'neo-
marxism' to the effect that it is 'liable to re-absorption' seems to
rest on a contrary notion that is itself both practically and conceptually unconvincing.

(d) It is claimed that 'neo-marxism' is the 'unhappy consciousness' of left intelligentsia.[129] This is an entirely plausible

claim; why it is a problem is rather less clear to us. We have repeated on several occasions that we take theorizing to be a practical activity that needs must reflect the circumstances of the
group doing the theorizing. Cumper, we noted, took Girvan's
'dependency' to be the self-serving ideology (pejorative) of
Third World intelligentsia. Cumper's criticisms we dismissed.
But the claim we granted might well be true; the fact that underdevelopment theory/'neo-marxism' has tended to tail off into a
variety of unarticulated, aspiring left, policy science efforts is
of interest. That 'neo-marxism' may be taken to reflect the circumstances of the theorist, we take to be proper. The real
question to ask is: just how well do they acknowledge their circumstances?

The matter of the general nature of social theorizing, and in
particular the issue of what it is proper for the 'Western' academic to say in respect of the Third World, will be pursued in
the final section of the study (Part V).

4.3 Summary note

This discussion of the 'Dynamic of theory II' was intended to
review 'marxian' debate on matters of the Third World. We have
been concerned to present the claims of the 'neo-marxists' and
the counter claims of their critics.

The central element of this area of discourse we have taken to
be the work of Baran, and the discourse itself the 'orthodoxy'
of the left. The object, 'neo-marxism', we introduced by reference to Palma who is concerned with the matter of the character
of argument in 'dependency'. 'Neo-marxism' is presented as the
third major effort to theorize the exchange of centre/periphery
within the marxian line. Originally we have Marx's scattered
writings, then Lenin's revisions, and finally the 'neo-marxian'
effort associated with Baran, Sweezy, and recently A.G. Frank.
The object 'neo-marxism' we constituted via a review of criticisms of it. The conventional objections, noted by Sutcliffe, we
have not treated; but the criticisms of the radicals we have. We
summarized them thus. The aggregative economic notion of surplus entails an affirmation of an economistic scheme of society.
This in turn involves a wrong historical schema of the rise of
capitalism, monopoly capitalism and underdevelopment. The resulting model of what counts as development is untenable and the
general moral critique of capitalism unhelpful. The political line
which follows from all this is, accordingly, wrong-headed.

These critics have tended to fall into the argument: 'Is underdevelopment theory/"neo-marxism" really marxian?' Palma's essay
implicitly makes the claim that this is an uninteresting question.
His preferred area of inquiry, and the area in which to search
for an answer to the question 'What counts as a marxian analysis
of the Third World?', is that of political economy. Political economy is taken as that characteristic nineteenth-century discipline
of which Marx was the foremost exponent.

Palma constructs these last noted claims via examination of
the work of Cardoso (with Faletto), who is taken to have provided, in his scheme of 'dependency', just such a 'political
economic analysis'. The key, so far as Palma's exegesis is concerned, is specificity of engagement:[130]

> It is thus through concrete studies of specific situations, and
> in particular of class relations and class structures in Brazil
> that Cardoso formulates the essential aspects of the depend-
> ency analysis .... In my view some of the most successful
> analyses within the dependency school have been those which
> analyse specific situations in concrete terms.

The theorists cited here, Cardoso and Faletto, and the mode of
inquiry invoked, political economy, will be treated in our final
part.

Part IV represents the last of the substantive parts of this
study. In Part V we return to the abstract level of theoretical
discussion adopted in our prologue. We will be concerned with
abstract issues - generally, social theorizing and the proper
nature of the 'Western' intellectual's involvement with the Third
World - and with redeeming the various promises we have made
throughout the study.

Part V

Concluding remarks

8 Social theorizing and the matter of the Third World

1.0 A STATEMENT OF THE CONCERNS OF CHAPTER 8

Our Prologue began by noting that it had been claimed that the 'discovery of the Third World' was as significant for present-day social theorizing as was the nineteenth-century 'discovery of industrialization' for the classical theorists of political economy and the 'founding fathers' of sociology. It has been towards an elucidation of this claim that our study has been directed. The particular 'object' of inquiry has been taken to be the 'career' of 'development studies' in the post-Second World War period. This 'career' is taken to admit of the description that it involved the attempt to constitute an autonomous discipline, which project collapsed under the combined weight of shifting historical circumstance, on the one hand, and, on the other, both its own inherent implausibility and its success in occasioning refinement in argument. We have treated this history in the hope of displaying something of the nature of social theorizing.

The particular substantive elements of this history have been treated by means of the preparation of sociology-of-knowledge-informed analyses of exemplars, taken as representatives of 'schools' with 'development studies'. We have been concerned to display the characteristic argument-forms of these efforts, and this 'formal' aspect has provided a means whereby the study as a whole could be both integrated as a text and related to recent debate within the social sciences as to the precise nature of social theorizing.

Now, as regards social theorizing per se we have had comparatively little to say, save for some preliminary remarks in our Prologue and scattered comments and observations thereafter. This being so, the 'first main concern' of this concluding chapter will be with the issue of the nature of social theorizing. We wish to consider social theorizing as the practical activity of, in the prime instance, ideology(theory)-construction. We do so in the context of post-war treatments of the matter of the development of the Third World.

The idea that social theorizing was, in its central and most unequivocal guise, concerned with the construction of ideological schemas whereby action in the world might be ordered and legitimated we drew from Hawthorn, Gellner, Hollis and Nell, and others. Classical nineteenth-century efforts are paradigm cases of the business of the construction of ideological schemas; that is, political economy and marxian analysis. The argument mode of this tradition of thought we took to involve the 'deployment of a morally informed categorical frame'.

Now, if this indicates the prime conception of social-theoretical engagement used throughout this study, then we can see how the sociology of knowledge work can be taken to illustrate the claims made; that is, the substantive work offers specific examples of social-theoretical engagement. Thus 'growth theory' is seen to be derived from the efforts of the 'West' to theorize 'intervention' in the context of the multiple conflicts of the USA, UK, and USSR, and the nascent nationalisms of the Third World. Invoking Keynesian work, theorists construct 'growth theory'; that is, the legitimating and ordering theorem of an ideology of 'authoritative interventionism'. Empiricist in conception, this takes 'development' to be a technical matter. It further sees the presently developed nations as having access to the requisite technical expertise; that is, orthodox economics appropriately extended. A relationship of super- and sub-ordination is thus legitimated, and responsibility for the future reserved for the technical 'experts' of the 'West' and their agents. Similar analyses were prepared for the other identifiable 'schools' in the post-war 'career' of 'development studies'.

This preliminary strategy of inquiry has involved the distinction between conception and intent; it is under these two headings that our sociology-of-knowledge-informed critiques have been produced. This scheme of criticism is both an obvious derivation from our notion of ideology-construction and a fairly unambitious treatment of the idea of critique. Here the scheme of social theorizing can be extended. Thus the notion of ideology critique is a simple corollary of the notion of ideology-construction. Now, as the latter has been taken to be best exemplified in the tradition of political economy, where we lodge Marx as the most subtle practitioner, so we take the former to be best exemplified in that tradition of marxian theorizing called the Frankfurt School, which comes down to us with Habermas and critical theory. Within the scheme of critical theory the notion of ideology critique is extended. Here the ideas of democracy, critique, and ideology-ranking come together, in that the latter pair suppose an 'ideal-speech' situation which in turn supposes a democratic society. This notion of critique we take to be a circumstance- and problem-specific extension of marxian analysis, with continuing relevance to the circumstances of mature capitalism, and having implications for 'Western' thinkers' treatments of matters of the Third World. We take the critique of ideology to be complementary, and secondary, to political economic inquiry. Both derive from Marx.

We can now present a wider view of the scope of social theorizing. Social theorizing we take to be involved with the construction, and then the criticism and comparative ranking of ideological schemes. This stance informs our first main concern in this chapter.

As regards our 'first main concern', we want to consider, in the company and in the light of our substantive investigations, the nature of the prime case of social theorizing. Originally given by the circumstances and problems attendant upon nineteenth-century industrialization, we confront the business of ideology-construction, characterized as entailing the 'deployment of a morally informed categorical frame', and discuss the mode of argument called 'political economy'. Following on from this, we consider the logical corollary of ideology critique, and the attached issue of comparative ranking. We look at the notion of critique in the tradition of the Frankfurt School. Again we make these notes in the company of illustrative material drawn from our substantive analyses.

From this point we turn to our 'second main concern', which is the question of social-theoretical engagement with matters of the Third World. Thus Palma has advocated the mode of argument called 'political economy' for those who would grasp the circumstances of Third World societies: it is implicit that this is the business of Third World theorists and their allies. (This notion of 'allies' is ambiguous with regard to the nature of the social-theoretical engagement being involved. We can here recall the link, pointed out by dependency theorists, between centres of metropolitan power and their peripheral 'agents': here there was an obvious economic coincidence of interests. But in the case of 'allies', invoked by Palma, the link is not the same; it is, rather, political sympathy most directly. The role of the 'allies' would seem to be distant and, in terms of engagement, attenuated.) Political-economic work according to Palma is to replace current varieties of mechanico-formal theorizing.

Our second area of concern in regard to treating matters of the Third World involves asking after the 'Western' thinkers' engagement with all these issues. Asking, 'Just what does it make sense to say?' the general strategy of reply must be to invoke those dictums we have prepared in the light of reflection upon social theorizing as such, and granting these (reflexivity, problem specificity, circumstance relevance, etc.) endeavour to indicate what this means in practical terms. Thus we may recall that Habermas's scheme of critical theory bids us recreate the sphere of the 'public'. This rather implies that the task of the 'Western' thinker is the critical scrutiny of specific exchanges between rich and poor, and the dissemination of the results of such inquiries.

Diagrammatically we have this:
(The numbers in brackets indicate sections in the chapter)

Social theorizing

Abstract points   Matters of Third World
(First main concern)   (Second main concern)

(2) Prime case .... Political economy of (4)
    (Political economy)   Third World
                                 (Cardoso and Faletto)

(3) Specific case .... Democratic critical
    (Critique of ideology)   scrutiny (5)

Illuminated by examples from our substantive analyses.

    In sum, having at the outset of the study undertaken to con-
sider the post-war history of 'development studies' in such a
fashion as to reveal something of the nature of social theorizing
itself, we are now obliged to redeem that promise. We attempt to
do this in two ways: by recording, in the company of illustrative
material drawn from our substantive analyses, our general views
on the nature of social theorizing; and by noting, again with
reference to our stocks of examples, the implications of these
views on social theorizing for those treating matters of the 'development' of the Third World.
    By way of a disclaimer, it should be made clear that the re-
marks in this chapter are tentative only. That the remarks in the
Prologue, those scattered through the study, and those presented here, together imply a developed scheme, covering the
nature of social theorizing and its deployment in matters of the
Third World, we grant. That the remarks in this chapter constitute a first approximation to such a general scheme we deny.
Our observations on the 'career' of 'development studies' serve
to indicate only in very general terms how the lessons of this
episode for ideas about the nature of social theorizing might be
set out.

2.0 POLITICAL ECONOMY

We now discuss what we take to be the central, paradigm, case
of social-theoretical engagement; that is, political economy. It
should be made clear at the outset that our remarks are limited;
we come at political economy, as an argument mode, from our
readings of the 'career' of 'development studies'. As with Palma
we take the 'career' of 'development studies' to have resulted in
the requirement that we consider the broadest and richest intellectual tradition available: this we suppose to be political economy.
We do not claim the status of Marx-scholar, nor do we claim to be

widely familiar with the history of economics; consequently, our
approach to the detail of political-economic argument is specific
also. We follow the lines of interest seemingly growing within
the ambit of 'development studies' (or, if you like, on the ruins
of 'development studies') rather than tackling the exegetical
works of the more straightforwardly political-economic writing,
be it orthodox or Marxian. Thus our view of the mode of argument at issue will be distinctly 'sociological', and will focus upon
methodology.

We have taken political economy as representing the central
guise of social-theoretical engagement, and have said that this
ideology-construction involves the 'deployment of a morally informed categorical frame'. This slogan is the 'real' which we
here wish to 'reconstruct'. We tackle the problem via three interrelated issues: (i) just what is special about the mode of inquiry
called political economy? (ii) What is there to note in respect of
this tradition of inquiry? (iii) How do the various efforts we
have treated in our substantive analyses stand up to the criteria
of explanatory adequacy implied?

2.1 The style of political economy

Political economy as a general style is touched upon by Carver.
He notes that 'much of the effort of the political economists went
into what appears today to be a very general enquiry, with
statements and defences of their views on definitional questions,
and some of the moral and political issues entailed'.[1] In addition to this catholicity of intellectual interest involved in the
construction of their effort[2] we must also note their thoroughgoing practical intent. Thus, of Marx's work, Carver, whom we
here take to be offering a contrast with abstract and general
work, observes that 'Marx does not seem to have set out to write
a work of political economy ... rather he aimed to study social
production ... by looking critically at the contemporary science
of social production.'[3] It is reported that the critique of the
orthodox had a two-fold aim: to contribute to the central problems of the tradition, and to reveal the logic of inquiry in concert with deciphering the 'mysterious' categories of the orthodox.
In connection with this second aspect, Carver offers a summation
which will stand as general. Noting that Marx's critique is subtle
and allusive and consequently none too easy to follow, he remarks:
'Also, he does not limit himself to criticism, but investigates the
questions which interest him, and then develops his own point of
view - a characteristic Marxian procedure.'[4]

This characteristic breadth of scope is picked up by those who
would affirm the propriety of this mode of inquiry. The explicit
contrast is often drawn with the restricted, partial, institutionalized discourses of the various orthodox sciences of the social.
This rejection of compartmentalism is the most general starting
point for Cardoso and Faletto, who in recording in most general

terms their intellectual history, take note of the impact of US
academic social science and detail their response to it. They
state: 'We attempt to re-establish the intellectual tradition based
on a comprehensive social science. We seek a global and dynamic
understanding of social structures.'[5] Beyond this they lodge
themselves specifically within a tradition; thus 'we stress the
socio-political nature of the economic relations of production,
thus following the nineteenth century tradition of treating economy as political economy... which found its highest expression
in Marx.[6]

This point in respect of breadth of scope is echoed by Palma,
who reviews the 'school of dependency' and accords Cardoso
pride of place. At the end of the review it is observed that:[7]

> The principal common element in these approaches is the
> attempt to analyse Latin American societies through a 'com-
> prehensive social science', which stresses the socio-political
> nature of the economic relations of production; in short the
> approach is one of *political economy*, and thus an attempt to
> revive the 19th century tradition in this respect.

Political economy not only differs from orthodox social science
in the case of the catholicity of its intellectual interest and practicality of intent, but it also differs in the overall 'shape' of its
method. According to Carver, Marx draws a distinction between
logical analysis 'in which something complex is resolved or broken
up into simple elements',[8] on the one hand, and, on the other,
logical synthesis which 'proceeds in the opposite direction in
order to reproduce the concrete in a conception'.[9] It is the
second procedure that is taken by Marx to represent the proper
direction of inquiry for political economy.

The effort is one of the intellectual 'reconstruction of the real'.
Thus it is noted that:[10]

> Marx develops the view that this concrete result, achieved by
> a process of synthesis, is also the 'actual starting point', the
> starting point which actually exists; in other words to perform
> the synthesis properly he must, at the beginning, presuppose
> actuality in order to arrive at the summarized conceptualized
> concrete.

It would seem that Cardoso and Faletto have absorbed this point,
a sort of strategic teleology of argument, for they use the otherwise curious phrase 'Our approach of course *assumes and demon-
strates* that ...'(our emphasis).[11] We take them to be invoking
the idea of logical synthesis: they reconstruct the real in a disciplined fashion in the hope of uncovering its inherent possibility
for the future, and the 'real' they identify is an inegalitarian
and exploitative social organization of dependent capitalism.

As a scheme of inquiry/explanation, political economy is clearly
sharply distinct from the orthodoxy. Inquiry does not proceed by

abstraction from the given, generalization and model-building;
nor is explanation linked with, or made in, some fashion analogous to, causal predictiveness. Instead, inquiry proceeds by
the technically explicit, categorical 'reconstruction of the real'.
To explain is to make sense. Of Marx's notion of 'science',
Carver notes: 'The searching process for Marx was essentially
active, investigative, critical and practical; a scientific presentation, in his view, seems to have been one which solved conceptual mysteries and presented the human world accurately,
intelligibly and politically.'[12]

The differences just noted have been represented in recent
critical-theory-inspired work in the guise of a distinction between validation and authentication, which notions we took note
of in our Prologue. Cardoso and Faletto seemingly anticipate this
distinction when they treat the issue of 'measurement'. They
reject the model of social scientific explanation presented in
orthodox US work, and assert that 'The accuracy of a historical-
structural interpretation has to be checked by confronting its
delineation of structural conditions and trends of change with
actual socio-political processes.'[13] They speak of two elements
'construction of interpretation and... its practical validation',[14]
and note that:[15] 'the demonstration of an interpretation follows
real historical process very closely and depends to some extent
on its own ability to show socio-political actors the precise solution to contradictory situations'.[16]

2.2 The character of argument in political economy

If we note briefly the detailed character of argument in political
economy, we can introduce a discussion of the substantive efforts
we have treated earlier in the study and show the link to our
third concern for this chapter: the political economy of dependent
capitalism. At the same time we can add some more specific criteria of evaluation to our 'examples'.

Here Rockmore can aid us. We have seen earlier that he is
concerned with the extent to which philosophy informs Marx's
work, and at one point he asserts that in order to grasp the
scope of Marx's effort it is proper to regard it 'as a unity in
terms of its philosophical aspect'.[17] Reviewing these matters
moves him to the conclusion that 'three of marxian philosophy's
distinctive characteristics are monism, a categorical scheme and
philosophical anthropology, all of which are general features of
19th century philosophy'.[18] Expanding upon these points,
Rockmore moves to consider the realization of philosophy: a matter necessitating, as a prerequisite, an analysis of social circumstance. The shape of this, so far as he is concerned, flows from
the philosophical scheme just noted: it is observed that 'Marxian
politico-economic theory in general can be accounted for solely
in terms of two elements drawn from Marxian philosophy, the
general categorical approach and the specific category of activity,

which derives from his philosophical anthropology.'[19] With regard to this category 'activity', we read it as invoking the notion
of homo faber,[20] presented in capitalist society as alienated
labour. This scheme for encapsulating the fundamental character
of marxian (and thereby all, if it is good) political economy we
have borrowed and presented in the simplified form of the slogan
'deployment of a morally informed categorical frame', which we
take to describe the general process of this style of theorizing.

The matter of the politico-ethical orientation of the distinguishable efforts within the 'career' of 'development studies' was dealt
with in chapter 2. Hence we will not ask after Marx's philosophical anthropology; the locus, we have supposed, of his ethic.
However, we can ask after the 'categories' used in 'reconstructing the real'. What is their character, just what categories are
used, and where do they come from? Much of this has been anticipated above.

Carver notes of Marx's 'Introduction' (1857) that 'A great deal
of his work in this text is an effort to investigate a number of
fundamental questions - particularly questions about the logical
relations that obtain among the concepts and "categories" of political economy.'[21] Of the term 'category' itself we find, in a
note, that 'Marx sometimes uses "category" to cover both the
sense of "concept" as the idea of a thing in general and in the
sense of the more specific term "category" as a class or division
formed for a particular discussion or inquiry.'[22] This double
aspect seems to come out in the section of the 'Introduction'
(1857) which treats the method of political economy: the generality of ideas and their specificity in respect of some particular
economic form.

This treatment of the method of political economy presents, as
we have seen, the idea of logical synthesis as the proper direction of explanation. This direction of explanation reconstructs
the real, from the simple and abstract to the complex and concrete, but it is not to be confused with the actual genesis of the
real. These two aspects, explanatory categorical reconstruction
of the real and the actual history of the real, are 'related' in
subtle and diverse ways: the relation is occasioned by Marx's
view ('language is practical consciousness') that economic categories are expressions of social relations. The scope for confusion is wide; Marx concludes that economic categories can
appear more or less elaborated in more or less developed economies, but clarity in formulation and grasp of simple categories
only comes in modern, industrial, society.

Marx discusses 'labour', and indicates that discovering economic categories is not just an intellectual effort: it depends upon
change in society. Carver sees this as a 'specification of his
general thesis on social determination of ideas'.[23] Marx con-
gratulates Adam Smith on coming up with the idea of 'labour',
but adds: 'Indifference towards any specific kind of labour presupposes a very developed totality of real kinds of labour of
which no single one is any longer predominant.'[24] Labour, as

such, only becomes a plausible element of discourse when actual social labour attains a certain character - a general interchange-ability within the division of labour. Marx notes:[25]

> This example of labour shows how even the most abstract cate-gories despite their validity - precisely because of their abstractness - for all epochs, are nevertheless, in the spec-ific character of this abstraction, themselves likewise a product of historic relations, and possess their full validity only for and within these relations.

Cardoso and Faletto grant this notion of specificity of concepts, and read it as an injunction to specificity in their inquiries; they seek the intellectual frame of dependency in specific economic forms. Presuming a comprehensive social science, they note that 'the crucial methodological question was to delineate moments of significant structural change in countries characterized by dif-ferent situations of dependency'.[26] Or, again, 'Our analyses of concrete situations requires us to find out what forms of social and economic exploitation there are.'[27] Of their entire effort they observe that:[28]

> If the analytical effort succeeds, general platitudes and reaf-firmations about the role of capitalist modes of production can turn into a lively knowledge of real problems. It is necessary to elaborate concepts and explanations able to show how gen-eral trends of capitalist expansion turn into concrete relations among men, classes and states in the periphery. This is the methodological movement constituting what is called the pas-sage from an 'abstract' style of analysis into a 'concrete' form of historical knowledge.

It is this element - specific inquiry, for the intellectual means to reconstruct the real - that is heavily stressed by Palma. As he says: 'In my view some of the most successful analyses within the dependency school have been those which analyse specific situations in concrete terms.'[29]
Carver summarizes thus:[30]

> Marx declares that the most abstract categories though valid (in the sense that they are logical universals) for all forms of society are nevertheless very much the products of a long historical process of development. They can only be formulated at a late historical stage when social life has become diverse and complex, and only in a developed society do they possess their 'full validity', their full range of connotations and de-notations.

> The vantage point of a developed society permits the analysis of the economic forms of the less developed:
> 'The bourgeois economy thus supplies the key to the ancient,

etc. But not at all in the manner of those economists who smudge over all historical differences and see bourgeois relations in all forms of society.'[31] Marx, quite clearly, would not have been too pleased with 'modernizers' such as Rostow:[32]

> The so called historical presentation of development is founded, as a rule, on the fact that the latest form regards the previous ones as steps leading up to itself, and since it is only rarely and only under quite specific conditions able to criticise itself ... it always conceives them one-sidedly.

Marx concludes his discussion of the method of political economy by noting that in any society one particular form of production is the key to grasping the essence of that society. He says, 'In all forms of society there is one specific kind of production which predominates over the rest, whose relations thus assign rank and influence to the others.'[33] With regard to modern society 'capital is the all dominating economic power of bourgeois society. It must form the starting point as well as the finishing point.'[34] The detail of Marx's political economy is beyond our scope, but we may note with Rockmore that 'Marx began his investigations with commodity analysis, out of which he then generated the remaining portions of his politico-economic theory.'[35] Here the notion of commodity analysis is taken to derive from the 'general categorical approach and the specific category of activity'.[36] If the notion of 'commodity' seems to be the key Marx uses for grasping the nature of the capitalist economy, then Cardoso and Faletto similarly pursue an essential characterization of their task. Thus granting the notions of a 'comprehensive social science' of political economy, and taking Marx as the pre-eminent figure in the tradition, they seek to understand the set of social relationships typical of dependent capitalism as these present themselves in particular specific circumstances.

In the light of Marx's notion of social determination of ideas, and his view of the core of his society, we can understand his undertaking the critique of political economy. As Carver says:[37]

> There were two advantages for him in starting his study of capitalist production by investigating, in a critical way, the concepts and theories of political economy: they attempted, with a certain amount of success to describe and explain economic activity in capitalist society; at the same time they were marked, in his view, as products of that society.

Carver takes Marx to have a dual objective: he is aiming to improve political economy, actually to comprehend in an adequate fashion the dynamic of social production in bourgeois society; and concomitantly, he is aiming to unravel the intellectual machineries of the bourgeois theorist, to reveal their conceptual equipment as being adequate, at least to some extent, to a social world itself misshapen.[38] This intellectual/practical discovery

is Marx's contribution to the struggle of the historically progressive class, the proletariat. The effort, in the end, is resolutely practical in intent. In this vein, Nicolaus argues that
Marx began his theoretical researches after the failure of the
revolutions of 1848 under the leadership of the petit-bourgeoisie:
'the defeat of this influence, next time, and the elevation of the
working class to the position of leadership of the revolutionary
camp as a whole, next time, was the overriding aim of Marx's
studies'.[39]

Cardoso and Faletto appear similarly practical. After the failure
of nationalist developmentalism in Latin America in the early
1960s, and in the case of Cardoso's homeland, Brazil, the anticipated collapse into authoritarianism, they seek to identify the
possibilities for the future. In sum, they aver that:[40]

> It is not realistic to imagine that capitalistic development will
> solve basic problems for the majority of the population. In the
> end, what has to be discussed as an alternative is not the con-
> solidation of the state and the fulfilment of 'autonomous cap-
> italism', but how to supersede them. The important question
> then, is how to construct paths towards socialism.[41]

2.3 Implied criteria of explanatory adequacy

From the foregoing notes on the matter of the nature of the mode
of inquiry called political economy, taken here as the central example of social-theoretical engagement, we can derive a set of
criteria of adequacy with which to judge such efforts. This issue
of judging competing ideological schemes has been touched upon
earlier. At the very outset of the study (in chapter 2) we contrived a 'model of the crude' as a reference point around which
distinguishable efforts in the 'career' of 'development studies'
could be placed. This 'model of the crude' was generated by
negating, on a most general level, the requirements of reflexivity of thinking of matters social. Thus a 'crude' effort was unreflective in matters of conception and intent. This is how we
'located' various efforts relative to one another.

The notions of conception and intent were deployed throughout
the study as the (sociology-of-knowledge-informed) keys to the
analysis of specific social-theoretical efforts. At the same time
our Prologue had established the idea that social theorizing entailed the 'deployment of a morally informed categorical frame'.
We ran these together at the end of chapter 6 and we identified
three sorts of reflexivity in conception: value-sensitivity, engagement (a notion of agent of theory-execution was involved),
and self-disclosure (the effort explains itself). In respect of the
exchange between conception and intent, we gestured to notions
of conceptual richness and appropriateness of categorical frame.
In the case of intent, we read this as a matter of practicality: is
the intent tenable, is it proper? It was with reference to this set

that we suggested that ideologies might be ranked according to rational criteria. We now have a third line of approach to this general issue of weighting competing alternatives; it flows from our notes on political economy. Appropriately, given the 'balance' of the earlier work (that is, moral intent has been discussed at length, especially in chapter 2; self-reflexivity was stressed in chapter 1), this lets us focus on the 'categorical' part of the slogan 'deployment of a morally informed categorical frame'.

The criteria of adequacy implied in our discussion of political economic argument can be taken as treating the matters of the problem appropriateness and conceptual richness of categorical frames of inquiry. Thus the first criterion to be drawn from discussion is that of breadth of scope. We have, in political-economic inquiry, typically, the pursuit of 'comprehensive social science': the approach is general in the sense of its 'level' of treatment and in the sense of the resource base used. The second criterion indicates that political-economic argument must be practical in intent; the attempt to construct abstract and neutral social technologies is deemed unsatisfactory. The third criterion of ranking which derives from our discussion of political economy concerns the strategy of argument adopted: the 'reconstruction of the real' is taken as appropriate and scientific, and consequently familiar scientistic modelling schemes are rejected as falsely conceived. The above-noted criteria may be taken as somewhat 'formal'. To these we add two further criteria, which involve wider commitments in respect of the nature of the world and the relation of thought to it. The fourth criterion recalls that concepts are occasioned by specific economic forms; and that whilst their application is inevitably going to be general, their fullest expression is going to be specific to some historical economic form. The fifth criterion derives from the argument that the economic form 'bourgeois capitalism' is complex enough to occasion a set of economic categories adequate to the comprehension of all other, existing and preceding, economic forms.

We can consider our illustrative material, in the light of the above, around the questions of (a) practicality of intent (engagement); (b) strategy of explanation; (c) substantive categories used (where the use of such notions as 'capitalism' is taken as proper).

(a) Practicality of intent we have come across at several stages in the study. We have argued that a social-theoretical effort of ideology-construction needs must specify an agent of theory-execution, or else the effort does not engage with the world; it becomes ideological in the familiar pejorative sense, or (as we should say) tends to 'low-grade ideology'. In the 'career' of 'development studies' a variety of 'engagements' have been noted, and in the ambit of the orthodox interventionist schemes this is typically a matter of adopting the role of 'the expert'. So we have the expert as technician in the case of the Harrod-Domar-informed 'growth theory'. Development is equated with economic growth, identified by the movement of statistical economic indices, and is

to be secured by the implementation of policies identified in
accord with the results of the (natural) science of economics.
Policy-generation tends to become a simple (if hugely elaborated)
technical matter of professional problem-solving. This general
pattern is repeated, in more grandiose fashion, in the case of
'modernization theory'. Here engagement is conceived of as technical but the role is that of expert as master scientist. Development is still taken as a matter of promoting economic growth,
but this is lodged within a frame claiming to treat wider matters
of social change.

We have argued that the role of 'the expert' is an evasion of
matters of valuation: writers using this stratagem neither pretend to complete neutrality - for that would be both immediately
implausible and, taken more theoretically, manifestly absurd (involving a denial of relevance) - nor do they explicitly argue a
case. The role of expert, as a claim to a particular status in the
political process, is grasped as the social science analogue of
the role of the natural scientist; it serves to provide a legitimating scheme allowing the 'expert' to adopt, or aspire to, the position of extra-systemic cause [42] 'Theory' becomes the technical
manipulative summary of the results of modelling the world.

With 'Neo-institutional social theory' (NIST) we confronted a
third variety of the role of the expert, and this time we also find
an argued case. With 'NIST' the 'expert as planner' was lodged
within a view of the world which argued that in periods of social
crisis valuation matters become obvious, and indeed politics reduces to planning. This scheme was found to be the most plausible of all these earlier efforts, but at the same time deeply
flawed. Its solution to the problem of values - that is, the appeal
to crisis-occasioned 'obviousness' - was deemed to be sophistry;
and the engagement of the scheme, via the actions of the 'reasonable men' in charge of a reforming state, was taken to be implausible, an implausibility that was announced by the notion of
the 'soft state'.

With 'dependency' the engagement issue was rather more involved. Thus Furtado (our exemplar) begins by affirming the
pursuit of relevance (problem-specificity) and casts the effort
within the frame of an orthodox empiricism. His early work is
dominated by the idea of a typology of models of structures of
dependent economies. The later work broadens the project: thus
Marx is invoked in a distant fashion, and the 'historical/institu-
tional/structural method' is affirmed. The familiar 'dependency'
line now emerges. Furtado conceives of his effort as an interpretative interventionism; the engagement is thus close to that
of the expert, yet also politically nationalist in a general way.
More difficulties of interpretation arise when we discover that
this 'dependency' scheme is taken by Furtado to be the basis not
only of an economics relevant to Latin America, but also of an
economics relevant to the circumstances of the developed countries, in contradistinction to an orthodoxy perceived as generally
irrelevant. The vacillation in Furtado's work between problem-

specificity, on the one hand, and the urge to generality (taken, it seems, from orthodox notions of propriety of scientific explanation) recurs throughout his work and throughout the work of the 'school' of which we have taken him as exemplar.

This slide to the general reappears, it may be argued, in the related line which we labelled 'underdevelopment theory'. Here our exemplar was A.G. Frank and his surplus appropriation scheme, and the Baran-inspired line of which it is a part. Palma argues that this is 'mechanico-formal', in the end an inversion of the orthodox. This criticism has some point; yet contrariwise we have argued that Frank's earlier work, in particular, is coherently engaged, in the mode of the pamphleteer. That is, Frank's agent of theory-execution is the political activist, who is omnipresent in his work precisely because he casts himself in that role. Frank's work is transitional, between an orthodoxy-derived 'structuralism' and a marxian-inspired scheme of 'dependent capitalism'; and it seems to us that both readings, though apparently contradictory, are tenable in that the work of any one theorist must present itself in diverse aspects. Palma is concerned less with the immediate circumstances of production of work and more with an abstract and general discussion of method. Indeed this last point is perhaps the key to the cogency of Palma's attack. For in his later work Frank is, it would seem, concerned to reconstruct the marxian-theoretical base invoked (in very general terms) in the early work; there is, that is to say, a shift from activism to scholarship. It is in connection with the later area that Palma's attack strikes home.

With the later work of Frank we come across the last area of effort in the history presented in this study: 'neo-marxism'. The matter of engagement is again complex: with Debray/Fanon we found it useful to distinguish the three roles of practitioner, theorist and commentator, and argued that with the later Frank and 'neo-marxism' there was a shift from activists to scholars, where scholarship was taken as a variety of commentary. The engagement of the scholar we suggested, following Habermas, centred upon the critique of ideology; but in the work of the 'neo-marxists' we found evidence of a slide to generality that issued in what resembled, in some cases, a nascent 'left policy science' (see the critic Taylor, for example); which notion clearly is not marxian. As regards political economy, it would seem that the adoption of this mode of inquiry in the circumstances of mature capitalism would constitute, on the critical theory line's view, an indirect engagement at best. And when this mode is adopted in respect of the Third World, it involves, it might be argued, the not altogether obviously satisfactory analogy of agent/ally. Thus it is implied that Third World theorists and their allies needs must use political-economic argument. But how plausible is this role of ally?

(b) The efforts of the orthodox and, in various ways, of those calling themselves marxist, adopt what Hindess dubs the 'epistemology of models'. In our substantive analyses this matter of the

impact of the common-sense notion of scientific explanation was
a principal concern. Again, as we move through the period of
our history, the examples of the unfortunate effects of this mistaken acknowledgment of the supposed procedures of natural
science become increasingly subtle.

Thus the earliest efforts at grasping the nature of the exchange of rich and poor nations revolve around the Harrod-
Domar model. We argued that H-D was a narrowly conceived
effort in that its empiricism and aprioristic model-building, together with its use of the syntax of natural science, issues in
policy science. Modelling - the pursuit of some analogue of reality, corresponding to how things really are - we take to be a
fallacious procedure because descriptions of the world are theory-
informed; that is, 'facts' are 'brute-relative'. Consequently a
'general description' or 'model', properly conceived, can only be
regarded as the sum of the commitments entered into by the theorist in so far as he affirms some frame or other of analysis. If
his effort is to be plausible this, we might expect, would encompass the world of common sense (that is, what the realistic model-
builders begin and end with), but it would not be bound by it
In the present case, via a formal consideration of certain aspects
of the Keynesian scheme, Harrod proceeds to execute an elaborate series of manipulations of certain notions and to derive
from them policy conclusions. We have noted Robinson's scepticism, both of Harrod's effort and the strategy itself as sympto-
matic of certain bad habits in economics. The scientism of
modelling was something we have stressed: abstraction and generalization from common-sensically read experience, coupled with
formalism in presentation and more or less explicit claims to the
status of (natural) science, all issue in efforts that are scientistic. The syntax of natural science compounds errors of conception,
and any residual sensitivity on the part of the theorist as to what
is involved in social theoretic work is dissipated. The theorist
comes to take his efforts as analogous to those of the natural
scientist, and the 'role of the expert' thus emerges.

To our mind this is all very low-grade ideology. This is very
clear in the case of 'modernization theory', where a model of the
modern is affirmed that is transparently a general characterization
of the US, according to the orthodox view. This model of the modern is contrasted with a model of traditional society - called forth
by negating the former - and this fundamental dichotomy is elucidated by reference to a further set of dichotomies: rural/
urban, agrarian/industrial, etc. The process of 'modernizing'
entails losing one set of attributes and gaining the other, thus
effecting the shift from 'traditional' to 'modern'. The basic crudity
is appalling, even in its elaborated versions.

More sophisticated in comparison are the efforts of 'NIST'.
Again modelling is the basic approach, but here there are additional stresses on problem-specificity, realism in modelling and
reflexivity in engagement. 'NIST' represents what can be called
a 'sociologized economics', and we considered at some length the

use made by 'NIST' of the resources of social science. We found that, epistemologically, fine-grained data was necessary for the construction and checking of concepts; methodologically, social science data establishes the possibility of realistic models and social science concepts their general structure; and finally, procedurally, the habit of reflexive scepticism is used to generate criticisms of proffered formulations. This reflexivity does not extend to reading social theorizing as a matter of ideology-making, but rather it is a partial effort: reflexivity appears as an additional technique which serves to permit better modelling. We reported that we took this to be the most sophisticated and plausible interventionist scheme.

When it comes to marxian-informed exercises, the issue of whether or not a correct strategy of explanation is being used becomes rather more cloudy. With Furtado, who makes play in his late work with a rehabilitated Marx, the tensions between problem-specificity and generality of formulation colour his entire approach. In the end, what began as the search for an economics relevant to Latin America is taken to issue in the construction of a new, and generally applicable, economics. The effects of the epistemology of models conception of inquiry continues in avowedly marxian efforts. Frank, for example, is taken to be pursuing 'mechanico-formal models' by Palma; and Frank's use of a simple explanatory frame and the syntax of the natural science orthodoxy permits this reading. An analogous slide to the general can be detected, it would seem, in some academic marxian scholarship; there is a retrogressive collapse into the orthodoxy, which issues in general schemes that ignore the matter of the necessary specificity of the theorist's engagement. General models of 'the one revolutionary path' are of little use.

Turning directly to the matter of the procedure of the 'reconstruction of the real', in contrast to modelling, then in respect of the strategy of explanation adopted by 'neo-marxism' we find ourselves in a quandary. In respect of the (sometimes furious) debate about whether or not Baran et al. are really marxists we are agnostic. Baran, the 'father' of the 'neo-marxist' approach, begins with the notion of surplus, which is both an economic and an ethico-political evaluative notion, and proceeds to account for the present circumstances and future possibilities of Third World 'dependent capitalism'. This on the face of it looks like logical synthesis; but Baran has been called a 'left-Keynesian', and the effort of 'neo-marxism' subjected to detailed and extensive criticism. Equally, these criticisms tend to focus on showing how Baran's substantive analytical machineries diverge from those deployed by Marx; which strictly would seem to be a largely irrelevant issue unless we are to suppose that the world has more or less stood still over the last century. The more appropriate question, suggested by Palma, is not whether or not this or that approach closes with, or diverges from the detail of Marx's work, but rather whether the effort is good or bad political economy. It would seem to be difficult to deny that Baran's work is political economy; and if its reception says anything about its problem appropriateness, then evidently we must grant it that also.

(c) In respect of the substantive categories deployed we can, at a most general level, note a shift from narrowly conceived technical schemes of economics-based work (growth theory, modernization) through elaborated sociologized economics (NIST, dependency) to full-blown marxian-informed efforts. The sequence 'orthodox', 'radical', 'marxist' is taken by us to represent an increasing richness of elements of categorical frame. The ideological schemes become subtler as attempts to constitute an autonomous discipline of 'development studies' fail.

2.4 Summary note

We have said that social theorizing as it presents itself in the business of the construction of ideological schemes, considered here in the context of the prime case of political economy, may be taken to entail the 'deployment of a morally informed categorical frame'. In terms of a simple checklist of attributes that slogan can be unpacked as follows: theorizing must be (i) problem-centred; the pursuit of academically bounded, scientistically conceived, general schemes is disavowed; (ii) circumstance-specific, that is, acknowledging that its business is with particular problems in particular places at particular times; (iii) reflexive (and this can be read as the methodological corollary of (ii)), as a routine matter of course rather than occasionally or as technique for improving orthodox efforts; (iv) engaged, (where this can be read as a methodological corollary of (i)); unless the theoretical efforts specify an agent of theory execution, the work cannot be taken to latch onto the world; (v) categorical-morally informed; so most generally we affirm that 'theory' is central to explanation.

3.0 CRITIQUE

If the foregoing indicates what can be taken as the prime conception of social-theoretical engagement, then what of the corollary, ideology critique? Ideology critique, as it presents itself in the tradition of the Frankfurt School, may be taken as a circumstance/problem-specific extension of marxian inquiry: it is, moreover, well suited to the academic institutional location of many 'Western' social theorists. Three elements order our remarks: (a) the backdrop of this tradition of critique, (b) the critique of ideology, (c) comparative ranking. As we have already had occasion to make reference to Habermas, we will approach these matters through considering his work, and only thereafter will we make any wider references to the Frankfurt School or 'humanist' marxisms. Yet at this point it must be clearly understood that our remarks are preliminary, tentative and largely

untutored; that is, we make no pretence to a developed grasp
of Habermas, much less do we take ourselves to be contributing
to the further elucidation of the ideas of this tradition.

(a) The nature of the exchange between theory and practice
is a central concern of Habermas. Rejecting the (recently) dominant 'positivist' scheme which affirms a self-understanding
which divorces knowledge and human interests, Habermas displays a series of strategic cases of the exchange of theory and
practice. He considers the historical and formal character of
each case's self-understanding and identifies the particular
relationship of interest and knowledge that informs or structures
them. The tripartite schema of knowledge-constitutive interests
was introduced in our Prologue and we sketch it below. First,
however, we can note Habermas's strategic, political, concern.

The classical notion of politics is taken to be presented by
Aristotle. In Aristotle's work politics did not pursue the rigorous understanding associated now with natural science, rather
it sought phronesis – a prudent understanding. Habermas takes
the view that this classical conception has decayed into positivist-
informed schemes of technical control. He speaks of a 'technocratic consciousness' where this pursues an ideal of the effective
abolition of politics in favour of a schema which would have policy scientific work disclosing objective (social scientific) necessity. This 'necessity' would be the province of the expert (and
we have seen throughout this study of development that the role
of the expert is often embraced). The crucial question becomes
the establishment of a politics appropriate to scientific civilization. The key to this would seem to be the reconstruction of
the public, a sphere of free discussion. This task presents itself most generally as the critical dissolution of distortions in
communication – we pursue the matter in the restricted context
of the critique of ideology.

An outline of Habermas's scheme of knowledge-constitutive
interests is to be found in his 'Knowledge and Human Interests'.
Here we find the tripartite scheme of 'interests'. The technical
interests of the empirical analytic, presently cast in logical empiricist (positivist) guise. The practical interest of the historical hermeneutic sciences concerned with rendering the social
world intelligible. Finally, and in contrast to these scientistic
inquiries (both take their task to involve treating a given set of
objects in a descriptive mode), we have the emancipatory interest of critical theory. Now of this last, Habermas makes Marx's
materialist presentation of the Enlightenment's stress on reason
the prototype – although never developed by Marx who, regret-
tably, collapsed into scientistic political economy. At this point
we may note two areas of criticism of Habermas's schemes.

First, it has been suggested that Habermas, and the Frankfurt
School, have regressed intellectually and are now pre-, rather
than post-marxian. Of Habermas's fellow Frankfurt School marxist, Marcuse, MacIntyre has suggested that far from 'up-dating'
Marx, what Marcuse accomplished is the reinvention of that

Young Hegelian 'critical criticism' which Marx was at pains to break from.[43] This or some analogous suspicion must attach to the work of Habermas. If, as seems to be the case, Habermas wants to make 'criticism' not only the presently relevant mode of social-theoretical engagement for the European left, but also, further, the paradigm of social-theoretical engagement, then this must be regarded as problematical.

The second, linked, note concerns Marx's dealings with political economy. In contrast to Carver et al., treated above, who make Marx's work a unity, Habermas seems to present a distinction between the critical and the political-economic. The latter is read as scientistic reduction; that is, we have the familiar Frankfurt School motif of the division between genuine marxists concerned with praxis and the mechanistic and wrong-headed followers of the Engelsian line of 'scientific marxism'. This reading of Marx - that in so far as he is involved with political economy he is tainted - is one that, in the light of our notes on political economy, and in the light of our arguments (illustrated from the 'career' of 'development studies') to the centrality of political economy in ideology making, we cannot share.

Returning to the project of Habermas's critical theory, drawn from undeveloped elements of Marx, we find that this is accomplished with a Freudianized historical materialism. Thus 'distorted communication', ideology, is regarded as a block to rational behaviour and supportive of the status quo. The critique of ideology functions such common sense and contributes to change in society. Moreover, the ideal of an autonomous selfhood and free exchange is anticipated in the structure of language itself; so communication anticipates and implies free communication. The pursuit of open debate, a reconstructed 'public', is compatible with scholarship, appropriate to scientific civilization, and tends to the realization of democracy.

Giddens treats this in the following way. In respect of Habermas's notion of ideology as distorted communication, he notes: 'There are two strands in Habermas' writing relevant to the characterization of ideology - and its critique.... The first is part of Habermas' discussion of the development of modern society and politics, the second locates ideology on the level of methodological analysis.'[44] The former is the critique of technocratic consciousness, the reduction of politics to technical expertise; whilst the second presents ideology critique as the central mode of inquiry for social science.

The social scientist analyses the process of creation and maintenance of structures of meaning, and their extension in the social world. These procedures and their results are presented in a fashion analogous to the therapeutic exchange of psychiatry. In this 'second phase', matters of plausibility, accessibility and problem appropriateness will be relevant to the acceptance (authentication) of the proffered schemes. The therapeutic process is governed by the notion of an 'ideal speech situation', intrinsic to language, which serves as a regulative ideal for discourse (as opposed to speech where consensus holds), and as an ethico-political engagement in that an 'ideal speech situation' supposes free debate, an 'open society'.

The subsequent progress of Habermas's thought is reviewed by McCarthy,[45] who regards the increasingly abstract treatment of these issues as resulting in a situation where an 'early' and a 'late' Habermas can be identified. It is suggested that only the former has much claim to any obvious contact with either the world or the marxian tradition. Bernstein too sees this problem. He notes:[46]

> the very self-understanding of the nature of a theory with practical intent by critical theorists requires the existence of a group or class of individuals to whom it is primarily addressed, and who will be the agents of revolution. But as critical theory became more sophisticated, this central political demand played less and less of a role. No critical theorist, including Habermas, has been absolutely clear on this point in the way Marx was. To whom is critical theory addressed .... What difference is there between the rarefied conception of critical theory, and the errors of the Young Hegelians that Marx so ruthlessly attacked and exposed?

So much for the most recent and elaborated scheme of critique: in terms of the division identifiable in Habermas's efforts, we consider the early notions of critique. In particular, we wish to see if they extend the ideas of criticism, developed in treating substantive work in a sociology-of-knowledge-informed fashion, in any useful ways.

(b) With regard to the 'critique of ideology', we need to take note that the term ideology figures in this area of debate in several senses. Thus in the Prologue to this study we made the notion of ideology the key methodological device for social theorizing. We began by citing MacIntyre's view that the limits of thought equal the limits of my world, and the limits of thought represent my exchange with my social world. Social inquiry thus appears as the investigation of language games, in the first instance. This scheme is affirmed in contrast to orthodox scientistic schemes of modelling. From this point two lines diverge. First, there is the methodology adopted in this study; that is, we have attempted to grasp the nature of a series of 'language games' via a sociology-of-knowledge-informed scheme; we have asked after the nature of a series of ideological statements. The second line involves a stronger development of the ontological aspects of the ideas; that is, rather than treating 'ideology' as an investigative key, it is used as a means of constituting more general characterizations of the social world. We took note of this when we referred to Giddens in our Prologue. In his work we find that the notion of 'language constituting the world' can be reinterpreted in a sociological and dynamic fashion: thus we have the cluster

of notions affirming that reality is structured, that these structures are the product and ground of social interaction, that
these structures are maintained and change, and that ordinary
language itself reflects power distributions. Clearly, in this
fashion our simple sociology-of-knowledge-informed scheme of
criticism, in terms of the conception and intent of identifiable
social-theoretical efforts, can be extended into a scheme that is
radically different. In nuce, the difference appears to be between a delimited-formal notion of ideology, which attaches to
those efforts of political economy we have instanced as paradigmatically social-theoretical engagement, on the one hand; whilst,
on the other, we have a pervasive-informal notion of ideology
which permits the ideological aspects of diverse language games
within society to be uncovered.

We have not had occasion to use an extended notion of critique,
one resting upon this 'pervasive-informal' notion of ideology. In
the Frankfurt School line the critique of ideology is taken as a
prerequisite of social change where culture is repressive and the
economic form advanced; in such circumstances (mature Western
capitalism) the critique of ideology in this elaborated sense does
indeed make sense as a proposal. In the Third World, where the
economic form of capitalism is of a different, 'dependent', type
and the polity is rarely equivalent to that of the 'West', the critique of ideology in a more classically marxian guise seems to make
better sense. Thus Cardoso and Faletto, treating Latin America,
invoke a tradition of political economy best exemplified in the
work of Marx. They do not invoke the language-sensitive schemes
of critique as treated by Giddens and the other thinkers we have
noted.

In a recent essay, Giddens[47] reports that the notion of ideology appears in Marx's work in two guises. One revolves around
the ideology versus science polarity, and the other (if we understand Giddens rightly) revolves around the sectional interest
versus ideology (pejorative) polarity. Now, in our sociology-of-
knowledge-informed critiques we have followed a line which reflects this division. We have been interested in conception and
intent. Of the former, we have considered scientism, concerning
ourselves with the pervasive impact upon social theorizing of the
image of the natural sciences; and with the latter, we have asked
to what extent do our exemplars of schools actually come clean
and argue coherent cases.

In terms of judging what is good and what is not so good in
the way of analyses of the circumstances of peripheral economies
within the world capitalist system, that is, 'development' - then
it seems to us, in the light of the foregoing reflections, that the
line of critical theory which culminates in Habermas is overly concerned with the subtleties of the investigation of meaning systems within the developed countries. If, however, our aim is to
grasp the issue of 'development', then the simpler notions of
critique - those flowing from consideration of ideology-making -
are likely to be more fruitful.

(c) With regard to the matter of the comparative ranking of ideological efforts to grasp the nature of 'development' we would argue for the replacement of the pervasive, and to our mind pernicious, image of the natural sciences. That the pursuit of a mode of inquiry cast in natural-science-aping terms has either served as a useful cover for ideological (pejorative) efforts or has sown confusion in otherwise laudable efforts are views that have been expounded at length. The varieties of claims to the status of expert noted fall within the first class and the various slides-to-the-general in formulations fall within the second class.

The contrary position which we have advocated is that distinguishable 'lines' within development studies should be taken as ideologies quite properly arguing a case for some client group or other. They may be analysed in terms of the manner of their construction and the nature of their claims/proposals and ranked accordingly.

In summary: we have taken the production of delimited and formal ideological schemes to be the prime case of social theorizing. The efforts of the nineteenth-century political economists are taken as best examples, with Marx pre-eminent. This mode of engagement is displayed in the work of Cardoso and Faletto, to whom we will shortly turn. The notion of ideology-construction readily calls forth the notion of critique, and we have been concerned to look at this. In the Frankfurt School-derived scheme of critical theory, we have taken note of what claims to be both a circumstance-specific extension of Marx and the establishment of a sophisticated scheme of critique. Both claims are problematical; and whilst the questions raised are absorbing, we tend to the view that discussion has become increasingly detached from the 'real world', and is, in any case, overly self-absorbed in so far as matters of the development of the Third World are concerned. (For example, a democrat confronted by, say, a General Somoza might be well advised to set aside anxieties in respect of elucidations of Habermas in favour of securing a ready supply of Kalashnikovs. We do not want to say that the pervasive-informal idea of ideology cannot be used in Third World polities; but that if theorizing is practical, then maybe delimited-formal schemes will be more immediately useful.) However, there may be one area of inquiry where a critical-theory-informed line might be appropriate. This is the area, internal to the developed, of 'popular perceptions' of the Third World and the relationship of these perceptions to the behaviour of rich world governments/business. This question we treat in section 5.0 of this chapter.

4.0 THE POLITICAL ECONOMY OF DEPENDENT CAPITALISM

A matter that we have had occasion to touch upon earlier reappears at this point. It is the question of what is to count as a properly marxian analysis of the Third World. Debate is occasioned by the blurred lines between 'dependency' and 'neo-marxism', and by the questioned status of the latter scheme.

With regard to discussions of 'dependency', which for Palma is an embracing term, he argues that the line's 'roots in the tradition of marxist thought'[48] have not been properly brought out. This tradition he then proceeds to review. It is an illuminating effort and presents the analysis of the exchange of centres/peripheries as a legitimate area of inquiry into the dynamic of capitalism. Three attempts to theorize the exchange are identified. First we have those of Marx and Engels, where 'capitalism (is seen) as a historically progressive system which will be transmitted from the advanced countries ... and which will spread through the backward nations'.[49] Following this we have the 'classic' theorists of imperialism, treating the circumstances of Russia and regarding Third World possibilities as 'limited by the new imperatives of the advanced economies'.[50] Third in this schema we have the work of the 'neo-marxists' following, preeminently, Baran. These works are pessimistic with regard to the possibilities of development of Third World economies so long as they remain incorporated within the world capitalist economy.

Of this last group, Palma notes:[51]

> It is in this third phase that the analyses of the dependency school emerge .... The core of these analyses is the study of the dynamics of individual Latin American societies through the concrete forms of articulation between 'external factors' .. .. and 'internal factors'.... They are therefore a part of the theory of imperialism.

Thus does Palma locate 'dependency', as fathered by Baran, in the line of marxian efforts to grasp the exchange of centres/peripheries.

The central figure, for Palma, in this 'dependency' line is Cardoso. We saw above that Marx could be regarded as the preeminent figure in the important line of inquiry called political economy. This was a view that Palma took: he goes on to claim that Cardoso (with Faletto) is a political economist treating 'dependency'. That Cardoso and Faletto, whose joint text we have looked at, are treating 'dependency' is evidently the case. Whether they are adopting the mode of political economy raises less obviously soluble questions. That they take themselves to be political economists working within a marxian line seems on the face of it to be clear. Thus they remark that they are 'following the nineteenth century tradition of treating economy as political economy'.[52] They continue: 'This methodological approach ... assumes that the hierarchy that exists in society is the result of established ways of organising the production of material and spiritual life ... we attempt to analyse domination in its connection with economic expansion.'[53] So where is the problem; have we not found the properly marxian approach to theorizing development? The problem presents itself via two thoughts: the one concerning Baran and 'mechanico-formal analysis', and the other concerning Cardoso and Faletto's self-positioning in respect of Marx.

Palma, in his treatment of the third distinguishable line of inquiry into the exchange between rich and poor within the marxian tradition, has occasion to argue that Baran, Frank, Wallerstein, et al., present impoverished and therefore questionable explanations. Briefly sketching the Frankian scheme of the 'surplus extraction chain', established over centuries and now serving to fix peripheral economies in a condition of underdevelopment, Palma raises objections in respect of the argument strategy. He observes that:[54]

> Frank's error... lies in his attempt to explain this phenomenon using the same economic determinist framework of the model he purports to transcend; in fact he merely turns it upside down: the development of the 'core' necessarily requires the underdevelopment of the 'periphery'... he constructs a mechanico-formal model.

Contrasting this with the Cardoso line, Frank's approach is condemned for a failure to analyse these matters in terms of the specific characteristics of such societies. This call for attention to the specificity of the intersection of particular peripheral economies with the world capitalist economy is repeatedly made by Palma; and recalling our earlier remarks on Cardoso and Faletto it evidently derives from them. Additionally, it is clear that in the light of our review of the nature of political economy, calls for circumstance/problem-specific formulations are appropriate. If we take Frank straightforwardly as a political economist then Palma's critique is apposite; but, as we have seen, Frank's work is a little more complex than this simple view allows. With regard to Palma's exposition, it seems that he pursues a sociologist's political economy, concerned that analyses should display the exchanges through time of identifiable class groupings. If we now turn to economics-minded thinkers, these objections to what we have termed 'neo-marxism' are presented in considerably more abrupt fashion.

Kay takes the whole 'neo-marxian' effort to have been incorrectly formulated: the claims of the orthodoxy that underdevelopment was an 'original condition' and that the historical development of capitalist metropoles had nothing to do with it were disproved. 'But this is as far as it went. As none of the major works produced by this school was firmly based on the law of value which Marx discovered and elaborated, little progress could be made beyond this point.'[55] This concern for the deployment of the 'theory of value' is also shown by Desai: of the general 'neo-marxian' stance of Baran it is observed that 'Baran and Sweezy in the *Monopoly Capital* do not use the value system at all.'[56] Desai, like Kay, takes this as the key to marxian economics. The following dismissive conclusion is offered:[57]

Baran and Sweezy's analysis is then a combination of Neoclassical micro-economics, without the assumption of perfect competition, and orthodox macroeconomics. The question whether Marxian economic theory is relevant to contemporary capitalism can easily be answered in the negative after reading *Monopoly Capital*.

If Cardoso and Faletto are in the line of Baran then they must be making large alterations to the economics and procedural aspects of that scheme. The procedural shifts, from 'mechanico-formal' generality to circumstance and problem-specificity, we have noted. But Cardoso and Faletto are, so far as can be seen, silent on matters of economics. The procedural and sociological (class analysis) and political revisions to 'neo-marxism' made by Cardoso and Faletto seem, at least in outline, to be clear; but what they would use to replace the economic substance of the dismissed 'mechanico-formal' surplus extraction scheme with is not clear. A doubt arises then, at this point, as to whether or not the scheme advocated by Palma is in fact marxian.

If we shift to our second area of unease we note that Cardoso and Faletto do not, so far as can be seen, actually claim to be marxists. They distance themselves, in a way that the academic Althusserian critics of Baran noted in chapter 7 do not, from Marx's detailed engagement with the economic substance of the classical tradition of political economy. Marx is taken as an exemplar of a procedure which they would affirm to be appropriate to grasping the nature of Latin American economies. They subsume him within a tradition of inquiry in which they lodge themselves. However, the political economy presented by Cardoso and Faletto seems devoid of any economics, save for general elements invoked from time to time in a treatment that seems heavily 'sociological'; thus they discuss the behaviour of interacting groups through history.

Now this is a problem for this study also. We have come to take up a position that resembles Cardoso and Faletto's vis à vis Marx and method. So Marx is taken as exemplar of a tradition of inquiry into which we lodge ourselves, in so far as that tradition and that exemplar are made the paradigm case of social theoretic engagement; against which we locate our own different and restricted critical efforts. Concomitantly, we may note that we have come at these matters of political economy out of 'dependency' debates, and not by considering economists on political economy. The suspicion must remain, for the present, that a fully explored political economic analysis of some circumstance or other must involve a significantly larger element of the familiarly economic than Cardoso and Faletto, or ourselves (so far as it might be appropriate) have displayed.

To recapitulate, briefly: given our remarks on Marx and on political economy, the treatment of the detailed economic aspects of Marx and the marxian tradition, and present discussions of these and their extension to matters of Third World, are out-

standing questions. Nevertheless, if we consider the business
of revising/recasting/fitting to new circumstances an intellectual
scheme, then the work of Baran et al. would seem, prima facie,
to have been seminal. Palma, let us recall, for all his doubts,
does make the 'neo-marxian' scheme the third major effort to
comprehend the nature of peripheral economies in the history of
the marxian tradition. Subsequent to Baran's early formulations,
the 'neo-marxian' line has been revised, polished and adjusted
over some considerable length of time. That all this work is in
error, or is a passing intellectual fashion, seem to be implausible
claims. Rather, in line with our above remarks on the nature of
social-theoretical engagement, we would wish to take the variant
of the 'neo-marxist' line presented by Cardoso and Faletto as
having established – at least in political, sociological and general
economic respects – the essential nature of an elaborated ideological engagement with the Third World. We can now turn to the
work of Cardoso and Faletto directly, and take note of Cardoso's
career via the exegesis provided by Kahl.

Palma characterizes what he takes to be the third, and most
convincing, type of 'dependency' analysis (the others being
Baran et al., and the reformulations of ECLA, Furtado and Sunkel) by noting three points. First, that this approach slots the
Latin American economies into the world economy, and takes itself to be a reworked theory of imperialism. Second, the internal
dynamics of dependency are treated at greater length. Third,
there is a thoroughgoing insistence upon the importance of
specificity in inquiry. In respect of this third point, Palma criticizes preceding efforts as 'partial', and urges that attention
must be focused on 'how the general and specific determinants
interact in particular and concrete situations'.[58]

The career of Cardoso we can briefly present by citing the
sketch made by Kahl, who is an American sociologist. His stance
towards Cardoso recalls strongly that of Gruchy to the 'institutionalists'; that is, the treatment is suffused with an apology for
his subject's radicalism. None the less, it provides a convenient
thumb-nail sketch.

Of Cardoso's early work, Kahl says: 'Three major influences
converged during those years in the mid-1950's. The first was
the direct study of the Negro situation in Brazil; the second
was a theoretical study of Marxist literature; and the third was
participation in radical politics.'[59] The early (more orthodox)
work treated the position of the Negro in Brazil, but in the early
1960s it is reported that Cardoso's interests shifted. At this time
there was a spell of vigorous growth and high optimism. Kahl
notes: 'Many believed that the business leaders of "national
bourgeoisie" were heroes who were moving the country... toward... an independent industrial economy and a modernized
democratic polity.'[60] In this period Cardoso investigated the
community of entrepreneurs who were, according to the orthodoxy of development theory, the key groups in matters of economic progress. It is reported that all this material persuaded

Cardoso that the position of the entrepreneurial group in respect of other major groups was fundamentally unstable. When the US-backed coup of 1964 came Cardoso was not surprised. The next three years were spent with an ECLA group in Chile where Cardoso worked with Faletto. In parallel with a general reworking of the survey material gathered in respect of the study of industrialists, the notion of 'dependency' was revised and elaborated. In 1967 Cardoso and Faletto published their work 'Dependency and Development in Latin America'.

Turning to that inquiry we will now consider specimens of their writing, rather than go on with any more general exegesis. We can look at their study and see how it presents a political economic analysis of the circumstances of Latin America (as seen by theorists actually resident there). In the new (1976) preface to their book, the authors remark that: (1) 'If the analytical effort succeeds, general platitudes and reaffirmations about the role of capitalist modes of production can turn into a lively knowledge of real processes'; (2) 'It is necessary to elaborate concepts and explanations able to show how general trends of capitalist expansion turn into concrete relations among men, classes and states in the periphery .... This is the methodological movement constituting what is called the passage from an "abstract" style of analysis into a "concrete" form of historical knowledge.'[61] We treat the two elements we have marked in turn.

An example of (1) might be this. Discussing the post-Second World War adjustments in societies to shifts in pre-war class alliances occasioned by changes in relations with the world economy, Cardoso and Faletto make the following report[62]

In Argentina, where the agro-export sector continued to be economically important, industrialization, although accompanied by substantial redistribution, was not significant, especially in the basic industries. The new situation of the world market presented the alternatives most dramatically: to hold down wages and public expenditures at the expense of the working-popular classes; or to re-organise and raise the productivity of the agro-export economy in order to use it to continue long term financing of the modern industrial sector. After the fall of Peron in 1955, the anti-populist opposition chose the latter policy. Nevertheless, the export sector could not by itself impose this objective on the rest of the country, nor could it counteract the pressure of the masses through an alliance with the politically weak industrial sectors, as was attempted by the Frondizi government (1958-62). Military intervention became frequent both as a form of arbitration and as an open reaction against a return to populism. This course of economic development was vigorously blocked by broad sectors of wage earners. It could not be imposed as a policy that, if not legitimate, was at least efficient. Therefore, there was neither development nor political stability.

An example of (2) might be found in their effort to characterize 'the new dependency'. Of this they note that it could be the
'most significant contribution by "dependistas" to the theory of
capitalistic societies'.[63] They offer the following:[64]

> peripheral industrialization is based on products which in
> the centre are mass consumed, but which are typically lux-
> urious consumption in dependent societies. Industrialization
> in dependent economies enhances income concentration as it
> increases sharp differences in productivity without general-
> izing this trend to the whole of the economy... accentuating
> what has been called in Latin America structural heterogeneity.

The elucidation of the various emerging class positions and
their relationships over time constitutes the key to Cardoso and
Faletto's effort. So they argue as follows:[65]

> Inward development in Latin America depended on an improve-
> ment in the terms of trade and on some participation by the
> population in the benefits of development. Momentarily favour-
> able circumstances made it possible to incorporate the masses
> without excluding the dominant sectors and strata of the
> period of outward expansion. This incorporation took place
> through the national populist version of the 'developmentalist
> alliance' in Brazil under Vargas, and in Argentina under
> Peron, and through the 'developmentalist state' in Mexico.
> When an attempt was made to satisfy the pressures from the
> peasant and urban popular sectors for greater incorporation,
> the capacity of accumulation was lowered. This broke an im-
> portant link in the alliance of political hegemony: the agrarian
> sector, especially the latifundista, turned against those urban
> industrial sectors that might support the demands of the
> masses; at the same time, the agrarian groups found allies in
> the industrial and financial groups that could not meet the
> pressures of the urban popular sectors for higher wages.

Thus do Cardoso and Faletto trace the tensions within the typical Latin American economy: a shifting scene of competing, co-
operating, cohabiting, and mutually unconnected groups, the
whole subject to the impact of the world economy, largely beyond
any group's control.

This ostensive presentation of Cardoso and Faletto follows our
earlier remarks on political economy. Excepting the two problematical points noted, these specimens reveal a marxian argument
strategy: particularly, class analysis. And Cardoso's recent
concerns (if Kahl's reports are true) – with the spontaneous
modes of organization of the masses, their potential for effecting
change, and the intellectuals' order/interpreting task – recall the
classic statements of the 1848 'manifesto' on the role of the communist party. It is such specificity of engagement – the element
stressed by Palma – which is surely the key to political-economic
analysis of Third World societies.

5.0 DEMOCRATIC-CRITICAL ENGAGEMENT

This section will be the most programmatic and speculative of
this chapter. The earlier sections have been ordered by discussions of particular materials, but here our effort is more
prospective. We seek to offer a first approximation of what, in
effect, is a frame whereby present engagements might be ordered
in the form of a series of study-derived prescriptions as to how
democratic-critical engagement treating Third World matters
should proceed.

Phrasing a starting question is difficult. If, on the one hand,
we proceed by asking just what does it make sense for the
'Western' thinker (who will be an academic as like as not) to say
about matters of the Third World, then discussion will tend to
the epistemic. It will recall the issues associated with our 'first
main concern' of this chapter. If, on the other hand, we ask just
what is the nature of the social-theoretical engagement with the
Third World that could call itself (scholarship-relevant) 'democratic-critical', then discussion tends to the practical. It invites
concentration on points falling within the ambit of our 'second
main concern'. Here we elect to focus upon the 'practical'; and
the 'epistemic' remarks we have made at various times above are
here supposed. We will take note of four issues: (1) ideology
critique, (2) counter-information, (3) left scientism, and (4)
political economy and the matter of agents/allies.

(1) We have taken social theorizing to be a generic term, and
would regard the examples and instances of social theorizing to
be many and diverse. Each mode we take, ideally, to be circumstance-specific, problem-centred and occasioning its own typical
manner of inquiry. To help us 'fix' debate in position we have
offered, and made use of, two exemplars. The idea that social
theorizing was, in its most central and unequivocal guise, the
construction of ideological schemes whereby action in the world
might be ordered and legitimated, we drew from Hawthorn,
Gellner, Hollis and Nell, Carver and Giddens. Classical nineteenth-century efforts are paradigm cases of the business of
constructing ideological schemas: political economy and marxian
analysis. Our second exemplar was the mode of social-theoretical
engagement called critique. This was taken to be the mode appropriate to mature capitalism, and best instanced in the Marx-
derived work of the Frankfurt School.

If we consider the notion of critique, then its character has
been approached from several directions in the course of this
study. The principal reading of critique was established with
reference to a simple, sociology-of-knowledge-informed, scheme
of conception and intent. A straightforward corollary of the
notion of ideology-construction which we drew from the above-
noted theorists. This reading was subsequently joined by schemes
serving to enrich the notion of critique thus far used. The work
of Habermas and the commentator Bernstein was noted, as was
the analysis of the nature of political economy offered by Carver.

Although these three, or four, lines were not assembled into one
coherent statement, we have taken them to be compatible. However, we have granted one distinction which does seem pertinent
to the present discussion.

Critique, substantively, we took to be best exemplified by
'critical theory'; taking this to be the circumstance-sensitive
and problem-relevant extension of Marx to the situation of mature
(hegemonic) capitalism. The specificity of this Marx-derived
effort is evidenced not only in its chosen 'target', cultural criticism, but also in its mode of inquiry. The simple notion of
ideology invoked above is capable, when coupled up to analyses
of language, of pervasive deployment. The critique of ideology,
in our examination of particular distinguishable elements in the
'career' of 'development studies', we have taken to mean the
more familiar examination of self-conscious (more or less) delimited schemes of ideology. The critique of ideology can thus proceed by considering either the delimited and formally elaborated
schemes ordinarily understood as ideologies, or it can proceed
by considering the pervasive and informal ideological schemes
which present themselves as unremarkable common sense.

In the body of this study we have concerned ourselves with
the elucidation of a series of ideologies, taken as delimited formal efforts. So we looked at: 'growth theory', 'modernization',
'neo-institutionalism', and so on. This seems to be a perfectly
proper exercise for a 'Western' thinker. In terms of judging what
is good and what is bad analysis of the Third World, the narrow
notion of critique of ideology seems appropriate and the scheme
associated with Habermas seems over-subtle. However, we can
also note an area of inquiry where attention to pervasive informal
ideology critique might be useful.

If we were to consider 'development', 'aid', 'the underdeveloped', etc., just as elements of contemporary societies' common-
sense explanations of how the world is, then the richer schemes
of critique might be useful. We could ask from whence came
'popular' notions of the exchange of 'rich' and 'poor'? How were
these images maintained? Which groups' interests do prevalent
notions serve, if any? The pursuit of possible means of changing
stereotypical views would be the practical intent of these enquir-
ies. To put this another way: whilst the realm of political economy continues to present itself as the crucial explanatory area
in treating matters of the Third World, it is none the less possible to conceive of an emancipatory critique of 'popular' views
of the Third World; seeing this as a pre-requisite to effecting
change in the behaviour of powerful groups in society.

(2) A question that follows from the above remarks concerns
the extent of critical work. Does the critique of (delimited formal)
ideology imply that we should move beyond the displaying of
elements of ideologies to the presentation of 'corrected' schemes?
That is, should we move from scholarly critique of the efforts of
the conventional wisdom to the preparation and dissemination of
counter-information?

Counter-information could include, for example, treating the involvement of the UK with the Third World. Here it would seem that four areas of inquiry present themselves. (a) The UK as an element of the world economy; here political and trading links to the Third World might be examined. For example, in the case of UK firms working in South Africa, this is often done. (b) The UK as a member of the Commonwealth; here the political and trade links to the Third World can be read in the context of 'residues' of empire. Recalling the work of some of the historians of colonialism we noted, who spoke of periodic reworkings of the relationship of centres and peripheries, this might be a fairly central area of inquiry. (c) More prospectively, we have the UK as a member of the EEC, a group having extensive contacts with colonial residues, formalized through the Lomé Convention. (d) The UK as a member of the UN. Here we have the 'international-general' level of debate around development issues. We have noted such instances as Bretton Woods, IMF and World Bank; and to these we can add a series of UNCTAD conferences and so on. This is an entire area of rich/poor exchange which we have not treated, save in passing.

Bernstein's list of elements of the critique of ideology might be taken to permit such an extension. It was indicated that the critique of ideology involved: (a) a characterization of the effort in question plus a detailing of the means whereby it was sustained; (b) this analysis served to permit efforts to destroy the legitimizing power of the ideology. Indeed, it would seem curious to restrict the efforts of scholarship to the narrowly academic realm. Critical theory, as propounded by Bauman and Fay (amongst others we have mentioned), would certainly expect this mode of social-theoretical engagement to present the fruits of its inquiries, at least in the end, in a generally assimilable form. This is essential if the reconstitution of the 'public' is to be effected.

(3) The critique of the ideologies of the orthodoxy of 'development studies', and the suggestion above that counter-information schemes might consider the position of the UK in the world economy, recalls the matter of general schemes. We have seen that Cardoso and Faletto argue strongly for specificity in economic/political/social inquiry and reject the pursuit of general explanations. In this we would agree with them. In the light of this we can present one mode of scholarly engagement with the Third World which is spurious.

The manoeuvre of 'exemplification-denial' has been noted in chapter 7, when we looked at some marxian-informed work. We suggested that these scholars exemplified their circumstances in offering subtle and detailed analyses, but then denied their circumstances by collapsing, apparently, into a wholly mechanical politics. Hugely elaborate analyses were taken to have practical lessons, where the measure of practicality was, it seemed, provided by the invocation of the model of 'the one revolutionary sequence'.

The worst case of what might be called 'left-scientism' was exemplified by Taylor. Foster-Carter drew our attention to Taylor's self-conception of academic inquiry as being concerned with the provision of the best possible tools of revolutionary analysis to the theoretically under-developed revolutionists of the Third World. This problem of the ease with which the 'slide to the general' can be effected - even if we do not, like Taylor, embrace it - crops up in our last issue: that of the use of the analogy 'agents/allies'.

(4) The notion of 'agents' is presented in dependency analysis. It serves to underline an obvious, but nevertheless crucial, coincidence of interests between two groups: on the one hand the managements of major multi-national firms; and, on the other, those members of Third World bourgeois industrial and commercial groups with whom they deal. The coincidence of interests admits of a general description based on resemblance; but the crucial point is that this mutuality of interest is occasioned by, and cemented in, their routine business practices. So much for 'agents'; what about 'allies'?

This question arises from considering the efforts of Cardoso and Faletto. They produce a political economic analysis of the circumstances of Latin American economies; and, finding that their present dependent incorporation offers little scope for the future, they turn to the spontaneous organizations of the mass of the populace and ask how these might aid the movement toward socialist change. So who can take on this particular role, this engagement? That their effort is engaged has to be granted; and if we take engagement to be circumstance-specific and problem-relevant, then it is difficult to see a theorist based in the 'West' being engaged in quite the same way as Cardoso and Faletto.

If we recall the schema of roles which we drew from Debray (in chapter 7), then given the trio 'theorist', 'practitioner', 'commentator', the work of Cardoso and Faletto entails taking the first two roles; whereas it is at least plausible to suggest that the thinker based in the 'West' will tend to have open only the role of 'commentator'. So even if both pursue the 'political economy of Latin America' they must do so in different ways. At this point the notion of allies might be introduced; as the multinationals have local agents, might not the locally based political economists have international allies? How might this relationship be occasioned and cemented in routine practice? One reply might be to invoke the notion of an international community of scholarship. But this seems dubious: we may grant that there is a single world economy, but we are, none the less, fixed in specific situations. Invoking such general and abstract coincidences of circumstances runs the risk of turning into an excuse for academicism. If we recall our discussion of Young's attack on the New Left co-option of liberation struggles, we can also point out that in rejecting Young's attack we none the less insisted upon the significance of the analogies asserted by the New Left. Yet the notion of an 'ally' clearly is a matter of political sympathy rather than any immediate, routine, coincidence of interest based on routine interaction.

The pursuit of political-economic inquiry, it seems to us, must be restrained by insistence upon circumstance-specificity and problem-relevance if the tempting error of the pursuit of the general is to be avoided. This rather suggests that for all the international traffic in ideas that undoubtedly exists, general statements to the effect that 'we are all concerned with world capitalism' must be regarded as declarations of solidarity rather than the basis of a potentially unified programme of inquiry and action.

In summary, the burden of this section is that social theoretic efforts needs must be sensitive to what makes sense to say. In political economy this rather implies, in respect of Third World material, adopting a role of commentator and eschewing claims to status of superior theorist. It is true that Marx argued that the more advanced economic form offered the more subtle conceptual armoury; but we cannot see that the circumstances of, say, Cardoso and Faletto, on the one hand, and Taylor on the other are that different. If we want a general summary, then as regards political economic analyses (and excluding the work that fails for the sorts of reasons discussed throughout the study), we are left with a family of them. To attempt to reduce these to one all-inclusive effort would seem to us to miss the point - they are practical, first and last.

With this injunction in mind, we can see that our history of the 'career' of 'development studies' has shown that a fairly simple notion of critique is usable. However - and here is the corollary of the above notes - if we sharpen this engagement and affirm our insistence on specificity of engagement, then the extended scheme of critical-theory invites study of the obfuscating character of the common-sense view of matters of the development of the Third World. The themes are familiar: the Third World is starving, incompetent, tribal, ungrateful, etc. It would seem to be appropriate to ask: from whence came these images? How are they maintained, and whose interests do they serve? Again this presentation of critical theory casts the engagement as circumstance-specific and problem-centred: that is, practical.

6.0 EPILOGUE

We began this study by undertaking to prepare an analytical history of the post-war 'career' of 'development studies' in such a way as to reveal something of the nature of social theorizing itself. This has been our strategy for elucidating the claims made by Hilal to the importance, for sociological inquiry, of the 'discovery' of the Third World. The substantive work of the study has been concerned with the preparation of sociology-of-know-

ledge-informed analyses of identifiable 'schools' via exemplars.
In this present, concluding, chapter we have tried to go some
way towards redeeming our general promises.

What are the main lessons of our inquiry? Considering the
question most generally we can briefly note the following.

(1) That social theorizing is practical

We grounded our study (in the 'Prologue') in a set of claims that
made social theorizing concerned with 'making sense'. Subsequently we have (a) illustrated this claim with our substantive
work, and (b) used this claim to give shape to our treatments of
the historical material.

The practicality of social theorizing is revealed in the substantive work. Each 'school' has been shown to have been producing situation sensitive and problem specific efforts. We have
taken this situation/problem specificity to be both (a) the key to
displaying the nature of the practicality of the various efforts
and (b) as requiring discussion and legitimation in its own appropriate terms and not in terms borrowed from the natural sciences.
In general we want to claim that circumstances and problems call
forth engagements and that particular sorts of engagements have
corresponding forms of inquiry.[66]

(2) That social-theoretic efforts are assembled or constructed

We take the business of social theorizing to be with 'making sense'
and this manufacture is effected by particular theorists in particular places, at particular times, in response to particular demands. Consequently, we think it most fruitful to analyse each
distinguishable effort with this in mind. Any effort is taken to
be reducible to more or less clear 'pieces of argument'. The reflexive corollary is that as our present works are similarly 'lodged
in history' so they too are composed of 'pieces of argument' and
that intra-disciplinary, or academic, or 'theoretical' treatment of
any given issue should be pursued in a way that makes this obvious.

We take this stance to run counter to the, arguably essentially
scientistic, common sense of sociology in that the pursuit of a
smooth seamless web of description and analysis of the social
world is not sought. Instead, we look to a mode of inquiry that
displays its own presently deployed 'pieces of argument'. Crudely,
we take social theorizing to be more like philosophical than natural scientific inquiry.

Given this dis-integrating view we need to either (a) identify
exemplars so as to 'fix' debate (this casts the business voluntar-
istically) or (b) identify those exemplars which our given social
world, or, more narrowly, disciplinary tradition, bequeaths to
us. In this second vein, we have identified, on the one hand,

Marx and classical political economy and, on the other, Habermas and the tradition of critical theory. These we have taken as our two main examples of social-theoretical engagement. They locate particular argument forms in history as a means to 'fix' subsequent, present, discussions. It is principally with the material provided by these two argument strategies that we have analysed our series of substantive efforts within 'development studies'.

(3) That treatments of Third World material should proceed in a similar fashion

As regards social-theoretical engagement with matters of the Third World this too should be specific. Directly engaged work, we want to claim, should specify the problems it addresses, the methods of inquiry adopted and what could count as a solution. (Work claiming to offer ways of effecting social change needs must order itself in accord with a specified agent.) On the other hand, intra-disciplinary or 'theoretical work', ordinarily understood, must eschew the pursuit of the general and attend to arguments.

Notes

1 THE SCOPE AND CONCERNS OF THE STUDY

1 Given that we take inquiry to be a complex exchange between theorist, discipline and society, the language of 'objects' is perhaps unhelpful. The implicit dualism of subject/object, and its requirement that the exchange of subject/object be taken to be essentially one of the accommodation of the former to the dictates of the nature of the latter, is here denied. The review we present of the process of 'object' constitution aims precisely to exemplify our claims in respect of theory-informing analysis.

2 Bauer (1971).

3 Seers, The Limitations of the Special Case, 'Oxford Bulletin of Statistics', 1963. (Reprinted in 'The Teaching of Development Economics', ed. K. Martin and J. Knapp, 1967.)

4 Streeten (1972).

5 Girvan (1973).

6 See Girvan (1973), pp. 23-4.

7 Leys (1977). It might also be noted that our treatment of A.G. Frank might be thought confusing in that he appears in this history of ours in two places. As the representative of 'underdevelopment theory' - a position transitional (casting this note in history of ideas fashion) between the sceptical orthodoxy of Furtado's 'dependency' and the critical marxism associated with Baran - and as one figure in the 'neo-marxian' scheme inspired by Baran. Frank's work is not treated in this study as a straightforwardly unified body of inquiry. It seems to us that there are diverse strands running through it, and different aspects of Frank's work are highlighted as we pursue various issues in his company.

8 MacIntyre (1962). Also in MacIntyre (1971).

9 Giddens (1976).

10 Hawthorn (1976), p. 86.

11 Gellner (1964), p. 52.

12 Hawthorn (1976), p. 255.

13 Ibid.

14 Fay (1975), pp. 15-16.

15 Bauman (1976).

16 Horkheimer and Adorno (1972).

17 Goldmann (1973).

18 Bauman (1976), p. 105.

19 Hollis and Nell (1975), p. 176.

20 Ibid., p. 159.

21 Ibid., p. 170.

22 Ibid.

23 The questions revolve around the status Hollis and Nell would accord to abstract theorizing of the sort they execute. Are we to take philosophical reflection as a preliminary, that is, as a means to the construction of analytical machineries which are thereafter applied to the world? Hollis and Nell's arguments rather seem to suggest this. If this is so then we would want to say that they have stood the business of social theorizing on its head. We take practicality as the key to grasping the nature of social theorizing: routine philosophical reflection is made secondary. Issues of 'grounding' have to be settled but they are 'matters arising' and not (intellectually privileged) starting points.

24 Rockmore (1976), p. 442.
25 Ibid., p. 442.
26 Ibid.
27 Ibid., p. 445.
28 Giddens (1979).
29 What we do not treat is the collapse of these various efforts back into what we might suppose is an eclectic brew of elements drawn from all the schemes (except Marxist) noted – that is, the present 'conventional wisdom'.

2 THE IDEA OF DEVELOPMENT

1 'Anticipate' in the sense of 'introduce early', and not in the sense of 'declaring before the event' what we think results will be. This second sense of anticipate would open up questions of circularity of argument.
2 Passmore (1970).
3 Pollard (1971).
4 Ibid., p. 30.
5 Passmore (1970), p. 193.
6 Berlin (1969), p. 131.
7 Macpherson: see particularly (1973).
8 Lukes (1974).
9 Phrased thus, it rather seems as if we might consider plunging into the sorts of debate that surround, for example, Winch and his claims vis à vis Azande culture; but this is not so. The 'European categories of thought' we have in mind are those of social analysis, the politico-ethical.
10 Ehrensaft (1971).
11 Sachs, 'The Discovery of the Third World', 1976.
12 Hetherington (1978), pp. 103-4.
13 Ibid., p. 104.
14 NIST = 'neo-institutional social theory'.
15 Palma (1978), p. 885.

PART II INTRODUCTORY REMARKS

1 Ehrensaft (1971).
2 United Nations (1951).
3 Brookfield (1975), p. 32.
4 Ibid., p. 24.
5 Zeylstra (1977).
6 Brookfield (1975), p. 76.
7 Dobb (1973).
8 There is an ambiguity here: is the first occurrence of 'problem' to be taken to be designating a theoretician's problem, whilst the second occurrence of 'problem' designates a problem ordinarily understood, one general to society or its ruling groups? It seems as if Dobb might be fusing these two; whereas if we follow Giddens with his 'double hermeneutic', we would want to distinguish the two occurrences and make two sorts of problems. The ordinarily accepted problem being simply raw material, predigested, for the theorist who treats it with reference to his own discipline-ruled realm of meanings, which are to be taken as distinct even if they cross-cut with common-sense lines.
9 Dobb (1973), p. 16.
10 Ibid., p. 17.
11 Ibid.

3 THE CRYSTALLIZATION OF THE POSITIVIST ORTHODOXY, 1943-55

1 Kiernan (1974), p. 126.
2 Clairmonte (1960).
3 Hobsbawm (1968).
4 Clairmonte (1960), p. 4.
5 Ibid., p. 7.
6 Lichtheim (1972).
7 Clairmonte (1960), p. 8.

8   Kurihara (1968), p. 127.
9   Napoleoni (1972), p. 64.
10 As regards Keynes's personal views, his milieu was the English establishment whose 'major unspoken premise ... is that capitalism is the only possible form of civilized society'. Sweezy goes on: 'in Keynes' eyes, Marx inhabited a theoretical underworld ... and there is no evidence that he ever thought of any of Marx's followers as anything but propagandists and agitators'. Keynes's work grows out of neo-classicism and is in terms of structural-political, that is, class analysis, impoverished. Keynes invokes the intervention of the State whenever the market goes awry; and the intervention is 'Olympian' remarks Sweezy. Sweezy in Eagly (1968), pp. 106-8.
11 Cf. with Graham (1976), who takes note of a variety of 'liberalisms' in the US establishment: 1 Roosevelt's 'liberalism', a modernist stance favouring co-operation of government and industry regulation by planning machinery. 2 Wilsonian liberalism, favouring a variety of laissez-faire which is informed by notions of the moral stature of early US farmers, that is, the myth of US 'small town'. 3 Secretary Hull's version of this, coloured by depression and equating US interest with both economic liberalism and best interests of world economy. 4 Economic liberalism of the nineteenth century, constructed in UK; this may be taken as the reference point for the various versions present. 5 Modernist liberalism of Keynesian ideas, prima facie close to Roosevelt's line.
12 Kolko (1968), p. 4.
13 Ibid., p. 254.
14 Ibid., p. 257.
15 Ibid., p. 265.
16 Thus Zeylstra, treating these issues, presents what we might suppose is the orthodoxy when he avers that: 'Soon, however, it became evident that the reconstruction of Europe and the development of backward areas were tasks of altogether different dimensions from those foreseen in Bretton Woods, and would require efforts far beyond the possibilities entrusted to IBRD and IMF. Moreover as a result in particular of the Soviet Union's attitude the spirit of solidarity among the allies did not long survive the end of hostilities, and its weakening dimmed the prospect of a collective approach to world problems as envisaged in Bretton Woods and San Francisco' (1977) p. 27.
17 Fleming (1961).
18 Lichtheim (1972), p. 293.
19 Kolko (1968), p. 620.
20 Ibid., p. 622.
21 Ibid., p. 624.
22 Streeten (1972).
23 Postan (1967), p. 12.
24 This is a curious report to make, in that (a) it rather denies the implicit point of calling his phase two 'recovery proper'; and (b) it clearly runs against the view of the US economist Harris, who makes much of a 'crisis' in 1947 as the occasion for establishing the ERP.
25 This is ambiguous: is he saying (1) aid did do the job; or (2) the announcement of aid contributed to the establishment of general attitudes in Europe conducive to growth, which subsequently followed?
26 Postan (1967), p. 14.
27 Harris (1948), p. 3.
28 Fleming (1961), p. 447.
29 Ibid., p. 501.
30 Zeylstra (1977), p. 31.
31 Postan (1967), p. 24.
32 Ibid.
33 Ibid., p. 49.
34 Brookfield (1975), p. 29.
35 Zeylstra (1977), p. 84.

36   Ibid., p. 86
37   Fay (1975), p. 19.
38   Both ontologically, as his alteration to the 'array' is not, usually, taken to
     alter him; and methodologically, in that his 'self' is no part of the manip-
     ulation (though he may for other reasons be pleased/distressed; thus a
     successful experiment, for example, might advance career prospects as
     well as human knowledge).
39   The subject/object dualism, coupled to an empiricist ontology of things,
     can have clearly unfortunate consequences in analysis. The priority of the
     'thing' seems to entail the priority of the 'static'. Thus, for example,
     A.D. Smith, in his book 'Social Change' (1976), argues for the logical
     priority of 'persistence' over 'change' on the grounds that change is always
     predicated of a pattern or object. The methodological consequence is taken
     to be that we must start with a given (static) pattern or object. Now here
     is a movement from logic to method, so where is the link seen by Smith?
     What he seems to be doing is arguing from the grammar of language to an
     ontology of things and then back down to method. We can, however, re-
     tort that by accepting an ontology of things he thereby accepts the priority
     of the 'static'. This being so, invoking 'predication of change to objects'
     as the basis for asserting the priority of the 'static' is a circular argument.
     Smith does not establish his preference, as he thinks; he merely announces
     it. Moreover, his announcement rests on a reading of the common sense of
     ordinary language which, as in this example, can clearly have unfortunate
     consequences. Smith does not actually say anything about the issue of
     static versus process explanations.
40   Napoleoni (1972), p. 33.
41   Ibid.
42   These manipulations were certainly 'ingenious', but quite how 'instructive'
     they were is rather open to doubt. Brookfield argues that 'growth-theory'
     quickly became hugely elaborated and wholly out of touch with reality.
     This mode of inquiry - mechanical and formal - is prone to such manip-
     ulations and must suffer as a result. These thoughts we return to below.
43   Friedman, 'The Methodology of Positive Economics', 1953, reprinted in Hahn
     and Hollis (1979).
44   Hutchinson (1977).
45   Solow (1970) cited in Jones (1975), p. 19.
46   Kurihara (1968), p. 137.
47   Ibid.
48   Actually, we use Harrod. Domar's work is roughly the same in spirit and
     conclusion, but begins at a different place and uses differing arguments.
49   Brookfield (1975), p. 30.
50   Zeylstra (1977), p. 85.
51   Brookfield (1975), p. 30.
52   Jones (1975), p. 66.
53   Zeylstra (1977), p. 88.
54   Kregel (1972).
55   Jones (1975), p. 123.
56   Ibid., p. 44.
57   Domar sets out from the observation that investment has a dual role. It
     raises the level of aggregate demand, and it raises absolute level of an
     economy's productive capacity. Domar wants to discover the conditions
     under which the effects of raising aggregate demand fit with the effects
     of raising productive capacity levels. He identifies a required rate of
     growth, that which Harrod calls the warranted rate.
58   This notion of 'Vr' ($Gw = \frac{s}{Vr}$) is confusing. Jones expresses it thus: 'The
     increment in the capital stock associated with an increment in output that
     is required by entrepreneurs if, at the end of the period, they are to be
     satisfied that they have invested the correct amount, ie, if the new cap-
     ital stock is to equal the amount that they consider appropriate for the new
     level of output and income' (1975), p. 48.
59   Ibid., p. 53.

60 Harrod (1939), p. 23: 'The dynamic theory so far stated may be summed up in two propositions. (1) A unique warranted line of growth is determined jointly by the propensity to save and the quantity of capital required by technological and other considerations per unit increment of total output. Only if producers keep to this line will they find that on balance their production in each period has been neither excessive nor deficient. (2) On either side of this line is a "field" in which centrifugal forces operate the magnitude of which varies directly as the distance of any point in it from the warranted line. Departure from the warranted line sets up an inducement to depart farther from it. The moving equilibrium of advance is thus a highly unstable one.'

61 Jones (1975), p. 53.

62 In the notation of the economists, what has to happen for there to be steady growth of the system is that Ga=Gw=Gn (where Ga is the actual rate of growth, Gw the warranted rate, and Gn the natural rate). If the equation has its determinants inserted then the problem becomes clear. The elements that determine the three growth rates are independently set, and only accident will bring them into the relation demanded by steady growth at full employment. This is the 'First Harrod Problem', and is a step towards his aim of showing that the system tends to stagnate. The 'Second Harrod Problem' might better be called a paradox. It is the problem of stability. If Ga diverges from Gw then it is likely to carry on doing so (within limits; presumably there is a minimum Ga below which an economy cannot fall, given rising population and improving technology). Once the growth path is lost, the rational corrective behaviour of the entrepreneur is such that things get worse, not better. This problem is referred to as the 'knife edge'. Jones summarizes thus: 'Three central issues have been noted: a. The *possibility* of steady state growth at full employment. b. The *improbability* of steady state growth at full employment. c. The *instability* of the warranted rate of growth' (1975), p. 59.

63 Ibid., p. 69.

64 Ibid., p. 89. 'We can summarize the relationships between the Harrod problems and the simple neoclassical model discussed in this chapter: (1) The first Harrod problem is removed by the assumption of a neoclassical aggregate production function implying a variable capital output ratio, v, together with the assumption of perfect factor markets. (2) The second Harrod problem is by-passed as a result of the absence in the neoclassical model of an independent investment function such that the expectations of entrepreneurs have no influence on the economy in general and on the determination of aggregate demand in particular.' Now whilst these matters are interesting in themselves, we are not trying to write an economic treatise. The reasons for looking at them are: first, to show that neoclassical and neo Keynesian lines of growth theory exist, contrary to Brookfield; and second, to show that in economics careful choice of assumptions gets you any desired answer. That being the case, the epistemology of models becomes very important as we ask: just what is the status of such efforts?

65 Cigno in Napoleoni (1972), p. 117.

66 Streeten (1972), p. 62.

67 Napoleoni (1972), p. 33. As regards (b), we can anticipate the matters to be looked at in Part III, by quoting from Seers and Colin Leys, writing in 1969 for an IDS seminary, 'The Crisis in Planning'. Seers notes that 'economists as a profession have contributed substantially to the unreality of planning' (p. 17). He points to the economist's training, it will have focused on models, formally elaborate and elegant; 'he is hardly prepared, therefore, to look at the economic, let alone the social realities and ask how the resources of the country might be mobilized for change' (p. 25). Seers details the errors and inadequacies built into economic modelling and we pursue these issues throughout this study. Leys argues from the damaging starting point that 'the underlying concept of planning contradicts the basic concept of politics' (p. 62), and then proceeds to present a structural-

functionalist analysis of policy-making in a political environment; his conclusions being that elaborate models are an elaborate waste of effort.

68 The issue of models and science/mathematics is taken up by Hindess; he
looks at the 'epistemology of models' and makes the following claim: 'This
epistemology shares nothing but the word "model" with the theory of models
in mathematical logic. By no stretch of the imagination can it be said to
represent the place and function of models in mathematics or the natural
sciences' (1977, p. 158).

69 Ibid., p. 144.
70 Ibid., p. 157.
71 Ibid.
72 Ibid., p. 158.
73 Ibid., p. 159.
74 Ibid., p. 142.
75 Ibid., p. 143.
76 Brookfield (1975), p. 26.
77 The confidence did not last, and by 1967 Mishan can openly condemn the
pursuit of growth.
78 Napoleoni (1972), p. 20.
79 Ibid., p. 134.
80 Turner and Collis (1977).
81 See for example, Jewkes (1948) or Hayek (1944).
82 Brookfield (1975), p. 25.
83 Clairmonte (1960), p. 225.
84 Thus, for the UK, Addison (1977) and D. Coates (1975) argue that the
Labour Party's 'golden age' - that is, the period 1945 to 1951 - was not that
of the foundation of socialism but rather of the dismantling of a wartime
socialist economy. Certainly, the establishment of the welfare state was
liberal business; consider, Beveridge. Whether the wartime economy was
'socialist' or just a 'wartime economy' is debatable; see, for example, Joan
Mitchell (1966).
85 Postan (1967), p. 29.
86 Ibid., p. 30.
87 Sweezy in Eagly (1968).
88 Waterson in Faber and Seers (1972).
89 Some trace back ideas of aid further; thus Brookfield cites pre-war efforts
of colonial governments. This sense of 'aid' is, however, somewhat remote
from our use, and although this colonial history is touched upon we do not
pursue this line.
90 R. Mikesell (1968), p. 70. In this sentence, the numbers are ours; we note
that (1) is general to 'intervention' per se, whereas (2) is specific to a US
style of growth economics.
91 Ibid., p. 4.
92 White (1974).
93 Streeten (1972), p. 297.
94 Zeylstra (1977), p. 15.
95 Ibid., p. 16.
96 Ibid., p. viii.
97 Ibid., p. 16.
98 Ibid.
99 Ibid.
100 Ibid.
101 Ibid., p. 19.
102 White (1974), p. 13.
103 Ibid., p. 105.
104 Ibid., p. 106. The full categorization is four-fold: 1 economic transfer
theories of two kinds: supplemental transfers, displacement transfers;
and 2 political transaction theories of two types: recipient-oriented comparative politics type, and donor-oriented international relations type.
See White, ch. 4.
105 Ibid., p. 109.

106 Ibid., p. 121.
107 Ibid., p. 112.
108 Ibid., p. 114.
109 Kurihara (1968), pp. 137-8.
110 Ibid., p. 138.
111 Kurihara refers back to a 1954 review of his of the 1951 UN report, in this he mentions Robinson. See 'Indian Economic Journal', April 1954, p. 346.
112 Robinson (1949).
113 UN (1951), p. 3.
114 Ibid.
115 Ibid., p. 9.
116 Ibid., p. 38.
117 Ibid., p. 41.
118 Ibid.
119 Rao we present simply as an example of reflection upon the export of Keynes. He has published a collection of essays under the title 'Essays in Economic Development' (1964), and in a series of articles which were produced in the early 1950s he takes issue with various points in the Keynesian lexicon as they are applied to matters of the underdeveloped economies.
120 V. Rao (1952b), p. 56.
121 Ibid.
122 Ibid.
123 Ibid., p. 65.
124 Brookfield (1975), p. 32.
125 UN (1951), p. 49.
126 Robinson (1949), p. 83.
127 UN (1951), p. 45.
128 Ibid., p. 49.
129 Ibid.
130 Ibid.
131 Ibid., p. 50.
132 Ibid., p. 85.
133 Lewis worked at various development-related inquiries; and Cumper notes that 'A true assessment of Lewis' contribution to the economics of development is admittedly difficult because he has operated at so many levels – as a general theorist, as an academic advocate of specific policies, and as an advisor on the execution of these policies .... However ... his main concern has been with the strategy of development.' This we take to mean the general theoretical work that Lewis undertook. Cumper is in 'Social and Economic Studies', p. 465, vol. 23, 1974.
134 Lewis (1955), preface.
135 Ibid., p. 9.
136 Ibid., p. 15.
137 Ibid., p. 18.
138 Ibid., p. 11.
139 Gellner (1964), p. 179.
140 Lewis (1955), p. 201.
141 Ibid., p. 207.
142 Ibid.
143 Ibid., p. 213.
144 Ibid., p. 214.
145 Ibid.

4 THE POSITIVIST HIGH TIDE: 'MODERNIZATION THEORY'

 1 United Nations (1951) (Referred to in the text as Lewis et al., 1951).
 2 Lewis (1955).
 3 Rostow (1960).
 4 White (1974).
 5 The 20th Party Congress is usually noted because it saw Khrushchev offering a partial critique of Stalin. This was, argues Lichtheim (1972, p. 300), the start of 'de-Stalinization' which was brought to a climax in the public speech to the 22nd Congress of October 1961.

6 White (1974), p. 204.
7 Kolko (1968), p. 619.
8 Aron (1973).
9 Steel (1977), p. 4.
10 Tipps (1976).
11 D.F. Fleming (1961), p. 740.
12 G. Lichtheim (1972), p. 294.
13 D. Caute (1978).
14 Ibid., p. 25.
15 Ibid., p. 28.
16 G. Hawthorn (1976); see ch. 9.
17 V. Kiernan (1978), p. 205.
18 Steel (1977), p. 16.
19 Quoted in Caute (1978), p. 30.
20 Ibid., p. 21.
21 Ibid., p. 22.
22 This theme of the contribution to disaster of the US intelligentsia is picked up by E. Young, when she argues from the misplaced confidence in 'crisis management' of Kennedy's apparatchiks in the wake of the Cuban crisis, to the commitment of troops to Vietnam. Their confidence is traced back to the idea that a truly scientific grasp of politics had been achieved (Young, 1972, chs. 9 and 10).
23 Caute (1978), p. 29.
24 There is a germ of truth here; thus Kolko notes that the US took Soviet behaviour in 1945-7 to be contrary to the Yalta agreements. However, he goes on to argue that these agreements and the 'betrayal' of Yalta are largely matters of US myth, even if the subsequent disillusionment was acute (Kolko, 1968, ch. 14).
25 Aron (1973), p. 304.
26 Kiernan echoes Aron's words: 'Anti-communism as an ideology was America's substitute for the "civilizing mission" of earlier imperialism. It could be grafted onto the ostensible purpose of the Second World War, defence of democracy' (p. 215). 'In Washington's eyes, since the ultimate goal, preservation of democracy, was righteous, all means toward it were warrantable, including suppression of democracy' (p. 216). 'No nation was to be allowed to quit the capitalist, or feudal, camp, whether it wanted to or not' (p. 212).
27 See Kiernan (1978), pt. 6, for detail.
28 Jones (1975), p. 53.
29 Ibid., p. 123.
30 Robinson (1962), p. 93.
31 Jones (1975), p. 124.
32 Implicit in these remarks is a further distinction between the way in which Keynes was received in US, UK and rest of Europe. Thus in the US his interventionism was ideologically incompatible with the tone of 'cold war' and reaction to the New Deal; although, as Graham makes clear, the US has shifted towards interventionism throughout the post-war period. These two aspects are caught by Harris's story of a conversation with Kennedy; where the latter, described by Harris as a Keynesian, wonders if it's a good idea, politically, to let Harris so label him. In the UK, on the other hand, Keynesian reformism can be seen to be fully within the style of the liberal establishment: thus Beveridge and Keynes are two of the architects of post-war Britain according to Paul Addison (1977). Though here, too, the reformism is restricted; as Postan notes, there is a slide from demands for full employment to the doctrine of growth, with all the functional benefits to the status quo that this entails (Postan, 1967, ch. 2).
33 Graham (1976), pp. 93-5.
34 Sweezy in Eagly (ed.) (1968), p. 147.
35 Ibid., p. 148.
36 Harris (1964), p. 197.
37 Brookfield (1975), p. 30.

38 Mikesell (1968), p. 32.
39 Ibid., p. 32.
40 Ibid., p. 33.
41 We shall ask if it is not the case that many of the curious debates about the 'extension' of economics into the Third World do not just flow from taking economics to be a sort of natural science.
42 Tipps (1976), p. 63.
43 Ibid., p. 64.
44 Ibid.
45 Ibid., p. 69.
46 Ibid., p. 71.
47 Ibid.
48 Hawthorn (1976), p. 242.
49 Ibid.
50 Ibid.
51 See 'Philosophy, Politics and Society', Series III, ed. P. Laslett and W.G. Runciman, Oxford, Blackwell, 1967.
52 Tipps (1976), p. 72
53 B. Fay (1975); see chs. 2 and 3.
54 Tipps (1976), p. 73.
55 Recalling our Prologue, we note that the 'interventions' of the positivist policy scientist are not like those of the critical theorist. The former is manipulative/authoritative, in conception/intent; whereas the latter is best read as moral persuasion, that is, emancipatory/participatory in conception/intent.
56 Tipps (1976), p. 73.
57 Brookfield (1975), p. 53.
58 Ibid., p. 77.
59 Ibid.
60 Huntington (1971), p. 30.
61 Ibid.
62 Ibid., p. 28.
63 Bernstein (1971), p. 143.
64 Hilal (1970), p. 5.
65 Roxborough (1979), p. 14.
66 Palma (1978), p. 899.
67 Frank (1969b), p. 75.
68 Ibid.
69 Hilal (1970), p. 7.
70 Ibid., p. 8.
71 Hawthorn (1976), p. 242.
72 Rhodes (1968), p. 384.
73 Brookfield (1975), p. 54.
74 Frank (1969b), p. 5.
75 Brookfield (1975), p. 54.
76 Ibid.
77 Ibid., p. 58.
78 Ibid.
79 Ibid., p. 60.
80 Girvan (1973).
81 Huntington (1974), p. 30.
82 Hilal (1970), p. 4.
83 Ibid., p. 5.
84 Ibid.
85 Huntington (1971), p. 35.
86 Bernstein (1971), p. 146.
87 Huntington (1971), p. 37.
88 Ibid.
89 Ibid.
90 Frank (1969b), p. 40.
91 Griffin (1969), p. 33.

92 Smith (1973), p. 87.
93 Gellner (1964).
94 White (1974), p. 202.
95 Graham (1976).
96 Young (1972).
97 Kiernan (1978).
98 Charlton and Montcrieff (1978), p. 82.
99 White (1974), p. 215.
100 Ibid., p. 212.
101 Mikesell (1968), p. 41.
102 Brookfield (1975), p. 35.
103 Hagen (1962), p. 514.
104 Ibid., p. 515.
105 Brookfield (1975), p. 38.
106 Baran and Hobsbawm (1961), p. 236.
107 Gellner (1964), p. 1.
108 Ibid., p. 5.
109 Ibid., p. 40.
110 Ibid., p. 34.
111 Ibid., p. 35.
112 Ibid., p. 37.

PART III INTRODUCTORY REMARKS

1 D. Seers (1963).
2 Girvan (1973).
3 R. Prebisch, head of ECLA in this period.
4 This is perhaps misleading: the genesis is in Prebisch's theorizing, though arguably the scheme was not fully worked out until the debate over inflation.
5 Girvan (1973), p. 12.
6 With regard to Latin American work, our sociology of knowledge approach points up relevant differences in the circumstances of theorizing, but there is a body of shared concepts.

5 THE CONTRIBUTION OF THE 'NEO-INSTITUTIONALISTS'

1 Nafziger (1976), p. 18.
2 Mandel (1968), p. 7.
3 Schurmann (1970), p. 74.
4 Ibid., p. 76.
5 Kiernan (1978), p. 258.
6 Ibid.
7 Barraclough (1967), p. 153.
8 Ibid.
9 Skillen (1977).
10 Worsley (1964).
11 To do so would be to turn our 'point of departure', the problem as seen by the colonial power, and our 'frame of possibility', into the bases of a set of ideal-typical responses to nationalist-developmentalism. However, we do not want any systematic ideal-typical analysis, so we use the notion 'minimum necessary change' as a reference point around which history may be ordered.
12 Grimal (1978), p. 224.
13 White (1974).
14 Zeylstra (1977).
15 White (1974), p. 210
16 Hargreaves (1979).
17 White (1974), p. 210.
18 Zeylstra (1977), p. 48.
19 White (1974), p. 211.
20 Ibid., p. 213.
21 Grimal (1978), p. 49.

22   P. Hetherington in her book 'British Paternalism and Africa: 1920-1940'
     (1978), traces the emergence of a reformist line. 'The writers of the 1920's
     were still bemused by notions of Britain's civilizing mission and the small
     voice of criticism was stilled by the authoritative tones of Lord Lugard.
     By the late 1930's the volume of criticism had swelled to a chorus. The
     theory of the dual mandate, which had earlier been surrounded by an aura
     of respectability, was now widely regarded with suspicion whilst the policy
     of indirect rule was under attack for a variety of reasons .... A new form
     of paternalism was now apparent. This time it was led by the reformers
     who stressed the importance of education, development and preparation
     for eventual independence. It was Lord Hailey who distilled these views into
     respectable form and provided a new orthodoxy which would justify Brit-
     ish presence in Africa' (p. 19).
23   Grimal (1978), p. 50.
24   In respect of these remarks, we can elucidate briefly. With regard to 'mod-
     ernization theory', the general milieu was of hostility to the 'left' in gen-
     eral and the USSR in particular. This provided the frame within which an
     affirmation of the model of the US could issue in the moral core of 'modern-
     ization theory', what D. Caute (1978, p. 21) calls the 'patriotic imperative'.
     The available resources of this predominantly US theoretical effort were
     growth theories and social science policy-relevant work. The demand for
     a revised theory of intervention flows from aid-donor competition with the
     USSR; the competition necessitates aid being presented as 'for develop-
     ment' rather than as 'for allies', as had been the case. The moral core is
     disguised – not altered.
25   Anticipating later concerns; on this matter of 'values', if we extend these
     remarks slightly we can usefully note the efforts of the theorist Myrdal.
     His work is suffused with a concern for 'values', and he makes central to
     his efforts what Zeylstra identifies as being typical of efforts in the first
     half of the twentieth century; that is, 'a paternalistic idealism born of
     western social philosophy' (p. 50). Streeten describes Myrdal as an inter-
     national figure and says of his career that it 'might be an exercise in prac-
     tical methodology' (Streeten in Myrdal, 1958, p. ix). This work was all
     bent towards the pursuit of a 'world welfare state'. Gould (1974, p. 408)
     takes him to be the bourgeois development theorist whose work is free of
     any latent imperialist apology. He is the 'best' example of this style of
     European thinking; Gould suggests that 'a critical reading of Myrdal pre-
     sents an exceptional opportunity to assess the structure and explanational
     potency of a bourgeois development theory largely disentangled from the
     thicket of covert imperialist apologetics'.
26   Grimal (1978).
27   White (1974), p. 203.
28   G. Hawthorn (1976), ch. 9.
29   The precise nature of the political/social changes attendant upon achieving
     independence is a matter of continuing debate. Hargreaves (1979) goes so
     far as to use the somewhat sensitive term 'collaborators'. This is lodged
     within a historian's treatment that identifies two periods of 'reconstruction
     of collaboration' (p. 81); the first being the institution of formal colonial
     authority, and the second its removal, that is decolonization. In respect
     of this second, it is argued that after the dislocation of the war years 'the
     effects, experienced not only in London and Paris, but in colonial capitals
     where African resistance began to seem an increasing danger, made it
     necessary to undertake one more "reconstruction of collaboration", to move
     back from a formal relationship of dominance towards systems which implied
     political equality between freely contracting partners' (p. xii).
30   Graham (1976).
31   Gruchy (1973).
32   G. Myrdal (1958), p. 225.
33   Dorfman (1963).
34   We may note that Dorfman lists some influences upon early institutionalist
     efforts. Thus in addition to some early anthropological work he cites Lester

Ward, an early US sociologist who provided counter-arguments to the social
Darwinists. Also, in philosophy the emergence of what is now termed 'pragmatism' was a major influence, as was that line of economic thought known
as the German Historical School.

35 Dorfman (1963), p. 13.
36 Ibid., p. 37.
37 Gruchy (1973), p. 79.
38 Ibid., p. 36.
39 Dorfman (1963), p. 9.
40 Gordon (1963), p. 146.
41 Gruchy noted: 'In effect what these post Veblenians did was to substitute
   John Dewey for Karl Marx and pragmatism for Hegelianised Marxism. The
   social philosophy of John Dewey is pluralistic, optimistic and activist in
   nature.' Going on to characterize them, he says: 'They are optimistic about
   the possibility of mankind solving its problems in an orderly, gradualistic
   and non-revolutionary manner. They are also activists where enthusiasm
   for social and economic reform leads them to work for the creation of a
   more reasonable social and economic system' (p. 81).
42 Gruchy (1973), p. 19.
43 Ibid., p. 3.
44 Sweezy in Eagly (1968).
45 Gruchy (1972): 'The neo-institutionalist as a scientist has no concern with
   "what ought to be". As a scientist he analyses the existing wants or goals
   held by individuals, groups and nations and enquires into how these
   values or goals were created and how they influence the course of economic activity.... If the neo-institutionalist wishes to advocate the acceptance of certain wants or goals, and many of them do not hesitate to do so,
   they understand that they are no longer acting in the capacity of scientific
   investigators but instead are advocates of reform' (p. 292).
46 Gruchy (1973), p. vi.
47 Gordon (1963), p. 124.
48 Ibid.
49 Ibid.
50 Ibid., p. 125.
51 Ibid.
52 Ibid.
53 Gruchy (1973), p. 177.
54 Myrdal (1958), p. 242.
55 Ibid., p. 249.
56 Ibid., p. 255.
57 Gruchy (1973), p. 178.
58 Ibid., p. 199.
59 Myrdal (1970a), p. 268.
60 Mikesell (1968).
61 Huntington (1971), p. 30.
62 Mikesell (1968), p. 43.
63 Gordon (1963), p. 124.
64 Streeten (1970a), p. 69.
65 Streeten (1972), p. 52.
66 Hindess (1977). If we follow Hindess we can argue that the first sentence -
   'All thought presupposes implicit model building and model using' - is
   either false (if we take, as does Hindess, mathematics to be the paradigmatic model-using discipline), or banal if we regard it as a metaphor for
   considered reflection. The second sentence expresses the core of the
   style's procedure: 'Rigorous abstraction, simplification and quantification
   are necessary conditions of analysis and policy' - and we can say that this
   is false if taken to imply that abstraction, etc., is the starting point of
   analysis (not even Myrdal would claim this) or, if it is merely an injunction
   about how to treat data, it is overly simplistic and maybe false.
67 Streeten (1970a), p. 69.
68 Streeten (1972), p. 52.

69 Ibid.
70 The procedures and habits of their own discipline are regular targets for the institutionalists. We can see this as reflexivity.
71 Streeten (1972), p. 54.
72 Two issues come out of this: (1) that theorists have fashions is worth noting, theorists are more than 'epistemic beings' and this is certainly worth bringing out; (2) more problematic is the line Streeten seems to take whereby matters of the logic of argument are tackled by reference to fashion. The sociology of knowledge point is excellent, but that it is presented as germane to matters of the logic of arguments seems to be (partially) wrong. We must distinguish between origin and validity, not so as to dismiss the insights of the sociology of knowledge in favour of some timeless universality of concepts and of logic (as is usually done), but so as to be able to construct practical, that is, useful, criticisms. We can grant the relativism of the sociology of knowledge - that is, that concepts and rules of evidence are historico-situation bound - but deny that anything of devastating practical import follows. It does not follow that 'all points of view are equally valid'. Criticisms of formulations having such and such an origin must continue, using the tools we have got, those of critical reason.
73 Streeten (1972), p. 55.
74 Myrdal (1958), p. 238.
75 Streeten in ibid., p. ix.
76 Ibid., p. 254.
77 Myrdal (1958), p. 256.
78 Streeten in ibid., p. xiv.
79 Ibid.
80 Ibid.
81 Ibid.
82 Ibid.
83 Ibid., p. xvii.
84 Ibid.
85 Ibid., p. xxi.
86 Streeten's effort seems to be predicated on the basis of the assumption that 'reflexivity' permits a 'better' neutrality. But if all this is presented as rules of thumb for scholars, then it is no good. The most orthodox can confront the list and say that they take 'appropriate note' of these matters, only to continue just as before. On the other hand, if Streeten's arguments are taken as a call for a more thoroughgoing change (a new self-conception of the theorist's role, and consequent adjustment in method), then what sustains this new self-conception of role and rule? The answer would seem to be some (new) more general schema explaining the need for, and scope of, the change. But in this case the orthodox will reject it; indeed, necessarily, since, after Dobb, their activities and views will be a negative defining feature of the new scheme. The Streeten/Myrdal 'improved theory' seems to fall between two stools. It is empiricist, and thus not really new; and what novelty it has is not such as to issue inevitably in any improvements in practice. Their critique seems to remain within the ambit of that which they criticize and is thus liable to 're-absorption', so to say. The improvement that is visible apparently in their efforts, we can suggest, flows from their presenting an adequate (or plausible) empiricism in place of an absurd empiricism. However, given our view of 'social theory' as being something other than empiricist, quite what status we accord to this 'improvement' is by no means obvious.
87 Gellner presents this argument in his book 'Thought and Change' (1964).
88 Streeten in Myrdal (1958), p. xxxiv.
89 Ibid.
90 Ibid., p. xxxv.
91 Gruchy (1973), p. 86.
92 Myrdal (1970a), p. 21.
93 G. Myrdal, The Soft State in Underdeveloped Countries in Streeten (1970b), p. 229.

94 Whether this is taken as some model of a Third World state established with all due care, or alternatively whether it is not just a list of divergences observed, is a moot point. It seems to be just a rough list.
95 Myrdal in Streeten (1970b), p. 241.
96 Ibid., p. 242.
97 Ibid.
98 Ibid., p. 248.
99 Which, accepting its impossibility (claim to fact), would issue in the construction of a social theory which did not touch the ground, that is, a perfectly irrelevant theory. This notion, at first glance, looks as though it is incoherent (claim to logic); thus the pursuit of 'value neutrality' is doubly futile.
100 Aside, during departmental seminar – Leeds.
101 Myrdal in Streeten (1970b), p. 242.
102 Passmore, (1970).
103 Ibid., p. 172.
104 Myrdal (1970a), p. 435.
105 Ehrensaft (1971).
106 Myrdal (1970a), p. 21.
107 Streeten (1972), p. 297.
108 Ibid., p. 298.
109 Coldmann (1969)
110 R. Bernstein (1976).
111 Ehrensaft (1971), p. 41.
112 Thus we set aside what is really the body of Gellner's work, that is, the substance, as this is all philosophically derived reflection which is not in any very ready way directly comparable to the Myrdalian work. To put this another way, there is the narrow issue of the pursuit of an adequate development studies, in this respect the two theorists are really rather similar and in the end both are unsatisfactory. In addition there is the wider issue, which interests us, of the advance of conceptions of what development studies is about; this is, properly, a matter of the philosophy of social science and in this respect Gellner is vastly more sophisticated than Myrdal (though equally, qua philosopher, he becomes rather unrepresentative as a revisionist modernization theorist).

6 DISCIPLINARY INDEPENDENCE AND THEORETICAL PROGRESSIVITY
1 Girvan (1973), p. 12.
2 'NIST' = 'neo-institutional social theory'.
3 That distinctive efforts in social theory (i.e. 'theories', ordinarily understood) are properly and most fruitfully to be regarded as ideologies is a position that has been argued for in our study's Prologue, and is thus an assumption of our more substantive analyses. In formal terms we offer here a further example of, and it is hoped a further elucidation of, that view.
4 We present this ideology ('dependency') with a view to considering its claims (and similar ones from other sources) to independence as a discipline. The effort is illustrative, and it can only be illustrative as we have denied at the outset claims to independence by treating it as ideology, in a double sense: (i) of the ideology in itself and (ii) of the explanatory characteristics of our stance. That our stance has been argued for in the study Prologue is all that disarms a charge of question begging in respect of the strategy of this part.
    In section 2.14 we ask whether or not our sketch offers any reasons to treat 'dependency' as independent and adequate. If we go on to ask independent of what? and adequate for what?, we open a route to a treatment of the ideology of 'dependency' that is comparative. Thus we slide towards the question of ranking ideologies, which we have reserved for section 3 of this chapter. It is very easy to slip from considering these odd claims to disciplinary independence to the intelligible matters of ranking, but the two are distinct issues. We must first establish the plausibility

of taking 'dependency' as an ideology (and thus not intelligibly independent) before going on to treat the matter of ranking.
5   O'Brien, in Oxaal et al. (1975), p. 9.
6   Furtado (1976), p. 298.
7   Ibid., p. 299.
8   Ibid.
9   Girvan (1973), p. 8.
10 Whether Brookfield is right to stress this shift quite as much as he does is debatable. Brookfield presents his exegesis under the sub-heading 'Towards a new paradigm: Prebisch, ECLA and industrialization'; which rather suggests that he follows, say, O'Brien, in regarding the 'dependency' position as representing some sort of break with the earlier structuralist line. It is not clear that this is so – the change in tone that Brookfield rightly picks up could as easily be taken to reflect Furtado's diminishing worries with regard to the presentation of the other than orthodox elements inherent in the original centre/periphery motif.
11 Furtado (1976), p. 126.
12 Brookfield (1975), p. 147.
13 Furtado (1976), p. 300.
14 Girvan (1973), p. 12.
15 Furtado (1964), p. 1.
16 Ibid.
17 Ibid.
18 Ibid., p. 4.
19 Ibid., p. 1.
20 Ibid., p. 3.
21 Ibid.
22 Ibid., p. 4.
23 Ibid., p. vii.
24 Ibid.
25 Ibid., p. 127.
26 Ibid.
27 Ibid.
28 Ibid., p. 129.
29 Ibid., p. 127.
30 Ibid., p. 136.
31 Ibid.
32 Ibid., p. 138.
33 Ibid.
34 Furtado's early work comes from his time as an ECLA economist, and the expectation of the nature of policy prescription resembles the Myrdalian scheme. Thus in policy terms the focus is on the government's planning and organization of 'industrialization', where this is a notion flowing from a revised orthodox definition of an underdeveloped country. Thus Furtado argues, 'we may define an underdeveloped structure as one in which full utilization of available capital is not a sufficient condition for complete absorption of the workforce at a level of production corresponding to the technology prevailing in the dynamic sector of the system' (1964, p. 141). Subsequent discussion of policy is couched in familiar ECLA terms, with a focus on import bottlenecks and balance of payments/inflation problems attendant upon rapid structural change.
35 Brookfield (1975), p. 145.
36 Furtado (1965), p. 47.
37 Furtado's treatment of Marx seems to involve two somewhat incompatible aspects: first, at a very general level there is an affirmation of what Furtado takes to be the basic marxian project – that is, a developmental reading of history which utilizes the base/superstructure distinction in providing the social dynamic; and second, and subsequently, a systematic rejection of distinctively marxian notions and argument in favour of an apparently simple and fairly orthodox sociology presented in the guise of political economy.

38 Furtado (1965), p. 62.
39 Furtado (1976), p. 300.
40 Ibid.
41 Ibid.
42 Ibid., p. 301.
43 Ibid.
44 Furtado and Girvan claim that 'dependency' is the basis of a 'truly ade-
    quate' economics, just as Myrdal did in respect of his own work. These
    'radicals' present the second general answer to the question in the Pro-
    logue about the nature of 'development studies': they take themselves to
    have established it as an independent discipline adequate to its object.
45 G. rvan (1973), p. 4.
46 O'Brien in Oxaal et al. (1975), p. 46.
47 Ibid., p. 47.
48 One comparison that we have not spelt out is that between circumstances
    of production in respect of the two theories 'NIST' and 'dependency'. Fur-
    tado touches upon this when he observes: 'Within the group of nations
    termed the Third World ... Latin America occupies a special position in
    view of the peculiarity of its relations with the US' (p. 61, in 'Latin Am-
    erican Radicalism' ed. Horowitz, 1969). The optimism of the newly inde-
    pendent is contrasted with the Latin American pessimism. More clearly
    impressed is the view of I. I. Horowitz: 'Liberation from colonialism is
    radically different from liberation from imperialism' (ibid., p. 21 as above).
    If we regard the histories of the two areas over the last century then we
    can record that colonialism and decolonization in Africa and Asia are not
    the same sort of historical experience as that nominal independence ex-
    periences by Latin America.
49 See Girvan (1973), pp. 23-4. Also Brookfield notes this debate. 'Classic'
    dualists, Boeke and Furnival, argue for a special, second, economics des-
    igned specifically for the Third World; the reply from the 'Economic' dual-
    ists (Arthur Lewis is cited as an early voice) involves a return to classical
    notions and macro-economic aggregative analysis, this is the work Kregel
    treats in his discussion of 'growth'. Furtado clearly places himself in this
    line, so this is where we must place 'dependency'. It is the manner in which
    the nature of this line is conceived, and subsequent claims made, that
    cause the problems.
50 The locution 'must involve the comprehension' is, on our part, an evasion
    of the issue of the dubious logic of this argument. If we recast this in terms
    of the schema of ideology construction, then the requirement to compre-
    hend the 'whole' which governs the 'part' that we are interested in can be
    satisfied with a series of general declarations or statements. Casting the
    effort in a natural-science-aping style makes for terrible problems - how
    independent is this sub-system, do system and sub-system share a set of
    common laws, how do they interact? ....etc. - which fortunately we do not
    have to pursue.
51 See O'Brien in Oxaal et al. (1975), p. 9.
52 Girvan (1973), p. 24.
53 The notion that generality of formulation is to be pursued is, as we saw in
    the case of Furtado's work, best regarded as an ill-digested borrowing
    from the common image of the natural sciences. What the role of general
    theory might be in social theorizing we have yet to determine.
54 Cumper (1974), p. 467.
55 That some argument-schemes are better than others is undoubtedly true;
    but this we take to be a matter of ranking ideologies, and not of record-
    ing some developmental sequence. Any example of this latter phenomenon
    could only be historical, and this is not the time-scale characteristically
    invoked by those who argue for progressivity in argument. Thus, for ex-
    ample, the sociology of the present day is, generally speaking, taken to be
    better than that of the philosophes, say.
56 Or, at least, its general shape may be derived. The basic conception of
    the exchange of rich and poor is transmitted. Emphasis on this or that

element in the set of arguments comprising the conception, plus the presentation of this or that set of data, can result in a variety of developed
lines of argument.

57 Girvan (1973), p. 4.
58 Ehrensaft (1971), p. 40.
59 Ibid., p. 41.
60 Ibid.
61 Ibid., p. 60.
62 Alternatively, instead of trying to make essentially practical sense of the
idea of progressivity, we could look for an entirely formal sense. Thus any
movement from premises via deductions to a conclusion would be counted
as evincing progressivity. Yet, clearly, such a formal notion would be no
basis for claims to the status of end products of progressive sequences.
63 R. Bernstein (1976), p. 90.
64 Ibid.
65 Bernstein's examples happen to be political science but his point is general
to social science.
66 Bernstein (1976), p. 98.
67 Again, the material used in preparing this sketch is derived from those
same writers who provided the material for the analogous exposition of
Furtado's work.
68 Brookfield (1975), p. 163. See also Booth (1975): 'A brief spell of teaching and research in Latin America in the early 1960's sufficed to convey to
Frank the largely fictional character of what he had been taught... and to
convince him of the importance of familiarity with the actual structure and,
still more important, the history of underdeveloped economies' (p. 61).
69 We follow Leys (1977).
70 Frank (1975), p. 96.
71 Ehrensaft (1971), p. 50.
72 Frank (1969b), p. 9.
73 Ibid., p. 16.
74 This resemblance of Frank to the structuralist line is close. Indeed, Frank's
early work can to some extent be seen as sketching one version of what
Furtado's early programme might have looked like if it were executed. Furtado observes that a most important task is the 'progressive identification
of factors that are specific for each structure. That effort will subsequently serve as a basis for establishing a typology of structures' (Furtado, 1964, p. vii). Frank's scheme rests on the location of each subsystem within the world system; as Brookfield notes: 'In one sense, Frank
elaborates dependency economics into a world wide interdependent system'
(Brookfield, 1975, p. 164). Brookfield also refers to the marxian aspects
of Frank's work as 'a derived framework' (ibid., p. 165). Frank's scheme
can readily take on the guise of an outline for a set of models.
75 How marked these differences are is a matter for debate. On this point
Booth, quoting an ECLA document that takes note of the restrictions placed
upon its proposals by present institutional structures, comments that: 'it
is only necessary to lift the veil of diplomatic language which enshrouds
statements of this type to understand why it is that ECLA's studies have
influenced revolutionaries as well as reformers' (Booth, 1975, p. 57). This
hints at ideological convergence.
76 On this point, see Booth (1975), pp. 65-66. Booth reports that the first
conference of OLAS (Latin American Solidarity Organisation) held in Havana
in 1967 propounded the view that the Latin American bourgeoisie were incapable of ordering development, and that a socialist route to development
was the only possibility. Booth notes that: 'It was with the theoretical
elaboration and documentation of this proposition that Frank's work was
very largely concerned' (p. 66.) This is to locate the germ of the characteristically Frankian effort in a political stance whose derivation is precisely mapped. This is the key to Booth's reading of Frank. That Frank's
effort is crucially determined by its political engagement is a line we affirm.
77 Frank (1969), p. ix.

78 Frank (1972), p. 145.
79 See Parkin on the role of 'left intelligentsia'; for example (1972).
80 As Myrdal's agent of theory-execution was modelled upon himself in the
    sense that his agent was an instantiation of the principle of 'reasonable-
    ness'; so Frank is his effort's own agent, a political activist; and this
    concurrence explains the omnipresence of the Frankian agent and the
    reason for labelling him a pamphleteer.
81 Compared with our treatment of the idea of development, or again, if we re-
    call Hobsbawm (1964) and his introduction to 'Pre-Capitalist Economic
    Formations', and the way in which chapter 2 translated an ethical question
    into a practical one, then we can say that there is a way of treating moral/
    political engagement as, so to say, an empirical matter; but not the way
    Frank does it, or says he is doing it.
82 We can see this seemingly 'ready-made' view presented in Frank very
    clearly. His general orientation, 'vision', emerges apparently from no-
    where; though he rather seems to want to claim it emerges from either a
    critique of the orthodox or historical analysis or both. Frank, adopting
    the syntax of science, wrongly presents his gestalt as a hypothesis: that
    is, as something to be tested via derived empirical propositions. We want
    to say that analysis of the gestalt is in large measure internal; that is, it is
    a matter of elucidating the moral and categorical frame that is supposed by
    the gestalt - it just is not an empirical matter, in this sense, at all. Again,
    it is arguably clear in the case of Frank since throughout the period of
    his early work the fundamental analytical orientation, the 'vision', is not
    revised in any significant way - notwithstanding a plethora of empirical/
    historical researches.
83 In the case of Frank, this 'vision', in so far as it entails an argument
    structure, is minimally developed; hence, perhaps, all the criticisms of
    Frank's 'simplistic schemas'.
84 Giddens (1979), p. 175.
85 Girvan (1973), p. 12.
86 Bernstein (1976), p. 114.
87 Giddens (1979), p. 188.
88 Bernstein (1976), p. 108.
89 Ibid.
90 Ibid., p. 209.
91 Bauman (1976), p. 105.
92 MacIntyre (1962).

PART IV INTRODUCTORY REMARKS
   1 This notion we use here for purposes of offering a general résumé: our
      history has treated the construction of a series of ideological efforts; and
      whilst they can be distinguished and lodged in a sequence, they cannot,
      without doing absurd violence to the material, be designated a fixed series
      of 'stages'.

7 ELEMENTS OF THE RENEWAL OF INTEREST IN MARXIAN SCHOLARSHIP:
THE TREATMENTS OF THE THIRD WORLD
   1 Kay (1975), p. 18.
   2 Compare with A. Arblaster ('New Statesman', 30/11/1979) who observes
      that there is an 'old New Left' and a 'new New Left'. It is the second
      grouping that we are concerned with. Crouch, writing in 1970, observes
      that: 'Although political philosophies are couched in universal language,
      their contents are usually much influenced by major incidents' (p. 18).
      Referring back to Arblaster, the proximate sources of action would be
      Hungary/CND for the 'old New Left', and Vietnam plus disillusionment with
      institutionalized socialist parties for the 'new New Left'. The general line
      must remain the same and Crouch's list of formative elements will serve,
      thus he reports that: 'The New Left stands very firmly in the localist
      community-oriented, near anarchist tradition of left wing politics, in firm
      opposition to the other dominant theme - that of the strong centralized
      state' (p. 18).

3   Birnbaum (1969), p. 142.
4   Ibid., p. 143.
5   Ibid.
6   Ibid., p. 144.
7   Ibid.
8   Goode (1974), p. 33.
9   Birnbaum (1969), p. 149.
10 Ibid.
11 Also noted are the students in Frankfurt, though they are described as being more 'theoretical'.
12 Presumably Statera means marxian socialism, for the SPD at least claims to be socialist.
13 G. Statera (1975), p. 88.
14 Ibid., p. 97.
15 Gross, 'France, May 1968' in Nagel (1969), p. 96.
16 Ibid., p. 91.
17 Young (1977), p. 27.
18 Statera (1975), p. 89.
19 Ibid., p. 93.
20 Hargreaves (1979), p. 83.
21 Ibid.
22 Ibid.
23 Davidson (1978), p. 178.
24 Ibid., p. 201.
25 Ibid., p. 227.
26 Ibid.
27 Ibid., p. 295.
28 See, for example, Macpherson (1966).
29 Davidson (1978), p. 328.
30 Ibid., p. 353.
31 G. Chaliand (1977), p. xiv.
32 Ibid., p. 23.
33 Ibid., p. 184.
34 Ibid.
35 Young (1977), p. 133.
36 Ibid., p. 166.
37 Fanon (1967), p. 29.
38 Ibid.
39 Ibid., p. 30.
40 Indeed, Davidson, (1978) observing that the imported political models collapsed spectacularly, explicitly makes this unsurprising and uninteresting. The real area of interest lies in the 'resultant development of ideas concerned with searching for a different model' (p. 295), which introduces the interest of the New Left noted below.
41 Davidson (1978), p. 227.
42 Ibid., p. 293.
43 Ibid., p. 328.
44 Chaliand (1977), p. 101.
45 Ibid.
46 Young (1977), p. 28.
47 Ibid., p. 48.
48 Ibid.
49 Cranston (1970), p. 7.
50 Young (1977), p. 1.
51 Ibid., p. 16.
52 Caute (1970), p. 70.
53 Blackburn (ed.) in Debray (1970), p. 9.
54 Young (1977), p. 132.
55 Ibid., p. 133.
56 Ibid., p. 254.
57 Again the question of whom to treat presents itself. With Debray or Chal-

iand we can see that there were many active groups of revolutionaries. We are interested in those invoked by New Left theorists. We can here claim that they fall into three sets: (1) Fanon (2) Guevara/Debray (3) Mao/ Giap; of which we will look at 1 and 2, as they seem to be the principal 'theoretical' influences; where (3) rather tends to become assimilated to the circumstances of the Vietnam war.

58 This is a stratagem to illustrate a point, not the first anticipation of an abstract theory: though the distinctions we use here might well form an element of an abstract theory of social theorizing.

59 K. Minogue in Cranston (1970), p. 26.

60 Ibid.

61 This introduces a second issue; if the first is about the matter of learning the lessons of experience, then the second is about presenting these insights as a theory.

62 Minogue in Cranston (1970), p. 28.

63 Debray (1967), p. 17.

64 Ibid., p. 21.

65 Minogue in Cranston (1970), p. 28.

66 Debray (1970), p. 27.

67 Minogue in Cranston (1970), p. 28.

68 Ibid., p. 26.

69 Blackburn in Debray (1970), p. 13.

70 Ibid., p. 22.

71 Debray (1970), p. 28.

72 Ibid., p. 33.

73 Ibid.

74 Caute (1970), p. 41.

75 Ibid.

76 Worsley (1969), p. 32.

77 Caute (1970), p. 68.

78 Fanon (1967), p. 30.

79 Ibid., p. 39.

80 Caute (1970), p. 61.

81 Fanon (1967), pp. 117–18.

82 Ibid., p. 47.

83 This is one line of criticism that is developed with regard to the 'neo-marxism' we treat below. Roxborough (1979) exemplifies the criticism. 'The final abandonment of revolutionary theory conceived as an analysis of the dynamics of the social structure which could serve as a guide for revolutionary action, came in the aftermath of the Cuban Revolution and the Algerian independence movement. It was the task of theorists like Franz Fanon and Regis Debray to divorce revolutionary practice totally from revolutionary theory' (p. 134). This judgment we find bizarre.

84 Neither present detailed academic-type revisions. Debray offers a systematic rewrite around the notion of the foco, but it is a 'reading' of the marxist canon rather than general revision. Fanon's work is even less of a 'revision of Marx'.

85 Foster-Carter (1964), p. 68.

86 Taylor (1974).

87 In their defence, it should be said that in each case they could reply that (a) these criticisms we have presented are not enough to 'secure conviction'; they are really just notes – precisely who, for example, do we have in mind?; (b) in any case the authors cited had fairly narrowly technical issues to debate and were, understandably, not bothered about displays of reflexive consistency; (c) anyway, the sorts of points we have made are routinely granted in these sorts of discussions: it is a part of disciplinary common sense.

88 Frank (1978), p. xiii.

89 Ibid., p. 1.

90 Ibid.

91 Ibid., p. 2.

92   Ibid.
93   There seems to be another point to be made in this connection: that is
     that philosophical reflection upon assumptions (governing method and pro-
     cedure and purpose) cannot be initiated simply by abstracting from work
     that has been routinely engaged with the world (that is, more or less em-
     piricist). The impulse to philosophical type reflection is understandable
     (given that these people are scholars, and that the 'movement' they con-
     sider has seemingly lost impetus), and to our mind appropriate (given our
     scheme of construction/criticism/ranking). But it has to be acknowledged
     as a distinct intellectual endeavour which requires, pre-eminently, that
     specific questions be put. Treating philosophical-type analysis as glorified
     tinkering with presently unhappily regarded 'models of reality' cannot gen-
     erate any useful answers. Roxborough's effort is maybe a case in point
     here; he presents a very abstract and general treatment of the pursuit of
     a model of development, but he never manages to pose a specific question,
     or set of them, which would get his aspiring philosophizing going.
94   Dependency is taken, by Palma, to emerge in phase III of marxian treat-
     ments of centre-periphery relations. Whether 'dependency' is or is not
     taken as marxian is not stated. In the end it seems as if Palma sidesteps
     the issue by (1) making 'dependency' a school, that is, a collection of dif-
     fering analyses; and (2) making the school one of political economy. Marx
     is subsumed under the tradition of political economy, though granted a
     major place in that tradition, and 'dependency' is taken as a modern
     specimen of political economy. The question 'is dependency marxian?' is
     sidestepped. Additionally, there is a somewhat confusing tension between
     'dependency' as a variety of (necessarily) marxian-informed political
     economy, on the one hand, and 'dependency' as an analysis of Latin Am-
     erica on the other.
95   Palma (1978), p. 884.
96   Palma says this division is logical rather than temporal. He then quotes
     Sutcliffe who certainly seems to take the division as temporal. Why does
     Palma insert this proviso? To prepare a formal set of assumptions as a
     basis for questions about method?
97   Palma (1978), p. 885
98   Ibid., p. 886.
99   Ibid., p. 899.
100 Brenner (1977), p. 53.
101 Leys (1977), p. 93.
102 Ibid.
103 Culley (1978), p. 102.
104 Ibid., p. 103.
105 Ibid., p. 110.
106 Bernstein (1979), p. 94.
107 Marcuse (1955) and (1970).
108 Macpherson (1964).
109 Brenner (1977), p. 48
110 Ibid.
111 Ibid., p. 53.
112 Ibid., p. 61.
113 Ibid., p. 67.
114 Ibid., p. 68.
115 Ibid., p. 27.
116 Palma (1978), p. 900.
117 Sutcliffe (1973), pp. 90-1.
118 Culley (1978), p. 107.
119 We might note, finally, that this issue of 'value theory' has occasioned
     much abstruse debate amongst those conversant with the detail of Marx's
     political economy; but it is an area we have not treated here.
120 Phillips (1977), p. 9.
121 Ibid., p. 11.
122 Ibid., p. 17.

123 Kay (1975), p. x.
124 Brenner (1977), p. 27.
125 Ibid., p. 29.
126 Indeed, it might be noted that with regard to issues revolving around the nature of the dynamic of capitalism, debate in the area of development studies coincides with discussion of history. Thus we have not in this section treated economics informed discussion, and we must also note and leave aside history-informed work.
127 Palma (1978), p. 900.
128 Middlemas (1979).
129 Leys (1977).
130 Palma (1978), p. 911.

8 SOCIAL THEORIZING AND THE MATTER OF THE THIRD WORLD
 1 Carver (1975), p. 7.
 2 See ibid., pp. 11-17 for a sketch of the breadth of Marx's reading.
 3 Ibid., pp. 8-9.
 4 Ibid., p. 88.
 5 Cardoso and Faletto (1979), p. ix.
 6 Ibid.
 7 Palma (1978), p. 911.
 8 Carver (1975) p. 129
 9 Ibid., p. 130.
10 Ibid., p. 132.
11 Cardoso and Faletto (1979), p. x.
12 Carver (1975), pp. 40-1.
13 Cardoso and Faletto (1979), p. xiv.
14 Ibid.
15 Ibid.
16 Thus far the criteria of adequacy implied, against which we might review some of our 'examples', are general: (i) breadth of scope, the pursuit of a 'comprehensive social science'; here the approach is both general in the sense of level of treatment and general in the sense of its intellectual resource base, a global explanation that bursts given disciplinary boundaries; (ii) practicality of intent, the point we drew from Dobb is crucial and if the effort in question does not specify an agent of theory-execution then it is not grounded; (iii) strategy of explanation, thus reconstruction of the real and not modelling.
17 Rockmore (1976), p. 438.
18 Ibid., p. 442.
19 Ibid., p. 444.
20 See S. Avineri (1968), pp. 77-86.
21 Carver (1975), p. 3.
22 Ibid., p. 4n.
23 Ibid., p. 147.
24 Marx (1973), p. 104.
25 Marx (1973), p. 105.
26 Cardoso and Faletto (1969), p. xiv.
27 Ibid.
28 Ibid., p. xviii.
29 Palma (1978), p. 911.
30 Carver (1975), p. 147.
31 Marx (1973), p. 105.
32 Ibid., p. 106.
33 Ibid.
34 Ibid., p. 107.
35 Rockmore (1976), p. 444.
36 Ibid.
37 Carver (1975), p. 9.
38 This, we may note, is all problematical; see for example Kilminster's (1980) discussion of Lukács.

39   Nicolaus (1973), p. 10.
40   Cardoso and Faletto (1979), p. xxiv.
41   What lessons can we take from this in regard to weighing the merits of our discussed examples? Three points: 1 concepts are specific to economic forms; 2 form bourgeois capitalism is developed enough to spawn a rich and subtle set of categories, applicable, with caution, to simpler forms; 3 inquiry is always, ultimately, practical. Thus Marx sought to uncover the dynamic of society to his agents of change the proletariat. Cardoso and Faletto concede status of dependent economies, grant internal political stasis, and in practice look to forms of organization spontaneous to working class/peasant groupings; seeing this as area to introduce their efforts of theorizing. See Kahl (1976), p. 17.
42   It is for this reason, the aim of 'interventionists' to render their behaviour non-causal, that is, extra-systemic, that modern states are concerned with protecting 'official secrets'. If the state's behaviour is hidden, then it tends to equivalence to the extra-system status its self-conception aspires to. State secrecy, in the case of UK, is not an unfortunate bad habit developed by bureaucrats in the wake of Edwardian anti-German scares; it is a functional prerequisite of present mode of state power - 'interventionism'.
43   A. MacIntyre (1970), pp. 22, 40, 61, 92.
44   Giddens (1979), p. 175.
45   T. McCarthy (1978).
46   R. Bernstein (1976), p. 206.
47   'Ideology and consciousness' in Giddens (1979).
48   Palma (1978), p. 882.
49   Ibid., p. 885.
50   Ibid., p. 886.
51   Ibid. Palma notes several different ways of reading this claim, depending upon how the term 'imperialism' is construed. He is at pains to deny that 'dependency', as he regards it, can be taken as being in competition with theories of imperialism.
52   Cardoso and Faletto (1979), p. ix.
53   Ibid.
54   Palma (1978), p. 900.
55   Kay (1975), p. x.
56   Desai (1974), p. 114.
57   Ibid., p. 116.
58   Palma (1978), p. 910.
59   Kahl (1976), p. 132.
60   Ibid., p. 133.
61   Cardoso and Faletto (1979), p. xviii.
62   Ibid., p. 151.
63   Ibid., p. xxii.
64   Ibid.
65   Ibid., p. 154.
66   Indeed, when discussing Debray, in chapter 7, we hinted at a way in which an extended, richer, version of this scheme, treating the aspect of activity rather than simply inquiry, might be approached, when we distinguished 'commentators', 'theorists' and 'practitioners'.

Bibliography

Addison, P. (1977), 'The Road to 1945', London, Cape.
Ali, T. (ed.) (1969), 'New Revolutionaries: Left Opposition', London, Peter Owen.
Allen, V.L. (1975), 'Social Analysis: a Marxist Critique and Alternative', London, Longman.
Aron, R. (1973), 'The Imperial Republic: the US and the World, 1945-1973', London, Weidenfeld & Nicolson.
Avineri, S. (1968), 'The Social and Political Thought of Karl Marx', Cambridge University Press.
Baran, P. (1973), 'The Political Economy of Growth', Harmondsworth, Penguin.
Baran, P., and Hobsbawm, E. (1961), The Stages of Economic Growth, in 'Kyklos', vol. 14.
Barraclough, G. (1967), 'An Introduction to Contemporary History'. Harmondsworth, Penguin.
Bauer, P.T. (1953), The United Nations Report on the Economic Development of Under-Developed Countries, 'Economic Journal', March.
Bauer, P.T. (1971), 'Dissent on Development', London, Weidenfeld & Nicolson.
Bauman, Z. (1972), Praxis: the controversial culture-society paradigm, in T. Shanin (ed.), 'The Rules of the Game: Cross-Disciplinary Essays on Models in Scholarly Thought', London, Tavistock.
Bauman, Z. (1976), 'Towards a Critical Sociology', London, Routledge & Kegan Paul.
Bendix, R. (1967), Tradition and Modernity Reconsidered, 'Comparative Studies In Society and History', vol. 9, no. 3.
Benton, T. (1977), 'The Philosophical Foundations of the Three Sociologies', London, Routledge & Kegan Paul.
Berlin, I. (1969), 'Four Essays on Liberty', London, Oxford University Press.
Bernstein, H. (1971), Modernization Theory and the Sociological Study of Development, 'Journal of Development Studies', no. 7.
Bernstein, H. (ed.) (1976), 'Underdevelopment and Development', Harmondsworth, Penguin.
Bernstein, H. (1979), Sociology of Underdevelopment Versus Sociology of Development, in D. Lehmann (ed.), 'Development Theory', London, Cass.
Bernstein, R. (1976), 'The Restructuring of Social and Political Theory', Oxford, Blackwell.
Birnbaum, N. (1969), The Staggering Colossus, in J. Nagel (ed.), 'Student Power', London, Merlin Press.
Black, C.E. (ed.) (1976), 'Comparative Modernization', London, Collier-Macmillan.
Blackburn, R. (1979), Was this the birth of anglo-marxism? 'Times Higher Education Supplement' 7/12/79/
Booth, D. (1975), Andre Gunter Frank: an introduction and appreciation, in Oxaal et al. (1975).
Brenner, R. (1977), The Origins of Capitalist Development: a Critique of Neo-Smithian Marxism, 'New Left Review', 104.
Brookfield, H. (1975), 'Interdependent Development', London, Methuen.
Brookings Institution (1962), 'Development of the Emergent Countries', Washington.
Buchanan, K. (1963), The Third World – its emergence and contours, 'New Left Review', 18.

Cardoso, F.H. and Faletto, E. (1979), 'Dependency and Development in Latin America', Berkeley and Los Angeles, University of California Press.
Carver, T. (1975), 'Karl Marx: Texts on Method', Oxford, Blackwell.
Caute, D. (1970), 'Fanon', London, Fontana.
Caute, D. (1978), 'The Great Fear: The Anti-Communist Purges under Truman and Eisenhower', London, Secker & Warburg.
Chaliand, G. (1977), 'Revolution in the Third World', Hassocks, Harvester.
Charlton, M. and Montcrieff, H. (1978), 'Many Reasons Why', New York, Hill & Wang.
Clairmonte, F.A. (1960), 'Economic Liberalism and Underdevelopment', Bombay, Asia Publishing House.
Coates, D. (1975), 'The Labour Party and the Struggle for Socialism', Cambridge University Press.
Cochran, T.C. (1960), Cultural factors in economic growth, 'Journal of Economic History', vol. xx.
Collingwood, C. (1970), Reflections on Myrdal, 'Journal of Contemporary Asia', vol. 1.
Cranston, M. (ed.) (1970), 'The New Left', London, Bodley Head.
Crouch, C. (1970), 'The Student Revolt', London, Bodley Head.
Culley, L. (1978), Economic Development in Neo-Marxist Theory, in B. Hindess (ed.), 'Sociological Theories of Economy', London, Macmillan.
Cumper, G. (1974), Dependence, Development, and the Sociology of Economic Thought, 'Social and Economic Studies', vol. 23.
David-Garson, G. (1970), The Ideology of the New Student Left, in J. Foster and D. Long (eds), 'Protest: Student Activism in America', New York, Morrow.
Davidson, B. (1978), 'Africa in Modern History', London, Allen Lane.
Debray, R. (1967), 'Revolution in the Revolution', London, Monthly Review Press.
Debray, R. (1970), 'Strategy for the Revolution', ed. R. Blackburn, London, Cape.
Desai, M. (1974), 'Marxian Economic Theory', London, Gray Mills.
DiMarco, L.E. (1972), 'International Economics and Development: Essays in Honour of Raul Prebisch', London, Academic Press.
Dobb, M. (1973), 'Theories of Value and Distribution since Adam Smith', Cambridge University Press.
Dorfman, J. (ed.) (1963), 'Institutional Economics: Veblen, Commons and Mitchell Reconsidered', Berkeley and Los Angeles, University of California Press.
Draper, T. (1969), 'Abuse of Power: US foreign policy from Cuba to Vietnam', Harmondsworth, Penguin.
Eagly, R.V. (ed.) (1968), 'Events, Ideology and Economic Theory', Detroit, Wayne State University Press.
Ehrensaft, P. (1971), Semi-Industrial Capitalism in the Third World: implications for social research in Africa, 'Africa Today', January.
Faber, M. and Seers, D. (eds) (1972), 'The Crisis of Planning', London, Chatto & Windus,
Fanon, F. (1967), 'The Wretched of the Earth', Harmondsworth, Penguin.
Fay, B. (1975), 'Social Theory and Political Practice', London, George Allen & Unwin.
Fleming, D.F. (1961), 'The Cold War and its Origins', New York, Doubleday.
Foster-Carter, A. (1979), Marxism versus Dependency Theory? a Polemic, in 'Leeds Occasional Papers in Sociology', no. 8.
Foster-Carter, A. (1964), Neo-Marxist Approaches to Development and Underdevelopment, in E. De Kadt and G. Williams (eds), 'Sociology and Development', London, Tavistock.
Frank, A.G. (1969b), 'Capitalism and Underdevelopment in Latin America', New York, Monthly Review Press.
Frank, A.G. (1969b), 'Latin America: Underdevelopment or Revolution', New York, Monthly Review Press.
Frank, A.G. (1972), 'Lumpenbourgeoisie-Lumpendevelopment', New York, Monthly Review Press.
Frank, A.G. (1975), 'On Capitalist Underdevelopment', Bombay, Oxford University Press.

Frank, A.G. (1978), 'Dependent Accumulation and Under-Development', London, Macmillan.
Furtado, C. (1964), 'Development and Underdevelopment', Berkeley and Los Angeles, University of California Press.
Furtado, C. (1965), 'Diagnosis of the Brazilian Crisis', Berkeley and Los Angeles, University of California Press.
Furtado, C. (1976), 'Economic Development of Latin America: a survey from colonial times to the Cuban Revolution', Cambridge University Press, 2nd edn.
Gellner, E. (1964), 'Thought and Change', London, Weidenfeld & Nicolson.
Gibbs, B. (1976), 'Freedom and Liberation', London, Sussex University Press.
Giddens, A. (1976), 'New Rules of Sociological Method', London, Hutchinson.
Giddens, A. (1979), 'Central Problems in Social Theory', London, Macmillan.
Girvan, N. (1973), The Development of Dependency Economics in the Caribbean and Latin America: review and comparison, in 'Social and Economic Studies', vol. 22.
Goldmann, L. (1969), 'The Human Sciences and Philosophy', London, Cape.
Goldmann, L. (1973), 'The Philosophy of the Enlightenment', London, Routledge & Kegan Paul.
Goode, S. (1974), 'Affluent Revolutionaries: A Portrait of the New Left', New York, New Viewpoints.
Gordon, R.A. (1963), Institutional Elements in Contemporary Economics, in Dorfman (1963)
Gould, J. (1974), Myrdal's Dilemma and Soviet Development Studies, 'Acta Sociologica', vol. 17.
Graham, O. (1976), 'Toward a Planned Society', New York, Oxford University Press.
Griffin, K. (1969), 'Underdevelopment in Spanish America: An Interpretation', London, Allen & Unwin.
Grimal, H. (1978), 'Decolonization: The British, French, Dutch and Belgian Empires 1919-1963', London, Routledge & Kegan Paul. First published 1965.
Gruchy, A. (1973), 'Contemporary Economic Thought: The Contribution of Neo-Institutional Economics', London, Macmillan.
Habermas, J. (1971), 'Knowledge and Human Interests', Boston, Beacon Press.
Habermas, J. (1974), 'Theory and Practice', London, Heinemann.
Hagen, E. (1962), 'The Theory of Social Change', Homewood, Ill., Dorsey.
Hahn, F. and Hollis, M. (eds) (1979), 'Philosophy and Economic Theory', Oxford University Press.
Hargreaves, J.D. (1979), 'The End of Colonial Rule in West Africa', London, Macmillan.
Harris, S. (1948), 'The European Recovery Programme', Cambridge, Mass., Harvard University Press.
Harris, S. (1964), 'The Economics of the Kennedy Years', London, Harper & Row.
Harrod, R. (1939), An Essay in Dynamic Theory, in 'Economic Journal', March.
Hawthorn, G. (1976), 'Enlightenment and Despair', Cambridge University Press.
Hayek, F. (1944), 'Road to Serfdom', London, Routledge & Kegan Paul.
Hayter, T. (1971), 'Aid as Imperialism', Harmondsworth, Penguin.
Heiman, E. (1952), Marxism and underdeveloped countries, in 'Social Research', September.
Hetherington, P. (1978), 'British Paternalism and Africa: 1920-1940', London, Cass.
Hilal, J. (1970), Sociology and Underdevelopment, Durham University (mimeo).
Hindess, B. (1977), 'Philosophy and Methodology in the Social Sciences', Hassocks, Harvester.
Hindess, B. (ed.) (1978), 'Sociological Theories of the Economy', London, Macmillan.
Hirst, P. (1976), 'Social Evolution and Sociological Categories', London, Allen & Unwin.
Hobsbawm, E.J. (1964), Introduction to K. Marx, 'Pre-Capitalist Economic Formations', London, Lawrence & Wishart.

Hobsbawm, E.J. (1968), 'Industry and Empire', Harmondsworth, Penguin.
Hollis, M. (1977), 'Models of Man', London, Cambridge University Press.
Hollis, M. and Nell, E.J. (1975), 'Rational Economic Man', London, Cambridge University Press.
Horkheimer, M. and Adorno, T. (1972), 'Dialectic of Enlightenment', New York, Herder & Herder.
Horowitz, I.L. (ed.) (1969), 'Latin American Radicalism', New York, Random House.
Hoselitz, B.F. (1960), 'The Sociological Aspects of Economic Growth', Chicago, Ill., Free Press.
Hoselitz, B.F. (ed.) (1971), 'The Progress of the Underdeveloped Areas', Chicago and London, University of Chicago Press.
Howard, M.C. and King, J.E. (1975), 'The Political Economy of Marx', Harlow, Longman.
Huntington, S. (1971), The Change to Change: modernization, development, and politics, in C.E. Black (1976).
Hutchinson, T.W. (1977), 'Knowledge and Ignorance in Economics', Oxford, Blackwell.
Jewkes, J. (1948), 'Ordeal by Planning', London, Macmillan.
Jones, H. (1975), 'An Introduction to Modern ""heories of Economic Growth', London, Nelson.
Kahl, J.H. (1976), 'Modernization, Exploitation and Dependency in Latin America', New Jersey, Transaction Books.
Kamenka, E. (1969), 'Marxism and Ethics', London, St Martin.
Kay, G. (1975), 'Development and Underdevelopment: a Marxist Analysis', London, Macmillan.
Kerr, C. (1973), 'Industrialism and Industrial Man', Harmondsworth, Penguin.
Kidron, M. (1968), 'Western Capitalism since the War', London, Weidenfeld & Nicolson.
Kiernan, V.G. (1974), 'Marxism and Imperialism', London, Arnold.
Kiernan, V.G. (1978), 'America: The New Imperialism', London, Zed Press.
Kilminster, R. (1980), 'Praxis and Method', London, Routledge & Kegan Paul.
Kolko, G. (1968), 'The Politics of War: US Foreign Policy 1943-1945', New York, Vintage Books.
Kregel, J.A. (1972), 'The Theory of Economic Growth', London, Macmillan.
Kurihara, K. (1954), The United Nations and Economic Development, 'Indian Economic Journal', April.
Kurihara, K. (1968), The Dynamic Impact of History on Keynesian Theory, in R.V. Eagly (1968).
Laclau, E. (1971), Feudalism and Capitalism in Latin America, 'New Left Review', 67.
Lehmann, D. (ed.) (1979), 'Development Theory', London, Cass.
Lévi-Strauss, C. (1968), 'Structural Anthropology', London, Allen Lane.
Lewis, W.A. et al. (1951), see under United Nations.
Lewis, W.A. (1954), Economic Development with Unlimited Supplies of Labour, 'Manchester School', May.
Lewis, W.A. (1955), 'The Theory of Economic Growth', London, Allen & Unwin.
Leys, C. (1975), 'Underdevelopment in Kenya', London, Heinemann.
Leys, C. (1977), Underdevelopment and Dependency: Critical Notes, 'Journal of Contemporary Asia', vol. 7:1.
Lichtheim, G. (1972), 'Europe in the Twentieth Century', New York, Praeger.
Lichtheim, G. (1977), 'Imperialism', Harmondsworth, Penguin.
Lieuwen, E. (1965), 'US Policy in Latin America: A Short History', London, Praeger.
Lipton, M. (1962), Balanced and Unbalanced Growth in Under-Developed Countries, 'Economic Journal', September.
Lukes, S. (1973), 'Individualism', Oxford, Blackwell.
Lukes, S. (1974), 'Power: a radical view', London, Macmillan.
McCarthy, T. (1978), 'The Critical Theory of Jurgen Habermas', London, MIT Press.
MacIntyre, A. (1962), A mistake about causality in social science, in P. Laslett

and W.G. Runciman (eds) (1962) 'Politics, Philosophy and Society', Series 2, Oxford, Blackwell.

MacIntyre, A. (1970), 'Marcuse', London, Fontana.

MacIntyre, A. (1971), The Idea of a Social Science, in 'Against the Self-Images of the Age', London, Duckworth.

Macpherson, C.B. (1964), 'The Political Theory of Possessive Individualism', Oxford University Press.

Macpherson, C.B. (1966), 'The Real World of Democracy', Oxford University Press.

Macpherson, C.B. (1973), 'Democratic Theory: Essays in Retrieval', Oxford University Press.

Maddison, A. (1971), 'Class Structure and Economic Growth', New York, Norton.

Magdoff, H. (1969), 'The Age of Imperialism', New York, Monthly Review Press.

Mandel, E. (1968), 'Europe versus America', London, New Left Books.

Mandel, E. (1969), The New Vanguard, in T. Ali (1969).

Marcuse, H. (1955), 'Eros and Civilization', Boston, Beacon Press.

Marcuse, H. (1970), 'Five Lectures', London, Allen Lane.

Marx, K. (1973), 'Grundrisse', Harmondsworth, Penguin.

Middlemas, K. (1979), 'The Politics of Industrial Society', London, Deutsch.

Mikesell, R.F. (1968), 'The Economics of Foreign Aid', London, Weidenfeld & Nicolson.

Mishan, E.J. (1969), 'The Costs of Economic Growth', Harmondsworth, Penguin.

Mishan, E.J. (1977), 'The Economic Growth Debate', London, Allen & Unwin.

Mitchell, J. (1900), 'Groundwork to Economic Planning', London, Secker & Warburg.

Myint, H. (1967), Economic Theory and the Underdeveloped Countries, in K. Martin and J. Knapp (eds) (1967), 'The Teaching of Development Economics', London, Cass.

Myrdal, G. (1957), 'Economic Theory and Underdeveloped Regions', London, Duckworth.

Myrdal, G. (1958), 'Value in Social Theory' (ed. Paul Streeten), London, Routledge & Kegan Paul.

Myrdal, G. (1970a), 'The Challenge of World Poverty', London, Allen Lane.

Myrdal, G. (1970b), 'Objectivity in Social Research', London, Duckworth.

Nafziger, E.W. (1976), A Critique of Development Economics in the US, 'Journal of Development Studies', vol. 13.

Nagel, J. (ed.) (1969), 'Student Power', London, Merlin Press.

Napoleoni, C. (1972), 'Economic Thought of the Twentieth Century', London, Martin Robertson.

Nell, E.J. (1972), The Revival of Political Economy, 'Social Research', vol. 39.

Nicolaus, M. (1973), Foreword to Marx (1973).

Nisbet, R. (1970), 'Developmentalism: a critical analysis', in J. McKinney and E. Tiryakian (eds), 'Theoretical Sociology', New York, Appleton-Century-Crofts.

O'Brien, D. (1972), Modernization, Order, and the Erosion of a Democratic Ideal: American Political Science 1960-70, 'Journal of Development Studies', vol. 8.

O'Brien, P.J. (1975), A Critique of Latin American Theories of Dependency in Oxaal et al. (1975).

Oxaal, I., Barnett, T. and Booth, D. (eds) (1975), 'Beyond the Sociology of Development', London, Routledge & Kegan Paul.

Palma, G. (1978), Dependency: a formal theory of underdevelopment or a methodology for the analysis of concrete situations of underdevelopment, 'World Development', vol. 6.

Parkin, F. (1972), 'Class Inequality and Political Order', St Albans, Paladin.

Passmore, J. (1970), 'The Perfectibility of Man', London, Duckworth.

Phillips, A. (1977), The Concept of Development, 'Review of African Political Economy', vol. 8.

Pollard, S. (1971), 'The Idea of Progress', Harmondsworth, Penguin.

Postan, M.M. (1967), 'An Economic History of Western Europe 1945-1964', London, Methuen.

Rao, V.K.R.V. (1952a), Full Employment and Economic Development, 'Indian

Economic Review', August.
Rao, V.K.R.V. (1952b), Investment, Income and the Multiplier in an Under-Developed Economy, 'Indian Economic Review', February.
Rao, V.K.R.V. (1953), Deficit Financing, Capital Formation and Price Behaviour in an Under-Developed Economy, 'Indian Economic Review', February.
Rao, V.K.R.V. (1964), 'Essays in Economic Development', Bombay, Asia Publishing House.
Rhodes, R.I. (1968), The Disguised Conservatism in Evolutionary Development Theory, 'Science and Society', vol. 32.
Robbins, L. (1932), 'Essay on the nature and significance of economic science', London, Macmillan.
Robinson, J. (1949), Mr Harrod's Dynamics, 'Economic Journal', March.
Robinson, J. (1962), 'Economic Philosophy', Harmondsworth, Penguin.
Rockmore, T. (1976), Radicalism, Science and Philosophy in Marx, 'Cultural Hermeneutics', 3.
Rostow, W.W. (1960), 'The Stages of Economic Growth', Cambridge University Press.
Roxborough, I. (1979), 'Theories of Underdevelopment', London, Macmillan.
Sachs, I. (1976), 'The Discovery of the Third World', London, MIT Press.
Schurmann, F. (1970), The Waning of the American Empire, 'Journal of Contemporary Asia', vol. 1.
Seers, D. (1963), The Limitations of the Special Case, reprinted in Martin, K. and Knapp, J. (eds) (1967), 'The Teaching of Development Economics', London, Cass.
Seers, D. (1979), What are we trying to measure? in Lehmann (1979).
Shaw, M. (1975), 'Marxism and Social Science: The Roots of Social Knowledge', London, Pluto Press.
Skillen, A. (1977), 'Ruling Illusions: Philosophy and the Social Order', Hassocks, Harvester.
Smith, A.D. (1973), 'The Concept of Social Change: A critique of the Functionalist Theory of Social Change', London, Routledge & Kegan Paul.
Smith, A.D. (1976), 'Social Change: Social Theory and Historical Processes', London, Longman.
Solow, R. (1956), A contribution to the theory of economic growth, 'The Quarterly Journal of Economics', pp. 65-94.
Statera, G. (1975), 'Death of a Utopia', Oxford University Press.
Steel, R. (1977), 'Pax Americana', Harmondsworth, Penguin.
Strawson, P. (1959), 'Individuals', London, Methuen.
Streeten, P. (1970a), An Institutional Critique of Development Concepts, 'Journal of European Sociology', vol. 11.
Streeten, P. (ed.) (1970b), 'Unfashionable Economics: Essays in Honour of Lord Balogh', London, Weidenfeld & Nicolson.
Streeten, P. (1972), 'The Frontiers of Development Studies', London, Macmillan.
Sutcliffe, R. (1973), Introduction to Baran (1973).
Taylor, J. (1974), Neo-Marxism and Underdevelopment: A Sociological Phantasy, 'Journal of Contemporary Asia', vol. 4.
Tipps, D.C. (1976), Modernization Theory and the Comparative Study of Societies: A Critical Perspective, in C.E. Black (ed.) (1976).
Turner, R.K. and Collis, C. (1977), 'The Economics of Planning', London, Macmillan.
United Nations (1951), 'Measures for the Economic Development of Under-Developed Countries', E/1968 ST/ECA/10, 3 May 1951.
White, J. (1974), 'The Politics of Foreign Aid', London, Bodley Head.
Wilson, H. (1977), 'The Imperial Experience in Sub-Saharan Africa Since 1870', Minneapolis, University of Minnesota Press.
Worsley, P. (1964), 'The Third World', London, Weidenfeld & Nicolson.
Worsley, P. (1969), Revolutionary Theories, 'Monthly Review', May.
Young, E. (1972), 'A Farewell to Arms Control', Harmondsworth, Penguin.
Young, N. (1977), 'An Infantile Disorder? The Crisis and Decline of the New Left', London, Routledge & Kegan Paul.
Zeylstra, G. (1977), 'Aid or Development?', Leyden, A.W. Sijthoff.

Index

294 *Index*

Routledge Social Science Series

Routledge & Kegan Paul   London, Henley and Boston

39 Store Street,
London WC1E 7DD
Broadway House,
Newtown Road,
Henley-on-Thames,
Oxon RG9 1EN
9 Park Street,
Boston, Mass. 02108

Contents

*Authors wishing to submit manuscripts for any series
in this catalogue should send them to the Social Science Editor,
Routledge & Kegan Paul Ltd, 39 Store Street,
London WC1E 7DD.*
● *Books so marked are available in paperback.*
○ *Books so marked are available in paperback only.*
*All books are in metric Demy 8vo format (216 × 138mm approx.)
unless otherwise stated.*

International Library of Sociology
General Editor John Rex

GENERAL SOCIOLOGY

Barnsley, J. H. The Social Reality of Ethics. *464 pp.*
Brown, Robert. Explanation in Social Science. *208 pp.*
● Rules and Laws in Sociology. *192 pp.*
Bruford, W. H. Chekhov and His Russia. *A Sociological Study. 244 pp.*
Burton, F. and **Carlen, P.** Official Discourse. *On Discourse Analysis, Government Publications, Ideology. About 140 pp.*
Cain, Maureen E. Society and the Policeman's Role. *326 pp.*
● **Fletcher, Colin.** Beneath the Surface. *An Account of Three Styles of Sociological Research. 221 pp.*
Gibson, Quentin. The Logic of Social Enquiry. *240 pp.*
Glassner, B. Essential Interactionism. *208 pp.*
Glucksmann, M. Structuralist Analysis in Contemporary Social Thought. *212 pp.*
Gurvitch, Georges. Sociology of Law. *Foreword by Roscoe Pound. 264 pp.*
Hinkle, R. Founding Theory of American Sociology 1881–1913. *About 350 pp.*
Homans, George C. Sentiments and Activities. *336 pp.*
Johnson, Harry M. Sociology: *A Systematic Introduction. Foreword by Robert K. Merton. 710 pp.*
● **Keat, Russell** and **Urry, John.** Social Theory as Science. *278 pp.*
Mannheim, Karl. Essays on Sociology and Social Psychology. *Edited by Paul Keckskemeti. With Editorial Note by Adolph Lowe. 344 pp.*
Martindale, Don. The Nature and Types of Sociological Theory. *292 pp.*
● **Maus, Heinz.** A Short History of Sociology. *234 pp.*
Myrdal, Gunnar. Value in Social Theory: *A Collection of Essays on Methodology. Edited by Paul Streeten. 332 pp.*
Ogburn, William F. and **Nimkoff, Meyer F.** A Handbook of Sociology. *Preface by Karl Mannheim. 656 pp. 46 figures. 35 tables.*
Parsons, Talcott and **Smelser, Neil J.** Economy and Society: *A Study in the Integration of Economic and Social Theory. 362 pp.*
Payne, G., Dingwall, R., Payne, J. and **Carter, M.** Sociology and Social Research. *About 250 pp.*
Podgórecki, A. Practical Social Sciences. *About 200 pp.*
Podgorecki, A. and **Łos, M.** Multidimensional Sociology. *268 pp.*
Raffel, S. Matters of Fact. *A Sociological Inquiry. 152 pp.*
● **Rex, John.** Key Problems of Sociological Theory. *220 pp.*
Sociology and the Demystification of the Modern World. *282 pp.*
● **Rex, John.** (Ed.) Approaches to Sociology. *Contributions by Peter Abell, Frank Bechhofer, Basil Bernstein, Ronald Fletcher, David Frisby, Miriam Glucksmann, Peter Lassman, Herminio Martins, John Rex, Roland Robertson, John Westergaard and Jock Young. 302 pp.*
Rigby, A. Alternative Realities. *352 pp.*
Roche, M. Phenomenology, Language and the Social Sciences. *374 pp.*
Sahay, A. Sociological Analysis. *220 pp.*
Strasser, Hermann. The Normative Structure of Sociology. *Conservative and Emancipatory Themes in Social Thought. About 340 pp.*
Strong, P. Ceremonial Order of the Clinic. *267 pp.*
Urry, John. Reference Groups and the Theory of Revolution. *244 pp.*
Weinberg, E. Development of Sociology in the Soviet Union. *173 pp.*

FOREIGN CLASSICS OF SOCIOLOGY

● **Gerth, H. H.** and **Mills, C. Wright.** From Max Weber: *Essays in Sociology. 502 pp.*

● **Tönnies, Ferdinand.** Community and Association *(Gemeinschaft und Gesellschaft).|Translated and Supplemented by Charles P. Loomis. Foreword by Pitirim A. Sorokin. 334 pp.*

SOCIAL STRUCTURE

Andreski, Stanislav. Military Organization and Society. *Foreword by Professor A. R. Radcliffe-Brown. 226 pp. 1 folder.*

Broom, L., Lancaster Jones, F., McDonnell, P. and **Williams, T.** The Inheritance of Inequality. *About 180 pp.*

Carlton, Eric. Ideology and Social Order. *Foreword by Professor Philip Abrahams. About 320 pp.*

Clegg, S. and **Dunkerley, D.** Organization, Class and Control. *614 pp.*

Coontz, Sydney H. Population Theories and the Economic Interpretation. *202 pp.*

Coser, Lewis. The Functions of Social Conflict. *204 pp.*

Crook, I. and **D.** The First Years of the Yangyi Commune. *304 pp., illustrated.*

Dickie-Clark, H. F. Marginal Situation: *A Sociological Study of a Coloured Group. 240 pp. 11 tables.*

Giner, S. and **Archer, M. S.** (Eds) Contemporary Europe: *Social Structures and Cultural Patterns, 336 pp.*

● **Glaser, Barney** and **Strauss, Anselm L.** Status Passage: *A Formal Theory. 212 pp.*

Glass, D. V. (Ed.) Social Mobility in Britain. *Contributions by J. Berent, T. Bottomore, R. C. Chambers, J. Floud, D. V. Glass, J. R. Hall, H. T. Himmelweit, R. K. Kelsall, F. M. Martin, C. A. Moser, R. Mukherjee and W. Ziegel. 420 pp.*

Kelsall, R. K. Higher Civil Servants in Britain: *From 1870 to the Present Day. 268 pp. 31 tables.*

● **Lawton, Denis.** Social Class, Language and Education. *192 pp.*

McLeish, John. The Theory of Social Change: *Four Views Considered. 128 pp.*

● **Marsh, David C.** The Changing Social Structure of England and Wales, 1871–1961. *Revised edition. 288 pp.*

Menzies, Ken. Talcott Parsons and the Social Image of Man. *About 208 pp.*

● **Mouzelis, Nicos.** Organization and Bureaucracy. *An Analysis of Modern Theories. 240 pp.*

● **Ossowski, Stanislaw.** Class Structure in the Social Consciousness. *210 pp.*

● **Podgórecki, Adam.** Law and Society. *302 pp.*

Renner, Karl. Institutions of Private Law and Their Social Functions. *Edited, with an Introduction and Notes, by O. Kahn-Freud. Translated by Agnes Schwarzschild. 316 pp.*

Rex, J. and **Tomlinson, S.** Colonial Immigrants in a British City. *A Class Analysis. 368 pp.*

Smooha, S. Israel: Pluralism and Conflict. *472 pp.*

Wesolowski, W. Class, Strata and Power. *Trans. and with Introduction by G. Kolankiewicz. 160 pp.*

Zureik, E. Palestinians in Israel. *A Study in Internal Colonialism. 264 pp.*

SOCIOLOGY AND POLITICS

Acton, T. A. Gypsy Politics and Social Change. *316 pp.*

Burton, F. Politics of Legitimacy. *Struggles in a Belfast Community. 250 pp.*

Crook, I. and **D.** Revolution in a Chinese Village. *Ten Mile Inn. 216 pp., illustrated.*

Etzioni-Halevy, E. Political Manipulation and Administrative Power. *A Comparative Study. About 200 pp.*

Fielding, N. The National Front. *About 250 pp.*

● **Hechter, Michael.** Internal Colonialism. *The Celtic Fringe in British National Development, 1536–1966. 380 pp.*

Kornhauser, William. The Politics of Mass Society. *272 pp. 20 tables.*

Korpi, W. The Working Class in Welfare Capitalism. *Work, Unions and Politics in Sweden. 472 pp.*

Kroes, R. Soldiers and Students. *A Study of Right- and Left-wing Students. 174 pp.*

Martin, Roderick. Sociology of Power. *About 272 pp.*

Merquior, J. G. Rousseau and Weber. *A Study in the Theory of Legitimacy. About 288 pp.*

Myrdal, Gunnar. The Political Element in the Development of Economic Theory. *Translated from the German by Paul Streeten. 282 pp.*

Varma, B. N. The Sociology and Politics of Development. *A Theoretical Study. 236 pp.*

Wong, S.-L. Sociology and Socialism in Contemporary China. *160 pp.*

Wootton, Graham. Workers, Unions and.the State. *188 pp.*

CRIMINOLOGY

Ancel, Marc. Social Defence: *A Modern Approach to Criminal Problems. Foreword by Leon Radzinowicz. 240 pp.*

Athens, L. Violent Criminal Acts and Actors. *104 pp.*

Cain, Maureen E. Society and the Policeman's Role. *326 pp.*

Cloward, Richard A. and **Ohlin, Lloyd E.** Delinquency and Opportunity: *A Theory of Delinquent Gangs. 248 pp.*

Downes, David M. The Delinquent Solution. *A Study in Subcultural Theory. 296 pp.*

Friedlander, Kate. The Psycho-Analytical Approach to Juvenile Delinquency: *Theory, Case Studies, Treatment. 320 pp.*

Gleuck, Sheldon and **Eleanor.** Family Environment and Delinquency. *With the statistical assistance of Rose W. Kneznek. 340 pp.*

Lopez-Rey, Manuel. Crime. *An Analytical Appraisal. 288 pp.*

Mannheim, Hermann. Comparative Criminology: *A Text Book. Two volumes. 442 pp. and 380 pp.*

Morris, Terence. The Criminal Area: *A Study in Social Ecology. Foreword by Hermann Mannheim. 232 pp. 25 tables. 4 maps.*

Rock, Paul. Making People Pay. *338 pp.*

● **Taylor, Ian, Walton, Paul** and **Young, Jock.** The New Criminology. *For a Social Theory of Deviance. 325 pp.*

● **Taylor, Ian, Walton, Paul** and **Young, Jock.** (Eds) Critical Criminology. *268 pp.*

SOCIAL PSYCHOLOGY

Bagley, Christopher. The Social Psychology of the Epileptic Child. *320 pp.*

Brittan, Arthur. Meanings and Situations. *224 pp.*

Carroll, J. Break-Out from the Crystal Palace. *200 pp.*

● **Fleming, C. M.** Adolescence: Its Social Psychology. *With an Introduction to recent findings from the fields of Anthropology, Physiology, Medicine, Psychometrics and Sociometry. 288 pp.*

● The Social Psychology of Education: *An Introduction and Guide to Its Study. 136 pp.*

Linton, Ralph. The Cultural Background of Personality. *132 pp.*

● **Mayo, Elton.** The Social Problems of an Industrial Civilization. *With an Appendix on the Political Problem. 180 pp.*

Ottaway, A. K. C. Learning Through Group Experience. *176 pp.*

Plummer, Ken. Sexual Stigma. *An Interactionist Account. 254 pp.*

● **Rose, Arnold M.** (Ed.) Human Behaviour and Social Processes: *an Interactionist Approach. Contributions by Arnold M. Rose, Ralph H. Turner, Anselm Strauss, Everett C. Hughes, E. Franklin Frazier, Howard S. Becker et al. 696 pp.*

Smelser, Neil J. Theory of Collective Behaviour. *448 pp.*

Stephenson, Geoffrey M. The Development of Conscience. *128 pp.*

Young, Kimball. Handbook of Social Psychology. *658 pp. 16 figures. 10 tables.*

SOCIOLOGY OF THE FAMILY

Bell, Colin R. Middle Class Families: *Social and Geographical Mobility. 224 pp.*
Burton, Lindy. Vulnerable Children. *272 pp.*
Gavron, Hannah. The Captive Wife: *Conflicts of Household Mothers. 190 pp.*
George, Victor and **Wilding, Paul.** Motherless Families. *248 pp.*
Klein, Josephine. Samples from English Cultures.
    1. Three Preliminary Studies and Aspects of Adult Life in England. *447 pp.*
    2. Child-Rearing Practices and Index. *247 pp.*
Klein, Viola. The Feminine Character. *History of an Ideology. 244 pp.*
McWhinnie, Alexina M. Adopted Children. *How They Grow Up. 304 pp.*
● **Morgan, D. H. J.** Social Theory and the Family. *About 320 pp.*
● **Myrdal, Alva** and **Klein, Viola.** Women's Two Roles: *Home and Work. 238 pp.*
    27 tables.
Parsons, Talcott and **Bales, Robert F.** Family: Socialization and Interaction Process.
    In collaboration with James Olds, Morris Zelditch and Philip E. Slater. 456 pp.
    50 figures and tables.

SOCIAL SERVICES

Bastide, Roger. The Sociology of Mental Disorder. *Translated from the French by*
    Jean McNeil. 260 pp.
Carlebach, Julius. Caring For Children in Trouble. *266 pp.*
George, Victor. Foster Care. *Theory and Practice. 234 pp.*
    Social Security: *Beveridge and After. 258 pp.*
George, V. and **Wilding, P.** Motherless Families. *248 pp.*
● **Goetschius, George W.** Working with Community Groups. *256 pp.*
Goetschius, George W. and **Tash, Joan.** Working with Unattached Youth. *416 pp.*
Heywood, Jean S. Children in Care. *The Development of the Service for the Deprived*
    Child. Third revised edition. 284 pp.
King, Roy D., Ranes, Norma V. and **Tizard, Jack.** Patterns of Residential Care.
    356 pp.
Leigh, John. Young People and Leisure. *256 pp.*
● **Mays, John.** (Ed.) Penelope Hall's Social Services of England and Wales.
    368 pp.
Morris, Mary. Voluntary Work and the Welfare State. *300 pp.*
Nokes, P. L. The Professional Task in Welfare Practice. *152 pp.*
Timms, Noel. Psychiatric Social Work in Great Britain (1939–1962). *280 pp.*
●   Social Casework: *Principles and Practice. 256 pp.*

SOCIOLOGY OF EDUCATION

Banks, Olive. Parity and Prestige in English Secondary Education: a Study in
    Educational Sociology. *272 pp.*
● **Blyth, W. A. L.** English Primary Education. *A Sociological Description.*
    2. Background. *168 pp.*
Collier, K. G. The Social Purposes of Education: *Personal and Social Values in*
    Education. 268 pp.
Evans, K. M. Sociometry and Education. *158 pp.*
● **Ford, Julienne.** Social Class and the Comprehensive School. *192 pp.*
Foster, P. J. Education and Social Change in Ghana. *336 pp. 3 maps.*
Fraser, W. R. Education and Society in Modern France. *150 pp.*
Grace, Gerald R. Role Conflict and the Teacher. *150 pp.*
Hans, Nicholas. New Trends in Education in the Eighteenth Century. *278 pp.*
    19 tables.
●   Comparative Education: *A Study of Educational Factors and Traditions. 360 pp.*
● **Hargreaves, David.** Interpersonal Relations and Education. *432 pp.*
●   Social Relations in a Secondary School. *240 pp.*
    School Organization and Pupil Involvement. *A Study of Secondary Schools.*

● **Mannheim, Karl** and **Stewart, W. A. C.** An Introduction to the Sociology of
   Education. *206 pp.*
● **Musgrove, F.** Youth and the Social Order. *176 pp.*
● **Ottaway, A. K. C.** Education and Society: An Introduction to the Sociology of
   Education. *With an Introduction by W. O. Lester Smith. 212 pp.*
   Peers, Robert. Adult Education: *A Comparative Study. Revised edition. 398 pp.*
   Stratta, Erica. The Education of Borstal Boys. *A Study of their Educational
   Experiences prior to, and during, Borstal Training. 256 pp.*
● **Taylor, P. H., Reid, W. A.** and **Holley, B. J.** The English Sixth Form. *A Case Study in
   Curriculum Research. 198 pp.*

SOCIOLOGY OF CULTURE

   Eppel, E. M. and **M.** Adolescents and Morality: *A Study of some Moral Values and
   Dilemmas of Working Adolescents in the Context of a changing Climate of
   Opinion. Foreword by W. J. H. Sprott. 268 pp. 39 tables.*
● **Fromm, Erich.** The Fear of Freedom. *286 pp.*
●   The Sane Society. *400 pp.*
   Johnson, L. The Cultural Critics. *From Matthew Arnold to Raymond Williams.
   233 pp.*
   Mannheim, Karl. Essays on the Sociology of Culture. *Edited by Ernst Mannheim in
   co-operation with Paul Kecskemeti. Editorial Note by Adolph Lowe. 280 pp.*
   Merquior, J. G. The Veil and the Mask. *Essays on Culture and Ideology. Foreword
   by Ernest Gellner. 140 pp.*
   Zijderfeld, A. C. On Clichés. *The Supersedure of Meaning by Function in Modernity.
   150 pp.*

SOCIOLOGY OF RELIGION

   Argyle, Michael and **Beit-Hallahmi, Benjamin.** The Social Psychology of Religion.
   256 pp.
   Glasner, Peter E. The Sociology of Secularisation. *A Critique of a Concept.
   146 pp.*
   Hall, J. R. The Ways Out. *Utopian Communal Groups in an Age of Babylon. 280 pp.*
   Ranson, S., Hinings, B. and **Bryman, A.** Clergy, Ministers and Priests. *216 pp.*
   Stark, Werner. The Sociology of Religion. *A Study of Christendom.*
      Volume II. *Sectarian Religion. 368 pp.*
      Volume III. *The Universal Church. 464 pp.*
      Volume IV. *Types of Religious Man. 352 pp.*
      Volume V. *Types of Religious Culture. 464 pp.*
   Turner, B. S. Weber and Islam. *216 pp.*
   Watt, W. Montgomery. Islam and the Integration of Society. *320 pp.*

SOCIOLOGY OF ART AND LITERATURE

   Jarvie, Ian C. Towards a Sociology of the Cinema. *A Comparative Essay on the
   Structure and Functioning of a Major Entertainment Industry. 405 pp.*
   Rust, Frances S. Dance in Society. *An Analysis of the Relationships between the Social
   Dance and Society in England from the Middle Ages to the Present Day. 256 pp.
   8 pp. of plates.*
   Schücking, L. L. The Sociology of Literary Taste. *112 pp.*
   Wolff, Janet. Hermeneutic Philosophy and the Sociology of Art. *150 pp.*

SOCIOLOGY OF KNOWLEDGE

   Diesing, P. Patterns of Discovery in the Social Sciences. *262 pp.*

● **Douglas, J. D.** (Ed.) Understanding Everyday Life. *370 pp.*
● **Hamilton, P.** Knowledge and Social Structure. *174 pp.*
Jarvie, I. C. Concepts and Society. *232 pp.*
Mannheim, Karl. Essays on the Sociology of Knowledge. *Edited by Paul Kecskemeti. Editorial Note by Adolph Lowe. 353 pp.*
Remmling, Gunter W. The Sociology of Karl Mannheim. *With a Bibliographical Guide to the Sociology of Knowledge, Ideological Analysis, and Social Planning. 255 pp.*
Remmling, Gunter W. (Ed.) Towards the Sociology of Knowledge. *Origin and Development of a Sociological Thought Style. 463 pp.*
Scheler, M. Problems of a Sociology of Knowledge. *Trans. by M. S. Frings. Edited and with an Introduction by K. Stikkers. 232 pp.*

URBAN SOCIOLOGY

Aldridge, M. The British New Towns. *A Programme Without a Policy. 232 pp.*
Ashworth, William. The Genesis of Modern British Town Planning: *A Study in Economic and Social History of the Nineteenth and Twentieth Centuries. 288 pp.*
Brittan, A. The Privatised World. *196 pp.*
Cullingworth, J. B. Housing Needs and Planning Policy: *A Restatement of the Problems of Housing Need and 'Overspill' in England and Wales. 232 pp. 44 tables. 8 maps.*
Dickinson, Robert E. City and Region: *A Geographical Interpretation. 608 pp. 125 figures.*
  The West European City: *A Geographical Interpretation. 600 pp. 129 maps. 29 plates.*
Humphreys, Alexander J. New Dubliners: *Urbanization and the Irish Family. Foreword by George C. Homans. 304 pp.*
Jackson, Brian. Working Class Community: *Some General Notions raised by a Series of Studies in Northern England. 192 pp.*
● **Mann, P. H.** An Approach to Urban Sociology. *240 pp.*
Mellor, J. R. Urban Sociology in an Urbanized Society. *326 pp.*
Morris, R. N. and **Mogey, J.** The Sociology of Housing. *Studies at Berinsfield. 232 pp. 4 pp. plates.*
Mullan, R. Stevenage Ltd. *About 250 pp.*
Rex, J. and **Tomlinson, S.** Colonial Immigrants in a British City. *A Class Analysis. 368 pp.*
Rosser, C. and **Harris, C.** The Family and Social Change. *A Study of Family and Kinship in a South Wales Town. 352 pp. 8 maps.*
● **Stacey, Margaret, Batsone, Eric, Bell, Colin** and **Thurcott, Anne.** Power, Persistence and Change. *A Second Study of Banbury. 196 pp.*

RURAL SOCIOLOGY

Mayer, Adrian C. Peasants in the Pacific. *A Study of Fiji Indian Rural Society. 248 pp. 20 plates.*
Williams, W. M. The Sociology of an English Village: *Gosforth. 272 pp. 12 figures. 13 tables.*

SOCIOLOGY OF INDUSTRY AND DISTRIBUTION

Dunkerley, David. The Foreman. *Aspects of Task and Structure. 192 pp.*
Eldridge, J. E. T. Industrial Disputes. *Essays in the Sociology of Industrial Relations. 288 pp.*
Hollowell, Peter G. The Lorry Driver. *272 pp.*
● **Oxaal, I., Barnett, T.** and **Booth, D.** (Eds) Beyond the Sociology of Development.

8

Economy and Society in Latin America and Africa. 295 pp.
Smelser, Neil J. Social Change in the Industrial Revolution: *An Application of Theory to the Lancashire Cotton Industry, 1770–1840. 468 pp. 12 figures. 14 tables.*
Watson, T. J. The Personnel Managers. *A Study in the Sociology of Work and Employment, 262 pp.*

ANTHROPOLOGY

Brandel-Syrier, Mia. Reeftown Elite. *A Study of Social Mobility in a Modern African Community on the Reef. 376 pp.*
Dickie-Clark, H. F. The Marginal Situation. *A Sociological Study of a Coloured Group. 236 pp.*
Dube, S. C. Indian Village. *Foreword by Morris Edward Opler. 276 pp. 4 plates.*
India's Changing Villages: *Human Factors in Community Development. 260 pp. 8 plates. 1 map.*
Fei, H.-T. Peasant Life in China. *A Field Study of Country Life in the Yangtze Valley. With a foreword by Bronislaw Malinowski. 328 pp. 16 pp. plates.*
Firth, Raymond. Malay Fishermen. *Their Peasant Economy. 420 pp. 17 pp. plates.*
Gulliver, P. H. Social Control in an African Society: a Study of the Arusha, Agricultural Masai of Northern Tanganyika. *320 pp. 8 plates. 10 figures.*
Family Herds. *288 pp.*
Jarvie, Ian C. The Revolution in Anthropology. *268 pp.*
Little, Kenneth L. Mende of Sierra Leone. *308 pp. and folder.*
Negroes in Britain. *With a New Introduction and Contemporary Study by Leonard Bloom. 320 pp.*
Tambs-Lyche, H. London Patidars. *About 180 pp.*
Madan, G. R. Western Sociologists on Indian Society. *Marx, Spencer, Weber, Durkheim, Pareto. 384 pp.*
Mayer, A. C. Peasants in the Pacific. *A Study of Fiji Indian Rural Society. 248 pp.*
Meer, Fatima. Race and Suicide in South Africa. *325 pp.*
Smith, Raymond T. The Negro Family in British Guiana: *Family Structure and Social Status in the Villages. With a Foreword by Meyer Fortes. 314 pp. 8 plates. 1 figure. 4 maps.*

SOCIOLOGY AND PHILOSOPHY

Adriaansens, H. Talcott Parsons and the Conceptual Dilemma. *About 224 pp.*
Barnsley, John H. The Social Reality of Ethics. *A Comparative Analysis of Moral Codes. 448 pp.*
Diesing, Paul. Patterns of Discovery in the Social Sciences. *362 pp.*
● **Douglas, Jack D.** (Ed.) Understanding Everyday Life. *Toward the Reconstruction of Sociological Knowledge. Contributions by Alan F. Blum, Aaron W. Cicourel, Norman K. Denzin, Jack D. Douglas, John Heeren, Peter McHugh, Peter K. Manning, Melvin Power, Matthew Speier, Roy Turner. D. Lawrence Wieder, Thomas P. Wilson and Don H. Zimmerman. 370 pp.*
Gorman, Robert A. The Dual Vision. *Alfred Schutz and the Myth of Phenomenological Social Science. 240 pp.*
Jarvie, Ian C. Concepts and Society. *216 pp.*
Kilminster, R. Praxis and Method. *A Sociological Dialogue with Lukács, Gramsci and the Early Frankfurt School. 334 pp.*
● **Pelz, Werner.** The Scope of Understanding in Sociology. *Towards a More Radical Reorientation in the Social Humanistic Sciences. 283 pp.*
Roche, Maurice. Phenomenology, Language and the Social Sciences. *371 pp.*
Sahay, Arun. Sociological Analysis. *212 pp.*
● **Slater, P.** Origin and Significance of the Frankfurt School. *A Marxist Perspective. 185 pp.*

Spurling, L. Phenomenology and the Social World. *The Philosophy of Merleau-Ponty and its Relation to the Social Sciences. 222 pp.*

Wilson, H. T. The American Ideology. *Science, Technology and Organization as Modes of Rationality. 368 pp.*

International Library of Anthropology
General Editor Adam Kuper

● **Ahmed, A. S.** Millennium and Charisma Among Pathans. *A Critical Essay in Social Anthropology. 192 pp.*
Pukhtun Economy and Society. *Traditional Structure and Economic Development. About 360 pp.*

Barth, F. Selected Essays. *Volume I. About 250 pp.* Selected Essays. *Volume II. About 250 pp.*

Brown, Paula. The Chimbu. *A Study of Change in the New Guinea Highlands. 151 pp.*

Foner, N. Jamaica Farewell. *200 pp.*

Gudeman, Stephen. Relationships, Residence and the Individual. *A Rural Panamanian Community. 288 pp. 11 plates, 5 figures, 2 maps, 10 tables.*
The Demise of a Rural Economy. *From Subsistence to Capitalism in a Latin American Village. 160 pp.*

Hamnett, Ian. Chieftainship and Legitimacy. *An Anthropological Study of Executive Law in Lesotho. 163 pp.*

Hanson, F. Allan. Meaning in Culture. *127 pp.*

Hazan, H. The Limbo People. *A Study of the Constitution of the Time Universe Among the Aged. About 192 pp.*

Humphreys, S. C. Anthropology and the Greeks. *288 pp.*

Karp, I. Fields of Change Among the Iteso of Kenya. *140 pp.*

Lloyd, P. C. Power and Independence. *Urban Africans' Perception of Social Inequality. 264 pp.*

Parry, J. P. Caste and Kinship in Kangra. *352 pp. illustrated.*

Pettigrew, Joyce. Robber Noblemen. *A Study of the Political System of the Sikh Jats. 284 pp.*

Street, Brian V. The Savage in Literature. *Representations of 'Primitive' Society in English Fiction, 1858–1920. 207 pp.*

Van Den Berghe, Pierre L. Power and Privilege at an African University. *278 pp.*

International Library of Phenomenology and Moral Sciences
General Editor John O'Neill

Apel, K.-O. Towards a Transformation of Philosophy. *308 pp.*

Bologh, R. W. Dialectical Phenomenology. *Marx's Method. 287 pp.*

Fekete, J. The Critical Twilight. *Explorations in the Ideology of Anglo-American Literary Theory from Eliot to McLuhan. 300 pp.*

Medina, A. Reflection, Time and the Novel. *Towards a Communicative Theory of Literature. 143 pp.*

International Library of Social Policy
General Editor Kathleen Jones

Bayley, M. Mental Handicap and Community Care. *426 pp.*

Bottoms, A. E. and **McClean, J. D.** Defendants in the Criminal Process. *284 pp.*

Bradshaw, J. The Family Fund. *An Initiative in Social Policy. About 224 pp.*

Butler, J. R. Family Doctors and Public Policy. *208 pp.*
Davies, Martin. Prisoners of Society. *Attitudes and Aftercare. 204 pp.*
Gittus, Elizabeth. Flats, Families and the Under-Fives. *285 pp.*
Holman, Robert. Trading in Children. *A Study of Private Fostering. 355 pp.*
Jeffs, A. Young People and the Youth Service. *160 pp.*
Jones, Howard and Cornes, Paul. Open Prisons. *288 pp.*
Jones, Kathleen. History of the Mental Health Service. *428 pp.*
Jones, Kathleen with **Brown, John, Cunningham, W. J., Roberts, Julian** and
     Williams, Peter. Opening the Door. *A Study of New Policies for the Mentally
     Handicapped. 278 pp.*
Karn, Valerie. Retiring to the Seaside. *400 pp. 2 maps. Numerous tables.*
King, R. D. and **Elliot, K. W.** Albany: Birth of a Prison—End of an Era. *394 pp.*
Thomas, J. E. The English Prison Officer since 1850: *A Study in Conflict. 258 pp.*
Walton, R. G. Women in Social Work. *303 pp.*
● **Woodward, J.** To Do the Sick No Harm. *A Study of the British Voluntary Hospital
     System to 1875. 234 pp.*

International Library of Welfare and Philosophy
General Editors   Noel Timms and David Watson

● **McDermott, F. E.** (Ed.) Self-Determination in Social Work. *A Collection of Essays
     on Self-determination and Related Concepts by Philosophers and Social Work
     Theorists. Contributors: F. P. Biestek, S. Bernstein, A. Keith-Lucas, D. Sayer,
     H. H. Perelman, C. Whittington, R. F. Stalley, F. E. McDermott, I. Berlin, H. J.
     McCloskey, H. L. A. Hart, J. Wilson, A. I. Melden, S. I. Benn. 254 pp.*
● **Plant, Raymond.** Community and Ideology. *104 pp.*
Ragg, Nicholas M. People Not Cases. *A Philosophical Approach to Social Work.
     168 pp.*
● **Timms, Noel** and **Watson, David.** (Eds) Talking About Welfare. *Readings in
     Philosophy and Social Policy. Contributors: T. H. Marshall, R. B. Brandt, G. H.
     von Wright, K. Nielsen, M. Cranston, R. M. Titmuss, R. S. Downie, E. Telfer, D.
     Donnison, J. Benson, P. Leonard, A. Keith-Lucas, D. Walsh, I. T. Ramsey.
     320 pp.*
● Philosophy in Social Work. *250 pp.*
● **Weale, A.** Equality and Social Policy. *164 pp.*

Library of Social Work
General Editor   Noel Timms

● **Baldock, Peter.** Community Work and Social Work. *140 pp.*
○ **Beedell, Christopher.** Residential Life with Children. *210 pp. Crown 8vo.*
● **Berry, Juliet.** Daily Experience in Residential Life. *A Study of Children and their
     Care-givers. 202 pp.*
○ Social Work with Children. *190 pp. Crown 8vo.*
● **Brearley, C. Paul.** Residential Work with the Elderly. *116 pp.*
● Social Work, Ageing and Society. *126 pp.*
● **Cheetham, Juliet.** Social Work with Immigrants. *240 pp. Crown 8vo.*
● **Cross, Crispin P.** (Ed.) Interviewing and Communication in Social Work.
     *Contributions by C. P. Cross, D. Laurenson, B. Strutt, S. Raven. 192 pp. Crown
     8vo.*

● **Curnock, Kathleen** and **Hardiker, Pauline.** Towards Practice Theory. *Skills and Methods in Social Assessments. 208 pp.*
● **Davies, Bernard.** The Use of Groups in Social Work Practice. *158 pp.*
● **Davies, Martin.** Support Systems in Social Work. *144 pp.*
 Ellis, June. (Ed.) West African Families in Britain. *A Meeting of Two Cultures. Contributions by Pat Stapleton, Vivien Biggs. 150 pp. 1 Map.*
● **Hart, John.** Social Work and Sexual Conduct. *230 pp.*
● **Hutten, Joan M.** Short-Term Contracts in Social Work. *Contributions by Stella M. Hall, Elsie Osborne, Mannie Sher, Eva Sternberg, Elizabeth Tuters. 134 pp.*
 Jackson, Michael P. and **Valencia, B. Michael.** Financial Aid Through Social Work. *140 pp.*
● **Jones, Howard.** The Residential Community. *A Setting for Social Work. 150 pp.*
● (Ed.) Towards a New Social Work. *Contributions by Howard Jones, D. A. Fowler, J. R. Cypher, R. G. Walton, Geoffrey Mungham, Philip Priestley, Ian Shaw, M. Bartley, R. Deacon, Irwin Epstein, Geoffrey Pearson. 184 pp.*
 Jones, Ray and **Pritchard, Colin.** (Eds) Social Work With Adolescents. *Contributions by Ray Jones, Colin Pritchard, Jack Dunham, Florence Rossetti, Andrew Kerslake, John Burns, William Gregory, Graham Templeman, Kenneth E. Reid, Audrey Taylor. About 170 pp.*
 Jordon, William. The Social Worker in Family Situations. *160 pp. Crown 8vo.*
● **Laycock, A. L.** Adolescents and Social Work. *128 pp. Crown 8vo.*
● **Lees, Ray.** Politics and Social Work. *128 pp. Crown 8vo.*
● Research Strategies for Social Welfare. *112 pp. Tables.*
○ **McCullough, M. K.** and **Ely, Peter J.** Social Work with Groups. *127 pp. Crown 8vo.*
● **Moffett, Jonathan.** Concepts in Casework Treatment. *128 pp. Crown 8vo.*
 Parsloe, Phyllida. Juvenile Justice in Britain and the United States. *The Balance of Needs and Rights. 336 pp.*
● **Plant, Raymond.** Social and Moral Theory in Casework. *112 pp. Crown 8vo.*
 Priestley, Philip, Fears, Denise and **Fuller, Roger.** Justice for Juveniles, *The 1969 Children and Young Persons Act: A Case for Reform? 128 pp.*
● **Pritchard, Colin** and **Taylor, Richard.** Social Work: Reform or Revolution? *170 pp.*
○ **Pugh, Elisabeth.** Social Work in Child Care. *128 pp. Crown 8vo.*
● **Robinson, Margaret.** Schools and Social Work. *282 pp.*
○ **Ruddock, Ralph.** Roles and Relationships. *128 pp. Crown 8vo.*
● **Sainsbury, Eric.** Social Diagnosis in Casework. *118 pp. Crown 8vo.*
● Social Work with Families. *Perceptions of Social Casework among Clients of a Family Service. 188 pp.*
 Seed, Philip. The Expansion of Social Work in Britain. *128 pp. Crown 8vo.*
● **Shaw, John.** The Self in Social Work. *124 pp.*
 Smale, Gerald G. Prophecy, Behaviour and Change. *An Examination of Self-fulfilling Prophecies in Helping Relationships. 116 pp. Crown 8vo.*
 Smith, Gilbert. Social Need. *Policy, Practice and Research. 155 pp.*
● Social Work and the Sociology of Organisations. *124 pp. Revised edition.*
● **Sutton, Carole.** Psychology for Social Workers and Counsellors. *An Introduction. 248 pp.*
● **Timms, Noel.** Language of Social Casework. *122 pp. Crown 8vo.*
● Recording in Social Work. *124 pp. Crown 8vo.*
● **Todd, F. Joan.** Social Work with the Mentally Subnormal. *96 pp. Crown 8vo.*
● **Walrond-Skinner, Sue.** Family Therapy. *The Treatment of Natural Systems. 172 pp.*
● **Warham, Joyce.** An Introduction to Administration for Social Workers. *Revised edition. 112 pp.*
● An Open Case. *The Organisational Context of Social Work. 172 pp.*
○ **Wittenberg, Isca Salzberger,** Psycho-Analytic Insight and Relationships. *A Kleinian Approach. 196 pp. Crown 8vo.*

Primary Socialization, Language and Education
General Editor Basil Bernstein

Adlam, Diana S., *with the assistance of Geoffrey Turner and Lesley Lineker.* Code in *Context. 272 pp.*
Bernstein, Basil. Class, Codes and Control. *3 volumes.*
●   1. *Theoretical Studies Towards a Sociology of Language. 254 pp.*
    2. *Applied Studies Towards a Sociology of Language. 377 pp.*
●   3. *Towards a Theory of Educational Transmission. 167 pp.*
Brandis, W. and Bernstein, B. Selection and Control. *176 pp.*
Brandis, Walter and Henderson, Dorothy. Social Class, Language and Communication. *288 pp.*
Cook-Gumperz, Jenny. Social Control and Socialization. *A Study of Class Differences in the Language of Maternal Control. 290 pp.*
● Gahagan, D. M. and G. A. Talk Reform. *Exploration in Language for Infant School Children. 160 pp.*
Hawkins, P. R. Social Class, the Nominal Group and Verbal Strategies. *About 220 pp.*
Robinson, W. P. and Rackstraw, Susan D. A. A Question of Answers. *2 volumes. 192 pp. and 180 pp.*
Turner, Geoffrey J. and Mohan, Bernard A. A Linguistic Description and Computer Programme for Children's Speech. *208 pp.*

Reports of the Institute of Community Studies

Baker, J. The Neighbourhood Advice Centre. A Community Project in Camden. *320 pp.*
● Cartwright, Ann. Patients and their Doctors. *A Study of General Practice. 304 pp.*
Dench, Geoff. Maltese in London. *A Case-study in the Erosion of Ethnic Consciousness. 302 pp.*
Jackson, Brian and Marsden, Dennis. Education and the Working Class: *Some General Themes Raised by a Study of 88 Working-class Children in a Northern Industrial City. 268 pp. 2 folders.*
Marris, Peter. The Experience of Higher Education. *232 pp. 27 tables.*
●   Loss and Change. *192 pp.*
Marris, Peter and Rein, Martin. Dilemmas of Social Reform. *Poverty and Community Action in the United States. 256 pp.*
Marris, Peter and Somerset, Anthony. African Businessmen. *A Study of Entrepreneurship and Development in Kenya. 256 pp.*
Mills, Richard. Young Outsiders: *a Study in Alternative Communities. 216 pp.*
Runciman, W. G. Relative Deprivation and Social Justice. *A Study of Attitudes to Social Inequality in Twentieth-Century England. 352 pp.*
Willmott, Peter. Adolescent Boys in East London. *230 pp.*
Willmott, Peter and Young, Michael. Family and Class in a London Suburb. *202 pp. 47 tables.*
Young, Michael and McGeeney, Patrick. Learning Begins at Home. *A Study of a Junior School and its Parents. 128 pp.*
Young, Michael and Willmott, Peter. Family and Kinship in East London. *Foreword by Richard M. Titmuss. 252 pp. 39 tables.*
  The Symmetrical Family. *410 pp.*

Reports of the Institute for Social Studies in Medical Care

Cartwright, Ann, Hockey, Lisbeth and Anderson, John J. Life Before Death. *310 pp.*
Dunnell, Karen and Cartwright, Ann. Medicine Takers, Prescribers and Hoarders.
  190 pp.
Farrell, C. My Mother Said. . . *A Study of the Way Young People Learned About Sex and Birth Control. 288 pp.*

Medicine, Illness and Society
General Editor W. M. Williams

Hall, David J. Social Relations & Innovation. *Changing the State of Play in Hospitals.*
  232 pp.
Hall, David J. and Stacey, M. (Eds) Beyond Separation. *234 pp.*
Robinson, David. The Process of Becoming Ill. *142 pp.*
Stacey, Margaret *et al.* Hospitals, Children and Their Families. *The Report of a Pilot Study. 202 pp.*
Stimson, G. V. and Webb, B. Going to See the Doctor. *The Consultation Process in General Practice. 155 pp.*

Monographs in Social Theory
General Editor Arthur Brittan

● Barnes, B. Scientific Knowledge and Sociological Theory. *192 pp.*
Bauman, Zygmunt. Culture as Praxis. *204 pp.*
● Dixon, Keith. Sociological Theory. *Pretence and Possibility. 142 pp.*
   The Sociology of Belief. *Fallacy and Foundation. About 160 pp.*
Goff, T. W. Marx and Mead. *Contributions to a Sociology of Knowledge. 176 pp.*
Meltzer, B. N., Petras, J. W. and Reynolds, L. T. Symbolic Interactionism. *Genesis, Varieties and Criticisms. 144 pp.*
● Smith, Anthony D. The Concept of Social Change. *A Critique of the Functionalist Theory of Social Change. 208 pp.*

Routledge Social Science Journals

The British Journal of Sociology. *Editor – Angus Stewart; Associate Editor – Leslie Sklair. Vol. 1, No. 1 – March 1950 and Quarterly. Roy. 8vo. All back issues available. An international journal publishing original papers in the field of sociology and related areas.*
Community Work. *Edited by David Jones and Marjorie Mayo. 1973. Published annually.*
Economy and Society. *Vol. 1, No. 1. February 1972 and Quarterly. Metric Roy. 8vo. A journal for all social scientists covering sociology, philosophy, anthropology, economics and history. All back numbers available.*

14

Social and Psychological Aspects of Medical Practice
Editor   Trevor Silverstone

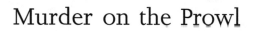

Murder on the Prowl

Murder on the Prowl

RITA MAE BROWN
& SNEAKY PIE BROWN

ILLUSTRATIONS BY WENDY WRAY

BANTAM BOOKS   NEW YORK • TORONTO • LONDON • SYDNEY • AUCKLAND

MURDER ON THE PROWL
A Bantam Book / April 1998

Library of Congress Cataloging-in-Publication Data

Brown, Rita Mae.
Murder on the prowl / by Rita Mae Brown and Sneaky Pie Brown.
p. cm.
ISBN 0-553-09970-1
I. Title.
PS3552.R698M88   1998
813'.54—dc21   97–31153
CIP

Published simultaneously in the United States and Canada

PRINTED IN THE UNITED STATES OF AMERICA
BVG   10 9 8 7 6 5 4 3 2 1

M

To Mr. Wonderful—sometimes
David Wheeler

Cast of Characters

Mary Minor Haristeen (Harry), the young postmistress of Crozet

Mrs. Murphy, Harry's gray tiger cat

Tee Tucker, Harry's Welsh corgi, Mrs. Murphy's friend and confidante

Pharamond Haristeen (Fair), veterinarian, formerly married to Harry

Mrs. George Hogendobber (Miranda), a widow who works with Harry in the post office

Market Shiflett, owner of Shiflett's Market, next to the post office

Pewter, Market's shamelessly fat gray cat, who now lives with Harry and family

Susan Tucker, Harry's best friend

Big Marilyn Sanburne (Mim), Queen of Crozet society

Rick Shaw, sheriff

Cynthia Cooper, police officer

Herbert C. Jones, pastor of Crozet Lutheran Church

Roscoe Fletcher, headmaster of the exclusive St. Elizabeth's private school

Naomi Fletcher, principal of the lower school at St. Elizabeth's. She supports her husband's vision 100%

Alexander Brashiers (Sandy), an English teacher at St. Elizabeth's who believes he should be headmaster

April Shively, secretary to the headmaster, whom she loves

Maury McKinchie, a film director who's lost his way, lost his fire, and seems to be losing his wife

Brooks Tucker, Susan Tucker's daughter. She has transferred to St. Elizabeth's

Karen Jensen, irreverent, a star of the field hockey team, and lusted after by most of the boys

Jody Miller, another good field hockey player, she seems to be suffering the ill effects of an evaporating romance with Sean Hallahan

Sean Hallahan, the star of the football team

Roger Davis, calm, quiet, and watchful, he is overshadowed by Sean

Kendrick Miller, driven, insular, and hot-tempered, he's built a thriving nursery business as he's lost his family . . . he barely notices them

Irene Miller, a fading beauty who deals with her husband's absorption in his work and her daughter's mood swings by ignoring them

Father Michael, priest at the Catholic church, a friend of the Reverend Herbert Jones

Jimbo Anson, owner of the technologically advanced car wash on Route 29

Coach Renee Hallvard, a favorite with the St. Elizabeth's students, she coaches the girls' field hockey team

Murder on the Prowl

1

Towns, like people, have souls. The little town of Crozet, Virginia, latitude 38°, longitude 78° 60′, had the soul of an Irish tenor.

On this beautiful equinox day, September 21, every soul was lifted, if not every voice—for it was perfect: creamy clouds lazed across a turquoise sky. The Blue Ridge Mountains, startling in their color, hovered protectively at the edge of emerald meadows. The temperature held at 72° F with low humidity.

This Thursday, Mary Minor Haristeen worked unenthusiastically in the post office. As she was the postmistress, she could hardly skip out, however tempted she was. Her tiger cat, Mrs. Murphy, and her corgi, Tee Tucker, blasted in and out of the animal door, the little flap echoing with each arrival or departure. It was the animals' version of teenagers slamming the door, and each whap reminded Harry that while they could escape, she was stuck.

Harry, as she was known, was industrious if a bit undirected.

Her cohort at the P.O., Mrs. Miranda Hogendobber, felt that if Harry remarried, this questioning of her life's purpose would evaporate. Being quite a bit older than Harry, Miranda viewed marriage as purpose enough for a woman.

"What are you humming?"

" 'A Mighty Fortress Is Our God.' Martin Luther wrote it in 1529," Mrs. H. informed her.

"I should know that."

"If you'd come to choir practice you would."

"There is the small matter that I am not a member of your church." Harry folded an empty canvas mail sack.

"I can fix that in a jiffy."

"And what would the Reverend Jones do? He baptized me in Crozet Lutheran Church."

"Piffle."

Mrs. Murphy barreled through the door, a large cricket in her mouth.

Close in pursuit was Pewter, the fat gray cat who worked days next door at the grocery store: nights she traveled home with Harry. Market Shiflett, the grocer, declared Pewter had never caught a mouse and never would, so she might as well go play with her friends.

In Pewter's defense, she was built round; her skull was round, her ears, small and delicate, were round. Her tail was a bit short. She thought of herself as stout. Her gray paunch swung when she walked. She swore this was the result of her having "the operation," not because she was fat. In truth it was both. The cat lived to eat.

Mrs. Murphy, a handsome tiger, stayed fit being a ferocious mouser.

The two cats were followed by the dog, Tee Tucker.

Mrs. Murphy bounded onto the counter, the cricket wriggling in her mouth.

"That cat has brought in a winged irritant. She lives to kill," Miranda harrumphed.

"A cricket doesn't have wings."

Miranda moved closer to the brown shiny prey clamped in the cat's jaws. "It certainly is a major cricket—it ought to have wings.

Why, I believe this cricket is as big as a praying mantis." She cupped her chin in her hand, giving her a wise appearance.

Harry strolled over to inspect just as Mrs. Murphy dispatched the insect with a swift bite through the innards, then laid the remains on the counter.

The dog asked, *"You're not going to eat that cricket, are you?"*

"No, they taste awful."

"I'll eat it," Pewter volunteered. *"Well, someone has to keep up appearances! After all, we are predators."*

"Pewter, that's disgusting." Harry grimaced as the rotund animal gobbled down the cricket.

"Maybe they're like nachos." Miranda Hogendobber heard the loud crunch.

"I'll never eat a nacho again." Harry glared at her coworker and friend.

"It's the crunchiness. I bet you any money," Miranda teased.

"It is." Pewter licked her lips in answer to the older woman. She was glad cats didn't wear lipstick like Mrs. Hogendobber. Imagine getting lipstick on a cricket or mouse. Spoil the taste.

"Hey, girls." The Reverend Herbert Jones strolled through the front door. He called all women girls, and they had long since given up hope of sensitizing him. Ninety-two-year-old Catherine I. Earnhart was called a girl. She rather liked it.

"Hey, Rev." Harry smiled at him. "You're late today."

He fished in his pocket for his key and inserted it in his brass mailbox, pulling out a fistful of mail, most of it useless advertisements.

"If I'm late, it's because I lent my car to Roscoe Fletcher. He was supposed to bring it back to me by one o'clock, and here it is three. I finally decided to walk."

"His car break down?" Miranda opened the backdoor for a little breeze and sunshine.

"That new car of his is the biggest lemon."

Harry glanced up from counting out second-day air packets to see Roscoe pulling into the post office parking lot out front. "Speak of the devil."

Herb turned around. "Is that my car?"

"Looks different with the mud washed off, doesn't it?" Harry laughed.

"Oh, I know I should clean it up, and I ought to fix my truck, too, but I don't have the time. Not enough hours in the day."

"Amen," Miranda said.

"Why, Miranda, how nice of you to join the service." His eyes twinkled.

"Herb, I'm sorry," Roscoe said before he closed the door behind him. "Mim Sanburne stopped me in the hall, and I thought I'd never get away. You know how the Queen of Crozet talks."

"Indeed," they said.

"*Why do they call Mim the Queen of Crozet?*" Mrs. Murphy licked her front paw. "*Queen of the Universe is more like it.*"

"*No, just the Solar System,*" Tucker barked.

"*Doesn't have the same ring to it,*" Mrs. Murphy replied.

"*Humans think they are the center of everything. Bunch of dumb Doras.*" Pewter burped.

The unpleasant prospect of cricket parts being regurgitated on the counter made Mrs. Murphy take a step back.

"How do you like your car?" Roscoe pointed to the Subaru station wagon, newly washed and waxed.

"Looks brand-new. Thank you."

"You were good to lend me wheels. Gary at the dealership will bring my car to the house. If you'll drop me home, I'll be fine."

"Where's Naomi today?" Miranda inquired about his wife.

"In Staunton. She took the third grade to see the Pioneer Museum." He chuckled. "Better her than me. Those lower-school kids drive me bananas."

"That's why she's principal of the lower school, and you're headmaster. We call you 'the Big Cheese.' " Harry smiled.

"No, it's because I'm a good fund-raiser. Anyone want to cough up some cash?" He laughed, showing broad, straight teeth, darkened by smoking. He reached into his pocket and pulled out a pack of Tootsie Rolls, then offered them around.

"You're not getting blood from this stone. Besides, I graduated from Crozet High." Harry waved off the candy.

"Me, too, a bit earlier than she did," Miranda said coyly.

"I graduated in 1945," Herb said boldly.

"I can't get arrested with you guys, can I? You don't even want my Tootsie Rolls." Roscoe smiled. He had a jovial face as well as manner. "Tell you what, if you win the lottery, give St. Elizabeth's a little bit. Education is important."

"*For what?*" Pewter stared at him. "*You-all don't do a damn thing except fuss at each other.*"

"*Some humans farm,*" Tucker responded.

Pewter glared down at the pretty corgi. "*So?*"

"*It's productive,*" Mrs. Murphy added.

"*It's only productive so they can feed each other. Doesn't have anything to do with us.*"

"*They can fish,*" Tucker said.

"*Big deal.*"

"*It's a big deal when you want your tuna.*" Murphy laughed.

"*They're a worthless species.*"

"*Pewter, that cricket made you out of sorts. Gives you gas. You don't see me eating those things,*" Mrs. Murphy said.

"You know, my car does look new, really." Herb again cast his blue eyes over the station wagon.

"Went to the car wash on Twenty-ninth and Greenbrier Drive," Roscoe told him. "I love that car wash."

"You love a car wash?" Miranda was incredulous.

"You've got to go there. I'll take you." He held out his meaty arms in an expansive gesture. "You drive up—Karen Jensen and some of our other kids work there, and they guide your left tire onto the track. The kids work late afternoons and weekends—good kids. Anyway, you have a smorgasbord of choices. I chose what they call 'the works.' So they beep you in, car in neutral, radio off, and you lurch into the fray. First, a yellow neon light flashes, a wall of water hits you, and then a blue neon light tells you your undercarriage is being cleaned, then there's a white light and a pink light and a green

light—why it's almost like a Broadway show. And"—he pointed
outside—"there's the result. A hit."

"Roscoe, if the car wash excites you that much, your life needs a
pickup." Herb laughed good-naturedly.

"You go to the car wash and see for yourself."

The two men left, Herb slipping into the driver's seat as Harry
and Miranda gazed out the window.

"You been to that car wash?"

"No, I feel like I should wear my Sunday pearls and rush right
out." Miranda folded her arms across her ample chest.

"*I'm not going through any car wash. I hate it,*" Tucker grumbled.

"*You hear thunder and you hide under the bed.*"

The dog snapped at Murphy, "*I do not, that's a fib.*"

"*Slobber, too.*" Since Murphy was on the counter, she could be as
hateful as she pleased; the dog couldn't reach her.

"*You peed in the truck,*" Tucker fired back.

Mrs. Murphy's pupils widened. "*I was sick.*"

"*Were not.*"

"*Was, too.*"

"*You were on your way to the vet and you were scared!*"

"*I was on my way to the vet because I was sick.*" The tiger vehemently
defended herself.

"*Going for your annual shots,*" Tucker sang in three-quarter time.

"*Liar.*"

"*Chicken.*"

"*That was two years ago.*"

"*Truck smelled for months.*" Tucker rubbed it in.

Mrs. Murphy, using her hind foot, with one savage kick pushed
a stack of mail on the dog's head. "*Creep.*"

"Hey!" Harry hollered. "Settle down."

"*Vamoose!*" Mrs. Murphy shot off the counter, soaring over the
corgi, who was mired in a mudslide of mail, as she zoomed out the
opened backdoor.

Tucker hurried after her, shedding envelopes as she ran.

Pewter relaxed on the counter, declining to run.

Harry walked to the backdoor to watch her pets chase one another through Miranda's yard, narrowly missing her mums, a riot of color. "I wish I could play like that just once."

"They are beguiling." Miranda watched, too, then noticed the sparkling light. "The equinox, it's such a special time, you know. Light and darkness are in perfect balance."

What she didn't say was that after today, darkness would slowly win out.

2

On her back, legs in the air, Mrs. Murphy displayed her slender beige tummy, the stripes muted, unlike the tiger stripes on her back, which were shiny jet-black. She heard the Audi Quattro a quarter of a mile down the driveway, long before Harry realized anyone had turned onto the farm drive.

Tucker, usually on guard, had trotted over to the creek that divided Harry's farm from Blair Bainbridge's farm on the southern boundary. A groundhog lived near the huge hickory there. Tucker, being a herding animal, possessed no burning desire to kill. Still, she enjoyed watching quarry, occasionally engaging a wild animal in conversation. She was too far away to sound a warning about the car.

Not that she needed to, for the visitor was Susan Tucker, Harry's best friend since toddler days. As Susan had traded in her old Volvo for an Audi Quattro, the tire sound was different and Tucker wasn't used to it yet. Mrs. Murphy possessed a better memory for such sounds than Tucker.

Pewter, flopped under the kitchen table, could not have cared less about the visitor. She was dreaming of a giant marlin garnished with mackerel. What made the dream especially sweet was that she didn't have to share the fish with anyone else.

Harry, on an organizing jag, was dumping the contents of her bureau drawers onto her bed.

Mrs. Murphy opened one eye. She heard the slam of the car door. A second slam lifted her head. Usually Susan cruised out to Harry's alone. Escaping her offspring saved her mental health. The back screen door opened. Susan walked in, her beautiful fifteen-year-old daughter, Brooks, following behind. No escape today.

"Toodle-oo," Susan called out.

Pewter, irritated at being awakened, snarled, "*I have never heard anything so insipid in my life.*"

Mrs. Murphy rested her head back down on her paw. "*Crab.*"

"*Well, that's just it, Murphy, I was having the best dream of my life and now—vanished.*" Pewter mourned the loss.

"Hi, Murphy." Susan scratched behind the cat's delicate ears.

"Oh, look, Pewts is underneath the kitchen table." Brooks, who loved cats, bent down to pet Pewter. Her auburn hair fell in a curtain across her face.

"*What I endure,*" the gray cat complained; however, she made no effort to leave, so the complaint was pro forma.

"I'm organizing," Harry called from the bedroom.

"God help us all." Susan laughed as she walked into the chaos. "Harry, you'll be up all night."

"I couldn't stand it anymore. It takes me five minutes to find a pair of socks that match and"—she pointed to a few pathetic silken remnants—"my underwear is shot."

"You haven't bought new lingerie since your mother died."

Harry plopped on the bed. "As long as Mom bought the stuff, I didn't have to—anyway, I can't stand traipsing into Victoria's Secret. There's something faintly pornographic about it."

"Oh, bull, you just can't stand seeing bra sizes bigger than your own."

"I'm not so bad."

Susan smiled. "I didn't say you were, I only hinted that you are a touch competitive."

"I am not. I most certainly am not. If I were competitive, I'd be applying my art history degree somewhere instead of being the postmistress of Crozet."

"I seem to remember one vicious field hockey game our senior year."

"That doesn't count."

"You didn't like BoomBoom Craycroft even then," Susan recalled.

"Speaking of jugs . . . I hear she seduced my ex-husband wearing a large selection of lingerie."

"Who told you that?"

"She did, the idiot."

Susan sat down on the opposite side of the bed because she was laughing too hard to stand up.

"She did! Can you believe it? Told me all about the black lace teddy she wore when he came out to the farm on a call," Harry added.

Pharamond Haristeen, "Fair," happened to be one of the best equine vets in the state.

"Mom, Pewter's hungry," Brooks called from the kitchen.

Tucker, having raced back, pushed open the screen door and hurried over to Susan only to sit on her foot. As it was Susan who bred her and gave her to Harry, she felt quite close to the auburn-haired woman.

"Pewter's always hungry, Brooks; don't fall for her starving kitty routine."

"Shut up," Pewter called back, then purred and rubbed against Brooks's leg.

"Mom, she's really hungry."

"Con artist." Walking back to the kitchen, Harry sternly addressed the cat, who was frantically purring. "If they gave Academy Awards to cats, you would surely win 'best actress.' "

"*I am so-o-o-o hungry*," the cat warbled.

"*If I could use the electric can opener, I'd feed you just to shut you up.*" Mrs. Murphy sat up and swept her whiskers forward, then back.

Harry, arriving at the same conclusion, grabbed a can of Mariner's Delight. "What's up?"

"We're having a family crisis." Brooks giggled.

"No, we're not."

"Mom." Brooks contradicted her mother by the tone of her voice.

"I'm all ears." Harry ladled out the fishy-smelling food. Pewter, blissfully happy, stuck her face in it. Mrs. Murphy approached her food with more finesse. She liked to pat the edge of her dish with her paw, sniff, then take a morsel in her teeth, carefully chewing it. She believed this was an aid to digestion, also keeping her weight down. Pewter gobbled everything. Calorie Kitty.

"I hate my teachers this year, especially Home Room." Brooks dropped on a brightly painted kitchen chair.

"Miss Tucker, you were not invited to sit down." Susan put her hands on her hips.

"Mom, it's Harry. I mean, it's not like I'm at Big Mim's or anything." She referred to Mim Sanburne, a fierce enforcer of etiquette.

"Practice makes perfect."

"Please have a seat." Harry invited her to the seat she already occupied.

"Thank you," Brooks replied.

"Just see that you don't forget your manners."

"Fat chance." Brooks laughed at her mother.

They strongly resembled each other, and despite their spats, a deep love existed between mother and daughter.

Danny, Susan's older child, was also the recipient of oceans of maternal affection.

Brooks abruptly got up and dashed outside.

"Where are you going?"

"Back in a flash."

Susan sat down. "I ask myself daily, sometimes hourly, whatever made me think I could be a mother."

"Oh, Susan." Harry waved her hand. "Stop trolling for compliments."

"I'm not."

"You know you're a good mother."

Brooks reappeared, Saturday newspaper in hand, and placed it on the table. "Sorry."

"Oh, thanks. I didn't get out to the mailbox this morning." She took the rubber band off the folded newspaper. The small white envelope underneath the rubber band contained the monthly bill. "I don't know why I pay for this damned paper. Half the time it isn't delivered."

"Well, they delivered it today."

"Hallelujah. Well—?" Harry shrugged. "What's the family crisis?"

"We're not having a family crisis," Susan replied calmly. "Brooks doesn't like her teachers, so we're discussing—"

"I hate my teachers, and Mom is getting bent out of shape. Because she graduated from Crozet High, she wants me to graduate from Crozet High. Danny graduates this year. That ought to be enough. Batting five hundred, Mom," Brooks interrupted.

Harry's eyes widened. "You can't drop out, Brooks."

"I don't want to drop out. I want to go back to St. Elizabeth's."

"That damned snob school costs an arm and a leg." Susan looked up at Pewter, who was eating very loudly. "That cat sounds like an old man smacking his gums."

Pewter, insulted, whirled around to face Susan, but she only proved the statement as little food bits dangled from her whiskers.

Susan smiled. "Like an old man who can't clean his mustache."

"Ha!" Mrs. Murphy laughed loudly.

"She really does look like that," Tucker agreed as she sat on the floor under the counter where Pewter chowed down. In case the cat dropped any food, Tucker would vacuum it up.

"Hey, I've got some cookies," Harry said.

"Thank you, no. We ate a big breakfast."

"What about coffee, tea?"

"No." Susan smiled.

"You don't think you can get along with your teachers or over-look them?" Harry switched back to the subject at hand.

"I hate Mrs. Berryhill."

"She's not so bad." Harry defended a middle-aged lady wid-owed a few years back.

"Gives me heaves." Brooks pretended to gag.

"If it's that bad, you aren't going to learn anything."

"See, Mom, see—I told you."

"I think it's important not to bail out before you've given it a month or two."

"By that time I'll have failed French!" She knew her mother espe-cially wanted her to learn French.

"Don't be so dramatic."

"Go on, be dramatic." Harry poked at Susan's arm while en-couraging Brooks.

"We need a little drama around here." Tucker agreed with Harry.

"I won't learn a thing. I'll be learning-deprived. I'll shrink into oblivion—"

Harry interrupted, "Say, that's good, Brooks. You must be read-ing good novels or studying vocabulary boosters."

Brooks smiled shyly, then continued. "I will be disadvantaged for life, and then I'll never get into Smith."

"That's a low blow," said Susan, who had graduated from Smith with Harry.

"Then you'll marry a gas station attendant and—"

"Harry, don't egg her on. She doesn't have to pay the bills."

"What does Ned say?" Harry inquired of Susan's husband, a lawyer and a likable man.

"He's worried about the money, too, but he's determined that she get a good foundation."

"St. Elizabeth's is a fine school even if I do think they're a bunch of snobs," Harry said forthrightly. "Roscoe Fletcher is doing a good job. At least everyone says he is. I can't say that I know a lot about education, but remember last year's graduating class put two kids in Yale, one in Princeton, one in Harvard." She paused. "I think everyone got into great schools. Can't argue with that."

"If I'm going to spend that much money, then I should send her to St. Catherine's in Richmond," Susan replied to Harry.

"Mom, I don't want to go away from home. I just want to get out of Crozet High. I'll be away soon enough when I go to college. Smith, Mom, Smith," she reminded her mother.

"Well—" Susan considered this.

"Call Roscoe Fletcher," Harry suggested. "Brooks has only been in school for two weeks. See if he'll let her transfer now or if she'll have to wait for the second semester."

Susan stood up to make herself a cup of tea.

"I asked you if you wanted tea," Harry said.

"I changed my mind. You want some?"

"Yeah, sure." Harry sat back down.

"I already called Roscoe. That officious bombshell of a secretary of his, April Shively, took forever to put me through. It's a contradiction in terms, bombshell and secretary." She thought a moment, then continued. "Of course, he said wondrous things about St. Elizabeth's, which one would expect. What headmaster won't take your money?"

"He has raised a lot of money, at least, that's what Mim says." Harry paused, "Mim graduated from Madeira, you know. You'd think she would have gone to St. Elizabeth's. Little Mim didn't graduate from St. Elizabeth's either."

"Mim is a law unto herself," Susan replied.

"Miranda will know why Big Mim didn't go there."

"If she chooses to tell. What a secret keeper that one is." Susan loved Miranda Hogendobber, being fully acquainted with her quirks. Miranda's secrets usually involved age or the petty politics of her various civic and church organizations.

"The big question: Can Brooks get in?"

"Of course she can get in," Susan replied in a loud voice. "She's carrying a three point eight average. And her record was great when she was there before, in the lower school."

"What about Danny? Will he be jealous?"

"No," Brooks answered. "I asked him."

Harry took her cup of tea as Susan sat back down.

"I just bought that Audi Quattro," Susan moaned. "How can I pay for all of this?"

"I can work after school," Brooks volunteered.

"I want those grades to stay up, up, up. By the time you get into college, you might have to win a scholarship. Two kids in college at the same time—when I got pregnant, why didn't I space them four years apart instead of two?" She wailed in mock horror.

"Because this way they're friends, and this way Danny can drive Brooks everywhere."

"And that's another thing." Susan smacked her hand on the table. "They'll be going to different after-school activities. He won't be driving her anywhere."

"Mom, half my friends go to St. Elizabeth's. I'll cop rides."

"Brooks, I am not enamored of the St. Elizabeth's crowd. They're too superficial, and I hear there's a lot of drugs at the school."

"Get real. There's a lot of drugs at Crozet High. If I wanted to take drugs, I could get them no matter where I went to school." She frowned.

"That's a hell of a note," Harry exclaimed.

"It's true, I'm afraid." Susan sighed. "Harry, the world looks very different when you have children."

"I can see that," Harry agreed. "Brooks, just who are your friends at St. Elizabeth's?"

"Karen Jensen. There's other kids I know, but Karen's my best friend there."

"She seems like a nice kid," Harry said.

"She is. Though she's also older than Brooks." Susan was frustrated. "But the rest of them are balls-to-the-wall consumers. I'm telling you, Harry, the values there are so superficial and—"

Harry interrupted her. "But Brooks is not superficial, and St. E isn't going to make her that way. It didn't before and it won't this time. She's her own person, Susan."

Susan dipped a teaspoon in her tea, slowly stirring in clover honey. She hated refined sugar. "Darling, go visit Harry's horses. I need a private word with my best bud."

"Sure, Mom." Brooks reluctantly left the kitchen, Tucker at her heels.

Putting the teaspoon on the saucer, Susan leaned forward. "It's so competitive at that school, some kids can't make it. Remember last year when Courtney Frere broke down?"

Trying to recall the incident, Harry dredged up vague details. "Bad college-board scores—was that it?"

"She was so afraid she'd disappoint her parents and not get into a good school that she took an overdose of sleeping pills."

"Now I remember." Harry pressed her lips together. "That can happen anywhere. She's a high-strung girl. She got into, uh, Tulane, wasn't it?"

"Yes." Susan nodded her head. "But it isn't just competitive between the students, it's competitive between the faculty and the administration. Sandy Brashiers is still fuming that he wasn't made upper-school principal."

"Politics exists in every profession. Even mine," Harry calmly stated. "You worry too much, Susan."

"You don't know what it's like being a mother!" Susan flared up.

"Then why ask my opinion?" Harry shot back.

"Because—" Susan snapped her teaspoon on the table.

"Hey!" Tucker barked.

"Hush, Tucker," Harry told her.

"What's the worst that can happen?" Harry grabbed the spoon out of Susan's hand. "If she hates it, you take her out of there. If she falls in with the wrong crowd, yank her out."

"This little detour could destroy her grade-point average."

"Well, she'll either go to a lesser college than our alma mater or she can go to a junior college for a year or two to pull her grades back up. Susan, it isn't the end of the world if Brooks doesn't do as well as you wish—but it's a hard lesson."

"I don't think Mrs. Berryhill is that bad."

"We aren't fifteen. Berryhill's not exactly a barrel of laughs even for us."

Susan breathed deeply. "The contacts she makes at St. Elizabeth's could prove valuable later, I suppose."

"She's a good girl. She'll bloom where planted."

"You're right." Susan exhaled, then reached over for the folded paper. "Speaking of the paper, let's see what fresh hell the world is in today."

She unfolded the first section of the paper, the sound of which inflamed Mrs. Murphy, who jumped over from the counter to sit on the sports section, the living section, and the classifieds.

"Murphy, move a minute." Harry tried to pull the living section out from under the cat.

"I enjoy sitting on the newspaper. Best of all, I love the tissue paper in present boxes, but this will do."

Harry gently lifted up Mrs. Murphy's rear end and pulled out a section of paper as the tail swished displeasure. "Thank you."

"I beg your pardon," Mrs. Murphy grumbled as Harry let her rear end down.

"Another fight in Congress over the federal budget," Susan read out loud.

"What a rook." Harry shrugged. "Nobody's going to do anything anyway."

"Isn't that the truth? What's in your section?"

"Car wreck on Twenty-ninth and Hydralic. Officer Crystal Limerick was on the scene."

"Anything in there about Coop?" She mentioned their mutual friend who was now a deputy for the Albemarle County Sheriff's Department.

"No." Harry flipped pages, disappointed that she didn't find what she was looking for.

"You've got the obit section, let's see who went to their reward."

"You're getting as bad as Mom."

"Your mother was a wonderful woman, and it's one's civic duty to read the obituary column. After all, we must be ready to assist in case—"

She didn't finish her sentence because Harry flipped open the section of the paper to the obituary page suddenly shouting, "Holy shit!"

3

"I just spoke to him yesterday." Susan gasped in shock as she read over Harry's shoulder the name Roscoe Harvey Fletcher, forty-five, who died unexpectedly September 22. She'd jumped up to see for herself.

"The paper certainly got it in the obit section quickly." Harry couldn't believe it either.

"Obit section has the latest closing." Susan again read the information to be sure she wasn't hallucinating. "Doesn't say how he died. Oh, that's not good. When they don't say it means suicide or—"

"AIDS."

"They never tell you in this paper how people die. I think it's important." Susan snapped the back of the paper.

" 'The family requests donations be made to the Roscoe Harvey

Fletcher Memorial Fund for scholarships to St. Elizabeth's. . . .'
What the hell happened?'' Harry shot up and grabbed the phone.

She dialed Miranda's number. Busy. She then dialed Dr. Larry
Johnson. He knew everything about everybody. Busy. She dialed the
Reverend Herbert Jones.

"Rev," she said as he picked up the phone, "it's Mary Minor."

"I know your voice."

"How did Roscoe die?"

"I don't know." His voice lowered. "I was on my way over
there to see what I could do. Nobody knows anything. I've spoken to
Mim and Miranda. I even called Sheriff Shaw to see if there had been
a late-night accident. Everyone is in the dark, and there's no funeral
information. Naomi hasn't had time to select a funeral home. She's
probably in shock."

"She'll use Hill and Wood."

"Yes, I would think so, but, well—" His voice trailed off a
moment, then he turned up the volume. "He wasn't sick. I reached
Larry. Clean bill of health, so this has to be an accident of some kind.
Let me get over there to help. I'll talk to you later."

"Sorry," Harry apologized for slowing him down.

"No, no, I'm glad you called."

"Nobody called me."

"Miranda did. If you had an answering machine you'd have
known early on. She called at seven A.M., the minute she saw the
paper."

"I was in the barn."

"Called there, too."

"Maybe I was out on the manure spreader. Well, it doesn't
matter. There's work to be done. I'll meet you over at the Fletchers'.
I've got Susan and Brooks with me. We can help do whatever needs to
be done."

"That would be greatly appreciated. See you there." He breathed
in sharply. "I don't know what we're going to find."

As Harry hung up the phone, Susan stood up expectantly.
"Well?"

"Let's shoot over to the Fletchers'. Herbie's on his way."

"Know anything?" They'd been friends for so long they could speak in shorthand to each other, and many times they didn't need to speak at all.

"No."

"Let's move 'em out." Susan made the roundup sign.

Tucker, assisted by Brooks, sneaked into the roundup. She lay on the floor of the Audi until halfway to Crozet. Mrs. Murphy and Pewter, both livid at being left behind, stared crossly as the car pulled out of the driveway.

Once at the Fletchers' the friends endured another shock. Fifty to sixty cars lined the street in the Ednam subdivision. Deputy Cynthia Cooper directed traffic. This wasn't her job, but the department was shorthanded over the weekend.

"Coop?" Harry waved at her.

"Craziest thing I've ever heard of," the nice-looking officer said.

"What do you mean?" Susan asked.

"He's not dead."

"WHAT?" all three humans said in unison.

Tucker, meanwhile, wasted no time. She walked in the front door, left open because of the incredible number of friends, acquaintances, and St. Elizabeth's students who were paying condolence calls. Tucker, low to the ground, threaded her way through the humans to the kitchen.

Brooks quickly found her friends, Karen Jensen and Jody Miller. They didn't know anything either.

As Harry and Susan entered the living room, Roscoe held up a glass of champagne, calling to the assembled, "The reports of my death are greatly exaggerated!" He sipped. "Bierce."

"Twain," Sandy Brashiers corrected. He was head of the English department and a rival for Roscoe's power.

"Ambrose Bierce." Roscoe smiled but his teeth were clenched.

"It doesn't matter, Roscoe, you're alive." Naomi, a handsome woman in her late thirties, toasted her husband.

April Shively, adoringly staring at her florid boss, clinked her glass with that of Ed Sugarman, the chemistry teacher.

"Hear, hear," said the group, which contained most of Harry's best friends, as well as a few enemies.

Blair Bainbridge, not an enemy but a potential suitor, stood next to Marilyn, or Little Mim, the well-groomed daughter of Big Mim Sanburne.

"When did you get home?" Harry managed to ask Blair after expressing to Roscoe her thanks for his deliverance.

"Last night."

"Hi, Marilyn." She greeted Little Mim by her real name.

"Good to see you." It wasn't. Marilyn was afraid Blair liked Harry more than herself.

Fair Haristeen, towering above the other men, strode over to his ex-wife, with whom he was still in love. "Isn't this the damnedest thing you've ever seen?" He reached into the big bowl of hard candies sitting on an end table. Roscoe always had candy around.

"Pretty weird." She kissed him on the cheek and made note that Morris "Maury" McKinchie, Roscoe Fletcher's best friend, was absent.

Meanwhile Tucker sat in the kitchen with Winston, the family English bulldog, a wise and kind animal. They had been exchanging pleasantries before Tucker got to the point.

"What's going on, Winston?"

"I don't know," came the grave reply.

"Has he gone to doctors in Richmond or New York? Because Harry heard from Herb Jones that he was healthy."

"Nothing wrong with Roscoe except too many women in his life."

The corgi cocked her head. *"Ah, well,"* she said, *"a prank, I guess, this obit thing."*

"Roscoe now knows how many people care about him. If people could attend their funerals, they'd be gratified, I should think," Winston said.

"Never thought of that."

"Umm." Winston waddled over to the backdoor, overlooking the sunken garden upon which Naomi lavished much attention.

"Winston, what's worrying you?"

The massive head turned to reveal those fearsome teeth. *"What if this is a warning?"*

"*Who'd do a thing like that?*"

"*Tucker, Roscoe can't keep it in his pants. I've lost count of his affairs, and Naomi has reached the boiling point. She always catches him. After many lies, he does finally confess. He promises never to do it again. Three months, six months later—he's off and running.*"

"*Who?*"

"*The woman?*" The wrinkled brow furrowed more deeply. "*April, maybe, except she's so obvious even the humans get it. Let's see, a young woman from New York, I forget her name. Oh, he's made a pass at BoomBoom, but I think she's otherwise engaged. You know, I lose count.*"

"Bet Naomi doesn't," the little corgi sagely replied.

4

That evening a heavy fog crept down Yellow Mountain. Harry, in the stable, walked outside to watch a lone wisp float over the creek. The wisp was followed by fingers spreading over the meadow until the farm was enveloped in gray.

She shivered; the temperature was dropping.

"Put on your down vest, you'll catch your death," Mrs. Murphy advised.

"What are you talking about, Miss Puss?" Harry smiled at her chatty cat.

"You, I'm talking about you. You need a keeper." The tiger sighed, knowing that the last person Harry would take care of would be herself.

Tucker lifted her head. Moisture carried good scent. "That bobcat's near."

"Let's get into the barn then." The cat feared her larger cousin.

As the little family plodded into the barn, the horses nickered. Darkness came as swiftly as the fog. Harry pulled her red down vest off a tack hook. She flipped on the light switch. Having stayed overlong at Roscoe Fletcher's to celebrate, she was now behind on her farm chores.

Tomahawk, the oldest horse in the barn, loved the advent of fall. A true foxhunting fellow, he couldn't wait for the season to begin. Gin Fizz and Poptart, the younger equines, perked their ears.

"*That old bobcat is prowling around.*" Mrs. Murphy leapt onto the Dutch door, the top held open by a nickel-plated hook.

Tomahawk gazed at her with his huge brown eyes. "*Mean, that one.*"

Two bright beady black eyes appeared at the edge of the hayloft. "*What's this I hear about a bobcat?*"

"*Simon, I thought you'd still be asleep,*" Tucker barked.

The opossum moved closer to the edge, revealing his entire light gray face. "*You-all make enough noise to wake the dead. Any minute now and Flatface up there will swoop down and bitterly chastise us.*"

Simon referred to the large owl who nested in the cupola. The owl disliked the domesticated animals, especially Mrs. Murphy. There was also a black snake who hibernated in the hayloft, but she was antisocial, even in summertime. A cornucopia of mice kept the predators fat and happy.

The hayloft covered one-third of the barn, which gave the space a lighter, airier feeling than if it had run the full length of the structure. Harry, using salvaged lumber, had built a hay shed thirty yards from the barn. She had painted it dark green with white trim; that was her summer project. Each summer she tried to improve the farm. She loved building, but after nailing on shingles in the scorching sun, she had decided she'd think long and hard before doing that again.

Mrs. Murphy climbed the ladder to the hayloft. "*Fog is thick as pea soup.*"

"*Doesn't matter. I can smell her well enough.*" Simon referred to the dreaded bobcat.

"*Maybe so, but she can run faster than anyone here except for the horses.*"

"*I'm hungry.*"

"*I'll get Mom to put crunchies in my bowl. You can have that.*"

Simon brightened. *"Goody."*

Mrs. Murphy walked the top beam of the stalls, greeting each horse as she passed over its head. Then she jumped down on the tall wooden medicine chest standing next to the tack-room door. From there it was an easy drop to the floor.

Harry, having fed the horses, knelt on her hands and knees in the feed room. Little holes in the wooden walls testified to the industry of the mice. She lined her feed bins in tin, which baffled them, but they gobbled every crumb left on the floor. They also ate holes in her barn jacket, which enraged her.

"Mother, you aren't going to catch one."

"Murphy, do something!"

The cat sat next to Harry and patted the hole in the wall. *"They've got a system like the New York subway."*

"You're certainly talkative," Harry commented.

"And you don't understand a word I'm saying." The cat smiled. *"I'm hungry."*

"Jeez, Murphy, lower the volume."

"Food, glorious food—" She sang the song from Oliver.

Tucker, reposing in the tack room, hollered, *"You sing about as well as I do."*

"Thanks. I could have lived my whole life without knowing that."

Her entreaties worked. Harry shook triangular crunchies out of the bag, putting the bowl on top of the medicine cabinet so Tucker wouldn't steal the food.

"Thanks," Simon called down, showing his appreciation.

"Anytime." Murphy nibbled a few mouthfuls to satisfy Harry.

"I suppose Pewter will be hungry." Harry checked her watch. "She's not an outdoor girl." She laughed.

"If she gets any fatter, you'll need to buy a red wagon so you can haul her gut around," Mrs. Murphy commented.

Harry sat on her old tack trunk. She glanced around. While there were always chores to be done, the regular maintenance ones were finished: feed, water, muck stalls, clean tack, sweep out the barn.

As soon as the horses finished eating, she would turn them out. With the first frost, usually around mid-October, she would flip their schedule. They'd be outside during the day and in their stalls at night. In the heat of summer they stayed inside the barn during the day; it was well ventilated from the breeze always blowing down the mountain. Kept the flies down, too.

She got up, her knees cracking, and walked to the open barn door. "You know, we could have an early frost." She returned to Fizz's stall. "I wonder if we should get on the new schedule now."

"*Go ahead. If there are a couple of hot days, we'll come inside during the day. We're flexible.*"

"*Let's stay inside.*" Poptart ground his sweet feed.

"*Who wants to argue with the bobcat? I don't,*" Tomahawk said sensibly.

Harry cupped her chin with her hand. "You know, let's go to our fall schedule."

"*Hooray!*" the horses called out.

"Nighty night," she called back, turning off the lights.

Although the distance between the stable and the house couldn't have been more than one hundred yards, the heavy fog and mist soaked the three friends by the time they reached the backdoor.

The cat and dog shook themselves in the porch area. Harry would pitch a fit if they did it in the kitchen. Even Harry shook herself. Once inside she raced to put on the kettle for tea. She was chilled.

Pewter, lounging on the sofa, head on a colorful pillow, purred, "*I'm glad I stayed inside.*"

"*You're always glad you stayed inside,*" Tucker answered.

Harry puttered around. She drank some tea, then walked back into her bedroom. "Oh, no." In the turmoil of the day, she'd rushed out with Susan and Brooks, forgetting the mess she had left behind. The contents of her bureau drawers lay all over her bed. "I will not be conquered by underpants."

She gulped her tea, ruthlessly tossing out anything with holes in it or where the fabric was worn thin. That meant she had only enough socks left for half a drawer, one satin bra, and three pairs of underpants.

"*Mom, you need to shop,*" said Mrs. Murphy, who adored shopping although she rarely got the opportunity for it.

Harry beheld the pile of old clothes. "Use it up, wear it out, make it do, or do without."

"*You can't wear these things. They're tired,*" Pewter, now in the middle of the pile, told her. "*I'm tired, too.*"

"*You didn't do anything.*" Murphy laughed.

Harry stomped out to the pantry, returning armed with a big scissors.

"*What's she going to do?*" Pewter wondered aloud.

"*Make rags. Mother can't stand to throw anything out if it can be used for something. She'll cut everything into squares or rectangles and then divide the pile between the house and the barn.*"

"*The bras, too?*"

"*No, I think those are truly dead,*" Mrs. Murphy replied.

"*Harry is a frugal soul,*" Pewter commented. She herself was profligate.

"*She has to be.*" Tucker cleaned her hind paws, not easy for a corgi. "*That post office job pays for food and gas and that's all. Luckily, she inherited the farm when her parents died. It's paid for, but she doesn't have much else. A little savings and a few stocks her father left her, but he wasn't a financial wizard either. Her one extravagance, if you can call it that, is the horses. 'Course, they help in 'mowing' the fields.*"

"*Humans are funny, aren't they?*" Pewter said thoughtfully. "*Big Mim wallows in possessions, and Harry has so little. Why doesn't Mim give things to Harry?*"

"*You forget, she gave her Poptart. She and Fair went halfsies on it.*"

"*I did forget. Still, you know what I mean.*"

Tucker shrugged. "*They're funny about things. Things mean a lot to them. Like bones to us, I guess.*"

"*I couldn't care less about bones. Catnip is another matter,*" the tiger said gleefully, wishing for a catnip treat.

"*Ever see that T-shirt? You know, the one that says 'He who dies with the most toys wins'?*" Pewter, snuggling in the new rag pile, asked.

"*Yeah. Samson Coles used to wear it—before he was disgraced by dipping into escrow funds.*" Tucker giggled.

"*Stupid T-shirt,*" Mrs. Murphy said briskly. "*When you're dead, you're dead. You can't win anything.*"

"*That reminds me. The bobcat's out there tonight,*" Tucker told Pewter.

"*I'm not going outside.*"

"*We know that.*" Mrs. Murphy swished her tail. "*Wonder if the Fletchers will find out who put that phony obituary in the paper? If they don't, Mother will. You know how nosy she gets.*"

The phone rang. Harry put down her scissors to pick it up. "Hi."

Blair Bainbridge's deep voice had a soothing quality. "Sorry I didn't call on you the minute I got home, but I was dog tired. I happened to be down at the café when Marilyn ran in to tell me about Roscoe dying. We drove over to his house, and I—"

"Blair, it's okay. She's crazy about you, as I'm sure you know."

"Oh, well, she's lonesome." Since he was one of the highest paid male models in the country, he knew perfectly well that women needed smelling salts in his presence. All but Harry. Therefore she fascinated him.

"Susan and I are riding tomorrow after church if you want to come along."

"Thanks. What time?"

"Eleven."

He cheerfully said, "I'll see you at eleven, and, Harry, I can tack my own horse. Who do you want me to ride?"

"Tomahawk."

"Great. See you then. 'Bye."

" 'Bye."

The animals said nothing. They knew she was talking to Blair, and they were divided in their opinions. Tucker wanted Harry to get back with Fair. She knew it wasn't unusual for humans to remarry after divorcing. Pewter thought Blair was the better deal because he was rich and Harry needed help in that department. Mrs. Murphy, while having affection for both men, always said that Mr. Right hadn't appeared. Be patient.

The phone rang again.

"Coop. How are you?"

"Tired. Hey, don't want to bug you, but did you have any idea who might have put that false obit in the papers?"

"No."

"Roscoe says he hasn't a clue. Naomi doesn't think it's quite as funny as he does. Herb doesn't have any ideas. April Shively thinks it was Karen Jensen since she's such a cutup. BoomBoom says Maury McKinchie did it, and he'll use our reactions as the basis for a movie. I even called the school chaplain, Father Michael. He was noncommittal."

"What do you mean?"

Father Michael, the priest of the Church of the Good Shepherd between Crozet and Charlottesville, had close ties to the private school. Although nondenominational for a number of years, St. Elizabeth's each year invited a local clergyman to be the chaplain of the school. This exposed the students to different religious approaches. This year it was the Catholics' turn. Apart from a few gripes from extremists, the rotating system worked well.

"He shut up fast," Coop replied.

"That's weird."

"I think so, too."

"What does Rick think?" Harry referred to Sheriff Shaw by his first name.

"He sees the humor in this, but he wants to find out who did it. If kids were behind this, they need to learn that you can't jerk people around like that."

"If I hear of anything, I'll buzz."

"Thanks."

"Don't work too hard, Coop."

"Look who's talking. See you soon. 'Bye."

Harry hung up the phone and picked up the small throw-out pile. Then she carefully divided the newly cut rags, placing half by the kitchen door. That way she would remember to take them to the barn in the morning. She noticed it was ten at night.

"Where does the time go?"

She hopped in the shower and then crawled into bed.

Mrs. Murphy, Pewter, and Tucker were already on the bed.

"What do you guys think about Roscoe's fake obituary?" she asked her animal friends.

Like many people who love animals, she talked to them, doing her best to understand. They understood her, of course.

"*Joke.*" Pewter stuck out one claw, which she hooked into the quilt.

"*Ditto.*" Tucker agreed. "*Although Winston said Naomi is furious with him. Mad enough to kill.*"

"*Humans are boring—*" Pewter rested her head on an outstretched arm.

"See, you think like I do." Harry wiggled under the blankets. "Just some dumb thing. For all I know, Roscoe did it himself. He's not above it."

"*Winston said Roscoe's running the women. Can't leave them alone.*" Tucker was back on her conversation with the bulldog.

"*Maybe this isn't a joke.*" Mrs. Murphy, who had strong opinions about monogamy, curled on Harry's pillow next to her head.

"*Oh, Murphy, it will all blow over.*" Tucker wanted to go to sleep.

5

The woody aroma of expensive tobacco curled up from Sandy
Brashiers's pipe. The leather patches on his tweed jacket were worn to
a perfect degree. His silk rep tie, stripes running in the English direction, left to right, was from Oxford University Motor Car Club. He
had studied at Oxford after graduating from Harvard. A cashmere V
neck, the navy underscoring the navy stripe in the tie, completed his
English-professor look.

However, the Fates or Sandy himself had not been kind. Not
only was he not attached to a university, he was teaching high-school
English, even if it *was* at a good prep school. This was not the future
his own professors or he himself had envisioned when he was a star
student.

He never fell from grace because he never reached high enough
to tumble. Cowardice and alcohol already marred his good looks at
forty-two. As for the cowardice, no one but Sandy seemed to know

why he hung back when he was capable of much more. Then again, perhaps even he didn't know.

He did know he was being publicly humiliated by headmaster Roscoe Fletcher. When the ancient Peter Abbott retired as principal of the upper school at the end of last year's term, Sandy should have automatically been selected to succeed Abbott. Roscoe dithered, then dallied, finally naming Sandy principal pro tem. He declared a genuine search should take place, much as he wished to promote from within.

This split the board of directors and enraged the faculty, most of whom believed the post should go to Sandy. If Roscoe was going to form a search committee each time a position opened, could any faculty member march assuredly into administration?

Fortunately for Brooks Tucker, she knew nothing of the prep school's politics. She was entranced as Mr. Brashiers discussed the moral turpitude of Lady Macbeth in the highly popular Shakespeare elective class.

"What would have happened if Lady Macbeth could have acted directly, if she didn't have to channel her ambition through her husband?"

Roger Davis raised his hand. "She would have challenged the king right in his face."

"No way," pretty Jody Miller blurted before she raised her hand.

"Would you like to expand on that theme after I call on you?" Sandy wryly nodded to the model-tall girl.

"Sorry, Mr. Brashiers." She twirled her pencil, a nervous habit. "Lady Macbeth was devious. It would be out of character to challenge the king openly. I don't think her position in society would change that part of her character. She'd be sneaky even if she were a man."

Brooks, eyebrows knit together, wondered if that was true. She wanted to participate, but she was shy in her new surroundings even though she knew many of her classmates from social activities outside of school.

Sean Hallahan, the star halfback on the football team, was called on and said in his deep voice, "She's devious, Jody, because she has to hide her ambition."

This pleased Sandy Brashiers, although it did not please Jody Miller, who was angry at Sean. Ten years ago the boys rarely understood the pressures on women's lives, but enough progress had been made that his male students could read a text bearing those pressures in mind.

Karen Jensen, blond and green-eyed, the most popular girl in the junior class, chirped, "Maybe she was having a bad hair day."

Everyone laughed.

After class Brooks, Karen, and Jody walked to the cafeteria—or the Ptomaine Pit, as it was known. Roger Davis, tall and not yet filled out, trailed behind. He wanted to talk to Brooks. Still awkward, he racked his brain about how to open a conversation.

He who hesitates is lost. Sean scooted by him, skidding next to the girls, secure in his welcome.

"Think the president's wife is Lady Macbeth?"

The three girls kept walking while Jody sarcastically said, "Sean, how long did it take you to think of that?"

"You inspire me, Jody." He cocked his head, full of himself.

Roger watched this from behind them. He swallowed hard, took two big strides and caught up.

"Hey, bean," Sean offhandedly greeted him, not at all happy that he might have to share the attention of three pretty girls.

If Roger had been a smart-ass kid, he would have called Sean a bonehead or something. Sean was bright enough, but his attitude infuriated the other boys. Roger was too nice a guy to put someone else down, though. Instead he smiled and forgot what he was going to say to Brooks.

Luckily, she initiated the conversation. "Are you still working at the car wash?"

"Yes."

"Do they need help? I mean, I'd like to get a job and—" Her voice faced away.

"Jimbo always needs help. I'll ask him," Roger said firmly, now filled with a mission: to help Brooks.

Jimbo C. Anson, as wide as he was tall, owned the car wash, the local heating-fuel company, and a small asphalt plant that he had bought when the owner, Kelly Craycroft, died unexpectedly. Living proof of the capitalist vision of life, Jimbo was also a soft touch. Brooks would be certain to get that after-school job.

Brooks was surprised when she walked through the backdoor of her house that afternoon to find her mother on the phone with Roger. He'd already gotten her the job. She needed to decide whether to work after school, weekends, or both.

After Brooks profusely thanked Roger, she said she'd call him back since she needed to talk to her mother.

"I guess you do." Susan stared at her after Brooks hung up the phone.

"Mom, St. Elizabeth's is expensive. I want to make money."

"Honey, we aren't on food stamps. At least, not yet." Susan sighed, loath to admit that the few fights she ever had with Ned were over money.

"If I can pay for my clothes and stuff, that will help some."

Susan stared into those soft hazel eyes, just like Ned's. Happy as she was to hear of Brooks's willingness to be responsible, she was oddly saddened or perhaps nostalgic: her babies were growing up fast. Somehow life went by in a blur. Wasn't it just yesterday she was holding this beautiful young woman in her arms, wondering at her tiny fingers and toes?

Susan cleared her throat. "I'm proud of you." She paused. "Let's go take a look at the car wash before you make a decision."

"Great." Brooks smiled, revealing the wonders of orthodontic work.

"Yeehaw!" came a holler from outside the backdoor.

"I'm here, too," Tucker barked.

Neither Mrs. Murphy nor Pewter was going to brazenly advertise her presence.

The Tuckers' own corgi, Tee Tucker's brother, Owen Tudor, raced to the backdoor as it swung open. Their mother had died of old age that spring. It was now a one-corgi household.

"Tucker," Owen kissed his sister. He would have kissed the two cats except they deftly sidestepped his advances.

"I didn't hear your truck," Susan said.

"Dead. This time it's the carburetor." Harry sighed. "One of these years I will buy a new truck."

"*And the cows will fly*," Pewter added sardonically.

"*Mom might win the lottery.*" Tucker, ever the optimist, pricked up her ears.

"Need a ride home?" Susan offered.

"I'll walk. Good for me and good for the critters."

"*It's not good for me*," Pewter objected instantly. "*My paws are too delicate.*"

"*You're too fat*," Mrs. Murphy said bluntly.

"*I have big bones.*"

"*Pewter—*" Tucker started to say something but was interrupted by Susan, who reached down to pet her.

"Why don't you all hop in the car, and we'll go to the car wash? Brooks took a job there, but I want to check it out. If you go with me, I'll feel better."

"Sure."

Everyone piled into the Audi. Mrs. Murphy enjoyed riding in cars. Pewter endured it. The two dogs loved every minute of it, but they were so low to the ground the only way they could see out the window was to sit on human laps, which were never in short supply.

They waved to Big Mim in her Bentley Turbo R, heading back toward Crozet.

Mrs. Murphy, lying down in the back window, watched the opulent and powerful machine glide by. "*She's still in her Bavarian phase.*"

"*Huh?*" Tucker asked.

"*Caps with pheasant feathers, boiled wool jackets. For all I know she's wearing lederhosen, or one of those long skirts that weigh a sweet ton.*"

"*You know, if I were German, I'd be embarrassed when Americans dress like that*," Pewter noted sagely.

"*If I were German, I'd be embarrassed if Germans dressed like that*," Owen Tudor piped up, which made the animals laugh.

"You-all are being awfully noisy," Harry chided them.

"They're just talking," Brooks protested.

"If animals could talk, do you know what they'd say?" Susan

then told them: "What's to eat? Where's the food? Can I sleep with it? Okay, can I sleep on it?"

"*I resent that,*" Mrs. Murphy growled.

"*Who cares?*" Pewter airily dismissed the human's gibe.

"*What else can they do but joke about their betters? Low self-esteem.*" Owen chuckled.

"*Yeah, and whoever invented that term ought to be hung at sundown.*" Mrs. Murphy, not one given to psychologizing, put one paw on Harry's shoulder. "*In fact, the idea that a person is fully formed in childhood is absurd. Only a human could come up with that one.*"

"*They can't help it,*" Tucker said.

"*Well, they could certainly shut up about it,*" Mrs. Murphy suggested strongly.

"*BoomBoom Craycroft can sure sling that crap around.*" Tucker didn't really dislike the woman, but then again, she didn't really like her either.

"*You haven't heard the latest!*" Pewter eagerly sat up by Brooks in the backseat.

"*What?*" The other animals leaned toward the cat.

"*Heard it at Market's.*"

"*Well!*" Mrs. Murphy imperiously prodded.

"*As I was saying before I was so rudely interrupted—*"

"*I did not interrupt you.*" Tucker was testy.

Owen stepped in. "*Shut up, Tucker, let her tell her story.*"

"*Well, BoomBoom was buying little glass bottles and a mess of Q-Tips, I mean enough Q-Tips to clean all the ears in Albemarle County. So Market asks, naturally enough, what is she going to do with all this stuff. Poor guy, next thing you know she launches into an explanation about fragrance therapy. No kidding. How certain essences will create emotional states or certain smells will soothe human ailments. She must have blabbed on for forty-five minutes. I thought I would fall off the counter laughing at her.*"

"*She's off her nut,*" Owen said.

"*Market asked for an example.*" Pewter relished her tale. "*She allowed as how she didn't have any essence with her but, for instance, if he felt a headache coming on, he should turn off the lights, sit in a silent room, and put a pot of water on the* stove with a few drops of sage essence. It would be even better if he had a wood-burning stove. Then he could put the essence of sage in the little humidifier on top."

"Essence of bullshit," Mrs. Murphy replied sardonically.

"Will you-all be quiet? This is embarrassing. Susan will never let you in her car again," Harry complained.

"All right by me," Pewter replied saucily, which made the animals laugh again.

Brooks petted Pewter's round head. "They have their own language."

"You know, that's a frightening thought." Susan glanced at her daughter in the rearview mirror, surrounded as she was by animals. "My Owen and poor dear departed Champion Beatitude of Grace—"

"Just call her Shortstop. I hate it when Susan uses Mom's full title." Owen's eyes saddened.

"She was a champion. She won more corgi firsts than Pewter and Murphy have fleas," Tucker said.

Murphy swatted at Tucker's stump. "If you had a tail, I would chew it to bits."

"I saw you scratching."

"Tucker, that was not fleas."

"What was it then, your highness? Eczema? Psoriasis? Hives?"

"Shut up." Mrs. Murphy bopped her hard.

"That is enough!" Harry twisted around in the front passenger seat and missed them because the car reached the entrance to the brand-new car wash, and the stop threw her forward.

Roger dashed out of the small glass booth by the entrance to the car-wash corridor.

"Hi, Mrs. Tucker." He smiled broadly. "Hi, Brooks. Hi, Mrs. Haristeen . . . and everybody."

"Is Jimbo here?"

"Yes, ma'am."

A car pulled up behind them, and one behind that. Roscoe Fletcher squirmed impatiently in the second car.

"Roger, I want to zip through this extravaganza." Susan reached in her purse for the $5.25 for exterior wash only.

"Mom, let's shoot the works."

"That's eleven ninety-five."

"I'll contribute!" Harry fished a five out of her hip pocket and handed it to Roger.

"Harry, don't do that."

"Shut up, Suz, we're holding up traffic."

"Here's the one." Brooks forked over a one-dollar bill.

"Okay then, a little to the right, Mrs. Tucker. There, you've got it. Now put your car in neutral and turn off the radio, if you have it on. Oh, and roll up the windows."

She rolled up the driver's side window as Roger picked up a long scrub brush to scrub her headlights and front grille while Karen Jensen worked the rear bumper. She waved.

"Hey, I didn't know Karen worked here. Jody, too." She saw Jody putting on mascara as she sat behind the cash register.

"Brooks, don't you dare open that window," Susan commanded as she felt the belt hook under the left car wheel. They lurched forward.

"*Hey, hey, I can't see!*" Pewter screeched.

"*Early blindness,*" Mrs. Murphy said maliciously as the yellow neon light flashed on, a bell rang, and a wall of water hit them with force.

Each cleansing function—waxing, underbody scrub and coat, rinsing—was preceded by a neon light accompanied by a bell and buzzer noise. By the time they hit the blowers, Pewter frothed at the mouth.

"Poor kitty." Brooks petted her.

"*Pewter, it really is okay. We're not in any danger.*" Mrs. Murphy felt bad that she had tormented her.

The gray kitty shook.

"Last time I take her through a car wash." Harry, too, felt sorry for the cat's plight.

They finally emerged with a bump from the tunnel of cleanliness. Susan popped the car in gear and parked it in a lot on the other side of the car wash.

As she and Brooks got out to meet with Jimbo Anson, Harry

consoled Pewter, who crawled into her lap. The other animals kept quiet.

A light rap on the window startled Harry, she was so intent on soothing the cat.

"Hi, Roscoe. You're right, it is like a Broadway show with all those lights."

"Funny, huh?" He offered her a tiny sweet, a miniature strawberry in a LaVossienne tin, French in origin. "Just discovered these. Les Fraises Bonbon Fruits pack a punch. Go on and try one."

"Okay." She reached in and plucked out a miniature strawberry. "Whooo."

"That'll pucker those lips. Naomi is trying to get me to stop eating so much sugar but I love sweetness." He noticed Brooks and Susan in the small office with Jimbo Anson. "Has she said anything about school?"

"She likes it."

"Good, good. You been to the vet?"

"No, we're out for a family drive."

"I can't remember the times I've seen you without Mrs. Murphy and Tucker. Now you've got Pewter, too. Market said she was eating him out of house and home."

"No-o-o," the cat wailed, shaken but insulted.

"*Hey, Pewter, we'll get even. We can pee on his mail before Mom stuffs it in his box,*" Murphy sang out gaily. "*Or we could shred it to bits, except the bills. Keep them intact.*"

St. Elizabeth's mail was delivered directly to the school. Personal mail was delivered to the Crozet post office.

"*Yeah.*" Pewter perked up.

"Good to see you, the animals, too." He waved and Harry hit the button to close the window.

Then she called after him, "Where'd you get the strawberry drops?"

"Foods of All Nations," he replied.

She noticed Karen Jensen making a face after he passed by. Roger laughed. "Kids," Harry thought to herself. Then she remembered the

time she stuck Elmer's Glue in the locks of her most unfavorite
teacher's desk drawer.

After ten minutes Susan and Brooks returned to the car.

Brooks was excited. "I'll work after school on Monday 'cause
there's no field hockey practice, and I'll work Saturdays. Cool!"

"Sounds good to me." Harry held up her hand for a high five as
Brooks bounced into the backseat.

Susan turned on the ignition. "This way she won't miss practice.
After all, part of school is sports."

"*Can we go home now?*" Pewter cried.

"Roscoe must live at this place," Susan said lightly as they pulled
out of the parking lot.

6

Little squeaks behind the tack-room walls distracted Harry from dialing. She pressed the disconnect button to redial.

Mrs. Murphy sauntered into the tack room, then paused, her ears swept forward. *"What balls!"*

"Beg pardon?" Pewter opened one chartreuse eye.

"Mouse balls. Can you hear them?"

Pewter closed her eye. *"Yes, but it's not worth fretting over."*

Harry, finger still on the disconnect button, rested the telephone receiver on her shoulder. "What in the hell are they doing, Murphy?"

"Having a party," the tiger replied, frustrated that she couldn't get at her quarry.

Harry lifted the receiver off her shoulder, pointing at the cat with it. "I can't put down poison. If you catch a sick mouse, then you'll die. I can't put the hose into their holes because I'll flood the tack room. I really thought you could solve this problem."

"*If one would pop out of there, I would.*" The cat, angry, stomped out.

"Temper, temper," Harry called out after her, which only made things worse.

She redialed the number as Murphy sat in the barn aisle, her back to Harry and her ears swept back.

"Hi, Janice. Harry Haristeen."

"How are you?" the bright voice on the other end of the line responded.

"Pretty good. And you?"

"Great."

"I hope you'll indulge me. I have a question. You're still editing the obituary page, aren't you?"

"Yep. Ninety-five cents a line. Five dollars for a photo." Her voice softened. "Has, uh—"

"No. I'm curious about how Roscoe Fletcher's obituary appeared in the paper."

"Oh, that." Janice's voice dropped. "Boy, did I get in trouble."

"Sorry."

"All I can tell you is, two days ago I received a call from Hallahan Funeral Home saying they had Roscoe's body as well as the particulars."

"So I couldn't call in and report a death?"

"No. If you're a family member or best friend you might call or fax the life details, but we verify death with the funeral home or the hospital. Usually they call us. The hospital won't give me cause of death either. Sometimes family members will put it in, but we can't demand any information other than verification that the person is dead." She took a deep breath. "And I had that!"

"Do you generally deal with the same people at each of the funeral homes?"

"Yes, I do, and I recognize their voices, too. Skip Hallahan called in Roscoe's death."

"I guess you told that to the sheriff."

"Told it to Roscoe, too. I'm sick of this."

"I'm sorry, Janice. I made you go over it one more time."

"That's different—you're a friend. Skip is being a bunghole, I can tell you that. He swears he never made the call."

"I think I know who did."

"Tell me."

"I will as soon as I make sure I'm right."

7

The high shine on Roscoe Fletcher's car surrendered to dust, red from the clay, as he drove down Mim Sanburne's two-mile driveway to the mansion Mim had inherited from her mother's family, the Urquharts.

He passed the mansion, coasting to a stop before a lovely cottage a quarter mile behind the imposing pile. Cars parked neatly along the farm road bore testimony to the gathering within.

Raising money for St. Elizabeth's was one of Little Mim's key jobs. She wanted to show she could be as powerful as her mother.

Breezing through Little Mim's front door, Roscoe heard Maury McKinchie shout, "The phoenix rises from the ashes!"

The members of the fund-raising committee, many of them alumnae, laughed at the film director's quip.

"You missed the resurrection party, my man." Roscoe clapped McKinchie on the back. "Lasted until dawn."

"Every day is a party for Roscoe," April Shively, stenographer's notebook flipped open at the ready, said admiringly.

April, not a member of the committee, attended all meetings as the headmaster's secretary, which saved the committee from appointing one of its own. It also meant that only information deemed important by Roscoe made it to the typed minutes. Lastly, it gave the two a legitimate excuse to be together.

"Where were you this time?" Irene Miller, Jody's mother, asked, an edge of disapproval in her voice since Maury McKinchie missed too many meetings, in her estimation.

"New York." He waited until Roscoe took a seat then continued. "I have good news." The group leaned toward him. "I met with Walter Harnett at Columbia. He loves our idea of a film department. He has promised us two video cameras. These are old models, but they work fine. New, this camera sells for fifty-four thousand dollars. We're on our way." He beamed.

After the applause, Little Mim, chair of the fund-raising committee, spoke. "That is the most exciting news! With preparation on our part, I think we can get approval from the board of directors to develop a curriculum."

"Only if we can finance the department." Roscoe folded his hands together. "You know how conservative the board is. Reading, writing, and arithmetic. That's it. But if we can finance one year— and I have the base figures here—then I hope and believe the positive response of students and parents will see us through the ensuing year. The board will be forced into the twentieth century"—he paused for effect—"just as we cross into the twenty-first."

They laughed.

"Is the faculty for us?" Irene Miller asked, eager to hitch on to whatever new bandwagon promised to deliver the social cachet she so desired.

"With a few notable exceptions, yes," Roscoe replied.

"Sandy Brashiers," April blurted out, then quickly clamped her mouth shut. Her porcelain cheeks flushed. "You know what a purist he is," she mumbled.

"Give him an enema," Maury said, and noted the group's

shocked expression. "Sorry. We say that a lot on a film shoot. If someone is really a pain in the ass, he's called the D.B. for douche bag."

"Maury." Irene cast her eyes down in fake embarrassment.

"Sorry. The fact remains, he is an impediment."

"I'll take care of Sandy," Roscoe Fletcher smoothly asserted.

"I wish someone would." Doak Mincer, a local bank president, sighed. "Sandy has been actively lobbying against this. Even when told the film department would be a one-year experimental program, totally self-sufficient, funded separately, the whole nine yards, he's opposed—adamantly."

"Has no place in academia, he says." Irene, too, had been lobbied.

"What about that cinematographer you had here mid-September? I thought that engendered enthusiasm." Marilyn pointed her pencil at Roscoe.

"She was a big hit. Shot film of some of the more popular kids, Jody being one, Irene."

"She loved it." Irene smiled. "You aren't going to encounter resistance from parents. What parent would be opposed to their child learning new skills? Or working with a pro like Maury? Why, it's a thrill."

"Thank you." Maury smiled his big smile, the one usually reserved for paid photographers.

He had enjoyed a wonderful directing career in the 1980s, which faded in the '90s as his wife's acting career catapulted into the stratosphere. She was on location so much that Maury often forgot he had a wife. Then again, he might have done so regardless of circumstances.

He had also promised Darla would lecture once a year at St. Elizabeth's. He had neglected to inform Darla, stage name Darla Keene. Real name Michelle Gumbacher. He'd cajole her into it on one of her respites home.

"Irene, did you bring your list of potential donors?" Little Mim asked. Irene nodded, launching into an intensely boring recitation of each potential candidate.

After the meeting Maury and Irene walked out to his country car, a Range Rover. His Porsche 911 was saved for warm days.

"How's Kendrick?" he inquired about her husband.

"Same old, same old."

This meant that all Kendrick did was work at the gardening center he had built from scratch and which at long last was generating profit.

She spied a carton full of tiny bottles in the passenger seat of the Rover. "What's all that?"

"Uh"—long pause—"essences."

"What?"

"Essences. Some cure headaches. Others are for success. Not that I believe it, but they can be soothing, I suppose."

"Did you bring this stuff back from New York?" Irene lifted an eyebrow.

"Uh—no. I bought them from BoomBoom Craycroft."

"Good God." Irene turned on her heel, leaving him next to his wildly expensive vehicle much favored by the British royals.

Later that evening when Little Mim reluctantly briefed her mother on the meeting—reluctant because her mother had to know everything—she said, "I think I can make the film department happen."

"That would be a victory, dear."

"Don't be so enthusiastic, Mother."

"I am enthusiastic. Quietly so, that's all. And I do think Roscoe enjoys chumming with the stars, such as they are, entirely too much. Greta Garbo. *That* was a star."

"Yes, Mother."

"And Maury—well, West Coast ways, my dear. Not Virginia."

"Not Virginia," a description, usually whispered by whites and blacks alike to set apart those who didn't measure up. This included multitudes.

Little Mim bristled. "The West Coast, well, they're more open-minded."

"Open-minded? They're porous."

8

"What have you got to say for yourself?" A florid Skip Hallahan glared at his handsome son.

"I'm sorry, Dad," Sean muttered.

"Don't talk to me. Talk to him!"

"I'm sorry, Mr. Fletcher."

Roscoe, hands folded across his chest, unfolded them. "I accept your apology, but did you really think phoning in my obituary was funny?"

"Uh—at the time. Guess not," he replied weakly.

"Your voice does sound a lot like your father's." Roscoe leaned forward. "No detentions. But—I think you can volunteer at the hospital for four hours each week. That would satisfy me."

"Dad, I already have a paper route. How can I work at the hospital?"

"I'll see that he does his job," Skip snapped, still mortified.

"If he falters, no more football."

"What?" Sean, horrified, nearly leapt out of his chair.

"You heard me," Roscoe calmly stated.

"Without me St. Elizabeth's doesn't have a prayer," Sean arrogantly predicted.

"Sean, the football season isn't as important as you learning: actions have consequences. I'd be a sorry headmaster if I let you off the hook because you're our best halfback . . . because someday you'd run smack into trouble. Actions have consequences. You're going to learn that right now. Four hours a week until New Year's Day. Am I clearly understood?" Roscoe stood up.

"Yes, sir.

"I asked you this before. I'll ask it one last time. Were you alone in this prank?"

"Yes, sir," Sean lied.

9

A ruddy sun climbed over the horizon. Father Michael, an early riser, enjoyed his sunrises as much as most people enjoyed sunsets. Armed with hot Jamaican coffee, his little luxury, he sat reading the paper at the small pine breakfast table overlooking the church's beautifully tended graveyard.

The Church of the Good Shepherd, blessed with a reasonably affluent congregation, afforded him a pleasant albeit small home on the church grounds. A competent secretary, Lucinda Payne Coles, provided much-needed assistance Mondays through Fridays. He liked Lucinda, who, despite moments of bitterness, bore her hardships well.

After her husband, Samson, lost all his money and got caught with his pants down in the bargain in an extramarital affair, Lucinda sank into a slough of despond. She applied when the job at the church became available and was happily hired even though she'd never worked a day in her life. She typed adequately, but, more important, she knew everyone and everyone knew her.

As for Samson, Father Michael remembered him daily in his prayers. Samson had been reduced to physical labor at Kendrick Miller's gardening business. At least he was in the best shape of his life and was learning to speak fluent Spanish, as some of his coworkers were Mexican immigrants.

Father Michael, starting on a second cup of coffee—two lumps of brown sugar and a dollop of Devonshire cream—blinked in surprise. He thought he saw a figure sliding through the early-morning mist.

That needed jolt of caffeine blasted him out of his seat. He grabbed a Barbour jacket to hurry outside. Quietly he moved closer to a figure lurking in the graveyard.

Samson Coles placed a bouquet of flowers on Ansley Randolph's grave.

Father Michael, a slightly built man, turned to tiptoe back to the cottage, but Samson heard him.

"Father?"

"Sorry to disturb you, Samson. I couldn't see clearly in the mist. Sometimes the kids drink in here, you know. I thought I could catch one in the act. I am sorry."

Samson cleared his throat. "No one visits her."

"She ruined herself, poor woman." Father Michael sighed.

"I know. I loved her anyway. I still loved Lucinda but . . . I couldn't stay away from Ansley." He sighed. "I don't know why Lucinda doesn't leave me."

"She loves you, and she's working on forgiveness. God sends us the lessons we need."

"Well, if mine is humility, I'm learning." He paused. "You won't tell her you saw me here, will you?"

"No."

"It's just that . . . sometimes I feel so bad. Warren doesn't visit her grave, and neither do the boys. You'd think at least once they'd visit their mother's grave."

"They're young. They think if they ignore pain and loss, it will fade away. Doesn't."

"I know." He turned, and both men left the graveyard, carefully shutting the wrought iron gate behind them.

At the northwest corner of the graveyard a massive statue of the Avenging Angel seemed to follow them with his eyes.

"I just so happen to have some of the best Jamaican coffee you would ever want to drink. How about joining me for a cup?"

"I hate to trouble you, Father."

"No trouble at all."

They imbibed the marvelous coffee and talked of love, responsibility, the chances for the Virginia football team this fall, and the curiousness of human nature as evidenced by the false obituary.

A light knock on the backdoor got Father Michael out of his chair. He opened the door. Jody Miller, one of his parishioners, wearing her sweats as she was on her way to early-morning field hockey practice, stood in the doorway, a bruise prominent on her cheek and a red mark near her eye that would soon blacken.

"Father Michael, I have to talk to you." She saw Samson at the table. "Uh—"

"Come on in."

"I'll be late for practice." She ran down the back brick walkway as Father Michael watched her with his deep brown eyes. He finally closed the door.

"Speaking of curious." Samson half smiled. "Everything is so important at that age."

It was.

Five minutes after Samson left, Skip Hallahan pulled into Father Michael's driveway with Sean in the passenger seat. Reluctantly, Sean got out.

"Father!" Skip bellowed.

Father Michael stuck his head out the backdoor. "Come in, Skip and Sean, I'm not deaf, you know."

"Sorry," Skip mumbled, then launched into Sean's misdeed before he'd taken a seat.

After Skip ranted for a half hour, Father Michael asked him to leave the room for a few minutes.

"Sean, I can see the humor in calling in the obituary. I really can. But can you see how you've upset people? Think of Mrs. Fletcher."

"I'm getting the idea," Sean replied ruefully.

"I suggest you call on Mrs. Fletcher and apologize. I also suggest you call Janice Walker, editor of the obituary page at the paper, and apologize, and lastly, write a letter of apology and send it to 'Letters to the Editor.' After that, I expect the paper will take your route away from you." The good priest tried to prepare him for retaliation.

Sean sat immobile for a long time. "All right, Father, I will."

"What possessed you to do this? Especially to your headmaster."

"Well, that was kind of the point." Sean suppressed a smile. "It wouldn't have been nearly as funny if I'd called in, uh, your obituary."

Father Michael rapped the table with his fingertips. "I see. Well, make your apologies. I'll calm down your father." He stood up to summon Skip Hallahan.

Sean stood also. "Thanks, Father."

"Go on. Get out of here." The priest clapped the young man on the back.

10

Every hamlet and town has its nerve centers, those places where people congregate to enjoy the delights of gossip. Not that men admit to gossiping: for them it's "exchanging information."

A small group of men stood outside the post office on the first Monday in October in buttery Indian-summer sunshine. The Reverend Herbert Jones, Fair Haristeen, Ned Tucker, Jim Sanburne—the mayor of Crozet—and Sandy Brashiers spoke forcefully about the football teams of Virginia, Tech, William and Mary, and, with a shudder, Maryland.

"Maryland's the one to beat, and it hurts me to say that," the Reverend Jones intoned. "And I never will say it in front of John Klossner."

John, a friend of Herb's, graduated from Maryland and never let his buddies forget it.

Another one of the "in" group, Art Bushey—absent this morning—had graduated from Virginia Military Institute, so there was no reason for argument there. Poor VMI's team couldn't do squat, a wretched reality for those who loved the institution and a sheer joy for those who did not.

"This is the year for Virginia, Herb. I don't care how hot Maryland has been up to now." Sandy Brashiers crossed his arms over his chest.

"Say, why aren't you in school today?" Herb asked.

"I've worked out a schedule with King Fletcher, so I don't go in until noon on Mondays." Sandy breathed in. "You know, I love young people, but they'll suck you dry."

"Too young to know what they're asking of us." Fair toed the gravel. "Now before we get totally off the subject, I want to put in a good word for William and Mary."

"Ha!" Jim Sanburne, a huge man in his middle sixties, almost as tall as Fair but twice as broad, guffawed.

"Give it up, Fair." Ned laughed.

"One of these days the Tribe will prevail." Fair, an undergraduate alumnus, held up the Victory V.

"How come you don't root for Auburn? That's where you went to veterinary school," Sandy said.

"Oh, I like Auburn well enough."

Harry, from the inside, opened the door to the post office and stood, framed in the light. "What are you guys jawing about? This is government property. No riffraff."

"Guess you'll have to go, Fair," Ned said slyly.

The other men laughed.

"We're picking our teams for this year." Jim explained the reasoning behind each man's choice.

"I pick Smith!"

"Since when does Smith have a football team?" Sandy Brashiers asked innocently.

"They don't, but if they did they'd beat VMI," Harry replied. "Think I'll call Art Bushey and torment him about it."

This provoked more laughter. Mrs. Murphy, roused from a midmorning catnap, walked to the open doorway and sat down. She exhaled, picked up a paw, and licked the side of it, which she rubbed on her face. She liked football, occasionally trying to catch the tiny ball as it streaked across the television screen. In her mind she'd caught many a bomb. Today football interested her not a jot. She ruffled her fur, smoothed it down, then strolled alongside the path between the post office and the market. She could hear Harry and the men teasing one another with outbursts of laughter. Then Miranda joined them to even more laughter.

Mrs. Murphy had lived all her life on this plot of Virginia soil. She watched the news at six and sometimes at eleven, although usually she was asleep by then. She read the newspapers by sitting right in front of Harry when she read. As near as she could tell, humans lived miserable lives in big cities. It was either that or newspapers worked on the Puritan principle of underlining misery so the reader would feel better about his or her own life. Whatever the reason, the cat found human news dull. It was one murder, car wreck, and natural disaster after another.

People liked one another here. They knew one another all their lives, with the occasional newcomer adding spice and speculation to the mix. And it wasn't as though Crozet never had bad things happen. People being what they are, jealousy, greed, and lust existed. Those caught paid the price. But in the main, the people were good. If nothing else they took care of their pets.

She heard a small, muffled sob behind Market Shiflett's store. She trotted to the back. Jody Miller, head in hands, was crying her heart out. Pewter sat at her sneakers, putting her paw on the girl's leg from time to time, offering comfort.

"*I wondered where you were.*" Murphy touched noses with Pewter, then stared at the girl.

Jody's blackening eye caught her attention when the girl removed her hands from her face. She wiped her nose with the back of her hand, blinking through her tears. "Hello, Mrs. Murphy."

"*Hello, Jody. What's the matter?*" Murphy rubbed against her leg.

Jody stared out at the alleyway, absentmindedly stroking both cats.

"*Did she say anything to you?*"

"No," Pewter replied.

"*Poor kid. She took a pounding.*" Mrs. Murphy stood on her hind legs, putting her paws on Jody's left knee for a closer look at the young woman's injury. "*This just happened.*"

"*Maybe she got in a fight on the way to school.*"

"*She has field hockey practice early in the morning—Brooks does, too.*"

"Oh, yeah." Pewter cocked her head, trying to capture Jody's attention. "*Maybe her father hit her.*"

Kendrick Miller possessed a vicious temper. Not that anyone outside of the family ever saw him hit his wife or only child, but people looked at him sideways sometimes.

The light crunch of a footfall alerted the cats. Jody, still crying, heard nothing. Sandy Brashiers, whose car was parked behind the market, stopped in his tracks.

"Jody!" he exclaimed, quickly bending down to help her.

She swung her body away from him. The cats moved out of the way. "I'm all right."

He peered at her shiner. "You've been better. Come on, I'll run you over to Larry Johnson. Can't hurt to have the doctor take a look. You can't take a chance with your eyes, honey."

"Don't call me honey." Her vehemence astonished even her.

"I'm sorry." He blushed. "Come on."

"No."

"Jody, if you won't let me take you to Dr. Johnson, then I'll have to take you home. I can't just leave you here."

The backdoor of the post office swung open, and Harry stepped out; she had heard Jody's voice. Miranda was right behind her.

"Oh, dear," Miranda whispered.

Harry came over. "Jody, that's got to hurt."

"I'm all right!" She stood up.

"That's debatable." Sandy was losing patience.

Miranda put a motherly arm around the girl's shoulders. "What happened?"

"Nothing."

"*She got pasted away,*" Pewter offered.

"I suggested that I take her to Larry Johnson—to be on the safe side." Sandy shoved his hands into his corduroy pockets.

Jody balefully implored Miranda with her one good eye. "I don't want anyone to see me."

"You can't hide for two weeks. That's about how long it will take for your raccoon eye to disappear." Harry didn't like the look of that eye.

"Now, Jody, you just listen to me," Miranda persisted. "I am taking you to Larry Johnson's. You can't play Russian roulette with your health. Mr. Brashiers will tell Mr. Fletcher that you're at the doctor's office so you won't get in trouble at school."

"Nobody cares about me. And don't call Mr. Fletcher. Just leave him out of it."

"People care." Miranda patted her and hugged her. "But for right now you come with me."

Encouraged and soothed by Miranda, Jody climbed into the older woman's ancient Ford Falcon.

Harry knitted her eyebrows in concern. Sandy, too. Without knowing it they were mirror images of one another.

Sandy finally spoke. "Coach Hallvard can be rough, but not that rough."

"Maybe she got into a fight with another kid at school," Harry said, thinking out loud.

"*Over what?*" Pewter asked.

"*Boys. Drugs. PMS.*" Mrs. Murphy flicked her tail in irritation.

"*You can be cynical.*" Pewter noticed a praying mantis in the crepe myrtle.

"*Not cynical. Realistic.*"

Tucker waddled out of the post office. Fast asleep, she had awakened to find no one in the P.O. "*What's going on?*"

"*High-school drama.*" The cats rubbed it in. "*And you missed it.*"

Larry Johnson phoned Irene Miller, who immediately drove to his office. But Jody kept her mouth shut . . . especially in front of her mother.

Later that afternoon, Janice Walker dropped by the post office.

"Harry, you ought to be a detective! How did you know it was Sean Hallahan? When you called me back yesterday to tell me, I wasn't sure, but he came by this morning to apologize. He even took time off from school to do it."

"Two and two." Harry flipped up the divider between the mail room and the public area. "He sounds like his dad. He can be a smart-ass, and hey, wouldn't it be wild to do something like that? He'll be a hero to all the kids at St. Elizabeth's."

"Never thought of it that way," Janice replied.

"You know, I was thinking of calling in BoomBoom Craycroft's demise." Harry's eyes twinkled.

Janice burst out laughing. "You're awful!"

11

Roscoe glanced out his window across the pretty quad that was the heart of St. Elizabeth's. Redbrick buildings, simple Federal style, surrounded the green. Two enormous oaks anchored either end, their foliage an electrifying orange-yellow.

Behind the "home" buildings, as they were known, stood later additions, and beyond those the gym and playing fields beckoned, a huge parking lot between them.

The warm oak paneling gave Roscoe's office an inviting air. A burl partner's desk rested in the middle of the room. A leather sofa, two leather chairs, and a coffee table blanketed with books filled up one side of the big office.

Not an academic, Roscoe made a surprisingly good headmaster. His lack of credentials bothered the teaching staff, who had originally wanted one of their own, namely Sandy Brashiers or even Ed Sugarman. But Roscoe over the last seven years had won over most of them. For one thing, he knew how to raise money as he had a "selling" personality and a wealth of good business contacts. For another, he was a good administrator. His MBA from the Wharton School at University of Pennsylvania stood him in good stead.

"Come in." He responded to the firm knock at the door, then heard a loud "Don't you dare!"

He quickly opened the door to find his secretary, April, and Sandy Brashiers yelling at each other.

April apologized. "He didn't ask for an appointment. He walked right by me."

"April, stop being so officious." Sandy brushed her off.

"You have no right to barge in here." She planted her hands on her slim hips.

Roscoe, voice soothing, patted her on her padded shoulder. "That's all right. I'm accustomed to Mr. Brashiers's impetuosity."

He motioned for Sandy to come in while winking at April, who blushed with pleasure.

"What can I do for you, Sandy?"

"Drop dead" was what Sandy wanted to say. Instead he cleared his throat. "I'm worried about Jody Miller. She's become withdrawn, and this morning I found her behind the post office. She had a bruised cheek and a black eye and refused to talk about it."

"There is instability in the home. It was bound to surface in Jody eventually." Roscoe did not motion for Sandy to sit down. He leaned against his desk, folding his arms across his chest.

"A black eye counts for more than instability. That girl needs help."

"Sandy," Roscoe enunciated carefully, "I can't accuse her parents of abuse without her collaboration. And who's to say Kendrick hit her? It could have been anybody."

"How can you turn away?" Sandy impulsively accused the florid, larger man.

"I am not turning away. I will investigate the situation, but I advise you to be prudent. Until we know what's amiss or until Jody herself comes forward, any accusation would be extremely irresponsible."

"Don't lecture *me*."

"Don't lecture me."

"You don't give a damn about that girl's well-being. You sure as hell give a damn about her father's contributions to your film project—money we could use elsewhere."

"I've got work to do. I told you I'll look into it." Roscoe dropped his folded arms to his sides, then pointed a finger in Sandy's reddening face. "Butt out. If you stir up a hornet's nest, you'll get stung worse than the rest of us."

"What's that shopworn metaphor supposed to mean?" Sandy clenched his teeth.

"That I know your secret."

Sandy blanched. "I don't have any secrets."

Roscoe pointed again. "Try me. Just try me. You'll never teach anywhere again."

Livid, Sandy slammed the door on his way out. April stuck her blond-streaked head back in the office.

Roscoe smiled. "Ignore him. The man thrives on emotional scenes. The first week of school he decried the fostering of competition instead of cooperation. Last week he thought Sean Hallahan should be censured for a sexist remark that I think was addressed to Karen Jensen—'Hey, baby!' " Roscoe imitated Sean. "Today he's frothing at the mouth because Jody Miller has a black eye. My God."

"I don't know how you put up with him," April replied sympathetically.

"It's my job." Roscoe smiled expansively.

"Maury McKinchie's on line two."

"Who's on line one?"

"Your wife."

"Okay." He punched line one. "Honey, let me call you back. Are you in the office?"

Naomi said she was, her office being in the building opposite his on the other side of the quad. He then punched line two. "Hello."

"Roscoe, I'd like to shoot some football and maybe field hockey practice . . . just a few minutes. I'm trying to pull together dynamic images for the alumni dinner in December."

"Got a date in mind?"

"Why don't I just shoot the next few games?" The director paused. "I've got footage for you to check. You'll like it."

"Fine." Roscoe smiled.

"How about a foursome this Saturday? Keswick at nine?"

"Great."

Roscoe hung up. He buzzed April. "You handled Sandy Brashiers very well," he told her.

"He gives me a pain. He just pushed right by me!"

"You did a good job. Your job description doesn't include tackling temporary principals and full-time busybodies."

"Thank you."

"Remind me to tell the coaches that Maury will be filming some football and hockey games."

"Will do."

He took his finger off the intercom button and sat in his swivel chair, feeling satisfied with himself.

12

Harry sorted her own mail, tossing most of it into the wastebasket. She spent each morning stuffing mailboxes. By the time she got to her own mail, she hadn't the patience to wade through appeals for money, catalogs, and flyers. Each evening she threw a canvas totebag jammed with her mail onto the bench seat of the old Ford truck. On those beautiful days when she walked home from work, she slung it over her shoulder.

She'd be walking for the next week regardless of weather because not only was the carburetor fritzed out on the truck, but a mouse had nibbled through the starter wires. Mrs. Murphy needed to step up her rodent control.

Harry dreaded the bill. No matter how hard she tried, she couldn't keep up with expenses. She lived frugally, keeping within a budget, but no matter how careful her plans, telephone companies

changed rates, the electric company edged up its prices, and the
county commissioners lived to raise Albemarle taxes.

She often wondered how people with children made it. They'd
make it better if they didn't work for the postal service, she thought
to herself.

Gray clouds, sodden, dropped lower and lower. The first big
raindrop splattered as she was about two miles from home. Tee
Tucker and Mrs. Murphy moved faster. Pewter, with a horror of
getting wet, ran ahead.

"I've never seen that cat move that fast," Harry said out loud.

A dark green Chevy half-ton slowly headed toward her. She
waved as Fair braked.

"Come on, kids," she called as the three animals raced toward
Fair.

As if on cue the clouds opened the minute Harry closed the
passenger door of the truck.

"Hope you put your fertilizer down."

"Back forty," she replied laconically.

He slowed for another curve as they drove in silence.

"You're Mary Sunshine."

"Preoccupied. Sorry."

They drove straight into the barn. Harry hopped out and threw
on her raincoat. Fair put on his yellow slicker, then backed the truck
out, parking at the house so Pewter could run inside. He returned to
help Harry bring in the horses, who were only too happy to get fed.

Mrs. Murphy and Tucker stayed in the barn.

"These guys look good." Fair smiled at Gin Fizz, Tomahawk,
and Poptart.

"Thanks. Sometimes I forget how old Tomahawk's getting to be,
but then I forget how old I'm getting to be."

"We're only in our thirties. It's a good time."

She scooped out the sweet feed. "Some days I think it is. Some
days I think it isn't." She tossed the scoop back into the feed bin.
"Fair, you don't have to help. Lucky for me you came along the road
when you did."

"Many hands make light work. You won't be riding tonight."

The rain, like gray sheets of iron, obscured the house from view.

"The weatherman didn't call for this, nor did Miranda."

"Her knee failed." He laughed. Miranda predicted rain according to whether her knee throbbed or not.

She clapped on an ancient cowboy hat, her rain hat. "Better make a run for it."

"Why don't you put me under your raincoat?" Mrs. Murphy asked politely.

Hearing the plaintive meow, Harry paused, then picked up the kitty, cradling her under her coat.

"Ready, steady, GO!" Fair sang out as he cut the lights in the barn.

He reached the backdoor first, opening it for Harry and a wet Tucker.

Once inside the porch they shook off the rain, hung up their coats, stamped their feet, and hurried into the kitchen. A chill had descended with the rain. The temperature plunged ten degrees and was dropping still.

She made fresh coffee while he fed the dog and cats.

Harry had doughnuts left over from the morning.

They sat down and enjoyed this zero-star meal. It was better than going hungry.

"Well—?"

"Well, what?" She swallowed, not wishing to speak with her mouth full.

"What's the matter?"

She put the rest of her glazed doughnut on the plate. "Jody Miller had a black eye and wouldn't tell anyone how she got it. The kid was crying so hard it hurt to see her."

"How'd you find out?"

"She cut classes and was sitting on the stoop behind Market's store."

"I found her first." Pewter lifted her head out of the food bowl.

"Pewter, you're such an egotist."

"Look who's talking," the gray cat answered Mrs. Murphy sarcastically. *"You think the sun rises and sets on your fur."*

"Miranda carried her over to Larry Johnson's. She stayed until Irene arrived. Irene wasn't too helpful, according to Miranda, a reliable source if ever there was one."

"Jody's a mercurial kid."

"Aren't they all?"

"I suppose." He got up to pour himself another coffee. "I'm finally warming up. Of course, it could be your presence."

"*I'm going to throw up.*" Pewter gagged.

"*You don't have a romantic bone in your body,*" Tucker complained.

"*In fact, Pewter, no one can see the bones in your body.*"

"*Ha, ha,*" the gray cat said dryly.

"Do you think it would be nosy if I called Irene? I'm worried."

"Harry, everyone in Crozet is nosy, so that's not an issue." He smiled. "Besides which, you and Miranda found her."

"*I found her,*" Pewter interjected furiously.

"You are not getting another morsel to eat." Harry shook her finger at the gray cat, who turned her back on her, refusing to have anything to do with this irritating human.

Harry picked up the old wall phone and dialed. "Hi, Irene, it's Mary Minor." She paused. "No trouble at all. I know Miranda was glad to help. I was just calling to see if Jody's all right."

On the other end of the line Irene explained, "She got into a fight with one of the girls at practice—she won't say which one—and then she walked into chemistry class and pulled a D on a pop quiz. Jody has never gotten a D in her life. She'll be fine, and thank you so much for calling. 'Bye."

" 'Bye." Harry hung up the receiver slowly. "She doesn't know any more than I do. She said the girls got into a fight at field hockey practice, and Jody got a D on a pop quiz in chemistry."

"Now you can relax. You've got your answer."

"Fair"—Harry gestured, both hands open—"there's no way that vain kid is going to walk into chemistry class with a fresh shiner. Jody Miller fusses with her makeup more than most movie stars. Besides, Ed Sugarman would have sent her to the infirmary. Irene Miller is either dumb as a stick or not telling the truth."

"I vote for dumb as a stick." He smiled. "You're making a

mountain out of a molehill. If Jody Miller lied to her mother, it's not a federal case. I recall you fibbing to your mother on the odd occasion."

"Not very often."

"Your nose is growing." He laughed.

Harry dialed Ed Sugarman, the chemistry teacher. "Hi, Ed, it's Mary Minor Haristeen." She paused a moment. "Do I need chemistry lessons? Well, I guess it depends on the kind of chemistry you're talking about." She paused. "First off, excuse me for butting in, but I want to know if Jody Miller came to your class today."

"Jody never came to class today," Ed replied.

"Well—that answers my question."

"In fact, I was about to call her parents. I know she was at field hockey practice because I drove by the field on my way in this morning. Is something wrong?"

"Uh—I don't know. She was behind Market's store this morning sporting a black eye and tears."

"I'm sorry to hear that. She's a bright girl, but her grades are sliding . . ." He hesitated. "One sees this often if there's tension in the home."

"Thanks, Ed. I hope I haven't disturbed you."

"You haven't disturbed me." He paused for a moment and then said as an aside, "Okay, honey." He then returned to Harry. "Doris says hello."

"Tell Doris I said hello also," Harry said.

Harry bid Ed good-bye, pressed the disconnect button, and thought for a minute.

"Want to go to a movie?"

"I'm not going out in that."

The rain pounded even harder on the tin roof. "Like bullets."

"I rented *The Madness of King George*. We could watch that."

"Popcorn?"

"Yep."

"If you'd buy a microwave, you could pop the corn a lot faster." He read the directions on the back of the popcorn packet.

"I'm not buying a microwave. The truck needs new starter

wires—the mice chewed them—needs new tires, too, and I'm even putting that off until I'm driving on threads." She slapped a pot on the stove. "And it needs a new carburetor."

After the movie, Fair hoped she'd ask him to stay. He made comment after comment about how slick the roads were.

Finally Harry said, "Sleep in the guest room."

"I was hoping I could sleep with you."

"Not tonight." She smiled, evading hurting his feelings. Since she was also evading her own feelings, it worked out nicely for her, temporarily, anyway.

The next morning, Fair cruised out to get the paper. The rain continued steady. He dashed back into the kitchen. As he removed the plastic wrapping and opened the paper, an eight-by-ten-inch black-bordered sheet of paper, an insert, fell on the floor. Fair picked it up. "What in the hell is this?"

13

"Maury McKinchie, forty-seven, died suddenly in his home October third," Fair mumbled as he read aloud Maury's cinematic accomplishments and the fact that he lettered in football at USC. He peered over Mrs. Murphy, who jumped on the paper to read it herself.

Both humans and the cat stood reading the insert. Pewter reposed on the counter. She was interested, but Murphy jumped up first. Why start the day with a fight? Tucker raced around the table, finally sitting on her mother's foot.

"What's going on?" Tucker asked.

"Tucker, Maury McKinchie is dead," Mrs. Murphy answered her.

"Miranda," Harry said when she picked up the phone, "I've just seen it."

"Well, I just saw Maury McKinchie jog down the lane between my house and the post office not ten minutes ago!"

"This is too weird." Harry's voice was even. "As weird as that rattail hair of his." She referred to the short little ponytail Maury wore at the nape of his neck. Definitely not Virginia.

"He wore a color-coordinated jogging suit. Really, the clothes that man wears." Miranda exhaled through her nostrils. "Roscoe was jogging with him."

"Guess he hasn't read the paper." Harry laughed.

"No." She paused. "Isn't this the most peculiar thing. If Sean's behind this again, he realized he can't phone in an obituary anymore. It can't be Sean, though—his father would kill him." She thought out loud.

"And he lost his paper route. Fired. At least, that's what I heard," Harry added.

"*Bombs away!*" Pewter launched herself from the counter onto the table and hit the paper, tearing it. Both cats and paper skidded off the table.

"Pewter!" Fair exclaimed.

"Aha!" Mrs. Hogendobber exclaimed when she heard Fair's voice in the background. "I knew you two would get back together," she gloated to Harry.

"Don't jump the gun, Miranda." Harry gritted her teeth, knowing a grilling would occur at the post office.

"See you at work," Miranda trilled.

14

"Not another prank!" the Reverend Herbert Jones said when he picked up his mail, commenting on the obituary insert in his paper that morning.

"A vicious person with unresolved authority-figure conflicts," BoomBoom Craycroft intoned. "A potent mixture of chamomile and parsley would help purify this tortured soul."

"Disgusting and not at all funny," Big Mim Sanburne declaimed.

"A sick joke," Lucinda Payne Coles said, picking up her mail and that of the Church of the Good Shepherd.

"Hasn't Maury been working with you on the big alumni fundraising dinner?" Harry inquired.

"Yes," Little Mim replied.

"What's going on at St. Elizabeth's?" Harry walked out front.

"Nothing. Just because Roscoe and Maury are associated with

the school doesn't make the school responsible for these—what should I call them—?" Little Mim flared.

Her mother, awash in navy blue cashmere, tapped Little Mim's hand with a rolled-up magazine.

"Premature death notices." Mim laughed. "Sooner or later they will be accurate. Sean Hallahan has apologized to everyone involved. At least, that's what his father told me. Who has the paper route? That's the logical question."

Marilyn sniffed. Her mother could get her goat faster than anyone on earth. "Roger Davis has the paper route."

"Call his mother," Mim snapped. "And . . . are you listening to me?"

"Yes, Mother."

"Whoever is writing these upsetting things knows a lot about both men."

"Or is a good researcher," Herb's grave voice chimed in.

"Don't look at me," Harry joked. "I never learned how to correctly write in footnotes. You have to do that to be a good researcher."

"Don't be silly. You couldn't have graduated from Smith with honors without learning how to do footnotes." Big Mim unrolled the magazine, grimaced at the photo of an exploded bus, and rolled it back up again. "I'll tell you what's worse than incorrect footnotes . . . lack of manners. Our social skills are so eroded that people don't write thank-you notes anymore . . . and if they did, they couldn't spell."

"Mother, what does that have to do with Roscoe's and Maury's fake obits?"

"Rude. Bad manners." She tapped the magazine sharply on the edge of the counter.

"Hey!" Little Mim blurted, her head swiveling in the direction of the door.

Maury McKinchie pushed through, beheld the silence and joked, "Who died?"

"You," Harry replied sardonically.

"Ah, come on, my last movie wasn't that bad."

"Haven't you opened your paper?" Little Mim edged toward him.

"No."

Herb handed the insert to Maury. "Take a look."

"Well, I'll be damned." Maury whistled.

"Who do you think did this?" Miranda zoomed to the point.

He laughed heartily. "I can think of two ex-wives who would do it, only they'd shoot me first. The obit would be for real."

"You really don't have any idea?" Herb narrowed his eyes.

"Not a one." Maury raised his bushy eyebrows as well as his voice.

Big Mim checked her expensive Schaffhausen watch. "I'm due up at the Garden Club. We vote on which areas to beautify today. A big tussle, as usual. Good-bye, all. Hope you get to the bottom of this."

" 'Bye," they called after her.

Maury, though handsome, had developed a paunch. Running would remove it, he hoped. Being a director, he had a habit of taking charge, giving orders. He'd discovered that didn't work in Crozet. An even bigger shock had befallen him when Darla became the breadwinner. He was searching for the right picture to get his career back on track. He flew to L.A. once a month and burned up the phone and fax lines the rest of the time.

"Mother wants to create a garden around the old railroad station. What do you bet she gets her way?" Little Mim jumped to a new topic. There wasn't anything she could do about the fake obituary anyway.

"The odds are on her side." Harry picked up the tall metal wastebasket overflowing with paper.

"I can do that for you." Maury seized the wastebasket. "Where does it go?"

"Market's new dumpster," Miranda said.

"Take me one minute."

As he left, Little Mim said, "He's a terrible flirt, isn't he?"

"Don't pay any attention to him," Harry advised.

"I didn't say he bothered me."

Maury returned, placing the wastebasket next to the table where people sorted their mail.

"Thank you," Harry said.

He winked at her. "My pleasure. You can say you've encountered an angel today."

"Beg pardon?" Harry said.

"If I'm dead, I'm living uptown, Harry, not downtown." He laughed and walked out with a wave.

Susan Tucker arrived just as Miranda had begun her third degree on the subject of Fair staying over.

"Miranda, why do you do this to me?" Harry despaired.

"Because I want to see you happy."

"Telling everyone that my ex-husband spent the night isn't going to make me happy, and I told you, Miranda, nothing happened. I am so tired of this."

"Methinks the lady doth protest too much." Mrs. Hogendobber coyly quoted Shakespeare.

"Oh, pul-lease." Harry threw up her hands.

Susan, one eyebrow arched, said, "Something did happen. Okay, maybe it wasn't sex, but he got his foot in the door."

"And his ass in the guest room. It was raining cats and dogs."

"*I beg your pardon,*" Mrs. Murphy, lounging in the mail cart, called out.

"All right." Harry thought the cat wanted a push so she gave her a ride in the mail cart.

"*I love this. . . .*" Murphy put her paws on the side of the cart.

"Harry, I'm waiting."

"For what?"

"For what's going on with you and Fair."

"NOTHING!"

Her shout made Tucker bark.

Pewter, hearing the noise, hurried in through the back animal door. "*What's the matter?*"

"*Mrs. H. and Susan think Mom's in love with Fair because he stayed at the house last night.*"

"Oh." Pewter checked the wastebasket for crumbs. "*They need to stop for tea.*"

Susan held up her hands. "You are so sensitive."

"Wouldn't you be?" Harry fired back.

"I guess I would."

"Harry, I didn't mean to upset you." Miranda, genuinely contrite, walked over to the small refrigerator, removing the pie she'd baked the night before.

Pewter was ecstatic.

Harry sighed audibly. "I want his attention, but I don't think I want him. I'm being perverse."

"Maybe vengeful is closer to the mark." Miranda pulled no punches.

"Well—I'd like to think I was a better person than that, but maybe I'm not." She glanced out the big front window. "Going to be a nice day."

"Well, my cherub is playing in the field hockey game, rain or shine," Susan said. "Danny's got football practice, so I'll watch the first half of Brooks's game and the last half of Danny's practice. I wish I could figure out how to be in two places at the same time."

"If I get my chores done, I'll drop by," Harry said. "I'd love to see Brooks on the attack. Which reminds me, got to call and see if my truck is ready."

"I thought you didn't have the money to fix it," Susan said.

"He'll let me pay over time." As she was making the call, Miranda and Susan buzzed about events.

"Miranda, do you think these false obituaries have anything to do with Halloween?" Harry asked as she hung up the phone.

"I don't know."

"*It's only the first week of October.*" Tucker thought out loud. "*Halloween is a long way away.*"

"*What about all those Christmas catalogs clogging the mail?*" Pewter hovered over the pie.

"*Humans like to feel anxious.*" Tucker declared.

"*Imagine worrying about Christmas now. They might not live to Christmas,*" Mrs. Murphy cracked.

The other two animals laughed.

"You know what I would do if I were one of them?" Pewter flicked off the dishcloth covering the pie. *"I'd go to an Arab country. That would take care of Christmas."*

"Take care of a lot else, too," Mrs. Murphy commented wryly.

Miranda noticed in the nick of time. "Shoo!"

Harry grabbed the phone. "Hello, may I have the obituary department?"

Miranda, Susan, the two cats, and the dog froze to listen.

"Obituary."

"Janice, have you heard about the insert?"

"Yes, but it's only in the papers of one route, Roger Davis's route. I can't be blamed for this one."

"I wouldn't want to be in Roger Davis's shoes right now," Harry said.

15

"I didn't do it." Roger, hands in his pants pockets, stared stubbornly at the headmaster and the temporary principal.

"You picked up the newspapers from the building at Rio Road?" Sandy questioned.

"Yes."

"Did you go through the papers?" Roscoe asked.

"No, I just deliver them. I had no idea that death notice on Mr. McKinchie was in there."

"Did anyone else go with you this morning? Like Sean Halla-han?"

"No, sir," Roger answered Roscoe Fletcher. "I don't like Sean."

Sandy took another tack. "Would you say that you and Sean Hallahan are rivals?"

Roger stared at the ceiling, then leveled his gaze at Sandy. "No. I don't like him, that's all."

"He's a bit of a star, isn't he?" Sandy continued his line of reasoning.

"Good football players usually are."

"No, I mean he's really a star now for putting the false obituary in the paper, Mr. Fletcher's obituary."

Roger looked from Sandy to Roscoe, then back to Sandy. "Some kids think it was very cool."

"Did you?" Roscoe inquired.

"No, sir," Roger replied.

"Could anyone have tampered with your papers without you knowing about it?" Roscoe swiveled in his chair to glance out the window. Children were walking briskly between classes.

"I suppose they could. Each of us who has a route goes to pick up our papers . . . they're on the landing. We've each got a spot because each route has a different number of customers. We're supposed to have the same number, but we don't. People cancel. Some areas grow faster than others. So you go to your place on the loading dock and pick up your papers. All I do is fold them to stick them in the tube. And on rainy days, put them in plastic bags."

"So someone could have tampered with your pile?" Roscoe persisted.

"Yes, but I don't know how they could do it without being seen. There are always people at the paper. Not many at that hour." He thought. "I guess it could be done."

"Could someone have followed after you on your route, pulled the paper out of the tube and put in the insert?" Sandy liked Roger but he didn't believe him. "One of your friends, perhaps?"

"Yes. It would be a lot of work."

"Who knows your paper route?" Roscoe glanced at the Queen Anne clock.

"Everyone. I mean, all my friends."

"Okay, Roger. You can go." Roscoe waved him away.

Sandy opened the door for the tall young man. "I really hope you didn't do this, Roger."

"Mr. Brashiers, I didn't."

Sandy closed the door, turning to Roscoe. "Well?"

"I don't know." Roscoe held up his hands. "He's an unlikely candidate, although circumstances certainly point to him."

"Damn kids," Sandy muttered, then spoke louder. "Have you investigated the Jody Miller incident further?"

"I spoke to Coach Hallvard. She said no fight occurred at practice. I'm going to see Kendrick Miller later today. I wish I knew what I was going to say."

16

Rumbling along toward St. Elizabeth's, Harry felt her heart sink lower and lower. The truck repairs cost $289.16, which demolished her budget. Paying over time helped, but $289 was $289. She wanted to cry but felt that it wasn't right to cry over money. She sniffled instead.

"*There's got to be a way to make more money,*" Mrs. Murphy whispered.

"Catnip," Pewter replied authoritatively. "*She could grow acres of catnip, dry it, and sell it.*"

"*Not such a bad idea—could you keep out of the crop?*"

"*Could you?*" Pewter challenged.

They pulled into the school parking lot peppered with Mercedes Benzes, BMWs, Volvos, a few Porsches, and one Ford Falcon.

The game was just starting with the captains in the center of the field, Karen Jensen for St. Elizabeth's and Darcy Kelly for St. Anne's Belfield from Charlottesville.

Roscoe had pride of place on the sidelines. Naomi squeezed next to him. April Shively sat on Roscoe's left side. She took notes as he spoke, which drove Naomi wild. She struggled to contain her irritation. Susan and Miranda waved to Harry as she climbed up to them. Little Mim sat directly behind Roscoe. Maury, flirtatious, amused her with Hollywood stories about star antics. He told her she was naturally prettier than those women who had the help of plastic surgery, two-hundred-dollar haircuts, and fabulous lighting. Little Mim began to brighten.

Pretty Coach Renee Hallvard, her shiny blond pageboy swinging with each stride, paced the sidelines. St. Anne's won the toss. While Karen Jensen trotted to midfield, the other midfielder, Jody Miller, twirled her stick in anticipation.

Irene and Kendrick Miller sat high in the stands for a better view. Kendrick had requested that he and Roscoe get together after the game. His attendance was noted since he rarely turned up at school functions, claiming work kept him pinned down.

People commented on the fact that Sean Hallahan and Roger Davis weren't at the game. Everyone had an opinion on that.

St. Anne's, a powerhouse in field hockey and lacrosse, worked the ball downfield, but Karen Jensen, strong and fast, stole the ball from the attacker in a display of finesse that brought the Redhawk supporters to their feet.

Brooks, an attacker, sped along the side, then cut in, a basic pattern, but Brooks, slight and swift, dusted her defender to pick up Karen's pinpoint pass. She fired a shot at the goalie, one of the best in the state, who gave St. Anne's enormous confidence.

The first quarter, speedy, resulted in no score.

"Brooks has a lot of poise under pressure." Harry was proud of the young woman.

"She's going to need it," Susan predicted.

"Quite a game." Miranda, face flushed, was remembering her days of field hockey for Crozet High in 1950.

The second quarter the girls played even faster and harder. Darcy Kelly drew first blood for St. Anne's. Karen Jensen, jogging back to the center, breathed a few words to her team. They struck back immediately with three razor-sharp passes resulting in a goal off the stick of Elizabeth Davis, Roger's older sister.

At halftime both coaches huddled with their girls. The trainers exhausted themselves putting the teams back together. The body checks, brutal, were taking their toll.

Sandy Brashiers, arriving late, sat on the corner of the bleachers.

"Jody's playing a good game." Roscoe leaned down to talk low to Sandy. "Maybe this will be easier than I thought."

"Hope so," Sandy said.

"Roscoe," Maury McKinchie teased him, "what kind of headmaster are you when a kid puts your obituary in the paper?"

"Looks who's talking. Maury, the walking dead," Roscoe bellowed.

"Only in Hollywood," Maury said, making fun of himself. "Oh, well, I've made a lot of mistakes on all fronts."

Father Michael, sitting next to Maury, said, "To err is human, to forgive divine."

"To err is human, to forgive is extraordinary." Roscoe chuckled.

They both shut up when Mrs. Florence Rubicon, the aptly, or perhaps prophetically, named Latin teacher, waved a red-and-gold Redhawks pennant and shouted, "*Carpe diem—*"

Sandy shouted back, finishing the sentence, "*Quam minimum credula postero.*" Meaning "Don't trust in tomorrow."

Those who remembered their Latin laughed.

A chill made Harry shiver.

"Cold?" Miranda asked.

"No—just"—she shrugged—"a notion."

The game was turning into a great one. Both sides cheered themselves hoarse, and at the very end Teresa Pietro scored a blazing goal for St. Anne's. The Redhawks, crestfallen, dragged off the field, hurt so badly by the defeat that they couldn't rejoice in how spectacularly they had played. It would take time for them to realize they'd participated in one of the legendary field hockey games.

Jody Miller, utterly wretched because Teresa Pietro had streaked by her, was stomping off the field, her head down. Her mother ran out to console her; her father stayed in the stands to talk to people and to wait for Roscoe, besieged, as always.

When Maury McKinchie walked over to soothe her, she hit him in the gut with her stick. He keeled over.

Irene, horrified, grabbed the stick from her daughter's hand. She looked toward Kendrick, who had missed the incident.

Coach Hallvard quickly ran over. Brooks, Karen, Elizabeth, and Jody's other teammates stared in disbelief.

"Jody, go to the lockers—NOW," the coach ordered.

"I think she'd better come home with me," Irene said tightly.

"Mrs. Miller, I'll send her straight home. In fact, I'll drive her home, but I need to talk to her first. Her behavior affects the entire team."

Jody, white-lipped, glared at everyone, then suddenly laughed. "I'm sorry, Mr. McKinchie. If only I'd done that to Teresa Pietro."

Maury, gasping for breath, smiled gamely. "I don't look anything like Teresa Pietro."

"Are you all right?" Coach Hallvard asked him.

"Yes, it's the only time I've been grateful for my spare tire."

Coach Hallvard put her hand under Jody's elbow, propelling her toward the lockers.

Roscoe turned around to look up to Kendrick, who was being filled in on the incident. He whispered to his wife, "Go see what you can do for Maury." Then he said to April, hovering nearby, "I think you'd better go to the locker room with Coach Hallvard and the team, right?"

"Right." April trotted across the field, catching up with Naomi, who pretended she was happy for the company.

Father Michael felt a pang for not pursuing Jody the morning she came to see him. He was realizing how much she had needed him then.

Brooks, confused like the rest of her teammates, obediently walked back to the locker room while the St. Anne's team piled on the bus.

Mrs. Murphy, prowling the bleachers now that everyone was down on the sidelines, jerked her head up when she caught a whiff, a remnant of strong perfume.

"*Ugh.*" Pewter seconded her opinion.

They watched Harry chat with her friends about the incident as Roscoe glided over to Kendrick Miller. Sandy Brashiers also watched him, his eyes narrow as slits.

The two men strolled back to the bleachers, not thinking twice about the cats sitting there.

Kendrick glanced across the field at a now upright Maury attended by Irene and Naomi. "He's got both our wives buzzing around him. I guess he'll live."

Roscoe, surprised at Kendrick's cool response, said, "Doesn't sound as if you want him to—"

Kendrick, standing, propped one foot on the bleacher higher than the one he was standing on. "Don't like him. One of those dudes who comes here with money and thinks he's superior to us. That posture of detached amusement wears thin."

"Perhaps, but he's been very good to St. Elizabeth's."

Quickly Kendrick said, "I understand your position, Roscoe, you'd take money from the devil if you had to. You're a good businessman."

"I'd rather be a good headmaster," Roscoe replied coolly. "I was hoping you could illuminate me concerning Jody."

"Because she hit Maury?" His voice rose. "Wish I'd seen it."

"No, although that's an issue now. She skipped school the other day with a black eye. She said she got it in practice, but Coach Hallvard said, no, she didn't and as far as she knew there were no fights after practice. Does she roughhouse with neighborhood kids or—?"

"Do I beat her?" Kendrick's face darkened. "I know what people say behind my back, Roscoe. I don't beat my daughter. I don't beat my wife. Hell, I'm not home enough to get mad at them. And yes—I have a bad temper."

Roscoe demurred. "Please, don't misunderstand me. My concern is the well-being of every student at St. Elizabeth's. Jody, a charming young girl, is, well, more up and down lately. And her grades aren't what they were last year."

"I'll worry about it when the first report card comes out." Kendrick leaned on his knee.

"That will be in another month. Let's try to pull together and get those grades up before then." Roscoe's smile was all mouth, no eyes.

"You're telling me I'm not a good father." Kendrick glowered. "You've been talking to my bride, I suppose." The word "bride" dripped with venom.

"No, no, I haven't." Roscoe's patience began to erode.

"You're a rotten liar." Kendrick laughed harshly.

"Kendrick, I'm sorry I'm wasting your time." He stepped down out of the bleachers and left a furious Kendrick to pound down and leave in the opposite direction.

Sandy Brashiers awaited Roscoe at the other end. "He doesn't look too happy."

"He's an ass." Roscoe, sensitive and tired, thought he heard implicit criticism in Sandy's voice.

"I waited for you because I think we need to have an assembly or small workshop about how to handle losing. Jody's behavior was outrageous."

Roscoe hunched his massive shoulders. "I don't think we have to make that big a deal out of it."

"You and I will never see eye to eye, will we?" Sandy said.

"I'll handle it," Roscoe said sternly.

A pause followed, broken by Sandy. "I don't want to make you angry. I'm not trying to obstruct you, but this gives us a chance to address the subject of winning and losing. Sports are blown out of proportion anyway."

"They may be blown out of proportion, but they bring in alumni funds." Roscoe shifted his weight.

"We're an institution of learning, not an academy for sports."

"Sandy, not now. I'm fresh out of patience," Roscoe warned.

"If not now, when?"

"This isn't the time or place for a philosophical discussion of the

direction of secondary education in general or St. Elizabeth's in particular.'' Roscoe popped a hard strawberry candy in his mouth and
moved off in the direction of the girls' locker room. Perhaps April
had some information for him. He noticed that Naomi had shep-
herded Maury toward the quad, so he assumed she would be serving
him coffee, tea, or spirits in her office. She had a sure touch with
people.

The cats scampered out from under the bleachers, catching up
with Harry, who was in the parking lot calling for them.

Late that night the waxing moon flitted between inky boiling clouds. Mrs. Murphy, unable to sleep, was hunting in the paddock closest to the barn. A sudden gust of wind brought her nose up from the ground. She sniffed the air. A storm, a big one, was streaking in.

Simon, moving fast for him, ran in from the creek. Overhead Flatface swooped low, banked, then headed out to the far fields for one more pass before the storm broke.

"That's it for me." Simon headed to the open barn door. "Besides, bobcat tracks in the creekbed."

"Good enough reason."

"Are you coming in?"

"In a minute." She watched the gray animal with the long rat tail shuffle into the barn.

A light wind rustled the leaves. She saw the cornstalks sway, then wiggle in Harry's small garden by the corner of the barn. This proved a handy repository for her "cooked" manure. A red fox, half grown, sashayed out the end, glanced over her shoulder, beheld Mrs. Murphy, put her nose up, and walked away.

Mrs. Murphy loved no fox, for they competed for the same game.

"*You stay out of my corn rows,*" she growled.

"*You don't own the world,*" came the belligerent reply.

A lone screech froze both of them.

"*She's a killer.*" The fox flattened for a minute, then got up.

"*You're between a storm and a bobcat. Where's your den?*"

"*I'm not telling you.*"

"*Don't tell me, but you'd better hike to it fast.*" A big splat landed on the cat. She thought about the fox's predicament. "*Go into the shavings shed until the storm blows over and the bobcat's gone. Just don't make a habit of it.*"

Without a word the fox scooted into the shavings shed, burrowing down in the sweet-smelling chips as the storm broke overhead.

The tiger cat, eyes widened, listened for the bobcat. Another more distant cry, like a woman screaming, told her that the beast headed back to the forest, her natural home. Since the pickings were so good in the fall—lots of fat mice and rats gorged on fallen grain plus fruits left drying on the vine—the bobcat ventured closer to the human habitation.

The wind stiffened, the trees gracefully bent lower. The field mouse Mrs. Murphy patiently tracked wanted to stay dry. She refused to poke her nose out of her nest.

More raindrops sent the cat into the barn. She climbed the ladder. Simon was arranging his sleeping quarters. His treasures, spread around him, included a worn towel, one leather riding glove, a few scraps of newspaper, and a candy bar that he was saving for a rainy day, which it was.

"*Simon, don't you ever throw anything out?*"

He smiled. "*My mother said I was a pack rat, not a possum.*"

The force of the rain, unleashed, hit like a baseball bat against the north side of the barn. Flatface, claws down, landed in her cupola. She glanced down at the two friends, ruffled her feathers, then shut her eyes. She disdained earthbound creatures.

"*Flatface,*" Simon called up to her, "*before you go to sleep, how big is the* bobcat?"

"*Big enough to eat you.*" She laughed with a whooing sound.

"*Really, how big?*" he pressed.

She turned her big head nearly upside down. "Thirty to forty pounds and still growing. She's quick, lightning-quick, and smart. Now, if you two peons don't mind, I'm going to sleep. It's turning into a filthy night."

Mrs. Murphy and Simon caught up on the location of the latest beaver dam, fox dens, and one bald eagle nest. Then the cat told him about the false obituaries.

"*Bizarre, isn't it?*"

Simon pulled his towel into his hollowed-out nest in the straw. "*People put out marshmallows to catch raccoons. Us, too. We love marshmallows. Sure enough, one of us will grab the marshmallow. If we're lucky, the human wants to watch us. If we're unlucky, we're trapped or the marshmallow is poisoned. I think a human is putting out a marshmallow for another human.*"

Mrs. Murphy sat a long time, the tip of her tail slowly wafting to and fro. "*It's damned queer bait, Simon, telling someone he's dead.*"

"*Not just him—everyone.*"

The storm lashed central Virginia for two days, finally moving north to discomfort the Yankees.

Harry's father said storms did Nature's pruning. The farm, apart from some downed limbs, suffered little damage, but a tree was down on the way to Blair Bainbridge's house.

On Saturday, Harry borrowed his thousand-dollar power washer. Merrily she blasted the old green-and-yellow John Deere tractor, her truck, the manure spreader, and, in a fit of squeaky-clean mania, the entire interior of the barn. Not a cobweb remained.

The three horses observed this from the far paddock. By now they were accustomed to Harry's spring and fall fits.

Other humans feeling those same urges worked on Saturday. Miranda aired her linens as she planted her spring bulbs. She'd need the rest of Sunday to finish the bulbs.

The Reverend Jones stocked his woodpile and greeted the chimney sweep by touching his top hat. A little superstition never hurt a pastor.

Fair Haristeen decided to run an inventory on equine drugs at the clinic only to repent as the task devoured the day.

BoomBoom Craycroft, adding orange zest to her list of essences, peeled a dozen of them.

Susan Tucker attacked the attic while Ned edged every tree and flower bed until he thought his fillings would fall out of his teeth from the vibrations of the machine.

Big Mim supervised the overhaul of her once-sunk pontoon boat.

Little Marilyn transferred the old records of St. Elizabeth's bene- factors to a computer. Like Fair, she was sorry she had started the job.

Sandy Brashiers made up the questions for a quiz on *Macbeth*.

Jody Miller worked at the car wash with Brooks, Karen, and Roger.

Because of the storm, the car wash was jam-packed. The kids hadn't had time for lunch, so Jody took everyone's order. It was her turn to cross Route 29 and get sandwiches at the gas station—deli on the southwest corner. The Texaco sat between the car wash and the intersection. If only that station had a deli, she wouldn't have to cross the busy highway.

Jimbo Anson slipped her twenty-five dollars for everyone's lunch, his included, as they were famished.

As the day wore on, the temperature climbed into the mid-sixties. The line of cars extended out to Route 29.

Roscoe Fletcher, his Mercedes station wagon caked in mud, pa- tiently waited in line. He had turned off Route 29 and moved forward enough to be right in front of the Texaco station. The car wash was behind the gas station itself, so the kids did not yet know their headmaster was in line and he didn't know how many cars were in front of him. The car stereo played *The Marriage of Figaro*. He sang aloud with gusto.

The line crept forward.

Jody headed down to the intersection. Five minutes later she dashed back into the office.

"Where's the food?" Roger, hungry, inquired as he reached in for another dry towel.

She announced, "Mr. Fletcher is in line! He hasn't seen me yet. I'll go as soon as he gets through the line."

"I'll starve by then," Roger said.

"He'll be cool." Karen stuck her head in the door as Roger threw her a bottle of mag washer for aluminum hubcaps.

"Maybe—but I don't want a lecture. I know I was wrong to hit Mr. McKinchie." Her voice rose. "I've had about all the help I can stand. I was wrong. Okay. I apologized. Guess you don't want to see him either." She pointed at Roger, who ignored her.

"Well, he's past the Texaco station. You'd better hide under the desk," Karen yelled. "Jeez, I think everyone in the world is here today." She heard horns beeping out on Route 29. Irene Miller had pulled in behind Roscoe, then Naomi Fletcher in her blue Miata. BoomBoom Craycroft, car wafting fragrances, was just ahead of him.

Roger waved up another car. He bent his tall frame in two as the driver rolled down the window. "What will it be?"

"How about a wash only?"

"Great. Put it in neutral and turn off your car radio."

The driver obeyed instructions while Karen and Brooks slopped the big brushes into the soapy water, working off the worst of the mud.

"Hey, there's Father Michael." Karen noticed the priest's black old-model Mercury. "You'd think the church would get him a better car." She yelled so Jody, scrunched under the desk, could hear her.

"It runs," Brooks commented on the car.

"How many are in the line now?" Roger wiped the sweat from his forehead with the back of his arm as Jimbo walked down to the intersection to direct drivers to form a double line. He needed to unclog the main north-south artery of Charlottesville.

"Number twenty-two just pulled in," Brooks replied.

"Unreal." Karen whistled.

Roscoe rolled down his window, flooding the car wash with Mozart. He was three cars away from his turn.

"You-all should learn your Mozart," he called to them. "Greatest composer who ever lived."

His wife shouted from her car, "It's the weekend, Roscoe. You can't tell them what to do."

"Right!" Karen laughed, waving at Naomi.

"I bet you listen to Melissa Etheridge and Sophie B. Hawkins," Roscoe said as he offered her strawberry hard candy, which she refused.

"Yeah." Karen turned her attention to the car in front of her. "They're great. I like Billy Ray Cyrus and Reba McEntire, too."

Irene rolled her window down. "Where's Jody?"

"She went to the deli to get our lunches, and I hope she hurries up!" Roger told a half-truth.

"What about Bach?" Roscoe sang out, still on his music topic.

"The Beatles," Karen answered. "I mean, that's like rock Bach."

"No, Bill Haley and the Comets are like rock Bach," Roscoe said as he sucked on the candy in his mouth. "Jerry Lee Lewis."

The kids took a deep breath and yelled and swung their hips in unison, "Elvis!"

By the time Roscoe put his left tire into the groove, everyone was singing "Hound Dog," which made him laugh. He noticed Jody peeking out of the office. The laughter, too much for her, had lured her from under the desk.

He pointed his finger at her. "You ain't nothin' but a hound dog."

She laughed, but her smile disappeared when her mother yelled at her. "I thought you were at the deli?"

"I'm on my way. We're backed up," she said since she'd heard what Roger told her mother.

"Mr. Fletcher, shut your window," Karen advised as the station wagon lurched into the car wash.

"Oh, right." He hit the electric button, and the window slid shut with a hum.

As the tail end of the Mercedes disappeared in a sheet of water, the yellow neon light flashed on and Karen waved Irene on. "He's so full of shit," she said under her breath.

BoomBoom hollered out her window, "Stress. Irene, this is too much stress. Come meet me at Ruby Tuesday's after the car wash."

"Okay," Irene agreed. Her left tire was in the groove now. "I want the works." Irene handed over fifteen dollars. Karen made change.

Roger, at the button to engage the track, waited for Roscoe to finish. The light telling him to put through the next vehicle didn't come on. Minutes passed.

"I'm in a hurry." Irene tried to sound pleasant.

"It's been like this all day, Mrs. Miller." Karen smiled tightly.

Brooks looked down the line. "Maybe Mr. Fletcher's out but the light didn't come on. I'll go see."

Brooks loped alongside the car wash, arriving at the end where the brown station wagon, nose out, squatted. The tail of the vehicle remained on the track. The little metal cleats in the track kept pushing the car.

Brooks knocked on the window. Roscoe, sitting upright, eyes straight ahead, didn't reply.

"Mr. Fletcher, you need to move out."

No reply. She knocked harder. Still no reply.

"Mr. Fletcher, please drive out." She waited, then opened the door. The first thing she noticed was that Mr. Fletcher had wet his pants, which shocked her. Then she realized he was dead.

19

It wasn't funny, but Rick Shaw wanted to laugh. Mozart blared through the speakers, and the car's rear end shone like diamonds after endless washings.

Naomi Fletcher, in shock, had been taken home by an officer.

Diana Robb, a paramedic with the rescue squad, patiently waited while Sheriff Shaw and Deputy Cooper painstakingly examined the car.

Jimbo Anson turned off the water when Rick told him it was okay.

Roger Davis directed traffic around the waiting line. He was relieved when a young officer pulled up in a squad car.

"Don't go yet," Tom Kline told Roger. "I'll need your help."

Obediently, Roger continued to direct traffic onto the Greenbrier side street. He wanted to comfort Brooks for the shock she had suffered, but that would have to wait.

Rick said under his breath to Coop, "Ever tell you about the guy who died on the escalator over in Richmond? I was fresh out of school. This was my first call as a rookie. No one could get on or off until cleared, and the store didn't turn off the motor. People were running in place. Super aerobics. 'Course the stiff rolled right up to the step-off, where his hair caught in the steps. By the time I reached him, he was half scalped."

"Gross." She knew that Rick wasn't unfeeling, but a law enforcement officer sees so much that a protective shell develops over emotions.

"Let's have the boys take photos, bag the contents of the station wagon." He reached in and, with his gloves on, snapped off the stereo. "Okay, we're done," he called over his shoulder to Diana Robb and Cooper behind him.

"Sheriff, what do you think?" the paramedic asked him.

"Looks like a heart attack. He's the right age for it. I've learned over the years, though, to defer to the experts. Unless Mrs. Fletcher objects, we'll send the body to Bill Moscowitz—he's a good coroner."

"If you don't stop smoking those Chesterfields, I'll be picking you up one of these days."

"Ah, I've stopped smoking so many times." He should have taken his pack out of his pocket and left it in the unmarked car; then she wouldn't have noticed. "Drop him at the morgue. I'll stop by Naomi's, so tell Bill to hold off until he hears from me." He turned to Coop. "Anything else?"

"Yeah, Roscoe's obituary was in the paper, remember?"

He rubbed his chin, the light chestnut stubble already appearing even though he'd shaved at six this morning. "We thought it was a joke."

"Boss, let's question a few people, starting with Sean Hallahan."

He folded his arms and leaned against the green unmarked car. "Let's wait—well, let me think about it. I don't want to jump the gun."

"Maury McKinchie's obituary was stuffed in the paper as well."

"I know. I know." He swept his eyes over the distressed Irene Miller and BoomBoom. Father Michael had administered the last rites. In the corner of his eye the lumpish figure of Jimbo Anson loomed. "I'd better talk to him before he runs to Dunkin' Donuts and eats another dozen jelly rolls." Jimbo ate when distressed. He was distressed a lot.

He half whispered, "Coop, take the basics from these folks, then let them go. I think BoomBoom is going to code on us." He used the medic slang word for "die."

Rick straightened his shoulders and walked the thirty yards to Jimbo.

"Sheriff, I don't know what to do. Nothing like this has ever happened to me. I just feel awful. Poor Naomi."

"Jimbo, death always upsets the applecart. Breathe deeply." He clapped the man on the back. "That's better. Now you tell me what happened."

"He went through the car wash, well I mean, I didn't see him, the kids were up front, and when the car didn't roll off she, I mean Brooks, ran around to see if the pedal hadn't released on the belt and, well, Roscoe was gone."

"Did you see him at all?"

"No, I mean, not until I came back with Brookie. Kid had some sense, I can tell you. She didn't scream or cry. She ran to my office, told me Roscoe was dead, and I followed her to there." He pointed.

"That's fine. I may be talking to you again, but it looks like a heart attack or stroke. These things happen."

"Business was great today." A mournful note crept into his voice.

"You'll be able to reopen before long. I'm going to impound the car, just routine, Jimbo. You won't have to worry about the vehicle being parked here."

"Thanks, Sheriff."

Rick clapped him on the back again and walked into the air-conditioned office—the day had turned unusually hot—where Brooks, Jody, and Karen sat. Cooper was already there.

"Sheriff, we were establishing a time line." Coop smiled at the three young women.

"One thirty, about," Brooks said.

"Mr. Anson said you showed presence of mind," Rick complimented Brooks.

"I don't know. I feel so bad for Mr. Fletcher. He helped me get into St. Elizabeth's after the semester started."

"Well, I'm not the Reverend Jones but I do believe that Roscoe Fletcher is in a better place. Much as you'll miss him, try to think of that."

"Jody, did you notice anything?" Coop asked.

"No. He said 'hi' and that was it. Karen and Brooks scrubbed down his bumpers. I think Roger pressed the button to send him in."

"Where is Roger?" Rick said.

"Directing traffic," Karen replied.

"Good man to have around."

This startled the two girls, who had never thought of Roger as anything other than a tall boy who was quiet even in kindergarten. Brooks was beginning to appreciate Roger's special qualities.

"Was there anything unusual about Mr. Fletcher or anyone else today?"

"No." Karen twirled a golden hair around her forefinger.

"Girls, if anything comes to mind, call me." He handed around his card.

"Is something wrong, something other than the fact that Mr. Fletcher is dead?" Brooks inquired shrewdly.

"No. This is routine."

"It's weird to be questioned." Brooks was forthright.

"I'm sorry you all lost Mr. Fletcher. I know it was a shock. I have to ask questions, though. I don't mean to further upset you. My job is to collect details, facts, like little pieces of a mosaic."

"We understand," Karen said.

"We're okay," Brooks fibbed.

"Okay then." He rose and Coop also handed her card to the three girls.

As she trudged across the blacktop to motion Roger from Greenbrier Drive, she marveled at the self-possession of the three high school girls. Usually, something like this sent teenage girls into a crying jag. As far as she could tell, not one tear had fallen, but then BoomBoom, never one to pass up the opportunity to emote, was crying enough for all of them.

20

Johnny Pop, the 1958 John Deere tractor, rolled through the meadow thick with goldenrod. Tucker pouted by a fallen walnut at the creek. Mrs. Murphy sat in Harry's lap. Tucker, a trifle too big and heavy, envied the tiger her lap status.

As the tractor popped by, she turned and gazed into the creek. A pair of fishy eyes gazed right back. Startled, Tucker took a step back and barked, then sheepishly sat down again.

The baking sun and two days of light winds had dried out the wet earth. Harry, determined to get one more hay cutting before winter, fired up Johnny Pop the minute she thought she wouldn't get stuck. She couldn't hear anything, so Mrs. Hogendobber startled her when she walked out into the meadow.

Tucker, intent on her bad mood, missed observing the black Falcon rumbling down the drive.

Miranda waved her arms over her head. "Harry, stop!"

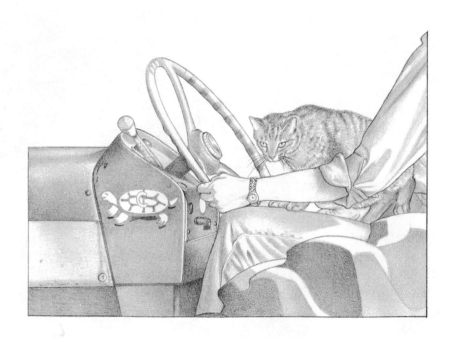

Harry immediately flipped the lever to the left, cutting off the motor. "Miranda, what's the matter? What are you doing out here on gardening day?"

"Roscoe Fletcher's dead—for real, this time."

"What happened?" Harry gasped.

Mrs. Murphy listened. Tucker, upon hearing the subject, hurried over from the creek.

Pewter was asleep in the house.

"Died at the car wash. Heart attack or stroke. That's what Mim says."

"Was she there?"

"No. I forgot to ask her how she found out. Rick Shaw told Jim Sanburne, most likely, and Jim told Mim."

"It's ironic." Harry shuddered.

"The obit?"

Harry nodded. Mrs. Murphy disagreed. "It's not ironic. It's murder. Wait and see. Cat intuition."

21

Sean Hallahan pushed a laundry cart along a hallway so polished it reflected his image.

The double doors at the other end of the corridor swung open. Karen and Jody hurried toward him.

"How'd you get in here?" he asked.

Ignoring the question, Jody solemnly said, "Mr. Fletcher's dead. He died at the car wash."

"What?" Sean stopped the cart from rolling into them.

Karen tossed her ponytail. "He went in and never came out."

"Went in what?" Sean appeared stricken, his face white.

"The car wash," Jody said impatiently. "He went in the car wash, but at the other end, he just sat. Looks like he died of a heart attack."

"Are you making this up?" He smiled feebly.

"No. We were there. It was awful. Brooks Tucker found him."

"For real," he whispered.

"For real." Jody put her arm around his waist. "No one's going to think anything. Really."

"If only I hadn't put that phony obituary in the paper." He gulped.

"Yeah," the girls chimed in unison.

"Wait until my dad hears about this. He's going to kill me." He paused. "Who knows?"

"Depends on who gets to the phone first, I guess." Karen hadn't expected Sean to be this upset. She felt sorry for him.

"We came here first before going home. We thought you should know before your dad picks you up."

"Thanks," he replied, tears welling in his eyes.

22

Father Michael led the assembled upper and lower schools of St. Elizabeth's in a memorial service. Naomi Fletcher, wearing a veil, was supported by Sandy Brashiers with Florence Rubicon, the Latin teacher, on her left side. Ed Sugarman, the chemistry teacher, escorted a devastated April Shively.

Many of the younger children cried because they were supposed to or because they saw older kids crying. In the upper school some of the girls carried on, whipping through boxes of tissues. A few of the boys were red-eyed as well, including, to everyone's surprise, Sean Hallahan, captain of the football team.

Brooks reported all this to Susan, who told Harry and Miranda when they joined her at home for lunch.

"Well, he ate too much, he drank too much, and who knows what else he did—too much." Susan summed up Roscoe's life.

"How's Brooks handling it?" Harry inquired.

"Okay. She knows people die; after all, she watched her grandma die by inches with cancer. In fact, she said, 'When it's my time I want to go fast like Mr. Fletcher.'"

"I don't remember thinking about dying at all at her age," Harry wondered out loud.

"You didn't think of anything much at her age," Susan replied.

"Thanks."

"Children think of death often; they are haunted by it because they can't understand it." Miranda rested her elbows on the table to lean forward. "That's why they go to horror movies—it's a safe way to approach death, scary but safe."

Harry stared at Miranda's elbows on the table. "I never thought of that."

"I know I'm not supposed to have my elbows on the table, Harry, but I can't always be perfect."

Harry blinked. "It's not that at all—it's just that you usually are—perfect."

"Aren't you sweet."

"Harry puts her feet on the table, she's so imperfect."

"Susan, I do not."

"You know what was rather odd, though?" Susan reached for the sugar bowl. "Brooks told me Jody said she was glad Roscoe was dead. That she didn't like him anyway. Now that's a bit extreme even for a teenager."

"Yeah, but Jody's been extreme lately." Harry got up when the phone rang. Force of habit.

"Sit down. I'll answer it." Susan walked over to the counter and lifted the receiver.

"Yes. Of course, I understand. Marilyn, it could have an impact on your fund-raising campaign. I do suggest that you appoint an interim headmaster immediately." Susan paused and held the phone away from her ear so the others could hear Little Mim's voice. Then she spoke again. "Sandy Brashiers. Who else? No, no, and no," she said after listening to three questions. "Do you want me to call anyone? Don't fret, doesn't solve a thing."

"She'll turn into her mother," Miranda predicted as Susan hung up the receiver.

"Little Mim doesn't have her mother's drive."

"Harry, not only do I think she has her mother's drive, I think she'll run for her father's seat once he steps down as mayor."

"No way." Harry couldn't believe the timid woman she had known since childhood could become that confident.

"Bet you five dollars," Miranda smugly said.

"According to Little Mim, the Millers are divorcing."

"Oh, dear." Miranda hated such events.

"About time." Harry didn't like hearing of divorce either, but there were exceptions. "Still, there is no such thing as a good divorce."

"You managed," Susan replied.

"How quickly you forget. During the enforced six months' separation every married couple and single woman in this town invited my ex-husband to dinner. Who had me to dinner, I ask you?"

"I did." Miranda and Susan spoke in chorus.

"And that was it. The fact that I filed for the divorce made me an ogre. He was the one having the damned affair."

"Sexism is alive and well." Susan apportioned out seven-layer salad, one of her specialties. She stopped, utensils in midair. "Did either of you like Roscoe Fletcher?"

"*De mortuis nil nisi bonum*," Miranda advised.

"Speak nothing but good about the dead," Harry translated although it was unnecessary. "Maybe people said that because they feared the departed spirit was nearby. If they gave you trouble while alive, think what they could do to you as a ghost."

"Did you like Roscoe Fletcher?" Susan repeated her question.

Harry paused. "Yes, he had a lot of energy and good humor."

"A little too hearty for my taste." Miranda found the salad delicious. "Did you like him?"

Susan shrugged. "I felt neutral. He seemed a bit phony sometimes. But maybe that was the fund-raiser in him. He had to be a backslapper and glad-hander, I suppose."

"Aren't we awful, sitting here picking the poor man apart?"
Miranda dabbed her lipstick-coated lips with a napkin.

The phone rang again. Susan jumped up. "Speaking of letting
someone rest in peace, I'd like to eat in peace."

"You don't have to answer it," Harry suggested.

"Mothers always answer telephones." She picked up the jan-
gling device. "Hello." She paused a long time. "Thanks for telling
me. You've done the right thing."

Little Mim had rung back to say St. Elizabeth's had held an
emergency meeting by conference call.

Sandy Brashiers had been selected interim headmaster.

23

Late that afternoon, a tired Father Michael bent his lean frame, folding himself into the confessional.

He usually read until someone entered the other side of the booth. The residents of Crozet had been particularly virtuous this week because traffic was light.

The swish of the fabric woke him as he half dozed over the volume of Thomas Merton, a writer he usually found provocative.

"Father, forgive me for I have sinned," came the formalistic opening.

"Go on, my child."

"I have killed and I will kill again." The voice was muffled, disguised.

He snapped to attention, but before he could open his mouth, the penitent slipped out of the booth. Confused, Father Michael pondered what to do. He felt he must stay in the booth for the confessional hours were well-known—he had a responsibility to his flock—but he wanted to call Rick Shaw immediately. Paralyzed, he grasped the book so hard his knuckles were white. The curtain swished again.

A man's voice spoke, deep and low. "Father forgive me for I have sinned."

"Go on, my child," Father Michael said as his mind raced.

"I've cheated on my wife. I can't help myself. I have strong desires." He stopped.

Father Michael advised him by rote, gave him a slew of Hail Marys and novenas. He kept rubbing his wristwatch until eventually his wrist began to hurt. As the last second of his time in the booth expired, he bolted out, grabbed the phone, and dialed Rick Shaw.

When Coop picked up the phone, he insisted he speak to the sheriff himself.

"Sheriff Shaw."

"Yes."

"This is Father Michael. I don't know"—sweat beaded on his forehead; he couldn't violate what was said in the confessional booth—"I believe a murder may have taken place."

"One has, Father Michael."

The priest's hands were shaking. "Oh, no. Who?"

"Roscoe Fletcher." Rick breathed deeply. "The lab report came back. He was poisoned by malathion. Not hard to get around here, so many farmers use it. It works with the speed of light so he had to have eaten it at the car wash. We've tested the strawberry hard candy in his car. Nothing."

"There couldn't be any mistake?"

"No. We have to talk, Father."

After Father Michael hung up the phone, he needed to collect his thoughts. He paced outside, winding up in the graveyard. Ansley Randolph's mums bloomed beautifully.

A soul was in peril. But if the confession he had heard was true, then another immortal soul was in danger as well. He was a priest. He should do something, but he didn't know what. It then occurred to him that he himself might be in danger—his body, not his soul.

Like a rabbit who hears the beagle pack, he twitched and cast his eyes around the graveyard to the Avenging Angel. It looked so peaceful.

24

His shirtsleeves rolled up, Kendrick Miller sat in his favorite chair to read the paper.

Irene swept by. "Looking for your obituary?" She arched a delicate eyebrow.

"Ha ha." He rustled the paper.

Jody, reluctantly doing her math homework at the dining-room table so both parents could supervise, reacted. "Mom, that's not funny."

"I didn't say it was."

"Who knows, maybe *your* obituary will show up." She dropped her pencil inside her book, closing it.

"If it does, Jody, you'll have placed it there." Irene sank gracefully onto the sofa.

Jody grimaced. "Sick."

"I can read it now: 'Beloved mother driven to death by child—and husband.' "

"Irene . . ." Kendrick reproved, putting down the paper.

"Yeah, Mom."

"Well"—she propped her left leg over an embroidered pillow—"I thought Roscoe Fletcher could have sold ice to Eskimos and probably did. He was good for St. Elizabeth's, and I'm sorry he died. I was even sorrier that we were all there. I would have preferred to hear about it rather than see it."

"He didn't look bad." Jody opened her book again. "I hope he didn't suffer."

"Too quick to suffer." Irene stared absently at her nails, a discreet pale pink. "What's going to happen at St. Elizabeth's?"

Kendrick lifted his eyebrows. "The board will appoint Sandy Brashiers headmaster. Sandy will try to kill Roscoe's film-course idea, which will bring him into a firefight with Maury McKinchie, Marilyn Sanburne, and April Shively. Ought to be worth the price of admission."

"How do you know that?" Jody asked.

"I don't know it for certain, but the board is under duress. And the faculty likes Brashiers."

"Oh, I almost forgot. Father Michael can see us tomorrow at two thirty."

"Irene, I have landscaping plans to show the Doubletree people tomorrow." He was bidding for the hotel's business. "It's important."

"I'd like to think I'm important. That this marriage is important," Irene said sarcastically.

"Then you pay the bills."

"You turn my stomach." Irene swung her legs to the floor and left.

"Way to go, Dad."

"You keep out of this."

"I love when you spend the evening at home. Just gives me warm fuzzies." She hugged herself in a mock embrace.

"I ought to—" He shut up.

"Hit me. Go ahead. Everyone thinks you gave me the shiner."
He threw the newspaper on the floor. "I've never once hit you."

"I'll never tell," she goaded him.

"Who did hit you?"

"Field hockey practice. I told you."

"I don't believe you."

"Fine, Dad. I'm a liar."

"I don't know what you are, but you aren't happy."

"Neither are you," she taunted.

"No, I'm not." He stood up, put his hands in his pockets. "I'm going out."

"Take me with you."

"Why?"

"I don't want to stay home with her."

"You haven't finished your homework."

"How come you get to run away and I have to stay home?"

"I—" He stopped because a determined Irene reentered the living room.

"Father Michael says he can see us at nine in the morning," she announced.

His face reddening, Kendrick sat back down, defeated. "Fine."

"Why do you go for marriage counseling, Mom? You go to mass every day. You see Father Michael every day."

"Jody, this is none of your business."

"If you discuss it in front of me, it is," she replied flippantly.

"She's got a point there." Kendrick appreciated how intelligent his daughter was, and how frustrated. However, he didn't know how to talk to her or his manipulative—in his opinion—wife. Irene suffocated him and Jody irritated him. The only place he felt good was at work.

"Dad, are you going to give St. E's a lot of money?"

"I wouldn't tell you if I were."

"Why not?"

"You'd use it as an excuse to skip classes." He half laughed.

"Kendrick"—Irene sat back on the sofa—"where do you get these ideas?"

"Contrary to popular opinion, I was young once, and Jody likes to—" He put his hand out level to the floor and wobbled it.

"Learned it from you." Jody flared up.

"Can't we have one night of peace?" Irene wailed, unwilling to really examine why they couldn't.

"Hey, Mom, we're dysfunctional."

"That's a bullshit word." Kendrick picked his paper up. "All those words are ridiculous. Codependent. Enabler. Jesus Christ. People can't accept reality anymore. They've invented a vocabulary for their illusions."

Both his wife and daughter stared at him.

"Dad, are you going to give us the lecture on professional victims?"

"No." He buried his nose in the paper.

"Jody, finish your homework," Irene directed.

Jody stood up. She had no intention of doing homework. "I hated seeing Mr. Fletcher dead. You two don't care. It was a shock, you know." She swept her books onto the floor; they hit with thuds equal to their differing weights. She stomped out the front door, slamming it hard.

"Kendrick, you deal with it. I was at the car wash, remember?"

He glared at her, rolled his paper up, threw it on the chair, and stalked out.

Irene heard him call for Jody. No response.

25

"You cheated!" Jody, angry, squared off at Karen Jensen.

"I did not."

"You didn't even understand *Macbeth*. There's no way you could have gotten ninety-five on Mr. Brashiers's quiz."

"I read it and I understand it."

"Liar."

"I went over to Brooks Tucker's and she helped me."

Jody's face twisted in sarcasm. "She read aloud to you?"

"No. Brooks gets all that stuff. It's hard for me."

"She's your new best friend."

"So what if she is?" Karen tossed her blond hair.

"You'd better keep your mouth shut."

"You're the one talking, not me."

"No, I'm not."

"You're weirding out."

Jody's eyes narrowed. "I lost my temper. That doesn't mean I'm weirding out."

"Then why call me a cheater?"

"Because"—Jody sucked in the cool air—"you're on a scholarship. You have to make good grades. And English is not your subject. I don't know why you even took Shakespeare."

"Because Mr. Brashiers is a great teacher." Karen Jensen glanced down the alleyway. She saw only Mrs. Murphy and Pewter, strolling through Mrs. Hogendobber's fall garden, a riot of reds, rusts, oranges, and yellows.

Taking a step closer, Jody leaned toward her. "You and I vowed to—"

Karen held up her hands, palms outward. "Jody, chill out. I'd be crazy to open my mouth. I don't want anyone to know I went to bed with a guy this summer, and neither do you. Just chill out."

Jody relaxed. "Everything's getting on my nerves . . . especially Mom and Dad. I just want to move out."

Karen noticed the tiger cat coming closer. "Guess everyone feels that way sometimes."

"Yeah," Jody replied, "but your parents are better than mine."

Karen didn't know how to answer that, so she said, "Let's go in and get the mail."

"Yeah." Jody started walking.

Pewter and Murphy, now at the backdoor of the post office, sat on the steps. Pewter washed her face. Mrs. Murphy dropped her head so Pewter could wash her, too.

"Didn't you think the newspaper's write-up of Roscoe's death was strange?" Murphy's eyes were half closed.

"You mean the bit about an autopsy and routine investigation?"

"If he died of a heart attack, why a routine investigation? Mom better pump Coop when she sees her—and hey, she hasn't been in to pick up her mail for the last two days."

"Nothing in there but catalogs." Pewter took it upon herself to check out everyone's mailbox. She said she wasn't being nosy, only checking for mice.

Shouting in the post office sent them zipping through the animal door.

They crossed the back section of the post office and bounded onto the counter. Both Harry and Mrs. Hogendobber were in the front section as were Jody, an astonished Samson Coles, and Karen Jensen. Tucker was at Harry's feet, squared off against Jody. The animals had arrived in the middle of an angry scene.

"You're the one!"

"Jody, that's enough," Mrs. Hogendobber, aghast, admonished the girl.

Samson, his gravelly voice sad, said quietly, "It's all right, Miranda."

"You're the one sleeping with Mom!" Jody shrieked.

"I am not having an affair with your mother." He was gentle.

"Jody, come on. I'll ride you home." Karen tugged at the tall girl's sleeve, at a loss for what to do. Her friend exploded when Samson put his arm around her shoulders, telling her how sorry he was that the headmaster had died.

"You cheated on Lucinda—everyone knows you did—and then Ansley killed herself. She drove her Porsche into that pond because of you . . . and now you're fucking my mother."

"JODY!" Mrs. Hogendobber raised her voice, which scared everyone.

Jody burst into tears and Karen pushed her out the front door. "I'm sorry, Mrs. Hogendobber and Mr. Coles. I'm sorry, Mrs. Haristeen. She's, uh . . ." Karen couldn't finish her thought. She closed the door behind her.

Samson curled his lips inward until they disappeared. "Well, I know I'm the town pariah, but this is the first time I've heard that I caused Ansley's death."

A shocked Miranda grasped the counter for support. "Samson, no one in this town blames you for that unstable woman's unfortunate end. She caused unhappiness to herself and others." She gulped in air. "That child needs help."

"*Help? She needs a good slap in the face.*" Pewter paced the counter.

Tucker grumbled. "*Stinks of fear.*"

"*They can't smell it. They only trust their eyes. Why, I don't know—their eyes are terrible.*" Mrs. Murphy, concerned, sat at the counter's edge watching Karen force Jody into her car, an old dark green Volvo.

"We'd better call Irene," Harry, upset, suggested.

"No." Samson shook his head. "Then the kid will think we're ganging up on her. Obviously, she doesn't trust her mother if she thinks she's having an affair with me."

"Then I'll call her father."

"Harry, Kendrick's no help," Mrs. Hogendobber, rarely a criticizer, replied. "His love affair with himself is the problem in that family. It's a love that brooks no rivals."

This made Harry laugh; Miranda hadn't intended to be funny, but she had hit the nail on the head.

Samson folded his arms across his chest. "Some people shouldn't have children. Kendrick is one of them."

"We can't let the child behave this way. She's going to make a terrific mess." Miranda added sensibly, "Not everyone will be as tolerant as we are." She tapped her chin with her forefinger, shifting her weight to her right foot. "I'll call Father Michael."

Samson hesitated, then spoke. "Miranda, what does a middle-aged priest know of teenage girls . . . of women?"

"About the same as any other man," Harry fired off.

"Touché," Samson replied.

"Samson, I didn't mean to sound nasty. You're probably more upset than you're letting on. Jody may be a kid, but a low blow is a low blow," Harry said.

"I could leave this town where people occasionally forgive but never forget. I think about it, you know, but"—he jammed his hands in his pockets—"I'm not the only person living in Crozet who's made a mistake. I'm too stubborn to turn tail. I belong here as much as the next guy."

"I hope you don't think I'm sitting in judgment." Miranda's hand fluttered to her throat.

"Me neither." Harry smiled. "It's hard for me to be open-minded about that subject, thanks to my own history . . . I mean,

BoomBoom Craycroft of all people. Fair could have picked someone—well, you know."

"That was the excitement for Fair. That BoomBoom was so
obvious." Samson realized he'd left his mail on the counter. "I'm
going back to work." He scooped his mail up before Pewter, recover-
ing from the drama, could squat on it. "What I really feel bad about
is tampering with the escrow accounts. That was rotten. Falling in
love with Ansley may have been imprudent, but it wasn't criminal.
Betraying a responsibility to clients, that was wrong." He sighed.
"I've paid for it. I've lost my license. Lost respect. Lost my house.
Nearly lost Lucinda." He paused again, then said, "Well, girls, we've
had enough soap opera for one day." He pushed the door open and
breathed in the crisp fall air.

Miranda ambled over to the phone, dialed, and got Lucinda
Coles. "Lucinda, is Father Michael there?"

He was, and she buzzed the good woman through.

"Father Michael, have you a moment?" Miranda accurately repeated the events of the afternoon.

When she hung up, Harry asked, "Is he going to talk to
her?"

"Yes. He seemed distracted, though."

"Maybe the news upset him."

"Of course." She nodded. "I'm going to clean out that refrigerator. It needs a good scrub."

"Before you do that, there's a pile of mail for Roscoe Fletcher.
Why don't we sort it out and run it over to Naomi after work?"

The two women dumped the mail out on the work table in the
back. A flutter of bills made them both feel guilty. The woman had
lost her husband. Handing over bills seemed heartless. Catalogs, mag-
azines, and handwritten personal letters filled up one of the plastic
boxes they used in the back to carry mail after sorting it out of the big
canvas duffel bags.

A Jiffy bag, the end torn, the gray stuffing spilling out, sent
Harry to the counter for Scotch tape.

Tucker observed this. She wanted to play, but the cats were
hashing over the scene they'd just witnessed. She barked.

"Tucker, if you need to go to the bathroom, there's the door."

"Can't we walk, just a little walk? You deserve a break."

"Butterfingers." Harry dropped the bag. The tiny tear in the cover opened wider.

Mrs. Murphy and Pewter stopped their gabbing and jumped down.

"Yahoo!" Mrs. Murphy pounced on the tear and the gray stuffing burst out.

"Aachoo." Pewter sneezed as the featherlight stuffing floated into the air.

"I've got it!" Mrs. Murphy crowed.

Pewter pounced, both paws on one end of the bag, claws out as the tiger cat ripped away at the other corner, enlarging the tear until she could reach into the bag with her paw.

If Mrs. Murphy had been a boxer, she would have been hailed for her lightning hands.

Lying flat on her side, she fished in the Jiffy bag with her right paw.

"Anything to eat?"

"No, it's paper, but it's crisp and crinkly."

The large gray cat blinked, somewhat disappointed. Food, the ultimate pleasure, was denied her. She'd have to make do with fresh paper, a lesser pleasure but a pleasure nonetheless.

"You girls are loony tunes." Tucker, bored, turned her back. Paper held no interest for her.

"Hooked it. I can get it out of the bag. I know I can." Murphy yanked hard at the contents of the package, pulling the paper partways through the tear.

"Look!" Pewter shouted.

Mrs. Murphy stopped for a second to focus on her booty. "Wow!" She yanked harder.

Tucker turned back around thanks to the feline excitement. "Give it to Mom. She needs it."

Mrs. Murphy ripped into the bag so fast the humans hadn't time to react, and the cat turned a somersault to land on her side, then put her paw into the bag. Her antics had them doubled over.

However funny she was, Mrs. Murphy was destroying government property.

"*Mom, we're rich!*" Mrs. Murphy let out a jubilant meow.

Harry and Miranda, dumbfounded, bent over the demolished bag.

"My word." Miranda's eyes about popped from her head. She reached out with her left hand, fingers to the floor, to steady herself.

The humans and animals stared at a stack of one-hundred-dollar bills, freshly minted.

"We'd better call Rick Shaw. No one sends that much money in the mail." Harry stood up, feeling a little dizzy.

"Harry, I don't know the law on this, but we can't open this packet."

"I know that," Harry, a trifle irritated, snapped.

"It's not our business." Miranda slowly thought out loud.

"I'll call Ned."

"No. That's still interfering in the proper delivery of the mail."

"Miranda, there's something fishy about this."

"Fishy or not, we are employees of the United States Postal Service, and we can't blow the whistle just because there's money in a package."

"We sure could if it were a bomb."

"But it's not."

"You mean we deliver it?"

"Exactly."

"Oh." Mrs. Murphy's whiskers drooped. "*We need that money.*"

26

Naomi Fletcher called Rick Shaw herself. She asked Miranda and Harry to stay until the sheriff arrived.

Mrs. Murphy, Pewter, and Tucker languished in the cab of the truck. When the sheriff pulled in with Cooper at his side, the animals set up such a racket that Cynthia opened the truck door.

"Bet you guys need to go to the bathroom."

"Sure," they yelled over their shoulders as they made a beeline for the front door.

"You'd better stop for a minute," Tucker advised the cats.

"I'm not peeing in public. You do it," the tiger, insulted, replied.

"Fine." The corgi found a spot under a tree, did enough to convince Cynthia that she had saved the interior of Harry's truck, then hurried to the front door.

Once inside they huddled under the coffee table while Cynthia dusted the bag and the bills for prints.

After an exhaustive discussion Rick told Roscoe Fletcher's

widow to deposit the money in her account. He could not impound the cash. There was no evidence of wrongdoing.

"There are no assumptions in my job, only facts." He ran his right hand through his thinning hair.

Naomi, both worried and thrilled, for the sum had turned out to be seventy-five thousand dollars, thanked the sheriff and his deputy for responding to her call.

Rick, hat in hand, said, "Mrs. Fletcher, brace yourself. The story will be out in the papers tomorrow. A coroner's report is public knowledge. Bill Moscowitz has delayed writing up the autopsy report for as long as he can."

"I know you're doing your best." Naomi choked up.

Harry and Miranda, confused, looked at each other and then back at Rick.

Naomi nodded at him, so he spoke. "Roscoe was poisoned."

"*What!*" Tucker exclaimed.

"*I told you,*" Mrs. Murphy said.

"*Don't be so superior,*" Pewter complained.

"Naomi, I'm sorry, so very sorry." Mrs. Hogendobber reached over and grasped Naomi's hand.

"*Who'd want to kill him?*" Pewter's long white eyebrows rose.

"*Someone who failed algebra?*" Mrs. Murphy couldn't resist.

"*Hey, where's Tucker?*" Pewter asked.

Tucker had sneaked off alone to find Winston, the bulldog.

Harry said, "I'm sorry, Naomi."

Naomi wiped her thin nose with a pink tissue. "Poisoned! One of those strawberry drops was poison."

Cooper filled in the details. "He ingested malathion, which usually takes just minutes to kill someone."

Harry blurted out, "I ate one of those!"

"When?" Rick asked.

"Oh, two days before his death. Maybe three. You know Roscoe . . . always offering everyone candy." She felt queasy.

"Unfortunately, we don't know how he came to be poisoned. The candy in his car was safe."

• • •

They squeezed back into Harry's truck, the cats on Miranda's lap. Tucker, between the two humans, told everyone what Winston had said. *"Naomi cries all the time. She didn't kill him. Winston's positive."*

"There goes the obvious suspect in every murder case." Pewter curled up on Miranda's lap, which left little room for Mrs. Murphy.

"You could move over."

"Go sit on Harry's lap."

"Thanks, I will, you selfish toad."

Tucker nudged Murphy. *"Winston said Sandy Brashiers is over all the time."*

"Why?" Pewter inquired.

"Trying to figure out Roscoe's plans for this school year. He left few documents or guidelines, and April Shively is being a real bitch—according to Winston."

"Secretaries always fall in love with their bosses," Pewter added nonchalantly.

"Oh, Pewter." Murphy wrinkled her nose.

"They do!"

"Even if she was in love with him, it doesn't mean she'd be an obstructionist—good word, huh?" Tucker smiled, her big fangs gleaming.

"I'm impressed, Tucker." The tiger laughed. *"Of course she's an obstructionist. April doesn't like Sandy. Roscoe didn't either."*

"Guess Sandy's in for a rough ride." Pewter noticed one of Herb Jones's two cats sitting on the steps to his house. *"Look at Lucy Fur. She always shows off after her visit to the beauty parlor."*

"That long hair is pretty, but can you imagine taking care of it?" Mrs. Murphy, a practical puss, replied.

"I don't know what this world is coming to." Miranda shook her head.

"Poison is the coward's way to kill someone." Harry, still shaken from realizing she had eaten Roscoe's candies, growled, "Whoever it was was chickenshit."

"That's one way to put it." Miranda frowned.

"The question is, where did he get the poison and is there a tin of lethal candies out there waiting for another innocent victim?" Harry stroked Murphy, keeping her left hand on the wheel.

"We know one thing," Miranda pronounced firmly. "Whoever killed him was close to him . . . if malathion kills as fast as Coop says it does."

"Close and weak. I mean it. Poison is the coward's weapon."

In that Harry was half right and half wrong.

27

A light wind from the southeast raised the temperature into the low seventies. The day sparkled, leaves the color of butter vibrated in the breeze, and the shadows disappeared since it was noon.

Harry, home after cub hunting early in the morning, had rubbed down Poptart, turned her out with the other two horses, and was now scouring her stock trailer. Each year she repacked the bearings, inspected the boards, sanded off any rust, and repainted those areas. Right now her trailer resembled a dalmatian, spots everywhere. She'd put on the primer but didn't finish her task before cub hunting started, which was usually in September. Cubbing meant young hounds joined older ones, and young foxes learned along with the young hounds what was expected of them. With today's good weather she'd hoped to finish the job.

Blair lent her his spray painter. As Blair bought the best of everything, she figured she could get the job done in two hours, tops.

She'd bought metallic Superman-blue paint from Art Bushey, who gave her a good deal.

"*That stuff smells awful.*" Tucker wrinkled her nose at the paint cans.

"*She's going to shoot the whole afternoon on this.*" Pewter stretched. "*I'll mosey on up to the house.*"

"*Wimp. You could sleep under the maple tree and soak up the sunshine,*" Mrs. Murphy suggested.

"*Don't start one of your outdoor exercise lectures about how we felines are meant to run, jump, and kill. This feline was meant to rest on silk cushions and eat steak tartare.*"

"*Tucker, let's boogie.*" Mrs. Murphy shook herself, then scampered across the stable yard.

"*I'm not going, and don't you come back here and make up stories about what I've missed,*" Pewter called after them. "*And I don't want to hear about the bobcat either. That's a tall tale if I ever heard one.*" Then she giggled. "*'Cept they don't have tails.*" By now she was heading toward the house, carrying on a conversation with herself. "*Oh, and if it isn't the bobcat, then it's the bear and her two cubs. And if I hear one more time about how Tucker was almost drug under by an irate beaver while crossing the creek . . . next they'll tell me there's an elephant out there. Fine, they can get their pads cut up. I'm not.*" She sashayed into the screened-in porch and through the open door to the kitchen. "Mmm." Pewter jumped onto the counter to gobble up crumbs of Danish. "*What a pity that Harry isn't a cook.*"

She curled up on the counter, the sun flooding through the window over the sink, and fell fast asleep.

The cat and dog trotted toward the northwest. Usually they'd head to the creek that divided Harry's land from Blair Bainbridge's land, but as they'd seen him this morning when he brought over the paint sprayer on his way to cubbing, they decided to sprint in the other direction.

"*Pewter cracks me up.*" Mrs. Murphy laughed.

"*Me, too.*" Tucker stopped and lifted her nose. "*Deer.*"

"*Close?*"

"*Over there.*" The corgi indicated a copse of trees surrounded by high grass.

"Let's not disturb them. It's black-powder season, and there's bound to be some idiot around with a rifle."

"I don't mind a good hunter. They're doing us a favor. But the other ones . . ." The dog shuddered, then trotted on. "Mom and Blair didn't have much to say to each other, did they?"

"She was in a hurry. So was he." Mrs. Murphy continued, "Sometimes I worry about her. She's getting set in her ways. Makes it hard to mesh with a partner, know what I mean?"

"She likes living alone. All that time I wanted Fair to come back, which he's tried to do—I really think she likes being her own boss."

"Tucker, she was hardly your typical wife."

"No, but she made concessions."

"So did he." Mrs. Murphy stopped a moment to examine a large fox den. "Hey, you guys run this morning?"

"No," came the distant reply.

"Next week they'll leave from Old Greenwood Farm."

"Thanks."

"Since when did you get matey with foxes?" Tucker asked. "I thought you hated them."

"Nah, only some of them."

"Hypocrite."

"Stick-in-the-mud. Remember what Emerson said, 'A foolish consistency is the hobgoblin of little minds.' "

"Where are we going?" Tucker ignored Murphy's reference.

"Here, there, and everywhere." Mrs. Murphy swished her tail.

"Goody." The dog loved wandering with no special plan.

They ran through a newly mown hayfield. Grasshoppers flew up in the air, the faint rattle of their wings sounding like thousands of tiny castanets. The last of the summer's butterflies swooped around. Wolf spiders, some lugging egg sacs, hurried out of their way.

At the end of the field a line of large old hickories stood sentinel over a farm road rarely used since the Bowdens put down a better road fifty yards distant.

"Race you!" the cat called over her shoulder as she turned left on the road heading down to a deep ravine and a pond.

"Ha!" The dog bounced for joy, screeching after the cat.

Corgis, low to the ground, can run amazingly fast when stretched out to full body length. Since Mrs. Murphy zigged and zagged when she ran, Tucker soon overtook her.

"I win!" the dog shouted.

"*Only because I let you.*"

They tumbled onto each other, rolling in the sunshine. Springing to their feet, they ran some more, this time with the tiger soaring over the corgi, dipping in front of her and then jumping her from the opposite direction.

The sheer joy of it wore them out. They sat under a gnarled walnut at the base of a small spring.

Mrs. Murphy climbed the tree, gracefully walking out on a limb. "*Hey, there's a car over that rise.*"

"*No way.*"

"*Wanna bet?*"

They hurried up and over the small rise, the ruts in the road deeper than their own height. Stranded in the middle of the road was a 1992 red Toyota Camry with the license plates removed. As they drew closer they could see a figure in the driver's seat.

Tucker stopped and sniffed. "*Uh-oh.*"

Mrs. Murphy bounded onto the hood and stared, hair rising all over her body. Quickly she jumped off. "*There's a dead human in there.*"

"*How dead?*"

"*Extremely dead.*"

"*That's what I thought. Who is it?*"

"*Given the condition of the body, your guess is as good as mine. But it was once a woman. There's a blue barrette in her hair with roses on it, little yellow plastic roses.*"

"*We'd better go get Mom.*"

Mrs. Murphy walked away from the Camry and sat on the rise. She needed to collect her thoughts.

"*Tucker, it won't do any good. Mother won't know what we're telling her. The humans don't use this road anymore. It might be days, weeks, or even months before anyone finds this, uh, mess.*"

"*Maybe by that time she'll be bones.*"

"*Tucker!*"

"*Just joking.*" The dog leaned next to her dear friend. "*Trying to lighten the moment. After all, you don't know who it is. I can't see that high up. Humans commit suicide, you know. Could be one of those things. They like to shoot themselves in cars or hotel rooms. Drugs are for the wimps, I guess. I mean, how many ways can they kill themselves?*"

"*Lots of ways.*"

"*I never met a dog that committed suicide.*"

"*How could you? The dog would be dead.*"

"*Smart-ass.*" Tucker exhaled. "*Guess we'd better go back home.*"

On the way across the mown hayfield Murphy said out loud what they both were thinking. "*Let's hope it's a suicide.*"

They reached the farm in twenty minutes, rushing inside to tell Pewter, who refused to believe it.

"*Then come with us.*"

"*Murphy, I am not traipsing all over creation. It's soon time for supper. Anyway, what's a dead human to me?*"

"*You'd think someone would report a missing person, wouldn't you?*" Tucker scratched her shoulder.

"*So many humans live alone, they aren't missed for a long time. And she's been dead a couple of weeks,*" Murphy replied.

28

Puce-faced Little Marilyn, hands on hips, stood in the middle of Roscoe Fletcher's office, as angry as April Shively.

"You hand those files over!"

Coolly, relishing her moment of power, April replied, "Roscoe told me not to release any of this information until our Homecoming banquet."

Little Mim, a petite woman, advanced on April, not quite petite but small enough to be described as perky. "I am chair of the fund-raising committee. If I am to properly present St. Elizabeth's to potential donors, I need information. Roscoe and I were to have our meeting today and the files were to be released to me."

"I don't know that. It's not written in his schedule book." April shoved the book across his desk toward Marilyn, who ignored it.

Marilyn baited her. "I thought you knew everything there was to know about Roscoe."

"What's that supposed to mean?"

"Take it any way you like."

"Don't you dare accuse me of improper conduct with Roscoe! People always say that. They say it behind my back and think I don't know it." Her words were clipped, her speech precise.

"You *were* in love with him."

"I don't have to answer that. And I don't have to give you this file either."

"Then you're hiding something. I will convene the board and request an immediate audit."

"What I'm hiding is something good!" She sputtered. "It's a large donation by Maury McKinchie for the film department."

"Then show it to me. We'll celebrate together." Little Mim reached out her left hand, with the pinkie ring bearing the crest of the Urquharts.

"No! I take his last words to me as a sacred duty."

Exasperated, tired, and ready to bat April silly, Little Mim left, calling over her shoulder, "You will hear from a lawyer selected by the board and from an accounting firm. Good or bad, we must know the financial health of this institution."

"If Roscoe were alive, you wouldn't talk to me this way."

"April, if Roscoe were alive, I wouldn't talk to you at all."

29

Little Mim was as good as her word. She convened an emergency board meeting chaired by Sandy Brashiers. Sandy had the dolorous duty of telling the group that he believed April had removed files from Roscoe's office: she refused to cooperate even with Sheriff Shaw. The suspicion lurked in many minds that she might have taken other items, perhaps valuable ones like Roscoe's Cartier desk clock.

Alum bigwigs blew like bomb fragments. Kendrick Miller called Ned Tucker at home, asking him to represent the board. Ned agreed. Kendrick then handed State Senator Guyot his mobile phone to call the senior partner of a high-powered accounting firm in Richmond, rousing him from a tense game of snooker. He, too, agreed to help the board, waiving his not inconsiderable fee.

Maury McKinchie, the newest member of the board, suggested

this unsettling news not be discussed until the Homecoming banquet. He made no mention of his large bequest.

Sandy Brashiers then made a motion to dismiss April from her post.

Fair Haristeen, serving his last year on the board, stood up. "We need time to think this over before voting. April is out of line, but she's overcome by grief."

"That doesn't give her the right to steal school records and God knows what else." Sandy leaned back in his chair. Underneath the table he tapped his foot, thrilled that revenge was so quickly his.

"Perhaps one of us could talk to her," Fair urged.

"I tried."

"Marilyn," Maury folded his hands on the table, "she may resent you because you're a strong supporter of Sandy."

"I am," Little Mim said forthrightly, as Sandy tried not to grin from ear to ear. "We have put our differences behind us."

"I don't want to open a can of worms—after all that has happened—but there had been tension inside the administration, two camps, you might say, and we all know where April's sympathies rest," Fair said.

"As well as her body," Kendrick said, a bit too quickly.

"Come on, Kendrick!" Fair was disgusted. "We don't know that."

"I'm sorry," Kendrick said, "but she's grieving more than Naomi."

"That's inappropriate!" Maury banged the table, which surprised them all.

"She spent more time with him than his wife did." Kendrick held up his hands before him, palms outward, a calm-down signal.

"Who then will bell the cat?" Sandy returned to business, secretly loving this uproar.

No one raised a hand. An uncomfortable silence hung over the conference room.

Finally Maury sighed. "I can try. I have little history with her, which under the circumstances seems an advantage. And Roscoe and I were close friends."

Little Mim smiled wanly. "Thank you, Maury, no matter what the consequences."

"Hear, hear!"

Sandy noticed the lights were on in the gymnasium after the meeting adjourned. He threw on his scarf and his tweed jacket, crossing the quad to see what activity was in progress. He couldn't remember, but then he had a great deal on his mind.

Ahead of him, striding through the darkness, was Maury McKinchie, hands jammed into the pockets of an expensive lambskin jacket.

"Maury, where are you going?"

"Fencing exhibition." Maury's voice was level but he had little enthusiasm for Sandy Brashiers.

"Oh, Lord, I forgot all about it." Sandy recalled the university fencing club was visiting St. Elizabeth's hoping to find recruits for the future. One of Coach Hallvard's pet projects was to introduce fencing at the secondary-school level. It was her sport. She coached field hockey and lacrosse, and had even played on the World Cup lacrosse team in 1990, but fencing was her true love.

Sandy jogged up to Maury. "I'm starting to feel like the absent-minded professor."

"Goes with the territory," came the flat reply.

"I know how you must feel, Maury, and I'm sorry. Losing a friend is never easy. And I know Roscoe did not favor me. We were just—too different to really get along. But we both wanted the best for St. Elizabeth's."

"I believe that."

"I'm glad you're on the board. We can use someone whose vision and experience is larger than Albemarle County. I hope we can work together."

"Well, we can try. I'm going to keep my eye on things, going to try to physically be here, too—until some equilibrium is achieved."

Both men sidestepped the volatile question of a film department.

And neither man yet knew that Roscoe had been poisoned, which would have cast a pall over their conversation.

Sandy smiled. "This must seem like small beer to you—after Hollywood."

Maury replied, "At least you're doing something important: teaching the next generation. That was one of the things I most respected about Roscoe."

"Ah, but the question is, what do we teach them?"

"To ask questions." Maury opened the gym door for Sandy.

"Thank you." Sandy waited as Maury closed the door.

The two men found places in the bleachers.

Sean Hallahan was practicing thrusts with Roger Davis, not quite so nimble as the football player.

Karen Jensen, face mask down, parried with a University of Virginia sophomore.

Brooks and Jody attacked each other with épées.

Jody flipped up her mask. "I want to try the saber."

"Okay." Coach Hallvard switched Roger and Sean from saber to épée, giving the girls a chance at the heavier sword.

"Feels good," Jody said.

Brooks picked up the saber, resuming her position. Jody slashed at her, pressing as Brooks retreated.

Hallvard observed this burst of aggression out of the corner of her eye. "Jody, give me the saber."

Jody hesitated, then handed over the weapon. She walked off the gym floor, taking the bleacher steps two at a time to sit next to Maury.

"How did you like it?" he asked her.

"Okay."

"I never tried fencing. You need quick reflexes."

"Mr. McKinchie." She lowered her voice so Sandy Brashiers wouldn't hear. His attention was focused on the UVA fencers. "Have you seen the BMW Z3, the retro sports car? It's just beautiful."

"It is a great-looking machine." He kept his eyes on the other students.

"I want a bright red one." She smiled girlishly, which accentuated her smashing good looks.

He held his breath for an instant, then exhaled sharply. She squeezed his knee, then jumped up gracefully and rejoined her teammates.

Karen Jensen flipped up her face mask, glaring at Jody, who glared right back. "Did you give out already?"

"No, Coach took away my saber."

Roger, in position, lunged at Brooks. "Power thighs."

"Sounds—uh—" Brooks giggled, not finishing her sentence.

"You never know what's going to happen at St. E's." With Sean in tow, Karen joined them. "At least this is better than shooting those one-minute stories. I hated that."

"If it's not sports, you don't like it," Jody blandly commented on Karen's attitude.

"Took too long." Karen wiped her brow with a towel. "All that worrying about light. I thought our week of film studies was one of the most boring things we ever did."

"When did this happen?" Brooks asked.

"First week of school," Karen said. "Lucky you missed it."

"That's why Mr. Fletcher and Mr. McKinchie are, I mean, were, so tight," Sean said. " 'Cause Mr. Fletcher said if we are to be a modern school, then we have to teach modern art forms."

"Stick with me, I'll make you a star." Jody mimicked the dead headmaster.

"Mr. McKinchie said he'd try to get old equipment donated to the school."

"I didn't think it was boring," Sean told Brooks.

"Mr. Fletcher said we'd be the only prep school in the nation with a hands-on film department," Karen added. "Hey, see you guys in a minute." She left to talk to one of the young men on the fencing team. Sean seethed.

"She likes older men," Jody tormented him.

"At least she likes men," Sean, mean-spirited, snarled at her.

"Drop dead, Hallahan," Roger said.

Jody, surprisingly calm considering her behavior the last two weeks, replied, "He can call me anything he wants, Roger. I couldn't care less. This dipshit school is not the world, you know. It's just his world."

"What's that supposed to mean?" Sean, angry, took it out on Jody.

"You're a big frog in a small pond. Like—who cares?" She smiled, a hint of malice in her eyes. "Karen's after bigger game than a St. Elizabeth halfback."

Sean's eyes followed Karen.

"She's not the only woman in the world." He feigned indifference.

"No, but she's the one you want," Jody said, needling him more.

Roger gently put his hand under Brooks's elbow, wheeling her away from the squabbling Jody and Sean. "Would you go with me to the Halloween dance?"

"Uh—" She brightened. "Yes."

30

Harry dropped the feed scoop in the sweet feed when the phone rang in the tack room.

She hurried in and picked up the phone. It was 6:30 A.M.

"Miranda, it had to be you."

"Just as Rick Shaw said, the story of Roscoe's poisoning is finally in the paper. But no one is using the word 'murder.' "

"Huh—well, what does it say?"

"There's the possibility of accidental ingestion, but deliberate poisoning can't be ruled out. Rick's soft-pedaling it."

"What has me baffled is the motive. Roscoe was a good headmaster. He liked the students. They liked him, and the parents did, too. There's just something missing—or who knows, maybe it was random, like when a disgruntled employee put poison in Tylenol."

"That was heinous."

"Except—I don't know—I'm just lost. I can't think of any reason for him to be killed."

"He wasn't rich. He appeared to have no real enemies. He had disagreements with people like Sandy Brashiers, but"—Miranda stopped to cough—"well, I guess that's why we have a sheriff's department. If there is something, they'll find it."

"You're right," Harry responded with no conviction whatsoever.

31

The repeated honking of a car horn brought Harry to the front window of the post office. Tucker, annoyed, started barking. Mrs. Murphy opened one eye. Then she opened both eyes.

"Would you look at that?" Harry exclaimed.

Miranda, swathed in an old cashmere cardigan—she was fighting off the sniffles—craned her neck. "Isn't that the cutest thing you ever saw?"

Pewter bustled out of Market's store. She had put in an appearance today, primarily because she knew sides of pork would be carried in to hang in the huge back freezer.

Jody Miller, her black eye fading, emerged from a red BMW sports car. The fenders were rounded, the windshield swept back at an appealing angle. She hopped up the steps to the post office.

Harry opened the door for her. "What a beautiful car!"

"I know." The youngster shivered with delight.

"Did your father buy you that?" Miranda thought of her little Ford Falcon. As far as she was concerned, the styling was as good as this far more expensive vehicle's.

"No, I bought it myself. When Grandpa died, he left money for me, and it's been drawing interest. It finally made enough to buy a new car!"

"Has everyone at school seen it?" Harry asked.

"Yeah, and are they jealous."

Since she was the first student to come in to pick up mail that day, neither woman knew what the kids' responses were to the newspaper story.

"How are people taking the news about Mr. Fletcher?" Miranda inquired.

Jody shrugged. "Most people think it was some kind of accident. People are really mad at Sean, though. A lot of kids won't talk to him now. I'm not talking to him either."

"Rather a strange accident," Miranda mumbled.

"Mr. Fletcher was kind of absentminded." Jody bounced the mail on the counter, evening it. "I liked him. I'll miss him, too, but Dad says people have a shelf life and Mr. Fletcher's ran out. He said there really aren't accidents. People decide when to go."

"Only the Lord decides that." Miranda firmly set her jaw.

"Mrs. Hogendobber, you'll have to take that up with Dad. It's"—she glanced at the ceiling, then back at the two women—"too deep for me. 'Bye." She breezed out the door.

"Kendrick sounds like a misguided man—and a cold-blooded one." Miranda shook her head as Pewter popped through the animal door, sending the flap whapping.

"Hey, I'd look good in that car."

"Pewter, you need a station wagon." Mrs. Murphy jabbed at her when she jumped on the counter.

"I am growing weary, very weary, of these jokes about my weight. I am a healthy cat. My bones are different from yours. I don't say anything about your hair thinning on your belly."

"Is not!"

"Mmm." The gray cat was noncommittal, which infuriated the tiger.

"*Do cats get bald?*" Tucker asked.

"*She is.*"

"*Pewter, I am not.*" Mrs. Murphy flopped on her back, showing the world her furry tummy.

Harry noticed this brazen display. "Aren't you the pretty puss?"

"*Bald.*"

"*Am not.*" Mrs. Murphy twisted her head to glare at Pewter.

"Wouldn't you love to know what this is about?" Harry laughed.

"Yes, I would." Miranda looked at the animals pensively. "How do I know they aren't talking about us?"

"And this coming from a woman who didn't like cats."

"Well—"

"You used to rail at me for bringing Mrs. Murphy and Tucker to work, and you said it was unclean for Market to have Pewter in the store."

Mrs. Hogendobber tickled Mrs. Murphy's stomach. "I have repented of my ways. 'O Lord, how manifold are thy works! In wisdom hast thou made them all: the earth is full of thy riches.' Psalm one hundred four." She smiled. "Cats and dogs are part of His riches."

As if on cue, the Reverend Herbert Jones strolled in. "Girls."

"Herb, how are you?"

"Worried." He opened his mailbox, the metal rim clicking when it hit the next box because he opened it hard. "Roscoe Fletcher murdered . . ." He shook his head.

"The paper didn't say he was murdered—just poisoned," Harry said.

"Harry, I've known you all your life. You think he was murdered, just as I do."

"I do. I wanted to see if you knew something I didn't," she replied sheepishly.

"You think his wife killed him?" Herb closed the mailbox, ignoring her subterfuge.

"I don't know," Harry said slowly.

"Fooling around, I'll bet you," Miranda commented.

"A lot of men fool around. That doesn't mean they're killed for it." Herb lightly slapped the envelopes against his palm.

Miranda shook her head. "Perhaps retribution is at work, but there's something eerie about Roscoe's obituary appearing in the paper. The murderer was advertising!"

"Some kind of power trip." He paused, staring at Mrs. Murphy. "And Sean Hallahan is the cat's-paw."

"Yes, Herb, just so." Miranda removed her half glasses to clean them. "I know I've harped to Harry about the obituary, but it upsets me so much. I can't get it out of my mind."

"So the killer, who I still say is a coward, is taunting us?"

"No, Harry, the killer was taunting Roscoe, although I doubt he recognized that. He thought it was a joke, I really believe that. The killer was someone or is someone he discounted." Herb waved his envelopes with an emphatic flourish. "And Sean Hallahan was the fall guy."

"In that case I wouldn't want to be in Maury McKinchie's shoes or Sean's."

"Me neither." Harry echoed Miranda.

"Then perhaps the killer is someone we've discounted." The Reverend Jones pointed his envelopes at Harry.

"You've got to be pushed to the edge to kill. Being ignored or belittled isn't a powerful enough motive to kill," Harry said sensibly.

"I agree with you there." Herb's deep voice filled the room. "There's more to it. You think Rick is guarding McKinchie?"

"I'll ask him." Miranda picked up the phone. She explained their thinking to Rick, who responded that he, too, had considered that Maury and Sean might be in jeopardy. He didn't have enough people in the department for a guard, but he sent officers to cruise by the farm. Maury himself had hired a bodyguard. Rick requested that Miranda, Harry, and Herb stop playing amateur detective.

Miranda then replayed this information minus the crack about being amateurs.

"Cool customer," Herb said.

"Huh?"

"Harry, Maury never said anything about a bodyguard."

"I'd sure tell—if for no other reason than hoping it got back to the killer. It'd put him on notice."

"Miranda, the killer could be in Paris by now," Herb said.

"No." Miranda pushed aside the mail cart. "We'd know who it is then. The killer can't go, and furthermore, he or she doesn't want to go."

"*The old girl is cooking today, isn't she?*" Pewter meowed admiringly.

"*That body in the Toyota has something to do with this,*" Mrs. Murphy stated firmly.

"*Nah.*"

"*Pewter, when we get home tonight, I'll take you there,*" Mrs. Murphy promised.

"*I'm not walking across all those fields in the cold.*"

"Fine." Mrs. Murphy stomped away from her.

Susan walked in the backdoor. "Harry, you've got to help me."

"Why?"

"Danny's in charge of the Halloween maze at Crozet High this year. I forgot and like an idiot promised to be a chaperon at the St. Elizabeth's Halloween dance."

"You still haven't figured out how to be in two places at the same time?" Harry laughed at her. As they had exhaustively discussed Roscoe's demise over the phone, there was no reason to repeat their thoughts.

"All the St. Elizabeth's kids will go through the maze and then go on to their own dance." Susan paused. "I can't keep everyone's schedules straight. I wouldn't even remember my own name if it wasn't sewn inside my coat."

"I'll do it"—Harry folded her arms across her chest—"and extract my price later."

"I do not have enough money to buy you a new truck." Susan caught her mail as Harry tossed it to her, a blue nylon belt wrapped around it. "Actually, your truck looks new now that you've painted it."

"*Everything on our farm is Superman blue,*" Murphy cracked, "*even the manure spreader.*"

That evening Mrs. Murphy and Tucker discussed how to lure a human to the ditched car. They couldn't think of a way to get Harry to follow them for that great a distance. A human might go one hundred yards or possibly even two hundred yards, but after that their attention span wavered.

"*I think we'll have to trust to luck.*" Tucker paced the barn center aisle.

"*You know, they say that killers return to the scene of the crime.*" Mrs. Murphy thought out loud.

"*That's stupid,*" Pewter interjected. "*If they had a brain in their head, they'd get out of there as fast as they could.*"

"*The emotion. Murder must be a powerful emotion for them. Maybe they go back to tap into that power.*" The tiger, on the rafters, passed over the top of Gin Fizz's stall.

Pewter, curled on a toasty horse blanket atop the tack trunk, disagreed. "*Powerful or not, it would be blind stupid to go down Bowden's Lane. Think about it.*"

"*I am thinking about it! I can't figure out how to get somebody out there.*"

"*You really don't want Mother to see it, do you?*" Tucker saw a shadowy little figure zip into a stall. "*Mouse.*"

"*I know.*" Mrs. Murphy focused on the disappearing tail. "*Does it to torment. Anyway, you're right. It's a grisly sight, and it would give Mother nightmares. Didn't like it much myself, and we're tougher about those things than humans.*"

"*In the old days humans left their criminals hanging from gibbets or rotting in cages. They put heads on the gates in London.*" Tucker imagined a city filled with the aroma of decay, quite pleasing to a dog.

"*Those days are long gone. Death is sanitized now.*" Pewter watched the mouse emerge and dash in the opposite direction. "*What is this, the Mouse Olympics?*"

A squeaky laugh followed this remark.

"*Those mice have no respect,*" Tucker grumbled.

32

Hands patiently folded in his lap, Rick sat in the Hallahan living room. Sean, his mother, father, and younger brother sat listening.

Cynthia had perched on the raised fireplace hearth and was taking notes.

"Sean, I don't want to be an alarmist, but if you did not act alone in placing that obituary, you've got to tell me. The other person may have pertinent information about Mr. Fletcher's death."

"So he was murdered?" Mr. Hallahan exclaimed.

Rick soothingly replied, opening his hands for effect, "I'm a sheriff. I have to investigate all possibilities. It could have been an accident."

Sean, voice clear, replied, "I did it. Alone. I wish I hadn't done it. Kids won't talk to me at school. I mean, some will, but others are acting like I killed him. It's like I've got the plague."

Sympathetically Cooper said, "It will pass, but we need your help."

Rick looked at each family member. "If any of you know anything, please, don't hold back."

"I wish we did," Mrs. Hallahan, a very pretty brunette, replied.

"Did anyone ever accompany your son on his paper route?"

"Sheriff, not to my knowledge." Mr. Hallahan crossed and uncrossed his legs, a nervous habit. "He lost the route, as I'm sure you know."

"Sean?" Rick said.

"No. No one else wanted to get up that early."

Rick stood up. "Folks, if anything comes to mind—anything—call me or Deputy Cooper."

"Are we in danger?" Mrs. Hallahan asked sensibly.

"If Sean is telling the truth—no."

33

Later that evening Sean walked into the garage to use the telephone. His father had phones in the bathrooms, bedrooms, kitchen, and in his car. Sean felt the garage was the most private place; no one would walk in on him.

He dialed and waited. "Hello."

"What do you want?"

"I don't appreciate you not talking to me at school. That's a crock of shit."

Jody seethed on the other end of her private line. "That's not why I'm ignoring you."

"Oh?" His voice dripped sarcasm.

"I'm ignoring you because you've got a crush on Karen Jensen. I was just convenient this summer, wasn't I?"

A pause followed this astute accusation. "You said we were friends, Jody. You said—"

"I know what I said, but I hardly expected us to go back to school and you try to jump Karen's bones. Jeez."

"I am not trying to jump her bones."

"You certainly jumped mine. I can't believe I was that stupid."

"Stupid. You wanted to do it as much as I did."

"Because I liked you."

"Well, I liked you, too, but we were friends. It wasn't a"—he thought for a neutral word—"like a hot romance. Friends."

"Friends don't sleep with each other's best friends . . . and besides, you wouldn't be the first."

"First what?"

"First guy to sleep with Karen. She tells me *everything*."

"Who did she sleep with?" Tension and a note of misery edged his voice.

"That's for me to know and for you to find out," she taunted. "I'm never letting you touch me again." As an afterthought she added, "And you can't drive my BMW either!"

"Do your parents know about the car?" he asked wearily, his brain racing for ways to get the information about Karen from Jody.

"No."

"Jody, if you had wanted . . . more, I wish you'd told me then, not now. And if you don't speak to me at school, people will think it's because of the obit."

"All you think about is yourself. What about me?"

"I like you." He wasn't convincing.

"I'm convenient."

"Jody, we have fun together. This summer was—great."

"But you've got the hots for Karen."

"I wouldn't put it like that."

"You'd better forget all about Karen. First of all, she knows you've slept with me. She's not going to believe a word you say. And furthermore, I can make life really miserable for you if I feel like it. I'll tell everyone you gave me my black eye."

"Jody, I never told anyone I slept with you. Why would you tell?" He ignored the black eye threat. Jody had told him her father gave her the black eye.

"Because I felt like it." Exasperated, she hung up the phone, leaving a dejected Sean shivering in the garage.

34

Larry Johnson removed his spectacles, rubbing the bridge of his nose where they pinched it. He replaced them, glanced over Jody Miller's file, and then left his office, joining her in an examining room.

"How are you?"

"I'm okay, I think." She sat on the examining table when he motioned for her to do so.

"You were just here in August for your school physical."

"I know. I think it's stupid that I have to have a physical before every season. Coach Hallvard insists on it."

"Every coach insists on it." He smiled. "Now what seems to be the problem?"

"Well"—Jody swallowed hard—"I, uh, I've missed my period for two months in a row."

"I see." He touched his stethoscope. "Have you been eating properly?"

"Uh—I guess."

"The reason I ask that is often female athletes, especially the ones in endurance sports, put the body under such stress that they go without their period for a time. It's the body's way of protecting itself because they couldn't bring a baby to term. Nature is wise."

"Oh." She smiled reflexively. "I don't think field hockey is one of those sports."

"Next question." He paused. "Have you had sexual relations?"

"Yes—but I'm not telling."

"I'm not asking." He held up his hand like a traffic cop. "But there are a few things I need to know. You're seventeen. Have you discussed this with your parents?"

"No," she said quickly.

"I see."

"I don't talk to them. I don't want to talk to them."

"I understand."

"No, you don't."

"Let's start over, Jody. Did you use any form of birth control?"

"No."

"Well, then"—he exhaled—"let's get going."

He took blood for a pregnancy test, at the same time pulling a vial of blood to be tested for infectious diseases. He declined to inform Jody of this. If something turned up, he'd tell her then.

"I hate that." She turned away as the needle was pulled from her arm.

"I do, too." He held the small cotton ball on her arm. "Did your mother ever talk to you about birth control?"

"Yes."

"I see."

She shrugged. "Dr. Johnson, it's not as easy as she made it sound."

"Perhaps not. The truth is, Jody, we don't really understand human sexuality, but we do know that when those hormones start flowing through your body, a fair amount of irrationality seems to flow with them. And sometimes we turn to people for comfort during difficult times, and sex becomes part of the comfort." He smiled.

"Come back on Friday." He glanced at his calendar. "Umm, make it Monday."

"All right." She paled. "You won't tell anyone, will you?"

"No. Will you?"

She shook her head no.

"Jody, if you can't talk to your mother, you ought to talk to another older woman. Whether you're pregnant or not, you might be surprised to learn that you aren't alone. Other people have felt what you're feeling."

"I'm not feeling much."

He patted her on the back. "Okay, then. Call me Monday."

She mischievously winked as she left the examining room.

35

Not wishing to appear pushy, Sandy Brashiers transferred his office to the one next to Roscoe Fletcher's but made no move to occupy the late headmaster's sacred space.

April Shively stayed just this side of rude. If Naomi asked her to perform a chore, retrieve information, or screen calls, April complied. She and Naomi had a cordial, if not warm, relationship. If Sandy asked, she found a variety of ways to drag her heels.

Although the jolt of Roscoe's death affected her every minute of the day, Naomi Fletcher resumed her duties as head of the lower school. She needed the work to keep her mind from constantly returning to the shock, and the lower school needed her guidance during this difficult time.

During lunch hour, Sandy walked to Naomi's office, then both of them walked across the quad to the upper school administration building—Old Main.

"Becoming the leader is easier than being the teacher, isn't it?" Naomi asked him.

"I guess for these last seven years I've been the loyal opposition." He tightened the school scarf around his neck. "I'm finding out that no matter what decision I make there's someone to 'yes' me, someone to 'no' me, and everyone to second-guess me. It's curious to realize how people want to have their own way without doing the work."

She smiled. "Monday morning quarterbacks. Roscoe used to say that they never had to take the hits." She wiggled her fingers in her fur-lined gloves. "He wasn't your favorite person, Sandy, but he was an effective headmaster."

"Yes. My major disagreement with Roscoe was not over daily operations. You know I respected his administrative skills. My view of St. Elizabeth's curriculum was one hundred eighty degrees from his, though. We must emphasize the basics. Take, for instance, his computer drive. Great. We've got every kid in this school computer literate. So?" He threw up his hands. "They stare into a lighted screen. Knowing how to use the technology is useless if you have nothing to say, and the only way you can have something to say is by studying the great texts of our culture. The computer can't read and comprehend *The Federalist Papers* for them."

"Teaching people to think is an ancient struggle," she said. "That's why I love working in the lower school . . . they're so young . . . their minds are open. They soak up everything."

He opened the door for her. They stepped into the administration building, which also had some classrooms on the first floor. A blast of warm radiator heat welcomed them.

They climbed the wide stairs to the second floor, entering Roscoe's office from the direction that did not require them to pass April's office.

She was on her hands and knees putting videotapes into a cardboard box. The tapes had lined a bottom shelf of the bookcase.

"April, I can do that," Naomi said.

Not rising, April replied, "These are McKinchie's. I thought I'd return them to him this afternoon." She held up a tape of *Red River*. "He lent us his library for film history week."

"Yes, he did, and I forgot all about it." Naomi noticed the girls of the field hockey team leaving the cafeteria together. Karen Jensen, in the lead, was tossing an apple to Brooks Tucker.

"April, I'll be moving into this office next week. I can't conduct meetings in that small temporary office. Will you call Design Interiors for me? I'd like them to come out here." Sandy's voice was clear.

"What's wrong with keeping things just as they are? It will save money." She dropped more tapes into the box, avoiding eye contact.

"I need this office to be comfortable—"

"This is comfortable," she interrupted.

"—for me," he continued.

"Well, you might not be appointed permanent headmaster. The board will conduct a search. Why spend money?"

"April, that won't happen before this school year is finished." Naomi stepped in, kind but firm. "Sandy needs our support in order to do the best job he can for St. Elizabeth's. Working in Roscoe's shadow"—she indicated the room, the paintings—"isn't the way to do that."

April scrambled to her feet. "Why are you helping him? He dogged Roscoe every step of the way!"

Naomi held up her hands, still gloved, in a gesture of peace. "April, Sandy raised issues inside our circle that allowed us to prepare for hard questions from the board. He wasn't my husband's best friend, but he has always had the good of St. Elizabeth's at heart."

April clamped her lips shut. "I don't want to do it, but I'll do it for you." She picked up the carton and walked by Sandy, closing the door behind her.

He exhaled, jamming his hands in his pockets. "Naomi, I don't ask that April be fired. She's given long years of service, but there's absolutely no way I can work with her or her with me. I need to find my own secretary—and that will bump up the budget."

She finally took off her gloves to sit on the edge of Roscoe's massive desk. "We'll have to fire her, Sandy. She'll foment rebellion from wherever she sits."

"Maybe McKinchie could use her. He has enough money, and she'd be happy in his little home office."

"She won't be happy anywhere." Naomi hated this whole subject. "She was so in love with Roscoe—I used to tease him about it. No one will ever measure up to him in her eyes. You know, I believe if he had asked her to walk to hell and back, she would have." She smiled ruefully. "Of course, she didn't have to live with him."

"Well, I won't ask her to walk that far, but I guess you're right. She'll have to go."

"Let's talk to Marilyn Sanburne first. Perhaps she'll have an idea—or Mim."

"Good God, Mim will run St. Elizabeth's if you let her."

"The world." Naomi swung her legs to and fro. "St. Elizabeth's is too small a stage for Mim the Magnificent."

April opened the door. "I know you two are talking about me."

"At this precise moment we were talking about Mim."

Sourly, April shut the door. Sandy and Naomi looked at each other and shrugged.

36

"How did I get roped into this?" Harry complained.

Her furry family said nothing as she fumbled with her hastily improvised costume. Preferring a small group of friends to big parties, Harry had to be dragged to larger affairs. Even though this was a high school dance and she was a chaperon, she still had to unearth something to wear, snag a date, stand on her feet, and chat up crashing bores. She thought of the other chaperons. One such would be Maury McKinchie, fascinating to most people but not to Harry. Since he was a chaperon, she'd have to gab with him. His standard fare, those delicious stories of what star did what and to whom on his various films, filled her with ennui. Had he been a hunting man she might have endured him, but he was not. He also appeared much too interested in her breasts. Maury was one of those men who didn't look you in the eye when he spoke to you—he spoke to your breasts.

Sandy Brashiers she liked until he grew waspish about the other faculty at St. Elizabeth's. With Roscoe dead he would need to find a new whipping boy. Still, he looked her in the eye when he spoke to her, and that was refreshing.

Ed Sugarman collected old cigarette advertisements. He might expound on the chemical properties of nicotine, but if she could steer him toward soccer, he proved knowledgeable and entertaining.

Coach Hallvard could be lively. Harry then remembered that the dreaded Florence Rubicon would be prowling the dance floor. Harry's Latin ebbed away with each year but she remembered enough Catullus to keep the old girl happy.

Harry laughed to herself. Every Latin teacher and subsequent professor she had ever studied under had been an odd duck, but there was something so endearing about them all. She kept reading Latin partly to bask in the full bloom of eccentricity.

"I can't wear this!" Harry winced, throwing off a tight pump. The patent leather shoe scuttled across the floor. She checked the clock, groaning anew.

"There's time," Mrs. Murphy said. "Can the tuxedo. It isn't you."

"I fed you."

"Don't be obtuse. Get out of the tuxedo." Murphy spoke louder, a habit of hers when humans proved dense. "You need something with imagination."

"Harry doesn't have imagination," Tucker declared honestly.

"She has good legs," Pewter replied.

"What does that have to do with imagination?" Tucker wanted to know.

"Nothing, but she should wear something that shows off her legs."

Mrs. Murphy padded into the closet. "There's one sorry skirt hanging in here."

"I didn't even know Mom owned a skirt."

"This has to be a leftover from college." The tiger inspected the brown skirt.

Pewter joined her. "I thought she was going to clean out her closet?"

"She organized her chest of drawers; that's a start."

The two cats peered upward at the skirt, then at each other.

"Shall we?"

"Let's." Pewter's eyes widened.

They reached up, claws unsheathed, and shredded the skirt.

"Wheee!" They dug in.

Harry, hearing the sound of cloth shredding, poked her head in the closet, the single light bulb swaying overhead. "Hey!"

With one last mighty yank, Mrs. Murphy scooted out of the closet. Pewter, a trifle slower, followed.

Harry, aghast, took out the skirt. "I could brain you two. I've had this skirt since my sophomore year at Crozet High."

"We know," came the titters from under the bed.

"Cats can be so destructive." Tucker's soulful eyes brimmed with sympathy.

"Brownnoser!" Murphy accused.

"I am a mighty cat. What wondrous claws have I. I can rip and tear and even shred the sky," Pewter sang.

"Great. Ruin my skirt and now caterwaul underneath the bed." Harry knelt down to behold four luminous chartreuse eyes peeking at her. "Bad kitties."

"Hee hee."

"I mean it. No treats for you."

Pewter leaned into Murphy. *"This is your fault."*

"Sell me out for a treatie." Mrs. Murphy bumped her.

Harry dropped the dust ruffle back down. She stared at the ruined skirt.

Murphy called out from her place of safety, *"Go as a vagabond. You know, go as one of those poor characters from a Victor Hugo novel."*

"Wonder if I could make a costume out of this?"

"She got it!" Pewter was amazed.

"Don't count your chickens." Mrs. Murphy slithered out from under the bed. *"I'll make sure she puts two and two together."*

With that she launched herself onto the bed and from the bed she hurtled toward the closet, catching the clothes. She hung there, swaying, then found the tattiest shirt she could find. She sank her claws in and slid down to the floor, the intoxicating sound of rent fabric heralding her descent.

"You're crazy!" Harry dashed after her, but Murphy blasted into the living room, jumped on a chair arm, then wiggled her rear end as though she was going to leap into the bookshelves filled not only with books but with Harry's ribbons and trophies. "Don't you dare."

"*Then leave me alone,*" Murphy sassed, "*and put together your vagabond costume. Time's a-wasting.*"

The human and the cat squared off, eye to eye. "You're in a mood, pussycat."

Tucker tiptoed out. Pewter remained under the bed, straining to hear.

"What's got into you?"

"*It's Halloween,*" Murphy screeched.

Harry reached over to grab the insouciant feline, but Mrs. Murphy easily avoided her. She hopped to the other side of the chair, then ran back into the bedroom where she leapt into the clothes and tore them up some more.

"*Yahoo! Banzai! Death to the Emperor!*"

"*Have you been watching those World War Two movies again?*" Tucker laughed.

"*Don't shoot until you see the whites of their eyes.*" Murphy leapt in the air, turning full circle and landing in the middle of the clothes.

"*She's on a military kick.*" Pewter snuck out from under the bed. "*If you get us both punished, Murphy, I will be really upset.*"

Murphy catapulted off the bed right onto Pewter. The two rolled across the bedroom floor, entertaining Harry with their catfight.

Finally Pewter, put out, extricated herself from the grasp of Murphy. She stalked off to the kitchen.

"*Fraidycat.*"

"*Mental case,*" Pewter shot back.

"Anything that happens tonight will be dull after this," Harry said with a sigh.

Boy, did she have a wrong number.

37

Little Mim, taut under her powdered face, wig bobbling, wandered across the highly polished gym floor to Harry. At least she thought it was Harry because the vagabond's escort, a pirate, was too tall to be anyone but Fair.

The dance was turning into a huge success, thanks to the band, Yada Yada Yada.

The curved sword, stuck through his sash, gave Fair a dangerous air. Other partyers wore swords. There was Stonewall Jackson and Julius Caesar. A few wore pistols that upon close examination turned out to be squirt guns.

Karen Jensen, behind a golden mask, drove the boys wild because she came as a golden-haired Artemis. Quite a bit of Karen was showing, and it was prime grade.

But then, quite a bit of Harry was showing, and that wasn't bad either.

Little Mim put her hand on Harry's forearm. "Could I have a minute?"

"Sure. Fair, I'll be right back."

"Okay," he replied from under his twirling mustache.

Marilyn pulled Harry into a corner of the auditorium. Madonna and King Kong were making out behind them. King Kong was having a hard time of it.

"I hope you aren't cross with me. I should have called you."

"About what?"

"I asked Blair to the dance. Well, it wasn't just that I needed an escort, but I thought I might interest him in the school and—"

"I have no claim on him. Anyway, we're just friends," Harry said soothingly.

"Thanks. I'd hoped you'd understand." Her wig wobbled. "How did they manage with these things?" She glanced around. "Can you guess who Stonewall Jackson is?"

"Mmm, the paunch means he's a chaperon," Harry stated.

"Kendrick Miller."

"Where's Irene? It isn't World War Three yet with those two, is it?"

"Irene's over there. It'd be a perfect costume if she were twenty years younger. Some women can't accept getting old, I guess." She indicated the woodland fairy, the wings diaphanous over the thin wire. Then, lowering her voice, "Did you see April Shively? Dressed as a witch. How appropriate."

"I thought you liked April?"

Realizing she might have said too much, Little Mim backtracked. "She's not herself since Roscoe's death, and she's making life difficult for everyone from the board on down to the faculty. It will pass."

"Or she will," Harry joked.

"Two bewitching masked beauties." Maury McKinchie complimented them from behind his Rhett Butler mask.

"What a line!" Harry laughed, her voice giving her away.

"May I have this dance?" Maury bowed to Harry, who took a turn on the floor.

Little Mim, happy she wasn't asked, hastened to Blair as fast as her wig would allow.

Sean Hallahan, dressed as a Hell's Angel, danced with Karen Jensen. After the dance ended, he escorted her off the floor. "Karen, is everyone mad at me?"

Jody, dragged along by her mother, glared at Sean. She was in a skeleton outfit that concealed her face, but Sean knew it was Jody.

"Jody is."

"Are you mad at me?"

"No."

"I feel like you've been avoiding me."

"Field hockey practice takes up as much time as football practice." She paused, clearing her throat. "And you've been a little weird lately—distant."

"Yeah, I know."

"Sean, you couldn't help the way things turned out—Mr. Fletcher's dying—and until then it was pretty funny. Even the phony obituary for Mr. McKinchie was funny."

"I didn't do that."

"I know, it was on Roger's paper route, and he says he didn't do it either."

"But I *really* didn't." He sensed her disbelief.

"Okay, okay."

"That's an incredible costume," he said admiringly.

"Thanks."

"Karen—do you like me a little?"

"A little," she said teasingly, "but what about Jody?"

"It's not—well, you know. We're close but not that way. We practiced a lot this summer and—"

"Practiced what?"

"Tennis. It's our spring sport." He swallowed hard.

"Oh." She remembered Jody's version of the summer.

"Will you go out with me next Friday after the game?"

"Yes," she said without hesitation.

He smiled, pushing her back out on the dance floor.

Coach Renee Hallvard, dressed as Garfield the cat, sidled up next to Harry.

"Harry, is that you?"

"Coach?"

"Yes, or should I say 'Meow'?"

"Wonder what Mrs. Murphy would say about this?"

Coach reached back, draping her tail over her arm. "Get a life."

They both laughed.

"She probably would say that."

"If you don't mind, I'll drop off this year's field hockey rule book on Monday."

"Why?" Harry murmured expectantly.

"I need a backup referee—just in case. You know the game."

"Oh, Coach. Make Susan do it."

"She can't." Coach Hallvard laughed at Harry. "Brooks is on the team."

"Well—okay."

Coach Hallvard clapped her on the back. "You're a good sport."

"Sucker is more like it."

Rhett Butler asked Harry to dance a second time. "You've got beautiful legs."

"Thank you," she murmured.

"I ought to give you a screen test."

"Get out of here." Harry thumped his back with her left hand.

"You're very attractive. The camera likes some people. It might like you." He paused. "What's so curious is that even professionals don't know who will be good on-screen and who won't."

"Rhett," she joked because she knew it was Maury, "I bet you say that to all the girls."

"Ha." He threw his head back and laughed. "Just the pretty ones."

"In fact, I heard you have a car full of vital essences, so you must have said something to BoomBoom."

"Oh!" His voice lowered. "What was I thinking?"

Part of Maury's charm was that he never pretended to be better than he was.

"Hey, I'll never tell."

"You won't have to. She will." He sighed, "You see, Harry, I'm a man who needs a lot of attention, female attention. I admit it."

Stonewall and Garfield, dancing near them, turned their heads. "You don't give a damn who you seduce and who you hurt. You don't need attention, you need your block knocked off," Kendrick Miller, as Stonewall, mumbled.

Rhett danced on. "Kendrick Miller, you're a barrel of laughs. I say what I think. You think being a repressed Virginian is a triumph. I think you're pathetic."

Kendrick stopped. Coach Hallvard stepped back.

"Guys. Chill out," Harry told them.

"I'll meet you after the dance, McKinchie. You say where and when."

"Are we going to fight a duel, Kendrick? Do I get the choice of weapons?"

"Sure."

"Pies. You need a pie in the face."

Harry dragged Maury backward. She had heard about Kendrick's flash temper.

"Since we can't use guns, we can start with fists," Kendrick called after him as Renee Hallvard pulled him in the direction opposite Maury.

As the dancers closed the spaces left by the vacating couples, a few noticed the minor hostilities. Fortunately, most of the students were wrapped up in the music and one another.

Jody put her hands on her hips, turned her back on her father, and walked to the water fountain. She had to take off the mask to drink.

"What a putz!" Maury shook his head.

"No one has ever accused Kendrick of having a good time or a sense of humor." Harry half laughed.

"Totally humorless." Maury emphasized the word. "Thank God his kid doesn't take after him. Funny thing, though, the camera liked Jody, and yet Karen Jensen is the more beautiful girl. I noticed that when we had our one-day film clinic."

"Hmm."

"Ah, the camera . . . it reveals things the naked eye can't see." He bowed. "Thank you, madam. Don't forget your screen test."

She curtseyed. "Sir." Then she whispered, "Where's your bodyguard?"

He winked. "I made that up."

Fair ambled over when he'd gone. "Slinging the bull, as usual?"

"Actually, we were talking about the camera . . . after he had a few words with Kendrick Miller. Testosterone poisoning."

"If you keep saying that, I'll counter with 'raging hormones.' "

"You do, anyway, behind our backs."

"I do not."

"Most men do."

"I'm not most men."

"No, you aren't." She slipped her arm through his.

The evening progressed without further incident, except that Sean Hallahan had a flask of booze in his motorcycle jacket. No one saw him drinking from it, but he swayed on his feet after each return from outside.

He got polluted, and when someone dressed as a Musketeer showed up at the party, sword in hand, and knocked him down, he couldn't get up.

As Yada Yada Yada played the last song of the evening, some of the kids began sneaking off. Roger and Brooks danced the last dance. They were a hit as Lucy and Desi.

A piercing scream didn't stop the dancers. After all, ghosts and goblins were about.

The piercing scream was followed by moans that seemed frightening enough. Finally, Harry and Fair left the dance to investigate. They found Rhett Butler lying bleeding on the hall floor, gasping for breath as the blood spurted from his throat and his chest. Bending over him, sword in hand, was a paunchy Stonewall Jackson.

38

Maury McKinchie died before the rescue squad arrived at St. Elizabeth's. Rick Shaw, sirens blaring, arrived seconds after his final gurgle.

Rick lifted Kendrick's bloodied sword from his hand.

"It wasn't me, it was the Musketeer. I fought him off, but it was too late," Kendrick babbled.

"Kendrick Miller, I am booking you under suspicion of murder. You have the right to remain silent . . ." Rick began.

Harry, Fair, Little Mim, and the other chaperons quickly cordoned off the hallway leading to the big outside doors, making sure that Irene was hurried out of the gym. Florence Rubicon ushered the dancers out by another exit at the end of the gym floor. Still, a few kids managed to creep in to view the corpse.

Karen and Sean, both mute, simply stared.

Jody walked up behind them, her mask off, her hair tousled, the horror of the scene sinking in. "Dad? Dad, what's going on?"

Cynthia flipped open her notebook and started asking questions.

Sandy Brashiers, in a low voice, said to Little Mim, "People are going to yank their kids out of here. By Monday this school will be a ghost town."

39

A light brown stubble covered Rick Shaw's square chin. As his thinning hair was light brown, the contrast amused Cynthia Cooper, although little was amusing at the moment.

The ashtray in the office overflowed. The coffee machine pumped out cup after cup of the stimulant.

Cynthia regretted Maury McKinchie's murder, not just because a man was cut down, literally, but because Sunday, which would dawn in a couple of hours, was her day off. She had planned to drive over to the beautiful town of Monterey, almost on the West Virginia border. She'd be driving alone. Her job prevented her from having much of a social life. It wasn't that she didn't meet men. She did. Usually they were speeding seventy-five miles per hour in a fifty-five zone. They rarely smiled when they saw her, even though she was easy on the eyes. The roundup of drunks at the mall furnished her with scores of men, and they fell all over her—literally. The occasional white-collar criminal enlivened her harvest of captive males.

Over the last years of working together she and Rick had grown close. As he was a happily married man, not a hint of impropriety tainted their relationship. She relied on his friendship, hard won because when she joined the force as the first woman Rick was less than thrilled.

The one man she truly liked, Blair Bainbridge, set many hearts on fire. She felt she didn't have a chance.

Rick liked to work from flow charts. He'd started three, ultimately throwing out each of them.

"What time is it?"

"Five thirty."

"It's always darkest before the dawn." Rick quoted the old saw. He swung his feet onto his desktop. "I hate to admit that I'm stumped, but I am."

"We've got Kendrick Miller in custody."

"Not for long. He'll get a big-money lawyer, and that will be that. And it had occurred to me that Kendrick isn't the kind of man to get caught committing a murder. Standing over a writhing victim doesn't compute."

"Could have lost his head." She emptied her cup. She couldn't face another swig of coffee. "But you're not buying, are you?"

"No." He paused. "We deal in the facts. The facts are, he had a bloody sword in his hand."

"And there were two other partyers wearing swords. One of whom vanished into thin air."

"Or knew where to hide."

"Not one kid there knew who the Musketeer was or had heard him speak." Cooper leaned against the small sink in the corner of the old room. She held her fingers to her temples, which throbbed. "Boss, let's back up. Let's start with Roscoe Fletcher."

"I'm listening."

"Sandy Brashiers coveted Roscoe's job. They never saw eye to eye."

He held up his hand. "Granted, but killing to become headmaster of St. Elizabeth's—is the game worth the candle?"

"People have killed for less."

"You're right. You're right." He folded his hands over his chest and made a mental note to dig into Sandy's past.

"Anyone could have poisoned Roscoe. He left his car unlocked, his office unlocked. It wouldn't take a rocket scientist to put a hard candy drenched in poison in his car or in his pocket or to hand it to him. Anyone could do it."

"Who would want to do it, though?" She put her hands behind her head, "Not one trace of poison was found in the tin of strawberry hard candies in his car. And the way he handed out candy, half the county would be dead. So we know the killer had a conscience, sort of."

"That's a quaint way of looking at it."

"I have a hunch Roscoe was sleeping with Irene Miller." Cynthia shook her feet, which were falling asleep in her regulation shoes. "That would be a motive for the first murder."

"We have no proof that he was carrying on an extramarital affair."

Cynthia smirked. "This is Albemarle County."

Rick half laughed, then stood up to stretch. "Everyone's got secrets, Coop. The longer I work this show, the more I realize that every single person harbors secrets."

"What about that money in the Jiffy bag?" Cynthia said.

"Too many prints on the bag and not a single one on the money." Rick sighed. "I am flat running into walls. The obvious conclusion is drug money, but we haven't got one scrap of evidence."

Cynthia shot a rubber band in the air. It landed with a flop on Rick's desk. "These murders are tied together, I'll bet my badge on that, but what I can't figure out is what an expensive school like St. Elizabeth's has to do with it. All roads lead back to that school."

"Roscoe's murder was premeditated. Maury's was not—or so it

appears. Kendrick Miller has a tie to St. Elizabeth's, but—" He shrugged.

"But"—Cooper shot another rubber band straight in the air— "while we're just postulating—"

"Postulating? I'm pissing in the wind."

"You do that." She caught the rubber band as it fell back. "Listen to me. St. Elizabeth's is the tie. What if Fletcher and McKinchie were filching alumni contributions?"

"Kendrick Miller isn't going to kill over alumni misappropriations." He batted down her line of thought.

The phone rang. The on-duty operator, Joyce Thomson, picked it up.

Cynthia said, "I've always wanted to pick up the phone and say, 'Cops and Robbers.' "

Rick's line buzzed. He punched in the button so Cynthia could listen. "Yo."

"Sheriff," Joyce Thomson said, "it's John Aurieano. Mrs. Berryhill's cows are on his land, and he's going to shoot them if you don't remove them."

Rick punched the line and listened to the torrent of outrage. "Mrs. Berryhill's a small woman, Mr. Aurieano. She can't round up her cattle without help, and it will take me hours to send someone over to help. We're shorthanded."

More explosions.

"Tell you what, I'll send someone to move them, but let me give you some friendly advice. . . . This is the country. Cows are part of the country, and I'll let you in on something quite shocking—they can't read 'No Trespassing' signs. You shoot the cows, Mr. Aurieano, and you're going to be in a lot more trouble than you can imagine. If you don't like the way things are, then move back to the city!" He put the phone down. "You know, there are days when this job is a real pain in the ass."

40

A subdued congregation received early-morning mass. Jody Miller and her mother, Irene, sat in a middle pew. The entire Hallahan family occupied a pew on the left. Samson Coles made a point of sitting beside Jody. Lucinda squeezed next to Irene. Whatever Kendrick Miller may or may not have done, the opprobrium shouldn't attach to his wife and child.

Still, parishioners couldn't help staring.

Rick and Cooper knelt in the back row. Rick's head bobbed as he started to drift off, and his forehead touched his hand. He jerked his head up. "Sorry," he whispered.

He and Cynthia waited in the vestibule while people shuffled out after the service. Curious looks passed among the churchgoers as everyone watched to see if the police would stop Irene. She and Jody passed Rick without looking right or left. The Hallahans nodded a greeting but kept moving.

Finally, disappointed, the rest of the congregation walked into the brisk air, started their cars, and drove away.

Rick checked his watch, then knocked on the door at the left of the vestibule.

"Who's there?" Father Michael called out, hearing the knock.

"Rick Shaw and Deputy Cooper."

Father Michael, wearing his robe and surplice, opened the door. "Come in, Sheriff, Deputy."

"I don't mean to disturb you on Sunday. I have a few quick questions, Father."

He motioned. "Come in. Sit down for a minute."

"Thanks." They stepped inside, collapsing on the old leather sofa. "We're beat. No sleep."

"I didn't sleep much myself. . . ."

"Have you been threatened, Father?" Rick's voice cracked from fatigue.

"No."

"In your capacity as chaplain to St. Elizabeth's, have you noticed anything unusual, say, within the faculty? Arguments with Roscoe? Problems with the alumni committee?"

Father Michael paused a long time, his narrow but attractive face solemn. "Roscoe and Sandy Brashiers were inclined to go at it. Nothing that intense, though. They never learned to agree to disagree, if you know what I mean."

"I think I do." Rick nodded. "Apart from the inviolate nature of the confessional, do you know or have you heard of any sexual improprieties involving Roscoe?"

"Uh—" The middle-aged man paused a long time again. "There was talk. But that's part and parcel of a small community."

"Any names mentioned?" Cynthia said. "Like Irene Miller, maybe?"

"No."

"What about Sandy Brashiers and Naomi Fletcher?"

"I'd heard that one. The version goes something like, Naomi tires of Roscoe's infidelities and enlists his enemy, or shall we say rival, to dispose of him."

Rick stood up. "Father, thank you for your time. If anything occurs to you or you want to talk, call me or Coop."

"Sheriff"—Father Michael weighed his words—"am I in danger?"

"I hope not," Rick answered honestly.

41

April Shively was arrested Monday morning at the school. She was charged with obstructing justice since she had consistently refused to hand over the school records, first to Sandy, then to the police. As she and Roscoe had worked hand in glove, not even Naomi knew how much April had removed and hidden.

Sandy Brashiers wasted no time in terminating her employment. On her way out of the school, April turned and slapped his face. Cynthia Cooper hustled her to the squad car.

St. Elizabeth's, deserted save for faculty, stood forlorn in the strong early November winds. Sandy and Naomi convened an emergency meeting of faculty and interested parties. Neither could answer the most important question: What was happening at St. Elizabeth's?

The Reverend Herbert C. Jones received an infuriating phone call from Darla McKinchie. No, she would not be returning to Albemarle County for a funeral service. She would be shipping her late husband's body to Los Angeles immediately. Would the Reverend please handle the arrangements with Dale and Delaney Funeral Home? She would make a handsome contribution to the church. Naturally, he agreed, but was upset by her high-handed manner and the fact that she cared so little for Maury's local friends, but then again, she seemed to care little for Maury himself.

Blue Monday yielded surprises every hour on the hour, it seemed. Jody Miller learned that yes, she was pregnant. She begged Dr. Larry Johnson not to call her mother. He wouldn't agree since she was under twenty-one, so she pitched a hissy fit right there in the examining room. Hayden McIntire, the doctor's much younger partner, and two nurses rushed in to restrain Jody.

The odd thing was that when Irene Miller arrived it was she who cried, not Jody. The shame of an out-of-wedlock pregnancy cut Irene to the core. She was fragile enough, thanks to the tensions inside her house and now outside it as well. As for Jody, she had no shame about her condition, she simply didn't want to be pregnant. Larry advised mother and daughter to have a heart-to-heart but not in his examining room.

At twelve noon Kendrick Miller was released on $250,000 bail into the custody of his lawyer, Ned Tucker. At one in the afternoon, he told his divorce lawyer not to serve papers on Irene. She didn't need that crisis on top of this one, he said. What he really wanted was for Irene to stand beside him, but Kendrick being Kendrick, he had to make it sound as though he were doing his wife a big favor.

At two thirty he blasted Sandy Brashiers on the phone and said he was taking his daughter out of that sorry excuse for a school until things got straightened out over there. By three thirty the situation was so volatile that Kendrick picked up the phone and asked Father Michael for help. For him to admit he needed help was a step in the right direction.

By four forty-five the last surprise of the day occurred when BoomBoom Craycroft lost control of her shiny brand-new 7 series BMW. She had roared up the alleyway behind the post office where she spun in a 360-degree turn, smashing into Harry's blue Ford.

Hearing the crash, the animals rushed out of the post office.

BoomBoom, without a scratch herself, opened the door to her metallic green machine, put one foot on the ground, and started to wail.

"Is she hurt?" Tucker ran over.

Mrs. Murphy, moving at a possum trot, declared, "Her essences are shaken."

In the collision the plastic case in which BoomBoom kept her potions slammed up against the dash, cracking and spilling out a concoction of rose, sage, and comfrey.

Harry opened the backdoor. "Oh, no!"

"I couldn't help it! My heel got stuck in the mat." BoomBoom wept.

Mrs. Hogendobber stuck her head out the door. Her body immediately followed. "Are you all right?"

"My neck hurts."

"Do you want me to call the rescue squad?" Harry asked, dubious but giving BoomBoom the benefit of the doubt.

"No. I'll go over to Larry's. It's probably whiplash." She viewed the caved-in side of the truck. "I'm insured, Harry, don't worry."

Harry sighed. Her poor truck. Tucker ran underneath to inspect the frame, which was undamaged. The BMW had suffered one little dent in the right fender.

Pewter, moving at a slower pace, walked around the truck. "We can still drive home in it. It's only the side that's bashed in."

"I'll call the sheriff's department." Miranda, satisfied that BoomBoom was fine, walked back into the post office.

Market Shiflett opened his backdoor. "I thought I heard something." He surveyed the situation.

Before he could speak, BoomBoom said, "No bones broken."

"Good." He heard the front door ring and ducked back into his store.

"Come inside." Harry helped her former rival out of the car. "It's cold out here."

"My heel stuck in that brand-new mat I bought." She pointed to a fuzzy mat with the BMW logo on it.

"BoomBoom, why wear high heels to run your errands?"

"Oh—well—" Her hand fluttered.

"Where have you been? You always come down to pick up your mail."

"I've been under the weather. These murders upset me."

Once inside, Mrs. Hogendobber brewed a strong cup of tea while they waited for someone to appear from the sheriff's department.

"I think it's dreadful that Darla McKinchie, that self-centered nothing of an actress, isn't having the service here." BoomBoom, revived by the tea, told them about Herb's phone call. She'd seen Herbie Jones at the florist.

"That is pretty cold-blooded." Harry bent down to tie her shoelaces. Mrs. Murphy helped.

"Someone should sponsor a service here."

"That would be lovely, BoomBoom, why don't you do it?" Miranda smiled, knowing she'd told BoomBoom to do what she wanted to do anyway.

After the officer left, having asked questions about the accident and taken pictures, the insurance agent showed up and did the same. Then he was gone, and finally BoomBoom herself left, which greatly relieved Harry, who strained to be civil to a woman she disliked. BoomBoom said she was too rattled to drive her car, so Lucinda Coles picked her up. BoomBoom left her car at the post office, keys in the ignition.

42

"April, cooperate, for Christ's sake." Cooper, exasperated, rapped her knuckles on the table.

"No, I'll stay here and live off the county for a while. My taxes paid for this jail." She pushed back a stray forelock.

"Removing documents pertinent to the murder of Roscoe Fletcher—"

April interrupted. "But they're not! They're pertinent to the operations of St. Elizabeth's, and that's none of your business."

Cooper slapped her hand hard on the table. "Embezzlement is my business!"

April, not one to be shaken by an accusation, pursed her lips. "Prove it."

Cynthia stretched her long legs, took a deep breath, counted to ten, and started anew. "You have an important place in this community. Don't throw it away to protect a dead man."

Folding her arms across her chest, April withdrew into hostile silence.

Cooper did likewise.

Twenty minutes later April piped up, "You can't prove I had an affair with him either. That's what everyone thinks. Don't give me this baloney about having an important place in the community."

"But you do. You're important to St. Elizabeth's."

April leaned forward, both elbows on the table. "I'm a secretary. That's nothing"—she made a gesture of dismissal with her hand— "to people around here. But I'm a damned good secretary."

"I'm sure you are."

"And"—she lurched forward a bit more—"Sandy Brashiers will ruin everything we worked for, I guarantee it. That man lives in a dream world, and he's sneaky. Well, he may be temporary headmaster, but headmaster of what! No one was at school today."

"You were."

"That's my job. Besides, no one is going to kill me—I'm too low on the totem pole."

"If you know why Roscoe was killed, they might."

"I don't know."

"If you did, would you tell me?"

A brief silence followed this question as a clap of thunder follows lightning.

Looking Cynthia square in the eye, April answered resolutely. "Yes. And I'll tell you something else. Roscoe had something on Sandy Brashiers. He never told me what it was, but it helped him keep Sandy in line."

"Any ideas—any ideas at all?"

"No." She gulped air. "I wish I knew. I really do."

43

Kendrick stared at Jody's red BMW as she exploded. "No! I paid for it with Grandpa K's money. He left the money to me, not you."

"He left it to pay for college, and you promised to keep it in savings." His face reddened.

Irene, attempting to defuse a full-scale blowup, stepped in. "We're all tired. Let's discuss this tomorrow." She knew perfectly well this was not the time to bring up the much larger issue of Jody's pregnancy.

"Stop protecting her," Kendrick ordered.

"You know, Dad, we're not employees. You can't order us around."

He slammed the side door of the kitchen, returning inside with the BMW keys in his hand. He dangled them under his daughter's nose. "You're not going anywhere."

She shrugged since she'd stashed away the second set of keys.

Kendrick calmed down for a moment. "Did you pick the car up today?"

"Uh—"

"No, she's had it for a few days."

"Three days."

Irene didn't know how long Jody had had the car, but that was hardly a major worry. She'd become accustomed to her daughter's lying to her. Other parents said their children did the same, especially in the adolescent years, but Irene still felt uneasy about it. Getting used to something didn't mean one liked it.

"If you've had this car three days, where was it?"

"I lent it to a friend."

"Don't lie to me!" The veins stood out in Kendrick's neck.

"Isn't it a little late to try and be a dad now?" she mumbled.

He backhanded her across the face hard. Tears sprang into her eyes. "The car goes back!"

"No way."

He hit her again.

"Kendrick, please!"

"Stay out of this."

"She's my daughter, too. She's made a foolish purchase, but that's how we learn, by making foolish mistakes," Irene pleaded.

"Where did you hide the car?" Kendrick bellowed.

"You can beat me to a pulp. I'll never tell you."

He raised his hand again. Irene hung on to it as Jody ducked. He threw his wife onto the floor.

"Go to your room."

Jody instantly scurried to her room.

Kendrick checked his watch. "It's too late to take the car back now. You can follow me over tomorrow."

Irene scrambled to her feet. "She'll lose a lot of money, won't she?"

"Twenty-one percent." He turned from Irene's slightly bedraggled form to walk into the kitchen, where he turned on the television to watch CNN.

He forgot or didn't care that Jody had a telephone in her room, which she used the second she shut her door.

"Hello, is Sean there?"

Moments later Sean picked up the phone.

"It's Jody."

"Oh, hi." He was wary.

"I just found out today that I'm pregnant."

A gasp followed. "What are you going to do?"

"Tell everyone it was you."

"You can't do that!"

"Why not? You didn't find me that repulsive this summer."

A flash of anger hit him. "How do you know it was me?"

"You asshole!" She slammed down the receiver.

A shaken, lonely Sean Hallahan put the receiver back on the cradle.

44

The front-office staff at Crozet High, frazzled by parental requests to accept transfers from St. Elizabeth's, stopped answering the phone. The line in the hall took precedence.

The middle school and grammar school suffered the same influx.

Sandy Brashiers took out an ad in the newspaper. He had had the presence of mind to place the full-page ad the moment Maury was killed. Given lag time, it ran today.

The ad stated that the board of directors and temporary head-master regretted the recent incidents at St. Elizabeth's, but these in-volved adults, not students.

He invited parents to come to his office at Old Main Building or to visit him at home . . . and he begged parents not to pull their children out of the school.

A few parents read the ad as they stood in line.

Meanwhile, the St. Elizabeth's students were thoroughly en-joying their unscheduled vacation.

Karen Jensen had called Coach Hallvard asking that the hockey team be allowed to practice with Crozet High in the afternoon until things straightened out.

Roger Davis used the time to work at the car wash. Jody said she needed money, so she was there, too.

Karen borrowed her daddy's car, more reliable than her own old Volvo, and took Brooks with her to see Mary Baldwin College in Staunton. She was considering applying there but wanted to see it without her mom and dad.

The college was only thirty-five miles from Crozet.

"I'd rather finish out at St. Elizabeth's than go to Crozet High." Karen cruised along, the old station wagon swaying on the highway. "Transferring now could mess up my grade-point average, and besides, we're not the ones in danger. So I'd just as soon go back."

"My parents are having a fit." Brooks sighed and looked out the window as they rolled west down Waynesboro's Main Street.

"Everybody's are. Major weird. BoomBoom Craycroft said it's karma."

"Karma is celestial recycling," Brooks cracked.

"Three points."

"I thought so, too." She smiled. "It is bizarre. Do you think the killer is someone at St. Elizabeth's?"

"Sean." Karen giggled.

"Hey, some people really think he did kill Mr. Fletcher. And everyone thinks Mr. Miller skewered Mr. McKinchie. He just got out of jail because he's rich. He was standing over him, sword in hand."

Brooks stared at the sumac, reddening, by the side of the road as they passed the outskirts of Waynesboro. "Did you hear April Shively's in jail? Maybe she did it."

"Women don't kill," Karen said.

"Of course they do."

"Not like men. Ninety-five percent of all murders are committed by men, so the odds are it's a man."

"Karen, women are smarter. They don't get caught."

They both laughed as they rolled into Staunton on Route 250.

45

November can be a tricky month. Delightful warm interludes cast a soft golden glow on tree limbs, a few still sporting colorful leaves. The temperature hovers in the high fifties or low sixties for a few glorious days, then cold air knifes in, a potent reminder that winter truly is around the corner.

This was one of those coppery, warm days, and Harry sat out back of the post office eating a ham sandwich. Sitting in a semicircle at her feet, rapturous in their attentions, were Mrs. Murphy, Pewter, and Tucker.

Mrs. Hogendobber stuck her head out the backdoor. "Take your time with lunch. Nothing much is going on."

Harry swallowed so she wouldn't be talking with her mouth full. "It's a perfect, perfect day. Push the door open and sit out here with me."

"Bring a sandwich," Pewter requested.

"Later. I am determined to reorganize the back shelves. Looks like a storm hit them."

"Save it for a rainy day. Come on," Harry cajoled.

"Well, it is awfully pretty, isn't it?" She disappeared quickly, returning with a sandwich and two orange-glazed buns, her specialty.

Although Mrs. Hogendobber's house was right across the alley from the post office, she liked to bring her lunch and pastries to work with her. A small refrigerator and a hot plate in the back allowed the two women to operate Chez Post, as they sometimes called it.

"The last of my mums." Miranda pointed out the deep russet-colored flowers bordering her fall gardens. "What is there about fall that makes one melancholy?"

"Loss of the light." Harry enjoyed the sharp mustard she'd put on her sandwich.

"And color, although I battle that with pyracantha, the December-blooming camellias, and lots of holly in strategic places. Still, I miss the fragrance of summer."

"*Hummingbirds.*"

"*Baby snakes.*" Mrs. Murphy offered her delectables.

"*Baby mice,*" Pewter chimed in.

"*You have yet to kill a mouse.*" Mrs. Murphy leaned close to Harry just in case her mother felt like sharing.

Pewter, preferring the direct approach, sat in front of Harry, chartreuse eyes lifted upward in appeal. "*Look who's talking. The barn is turning into Mouse Manhattan.*"

Tucker drooled. Mrs. Hogendobber handed her a tidbit of ham, to the fury of the two cats. She tore off two small pieces for them, too.

"*Mine has mustard on it,*" Mrs. Murphy complained.

"*I'll eat it,*" Tucker gallantly volunteered.

"*In a pig's eye.*"

"*Aren't we lucky that Miranda makes all these goodies?*" Pewter nibbled. "*She's the best cook in Crozet.*"

Cynthia Cooper slowly rolled down the alleyway, pulling in next to BoomBoom's BMW. "Great day."

"Join us."

She checked her watch. "Fifteen minutes."

"Make it thirty, and leave your radio on." Harry smiled.

"Good idea." Cynthia cut off the ignition, then turned the volume up on the two-way radio. "Mrs. H., did you make sandwiches for Market today?"

"Indeed, I did."

Cynthia sprinted down the narrow alley between the post office and the market. Within minutes she returned with a smoked turkey sandwich slathered in tarragon mayonnaise, Boston lettuce peeping out from the sides of the whole wheat bread.

The three sat on the back stoop. Every now and then the radio squawked, but no calls for Coop.

"Why did you paint your fingernails?" Harry noticed the raspberry polish.

"Got bored."

"Isn't it funny how Little Mim changes her hairdo? Each time it's a new style or color, you know something is up," Miranda noted.

Sean Hallahan ambled down the alleyway.

"You look like the dogs got at you under the porch." Harry laughed at his disheveled appearance.

"Oh"—he glanced down at his wrinkled clothes—"guess I do."

"Is the football team going to practice at Crozet High? Field hockey is," Harry said.

"Nobody's called me. I don't know what we're going to do. I don't even know if I'm going back to St. Elizabeth's."

"Do you want to?" Cynthia asked.

"Yeah, we've got a good team this year. And it's my senior year. I don't want to go anywhere else."

"That makes sense," Mrs. Hogendobber said.

He ran his finger over the hood of the BMW. "Cool."

"Ultra," Harry replied.

"Just a car." Pewter remained unimpressed by machines.

He bent over, shading his eyes, and peered inside. "Leather. Sure stinks, though."

"She spilled her essences," Harry said.

"*Don't be squirrelly,*" Mrs. Murphy advised.

Sean opened the door, and the competing scents rolled out like a wave. "I hope I get rich."

"Hope you do, too." Harry gave the last of her sandwich to the animals.

He turned on the ignition, rolled down the windows, and clicked on the radio. "Too cool. This is just too cool."

"Where is BoomBoom, anyway?" Cynthia drank iced tea out of a can.

"Who knows? She needs someone to follow her to the BMW dealer. She slightly dented her bumper, not even a dent actually—she rubbed off some of the finish." Harry indicated the spot.

Sean, paying no attention to the conversation, leaned his head back and turned up the radio a bit. He was surrounded by speakers. Then he let off the emergency brake, popped her in reverse, and backed out into the alleyway. He waved at the three women and three animals and carefully rolled forward.

"Should I yank his chain?" Cynthia craned her neck.

"Nah."

They waited a few moments, expecting him to go around the block and reappear. Then they heard the squeal of rubber.

Cooper put down what was left of her sandwich. She stood up. The car was pulling away.

Mrs. Hogendobber listened. "He's not coming back."

"I don't believe this!" Cooper hurried to the squad car as Tucker scarfed down the sandwich remains. She pulled out the speaker, telling the dispatcher where she was and what she was doing. She didn't ask for assistance yet because she thought he was taking a joyride. She hoped to catch him and turn him back before he got into more trouble—he was in enough as it was.

"Can I come?" Harry asked.

"Hop in."

Harry opened the door. Mrs. Murphy and Tucker jumped in with her. "Miranda, do you care?"

"Go on." She waved her off, then glanced down. "Pewter, are you staying with me?"

"*Yes, I am.*" The gray cat followed her back into the post office.

Cynthia turned left, heading toward Route 250. "Sounded like he was heading this way."

"Don't you think he'll make a big circle and come back?"

"Yeah, I do. Right under my nose. . . . Jeez, what a dumb thing to do." She shook her head.

"He hasn't shown the best judgment lately."

Mrs. Murphy settled in Harry's lap while Tucker sat between the humans.

As they reached Route 250, they noticed a lumber truck pulling off to the right side of the road. Cynthia slowed, putting on her flashers. "Stay here." She stepped out. Harry watched as the driver spoke to her and pointed toward the west. A few choice words escaped his tobacco-stained lips. Coop dashed back to the car.

She hit the accelerator and the sirens.

"Trouble?"

"Yep."

Other cars pulled off to the right as Cynthia's car screeched down Route 250 to the base of Afton Mountain. Then they started the climb to the summit, some 1850 feet.

"You think he got on Sixty-four?"

"Yeah. A great big four-lane highway. He's gonna bury the speedometer."

"Shit, Cooper, he's going to bury himself."

"That thought has occurred to me."

Mrs. Murphy leaned over Harry and said to Tucker, "*Fasten your seat belt.*"

"*Yeah,*" the dog replied, wishing there were seat belts made for animals.

Cynthia hurtled past the Howard Johnson's at the top of the mountain, turning left, then turning right to get onto Interstate 64. Vehicles jerked to the right as best they could but in some places on the entrance ramp the shoulder was inadequate. She swerved to avoid the cars.

The Rockfish Valley left behind was supplanted by the Shenandoah Valley. There was a glimpse of Waynesboro off to the right as they got onto I 64.

Remnants of fall foliage blurred. Cynthia negotiated the large sweeping curves on top of the Blue Ridge Mountains.

"What if he took the Skyline Drive?" Harry asked.

"I'm going to have to call in the state police and Augusta County's police, too. Damn!"

"He asked for it," Harry replied sensibly.

"Yes, he did." Cooper called the dispatcher, gave her location, and requested assistance as well as help on the Skyline Drive.

"*Doesn't compute.*" Mrs. Murphy snuggled as Harry held her in the curves.

"*That he stole the car?*"

"*That he did it right in front of them. He wants to get caught.*" Her eyes widened as they hung another curve. "*He's in on it, or he knows something.*"

"*Then why steal a car in front of Coop?*" Tucker asked the obvious question.

"*That's what I mean—something doesn't compute,*" Murphy replied.

Up ahead they caught sight of Sean. Cynthia checked her speedometer. She was hitting ninety, and this was not the safest stretch of road in the state of Virginia.

She slowed a bit. "He's not only going to hurt himself, he's going to hurt someone else." She clicked on the black two-way radio button. "Subject in sight. Just past Ninety-nine on the guardrail." She repeated a number posted on a small metal sign. "Damn, he's going one hundred." She shook her head.

As good as the BMW was, Sean was not accustomed to driving a high-performance machine in challenging circumstances. The blue flashing lights behind him didn't scare him as much as the blue flashing lights he saw in the near distance, coming from the opposite direction. He took his eyes off the road for a split second, but a split second at 100 miles an hour is a fraction too long. He spun out, steered hard in the other direction, and did a 360, blasting through the guardrail and taking the metal with him as he soared over the ravine.

"Oh, my God!" Harry exclaimed.

Cynthia screeched to a stop. The BMW seemed airborne for an eternity, then finally crashed deep into the mountain laurels below.

Both Cynthia and Harry were out of the squad car when it stopped. Mrs. Murphy and Tucker could run down the mountainside much better than the two humans could as they stumbled, rolled, and got up again.

"We've got to get him before the car blows up!" Mrs. Murphy shouted to the corgi, who realized the situation also.

The BMW had landed upside down. The animals reached it, and Tucker tried to open the door by standing on her hind legs.

"Impossible."

The tiger raced around the car, hoping windows would have been smashed to bits on the other side.

Harry and Cooper, both covered in mud, scratched, and torn, reached the car. Cooper opened the door. Sean was held in place upside down by the safety belt. She reached in and clicked the belt. Both she and Harry dragged him out.

"Haul," Cynthia commanded.

Harry grabbed his left arm, Cynthia his right, and Tucker grabbed the back of his collar. They struggled and strained but managed to get the unconscious, bloodied boy fifty yards up the mountainside. Mrs. Murphy scampered ahead.

The BMW made a definite clicking sound and then *boom*, the beautiful machine was engulfed in flames.

The two women sat for a moment, holding Sean so he wouldn't slide back down. Mrs. Murphy walked ahead, searching for the easiest path up. Tucker, panting, sat for a moment, too.

They heard more sirens and a voice at the lip of the ravine.

Tucker barked. *"We're down here!"*

Harry, still holding Sean, turned around to see rescue workers scrambling down to help. She felt for the vein in his neck; a faint pulse rippled underneath her fingertips. "He's alive."

Mrs. Murphy said under her breath, *"For how long?"*

46

The cherry wood in the fireplace crackled, releasing the heavy aroma of the wood. Tucker, asleep in front of the fire, occasionally chattered, dreaming of squirrels.

Mrs. Murphy curled up in Harry's lap as she sat on the sofa while Pewter sprawled over Fair's bigger lap in the other wing chair. Exhausted from the trauma as well as the climb back up the deep ravine, Harry pulled the worn afghan around her legs, her feet resting on a hassock.

Fair broke the stillness. "I know Rick told you not to reveal Sean's condition, but you can tell me."

"Fair, the sheriff has put a guard in his hospital room. And to tell the truth, I don't know his condition."

"He was mixed up in whatever is going on over at St. Elizabeth's?"

"I guess he is." She leaned her head against a needlepoint pillow. "In your teens you think you know everything. Your parents are out of it. You're invincible. Especially Sean, the football star. I wonder how he got mixed up in this mess, and I wonder what's really behind it."

"I heard April was released from jail today, and she didn't want to leave," Fair remarked. "She must know what's going on, too."

"That's so strange. She doesn't look like a criminal, does she?"

"I always thought she was in love with Roscoe and that he used her," Fair said.

"Slept with her?"

"I don't know. Maybe"—he thought a moment—"but more than that, he used her. She jumped through all his hoops. April was one of the reasons that St. E's ran so smoothly. Sure as hell wasn't Roscoe. His talents rested in directions other than details." He rose and tossed another log on the fire. "He ever offer you candy?"

"Every time he saw me."

"*Never offered me catnip,*" Pewter grumbled.

"*Mom's got that look on her face. She's having a brainstorm.*" Tucker closely observed Harry.

"*Humans are fundamentally irrational. They use what precious rationality they have justifying their irrational behavior. A brainstorm is an excuse not to be logical,*" Pewter said.

"*Amen.*" Murphy laughed.

Harry tickled Murphy's ears. "Aren't we verbal?"

"*I can recite entire passages from Macbeth, if you'd care to hear it. 'Tomorrow and tomorrow and tomorrow creeps—'*"

"*Show-off.*" Pewter swished her tail once. "*Quoting Shakespeare is no harder than quoting 'Katie went to Haiti looking for a thrill.'*"

"Cole Porter." Mrs. Murphy sang the rest of the song with Pewter.

"What's going on with these two?" Harry laughed.

"Mrs. Murphy's telling her about her narrow escape from death."

"*That's the first thing I did when we got home.*" Mrs. Murphy sat up now and belted out the chorus from "Katie Went to Haiti."

"*Jesus,*" Tucker moaned, flattening her ears, "*you could wake the dead.*"

Pewter, on a Cole Porter kick, warbled, *"When They Begin the Beguine."*

The humans shook their heads, then returned to their conversation.

"Maybe the link is Sean's connection to Roscoe and Maury." Harry's eyes brightened. "He could easily have stuffed Roger's newspapers with the second obituary. Those kids all know one another's schedules. They must have been using Sean for something—" Her brow wrinkled; for the life of her she couldn't figure out what a teenage boy might have that both men wanted.

"Not necessarily." Fair played devil's advocate. "It really could be coincidence. Just dumb luck."

Harry shook her head, "No, I really don't think so. Sean is up to his neck in this mess."

Fair cracked his knuckles, a habit Harry had tried to forget. "Kendrick Miller stabbed Maury. Maury's murder has nothing to do with Roscoe's. And the kid liberated the BMW, so to speak, and just got carried away. Started something he didn't know how to finish."

"But Rick Shaw's guarding him in the hospital." Harry came back to that very important fact.

"You're right—but connecting him to Roscoe's murder and Maury's seems so far-fetched."

Harry leapt off the sofa. "Sorry, Murphy."

"I was so-o-o comfortable," Murphy moaned angrily. *"Pewter, let's give it to them. Let's sing 'Dixie.'"*

The two cats blended their voices in a rousing version of the song beloved of some folks south of the Mason-Dixon Line.

"You're a veterinarian. You shut them up," Tucker begged.

Fair shrugged, laughing at the two performers.

"Here." Harry tossed Fair a bag of treats. "I know this works." It did, and she dialed Susan. "Hey, Suz."

"Miranda's here. Why didn't you tell me!"

"I am."

"How long have you been home? Oh, Harry, you could have been barbecued."

"I've been home an hour. Fair's here."

"Tell me what happened."

"I will, Susan, tomorrow. I promise. Right now I need to talk to Brooks. Are you sending her to St. Elizabeth's tomorrow?"

"No. Although she wants to go back." Susan called her daughter to the phone.

Harry got right to the point. "Brooks, do you remember who Roscoe Fletcher offered candy to when he waited in line at the car wash?"

"Everybody."

"Try very hard to remember, Brooks."

"Uh, okay . . . when I first saw him he was almost out on Route Twenty-nine. I don't think he talked to anyone unless it was the guys at the Texaco station. I didn't notice him again until he was halfway to the entrance. Uh—" She strained to picture the event. "Mrs. Fletcher beeped her horn at him. He got out to talk to her, I think. The line was that slow. Then he got back in. Mrs. Miller talked to him. Karen walked over for a second. He called her over. Jody, when she saw him, hid back in the office. She'd been reamed out, remember, 'cause of losing her temper after the field hockey game. Uh—this is hard."

"I know, but it's extremely important."

"Roger, once Mr. Fletcher reached the port—we call it the port."

"Can you think of anyone else?"

"No. But, I was scrubbing down bumpers. Someone else could have walked over for a second and I might not have seen them."

"I realize that. You've done a good job remembering."

"Want Mom back?"

"Sure."

"What are you up to?" Susan asked.

"Narrowing down who was offered candy by Roscoe at the car wash."

Susan, recognizing Harry was obsessed, told her she would see her in the morning.

Harry then dialed Karen Jensen's number. She asked Karen the same questions and received close to the same answers, although Karen thought Jody had been off the premises of the car wash, had walked back, seen Roscoe and ducked inside Jimbo's office. She remembered both Naomi and Irene waiting in line, but she couldn't recall if they got out of their cars. She wanted to know if Sean was all right.

"I don't know."

Karen's voice thickened. "I really like Sean—even if he can be a jerk."

"Can you think of any reason why he'd take Mrs. Craycroft's car?"

"No—well, I mean, he's sort of a cutup. He would never steal it, though. He just wouldn't."

"Thanks, Karen." Harry hung up the phone. She didn't think Sean would steal a car either. Joyride, yes. Steal, no.

She called Jimbo next. He remembered talking to Roscoe himself, then going back into his office to take a phone call. Harry asked if Jody was in the office with him. He said yes, she came in shortly after he spoke to Roscoe, although he couldn't be precise as to the time.

She next tried Roger, who thought Roscoe offered candy to one of the gas jockeys at the Texaco. He had glanced up to count the cars in the line. He remembered both Naomi and Irene getting out of their cars and talking to Roscoe as opposed to Roscoe getting out to talk to his wife. He was pretty sure that was what he saw, and he affirmed that Jody emphatically did not want to talk to Roscoe. He didn't know when Jody first caught sight of Roscoe. She was supposed to be picking up their lunch, but she never made it.

The last call was to Jody. Irene reluctantly called her daughter to the phone.

"Jody, I'm sorry to disturb you."

"That's okay." Jody whispered, "How's Sean? It's all over town that he wrecked BoomBoom Craycroft's new car."

"I don't know how he is."

"Did he say anything?"

"I can't answer that."

"But you pulled him out of the vehicle. He must have said something . . . like why he did it."

"Sheriff Shaw instructed me not to say anything, Jody."

"I called the hospital. They won't tell me anything either." A note of rising panic crept into her voice.

"They always do that, Jody. It's standard procedure. If you were in there with a hangnail, they wouldn't give out information."

"But he's all right, isn't he?"

"I can't answer that. I honestly don't know." Harry paused. "You're good friends, aren't you?"

"We got close this summer, playing tennis at the club."

"Did you date?"

"Sort of. We both went out with other people." She sniffed. "He's got to be okay."

"He's young and he's strong." Harry waited a beat, then switched the subject. "I'm trying to reconstruct how many people Mr. Fletcher offered strawberry drops to since, of course, anyone might have been poisoned." Harry wasn't telling the truth of what she was thinking, although she *was* telling the truth, a neat trick.

"Everyone."

Harry laughed. "That's the general consensus."

"Who else have you talked to?"

"Roger, Brooks, Karen, and Jimbo. Everybody says about the same thing although the sequence is scrambled."

"Oh."

"Did Mr. Fletcher offer you candy?"

"No. I chickened out and ran into Mr. Anson's office. I was in the doghouse."

"Yeah. Well, it was still a great game, and you played superbly."

"Really?" She brightened.

"You could make All-State. That is, if St. Elizabeth's has a season. Who knows what will happen with so many people taking their kids out of there."

"School's school." Jody confidently predicted, "I'm going back,

others will, too. I'd rather be there than"—she whispered again—
"here."

"Uh, Jody, are your mother and father near?"

"No, but I don't trust them. Dad's truly weird now that he's out
on bail. Mom could be on the extension for all I know."

"Only because she's worried about you."

"Because she's a snoop. Hear that, Mom? If you're on the line,
get off!"

Harry ignored the flash of bad manners. "Jody, can you tell me
specifically who Mr. Fletcher offered candy to, that is, if you were
watching from Jimbo's office?"

"Mr. Anson went out to talk to him. I sat behind the desk. I
didn't really notice."

"Did you see Mrs. Fletcher or your mom get out of their cars
and talk to Mr. Fletcher?"

"I don't remember Mom doing anything—but I wasn't really
watching them."

"Oh, hey, before I forget it, 'cause I don't go over there much
the kids said you were on lunch duty that day. Where do you get
good food around there?"

"You don't."

"You were on lunch duty?" Harry double-checked.

"Yeah, and Roger got pissed at me because he was starving and I
saw Mr. Fletcher before I crossed the road so I ran back. If I'd crossed
the road he would have seen me. The line was so long he was almost
out at the stoplight."

"Did he see you?"

"I don't think so. He saw me in the office later. He wasn't even
mad. He waved."

"Did you give Jim his money back?" Harry laughed.

"Uh—no." Jody's voice tightened. "I forgot. It was—uh—well,
I guess he forgot, too."

"Didn't mean to upset you."

"I'll pay him back tomorrow."

"I know you will." Harry's voice was warm. "Thanks for giving me your time. Oh, one more thing. I forgot to ask the others this. What do you, or did you, think of Mr. Fletcher's film department idea?''

'' 'Today St. Elizabeth's, tomorrow Hollywood,' that's what he used to say. It was a great idea, but it'll never happen now.''

"Thanks, Jody." Harry hung up the phone, returning to the sofa where she nestled in.

Mrs. Murphy crawled back in her lap. *"Now stay put."*

"Satisfied?" Fair asked.

"No, but I'm on the right track." She rested her hand on Mrs. Murphy's back. "I'm convinced. The real question is not who Roscoe offered candy to but who gave him candy. Rick Shaw must have come to the same conclusion." She tickled Murphy's ear. "He's not saying anything, though."

"Not to you."

"Mmm." Harry's mind drifted off. "Jody's upset over Sean. I guess they had a romance and I missed it."

"At that age you blink and they're off to a new thrill." He put his hands behind his head, stretching his upper body. Pewter didn't budge. "Everyone's upset. BoomBoom will be doubly upset." He exhaled, wishing he hadn't mentioned that name. "I'm surprised that you aren't more upset."

"I am upset. Two people are dead. Sean may well join them in the hereafter, and I can't figure it out. I hate secrets."

"That's what we pay the sheriff to do, to untie our filthy knots of passion, duplicity, and greed."

"Fair"—Harry smiled—"that's poetic."

He smiled back. "Go on."

"BoomBoom Craycroft." Harry simply repeated the name of Fair's former lover, then started laughing.

He smiled ruefully. "A brand-new BMW."

"She's such a flake. Pretty, I grant you that. I think I could have handled just about anyone else but BoomBoom." Harry took a side-swipe at Fair.

"That's not true, Harry, a betrayal is a betrayal, and it wouldn't have mattered who the woman was. You'd still feel like shit, and you'd say the same thing you're saying now but about her. I am rebuilding my whole life, my inner life. My outer life is okay." He paused. "I want to spend my life with you. Always did."

"Do you know why you ran around?"

"Fear."

"Of what?"

"Of being trapped. Of not living. When we married, I'd slept with three other women. I was a dutiful son. I studied hard. Kept my nose clean. Went to college. Went to vet school. Graduated and married you, the girl next door. I hit thirty and thought I was missing something. Had I married you at thirty, I would have gotten that out of my system." He softened his voice. "Haven't you ever worried that you're missing out?"

"Yeah, but then I watch the sunrise flooding the mountains with light and I think, 'Life is perfect.' "

"You aren't curious about other men?"

"What men?"

"Blair Bainbridge."

"Oh." She took her sweet time answering, thoroughly enjoying his discomfort. "Sometimes."

"How curious?"

"You just want to know if I'm sleeping with anyone, and that's my business. It's all about sex and possession, isn't it?"

"It's about love and responsibility. Sex is part of that."

"This is what I know: I like living alone. I like answering to no one but myself. I like not having to attend social functions as though we are joined at the hip. I like not having a knot in my stomach when you don't come home until two in the morning."

"I'm a vet."

She held up her hand. "With so many chances to jump ladies' bones, I can't even count them."

"I'm not doing that." He took her hand. "Our divorce was so painful, I didn't think I could live through it. I knew I was wrong. I didn't know how to make it right. Enough time has passed that I can be trusted, and I can be more sensitive to you."

"Don't push me."

"If I don't push you, you do nothing. If I ask anyone else to a party or the movies because I'd like to enjoy someone's companionship, you freeze me out for a week or more. I'm damned if I do and damned if I don't."

"*He's right, Mom,*" Mrs. Murphy agreed with Fair.

"*Yeah,*" Tucker echoed.

"*They talk too much.*" Pewter, weary from her singing and all the spoon bread she'd stolen, wanted to sleep.

"Cheap revenge, I guess." Harry honestly assessed herself.

"Does it make you happy?"

"Actually, it does. Anyone who underestimates the joy of revenge has no emotions." She laughed. "But it doesn't get you what you want."

"Which is?"

"That's just it. I don't really know anymore."

"I love you. I've always loved you, and I always will love you." A burst of passion illuminated his handsome face.

She squeezed his hand. "I love you, too, but—"

"Can't we get back together? If you aren't ready for a commitment, we can date."

"We date now."

"No, we don't. It's hit or miss."

"You're not talking about dating. You're talking about sleeping together."

"Yes."

"I'll consider it."

"Harry, that's a gray reply."

"I didn't say no, nor did I say maybe. I have to think about it."

"But you know how I feel. You know what I've wanted."

"Not the same as a direct request—you just made a direct request, and I have to think about it."

"Do you love me at all?"

"The funny part of all this is that I do love you. I love you more now than when we married, but it's different. I just don't know if I can trust you. I'd like to, truly I would, because apart from Susan,

Miranda, and my girlfriends, I know you better than anyone on the face of the earth, and I think you know me. I don't always like you. I'm sure I'm not likable at times, but it's odd how you can love someone and not like them." She hastened to add, "Most times I like you. Really, it's just when you start giving orders. I hate that."

"I'm working on that. Most women want to be told what to do."

"Some do, I know. Most don't. It's a big fake act they put on to make men feel intelligent and powerful. Then they laugh at you behind your back."

"You don't do that."

"No way."

"That's why I love you. One of the many reasons. You always stand up to me. I need that. I need you. You bring out the best in me, Harry."

"I'm glad to hear it," she replied dryly, "but I'm not on earth to bring out the best in you. I'm on earth to bring out the best in me."

"Wouldn't it be right if we could do that for each other? Isn't that what marriage is supposed to be?"

She waited a long time. "Yes. Marriage is probably more complicated than that, but I'm too tired to figure it out . . . if I ever could. And every marriage isn't the same. Our marriage was different from Miranda and George's, but theirs worked for them. I think you do bring out good things in me—after all, I wouldn't be having this conversation with anyone else, and that's a tribute to you. You know I loathe this emotional stuff."

He laughed. "Harry, I do love you."

She got up and kissed his cheek, disturbing a disgruntled Murphy one more time. "Let me think."

He mused. "I never knew love could be this complicated, or even that I could be this complicated!" He laughed. "I always knew you were complicated."

"See—and I think I'm simple."

Mrs. Murphy settled down in front of the fireplace to stare into the flames. "You know what worries me?"

"*What?*" Pewter yawned.

"*If Sean is part of Roscoe's murder, if he's in on this somehow, Mother was one of the last people to be with him. Only Cooper knows he didn't speak to her and Rick.*"

"*So?*" The gray cat fluttered her fur.

"*So, Pewter, the killer might think he told Mother what's what.*"

Pewter's eyes opened wide as did Tucker's. They said in unison, "*I never thought of that.*"

47

The antiseptic odor of hospitals turned Deputy Cooper's stomach. It stung her nostrils even though it wasn't as overpowering as, say, garbage. She wondered if the real offender was the associations she had concerning hospitals, or if truly she just hated the antiseptic.

Shorthanded though the department was, Rick was ferocious about maintaining vigilance over Sean. He'd broken half the bones in his body, his legs being the worst. His left arm was smashed in two places. His spleen was ruptured, and his left lung was punctured by his rib, which caved inward.

His right arm was fine. His skull was not crushed, but the force of the impact had created a severe concussion with some swelling in the brain. He had not regained consciousness, but his vital signs, though weak, had stabilized.

There was a good chance he'd live, although he'd never play

football again. Sean's mother and father took turns watching over him. His grandparents flew in from Olathe, Kansas, to help.

Cynthia half dozed on the hard-backed chair. On the other side of the bed his mother slept in another chair, equally uncomfortable.

A low moan alerted Cynthia. Her eyes opened, as did Sean's.

He blinked strongly to make sense of where he was.

"Sean," Cynthia said in a clear low voice.

His mother awakened with a start and leaned over her son. "Honey, honey, it's Mom."

He blinked again, then whispered, "I'm a father." His lips moved but no more sound escaped. Then, as if he had never spoken, he shut his eyes again and lost consciousness.

48

A howitzer ripped through Harry's meticulously planned schedule. Each night before retiring she would take a sheet of tablet paper, eight by eleven inches, fold it in half, and number her chores in order of priority. She used to watch her mother do it, absorbing the habit.

Harry was an organized person. Her disorganization involved major life questions such as "Whither thou goest?" She told herself Americans put too much emphasis on direction, management, and material success instead of just jumping into life.

Awaking each morning between five thirty and six, she first drank a piping hot cup of tea, fed the horses, picked out the stalls, stripping them on Saturdays, turned the horses out, fed Mrs. Murphy, Tucker, and now Pewter. Then she usually walked the mile out to the road to get her paper. That woke her up. If she was running behind or the weather proved filthy, she'd drive out in the blue truck.

Thanks to BoomBoom, the blue truck reposed again at the service station. Fortunately, BoomBoom's insurance really did cover the damages. And she'd get a new BMW since Sean had destroyed hers. Harry's worry involved the ever-decreasing life span of the 1978 Ford. She had to get a new truck. Paying for it, even a decent used one, seemed impossible.

The morning, crisp and clear at 36° F, promised a glorious fall day ahead. She jogged back, never opening the newspaper. Reading it with her second cup of tea and breakfast rewarded her for finishing the farm chores before heading off to the post office. She adored these small rituals of pleasure. Another concept she'd learned from her mother.

She bit into a light biscuit . . . then stopped, the biscuit hanging from her mouth. As she opened her mouth, the biscuit dropped onto the plate.

She knocked the chair over calling Susan. "You up?"

"Barely."

"Open the paper."

"Mmm. Holy shit! What's going on around here?" Susan exploded.

On the front page of the newspaper ran the story of the high-speed car chase. Harry was quoted as saying, "Another ten seconds and he'd have been blown to bits."

But what caused Susan's eruption was a story in the next column concerning April Shively's release on twenty thousand dollars' bail. That was followed by April's declaring she would not release the papers she had taken from St. Elizabeth's until the board of governors audited the current accounting books in the possession of the temporary headmaster, Sandy Brashiers. She all but accused him of financial misdeeds just this side of embezzlement.

As Harry and Susan excitedly talked in the background, Mrs. Murphy sat on the newspaper to read. Pewter joined her.

"Sean's not in the obit column, so we know he's still fighting." Murphy touched her nose to the paper.

"Going to be a hell of a day at the post office," Tucker predicted.

How right she was. A gathering place in the best and worst of times, it was packed with people.

Big Mim, hoisted up on the counter by the Reverend Jones, clapped her hands. "Order. Could I have some order, please?"

Accustomed to obeying the Queen of Crozet, they fell silent.

"Honeybun, we could move to city hall," her husband, the mayor, offered.

"We're here now, let's get on with it." Mim sat down and crossed her legs. Mrs. Murphy and Pewter flanked her. Tucker wandered among the crowd. The animals decided they would pay attention to faces and smells. Someone might give himself or herself away in a fashion a human couldn't comprehend.

Mim stared sternly at Karen, Jody, Brooks, and Roger. "Why aren't you in school?"

Karen answered for all of them. "Which school? We want to go back to St. Elizabeth's. Our parents won't let us."

"Then what are you doing here?" She pounded them like a schoolmarm.

"The post office is where everything happens, sort of," Brooks replied.

"*Smart kid*," Mrs. Murphy said.

Irene called out, "Marilyn, can you guarantee my child's safety?"

"Irene, no school can do that anymore, but within reason, yes." Marilyn Sanburne felt she spoke for the board.

Harry leaned across the counter. "Guys, I don't mind that you all meet here, but if someone comes in to get their mail, you have to clear a path for them. This is a federal building."

"The hell with Washington," Market Shiflett brazenly called out. "We had the right idea in 1861."

Cheers rose from many throats. Miranda laughed as did Harry. Those transplanted Yankees in the crowd would find this charming, anachronistic proof that Southerners are not only backward but incapable of forgetting the war.

What Southerners knew in their souls was that given half the chance, they'd leave the oppressive Union in a skinny minute. Let the Yankees tax themselves to death. Southerners had better things to do with their time and money, although it is doubtful those "better things" would be productive.

"Now we must remain calm, provoking as these hideous events have been." Mim turned to Harry. "Why don't you call Rick Shaw? He ought to be here."

"No." Herbie gently contradicted her. "If you'll forgive me, madam"—he often called Mim "madam"—"I think we'll all be more forthcoming without the law here."

"Yes." Other voices agreed.

Mim cast her flashing blue gaze over the crowd. "I don't know what's going on, I don't know why it's going on, but I think we must assume we know the person or persons responsible for Roscoe's demise as well as Maury's bizarre death. This community must organize to protect itself."

"How do we know the killer isn't in this room?" Dr. Larry Johnson asked.

Father Michael replied, "We don't."

"Well, Kendrick was found bending over Maury. Sorry, Irene, but it's true," Market said.

"Then we're telling the killer or killers our plans. How can we protect ourselves?" Lucinda Payne Coles, her brow furrowed, echoed what many others felt as well.

Harry raised her hand, a gesture left over from school.

"Harry." Mim nodded toward her.

"The question is not if the killer or killers could be in this room. The question is, why are people being killed? We'll worry ourselves into a fit if we think each of us is vulnerable."

"But we are!" Market exclaimed. "Two people are dead—and one seventeen-year-old boy who admitted planting the first obituary is in the hospital. Who or what next?"

Harry replied evenly, "Marilyn, I know you don't want to hear this, but everything points to St. Elizabeth's."

"Does that mean we're suspects?" Jody Miller joked.

Irene put her hand on her daughter's shoulder. "No one is

suspecting students, dear." She cast a knowing look at Larry Johnson. She needed to talk to him. Jody was in the first trimester of her pregnancy. A major decision had to be made. On the other hand, she watched Father Michael and thought maybe she should talk to him. It didn't occur to her that Jody was the one who needed to do the talking.

Neither Sandy Brashiers nor any faculty members from the school were there to defend themselves or the institution. They were holding back a tidal wave of questions, recriminations, and fear at their own faculty meeting. The reporters, like jackals, camped at the door.

"You must put aside April's absurd accusations," Marilyn said nervously, "and we will audit the books this week to lay her accusations to rest. She's only trying to divert our attention."

"It's true," Roger said in his quiet voice. "The problem is at St. E's."

Mim asked, "Do you have any idea, any idea at all, what is going on at your school? Is there a drug problem?"

"Mrs. Sanburne, drugs are everywhere. Not just at St. E's," Karen said solemnly.

"But you're rich kids. If you get in trouble, Daddy can bail you out." Samson Coles bluntly added his two cents even though many people shunned him.

"That's neither here nor there," Market said impatiently. "What are we going to do?"

"Can we afford more protection? A private police force?" Fair was pretty sure they couldn't.

"No." Jim, towering over everyone but Fair, answered that query. "We're on a shoestring."

"The rescue squad and other groups like the Firehouse gang could pitch in." Larry, getting warm, removed his glen plaid porkpie hat.

"Good idea, Larry." Mim turned to her husband. "Can we do that? Of course we can. You're the mayor."

"I'll put them on patrol. We can set up a cruise pattern. It's a start."

Mim went on. "While they're doing that, the rest of us can go over our contacts with Roscoe, April, Maury, and Sean. There may be a telling clue, something you know that seems unimportant but is really significant, the missing link, so to speak."

"Like, who gave Roscoe Fletcher candy at the car wash?" Miranda said innocently. "Harry thinks the killer was right there and gave him the poisoned candy right under everyone's nose."

"*She just let the cat out of the bag.*" Murphy's eyes widened.

"*What can we do?*" Tucker cried.

"*Pray the killer's not in this room,*" Mrs. Murphy said, knowing in her bones that the killer was looking her right in the face.

"*But Rick Shaw and Cynthia must have figured out the same thing.*" Pewter tried to allay their fears.

"*Of course they have, but until this moment the person who wiped out Roscoe didn't realize Mom had figured out most people were approaching Roscoe's murder backward. Now they'll wonder what else she's figured out.*"

"*It's Kendrick Miller.*" Pewter licked her paw, rubbing her ear with it.

"*If he is the one, he can get at Mom easily,*" Tucker responded. "*At least he's not here.*"

"*Don't worry, Irene will repeat every syllable of this meeting.*" Murphy's tail tip swayed back and forth, a sign of light agitation.

"*We need to ask Fair to stay with Mom.*" Tucker rightly assumed that would help protect her.

"*Fat chance.*" Murphy stood up, stretched, and called to her friends, "*Come on out back with me. Humans need to huff and puff. We've got work to do.*"

Tucker resisted. "*We ought to stay here and observe.*"

"*The damage is done. We need to hotfoot it. Come on.*"

Tucker threaded her way through the many feet and dashed through the animal door. Once outside she said, "*Where are we going?*"

"*St. Elizabeth's.*"

"*Murphy, that's too far.*" Pewter envisioned the trek.

"*Do you want to help, or do you want to be a wuss?*"

"*I'm not a wuss.*" Pewter defiantly swatted at the tiger cat.

"*Then let's go.*"

Within forty-five minutes they reached the football and soccer fields. Tired, they sat down for a minute.

"Stick together. We're going to work room to room."

"What are we looking for?"

"I'm not sure yet. If April took other books, they're truly cooked now. But none of these people thought they were going to be killed. They must have left unfinished business somewhere, and if the offices are clean as a whistle, then it means April knows the story—the whole story, doesn't it?"

49

Eerie quiet greeted the animals as they padded down the hallway of the Old Main Building, the administration building. The faculty meeting was heating up in the auditorium across the quad. Not one soul was in Old Main, not even a receptionist.

"Think the cafeteria is in Old Main?" Pewter inquired plaintively.

"No. Besides, I bet no one is working in the cafeteria." Tucker was anxious to get in and get out of the place before the post office closed. If Harry couldn't find them, she'd pitch a fit.

"Perfect." Mrs. Murphy read HEADMASTER in gold letters on the heavy oak door, slightly ajar. The cat checked the door width using her whiskers, knew she could make it, and squeezed through. Fatty behind her squeezed a little harder.

Tucker wedged her long nose in the door. Mrs. Murphy turned around and couldn't resist batting Tucker.

"No fair."

"Where's your sense of humor? Pewter, help me with the door."

The two cats pulled with their front paws as Tucker pushed with her nose. Finally the heavy door opened wide enough for the corgi to slip through. Everything had been moved out except for the majestic partner's desk and the rich red Persian carpet resting in front of the desk.

"Tucker, sniff the walls, the bottom of the desk, the bookcases, everything. Pewter, you check along the edge of the bookcases. Maybe there's a hidden door or something."

"What are you going to do?" Pewter dived into the emptied bookshelves.

"Open these drawers."

"That's hard work."

"Not for me. I learned to do this at home because Harry used to hide the fresh catnip in the right-hand drawer of her desk . . . until she found out I could open it."

"Where does she hide it now?" Pewter eagerly asked.

"Top of the kitchen cabinet, inside."

"Damn." Pewter rarely swore.

"Let's get to work." Mrs. Murphy flopped on her side, putting her paw through the burnished brass handle. Using her hind feet she pushed forward. The long center drawer creaked a bit, then rolled right out. Pens, pencils, and an avalanche of paper clips and engraved St. Elizabeth's stationery filled the drawer. She stuck her paws to the very back of the drawer. Mrs. Murphy shivered. She wanted so badly to throw the paper on the floor, then plunge into it headfirst. A paper bag was fun enough but expensive, lush, engraved laid bond—that was heaven. She disciplined herself, hopping on the floor to pull out the right-hand bottom drawer. The contents proved even more disappointing than the center drawer's: a hand squeezer to strengthen the hand muscles, a few floppy discs even though no computer was in the room, and one old jump rope.

"Anything?" She pulled on the left-hand drawer.

Tucker lifted her head, *"Too many people in here. I smell mice. But then that's not surprising. They like buildings where people go home at night—less interference."*

"*Nothing on the bookshelves. No hidden buttons.*"

Murphy, frustrated at not finding anything, jumped into the drawer, wiggling toward the back. Murphy's pupils, big from the darkness at the back of the drawer, quickly retracted to smaller circles as she jumped out. She noticed a small adhesive mailing label, ends curled, which must have fallen off a package. "*Here's an old mailing label. Neptune Film Laboratory, Brooklyn, New York—and three chewed pencils, the erasers chewed off. This room has been picked cleaner than a chicken bone.*"

"*We could go over to where Maury McKinchie was killed, in the hall outside the gymnasium,*" Tucker suggested.

"*Good idea.*" Mrs. Murphy hurried out the door.

"*She could at least wait for us. She can be so rude.*" Pewter followed.

The cavernous gymnasium echoed with silence. The click of Tucker's unretractable claws reverberated like tin drums.

"*Know what hall?*"

"No," Mrs. Murphy answered Tucker, "*but there's only one possibility. The two side halls go to the locker rooms. I don't think Maury was heading that way. He probably went through the double doors, which lead to the trophy hall and the big front door.*"

"*Then why did we come in the backdoor?*" Pewter grumbled.

"*Because our senses are sharper. We could pick up something in the lockers that a human couldn't. Not just dirty socks but cocaine lets off a sharp rancid odor, and marijuana is so easy a puppy could pick it up.*"

"*I resent that. A hound puppy is born with a golden nose.*"

"*Tucker, I hate to tell you this but you're a corgi.*"

"*I know that perfectly well, smart-ass.*" Ready to fight, she stopped in front of a battered light green locker. "*Wait a minute.*" She sniffed around the base of the locker, putting her nose next to the vent. "*Sugary, sticky.*"

"*Hey, look at that.*" Pewter involuntarily lifted her paw, taking a step back.

"Dead." Mrs. Murphy noted the line of dead ants going into the locker. She glanced up. "*Number one fourteen.*"

"*How do we get in there? I mean, if we want to?*" Pewter gingerly leapt over the ants.

"*We don't.*" Tucker indicated the big combination lock hanging on the locker door.

"*Why go to school if you have to lock away your possessions? Kids stealing from kids. It's not right.*"

"*It's not right, but it's real,*" Mrs. Murphy answered pragmatically. "*We aren't going to get anyone into this locker. Even the janitor has burnt rubber.*"

"*He rides a bicycle,*" Tucker said laconically, picturing Powder Hadly, thirties and simpleminded. He was so simpleminded he couldn't pass the written part of the driving test although he could drive just fine.

You get my drift." The tiger bumped into the corgi. Tucker bumped back, which made the cat stumble.

"*Twit.*"

"*It's all right if you do it. If I do anything you bitch and moan and scratch.*"

"*What are you doing then?*"

"*Describing your behavior. Flat facts.*"

"**The flat facts are, we can't do diddly.**" She halted. "*Well, there is one trick if we could get everyone to open their lockers. Not that the dead-ant locker has poison in it. That would be pretty stupid, wouldn't it? But who knows what's stashed in these things.*"

"*Do the faculty have lockers?*" Pewter asked.

"*Sure.*"

"*How do you know the faculty lockers from the kids'?*"

"*I don't know. We're on the girls' side. Maybe there's a small room we've missed that's set aside for the teachers.*"

They scampered down the hall and found a locker room for the female faculty. But there was nothing of interest except a bottle of Ambush perfume that had been left on the makeup counter. The men's locker room was equally barren of clues.

"*This was a wasted trip, and I'm famished.*"

"Not so wasted." Murphy trotted back toward the post office.

"*I'd like to know why. Roscoe's office was bare. We passed through April's office, nothing there. The sheriff has crawled over everything, fouling the scent. The gym is a tomb. And my pads are cold.*"

"*We found out that the killer had to have left the gym before Maury McKinchie to wait outside the front doors. They're glass so he could see Maury come out, or he waited behind one of the doors leading to the boys' locker room or the girls'. He dashed out and stabbed Maury and then either ran outside or he ran back into the gym. In costume, remember. He knew this setup.*"

"*Ah.*" Tucker appreciated Mrs. Murphy's reasoning. "*I see that, but if the killer had been outside, more people would have seen him because he was in costume—unless he changed it. No time for that, I think.*" Tucker canceled her own idea.

"*He was a Musketeer, if Kendrick is telling the truth. My hunch is he came from the side. From out of the locker rooms. No one had reason to go back there unless they wanted to smoke or drink, and they could easily do that outside without some chaperon or bush patrol. No, I'm sure he ran out the locker-room side.*"

"*You don't believe Kendrick did it?*" Pewter asked, knowing the answer but wanting to hear her friend's reasons.

"*No.*"

"*But what if Maury was sleeping with Irene?*" Tucker logically thought that was reason enough for some men to murder.

"*Kendrick wouldn't give a damn. A business deal gone bust, or some kind of financial betrayal might provoke him to kill, but he'd be cold-blooded about it. He'd plan. This was slapdash. Not Kendrick's style.*"

"*No wonder Irene mopes around,*" Pewter thought out loud. "*If my husband thought money was more important than me, I'd want a divorce, too.*"

"*Could Maury have been killed by a jilted lover?*"

"*Sure. So could Roscoe. But it doesn't fit. Not two of them back-to-back. And April Shively wouldn't have vacuumed out the school documents if it was that.*"

They reached the post office, glad to rush inside for warmth and crunchies.

"Where have you characters been?" Harry counted out change.

"*Deeper into this riddle, that's where we've been.*" Mrs. Murphy watched Pewter stick her face into the crunchies shaped like little fish. She didn't feel hungry herself. "*What's driving me crazy is that I'm missing something obvious.*"

"Murphy, I don't see how we've overlooked anything." Tucker was tired of thinking.

"No, it's obvious, but whatever it is, our minds don't want to see it." The tiger dropped her ears for a moment, then pricked them back up.

"Doesn't make sense," Pewter, thrilled to be eating, said between garbled mouthfuls.

"What is going on is too repulsive for our minds to accept. We're blanking out. It's right under our noses."

50

The uneasiness of Crozet's residents found expression in the memorial service for Maury McKinchie.

There was a full choir and a swelling organ but precious few people in Reverend Jones's church. Darla had indeed flown the body back to Los Angeles, so no exorbitantly expensive casket rested in front of the altar. Miranda, asked to sing a solo, chose "A Mighty Fortress Is Our God" because she was in a Lutheran church and because no one knew enough about Maury's spiritual life to select a more personal hymn. BoomBoom Craycroft wept in the front left row. Ed Sugarman comforted her, a full-time job. Naomi Fletcher, in mourning for Roscoe, sat next to Sandy Brashiers in the front right row. Harry, Susan, and Ned also attended. Other than that tiny crew, the church was bare. Had Darla shown her famous and famously kept face, the church would have been overflowing.

Back at the post office Harry thought about what constituted a life well lived.

At five o'clock, she gathered up April Shively's mail.

"Do you think she'll let you in?"

Harry raised her eyebrows. "Miranda, I don't much care. If not, I'll put it by her backdoor. Need anything while I'm out there? I'll pass Critzer's Nurseries."

"No, thanks. I've put in all my spring bulbs," came the slightly smug reply.

"Okay then—see you tomorrow."

Ten minutes later Harry pulled into a long country lane winding up at a neat two-story frame colonial. Blair Bainbridge had lent Harry his truck until hers was fixed. When she knocked on the door, there was no answer. She waited a few minutes, then placed the mail by the backdoor. As she turned to leave, the upstairs window opened.

"I'm not afraid to come in and get my mail."

"Your box was overflowing. Thought I'd save you a trip."

"Anybody know if Sean's going to make it?"

"No. The hospital won't give out information, and they won't allow anyone to visit. That's all I know."

"Boy doesn't have a brain in his head. Have you seen Sandy Brashiers or Naomi?" April half laughed. Her tone was snide.

Harry sighed impatiently. "I doubt they want to see you any more than you want to see them. Marilyn's not your biggest fan now either."

"Who cares about her?" April waved her hand flippantly. "She's a bad imitation of a bad mother."

"Big Mim's okay. You have to take her on her own terms."

"Think we can get inside?" Tucker asked.

"No," Murphy replied. "She's not budging from that window."

"What are they saying about me?" April demanded.

"Oh—that you hate Sandy, loved Roscoe, and you're accusing Sandy to cover your own tracks. If there's missing money, you've got it or know where it is."

"Ha!"

"But *you do know something, April. I know you do,*" Murphy meowed loudly.

"That cat's got a big mouth."

"*So's your old lady,*" Murphy sassed her.

"*Yeah!*" Pewter chimed in.

"April, I wish you'd get things right." Harry zipped up her jacket. "The school's like a tomb. Whatever you feel about Sandy—is it worth destroying St. Elizabeth's and everything Roscoe worked so hard to build?"

"*Good one, Mom.*" Tucker knew Harry had struck a raw nerve.

"Me destroy St. Elizabeth's! If you want to talk destruction, let's talk about Sandy Brashiers, who wants us to commit our energies and resources to a nineteenth-century program. He's indifferent to computer education, hostile to the film-course idea, and he only tolerates athletics because he has to—if he takes over, you watch, those athletic budgets will get trimmed and trimmed each year. He'll take it slow at first, but I know him! The two-bit sneak."

"Then come back."

"They fired me!"

"If you give back the papers—"

"Never. Not to Brashiers."

Harry held up her hands. "Give them to Sheriff Shaw."

"Fat lot of good that will do. He'll turn them over to St. Elizabeth's."

"He can impound them as evidence."

"Are you that dumb, or do you think I am?" April yelled. "Little Mim will whine, and Mommy will light the fires of hell under Rick Shaw's butt. Those papers will go to the Sanburne house if not St. Elizabeth's."

"How else can you clear your name?"

"When the time comes, I will. You just wait and see."

"I guess I'll have to." Harry gave up, walking back to the truck. She heard the window slam shut.

"*Time has a funny way of running out,*" Mrs. Murphy noted dryly.

51

Driving back into Crozet, Harry stopped and cajoled Mrs. Hogendobber to drive her through the car wash in her Falcon. Pewter, hysterical
at the thought, hid under the seat. Harry filled Miranda in on the
conversation with April, a belligerent April.

As they pulled right off Route 29, coasting past the Texaco station, Harry observed the distance between the gas pumps and the
port of the car wash. It was a quick sprint away, perhaps fifty yards at
the most. The Texaco station building blocked the view of the car
wash.

"Go slow."

"I am." Miranda scanned the setup, then coasted to a stop before the port.

Jimbo Anson rolled out, the collar of his jacket turned up against
the wind. "Welcome, Mrs. Hogendobber. I don't believe you've ever
been here."

"No, I haven't. I wash the car by hand. It's small enough that I can do it, but Harry wants me to become modern." She smiled as Harry reached across her and paid the rate for "the works."

"Come forward . . . there you go." He watched as Miranda's left wheel rolled onto the track. "Put her in neutral, and no radio." Jimbo punched the big button hanging on a thick electrical cord, and the car rolled into the mists.

A buzzer sounded, the yellow neon light flashed, and Miranda exclaimed, "My word."

Harry carefully noted the time it took to complete the cycle as well as how the machinery swung out from the side or dropped from above. The last bump of the track alerted them to put the car in drive. Harry mumbled, "No way."

"No way what?"

"I was thinking maybe the killer came into the car wash, gave Roscoe the poisoned candy, and ran out. I know it's loony, but the sight of someone soaking wet in the car wash, someone he knew, would make him roll down the window or open a door if he could. It was a thought. If you run up here from the Texaco station, which takes less than a minute, no one could see you if you ducked in the car wash exit. But it's impossible. And besides, nobody noticed anyone being all wet."

" 'Cain said to Abel, his brother, "Let us go out to the field." And when they were in the field, Cain rose up against his brother Abel, and killed him. Then the Lord said to Cain, "Where is Abel your brother?" He said, "I do not know; am I my brother's keeper?" And the Lord said, "What have you done? The voice of your brother's blood is crying to me from the ground." ' " Mrs. Hogendobber quoted Genesis. "The first murder of all time. Cain didn't get away with it. Neither will this murderer."

"Rick Shaw is working overtime to tie Kendrick to both murders. Cynthia called me last night. She said it's like trying to stick a square peg in a round hole. It's not working, and Rick is tearing his hair out."

"He can ill afford that." Mrs. Hogendobber turned south on Route 29.

"I keep coming back to cowardice. Poison is the coward's tool."

"Whoever killed McKinchie wasn't a coward. A bold run-through with a sword shows imagination."

"McKinchie was unarmed, though," Harry said. "The killer jumped out and skewered him. Imagination, yes, but cowardice, yes. It's one thing to plan a murder and carry it out, a kind of cold brilliance, if you will. It's another thing to sneak up on people."

"It is possible that these deaths are unrelated," Miranda said tentatively. "But I don't think so; that's what worries me." She braked for a red light.

She couldn't have been more worried than Father Michael, who, dozing in the confession booth, was awakened by the murmur of that familiar muffled voice, taking pains to disguise itself.

"Father, I have sinned."

"Go on, my child."

"I have killed more than once. I like killing, Father. It makes me feel powerful."

A hard lump lodged in Father Michael's thin throat. "All power belongs to God, my child." His voice grew stronger. "And who did you kill?"

"Rats." The disguised voice burst into laughter.

He heard the swish of the heavy black fabric, the light, quick footfall. He bolted out of the other side of the confession booth in time to see a swirl of black, a cloak, at the side door, which quickly closed. He ran to the door and flung it open. No one was there, only a blue jay squawking on the head of the Avenging Angel.

52

"Nobody?"

Lucinda Payne Coles, her heavy skirt draped around her legs to ward off the persistent draft in the old office room, said again, "Nobody. I'm at the back of the church, Sheriff. The only way I'll see who comes in and out of the front is if I walk out there or they park back here."

Cynthia, also feeling the chill, moved closer to the silver-painted radiator. "Have you noticed anyone visiting Father Michael lately, anyone unusual?"

"No. If anything it's quieter than normal for this time of year."

"Thanks, Mrs. Coles. Call me any time of the day or night if anything occurs to you."

Rick and Cynthia walked outside. A clammy mist enshrouded them in the graveyard. They bent down at the side door. Depressions on leaves could be seen, a slight smear on the moisture that they tracked into the cemetery.

"Smart enough to cover his tracks," Cynthia said.

"Or hers. That applies to every country person in the county," Rick replied. "Or anyone who's watched a lot of crime shows." He sat on a tombstone for a moment. "Any ideas?"

"Nope."

"Me neither."

"We know one thing. The killer likes to confess."

"No, Coop, the killer likes to brag. We've got exactly one hope in hell."

"Which is?" She told herself she wasn't really a smoker as she reached into her pocket for a pack.

"I'll take one of those." Rick reached out.

They lit up, inhaling.

"Wonder how many people buried here died of emphysema?"

"Don't know." He laughed. "I might be one of them someday."

"What's your one hope, boss?"

"Pride goeth before a fall."

53

Rick Shaw set up a temporary command post in April Shively's office. Little Mim and Sandy Brashiers requested over the radio and in the newspaper that students return to St. Elizabeth's for questioning.

Every hand Rick could spare was placed at the school. Little Mim organized and Sandy assisted.

"—the year started out great. Practice started out great—" Karen Jensen smiled at the sheriff. "Our class had a special film week. We wrote a story, broke it down into shots, and then Friday, we filmed it. Mr. McKinchie and Miss Thalman from New York directed us. That was great. I can't think of anything weird."

"Sean?"

"Oh, you know Sean, he likes playing the bad boy, but he seemed okay." She was relaxed, wanting to be helpful.

"If you think of anything, come on back or give me a call." Rick smiled reflexively. When Karen had left, he said to Cooper, "No running nose, no red eyes or dilated pupils or pupils the size of a pin. No signs of drug abuse. We're halfway through the class—if only Sean would regain consciousness."

"If he is going to be a father, that explains a lot."

"Not enough," Rick grumbled.

Cynthia flipped through her notes. "He used to run errands for April Shively. Jody Miller said Sean had a permanent pink pass." She flipped the notebook shut.

A bark outside the door confused them for a moment, then Cynthia opened the door.

Fur ruffled, Tucker bounded in. *"We can help!"*

With less obvious enthusiasm Mrs. Murphy and Pewter followed.

"Where's Harry?"

As if to answer Coop's question, Harry walked through the door carrying a white square plastic container overflowing with mail. "Roscoe's and Maury's mail." She plopped the box on the table. "I put Naomi's mail in her mailbox."

"Anything unusual?" Rick inquired.

"No. Personal letters and bills, no Jiffy bags or anything suspicious."

"Has she been coming to pick up her mail?"

"Naomi comes in each day. But not today. At least not before I left."

Cynthia asked, "Does she ever say anything at all?"

"She's downcast. We exchange pleasantries and that's it."

"Good of Blair to lend you his Dually." Coop hoped her severe crush on the handsome man wouldn't show. It did.

"He's a good neighbor." Harry smiled. "Little Mim's pegged him for every social occasion between now and Christmas, I swear."

"He doesn't seem to mind."

"What choice does he have? Piss off a Sanburne?" Her eyebrows rose.

"Point taken." Cynthia nodded, feeling better already.

"When you girls stop chewing the fat, I'd be tickled pink to get back to business."

"Yes, boss."

"Spoilsport," Harry teased him. "If we take our minds off the problem, we usually find the answer."

"That's the biggest bunch of bull I've heard since 'Read my lips: No new taxes,' " Rick snorted.

"*Read my lips: Come to the locker room.*" The tiger cat let out a hoot.

"Was that a hiccup?" Cynthia bent down to pat Mrs. Murphy.

"*Let's try the old run away—run back routine.*" Tucker ripped out of the room and ran halfway down the hall, her claws clicking on the wooden floor, then raced back.

"*Let's all do it.*" Mrs. Murphy followed the dog. Pewter spun out so fast her hind legs slipped away from her.

"Nuts." Rick watched, shaking his head.

"Playful." Coop checked the mail. There wasn't anything that caught her eye as odd.

Halfway down the hall the animals screeched to a halt, bumping into one another.

"*Idiots.*" Mrs. Murphy puffed her tail. The fur on the back of her neck stood up.

"*We could try again.*" Tucker felt that repetition was the key with humans.

"*No. I'll crawl up Mother's leg. That gets her attention.*"

"*Doesn't mean she'll follow us,*" Pewter replied pragmatically.

"*Have you got a better idea?*" The tiger whirled on the gray cat.

"*No, Your Highness.*"

The silent animals reentered the room. Mrs. Murphy walked over to Harry, rubbed against her leg, and purred.

"Sweetie, we'll go in a minute."

That fast Murphy climbed up Harry's legs. The jeans blunted the claws, yet enough of those sharp daggers pierced the material to make Harry yelp.

"*Follow me!*" She dropped off Harry's leg and ran to the door, stopping to turn a somersault.

"Show-off," Pewter muttered under her breath.

"*You can't do a somersault,*" Murphy taunted her.

"Oh, *yes*, I *can*." Pewter ran to the door and leapt into the air. Her somersault was a little wobbly and lopsided, but it was a somersault.

"You know, every now and then they get like this," Harry explained sheepishly. "Maybe I'll see what's up."

"I'll go with you."

"You're both loose as ashes." Rick grabbed the mail.

As Harry and Cynthia followed the animals, they noticed a few classrooms back in use.

"That's good, I guess," Cynthia remarked.

"Well, once you all decided to work out of the school to question students, some of the parents figured it would be safe to send the kids back." Harry giggled. "Easier than having them at home, no matter what."

"Are we on a hike?" Cynthia noticed the three animals had stopped at the backdoor to the main building and were staring at the humans with upturned faces.

When Harry opened the door, they shot out, galloping across the quad. "All right, you guys, this is a con!"

"No, it isn't." The tiger trotted back to reassure the two wavering humans. *"Come on. We've got an idea. It's more than any of you have."*

"I could use some fresh air." Cynthia felt the first snowflake of winter alight on her nose.

"Me, too. Miranda will have to wait."

They crossed the quad, the snowflakes making a light tapping sound as they hit tree branches. The walkway was slick but not white yet. In the distance between the main building and the gymnasium, the snow thickened.

"Hurry up. It's cold," Pewter exhorted them.

The humans reached the front door of the gym and opened it. The animals dashed inside.

Mrs. Murphy glanced over her shoulder to see if they were behind her. She ran to the girls' gym door at one corner of the trophy hall. The other two animals marched behind her.

"This is a wild-goose chase." Cynthia laughed.

"Who knows, but it gives you a break from Rick. He's just seething up there."

"He gets like that until he cracks a case. He blames himself for everything."

They walked into the locker room. All three animals sat in front of 114. The line of dead ants was still there.

Since each locker wore a combination lock like a ring hanging from a bull's nose, they couldn't get into the locker.

But it gave Cynthia an idea. She found Coach Hallvard, who checked her list. Number 114 belonged to Jody Miller. Cynthia requested that the coach call her girls in to open their lockers.

An hour later, Coach Hallvard, an engine of energy, had each field hockey player, lacrosse, basketball, track and field, anyone on junior varsity or varsity standing in front of her locker.

Harry, back at work, missed the fireworks. When 114 was opened, an open can of Coca-Cola was the source of the ant patrol. However, 117 contained a Musketeer costume. The locker belonged to Karen Jensen.

54

Rick paced, his hands behind his back. Karen sobbed that she knew nothing about the costume, which was an expensive one.

"Ask anybody. I was Artemis, and I never left the dance," she protested. She was also feeling low because a small amount of marijuana had been found in her gym bag.

Rick got a court order to open lockers, cutting locks off if necessary. He had found a virtual pharmacy at St. Elizabeth's. These kids raided Mom and Dad's medicine chest with regularity or they had a good supplier. Valium, Percodan, Quaaludes, speed, amyl nitrate, a touch of cocaine, and a good amount of marijuana competed with handfuls of anabolic steroids in the boys' varsity lockers.

Hardened though he was, he was unprepared for the extent of drug use at the school. When he pressured one of the football players, he heard the standard argument: if you're playing football against guys who use steroids and you don't, you get creamed. If a boy wants to excel at certain sports, he's got to get into drugs sooner or later. The drug of choice was human growth hormone, but none of the kids could find it, and it was outrageously expensive. Steroids were a lot easier to cop.

The next shocker came when Cynthia checked the rental of the Musketeer costume using a label sewn into the neck of the tunic. She reached an outfitter in Washington, D.C. They reported they were missing a Musketeer costume, high quality.

It had been rented by Maury McKinchie using his MasterCard.

55

The snow swirled, obscuring Yellow Mountain. Harry trudged to the barn, knowing that no matter how deep the snow fell, it wouldn't last. The hard snows arrived punctually after Christmas. Occasionally a whopper would hit before the holidays, but most residents of central Virginia could count on real winter socking them January through March.

The winds, stiff, blew the fall foliage clean off the trees. Overnight the riotous color of fall gave way to the spare monochrome of winter.

A rumble sent Tucker out into the white. Fair pulled up. He clapped his cowboy hat on his head as he dashed for the barn.

"Harry, I need your help."

"What happened?"

"BoomBoom is pitching a royal hissy. She says she has to talk to someone she can trust. She has a heavy heart. You should hear it."

"No, I shouldn't."

"What should I do?" He fidgeted. "She sounded really distressed."

Harry leaned against a stall door. Gin Fizz poked his white nose over the top of the Dutch doors, feed falling from his mouth as he chewed. Usually he'd stick his head out and chat. Today he was too hungry and the feed was too delicious.

"*Mom, go along. That will give BoomBoom cardiac arrest.*" Murphy laughed.

"I'll tell you exactly what I think. She was sleeping with Maury McKinchie."

"You don't know that for a fact." He removed his hat and shook his head.

"Woman's instinct. Anyway, if you don't want to hear what I have to say, I'll go back to work and you can do whatever."

"I want to know."

"The more I think about the horrible events around here, the more it points to the battle between Roscoe and Sandy Brashiers over the future direction of St. Elizabeth's." She held up her hand. "I know. Doesn't take a genius to figure that out."

"Well, I hadn't thought about it that way."

"Comfort BoomBoom—within reason. She might have a piece of the puzzle and not know it. Or she may be in danger. On the other hand, BoomBoom won't miss a chance to emote extravagantly." She smiled. "And, of course, you'll tell me everything."

56

What was working on BoomBoom was her mouth. She confessed to Fair that she had been having an affair with Maury McKinchie. She had broken it off when she discovered he was having affairs with other women or at least with one important woman. He wouldn't tell her who it was.

She thought that the Other Woman, not his wife, of course, might have killed him.

"What a fool I was to believe him." Her expressive gray-blue eyes spilled over with salty tears.

Fair wanted to hug her, console her, but his mistrust of her ran deep enough for him to throttle his best impulses. One hug from him and she'd be telling everyone they had engaged in deep, meaningful discussions. Gossip would take it from there.

"Did he promise to divorce Darla?"

"No. She was his meal ticket."

"Ah, then what was there to believe? I'm missing a beat here. I don't mean to be dense."

"You're not dense, Fair, darling, you're just a man." She forgot her misery long enough to puff up his ego. "Men don't look below the surface. Believe? I believed him when he said he loved me." She renewed her sobs and no amount of light sea kelp essence could dispel her gloom.

"Maybe he did love you."

"Then how could he carry on with another woman? It was bad enough he had a wife!"

"You don't know for certain—do you?"

"Oh, yes, I do." She wiped her eyes with her handkerchief. "I ransacked his car when he was 'taking a meeting,' as he used to say, with Roscoe. He kept everything important in that car. Here." She reached into her silk robe, a luscious lavender, and pulled out a handful of envelopes, which she thrust into his hands. "See for yourself."

Fair held the light gray envelopes, Tiffany paper, wrapped in a white ribbon. He untied the ribbon. "Shouldn't you give these to Rick Shaw?"

"I should do a lot of things; that's why I need to talk to you. How do I know Rick will keep this out of the papers?"

"He will." Fair read the first letter rapidly. Love stuff only interested him if it was his love stuff. His mood changed considerably when he reached the signature at the bottom of the next page. In lovely cursive handwriting the name of "Your Naomi" appeared. "Oh, shit."

"Killed him."

"You think Naomi killed him?"

"She could parade around in a Musketeer costume as easily as the rest of us."

"Finding that costume in Karen Jensen's locker sure was lucky for Kendrick." Fair raised an eyebrow. "I wouldn't let him off the hook yet myself. That guy's got serious problems."

"Heartless. Not cruel, mind you, just devoid of feeling unless there's a dollar sign somewhere in the exchange." BoomBoom tapped a long fingernail in the palm of her other hand. "Think how easy it would have been for Naomi to dump that costume in a kid's locker. Piece of cake."

"Maybe." Fair handed the envelopes back to BoomBoom.

"You aren't going to read the rest of them? They sizzle."

"It's none of my business. You should hand them over to Rick. Especially if you think Naomi killed McKinchie."

"That's just it. She must have found out about me and let him have it after offing Roscoe. Ha. She thought she was free and clear, and then she finds out there's another woman. I give him credit for energy. A wife and two lovers." She smirked, her deep dimple, so alluring, drawing deeper.

"I guess it's possible. Anything's possible. But then again, who's to say you didn't kill Maury McKinchie?" Fair, usually indirect in such circumstances, bluntly stated the obvious.

"Me? Me? I couldn't kill anyone. I want to heal people, bind their inner wounds. I wouldn't hurt anyone."

"I'm telling you how it looks to a—"

"A scumbag! Anyone who knows me knows I wouldn't kill, and most emphatically not over love."

"Sex? Or love?"

"I thought you'd be on my side!"

"I am on your side." He leveled his gaze at the distressed woman, beautiful even in her foolishness. "That's why I'm asking you questions."

"I thought I loved Maury. Now I'm not so sure. He used me. He even gave me a screen test."

"From a sheriff's point of view, I'd say you had a motive."

"Well, I didn't have a motive to kill Roscoe Fletcher!"

"No, it would appear not. Did anyone have it in for Roscoe? Anyone you know?"

"Naomi. That's what I'm telling you."

"We don't know that he was cheating on her."

"He gathered his rosebuds while he may. Don't all you men do that—I mean, given the opportunity, you're all whores."

"I was." His jaw locked on him.

"Oh, Fair, I didn't mean you. You and Harry weren't suited for each other. The marriage would have come apart sooner or later. You know I cherish every moment we shared, and that's why, in my hour of need, I called you."

How could he have ever slept with this woman? Was he that blinded by beauty? A wave of disgust rose up from his stomach. He fought it down. Why be angry at her? She was what she was. She hadn't changed. He had.

"Fair?" She questioned the silence between them.

"If you truly believe that Naomi Fletcher killed her husband because she wanted to be with Maury McKinchie and then killed him in a fit of passion because she found out about you, you must go to the sheriff. Turn over those letters."

"I can't. It's too awful."

He changed his tack. "BoomBoom, what if she comes after you—assuming your hypothesis is correct."

"No!" Genuine alarm spread over her face.

"What about April Shively?" he pressed on.

"A good foundation base would have changed her life. That and rose petals in her bathwater." BoomBoom's facial muscles were taut; the veins in her neck stood out. "O-o-o, I'm cramping up. A charley horse. Rub it out for me."

"Your calf is fine. Don't start that stuff with me."

"What stuff?" She flared her nostrils.

"You know. Now I'm calling the sheriff. You can't withhold evidence like this."

"Don't!"

"BoomBoom, for once put your vanity aside for the public good. A murderer is out there. It may be Naomi, as you've said, but"—he shrugged—"if news leaks out that you had a fling with Maury, it's not the end of the world."

"Easy for you to say."

"I thought the man was a perfect ass."

"He made me laugh. And I can act as well as half of those people you see on television."

"I would never argue that point." He paused a moment, a

flicker, a jolt to the brain. "BoomBoom, have you ever watched any of Maury's movies?"

"Sure. Every one."

"Did you like them? I mean, can you tell me something about them?"

"He used hot, hot leading ladies. He gave Darla her big break, you know."

"Hot? As in sex?"

"Oh"—she flipped her fingers downward, a lightning-fast gesture, half dismissal—"everything Maury did was about sex: the liberating power of sex and how we are transformed by it. The true self is revealed in the act. I mean, the stories could be about the Manhattan district attorney's office or about a Vietnamese immigrant in Los Angeles—that's my favorite, *Rice Sky*—but sex takes over sooner or later."

"Huh." He walked over to the phone.

"Don't leave me."

"I'm not." He called Harry first. "Honey, I'm waiting for Rick Shaw. I'll explain when I get to your place. Is your video machine working? Good. I'm bringing some movies. We're going to eat a lot of popcorn." Then he dialed Rick.

In fifteen minutes Rick and Cynthia arrived, picked up the envelopes, and left after commanding BoomBoom not to leave town.

When she begged Fair not to leave, he replied, not unkindly, "You need to learn to be alone."

"Not tonight! I'm scared."

"Call someone else."

"You're going back to Harry."

"I'm going to watch movies with her."

"Don't do it. It's a big mistake."

"Do what?"

"Fall in love with her."

"I never fell out of love with her. I lost me first, then I lost my wife. Sorry, BoomBoom."

57

"Girl, you'd better have a good explanation." Kendrick's eyes, blood-shot with rage, bored into his daughter.

"I told you. I paid with Grandpa's legacy."

"I checked the bank. You're a minor, so they gave me the information. Your account is not missing forty-one thousand dollars, which is what that damned BMW cost!"

"The check hasn't cleared yet," she replied coolly.

"Pegasus Motor Cars says you paid with a certified check. Who gave you the money!"

"Grandpa!" She sat on the edge of the sofa, knees together like a proper young lady.

"Don't lie to me." He stepped toward her, fists clenched.

"Dad, don't you dare hit me, I'm pregnant."

He stopped in his tracks. "WHAT?"

"I . . . am . . . pregnant."

"Does your mother know?"

"Yes."

If Irene had appeared at that moment, Kendrick might have killed her. Luckily she was grocery shopping. He transferred his rage to the man responsible.

"Who did this to you?"

"None of your business."

"It is my business. Whoever he is, he's going to make good on this deal. He'll marry you."

"I don't want to get married."

"Oh, you don't?" Venom dripped from his voice. "Well, what you want is irrelevant. You got into this mess by following your wants. My God, Jody, what's happened to you?" He sat down with a thud, the anger draining into fear and confusion.

"Don't be mad at Mom. She did what a mother is supposed to do. She went to the doctor with me—once I knew. We were going to tell you, Dad, but with everything that's happened to you—we put it off."

"Who is the father?"

"I'm not sure."

"How many boys have you slept with?" His voice cracked.

"A couple."

"Well, who do you think it is?"

"Sean Hallahan—maybe."

"Oh, shit."

58

"Don't lie to me." Susan hovered over Brooks.

"I'm not. I don't do drugs, Mom."

"You hang out with someone who does."

"Jensen's not a druggie. She had one joint in her bag. Chill out."

Ned stepped in. "I think it's time we all went to bed."

"Danny's already in bed." Brooks envied her brother, off the hook on this one.

"Now look, daughter, if you are hiding something, you'd better come clean. Whatever you're doing, we'll deal with it."

"I'm not doing anything."

"Susan." Ned rubbed his forehead. A headache nibbled at his temples.

"I want to get to the bottom of this. Sheriff Shaw asked each of you questions after the marijuana was found and after that costume showed up. I can't believe it. It's too preposterous. Karen Jensen."

"Mom, Karen didn't kill Mr. McKinchie. Really. It's nuts."

"How do you suppose the costume got in her locker?"

"Easy. Everyone on the team knows everyone else's combination. We're always borrowing stuff."

Susan hovered over Brooks. "What do you know about Karen Jensen that we don't?"

"Karen's okay. She's not a druggie. The only thing I know about Karen is that she was dating an older guy from UVA this summer and got a little too close. Really. She's okay."

Susan put her arm around her daughter's shoulders. "I hope you are, too."

Later Susan called Harry, relaying the conversation with Brooks. Harry treated her to a synopsis of *Rice Sky*.

"Sounds boring."

"Made a lot of money. I think the real reason Roscoe was pushing the film-department idea was to punch up Maury. He was so overshadowed by Darla. Roscoe was smart. Cater to Maury and good things would follow."

"Money. Tons of money."

"Sure. They'd name the department after Maury. He'd donate all his scripts, round up old equipment; the whole thing would be an ego trip."

"How much do you think an ego trip like that would cost?"

"It would take at least a million-dollar endowment, I'd think. Probably more." Harry scribbled on a brown paper bag. "I'm not too good at knowing what it would be worth, really, but it would have to be a lot."

"What's Fair think?"

"Millions," he called out.

"Sandy Brashiers can't be that stupid," Harry said. "For a couple of million dollars even he would cave in on the film-department idea."

"I doubt Roscoe put it in dollars and cents."

"Yeah. Maybe it's in April's books."

"Susan, if that's all that's in there, what's to hide?"

"Damned if I know. We called about Sean, by the way. No change."

"I called, too."

"That kid has to know something. Larry Johnson said he'd heard the main swelling was diminishing. Maybe he'll snap out of the coma once the swelling is down."

"He's lucky to be alive."

59

"Why don't you just tell me the truth?" Rick rapped his fingers on the highly polished table.

"You have no right to push me like this." Naomi Fletcher had her back up.

"You know more than you're telling me." He remained cool and professional.

"No, I don't. And I resent you badgering me when I'm in mourning."

Wordlessly, Cynthia Cooper slid the packet of envelopes, retied with a neat bow, across the table to Naomi. Her face bled bone white.

"How—?"

"The 'how' doesn't matter, Naomi. If you are in on these murders, come clean." Cynthia sounded sympathetic. "Maybe we can work a deal."

"I didn't kill anyone."

"You didn't kill Roscoe to clear the way for McKinchie to marry you?" Rick pressured her.

"Marry Maury McKinchie? I'd sooner have a root canal." Her even features contorted in scorn.

"You liked him enough to sleep with him." Cynthia felt the intimate information should best come from her, not Rick.

"That doesn't mean I wanted to spend my life with him. Maury was a good-time Charlie, and that's all he was. He wasn't marriage material."

"Apparently, neither was Roscoe."

She shrugged. "He was in the beginning, but men change."

"So do women." Cynthia pointed to the envelopes.

"What's good for the gander was good for the goose, in this instance. The marriage vows are quite lovely, and one would hope to live up to them, but they are exceedingly unrealistic. I didn't do anything wrong. I didn't kill anyone. I played with Maury McKinchie. You can't arrest me for that."

"Played with him and then killed him when you learned he wasn't serious about you and he was sleeping with another woman."

"BoomBoom." She waved her hand in the air as though at an irritating gnat. "I'd hardly worry about her."

"Plenty of other women have." Cynthia bluntly stated the truth.

"BoomBoom was too self-centered for Maury. One was never really in danger of a rival because he loved himself too much, if you know what I mean." She smiled coldly.

"You were at the car wash the day your husband died. You spoke to him. You could have easily given him poisoned candy."

"I could have, but I didn't."

"You're tough," Rick said, half admiringly.

"I'm not tough, I'm innocent."

"If I had a dollar for every killer who said that, I'd be a rich man." Rick felt in his coat pocket for his cigarettes. "Mind if I smoke?"

"I most certainly do. The whole house will stink when you leave, which I hope is soon."

Cynthia and Rick shared a secret acknowledgment. No Southern lady would have said that.

"How well did you know Darla?"

"A nodding acquaintance. She was rarely here."

"If you didn't kill Roscoe, do you know who did?"

"No."

"How does withholding evidence sound to you, Mrs. Fletcher?" Rick hunched forward.

"Like a bluff."

"For chrissake, Naomi, two men are dead!" Cynthia couldn't contain her disgust. Then she quickly fired a question. "Was your husband sleeping with April Shively?"

"God, no," Naomi hooted. "Roscoe thought April was pretty but deadly dull." Naomi had to admit to herself that dullness didn't keep men from sleeping with women. However, she wasn't going to admit that to Shaw and Cooper.

"Do you think Kendrick killed Maury?" Rick switched his bait.

"Unlikely." She closed her eyes, as if worn-out.

Cooper interjected. "Why?"

Naomi perked up. "Kendrick doesn't have the balls."

"Did you love your husband?" Rick asked.

She grew sober, sad even. "You live with a man for eighteen years, you tend to know him. Roscoe might wander off the reservation from time to time. He could indulge in little cruelties—his treatment of Sandy Brashiers being a case in point. He kept Sandy in the dark about everything." She paused, "Did I love him? I was accustomed to him, but I did love him. Yes, I did."

Cynthia mustered a smile. "Why?"

Naomi shrugged. "Habit."

"What did Roscoe have against Sandy Brashiers?"

"Roscoe always had it in for Harvard men. He said the arrogance of their red robes infuriated him. You know, during academic ceremonies only Harvard wears the crimson robe."

"Do you have any feeling about the false obituaries?" Cynthia prodded.

"Those?" Naomi wrinkled her brow. "Kids' prank. Sean apologized."

"Do you think he was also responsible for the second one?"

"No. I think it was a copycat. Sean got the luxury of being a bad dude. Very seductive at that age. Another boy wanted the glory. Is it that important?"

"It might be." Rick reached for his hat.

"Have you searched April Shively's house?" Naomi asked.

"House, car, office, even her storage unit. Nothing."

Naomi stood up to usher them out. "She doesn't live high on the hog. I don't think she embezzled funds."

"She could be covering up for someone else." Cynthia reached the door first.

"You mean Roscoe, of course." Naomi didn't miss a beat. "Why not? He's dead. He can be accused of anything. You have to find criminals in order to keep your jobs, don't you?"

Rick halted at the door as Naomi's hand reached the knob. "You work well with Sandy, don't you? Under the circumstances?"

"Yes."

"Did you know that Sandy got a student pregnant at White Academy, the school he worked at before St. Elizabeth's?"

Cooper struck next. "Roscoe knew."

"You two have been very busy." Her lips tightened.

"Like you said, Mrs. Fletcher, we have to find criminals in order to keep our jobs." Rick half smiled.

She grimaced and closed the door.

60

Mrs. Murphy leaned against the pillow on the sofa. She stretched her right hind leg out straight and held it there. Then she unsheathed her claws and stared at her toes. What stupendously perfect toes. She repeated the process with the left hind leg. Then she reached with her front paws together, a kitty aerobic exercise. Satisfied, she lay back on the pillow, happily staring into the fire. She reviewed in her mind recent events.

Harry dusted her library shelves, a slow process since she'd take a book off the shelf, read passages, and then replace it. A light snow fell outside, which made her all the happier to be inside.

Tucker snored in front of the fire. Pewter, curled in a ball at the other end of the sofa, dreamed of tiny mice singing her praise. "O Mighty Pewter, Queen of Cats."

"Lord of the Flies." Harry pulled the old paperback off the shelf. "Had to read it in college, but I hated it." She dropped to the next shelf. "Fielding, love him. Austen." She turned to Mrs. Murphy. "Literature is about sensibility. Really, Murphy, John Milton is one of the greatest poets who ever lived, but he bores me silly. I have trouble liking any art form trying to beat a program into my head. I suppose it's the difference between the hedgehog and the fox."

"*Isaiah Berlin.*" Mrs. Murphy recalled the important work of criticism dividing writers into hedgehogs or foxes, hedgehogs being fixed on one grand idea or worldview whereas foxes ran through the territory; life was life with no special agenda. That was how she thought of it anyway.

"What I mean is, Murphy, readers are hedgehogs or foxes. Some people read to remember. Some read to forget. Some read to be challenged. Others want their prejudices confirmed."

"*Why do you read, Mother?*" the cat asked.

"I read," Harry said, knowing exactly what her cat had asked her, "for the sheer exultant pleasure of the English language."

"*Ah, me, too.*" The tiger purred. Harry couldn't open a book without Mrs. Murphy sitting on her shoulder or in her lap.

Sometimes Pewter would read, but she favored mysteries or thrillers. Pewter couldn't raise her sights above genre fiction.

Mrs. Murphy thought the gray cat might read some diet books as well. She stretched and walked over to Harry. She jumped on a shelf to be closer to Harry's face. She scanned the book spines, picking out her favorites. She enjoyed biographies more than Harry did. She stopped at Michael Powell's *My Life In The Movies.*

She blinked and leapt off the shelf, cuffing Tucker awake. "*Come on, Tucker, come on.*"

"*I'm so comfortable.*"

"*Just follow me.*" She skidded out the animal door, Tucker on her heels.

"What in God's name gets into her?" Harry held *The Iliad.*

Forty-five minutes later both animals, winded, pulled up at Bowden's pond where the Camry and the grisly remains still sat, undiscovered by humans.

"*Tucker, you cover the east side of the pond. I'll cover the west. Look for a video or a can of film.*"

Both animals searched through the snow, which was beginning to cover the ground; still the shapes would have been obvious.

An hour later they gave up.

"Nothing," Tucker reported.

"*Me either.*"

A growl made their hair stand on end.

"*The bobcat!*" Mrs. Murphy charged up the slippery farm road, leaping the ruts. Tucker, fast as grease, ran beside her.

They reached the cutover hayfields, wide open with no place to hide.

"*She's gaining on us.*" Tucker's tongue hung out.

And she was, a compact, powerful creature, tufts on the ends of her ears.

"*This is my fault.*" The cat ached from running so hard.

"*Save your breath.*" Tucker whirled to confront the foe, her long fangs bared.

The bobcat stopped for a moment. She wanted dinner, but she didn't want to get hurt. She loped around Tucker, deciding Murphy was the better chance. Tucker followed the bobcat.

"*Run, Murphy, run. I'll keep her busy.*"

"*You domesticated worm,*" the bobcat spat.

Seeing her friend in danger, Murphy stopped panting. She puffed up, turning to face the enemy. Together she and Tucker flanked the bobcat about twenty yards from her.

The bobcat crouched, moving low toward Mrs. Murphy, who jumped sideways. The bobcat ran and flung herself in the air. Murphy sidestepped her. The big cat whirled and charged just as Tucker hurtled toward her. The dog hit the bobcat in the legs as she was ready to pounce on Murphy. The bobcat rolled, then sprang to her feet. Both friends were side to side now, fangs bared.

"In here!" a voice called from the copse of trees a spring away.

"*Let's back toward it,*" Murphy gasped.

"*Where are we going?*" Tucker whispered.

"*To the trees.*"

"*She's more dangerous there than in the open.*"

"*It's our only hope.*"

"*You two are worthless.*" The bobcat stalked them, savoring the moment.

"*That's your opinion.*" Mrs. Murphy growled deep in her throat.

"*You're the hors d'oeuvre, your canine sidekick is the main meal.*"

"*Don't count your chickens.*" Murphy spun around and flew over the snow.

Tucker did likewise, the bobcat closing in on her. She heard breathing behind her and then saw Mrs. Murphy dive into a fox hole. Tucker spun around and snapped at the bobcat's forelegs, which caught her completely by surprise. It gave Tucker the split second she needed to dive into the fox hole after her friend.

"*I can wait all night,*" the bobcat muttered.

"*Don't waste time over spilt milk,*" Mrs. Murphy taunted.

"*I'm glad some of you are big foxes.*" Tucker panted on the floor of the den. "*I'd have never gotten into your earth otherwise.*"

The slight red vixen said to Murphy, "*You told me once to stay in the shed during a bad storm. I owe you one.*"

"*You've more than repaid me.*" Murphy listened as the bobcat prowled around, unwilling to give up.

"*What were you two doing out here tonight?*"

"*Looking for a film or a video back where the dead human in the car is,*" Tucker said.

"*Nobody will find that human until deer-hunting season starts, and that's two weeks away,*" the vixen noted wisely.

"*Did you-all see anything?*"

"*No, although when we first found her at the end of September she'd only been dead a few weeks.*"

"*September! I think the killer threw the evidence in the pond.*" Murphy was a figuring cat.

"*How do you know?*" Tucker knew that the feline was usually a few steps ahead of her.

"*Because the murders are about film and Roscoe's film department. It was right in front of my face, but I didn't see it. Whoever is in that car is the missing link.*"

"Murphy," Tucker softly said, "*have you figured out what's going on?*"

"*Yes, I think I have, but not in time—not in time.*"

61

Kendrick and Jody sat on a bench outside the intensive care unit. An officer guarded Sean inside. His grandfather was there, too.

Kendrick stopped Dr. Hayden McIntire when he came out of the room. "How is he?"

"We're guardedly optimistic." He looked at Jody. "Quite a few of his friends have stopped by. He's a popular boy."

"Has Karen Jensen been here?" Jody asked.

"Yes. So were Brooks Tucker, Roger Davis, and the whole football team, of course. They can't go in, but it was good that they came."

"Well, that's nice." Kendrick smiled unconvincingly.

After Hayden left, Kendrick took his daughter by the elbow. "Come on, he isn't going to rise up and walk just because you're here."

She stared at the closed doors. "I wish he would."

"I'll attend to Sean in good time."

"Dad, you can't make anybody do anything. One mistake isn't cured by making a bigger one."

They walked down the hall. "That's a mature statement."

"Maybe I'm learning something."

"Well, learn this. I'm not having bastards in my house, so you're going to marry somebody."

"It's my body."

He grabbed her arm hard. "There is no other option."

"Let me go or I'll scream bloody murder right here at University of Virginia Hospital. And you're in enough trouble." She said this without rancor.

"Yes." He unhanded her.

"Did you kill Maury McKinchie?"

"What?" He was shocked that she asked.

"Did you kill Maury McKinchie?"

"No."

62

Neither Mrs. Murphy nor Tucker returned home all night. Harry had called and called. Finally she fed the horses and, last of all, Pewter.

Walking down to get the paper, she heard Tucker bark. *"We're safe!"*

"Yahoo!" Mrs. Murphy sped beside the dog, stopping from time to time to jump for joy, straight in the air, the snow flying up and catching the sunlight, making thousands of tiny rainbows.

"Where have you two been?" Harry hunched down to gather them both in her arms. "I was worried sick about you." She sniffed. "You smell like a fox."

"We spent the night with our hosts," Murphy said.

Tucker, turning in excited circles, interrupted. *"We think there's evidence in Bowden's pond, and then we stayed too late and the bobcat tracked us. Oh, it was a close call."*

"Tucker was brave!"

"*You, too.*"

"Such talk." Harry laughed at their unintelligible chatter. "You must be starving. Come on. We've got to hurry or I'll be late for work."

Driving Blair's Dually into Crozet, Harry noticed the snow lying blue in the deep hollows.

The three rushed into the post office, nearly getting stuck in the animal door. Mrs. Hogendobber, who usually greeted them, was so excited, she barely noticed their entry.

"Hi, Miranda—"

"Where have you been?" Miranda clapped her hands in anticipation of telling her the news.

"What is the matter?"

"Kendrick Miller confessed to Rick Shaw that he had killed Maury McKinchie and Roscoe Fletcher. He had made up the story about the Musketeer because he remembered the Musketeer was wearing a sword. The costume hanging in Jensen's locker was irrelevant to the case. He confessed last night at midnight."

"*I don't believe it,*" Mrs. Murphy exclaimed.

63

A crowd had gathered at Mim's . . . a good thing, since she put them to work stuffing and hand-addressing envelopes for the Multiple Sclerosis Foundation in which she was typically active.

Brooks, Roger, and Karen were relieved now that St. Elizabeth's could return to normal. Sandy Brashiers, at the head of the envelope line, told them to pipe down.

Gretchen, Mim's cook, served drinks.

When Cynthia walked through the door, everyone cheered. Accorded center stage, she endured question after question.

"One at a time." Cynthia laughed.

"Why did he do it?" Sandy Brashiers asked.

Cynthia waited a moment, then said, "These were crimes of passion, in a sense. I don't want to offend anyone but—"

"Murder is the offense," Sandy said. "We can handle his reasons."

"Well—Roscoe was carrying on an affair with Irene Miller and Kendrick blew up."

"*Roscoe?* What about Maury?" Fair Haristeen, tired from a day in the operating room, sat in a chair. Enough people were folding and stuffing. He needed a break.

"Kendrick has identified the poison used. He said Maury was on to him, knew he'd killed Roscoe, and was going to prove it. He killed him to shut him up."

Harry listened with interest. She felt such relief even as she felt sorrow for Irene and Jody. Irene had had an affair. No cheers for that, but to have a husband snap and go on a killing spree had to be dreadful. No wonder Jody had beaned Maury McKinchie at the hockey game. The tension in the Miller household must have been unbearable. "*Nouveau riche,*" Mim cried.

"I'd rather be *nouveau riche* than not *riche* at all," Fair rejoined, and since Mim adored her vet, he could get away with it.

Everyone truly laughed this time.

"How did Kendrick get such powerful poison?" Reverend Herb Jones wondered.

"The nursery and gardening business needs pesticides."

Harry noticed BoomBoom's unusual reticence. "Aren't you relieved?"

"Uh—yes," said the baffled beauty. She'd had no idea about Roscoe and Irene. Why didn't Maury tell her? He'd relished sexual tidbits.

Sandy Brashiers put his hands on his hips. "This still doesn't get April Shively off the hook. After all, she is withholding papers relevant to school operation."

"Maybe she will come forward now," Little Mim hoped out loud.

"How do you know for sure it was Mr. Miller?" Karen said to everyone's amazement.

Cynthia answered, "A detailed confession is about as close to a lock as you can get."

"Why'd he tell?" Harry wondered aloud.

Cynthia winked at her. "Couldn't live with the guilt. Said he confessed to Father Michael first, and over time realized he had to give himself up."

"Well, it's over. Let's praise the Lord for our deliverance," Miranda instructed them.

"Amen," Herb agreed and the others joined in.

"You know, I keep thinking about Irene and Jody sitting home alone. They must be wretched. We should extend our sympathy." Miranda folded her hands as if in prayer.

Everyone looked at Mrs. Hogendobber, thought for a moment, and then agreed that she had a point. It might not be fun to go over to the Millers', but it was the right thing to do.

After the work party, Harry, Fair, Big Mim, Little Mim, Herb Jones, Miranda, and Susan Tucker drove over. The kids piled into Roger's old car. Father Michael had been with the family since Kendrick gave himself up late that afternoon. It was the priest who answered the door. Surprised to see so many people, he asked Irene if she would be willing to see her neighbors. She burst into tears and nodded "yes."

The first person Irene greeted was Big Mim, who after the formalities offered them a sojourn in one of her farm dependencies if they should need privacy from the press.

Irene thanked her and began crying again.

Miranda put her arm around her. "There, there, Irene. This is too strange to contemplate. You must be feeling confused and terrible."

"Bizarre," Jody said forthrightly. "I can't believe he lost it like that."

Irene, not ready to give up on her husband, sputtered, "He's no murderer!"

"He confessed," Jody said flatly.

"We're your friends, no matter what." Softhearted Roger couldn't bear to see Jody's mother cry.

"Mom, I want to go back to school. I know this won't go away, but something in our lives has to be normal."

"Jody, that only puts more pressure on you." Irene worried about the reaction of the other students.

"Hey, I'm not responsible for Dad. I need my friends."

"We'll see."

"Mom, I'm going."

"We'll watch over her," Karen volunteered.

As this issue was hashed out, Father Michael and Herb Jones huddled in a corner. Father Michael, secure in the company of another cleric, whispered to him that he was tremendously relieved that Kendrick was behind bars. After all, he himself was likely to be the next victim.

"Bragging?"

"Not exactly. The first confession was straightforward. The second one, he said he liked killing. He liked the power. I can't say I ever recognized his voice."

"Was there a sense of vindication?" Herb inclined his head close to Father Michael's.

"I couldn't say."

"A touch dramatic."

"The entire episode was certainly that."

Later that evening Harry told Mrs. Murphy, Tucker, and Pewter all that had transpired at Big Mim's and then over at Irene Miller's. Angry though they were at not being included, they listened as she babbled while doing her chores.

"*They're so far away from the truth it hurts,*" Tucker said and Pewter agreed, since Mrs. Murphy had briefed them on what she felt was truly going on.

"*It's going to hurt a whole lot more.*" Mrs. Murphy stared out the window into the black night. Try as she might, she couldn't think of what to do.

64

Typical of central Virginia in late November, a rush of warm wind rolled up from the Gulf of Mexico. Temperatures soared into the low sixties.

Students were now back at St. Elizabeth's, thanks to Kendrick's midnight confession.

Harry and Miranda shoveled through the landslide of mail.

Jody Miller and Karen Jensen pulled in front of Market Shiflett's store.

"Things are finally settling down." Miranda watched the girls, smiling, enter the grocery store.

"Thank God." Harry tossed a catalog into the Tucker post box. "Now if my truck would just get fixed! I'm getting spoiled driving Blair's Dually and I don't want to wear out my welcome."

"Think of all the string and rubber bands they have to remove," Pewter quipped sarcastically. "What are Jody and Karen doing out of school?"

"Hookey," Tucker thought out loud.

Mrs. Murphy said, "*There's a big field hockey game after school today, and a huge football game Friday. Maybe their coach got them out of class.*"

"*Wish we'd get out of work early.*" Pewter rubbed the plastic comb Harry had just installed on the corner of the post boxes. It was advertised as a cat-grooming aid.

" *'Course St. E's won't be worth squat—they lost too much practice time, but Crozet High ought to have a good game.*" The tiger enjoyed sports.

"*St. E's practiced,*" Tucker said. "*Of course, how well they practiced with all the uproar is anyone's guess.*"

Jody and Karen came out of the store, placed a big carton in the back of Karen's old car, and drove off.

Susan zoomed into the post office through the backdoor. "Good news!"

"*What?*" came the animal and human chorus.

"Sean Hallahan has regained consciousness." She beamed. "He's not out of the woods yet, but he knows his name, where he is, he recognizes his parents. He's still in intensive care. Still no visitors."

"That's great news." Harry smiled.

"Once he's really clear, off some of the painkillers, he'll have other pains to deal with . . . still, isn't it wonderful?"

65

The deep golden rays of the late afternoon sun slanted over the manicured field hockey pitch. The high winds and snow of the previous week had stripped the trees of their leaves, but the mild temperature balanced the starkness of early winter.

Knowing how rapidly the mercury could fall, Harry tossed four blankets over her shoulder.

As she made her way to the bleachers, the Reverend Herb Jones called out, "You opening a trading post?"

"Four beaver pelts for one heavy blanket." She draped a royal-blue buffalo plaid blanket over her arm as if to display her wares.

Miranda, warm in her MacLeod tartan kilt with a matching tam-o'-shanter, soon joined them. She carried two hot thermoses, one of tea, the other of chocolate.

"You come sit by me." Herb patted the hard wooden bleacher seat next to him.

Sandy Brashiers, beaming, shook the hands of parents, telling each of them how grateful he was that St. Elizabeth's frightful ordeal was behind them. He thanked everyone for their support, and he promised the best for the remainder of the semester.

Coach Hallvard, about to face the formidable St. Catherine's team from Richmond, had not a second to glad-hand anyone.

Mim accompanied her daughter, which put Little Mim's nose out of joint because she wanted to be accompanied by Blair Bainbridge. He, however, had been roped into setting up the hot dog stand since his Dually, the newest in town, could pull the structure. Not only did Blair's Dually have a setup for a gooseneck trailer, he also had a Reese hitch welded to the frame.

"Mother, why don't you sit with the girls?" Little Mim waved broadly at Miranda in MacLeod tartan splendor.

Mim, sotto voce, replied, "Trying to get rid of me?"

"Why, Mother, whatever gave you such a silly idea?"

"Humph. You need me to extract money out of these tightwads, Marilyn. You haven't been a raging success."

"Considering all that's happened here, I've done pretty damn well, Mother. And I don't need you to advertise my shortcomings. I'm conversant with them."

"Well, aren't we testy?"

"Yes, we are." Little Mim gave her a sickeningly sweet smile.

These last two years Little Mim had found some backbone. Her mother enjoyed friction on the odd occasion, although she wasn't accustomed to receiving it from her formerly obsequious daughter. However, it did spice up the day.

"Mimsy," Miranda called out, knowing Mim hated "Mimsy." She felt devilish. "Sit with us."

Mim, throwing her alpaca shawl, deep raspberry, over her wildly overpriced Wathne coat, paraded grandly to the bleachers, leaving Little Mim to scoot to the hot dog stand where she found, to her dismay, Cynthia Cooper helping Blair set up shop.

The home team trotted across the field as the rhythm section of the band beat the drums.

Karen Jensen ran with Brooks. "Toni Freeman has moves like a snake," Karen said about the opponent who would be covering Brooks.

"I'll be a mongoose."

"This is going to be a tough game." Karen grew increasingly fierce before the game.

"Zone. You'll be in the zone."

"Yeah. There's Rog."

Brooks waved back at Roger.

"Tossed salad." Karen laughed, meaning Roger had flipped over Brooks.

Jody loped up from behind. "Let's skin 'em alive, pound 'em senseless! Yes!" She moved by them.

As the team approached the bench, the stands erupted in a roar. St. Catherine's also shouted. The entire senior class had trekked out from Richmond. This was a grudge match because St. Catherine's had edged out St. E's in the semifinals at last year's state tournament.

The three animal friends sat with the humans on the bleachers. Pewter hated the crowd noises. *"I'm going back to the car."*

"Miranda closed up the Falcon; you can't get in," Mrs. Murphy told her.

"Then I'll go to the hot dog stand." Pewter's eyes glistened.

"Stay with us," Murphy told her loudly.

"Will you two stop fussing at each other!" Harry commanded.

"She started it." Pewter oozed innocence.

A phone rang in Herb's pocket.

"What on earth?" Miranda exclaimed when he pulled a fold-up cellular out of his Norfolk jacket.

"The modern age, Miranda, the modern age." He pulled out the antenna, hit a button, and said, "Hello."

Susan answered, "Herb, tell the gang I'm on my way. Oh, and tell Harry I dropped off BoomBoom to pick up her truck. It's ready."

"Okay. Anything else?"

"No. Be there in ten minutes."

"Fine. 'Bye." He pressed the green button again, sliding the aerial down. "Harry, Susan will be here in ten minutes, and Boom-Boom is bringing your truck. Susan dropped her off."

"BoomBoom? Great. Now I have to be terminally grateful."

"No, you don't. After all, she wrecked your truck in the first place."

"Given the way she drives, she'll wreck it again."

"*Mother, you're irrational about BoomBoom.*" Mrs. Murphy scratched her neck.

"No, she won't," Herb answered. "Here we go!"

The game started with St. Catherine's racing downfield, taking a shot on goal, saved.

"Jeez, that was fast." Harry hoped St. Elizabeth's defense would kick in soon.

"May I see that?"

"Sure." Herb handed Miranda the cellular phone.

She slipped the aerial out and held it to her ear. "It's so light."

"I'll pick up my messages; listen to how clear it is." He punched in what must have been seventeen or more numbers and held the phone to Miranda's ear.

"Amazing." Suddenly her face changed. "Herbie, look."

Parading in front of the bleachers was April Shively wearing a St. Elizabeth's jacket. She was carrying three closed cartons that she dumped at Sandy Brashiers's feet.

Blair noticed this from the hot dog stand. Cynthia hurried over, Little Mim at her heels.

"Deputy Cooper." A surprised Sandy put his hand on the boxes. "Marilyn."

"I'll take those." Little Mim bent over and picked up a rather heavy carton.

"No." Sandy smiled falsely.

April, her grin widening, turned on her heel and left. "Ta-ta!"

"Damn her," Sandy said under his breath.

"Cynthia, you can't have these." Little Mim squared her shoulders.

"Why don't we examine them together? It will only help St. Elizabeth's if everything is aboveboard from the start." Cynthia made a strong argument.

"As headmaster, I'll take charge of those documents."

"Down in front!" a fan, oblivious to the drama, yelled at them.

"Without me you won't be headmaster for long." Little Mim clipped her words, then smiled at the deputy as she changed course. "Come on, Cynthia. You're absolutely right. We should do this together."

As they hauled off the cartons, the announcer blared over the loudspeaker, "We are happy to announce that St. Elizabeth's own Sean Hallahan has regained consciousness, and we know all your prayers have helped."

A huge cheer went up from the stands.

After the game, won by St. Elizabeth's, Jody, who'd played brilliantly, drove alone to the University of Virginia Hospital.

Sean, removed to a private room, no longer had a guard since Kendrick had confessed. His father was sitting with him when Jody, wearing a visitor's pass, lightly knocked on the door.

"May I come in?"

Sean turned his head toward her, stared blankly for a moment, then focused. "Sure."

"Hello, Mr. Hallahan."

"Hello, Jody. I'm sorry this is such a troubling time for you."

"It can't be as bad as what you're going through." She walked over to Sean. "Hey."

"Hey." He turned his head to address his father. "Dad, could we be alone?"

In that moment Mr. Hallahan knew Jody was the girl in question, for his wife had told him Sean's words during his first, brief moment of lucidity when Cynthia Cooper was on guard.

"I'll be just down the hall if you need me."

When he had left, Jody leaned over, kissing Sean on the cheek. "I'm sorry, I'm really sorry."

"I was stupid. It wasn't your fault."

"Yes, it was. I told you—well, the news—when I was pissed off at you and the world."

"I'll marry you if you like," he gallantly offered.

"No. Sean, I was angry because you were paying attention to Karen. I wanted to hurt you."

"You mean you aren't pregnant?" His eyes brightened.

"No, I am."

"Oh." He dropped his head back on the pillow. "Jody, you can't face this alone. Lying here has given me a lot of time to think."

"Do you love Karen?"

"No. I haven't even gone out with her."

"But you want to."

He drew a long breath. "Yeah. But that was then. This is now."

"Will you walk again?"

"Yes." He spoke with determination. "The doctors say I'll never play football again . . . but they don't know me. I don't care what it takes. I will."

"Everyone's back at school. My dad confessed to the murders."

"Mom told me." He didn't know what to say. "I wish I could be at Homecoming."

"Team won't be worth squat without you."

"Paul Briscoe will do okay. He's just a sophomore, but he'll be good."

"Do you hate me?" Her eyes, misty, implored him.

"No. I hate myself."

"Did you tell anyone—"

"Of course not."

"Don't."

"What are you going to do?"

"Get rid of it."

He breathed hard, remaining quiet for a long time. "I wish you wouldn't do that."

"Sean, the truth is—I'm not ready to be a mother. You're not ready to be a father, either, and besides—it may not be yours."

"But you said—"

"I wanted to hurt you. It may be yours and it may not. So just forget it. Forget everything. My dad's in jail. Just remember—my dad's in jail."

"Why would he kill Mr. Fletcher and Mr. McKinchie?"

"I don't know."

His pain medication was wearing off. Sweat beaded on Sean's forehead. "We were having such a good time." He pushed the button for the nurse. "Jody, I need a shot."

"I'll go. Don't worry. You're sure you didn't tell anyone anything?"

"I didn't."

"I'll see you later." She passed Mr. Hallahan, who walked back into Sean's room the minute she left.

"She's the one."

"No." Grimacing, Sean pleaded, "Dad, get the nurse, will you? I really hurt."

67

That same night Cynthia Cooper and Little Mim sifted through papers at Little Mim's beautiful cottage on her mother's vast estate.

"Why do you think April finally changed her mind?" Little Mim said.

"Had to be that she heard about Roscoe's affair with Irene," Coop answered. "Her hero suddenly had feet of clay."

The minutes from the various committee meetings provided no surprises.

Roscoe's record book containing handwritten notes made after informal meetings or calls on possible donors did pack some punch.

After a meeting with Kendrick Miller, Roscoe had scrawled, "Discussed women's athletics, especially a new training room for the girls. Whirlpool bath. Won't give a penny. Cheap bastard."

On Father Michael's long prayers during assembly: "A simple 'Bless us, dear Lord' would suffice."

After a particularly bruising staff meeting where a small but well-organized contingent opposed athletic expansion and a film department, he wrote concerning Sandy Brashiers, "Judas."

As Little Mim occasionally read pungent passages aloud, Cynthia, using a pocket calculator, went through the accounting books.

"I had no idea it cost so much money to run St. E's." She double-checked the figures.

"What hurts most is maintenance. The older buildings suck up money."

"Guess they were built before insulation."

"Old Main was put up in 1834."

Cynthia picked up the last book, a green clothbound book, longer than it was wide. She opened it to the figures page without checking the front. As she merrily clicked in numbers, she hummed. "Do you remember what cost five thousand dollars the first week of September? It says 'W.T.' " She pointed to the ledger.

"Doesn't ring a bell."

Cynthia punched in more numbers.

"Hey, here's a good one." Little Mim laughed, reading out loud. " 'Big Mim suggested I butter up Darla McKinchie and get her to pry money out of Kendrick. I told her Darla has no interest in St. Elizabeth's, in her husband's career and, as best I can tell, no affection for the state of Virginia. She replied, "How common!" ' "

Little Mim shook her head. "Leave it to Mother. She can't ever let me have something for myself. I'm on the board, she isn't."

"She's trying to help."

Marilyn's hazel eyes clouded. "Help? My mother wants to run every committee, organization, potential campaign. She's indefatigable."

"What cost forty-one thousand dollars?"

Little Mim put down Roscoe's record book to look at the ledger. "Forty-one thousand dollars October twenty-eighth. Roscoe was dead by then." She grabbed the ledger, flipping back to the front. "Slush fund. What the hell is this?"

Coop couldn't believe she'd heard Little Mim swear. "I suppose most organizations have a kitty, although this is quite a large one."

"I'll say." Little Mim glanced over the incoming sums. "We'll get to the bottom of this." She reached for the phone, punching numbers as she exhaled loudly. "April, it's Marilyn Sanburne." She pressed the "speaker" button so that Coop could hear as well.

"Are you enjoying yourself?"

"Actually, I am," came the curt reply. "Roscoe's record book is priceless. What is this green ledger?"

"I have no idea."

"April, don't expect me to believe you. Why else would you remove these papers and accounting books? You must have known about the slush fund."

"First of all, given everyone's temper these days, a public reading of Roscoe's record book is not a good idea. Second, I have no idea what the slush fund was. Roscoe never once mentioned it to me. I found that book in his desk."

"Could Maury have started giving St. Elizabeth's an endowment?"

"Without fanfare? He was going to give, all right, but we were going to have to kiss his ass in Macy's window."

Little Mim bit her lip. "April, I've misjudged you."

"Is that a formal apology?" April asked.

"Yes."

"I accept."

"Sandy Brashiers couldn't have handled this," Little Mim admitted.

"He'd have fumbled the ball. All we need is for the papers to get wind of this before we know what it's all about," April said.

"You have no idea?" Little Mim pressed.

"No. But you'll notice the incoming sums are large and regular. Usually between the tenth and fifteenth of each month."

"Let me see that." Coop snatched the green book out of Little Mim's hands. "Damn!"

"What?" Little Mim said.

Cynthia grabbed the phone. "April, seventy-five thousand dollars came in the week after Roscoe died. It's not reflected in the ledger, but there is a red dot by October tenth. For the other deposits, there's a red dot with a black line through it."

"Primitive but effective bookkeeping," April said.

"Did you know a Jiffy bag with seventy-five thousand dollars arrived in Roscoe's mailbox at Crozet on October"—she figured a moment—"twelfth. I'm pretty sure it was the twelfth."

"I didn't know a thing about it."

"But sometimes you would pick up Roscoe's personal mail for him?"

"Infrequently . . . but yes."

"Do you remember other Jiffy bags?"

"Cooper, most books are sent in bags like that."

"Do you swear to me you don't know what this money represents?"

"I swear, but I know it represents something not right. That's why I cleaned everything out. I didn't mind sitting in jail. I felt safe."

"One last question."

"Shoot."

"Do you believe that Kendrick Miller killed Roscoe and Maury?"

"Roscoe loathed him. But, no, I don't."

"He says he blew up in a rage."

"Show him the ledger."

"I'm going to do just that. One more question. I promise this is the last one. Do you think Naomi knows about the ledger?"

A pause. "If she did, we'd see the money. Even if just a pair of expensive earrings."

"Thanks, April."

"Are you going to prosecute me for obstructing justice?"

"I'm not the legal eagle, but I'll do what I can."

"Okay." April hung up, satisfied.

"Marilyn, I need this ledger. I won't publicize it, but I need to show it to Kendrick and Naomi. This is starting to look like money-laundering. Question is, was Kendrick Miller involved in it?"

The next day Kendrick examined the figures closely but said nothing. Cynthia could have bashed him.

Naomi appeared genuinely shocked by the secret bookkeeping.

All Rick Shaw said when he read through the book was, "Dammit to hell!"

68

"Stick Vicks VapoRub up your nose." Rick handed over the small blue glass jar to Cynthia Cooper as they cut the motor to the squad car.

She fished out a big dab, smoothing it inside each nostril. The tears sprang from her eyes.

"Ready?"

"Yep." She noticed that the photographer was already there. The rescue squad would soon follow. "Boy, George Bowden looks rough."

"Probably puked his guts out. Natural reaction."

"George." Rick walked over, leaves crunching underfoot. "Feel up to some questions?"

"Uh-huh." He nodded.

"What time did you discover the body?"

"Well, now, let me see. I set the alarm for four o'clock 'cause I wanted to be at the edge of the oat fields just on my way down to the hayfields. Good year for grouse, I can tell you. Anyway, uh"—he rubbed his back pockets in an upward motion—"got here about four forty-five, thereabouts. The kids set up a ruckus. Followed them." He indicated his hunting dogs as the kids.

Cynthia carefully walked around the car. The Vicks killed the stench but couldn't do much about the sight. She dusted each door handle. As she was quietly doing her job, another member of the department, Tom Kline, arrived. He gagged.

"Vicks." She pointed to the squad car.

He jammed the stuff up his nose, then returned, carefully investigating the car.

"Guys, I'm going to open the door. It'll be a real hit even with the Vicks. We need to dust the inside door handles, the glove compartment, just hope we're lucky. We aren't going to get anything off the body."

When the door was opened, George, although twenty yards away, stepped backward. "My God."

"Walk on back here with me." Rick led him out of olfactory range. "It's overpowering. The carbon cycle."

"What?"

"Carbon. The breakdown of flesh." Since George wasn't getting it, Rick switched back to business. "Did you notice anything unusual apart from the corpse? Footprints?"

"Sheriff, that thing's been out here so long, any footprints would be washed out."

"A month to six weeks. 'Course, we've had some cold spells. Bill Moscowitz can pinpoint the time for us. Bad as it is, the corpse would be torn apart if it had been out of the car. The fact that it's relatively intact may help us."

"Tire tracks washed out, too. I mean, I would have noticed tire tracks before. Would have come on down."

"You haven't been over here?"

"Been up on the mountain fields, no reason to come down here. Hay's not worth cutting this year anyway. Forgot to fertilize. Mostly I've been working on the mountainside of the farm because of the apples. Good year."

"What about grapes?"

"Got them in 'fore the rains. Be real sweet 'cause of the light drought this summer."

"Do you recognize that corpse?"

"How would I?"

"Odd though it may seem, if that body belonged to someone you knew, you would probably recognize it even in its current condition. Nine times out of ten people do."

"You mean, you show people something like that?"

"Only if we can't make an identification by any other means. Naturally, you try to spare the family as much pain as possible."

"I don't know that"—he gesticulated—"don't know the car. Don't know why she came down this lane. Don't know nothing."

"George, I'm sorry this has happened to you. Why don't you go on home? If I need you, I'll call or come by."

"You gonna take that outta here, aren't you?"

"As soon as we finish dusting the car and taking photos."

"Something in the air, Sheriff."

"I beg pardon?" Rick leaned forward as if to draw closer to George's meaning.

"Evil. Something in the air. The headmaster fella at the rich kids' school and then that Hollywood blowhard stabbed by Kendrick Miller. Sometimes I think a door to the underworld opens and bad spirits fly out."

"That's very interesting," said Rick, who thought George was slightly demented: nice but tilted.

"I was saying to Hilary the other day, evil flowing down the mountain with that cold wind. Life is an endless struggle between good and evil."

"I expect it is." Rick patted him on the back. "You go on home, now."

George nodded good-bye. The dogs tagged at his heels. George, not more than thirty-five, thought and acted like a man in his sixties.

"Boss, we're finished down here. You want a look before we wrap up?"

"Yeah." Rick ambled over. There were no weapons in the car or in the trunk, which ruled out a self-inflicted wound. There was no purse. Usually if someone committed suicide by drug overdose, the vial would be around. Given the body's state of decay, how she died would have to be determined by the coroner. "You satisfied?"

"Yes," Cooper replied, holding out the car registration. "Winifred Thalman."

"Okay." He nodded to the rescue squad.

Diana Robb moved forward with a net. When a body was decomposed, they placed a net around it to keep bones and disintegrating flesh together as much as possible.

"I'm going back to the office," Rick told Cynthia. "I'll call New York Department of Motor Vehicles and start from there. If there's a super at her address, I'll call him, too. I want you to make the rounds."

"You thinking what I'm thinking?"

"Yeah."

"She would have been killed close to the time of Roscoe's death."

He picked up a brittle leaf, pulling away the drying upper epidermis, exposing the veins. "Could have." He released the leaf to fall dizzily back to earth. "It's the why."

They looked at each other a long time. "Boss, how we gonna prove it?"

He shrugged. "Wait for a mistake."

69

The drive back from Richmond, hypnotic in its boredom, found Irene and Jody silent. Irene swung onto the exit at Manakin-Sabot.

"Why are you getting off sixty-four?"

"I'll stay more alert on two-fifty. More to see."

"Oh." Jody slumped back in her seat.

"Do you feel all right?"

"Tired."

"That's natural after what your body has just been through."

"Mom, did you ever have an abortion?"

Irene cleared her throat. "No."

"Would you?"

"I don't know. I was never in your position. Your father thinks it's murder." Her brow furrowed. "How are you going to break this to him?"

"He should talk."

"Don't start, today. He's a flawed man but he's not a killer. Now, I'm going to tell him you had a miscarriage. Leave it to me."

"We're lucky he's in jail." Jody smiled weakly, adding, "If he was home he'd kill us!"

"Jody!"

"I'm sorry, but, Mom, he's confused. People do have secret lives, and Dad is weird."

Irene raised her voice. "You think he did it, don't you? You think he killed Roscoe and McKinchie. I don't know why. You ought to give your father more support."

"Dad's got an evil temper."

"Not that evil."

"You were going to divorce him. All of a sudden he's this great guy. He's not so great. Even in jail he's not much different from when he was out of jail."

A strangled silence followed. Then Irene said, "Everyone can change and learn. I know your pregnancy shocked him into looking at himself. He can't change the past, but he can certainly improve the future."

"Not if he gets convicted, he can't."

"Jody, shut up. I don't want to hear another word about your father getting convicted."

"It's better to be prepared for the worst."

"I'm taking this a day at a time. I can't handle any more than I'm handling now, and you aren't helping. You know your father is innocent."

"I almost don't care." Jody sat up straight. "Just let me have what's left of this year, Mom, please."

Irene considered what her daughter said. Jody could seem so controlled on the outside, like her father, but her moods could also shift violently and quickly. Her outburst at the field hockey game, which now seemed years away, was proof of how unhappy Jody had been. She hadn't seen her daughter's problems because she was too wrapped up in her own. A wave of guilt engulfed her. A tear trickled down Irene's pale cheek.

Jody noticed. "We'll be okay."

"Yes, but we'll never be the same."

"Good."

Irene breathed in deeply. "I guess things were worse than I realized. The lack of affection at home sent you looking for it from other people . . . Sean in particular."

"It was nice being"—she considered the next word—"important."

They swooped right into the Crozet exit. As they decelerated to the stop sign, Irene asked, "Did you tell anyone else you were pregnant?"

"No!"

"I don't believe you. You can't resist talking to your girl friends."

"And you never talk to anyone."

"Not about family secrets."

"Maybe you should have, Mother. What's the big deal about keeping up appearances? It didn't work, did it?"

"Did you tell anyone?"

"No."

"You told Karen Jensen."

"I did not."

"You two are as thick as thieves."

"She hangs out with Brooks Tucker as much as she hangs out with me." A thin edge of jealousy lined Jody's voice. "Mom, hang it up."

Irene burst into tears. "This will come back to haunt you. You'll feel so guilty."

"It was the right thing to do."

"It violates everything we've been taught. Oh, why did I agree to this? I am so ashamed of myself."

"Mother, get a grip." Icy control and icy fury were in Jody's young face. "Dad's accused of murder. You're going to run the business. I'm going to college so I can come home and run the business. You can't take care of a baby. I can't take care of a baby."

"You should have thought of that in the first place," Irene, a hard edge now in her voice, too, shot back.

"Maybe you should have thought about your actions, too."
Jody's glacial tone frosted the interior of the car.

"What do you mean?" Irene paused. "That silly idea you had
that I was sleeping with Samson Coles. Where do you get those ideas?
And then to accuse the poor man in the post office."

"To cover your ass."

"What!" Irene's eyes bugged out of her head.

"You heard what I said—to cover your ass. You'd been sleeping
with Roscoe. You thought I didn't know."

Irene sputtered, her hands gripping the steering wheel until her
knuckles were white. "How dare you."

"Save it, Mom. I know because he told me."

"The bastard!"

"Got that right."

Irene calmed down a moment. "Why would he tell you?" She
still hadn't admitted to Jody the veracity of the accusation.

"Because I was sleeping with him, too."

"Oh, my God." Irene's foot dropped heavier on the gas pedal.

"So don't tell me right from wrong." Jody half smiled.

"I'm glad he's dead."

Jody smiled fully. "He didn't tell me, really—I figured it out for
myself."

"You—" Irene sputtered.

"It doesn't matter." Jody shrugged.

"The hell it doesn't." She slowed down a bit since the red
speedometer needle had surged past eighty. "Did you sleep with
him?"

"Yes. Each year Roscoe picked his chosen one. My turn, I
guess."

"Why?" Irene moaned.

"Because he'd give me anything I wanted and because I'd get
into whatever school I wanted. Roscoe would fix it."

"Jody, I'm having a hard time taking all this in." Irene's lower
lip trembled.

"Stop," Jody commanded.

"Stop what?"

"The car!"

"Why?"

"We need to pick up the mail."

"I'm too shook up to see people."

"Well, I'm not. So stop the damned car and I'll get the mail."

Irene parked at the post office, while Jody got out. Then she worried about what her daughter would say to Harry and Miranda, so she followed her inside.

Harry called out, "In the nick of time."

Miranda, busy cleaning, called out a hello.

"Irene, you look peaked. Come on back here and sit down. I'll make you a cup of tea."

Irene burst into tears at Miranda's kindness. "Everything is so awful. I want my husband out of jail."

"Mom, come on." Jody tugged at her, smiling weakly at Miranda and Harry.

"Poor Irene." Tucker hated to see humans cry.

"She's better off without him," Pewter stated matter-of-factly.

Two squad cars roared by the post office, sirens wailing, followed by the rescue squad. Cynthia trailed in her squad car. But she pulled away and stopped at the post office. She opened the door and saw Irene and Jody.

"What's going on?" Miranda asked.

"A corpse was found at Bowden's farm." She cleared her throat. "The car is registered to Winifred Thalman of New York City."

"I wonder who—" Miranda never finished her sentence.

"Mom, I'm really tired."

"Okay, honey." Irene wiped her eyes. "You can't accuse Kendrick of this one! He's in jail."

Cooper quietly replied, "I don't know about that, Mrs. Miller, she's been dead quite some time."

Tears of frustration and rage flooded Irene's cheeks. She slapped Cynthia hard.

"Mom!" Jody pulled her mother out of there.

"Striking an officer is a serious offense, isn't it?" Harry asked.

"Under the circumstances, let's just forget it."

"*They finally found the body.*" Tucker sighed.

"*Yes.*" The tiger squinted as the dying sun sparked off Irene's windshield as she pulled away from the post office. "*They're getting closer to the truth.*"

"*What is the truth?*" Pewter said philosophically.

"*Oh, shut up.*" Mrs. Murphy cuffed her friend's ears.

"*I couldn't resist.*" The gray cat giggled.

"*We might as well laugh now,*" Tucker said. "*We aren't going to laugh later.*"

70

Mrs. Murphy worked feverishly catching field mice, moles, shrews, and one sickly baby bunny, which she quickly put out of its misery. Pewter opened the kitchen cabinets while Harry slept. She had a knack for flipping open cabinet doors. She'd grab the knob and then fall back. She rooted around the shelf until she found a bottle of catsup. Fortunately, the bottle was plastic because she knocked it out of the cabinet, shoving it onto the floor for Tucker to pick up.

The corgi's jaws were strong enough to carry the oddly shaped object out to the truck.

"I can put all the kill here in the bed," Mrs. Murphy directed the other two. "If you'll help me, Pewter."

"Harry's going to find all this."

"Not if Tucker can drag out the old barn towel."

"How are we going to get it up in the bed of the truck?"

"Pewter, let me do the thinking. Just help me, will you?"

"What do you want me to do with this bottle of catsup?"

"Put it behind the front wheel of the truck. When Harry opens the door for us, pick it up and jump in the truck. Pewter and I will distract her. You can drop it and kick it under the seat. Remember, gang, she's not looking for this stuff. She won't notice."

Tucker hid the catsup behind the front wheel, then strolled into the barn and yanked the towel off the tack trunk with Harry's maiden initials on it, MM. She tripped over the towel as she walked to the truck, so she dragged it sideways.

Murphy and Pewter placed the small dead prey at the back corner of the truck bed.

"Pewter, perch on the bumper step."

"You'd better do it. You're thinner." Pewter hated to admit that she was overweight.

"All right." Murphy jumped down on the back bumper step while Pewter hoisted herself over the side of the tailgate. Tucker sat patiently, the towel in her mouth.

Simon, returning home in the early dawn from foraging, stopped to wonder at this activity. *"What are you-all doing?"*

"Trying to get the towel into the bed of the truck. It's too big to put in my mouth and jump in," Mrs. Murphy informed him. *"Okay, Tucker, stand on your hind legs and see if you can reach Pewter."*

Tucker put her paws on the bumper, her nose edging over the top.

Mrs. Murphy leaned down, grabbing the towel with her left paw. *"Got it."*

Pewter, half hanging over the tailgate, quickly snatched the towel before Murphy dropped it—it was heavy. With Pewter pulling and Mrs. Murphy pushing, the two cats dumped the towel into the truck bed. Mrs. Murphy gaily leapt in, and the two of them placed the towel over the kill, bunching it up to avoid its looking obvious.

"I'll be," Simon said admiringly.

"Teamwork," Mrs. Murphy triumphantly replied.

"What are you going to do with those bodies?" Simon giggled.

"Lay a trail to the killer. Mom's going over to St. Elizabeth's today, so I think we can get the job done."

The possum scoffed. "*The humans won't notice, or, if they do, they'll discount it.*"

The tiger and the gray cat peeped over the side of the truck. "*You might be right, but the killer will notice. That's what we want.*"

"*I don't know.*" Simon shook his head.

"*Anything is better than nothing,*" Murphy said forcefully. "*And if this doesn't work, we'll find something else.*"

"*Why are you so worried?*" Simon's furry nose twitched.

"*Because Mother will eventually figure out who the murderer really is.*"

"Oh." The possum pondered. "*We can't let anything happen to Harry.*" He didn't want to sound soft on any human. "*Who else will feed me marshmallows?*"

71

The animals, exhausted from running back and forth across the playing fields, sacked out immediately after eating.

Pewter and Mrs. Murphy curled up on either side of Tucker on the sofa in front of the fire. Pewter snored, a tiny little nasal gurgle.

Fair brought Chinese food. Harry, good with chopsticks, greedily shoved pork chow mein into her mouth. A light knock on the door was followed by Cynthia Cooper, sticking her head in. She pulled up a chair and joined them.

"Where are the critters?"

"Knocked out. Every time I called them, they were running across the football field today. Having their own Homecoming game, I guess. Can I get you anything else?"

"Catsup." She pointed at her plate. "My noodles."

"You're kidding me." Harry thought of catsup on noodles as

she opened her cabinet. "Damn, I had a brand-new bottle of catsup, and it walked away."

"Catsup ghost." Fair bit into a succulent egg roll, the tiny shrimp bits assaulting his taste buds.

"What were you doing at St. E's?"

"Like a fool, I agreed to help Renee Hallvard referee the field hockey games if she can't find anyone else. She can't for the next game, so I went over to review the rules. I wish I'd never said yes."

"I have a hard time saying no, too. The year I agreed to coach Little League I lost twenty pounds"—Fair laughed—"from worrying about the kids, my work, getting to practice on time."

"Is this a social call, Cynthia? Come on," Harry teased her.

"Yes and no. The corpse, Winifred Thalman, was a freelance cinematographer. I called April Shively before anyone else—after I stopped at the post office. She says Thalman was the person who shot the little movies the seniors made their first week back at school."

"Wouldn't someone have missed her in New York? Family?"

Cooper put down her egg roll. "She was estranged from her only brother. Parents dead. As a cinematographer, her neighbors were accustomed to her being absent for months at a time. No pets. No plants. No relationships. Rick tracked down the super in her building."

"You didn't stop at the post office to tell me the news first, did you?" Harry smiled.

"Saw Irene's car."

"Ah."

"Kendrick's got to be lying. Only reason we can come up with for him to do that is he's protecting his wife or his daughter."

"They killed Roscoe and Maury?" Fair was incredulous.

"We think one of them did. Rick's spent hours going over Kendrick's books and bank accounts, and there's just no evidence of any financial misdoing. Even if you buy the sexual jealousy motive, why would he have killed this Thalman woman?"

"Well, why would Irene or Jody have done it?" Harry asked.

"If we knew that, we'd know everything." Cynthia broke the

egg roll in two. "Irene will be at the field hockey game tomorrow. We'll have her covered by a plainclothesman from Waynesboro's department. You'll be on the field. Keep your eyes open."

"Irene or Jody stabbed Maury? Jeesh," Fair exclaimed. "Takes a lot of nerve to get that close at a public gathering."

"Wasn't that hard to do," Harry said. "Sometimes the easiest crimes are the ones committed in crowds."

"The killer confessed twice to Father Michael. Since Kendrick has confessed, Father Michael hasn't heard a peep. Nothing unusual about that—if you're a murderer and someone has taken the rap for you. Still, the impulse to confess is curious. Guilt?"

"Pride," Harry rejoined.

"Irene or Jody . . . I still can't get over it."

"Do you think they know? I mean, does one of them know the other is a killer?" Harry asked.

"I don't know. But I hope whoever it is gets sloppy or gets rattled."

"Guess this new murder will be on the eleven o'clock news"— Harry checked the old wall clock—"and in the papers."

"Whole town will be talking." Cynthia poured half a carton of noodles on her plate. "Maybe that'll rattle our killer. I don't know, she's been cold as ice."

"Yeah, well, even ice has a melting point." Fair tinkled the ice in his water glass.

"Harry, because you're in the middle of the field, you're secure. If it is Jody, she can't stab you or poison you without revealing herself. Are you willing to bait her? If we're wrong, there will be plenty of time to apologize."

"I'll do it." She nodded her head, "Can you set a trap for Irene?"

"Fair?"

"Oh, hell!" He put down his glass.

72

The colored cars and trucks filling the St. Elizabeth's back parking lot looked like jelly beans. The St. Elizabeth's supporters flew pennants off their antennas. So did the Chatham Hall fans. When the wind picked up, it resembled a used-car parking lot. All that was missing were the prices in thick grease crayon on the windshields.

Harry, despite all, read and reread the rule book in the faculty locker room. She knew the hardest part of refereeing would be blowing the whistle. Once she grew confident, she'd overcome that. And she had to establish her authority early on because if the kids thought they could get away with fouling, some would.

Mrs. Murphy sat on the wooden bench next to her. Pewter and Tucker guarded the door. Deputy Cooper waited in the hall.

The noise of a locker being pulled over, followed by shouting, reverberated down the hall.

"What the hell?" Harry ran out the door toward the commotion.

Cooper jerked her head in the direction of the noise. "It's World War Three in there, and the game hasn't even started."

"Well, it is the qualifier for state." Harry tucked her whistle in the whistle pocket.

Pewter giggled. *"She found it."*

The animals ran down the hall. Tucker, losing her hind footing on the slick waxed surface, spun around once. They reached the locker room and crept along the aisle.

"What a dirty trick! I'll kill whoever did this!" Jody kicked her locker again for good measure. Dead mice, moles, and shrews were scattered over the floor. A bottle of catsup, red stuff oozing out of the bite marks, splattered everywhere. Jody's stick had catsup on it, too.

"Gross." Karen Jensen jumped backward as the tiny dead animals spilled everywhere.

"You did this!" Jody lost her composure, accusing the last person who would do such a thing.

"You're crazy," Karen shot back.

Jody picked up her hockey stick and swung at Karen's head. Fortunately, Karen, the best player on the team and blessed with lightning reflexes, ducked. Brooks grabbed Jody from behind, but Jody, six inches taller, was hard to hold.

Coach Hallvard dashed into the room. "Cut it out!" She surveyed the mess. "All right. Out of here. Everyone out of here."

"Someone filled my locker with dead mice and catsup!" Jody shrieked. "And it's your fault. You won't let us keep locks on our lockers anymore!"

"We'll solve this after the game." Coach put her hands on her hips. "It could have been someone from Chatham Hall. It certainly would benefit them to rattle one of our best players and set this team fighting among ourselves, wouldn't it?"

The girls drank in this motivating theory, none of which Hallvard believed. However, it provided a temporary solution. She'd talk to Deputy Cooper after the game. Coach was intelligent enough to know that anything out of the ordinary at St. Elizabeth's must be treated with the utmost suspicion, and Cynthia had briefed her to be alert. She didn't identify Jody as a possible suspect.

"You're right, Coach." Jensen, the natural leader of the team, finally spoke. "Let's wipe them off the face of the earth!"

The girls cheered. As they grabbed their sticks and filed out of the room, Brooks noticed Mrs. Murphy.

"Murphy, hi, kitty."

"Keep your cool, Brooks, this will be a hell of a game."

When the home team ran across the field to the benches, the home crowd roared.

Fair sat next to Irene, as he promised Cynthia he would. The plainclothes officer from Waynesboro sat behind her, pretending to be a Chatham Hall supporter.

Miranda, also alerted, huddled with Mim in the center of the bleachers.

Cynthia stayed behind the Chatham Hall bench, which gave her a shorter sprint to the gym if need be. She knew Irene was well covered, so she watched Jody.

Herb Jones joined Sandy Brashiers and some of the faculty on the lower bench seats.

Harry met her co-official, Lily Norton, a former All-American, who drove over from Richmond.

"I'm a last minute fill-in, Miss Norton. Bear with me." Harry shook her hand.

"I was a freshman at Lee High the year you-all won state." She warmly returned the handshake. "You'll do fine, and please, call me Lily."

"Okay." Harry smiled.

They both synchronized their watches, then Lily put the whistle to her lips, blew, and the two captains trotted out to the center of the field.

Mrs. Murphy, Pewter, and Tucker, on the gym side of the field, watched closely, too.

"Tucker, stay on the center line on this side. You know what to do?"

"Yes," Tucker answered forcefully.

"Pewter, you hang out by the north goal. There's a maple tree about twenty

yards back from the goal. If you get up in there, you can see what's going on. If anything worries you, holler."

"You-all won't be able to hear me because of the crowd noise."

"Well"—Mrs. Murphy thought a minute—"about all you can do is run down the tree. We'll keep glancing in your direction."

"Why can't we stay on the edges of the field?" Tucker said.

"The referees will chase us off. Mom will put us in the truck. We've got to work with what we have."

"That field is a lot of territory to cover," Pewter, not the fastest cat in the world, noted.

"We'll do what we can. I'll stay under the St. Elizabeth's bench. If I get shooed away from there, I'll head down to the south goal. We clear?"

"Yes," they both said.

"Why can't Coop shoot if Jody or Irene goes nuts?"

"She can, but let's hope she doesn't need to do that." Murphy exhaled from her delicate nostrils. "Good luck."

The three animals fanned out to their places. Mrs. Murphy ducked feet and the squeals of the players who saw her. She scrunched up under the players' bench, listening intently.

The first quarter provided no fireworks but showed off each team's defensive skills. Jody blocked an onrushing Chatham Hall player but got knocked sideways in the process. She leapt up, ready to sock the girl, but Karen yelled at her, "Stay in your zone, Miller."

"Up yours," Jody shot back, but she obeyed.

The first half passed, back and forth but no real excitement.

Pewter wished she were under the bench because the wind was picking up. Her perch was getting colder and colder.

The second half opened with Brooks stealing a Chatham Hall pass and running like mad toward the goal where, at the last minute, now covered, she fired off a pinpoint pass to Karen Jensen, who blazed her shot past the goalie. A roar went up from the St. Elizabeth's bleachers.

Susan jumped up and down. Irene, too, was screaming. Even Sandy Brashiers, not especially interested in athletics, was caught up in the moment.

The big girl whom Jody had blocked took advantage of the run back to the center to tell Jody just what she thought of her. "Asshole."

"It's not my fault you're fat and slow," Jody needled her.

"Very funny. There's a lot of game left. You'd better watch out."

"Yeah, sure." Jody ignored her.

Chatham Hall grabbed the ball out of the knock-in. The big player, a midfielder, took the pass and barreled straight at Jody, who stepped out of the way, pretended to be hit, rolled, and flicked her stick out to catch the girl on the back of the leg.

Harry blew the whistle and called the foul.

Jody glared at Harry, and as Chatham Hall moved downfield, she brushed by Harry, close enough to make Harry step back and close enough for Harry to say, "Jody, you're the killer."

A hard shot on goal was saved by the St. Elizabeth's goalie. Another roar erupted on the sidelines. But the game became tougher, faster, and rougher. By the end of the third quarter both sides, drenched in sweat, settled in for a last quarter of attrition.

Whether by design or under the leadership of the big Chatham Hall midfielder, their team kept taking the ball down Jody's side. Jody, in excellent condition and built for running, couldn't be worn down, but they picked at her. Each time she'd lose her temper, they'd get the ball by her.

Finally Coach Hallvard took her off the field, substituting a talented but green sophomore, Biff Carstairs.

Jody paced in front of the bench, imploring Renee Hallvard, "Put me back in. Come on. Biff can't handle it."

True enough. As they flew down the right side of the field, Biff stayed with them, but she hadn't been in a game this good, this fast, or this physically punishing.

Chatham Hall scored on that series of plays, which made Jody scream at the top of her lungs. Finally, Hallvard, fearing another quick score, put Jody back in. The St. Elizabeth's side cheered anew.

Fair murmured in a low voice as the crowd cheered, "Irene, give yourself up. We all know it wasn't Kendrick."

She whirled around. "How dare you!"

A pair of hands behind her dropped to her shoulders so she

couldn't move. The plainclothesman ordered, "Stay very still." He removed one hand and slipped it inside his coat to retrieve a badge.

"I didn't kill those people." Irene's anger ebbed.

"Okay, just sit tight," the plainclothesman said quietly.

Perhaps Jody felt an extra surge of adrenaline. Whatever, she could do no wrong. She checked her woman, she stole the ball, she cracked the ball right up to her forwards. She felt invincible. She really could do no wrong. With Jody playing all out at midfield and Karen and Brooks lethal up front, St. Elizabeth's crushed Chatham Hall in the last quarter. The final score was four to two. The crowd ran off the bleachers and spilled onto the field. Mrs. Murphy streaked down the sidelines to escape the feet. Pewter climbed down from the tree, relieved that nothing dangerous had happened. The animals rendezvoused at the far sideline at center with Tucker.

"*I thought she'd whack at Mom with her stick. I thought we rattled her enough.*" Pewter was dejected that Jody had proved so self-possessed.

"*Oh, well.*" Tucker sat down.

Mrs. Murphy scanned the wild celebration. Harry and Lily slowly walked off the field. Jody watched out of the corner of her eye even as she jumped all over her teammates.

"Nice to work with you." Lily shook Harry's hand. "You did a good job."

"Thanks. Aren't you going back to change?"

"No, I'd better get on the road." Lily headed toward the parking lot behind the gym.

As Harry entered the gym, Jody drifted away from the group. There was nothing unusual in a player heading back to the gym.

Cynthia, caught in the crowd, fought to get through the bodies when she saw Jody leave.

The three animals raced across the grass, little tufts of it floating up in the wind as it flew off their claws. They reached the door just as Harry opened it.

"Hi, guys." She was tired.

Within a minute Jody, stick in hand, was also in the gym. As Harry turned right down the hall toward the faculty changing room,

Jody, on tiptoes now, moved down the hall, carefully listening for another footfall. Without speaking to one another, the animals ducked in doorways. Only Murphy stayed with Harry in case Tucker and Pewter failed.

Jody passed Pewter, who ran out and grabbed the back of her leg with her front claws. Jody howled, whirled around, and slapped at the cat, who let go just as Tucker emerged from the janitor's door. She ran hard at Jody, jumped up, and smashed into her knees. Dog and human collapsed in a heap, and the hockey stick clattered on the shiny floor.

"Goddammit!" Jody reached for her stick as Tucker grabbed the end of it.

They tugged from opposite ends. Tucker slid along the floor, but she wouldn't let go. Jody kicked at the dog, then twisted the stick to force her jaws loose. It didn't work. Pewter jumped on Jody's leg again as Harry, hearing the scramble, opened the locker room door and came back into the hall. Mrs. Murphy stuck with Harry.

"*Good work,*" the tiger encouraged her pals.

Jody, seeing Harry, dropped her hockey stick, lunging for Harry's throat.

Harry raised her forearm to protect herself. She stumbled back against the concrete wall of the gym, which gave her support. She lifted up her knee, catching Jody in the crotch. It slowed Jody, but not enough. Pewter, still hanging on to Jody's right leg, was joined by Murphy on the left. They sank their fangs in as deep as they'd go.

Jody screamed, loosening her grip on Harry's neck. The enraged girl lurched for her hockey stick. Tucker was dragging it down the hallway, but the corgi couldn't go fast, she being small and the stick being large.

Jody yanked the stick hard out of the dog's jaws. Tucker jumped for the stick, but Jody held it over her head and ran for Harry, who crouched. The hallway was long and narrow. She would use the walls to her benefit. Harry, a good athlete, steadied for the attack.

Jody swung the stick at her head. Harry ducked lower and

shifted her weight. The tip of the hockey stick grazed the wall. Harry moved closer to the wall. She prayed Jody would crack her stick on the wall.

Jody, oblivious to the damage the cats were doing to her legs, she was so obsessed, swung again. The stick splintered, and that fast Harry pushed off the wall and flung herself at Jody. The two went down hard on the floor as the cats let go of their quarry. Tucker ran alongside the fighting humans, waiting for an opening. Her fangs, longer than the cats', could do more damage.

Sounds down the hall stopped Jody for a split second. She wriggled from Harry's grasp and raced away from the noise. Tucker caught her quickly and grabbed her ankle. Jody stopped to beat off the dog just as Cynthia Cooper rounded the corner and dropped to one knee, gun out.

"Stop or I'll shoot."

Jody, eyes glazed, stared down the barrel of a .357, stared at the bloody fangs of Tucker, then held up her hands.

73

Because of their bravery, the animals were rewarded with filet mignon cooked by Miranda Hogendobber. Harry, Fair, Susan, Brooks, Cynthia, and the Reverend Jones joined them. The animals had place settings at the big dinner table. Miranda went all out.

"This is heaven," Pewter purred.

"I didn't know Pewter had it in her." Susan smiled at the plump kitty.

"There's a lion beneath that lard," Mrs. Murphy joked.

As the humans put together the pieces of the murderous puzzle, Tucker said, "Murphy, how did you figure it out?"

"Mother was on the right track when she said that whoever killed Roscoe Fletcher did it at the car wash. Any one of the suspects could have done it, but not one person recalled anyone giving Roscoe candy, although he offered it to them. Jody walked past the Texaco station on her way to the deli. The station blocks the view from the car wash. She gave him the candy; no one saw her, and no car was behind Roscoe yet. She could have worked fast, then run back to the office. It would give her a good alibi. She was waiting for an opportunity. She was smart enough to know this was a good shot. Who knows how long she carried that candy around?''

"I don't know whether to pity Jody or hate her," Susan Tucker mused.

" 'Behold, these are the ungodly, who prosper in the world; they increase in riches!' Psalm Seventy-three, verse twelve," Miranda recited. "Roscoe and Maury did increase in riches, but they paid for it. As for Jody, she was very pretty and vulnerable. But so are many other young people. She participated in her own corruption."

"The slush fund ledger gave me part of the motive—money—but I couldn't find the slushers. Drugs weren't it." Cynthia folded her arms across her chest. "Never would I have thought of porno movies."

"It is ghastly." The Reverend Jones shuddered.

"What tipped you off?" Pewter asked Murphy.

"It took me a long time to figure it out. I think finding that address label at the bottom of Roscoe's desk was my first inkling. Neptune Film Lab. And wonderful though it might be to have a film department at a private secondary school—it seemed like a great expense even if Maury was supposedly going to make a huge contribution."

"Kendrick was more of a man than we've given him credit for," Susan said.

"He guessed Jody was the killer. He didn't know why." Cynthia recalled the expression on his face when Jody confessed. "She'd told Irene and Kendrick that she was pregnant by Sean. It was actually Roscoe."

"I'd kill him myself." Fair's face flushed. "Sorry, Herb."

"Quite understandable under the circumstances."

"She had slept with Sean and told him he was the father of her child. That's when he stole the BMW. He was running away and asking for help at the same time," Cynthia continued. "But she now says the father might be Roscoe. And she said this is the second film made at St. Elizabeth's. Last year they used Courtney Frere. He'd pick one favorite girl for his films. We tracked her down at Tulane. Poor kid. That's what the sleeping pills were about, not low board scores. The film she was in was shot at Maury's house, but then Roscoe and

Maury got bolder. They came up with the bright idea of setting up shop at St. Elizabeth's. It certainly gave them the opportunity to troll for victims."

"Monsters." Miranda shook her head.

"There have always been bad people." Brooks surprised everyone by speaking up. "Bad as Mr. Fletcher and Mr. McKinchie were, she didn't have to kill them."

"She snapped." Susan thought out loud. "All of a sudden she must have realized that one mistake—that movie—could ruin the rest of her life."

"Exactly." Cynthia confirmed this. "She drove out with Winifred Thalman, thinking she could get the footage back, but Winifred had already mailed the rough cut to Neptune Lab. She only had outtakes with her, so Jody killed her. She threw the outtakes in the pond."

"How," Harry asked, "did she kill her?"

"Blow to the head. Maybe used her hockey stick. She walked across the fields after dark and arrived home in time for supper. After that she was driven by revenge. She wanted power over the people she felt had humiliated her—even though she'd agreed to be in these movies for money."

"The slush fund?" Harry asked.

"Right. Forty-one thousand dollars withdrawn by Maury, as it turns out. Forty-one thousand dollars for her BMW . . . it all added up. Imagine how Kendrick must have felt when he saw that figure in Roscoe's secret ledger. The deposits were from other films. Maury and Roscoe shot porno movies in New York, too. There they used professionals. Roscoe's fund-raising trips were successful on both counts," Cynthia said.

"How'd she kill Maury?" Brooks was curious.

"She slipped into the girls' locker room, put on the Musketeer outfit, and rejoined the party. She saw Maury start to leave and stabbed him, with plenty of time to get back to the locker and change into her skeleton costume. She may even have lured Maury out of the dance, but she says she didn't," Cynthia answered.

"Does she feel any remorse?" Miranda hoped she did.

"For killing three people? No, not a bit. But she feels terrible that she lied to Sean about being the father. About goading him into calling in the false obituary and about following Roger on his paper route and stuffing in the Maury obit. That's the extent of her remorse!"

"Do you believe she's crazy?" Fair said.

"No. And I am sick of that defense. She knows right from wrong. Revenge and power. She should be tried as an adult. The truth is: she enjoyed the killing." Cynthia stabbed her broccoli.

"*Why would a human pay to watch another human have sex?*" Pewter laughed.

"*Boredom.*" Tucker ate table scraps slipped her by Fair.

"*I wouldn't pay to watch another cat, would you?*" Pewter addressed Murphy.

"*Of course not, but we're cats. We're superior to humans.*" She glanced at Tucker.

"*I wouldn't do it, I'm superior, too,*" Tucker swiftly said, around a mouthful.

"*Yes—but not quite as superior as we are.*" Mrs. Murphy laughed.

Dear Highly Intelligent Feline:

Tired of the same old ball of string? Well, I've developed my own line of catnip toys, all tested by Pewter and me. Not that I love for Pewter to play with my little sockies, but if I don't let her, she shreds my manuscripts. You see how that is!

Just so the humans won't feel left out, I've designed a T-shirt for them.

If you'd like to see how creative I am, write to me and I'll send you a brochure.

Sneaky Pie's Flea Market
c/o American Artists, Inc.
P.O. Box 4671
Charlottesville, VA 22905

In felinity,

SNEAKY PIE BROWN

P.S. Dogs, get a cat to write for you!